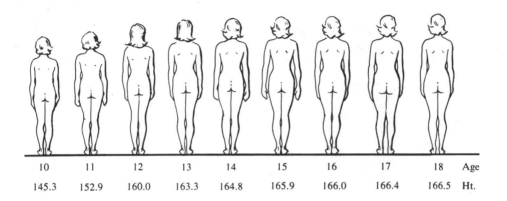

| | | | | | | | | | |
|---|---|---|---|---|---|---|---|---|---|
| 10 | 11 | 12 | 13 | 14 | 15 | 16 | 17 | 18 | Age |
| 145.3 | 152.9 | 160.0 | 163.3 | 164.8 | 165.9 | 166.0 | 166.4 | 166.5 | Ht. |

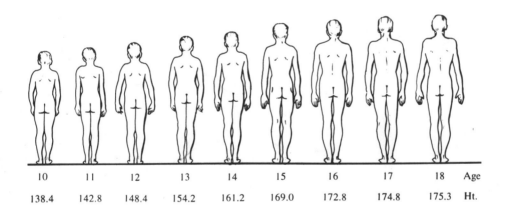

| | | | | | | | | | |
|---|---|---|---|---|---|---|---|---|---|
| 10 | 11 | 12 | 13 | 14 | 15 | 16 | 17 | 18 | Age |
| 138.4 | 142.8 | 148.4 | 154.2 | 161.2 | 169.0 | 172.8 | 174.8 | 175.3 | Ht. |

# Children

## Development and Relationships

# Children Development

Robert J. Izzo

## Mollie S. Smart & Russell C. Smart

Department of Child Development and Family Relations   University of Rhode Island

# and Relationships

**second edition**

Macmillan Publishing Co., Inc.
New York

Collier Macmillan Publishers
London

Copyright © 1972, Macmillan Publishing Co., Inc.
PRINTED IN THE UNITED STATES OF AMERICA

Earlier edition copyright © 1967 by Macmillan Publishing Co., Inc.

Macmillan Publishing Co., Inc.
866 Third Avenue, New York, New York 10022

Collier-Macmillan Canada, Ltd.


Library of Congress catalog card number: 71-151691

PRINTING        7 8 9 10 11        YEAR        5 6 7 8 9

# To Laura and Craig

# Preface
## to the Second Edition

The purposes of this book are threefold: to give basic information to students preparing for professional work with children, to map out the field and kindle the interest of students planning to specialize in child development or child psychology, and to contribute to the reader's liberal education by adding to his knowledge of man. While we do not consider a primary purpose of a college course to be parent education, we realize that students usually plan to apply their learning to their personal lives. This aim involves no conflict with the objectives stated above.

The field of child development traditionally includes physical as well as psychological development. It also includes consideration of the family and culture in which the child grows up. The explosion of knowledge in recent years has discouraged some teachers of child development from venturing outside the field of psychology. We believe, however, that it is both valuable and possible to study the child as a physical and psychological being who lives in a family in a culture.

The framework of this book comes from two great men, Erik Erikson and Jean Piaget. Erikson, the Vienna-born psychoanalyst, and Piaget, the Swiss psychologist, have contributed deeply and broadly to the study of children. Their viewpoints fit together and complement each other in such a way as to delight the student of child development. They give a sweeping view of human growth, Erikson painting a far-reaching picture of personality development, Piaget illumining the growth of the mind. The work of both men can be studied on many different levels of difficulty. In an introductory book, we cannot hope to examine either in depth, our main purpose in using the ideas of Erikson and Piaget being to integrate the book. The multiplicity of research on children, especially on relationships, makes confusing reading unless some threads of consistent theory tie it together.

Another great man who has influenced our thinking is Lawrence K. Frank, who has been called the father of child development. Frank's understanding and creativity gave beginning and shape to the field of child development and to the dynamic-developmental viewpoint.

And of course we are indebted to the hundreds of research workers whose products form the subject matter of this book. We have tried to include the basic research and the most recent research which presents children as interacting, developing, and relating.

"Where sciences meet, their growth occurs."* The field of child development is a place where sciences meet and hence where sciences also grow. Since the publi-

---

* F. G. Hopkins, Biological thought and chemical thought, *Lancet*, 1938, **1**, 1147–1150, 1201–1204.

cation of the first edition of this book, the sciences of psychology and nutrition have grown through their encounters in the bodies and minds of children. The children who have thus contributed to growth in psychology and nutrition are the poor of the world, the deprived children of our own United States of America and the children of underdeveloped countries. In them and in their parents, psychology and nutrition have encountered sociology and anthropology, genetics and obstetrics—and all have grown. The study of child development, which includes findings from all these fields and more, has been enriched by research stemming from problems of the poor and from attempts to solve them. The worldwide problem of population explosion makes *quality* of the individual a subject of increasing pertinence. Improved quality is possible through new knowledge of heredity, prenatal care, and delivery. New knowledge of development is available for improvements in relationships and education, although the applications lag. Studies of some segments of affluent societies have shown a new stage of development occupying a place between adolescence and adulthood.

In this edition we have focused on a wider range and broader sample of children and families than we did in the first edition. This expanded viewpoint reflects our own increasing awareness and also our students' growing capacities for caring about the world's children and for identifying themselves primarily as human beings.

We are indebted to Bernice Borgman, Claire Lehr, Duwayne Keller, and James Walters for their constructive criticism, and to Evelyn Omwake and her students for their helpful suggestions. Lucile Votta has given us advice in the field of health. Our research assistant, Elizabeth Lamberton, gave extensive, invaluable help. We appreciate the contributions of our photographers: Louise Boyle, Donna J. Harris, Robert J. Izzo, Halvar Loken, Ellen S. Smart, and Craig Szwed. We also want to thank our typists, Mary Fields and Deborah Petterson. Alta Gordon's aid was indispensable in the final stages.

M. S. S.
R. C. S.

Wharerata
Massey University
Palmerston North
New Zealand

# Contents

# Appendixes

# Appendixes

# Introduction

The concept of stages of development is used commonly in both popular and scientific thinking. We follow both Erikson and Piaget in our use of *stages*. A stage is a period during which certain changes occur. The achievements of each stage are built upon the foundation of developments of previous stages. At each stage, there are certain kinds of problems to be solved. When the child succeeds, he can and does go on to tackle new problems and to grow through solving them. Each stage is named after activities that the child carries on during that period. Erikson's stages are named after activities involving the whole personality, Piaget's after intellectual activities. While there are not exact chronological ages to mark the beginnings and ends of stages, there are rough averages for landmarks. For each of Erikson's childhood and adolescent stages, there is a corresponding one in Piaget's series. Often it is possible to see a close relationship between the behavior patterns described by the two men. Sometimes the personality development taking place can be seen to be an essential result of the intellectual abilities and limits at that time.

Some students may prefer to read Chapter 17 first rather than last, since it concerns the variety of ways in which the individual interacts with his environment. It includes theories and explanations of how these interactions take place and how the individual develops through them. The rest of the book is organized on an age-level basis in order to make children seem whole and real. We believe that a beginning student finds the subject matter more interesting when he can picture children as people. The disadvantage of an age-level organization is that the same topics have to be introduced in several different places. In doing this, we try not to repeat, but only to recapitulate enough to recall what has already been said. If a student wishes to study by topics rather than by age levels, he can do so by using the index or by grouping the chapters thus: 1; 2, 3, 6, 7, 10, 11, 14; 2, 3, 5, 9, 13; 4, 7, 8, 11, 12, 15, 16; 17.

Part 1 deals with the infant, from his conception to about 2 years of age. One stage of personality growth is almost completed during infancy, *almost* rather than *all*, because no stage of personality growth is ever entirely done. The development of the sense of trust is in its crucial period at this time, and the resolutions of the problems of trust are the stuff of which infant personality is built. Infant intellectual growth comprises the sensorimotor period of intelligence, during which the child learns to control his movements in space and establishes the idea that objects are permanent. He comes to realize that he is an object in space, and an object among objects. These achievements contribute largely to his sense of trust, since he thus learns to expect certain regularities in the world, and he learns that he can count on himself to accomplish certain acts. During the last stage of the sensorimotor period of intelligence, the toddler becomes involved in a new stage of personality growth, the development of the sense of autonomy. Problems of autonomy occupy him for about the first half of the preschool period, which is considered in Part II of this book. The time from 18 months to 2 years, when the child is called a *toddler*, is a transition period in both intellect and personality. Intellectually, the toddler enjoys the new ability to represent actions and objects to himself, through the use of mental images. He demonstrates that he can do so when he pretends and imitates. He can use very primitive foresight and planning. The growth of the sense of autonomy is facilitated by these new mental abilities, through which he begins to know himself as a person-among-persons. Growing physical powers and motor coordinations also contribute to his feelings of being an individual who can make decisions and who can succeed. His testing grounds and workshop include both objects and people. Through interactions with them, he develops in one direction or another. Our consideration of development and relationships therefore is very much concerned with those interactions.

The child from age 2 to 6 or 7, known as the preschool child, is the focus of Part II. *Preschool* is an accurate term in the sense that children are not required to go to school until the end of this period. It is a misleading term in its implication that education may not occur at this age. The preschool years are vastly significant for both personality and intellectual growth. With the problems of developing a sense of autonomy fairly well in hand by age 3½, the preschool child comes to grips with the development of a sense of initiative and imagination. Although he thinks very concretely and cannot go beyond his own limited point of view in controlled thought, his imagination catapults him far and wide. Personality develops now through starting new activities, getting new ideas and through exploration of every-thing—places, people, language, objects, art materials. New experiences give him not only starting points for flights of fancy, but the wherewithal for building his primitive, concrete concepts of the world. Repeated experiences are necessary, too, since only through repeated encounters with classes of objects can he pull abstrac-tions from them, and only through repeatedly checking his interpretations with other people can his thinking become socialized. Nor does he have to figure out everything for himself, through experience. Other people give him words with which to label his experiences, and then those experiences take on wider meanings, mean-ings that are valid in his culture. Other people show him how to feel in this or that situation, how to heal a hurt, how to see the funny side. They tell him what is important in life and how to get it. Although such messages often come through straight, they do not always do so. And often the behavior of the child is a language that adults find difficult to understand. The study of child development should help adults to interpret the language of behavior and to respond to it in ways that are meaningful to the child.

The elementary school child, considered in Part III, is quite different from the preschool child in body, mind, and personality. He has the physical advantages of slow growth, well-developed motor coordinations, and relatively few illnesses. His very admission to the world outside the family, the real world of school, proclaims that he is recognized as ready to go to work. Indeed, he is ready to give up much of the play which constituted his preschool business in order to learn the rules of his society and the fundamentals of being a worker. (He still needs to play, however.) Personality growth requires the development of a sense of industry. He accepts a great deal of repetitive practice, even appearing to enjoy doing the same thing over and over. Not only does he strive to learn reading, writing, and arithmetic, but much of his supposedly free time is spent practicing motor skills and learning the rules of social and intellectual games. The school-age phase of intellectual development, the period of concrete operations, is marked by faster, more flexible, and more accurate thinking. Instead of being limited by his own point of view, the schoolchild can inquire and imagine himself into the places of other people, which he does in much of his social interaction. His broader backlog of experience and his previous achievements with concepts supplement his emerging ability to consider several aspects of the situation before coming to a conclusion. Satisfactory personality development results from interactions in which his physical and mental powers develop, in which he does learn the skills and rules that other children his age are learning, and in which he gets the idea that he has performed satisfactorily. Since his field of interaction has broadened far beyond the family, people outside the family become increasingly important in contributing to success or failure, to a sense of industry or a sense of inferiority.

Part IV is concerned with adolescence, a time of life whose chronological age limits are very vague. A cycle of interrelated events begins shortly before puberty. If age 11 or 12 is considered as close to the beginning of adolescence, then most adolescents will be included. The end of adolescence is, of course, adulthood, however one defines it. The dominant personality problem is to develop a sense of identity. The intellectual stage typical of the period is that of formal operations, the same as it is for adults. The adolescent is faced with the problem of becoming a new, grown-up person who knows who he is, what he wants to become, what he could be, and where he is going. He has to realize that he is the same person who used to be a certain child and that there is continuity in his life. At the same time, much is different, and many more changes will be necessary in the near future. He must get used to a rapidly changing body which probably does not look just as he would like it to look. New emotions are hard to deal with. Intellectual advances make true logical thought possible. Not only can the adolescent deal with the abstract concepts required by his schoolwork, but he can think thoughts about how society ought to be, and what part he might play in bringing about all sorts of reforms. Often, even usually, the reality of his performance does not jibe with his plans and schemes. He has to work out a new identity in each area of his life, in study and work, in his family, with friends and sweethearts, and in religion or what represents his relationship to all of reality. He must determine the persons and institutions worthy of his fidelity and must pledge himself to be true to them. For a small proportion of adolescents, *youth*, an extended moratorium, intervenes before adulthood. Another stage of personality development, the development of the sense of intimacy, is begun toward the end of adolescence, when the sense of identity is quite well established.

Figure 17–2 represents Erikson's stages of personality development and Piaget's stages of intellectual development, in order that their corresponding age levels can be noted. We conceive of each stage of personality development as a rope which swells at the age level where its problems are most pressing. Each rope stretches throughout life to show that no stage is ever finished completely, no problems solved perfectly and finally. Problems of all types recur throughout life and are handled through interactions at the time of occurrence, determined by the personality already created and by the opportunities offered by the environment. Figure 17–2 shows the eight ropes separated. Since all life's problems and all aspects of development are closely related, we think also of personality as something like a rope with the eight strands interwined with each other. As one strand swells at its dominant time, the strains on the other strands are affected.

# Part I

# Infancy

# Introduction

In the brief period of two and a half years, the human being develops from a speck of fertilized ovum into a real person who can walk, talk, make decisions, and build relationships. Never again will he grow as fast as he grows during his first weeks of existence. Never again will he have such a wide range of potentialities and possibilities for development.

The dynamic interplay and interdependence of mother and baby are punctuated by the dramatic crisis of birth, when the relationship of the two must be reorganized on a different level. Both physical and emotional interaction continue while a new dimension is added. Cognitive stimulation and intellectual development occur in the give and take of mother and baby and also in the participation of other people in the infant's expanding social world. Although he does not speak his first recognizable words until near the end of the first year, the baby prepares for his achievement throughout the early months in a remarkable interweaving of motor, sensory, social, and emotional experiences. The end of infancy is marked by his beginning to use language for both communication and thinking.

The infant takes an active role in influencing his environment, at first through an impressive repertory of reflex behavior which is gradually modified and reorganized on more complex levels. The new baby makes his family into a different family, its members into new people. The development of the infant's sense of trust goes hand in hand with the development of a sense of generativity in his parents. The sense of autonomy develops rapidly in the latter half of the second year, requiring parents to restructure their own behavior. All of the infant's development takes place through interaction with a physical and social environment.

The first chapter in this part of the book deals with prenatal life and birth from the standpoints of both the baby and mother, stressing the natural mechanisms which promote the safety and well-being of both. Chapter 2 is concerned with the newborn and his adjustment to life. The next two chapters deal first with the baby's physical, motor, intellectual, and emotional development and then with care and guidance in relation to healthy development.

# Chapter 1

Halvar Loken

# Prenatal Development and Birth

The individual's first relationship is as a baby inside his mother. As an embryo and then a fetus, he influences his mother and is influenced by her. The stress in this chapter will be on the physical and psychological development of the baby, explained in the light of the mother's development and the mutuality of the two individuals.

9

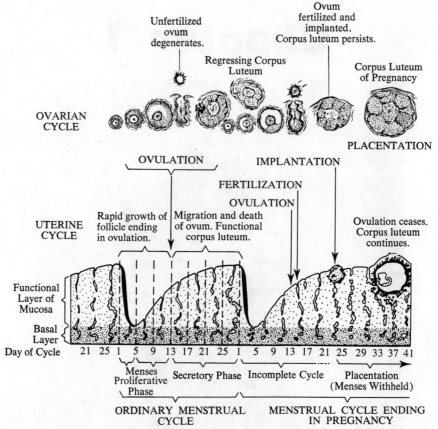

**Figure 1–1.** Changes taking place in the ovary and uterus during an ordinary menstrual cycle and during the beginning stage of a pregnancy. (Modified from Schroder in B. M. Patten, *Human Embryology*, 2nd edition. Copyright 1953. McGraw-Hill Book Company. Used by permission.)

## Stages of Prenatal Development

### From Fertilization to Implantation

The time when the baby can begin depends upon ovulation. At about the middle of each menstrual cycle (the thirteenth or fourteenth day of a 28-day cycle), a mature ovum reaches the middle of the Fallopian tube in its journey from the ovary to the uterus. Figure 1–1 shows the sequence and timing of events in the menstrual cycle.

The ovum is a little ball about the size of a dot which looks much like a chicken egg if seen under a microscope. It has a yellow yolk in the middle of clear fluid, surrounded by a gummy shell. Figure 1–2 shows a greatly magnified human egg. Unable to move by itself, the ovum is swept down the tube by suction, expansion, and contraction of the tube, and hairlike parts of the tube which lash back and forth. The sperm that must meet it partway down the tube if fertilization is to take place is one of 500 million, more or less, contributed by the father some time during the past 48 hours. Ever so much smaller than the egg, the sperm swims by lashing its long tail. Figure 1–3 shows several sperm cells. Probably many sperm bump against

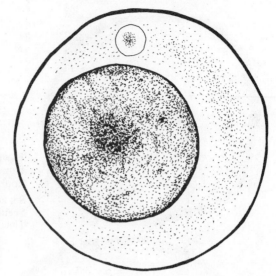

**Figure 1–2.** A human egg, about 800 times actual size. A tough membrane encloses a layer of whitish fluid, inside which is a yolk-like central portion. The little ball inside the white layer is a polar body, containing unused chromosomes.

SOURCE: After a photograph by Landrum Shettles in E. H. Haveman, *Birth control*. Time, Inc., 1967.

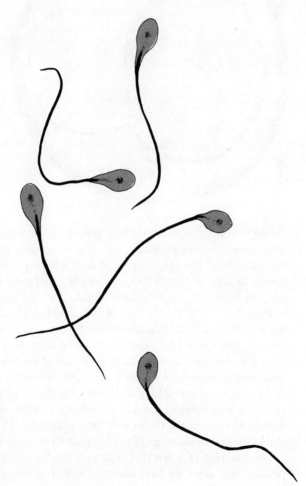

**Figure 1–3.** Several sperm cells magnified about 900 times.

SOURCE: After a photograph by Landrum Shettles in E. H. Haveman, *Birth control*. Time, Inc., 1967.

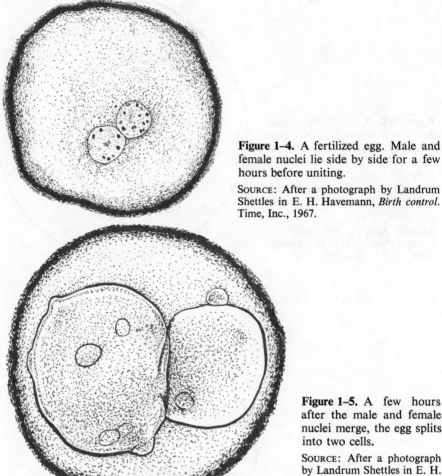

**Figure 1–4.** A fertilized egg. Male and female nuclei lie side by side for a few hours before uniting.

SOURCE: After a photograph by Landrum Shettles in E. H. Havemann, *Birth control.* Time, Inc., 1967.

**Figure 1–5.** A few hours after the male and female nuclei merge, the egg splits into two cells.

SOURCE: After a photograph by Landrum Shettles in E. H. Havemann,*Birth control.*Time, Inc., 1967.

the egg before one succeeds in penetrating the tough outer membrane. Although more than one may penetrate the membrane, only one sperm's nucleus unites with the nucleus of the egg. The male and female nucleus lie side by side for a few hours, as seen in Figure 1–4, before they merge to form the zygote, the fertilized egg, the beginning of a new individual. The egg splits into 2 cells, as can be seen in Figure 1–5. The 2 cells form 4 cells and the 4 cells 8. After 72 hours, the ovum has grown into 32 cells, as shown in Figure 1–6, and after four days, it consists of 90 cells and looks like Figure 1–7. Note that there is a cavity in the center, and cells are clustered around it. It is in this state that the organism, now called a blastocyst, leaves the Fallopian tube and enters the uterus, where it floats for one or two days before settling itself into the lining of the uterus. The outer layer of cells, the trophoblast, produces tendrils, or villi, which burrow into the uterine lining and connect the ovum with the uterine wall. This process, called implantation, marks the end of the stage of the ovum and the beginning of the stage of the embryo.

The question of when this organism can be considered a human being is an important one, since we have the means of diagnosing many abnormalities in utero.

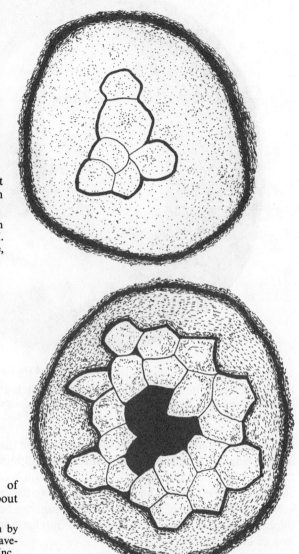

**Figure 1–6.** During the first 72 hours of life, the ovum grows into 32 cells.

SOURCE: After a photograph by Landrum Shettles in E. H. Havemann, *Birth control.*Time, Inc., 1967.

**Figure 1–7.** At four days of age, the ovum consists of about 90 cells.

SOURCE: After a photograph by Landrum Shettles in E. H. Havemann, *Birth control.* Time, Inc., 1967.

A properly performed abortion carries less risk than a tonsillectomy and a great deal less discomfort. In addition, a growing number of people are coming to believe that every woman has a right to decide for herself whether she shall bear a child. English common law and the laws of the Roman Catholic Church until the nineteenth century were permissive as long as the abortion took place before the quickening, the time when the fetus was first felt moving by the mother. During the nineteenth century, restrictive laws were passed, and the Roman Catholic Church redefined the point of humanity as being fertilization. More liberal trends are again in evidence. Scholars point out that before implantation, the ovum has no dependence on the mother and that the embryo is not an individual life until it becomes a fetus and produces hormones of its own [2]. Others say, "Scientifically,

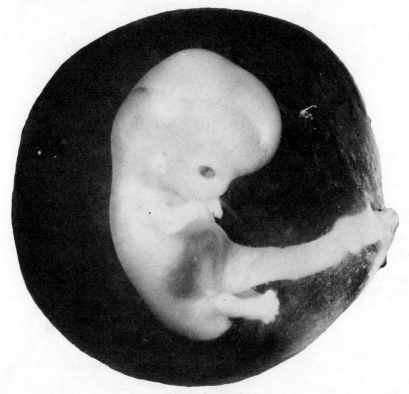

By courtesy of the Carnegie Institution of Washington.

**Figure 1–8.** The embryo at 7 weeks. This photograph is about four times life size. Notice the human-looking face, with eyes, ears, nose, and lips. The arms have hands, with fingers and thumbs. The legs have knees, ankles, and toes.

the fetus is not a human being for the simple reason that it cannot survive, even with outside help" [23]. The cultural definition of full human status varies throughout the world, from the notion of the fertilized ovum being human to the idea that the child is not a real person until several months after birth [37].

None of the events of the period of the ovum can be felt by the mother, not even implantation. Her offspring is well settled into her body before she has any indication of his presence.

## The Embryo

The individual is called an embryo during the time that the various organs and tissues are being differentiated and formed, from the end of the second week to the end of the second month. Mosslike villi extend from the embryo into the blood spaces of the maternal uterus, forming a means of exchanging body fluids. Protective and supportive membranes, the chorion and amnion, take form. The amniotic sac enclosing the embryo begins to fill with fluid.

The head comes first in the developmental timetable. The head of the embryo is one half of its total length; of the newborn, one quarter; of the adult, one tenth. These ratios illustrate the principle of developmental direction, described in Chapter 17, which holds for lower animals as well as for man and for function as well as for structure—that is, *development proceeds from anterior to posterior.*

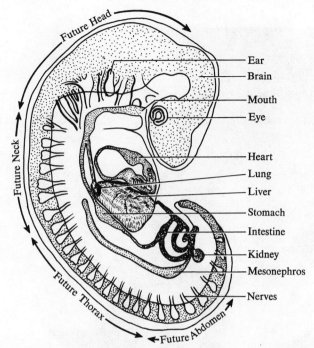

**Figure 1–9.** The month-old embryo has the foundations of many organs and systems.
SOURCE: Reproduced by permission from M. S. Gilbert, *Biography of the Unborn*. Baltimore: The Williams & Wilkins Co., 1938.

The 18-day embryo has the beginning of a heart, which begins to beat at the end of the third week. By 4 weeks the embryo has a system of blood vessels connected with the heart and two tubes which are the beginnings of the gastrointestinal tract and the cerebrospinal canal. He has eyeballs with lenses, pits which will be parts of the nose, semicircular canals, a primitive kidney, lung sacs, and limb buds. Figure 1–9 shows some of these structures.

Development is very rapid during the second 4 weeks. During this time the embryo comes to look a little like a human being. Figure 1–10 indicates how quickly length and weight increase. Since measurements of the embryo and fetus vary considerably from one study to another, these graphs should be taken as approximations and not as exact representations.

### The Fetus

At 8 weeks, the organism is recognizable, at least to the practiced eye, as a human being, and a new name is applied. From the end of the eighth week until he is born, the individual is called *fetus* instead of *embryo*. Complete with face, neck, arms, legs, fingers, toes, some calcification of his bones, functioning internal organs and muscles, the fetus is ready to build upon the basic form that has been laid down.

Development during the third month includes differentiation between the sexes, the tooth buds and sockets for the temporary teeth, the vocal chords and, of course,

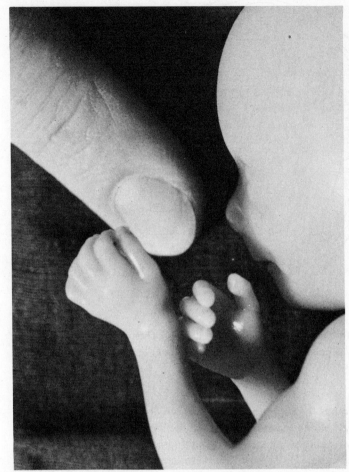

Ellen S. Smart

**Figure 1–10.** Fetus at about four months.

growth in size and complexity. The third and fourth months are a time of tremendous growth in size; 6 or 8 inches are added to his length. At 4 months the fetus has reached half of what its length will be at birth. At 6 months the vernix caseosa, formed from skin cells and a fatty secretion, protects the thin, delicate skin. The skin is red and wrinkled until subcutaneous fat is deposited under it, during the last 3 months of prenatal life. The fetus swallows, makes breathing movements, secretes enzymes and hormones, digests, and secretes urine. He makes hiccuplike movements and is thought to suck his thumb. All of these functions indicate the maturing of the nervous system.

The baby in utero is an aquatic creature who has been described as "a sort of combination astronaut and underwater swimmer" [35]. The surrounding amniotic fluid supports him in an almost weightless state, protects him from shocks and jarring, and gives him freedom to move. "His movements to and fro, round and round, up and down, have the wonderfully relaxed grace which we see in films of life under water . . . he is really very busy, swimming around in his private space capsule" [35].

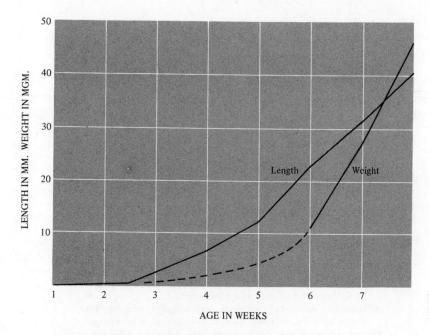

2. Flat embryonic disc with three germ layers
3. Disc arches to form cylinder, beginning alimentary canal, kidney, heart, nervous system, muscles.
4. C shape with large head end, tail, limb buds, gill slits, bulging beating heart.  Beginnings of eyes, nose pits, ears, lungs, jaws.
6. Face forming, with lips.  Eyes on sides.  Paddle-like limbs.  Cartilage beginning.  Brain growing rapidly, bending forward.
8. Looks human, with jaws, ears, fingers and toes.  Tail almost covered. Head about half of total length.  Forehead bulges with large brain. Ossification centers.  Testes and ovaries distinguishable.

**Figure 1–11a.** Summary of development during the period of the embryo.

SOURCES: G. S. Dodds, *The Essentials of Human Embryology*, 3rd edit., John Wiley & Sons, 1946. M. S. Gilbert, *Biography of the Unborn*, Williams & Wilkins, 1938. B. M. Patten, *Human Embryology*, 2nd edit., McGraw-Hill, 1953.

By 12 weeks the head extends when the trunk flexes, the rump flexes more rapidly, and one arm moves farther back than its opposite. To a lesser degree, the legs also move independently of the trunk and asymmetrically, suggesting the beginning of alternating movements. Thus the anterior portion shows more behavior than the posterior portion, illustrating again the principle that development proceeds from the anterior to posterior. Another principle specified in Chapter 17 is demonstrated also, namely that *development proceeds through differentiation and integration.* The generalized movement of the fetus at 8 weeks, when the limbs move along with the trunk, is differentiated to a unit of movement in which arms and legs are independent of the trunk but coordinated with it.

The fetus is 16 to 20 weeks old when his mother first feels him moving like a butterfly inside her. Before long, he will thump her interior instead of tickling it. Already he has a large repertory of movements which includes blinking, sucking, turning the head and gripping, and a wide variety of movements of limbs, hands, and feet.

The motor behavior of the baby before birth is related to his behavior after birth, as might be expected [61]. Thirty-five women kept records of fetal movements

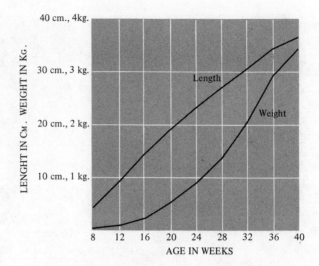

12. Sex distinguishable. Eyelids sealed shut. Buds for deciduous teeth. Vocal cords. Digestive tract, kidneys and liver secrete.
16. Head about one third of total length. Nose plugged. Lips visible. Fine hair on body. Pads on hands and feet. Skin dark red, loose, wrinkled.
20. Body axis straightens. Vernix caseosa covers skin as skin glands develop. Internal organs move toward mature positions.
24–28. Eyes open. Taste buds present. If born, can breathe, cry and live for a few hours.
28–40. Fat deposited. Rapid brain growth. Nails develop. Permanent tooth buds. Testes descend. Becomes viable.

**Figure 1–11b.** Summary of development during the fetal period.
SOURCES: As in 1–11a.

during the last three months of pregnancy. Gesell tests done on the babies at 12, 24, and 36 weeks showed positive relationships between amount of fetal activity and motor and total scores at each level.

The last half of prenatal life is a period of preparation for birth and independent living. Most important is the maturing of the nervous system, which must organize and coordinate all the other systems. The establishment of breathing, the most precarious step into the outside world, will be determined largely by the condition of the nervous system. Figure 1–11 shows growth in length and height during the prenatal period, along with some landmarks of development.

### The Placenta and Cord

The placenta, an organ that serves the unborn baby's growth needs, might be thought of as a part of the fetus which is discarded at birth. Derived from the trophoblast, which sends tendrils into the endometrial tissue (uterine lining) of the mother, the placenta grows into an inch-thick disc, about 7 inches across. One side of it is attached to the mother's uterus and the other side to the baby's umbilical cord. In the early stages of pregnancy, the placenta does the work of kidney, intestine, liver, endocrines, and lungs for the baby, adjusting its functions as the fetus grows its internal organs. Through the placenta the baby gets nutrients and oxygen from his mother and sends carbon dioxide and other waste products into her body for disposal. The baby's and mother's blood stream do not mix, however, except for the occasional escape of small amounts of the baby's blood into the mother's. They exchange products through the walls of tiny blood vessels which lie close to each other but do not run into each other. This system is the placental barrier. Bodies carrying immunity pass through the barrier from mother to fetus, thus protecting him for several months after birth from the diseases to which his mother is immune. The placenta makes hormones that affect both baby and mother, directing development of the mother's body in ways that nurture the fetus and prepare her body for birth and lactation.

The umbilical cord is derived from the body stock which is differentiated out of the trophoblast. Connecting the baby and placenta, the cord in utero looks like a stiff rope or tube, about 20 inches long. Blood flows through the cord at a high rate, as much as a half pint per minute [35]. Since the cord is under pressure, it is not flexible enough to knot in the uterus. Only during the birth processes, when it becomes slack, is there any possibility of danger from the baby entangling himself in it. At that point, of course, the physician or midwife will take care of such an emergency.

## Stages of Maternal Development and Experience

Since the zygote is free-floating and self-contained for about a week, the mother has no reactions to pregnancy until after implantation.

### Symptoms and Diagnosis

Failure to menstruate is usually the first symptom of pregnancy, although it is not a conclusive symptom. Absence of menses can be due to a variety of reasons, including age, illness, and emotional upset; menstruation during the first two or three months of pregnancy is possible. Breast changes may announce pregnancy: fullness, tingling, and hypersensitivity may occur even before the first period.

Nausea or queasiness may begin when the first period is overdue. For those who are nauseated, the common pattern is morning queasiness, which disappears gradually in about eight weeks. Recent studies indicate that about one out of two pregnant women has some nausea during pregnancy. The most common pattern is a mild disturbance, consisting of morning queasiness which disappears during the day. Such symptoms are most likely due to biochemical changes rather than to psychological maladjustment [21]. Severe, pathological vomiting, which occurs in a small percentage of women, is more likely to have some psychological origins. Research on nausea of pregnancy has yielded conflicting results, however, and these conclusions are only tentative [21]. Fatigue and the need for extra sleep, frequent during the early months of pregnancy, probably represent a protective mechanism for facilitating physical changes. Frequency of urination is another early symptom.

The physician can diagnose pregnancy through laboratory tests soon after the first missed period. The classic and conclusive signs are hearing the fetal heartbeat, feeling fetal movements, and seeing the fetal skeleton in an X ray—all possible between the sixteenth and twentieth weeks.

### Physical Changes

The whole body is affected by pregnancy. The first stage seems to be one of reorganization. The middle stage is normally one of smooth functioning, when the mother feels and looks blooming, settles into her job of supplying the fetus. Later stages involve more preparations for the birth process.

Foundations for childbearing are laid early in the mother's life, even at her conception, since pregnancy and birth are affected by the whole of her development and health [30]. The woman who begins pregnancy with a normal, fully mature, healthy, well-nourished body, in contrast to one in poor nutritional condition, is less likely to have complications in pregnancy, premature birth, and a baby in poor condition [46]. It is difficult to compensate for inadequacies in certain nutritional elements during pregnancy. For example, if the mother has a good supply of calcium already stored in her bones, she will be more likely to keep herself and her baby well supplied with calcium than will a mother with inadequate stores, even though both have a good diet during pregnancy. Similarly with nitrogen retention and hemoglobin level, a healthy condition in the beginning makes it easier to maintain good levels through pregnancy [57].

Special diets for the bride-to-be are a feature of some non-Western societies— a very functional feature. Even husbands-to-be have been known to receive nutritional supervision. Where a fat girl is beautiful, as in some African cultures, the standard of beauty may contribute to the nutritional preparation of mothers. In America, where slenderness is beautiful and high fashion models are scrawny, teen-age girls often eat inadequate diets which put them into poor condition for motherhood. Recent evidence pushes the important period for nutrition back into childhood, indicating that the adolescent years are only part of the time when a girl's nutrition has implications for her offspring: ". . . the mother's opportunity to grow during her childhood is perhaps the single strongest determining factor for her obstetrical and reproductive performance." [3].

**Reproductive System.** The uterus grows in weight from 2 ounces to over 2 pounds, in capacity from a half teaspoon to 4 or 5 quarts. Muscle fibers grow to 10 times their former length. The preparation of the muscular layer of the uterus is extremely important, since it will open the cervix, help to push the baby out, and form ligatures to cut off the blood vessels supplying the lining of the uterus. The lining provides the spot where the blastocyst implants and takes part in forming the placenta. It provides a mucous plug to close the entrance to the uterus. The cervix, or neck of the uterus, softens as its muscle fibers diminish in number and size, connective tissue grows thinner, and blood supply increases. The vagina increases in length and capacity as its muscle fibers hypertrophy, connective tissue loosens, and more blood is supplied. All perineal structures, the tissues surrounding the birth canal, are loosened, becoming more distensible. Vaginal secretions increase in quantity and in bacteriocidal action.

Hormones from the placenta prepare the breasts for lactation. The breasts increase in size due to an increase in mammary gland tissue and an increased blood supply. The pigmented area darkens. From the fourth month on, colostrum, a clear yellow fluid, is excreted from the nipple.

**Circulatory System.** The blood vessels supplying the uterus elongate, dilate, and become tortuous. The blood volume increases by one fifth, but has a progressively lower specific gravity and lower hemoglobin count. Although this condition is not true anemia, good hygiene is important in order to prevent anemia. Because of the changing specific gravity, the ordinary balance of fluids in the lymph system and certain veins may be upset. Balance is encouraged by breathing movements and muscular activity and upset by inactivity and gravity. When too much blood accu-

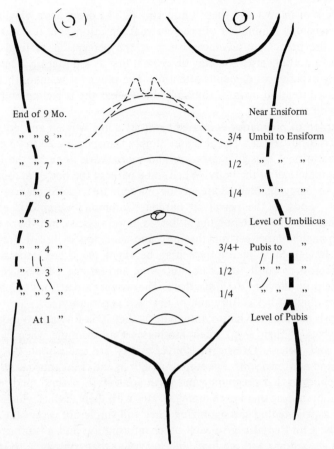

**Figure 1–12.** The height reached by the uterus at each successive month of pregnancy.
Source: Reproduced by permission from J. P. Greenhill. *Obstetrics* (13th ed.) Philadelphia: W. B. Saunders Company, 1965.

mulates in the vessels of the legs and the perineal and anal regions, drainage is improved by resting with the feet up.

**Systemic Functions.** Changes in the hormonal balance occur. Pregnancy affects various glands, including the thyroid, parathyroid, pituitary, and suprarenals. Metabolism is increased and improved after the third month. The capacity to store essential elements increases. The kidneys must work harder to take care of the products of increased metabolism and excretion of the fetus. The pelvis of the kidney dilates to double its former capacity. Sweat and sebaceous glands become more active.

*Psychological Aspects*

Pregnancy is a crisis period. New feelings go along with the pervading physical changes and reorganization. The first pregnancy brings sensations that a woman has not known before. Perhaps there has been something like it, but not exactly in this form. She has been tired before, but not so eager for an afternoon nap. She has experienced an upset stomach, but not the consistent daily cycle of hovering on the brink of nausea and then conquering it. The deep, alive, tingling sensation in the breasts may remind her of premenstrual sensations, but it is more than that. Then, as the pregnancy advances, there is the perception of fetal movements, which is like nothing else. She may describe it first as a fluttering. The spectrum of new bodily experiences demands attention. The pregnant woman, therefore, turns some of her attention inward, thinking about what she is feeling and about what is happening to her body.

The burden of pregnancy is carried easily by some women and not so easily by others. It is a burden in a literal sense. Simply transporting 20 to 25 extra pounds requires additional muscular exertion and more work done by the lungs, heart, kidneys—in fact, all of the body. When some parts of the body are found to be not quite up to carrying their share of the burden, their performance, resulting in discomfort, adds to the perceived burden. Common discomforts of pregnancy include varicose veins (the bulging of loaded blood vessels), heartburn (the product of the stomach's imperfect functioning), and shortness of breath (resulting from squeezed lungs). Such discomforts may be slight or severe, depending on such physical factors as bodily structure, nutrition, and fatigue. Medical care and good hygiene help to alleviate the difficulties. The woman's reactions to pregnancy are also the product of her culture and of her own personality.

Little girls are taught what to anticipate as they look forward to growing up and having babies of their own. Their mothers set an example when carrying baby brothers and sisters. Overheard conversations are influential. So are glances, nuances, and conversations that stop in midair as the child approaches. If mothers tell their children that pregnancy and birth are simple, natural, and beautiful and yet the children hear them exchanging stories with their friends which depict these processes as frightening and agonizing, they will surely not accept the first version confidently. Children also give each other information and misinformation. They may read news items and see films and television that contribute to their attitude toward pregnancy and child birth. The reality of the situation is not lost in those looking forward to pregnancy. They notice how pregnant women are regarded in their culture. The range and variety of attitudes toward pregnancy in the various cultures of the world are quite amazing. There are those who regard pregnancy as a time of illness and an abnormal condition, as do certain peoples in South, Central, and North America; other tribes in South America and in the Pacific regard it as very normal and natural; some African tribes think that pregnancy is the height of happiness. Birth may be considered defiling and unclean, so that a woman is dirty afterwards and must be purified by a religious ritual. Birth may be thought supernatural, a time when a woman hovers between life and death or is especially vulnerable to demons [37].

The wide diversity of cultures in America results in wide variation in attitudes toward pregnancy. While today, in contrast to half a century ago, there is no taboo on pregnant women appearing in public and carrying on their ordinary activities, substantial fears, superstitions, and anxieties linger on because of ignorance. Many a girl in a pretty maternity dress, unembarrassed at her bulge in front, is afraid of the unknown she will have to meet in the labor room. The luckier ones have had a good sex education and preparation for childbirth. An aspect of today's reality is the comparative ease and safety with which human reproduction occurs. Because of medical knowledge and techniques, drugs, nutrition, and health care, girls do not hear very often about women dying in childbirth or of their being almost frightened to death. They do hear, however, of children being born with physical and mental defects. They may be even more aware of these children than their grandmothers were, since there are more of them around. Modern medicine, although doing marvels to correct defects, maintains life in increasing numbers of defective children. Pregnant women commonly fear that their children will not be normal.

The personality of the expectant mother plays a large part in her reactions to pregnancy. If she has coped successfully with the problems of identity and has a marriage in which her sense of intimacy has developed, then, most likely, she welcomes parenthood with a feeling of confidence and happy anticipation. Nobody is unshakable in his self concepts, and nobody has perfect communication and sharing with another. Therefore, even the healthiest pregnant woman will have occasional doubts about herself: her potential as a mother and her ability to cope with the more complicated family which will result from the birth of her baby. The woman who had difficult problems before her pregnancy is likely to find life harder now. The demands upon her would understandably increase fears about sex, modesty, physical adequacy, and family difficulties. Sick role expectations have also been found to be associated with low social and educational status, low levels of aspiration, and disturbances in social relationships [47].

A pregnant mother's emotions are understandably affected by whether she wants the pregnancy or not. There is evidence that many pregnancies are unwelcome. For example, during the year in which abortions were legalized in Japan, it is estimated that about 2 million abortions were performed, approximately the same number as there were live births [22]. In the United States an estimate of between 1 and 2 million illegal abortions to 3½ million births does not accurately reflect the number of unwanted pregnancies but only those unwanted to the point of desperation. Poor Americans, much more than those on higher economic levels, are likely to have more children than they want [44]. These are the women on whom pregnancy would be the greatest burden, physically and emotionally. And of course the unhappy state of the mother during an unwanted pregnancy is only the beginning of an unfortunate and avoidable situation.

**The Expectant Father.** A man can contribute to the well-being of his unborn child through the help and support he gives to his wife. Feeling vulnerable as she does, her confidence in him as provider and protector is constructive in making her relaxed and secure. She appreciates reassurance that she is still attractive in spite of her increasing girth and decreasing agility. She may want some sympathy for the aches, pains, annoyances, and limitations on activity. If she has fears about the pain of delivery and the well-being of the baby or fears about her competence as a mother, she may seek reassurance from her husband. A mature man, who has coped successfully with his own personality growth, can give his pregnant wife a great deal of comfort through his understanding, sympathy, and confidence. Many men, even while trying to be supportive, find the role of expectant father a very difficult one to play.

With a first pregnancy, the natural turning inward of the woman's attention may constitute the first time in the marriage when the husband feels displaced in her thoughts. He may realize that the worst is yet to come, when the infant will require a great deal of the time and attention which used to belong to him. He may feel deprived sexually, since the doctor may limit intercourse. The father will probably feel added financial responsibility, since a new baby costs something even before birth and then costs more and more as the years go by. New, larger, costlier living quarters may be indicated. The thoughts of college expenses may cross his mind. If the pregnancy is an unwanted one, especially if it threatens the mother's health and the family's solvency, then the expectant father is likely to feel strong guilt.

The husband may find himself being the main, or even only, emotional support of his pregnant wife. When a young American couple move to another part of the country, leaving family and friends behind, they are dependent, at least for a while, on the resources they have as a pair. In contrast, an extended family offers vast aid and support to a pregnant woman. If not already living with the older generation, the young woman may go home to her mother's house, where she is surrounded with affectionate care until after her baby is born and adjusted to life. Or her mother may come to her, taking authoritative command of what is considered woman's affairs, thus relieving the young father of much of the burden he would have to carry in a nuclear family consisting of husband, wife, and child.

In order to fill in some of the emotional and technical gaps created by the change from extended to nuclear family life, many communities offer education for childbirth. Pregnant mothers, with the permission of their doctors, learn about the changes taking place within themselves, how delivery takes place, how to care for themselves and how to care for their babies. Fathers go to classes that focus on what they want to know, what is happening to mother and baby, their own hereditary contribution, what they can do psychologically, and something about infant care and development. Through discussions, both parents clarify their own feelings and share with other expectant parents. Thus they derive much of the security offered in other cultures by experienced family members, while they enjoy the added advantage of applying knowledge from modern research. The International Childbirth Education Association is a federation of groups and individuals interested in family-centered maternity and infant care. This association holds conferences and sponsors programs and provides educational materials on preparation for childbirth and breast feeding and promotes medical and hospital practices which support sound parent–child and husband–wife relationships. (The address of the association is 1840 South Elena, Suite 205, Redondo Beach, California 90277.)

**When There Is No Father.** With increasing numbers of out-of-wedlock pregnancies occurring in the United States, it is appropriate to wonder how a pregnant woman manages without a partner's help and love. Much depends on the woman's motivation for becoming pregnant and upon her social group's evaluation of illegitimate pregnancies. When the pregnancy represents rebellion against parents and/or society, then obviously the young woman is immature and in serious emotional conflict. When, on the other hand, an unmarried girl is pregnant in a social setting where illegitimate pregnancies are frequent and easily accepted, then she may have little or no psychological trauma. Her own mother may take over much responsibility, giving her the protection and security that a married woman would get from her husband. Out-of-wedlock pregnancy usually causes shame and anxiety to middle-class Americans, while some women in subcultures of poverty may accept it more casually [43]. Statistics concerning illegitimate pregnancies are hard to interpret because of the socioeconomic factors involved. However, studies of such pregnancies do show the following: they occur at all social levels, but in greater numbers at lower levels; the women tend to be young, many of them under 20; mothers are more likely to work late in pregnancy, to receive little or no prenatal

Halvar Loken

care, and to live in poor housing; death rates for mothers and babies are higher than in legitimate pregnancies; low birth weights and higher prematurity rates are more frequent [30].

## Prenatal Influence

The question of whether and how a woman can influence her unborn baby is one which has intrigued people since the dawn of history. Some societies have maintained that specific thoughts and experiences could mark the baby in specific ways, such as the notion that if a rabbit ran across the pregnant woman's path, she would bear a baby with a harelip, or if she squashed a strawberry, her baby would have a red birthmark. Less specific, but just as unfounded, is the notion that by listening to good music and viewing great paintings, a woman could confer talent upon the child within her. As scientific knowledge about pregnancy and birth became widespread, more and more people realized that the baby's blood system was separate from the mother's, exchanging nutrients and products of excretion through membranes, but not exchanging blood. As the old superstitions, such as those of the harelip and strawberry mark, were swept away, many people got the idea that nutrition was the *only* prenatal influence. It is now known that chronic or severe stress of the mother constitutes danger to the baby and that there are indeed additional ways in which an unborn baby can be affected through its mother.

### Nutrition

The woman who starts her pregnancy in good nutritional condition is fortunate, since she can thus provide the optimal environment for her baby right from the beginning. A nutritional defect is difficult to correct when the demands upon the body are increased by pregnancy. The very fact of being well nourished shows that the woman has established a pattern of eating an adequate selection of foods in amounts suited to her. She will not have to change her ways of eating other than to increase the amounts slightly as pregnancy advances.

While nearly all people in all parts of the world believe that diet during pregnancy is important, the nutritional adaptations prescibed for pregnant women are not always helpful. Meat and fish are often forbidden, as in the tribe who prohibited owl monkey meat for fear that that it would influence the baby to stay awake at night.

**Gross Results of Malnutritrition.** Until recently, adequacy of prenatal nutrition was estimated largely in rather gross terms, such as number of miscarriages and stillbirths, birth weight, and abnormalities of labor. These indices are still valuable in pointing up the importance of a good diet in pregnancy, but now there are additional pieces of evidence for the vital role of prenatal nutrition. One gross statistic, which is nevertheless impressive, comes from a study on infant mortality rates in 17 African tribes. Among those tribes who had adequate diets or who supplemented inadequate diets sufficiently during pregnancy, the infant mortality rate was 96.8 per thousand births; in tribes with inadequate diets and no supplementation, the rate was 181.1 deaths per thousand births [24]. Wars and other disasters have provided famine conditions under which the effects of serious nutritional deficiencies can be studied. Toward the end of World War II and immediately afterward, the birth weight of babies was reduced in parts of Holland, Germany, and Russia [12, 53]. The siege of Leningrad resulted in severe food restrictions for pregnant mothers who were already malnourished. In 1942 the stillbirth rate doubled, and premature births increased by 41 percent [57]. The effects of improving an inadequate diet were demonstrated by Canadian physicians who supplemented the diets of half of a group of nutritionally deficient pregnant women [16]. The experimental group of mothers (those with improved diets) had fewer cases of anemia, toxemia, miscarriages, and premature births. Their average length of labor was shorter. Their babies were in better condition at birth and were healthier infants than those of the control group. Another way of focusing on the problem of poor prenatal nutrition was to examine the histories of stillborn infants, infants who died in the first few days of life, prematures, and babies with congenital defects [6]. Almost all of the mothers of these infants had had very poor diets during pregnancy.

**Some Specific Results of Malnutrition.** Since nutrition deprivation studies cannot be done on human beings because of moral considerations, researchers use animals to study the effects of prenatal starvation and malnutrition. While results cannot be applied directly to human beings, they give insight into what happens when the developing baby does not have enough body-building materials. In the early stages of cleavage, when the fertilized ovum is first dividing, the ovum's use of oxygen is significantly retarded in animals on a low protein diet [41]. Baby rats whose mothers were underfed while pregnant did not show marked size reduction at birth, but their ultimate growth potential was reduced, they were unable to utilize food efficiently, and they showed abnormalities and delays in behavior and motor development [52]. When pregnant rats were fed low protein diets during the latter half of pregnancy, their offspring were slow learners [7].

**Feeding the Pregnant Woman.** Pregnant American women are often placed in conflict over what they should eat [37]. It is common medical practice to restrict weight gain. Doctors often give out a diet sheet prescribing a diet of good quality while restricting calories. The rationale for limiting weight gain is usually threefold: the mother will have less fat to lose after delivery and hence will look better;

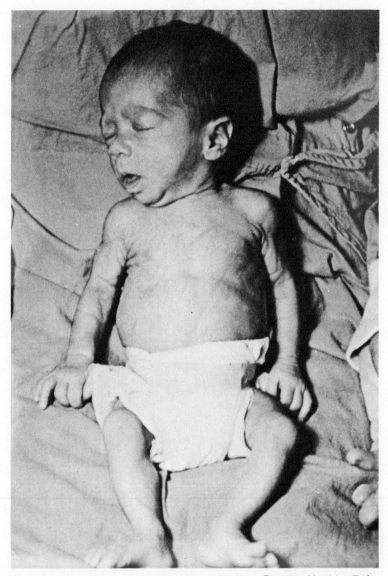

Courtesy *Nutrition Today*

**Figure 1–13.** Typical underweight newborn baby.
From R. E. Shank, "A Chink in Our Armor," *Nutrition Today*, 1970, **5**:2, p. 2. Copyright © 1970, Enloe, Stalvey and Associates.

chances of toxemia will be decreased; the baby will take what he needs, anyway. Sometimes a fourth is added: the baby will be smaller at birth and hence easier to deliver. A recent report of the Food and Nutrition Board of the National Research Council calls for important changes in the nutritional management of pregnancy [51]. The average optimal gain in pregnancy is 24 pounds, and there is no scientific reason for limiting it to lesser amounts. When well-fed, younger women will tend to gain a little more, thin women more, fat women less, and women having their first babies more. Pregnancy is not a time for fat women to try to reduce. Severe

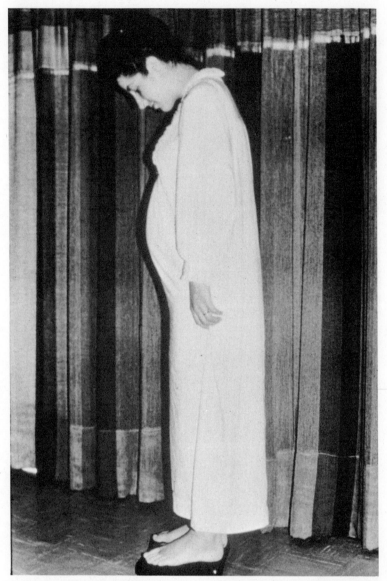

Halvar Loken

restriction of calories is potentially harmful to both mother and baby. The mother should eat what she wants, as long as her diet is balanced. There is no evidence that weight gain due to accumulation of fat is associated with toxemia. The committee also recommends supplements of iron and folic acid and cautions against routine restriction of salt. Normal weight gain and the distribution of the weight are shown in Figures 1–14a and 1–14b.

The notion that the baby will somehow draw what he needs out of his mother's body is an old wives' tale. Animal experiments show that calorie and protein restrictions in the mother's diet drastically affect litter size, survival, birth weight, growth patterns, and behavior of offspring [51]. Human studies have shown a strong association between weight gain of mother and birth weight of baby. Birth weight

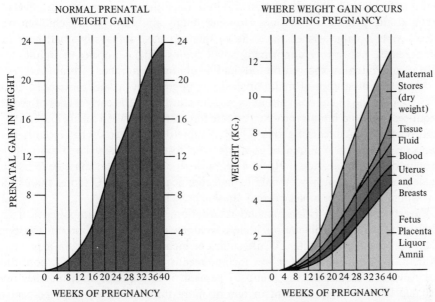

NORMAL PRENATAL
WEIGHT GAIN

WHERE WEIGHT GAIN OCCURS
DURING PREGNANCY

**Figure 1–14.** Normal prenatal weight gain and where weight gain occurs during pregnancy.

SOURCE: Reprinted by permission from R. E. Shank, "A Chink in Our Armor," *Nutrition Today*, 1970, **5**:2, p. 6. Copyright © 1970, Enloe, Stalvey and Associates.

of baby is linked to survival, normalcy, and health of the infant. A specific example of the baby's inability to get what he needs if the mother does not supply enough is that of 8-month-old babies whose mothers had had low iodine levels in their blood during pregnancies which were otherwise normal [27]. When compared with babies of mothers who had had normal iodine levels, the experimental group scored significantly lower on motor and mental tests and showed higher incidences of cerebral palsy, mental deficiency, visual and hearing loss and other impairments. A more drastic illustration of the importance of adequate *intake* is the case of pregnant rats that were deprived of zinc. Ninety percent of their babies had malformation, including cleft lip, missing limbs, brain anomalies, and curved spines [29]. Analyses of the mothers' bodies showed no losses of zinc from their bones and livers. The zinc was actually in the mothers' bodies, but the fetuses could not withdraw it. Apparently they had to get their supply from zinc in the current diet, not out of the mothers' reserves.

**Malnutrition and Mental Retardation.** A growing body of evidence links prenatal malnutrition to mental retardation in children. Brain growth is very rapid during the prenatal period for both animals and humans. Eighty percent of adult brain size is reached at 4 weeks by the rat, 8 to 10 weeks by pigs, and 3 years by human children [50]. When a human baby is born, his brain is gaining weight at the rate of 1 to 2 milligrams each minute. Because of such a rapid growth rate, the brain is especially sensitive to nutritional deprivation when the organism is very young. (The principle of critical periods, described in Chapter 17, is illustrated here.) Brain growth is thought to begin with increasing the number of cells (by cell division) and then to continue with increases in number of cells and size of cells, ending with a period of increase in size of cells [65]. Pregnant rats who were fed a low protein diet produced babies whose brains were different in weight, protein content, and number of cells [69]. In human children it is difficult to separate the effects of prenatal and postnatal nutrition. However, many studies of young children who were severely malnourished have shown them to have unusually small head circumferences, suggesting abnormally small brains [50]. Autopsies of infants who died of malnutrition showed that all had a subnormal number of brain cells [39].

A number of studies of malnourished young children in underdeveloped countries support the likelihood that malnourishment during the early stages of growth produces impaired intelligence, inadequate integration between seeing and hearing, apathy, and limited learning ability [10]. A more definitive study has recently been done on American children of mothers who lost abnormally large amounts of protein during pregnancy [39]. At 4 years these children, who must have had an inadequate protein supply prenatally, had significantly lower IQ scores than children whose mothers retained normal amounts of protein.

**Poverty and Malnutrition.** Mental retardation, apathy, and impaired learning ability are serious problems in underdeveloped countries and among the poor people in the United States. While sufficient income does not assure a pregnant woman of an adequate diet, a low income means virtual certainty of a poor diet. An American dietary survey found 37 percent of households with incomes over $10,000 to have diets deficient in one or more nutrients. Sixty-three percent of households with incomes under $3000 had deficient diets. Half of all the families surveyed had diets that did not meet all nutritional requirements. The nutrients most often lacking were calcium, vitamin A, and ascorbic acid [60]. Customs and knowledge are also important. In India, where the average income is $86 a year, and in much of Asia, for example, the wife eats after her husband and children have eaten. What is more, it is not easy to get enough protein from a vegetarian diet, and most Indians are vegetarians. In parts of Nigeria, pregnant women may not eat vegetables or fruits. After delivery, they are not supposed to eat soup containing meat or fish [8].

**Importance of Nutrition Education.** Even when enough good food is available, most women need education and guidance in planning their diets. Probably the best place to begin is in nutrition education for all high school girls. More specific guidance during pregnancy is offered by classes for mothers, often taught as part of a comprehensive maternal care program in a hospital or clinic, or by public health nurses in the community. Countries with strong maternal and child health programs, such as New Zealand and Sweden, teach and help a large proportion of pregnant women. Their infant and maternal mortality statistics reflect the value of such programs. (See Figures 1–15a and 1–15b.)

Requirements vary from one woman to another, and there are a variety of ways in which requirements can be met. When deficiencies occur, they can harm either mother or baby but they are likely to harm both. Dietary deficiencies can contribute to premature and otherwise abnormal births, stillbirth, death within the first few days of life, congenital defects, small size, and illnesses during infancy. The importance of adequate, individualized prenatal care is emphasized by the role of nutrition in assuring the health and safety of mother and baby.

*Sensory Stimuli*

The fetus responds to a wide variety of tones and to loud and sudden noises with increased motor activity and heart rate. Although this behavior has been

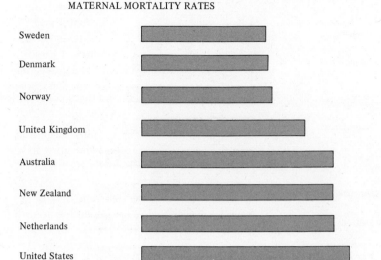

MATERNAL MORTALITY RATES

NUMBER OF DEATHS (PER 100,000 LIVE BIRTHS)

**Figure 1–15a.** Maternal mortality in prosperous countries.

Source: Data from *Statistical Bulletin*, Metropolitan Life Insurance Company, 1968, **49**, p. 4. Also from 1969 World Population Data Sheet, *Obstetrical and Gynecological News*, 1969, **4**:10, p. 28.

studied in detail [55], it is not known whether there are any lasting effects from stimulating the unborn baby in this way. Probably every baby receives some loud and sudden stimuli before birth—when his mother drops a pot in the kitchen, at a concert, in heavy traffic, when a siren blows, and so on. Mothers report that their fetuses do react to such noises by moving. The baby can be conditioned during the last two months of pregnancy to give a startle response. In one study, the primary stimulus, a loud noise, was paired with a vibrotactile stimulus (an electric doorbell with the gong removed). The latter called forth no fetal response when originally applied to the mother's abdomen, but after 15 or 20 trials with the loud noise, the vibrotactile stimulus alone elicited a startle response [56].

The baby's eyes open in utero. The mother's internal organs make noises that in all likelihood her baby can hear. Her breathing is rhythmic, too, with some tactile and kinesthetic stimulation along with auditory. An interesting suggestion is that "if she should drink a glass of champagne or a bottle of beer, the sounds, to her unborn baby, would be something akin to rockets being shot off all around" [35]. The baby surely hears his mother talking, coughing, sneezing, and swallowing. Her heartbeat is a rhythmic sound that may take on important significance at this time, when the infant receives steady auditory stimulation from it over a long period.

The following chapter includes a description of experiments with babies and toddlers, using a heartbeat sound. Because the sound was found soothing to infants and children, it seems worthwhile to consider what meaning it may have prenatally. The heartbeat sound has the criteria of an imprinting stimulus being intermittent and repetitious and occurring early in the life of the organism, before it experiences fear [48]. Later, when the organism is exposed to fear, it is reassured by the stimulus

INFANT MORTALITY RATES (BIRTH – 1 YEAR)

NUMBER OF DEATHS (PER 1,000 LIVE BIRTHS)

**Figure 1–15b.** Infant mortality in prosperous countries.
SOURCE: As in 1–15a.

to which it has been imprinted. Thus it seems quite possible that the unborn baby interacts with his environment in such a way that the rhythms of sounds and pressures prepare him for coping with some of the difficulties he will encounter after he is born. Seeking to comfort his distress and express their love, his parents and other people will hold him in their arms and walk with him or rock and jiggle him. The resulting sounds and pressures will reassure him, perhaps because he was imprinted prenatally to such stimuli.

*Maternal Emotions*

Fetal behavior has been studied at the Fels Institute for several decades. Emotional disturbances in the mother have been shown to be associated with high activity in the fetus [54]. Infants of mothers who had suffered emotional upsets during pregnancy were likely to show frequent irritability, excessive crying, and gastrointestinal disturbances, such as regurgitation, dyspepsia, and diarrhea. These difficulties are thought to be of autonomic origin and to be caused by intra-uterine conditions.

Severe stress of the pregnant mother is associated with complications of pregnancy and with poor condition and abnormality of the baby. When a stress is measured by objective situations, such as marriage problems, injury, death or illness of the husband or a child, severe housing problems, or economic difficulties, some studies have shown an association between maternal shock and defects in babies [21]. Stress may be more or less harmful at different stages occurring between fertilization and implantation and may result in death of the fertilized ovum [45].

Further evidence of the significance of maternal emotional upset comes from a study of factors connected with birth difficulties and infant abnormalities. A highly anxious group of mothers was found to experience more complications of delivery and abnormalities in their babies [11]. A state of general moodiness, depression, and overdependency in pregnant mothers was found to be associated with physical complications of childbirth [26]. Another group of mothers who indicated negative attitudes on a questionnaire produced babies whose behavior was deviant during a rating period of the first five days of life, in terms of amount of crying, sleeping, bowel movements, feeding, and irritability [19]. The connection between maternal emotions and fetal upset is made through several steps, but it can be explained in physical terms [38].

The nervous and endocrine systems communicate through the blood. An experience of the mother is registered in her cerebral cortex from which impulses pass to the thalamus, hypothalamus, and into the autonomic nervous system. The autonomic system acts on the endocrines, which pour their products into the blood. The blood takes the products of the endocrines to the placenta, through which some of them pass to the fetal blood and to the nervous system of the fetus.

Another explanation is suggested by Salk's [48] explorations with a gallop heartbeat rhythm and a very fast heartbeat. The newborn infants who had quieted to the sound of a normal heartbeat showed an immediate increase in crying and disturbance to these unusual heartbeats and also to a hissing sound which the machine accidentally developed. A frightened or disturbed pregnant mother could be expected to show variations from the normal pattern of heartbeat and breathing. Her baby then might be disturbed by the resulting tactile, auditory, and kinesthetic stimuli. Either by themselves, or added to the effects of the endocrines in the blood, these stimuli could be a significant prenatal influence. Proof of their influence awaits further research.

If an unborn baby can suffer from his mother's extreme emotional upset, then could the opposite be true? What happens to the fetus whose mother has an unusually happy, safe, secure time? At birth, is he different from babies whose mothers have had an average or disturbed pregnancy? Definitive answers to these questions are not available. However, the multiplicity of studies on harmful influences makes one very much aware of what can go wrong prenatally. Perhaps a happy, relaxed pregnancy contributes physical and mental health to the baby. There is nothing to lose and possibly much to gain when the father and other family members are understanding, considerate, and affectionate with the expectant mother, not only for her sake, but also for the baby's. This is not to say that the pregnant mother cannot safely deal with everyday problems and work, but only that she benefits from having the general tone of her life a positive one.

### Physical and Chemical Agents

Heavy labor during pregnancy constitutes a stress on the fetus as well as on the mother. Extreme summer heat is another kind of stress [40]. Massive X-ray doses are lethal or seriously damaging to the unborn child. After World War II, effects of atom bomb radiation on children who had been in utero at the time included increased anomalies and morbidity [42, 67].

Many drugs taken by the pregnant mother can affect the baby, some apparently temporarily and some drastically and permanently. Quinine can cause deafness. At least five studies show that smoking during pregnancy increases the risk of producing a premature baby or a baby of low birth weight [40]. There is some evidence that the lower the socioeconomic status, the greater the effect of smoking during pregnancy. A possible explanation is that the very poor mothers lower their protein intake significantly when they smoke, whereas protein intake is not much affected by smoking in the upper economic brackets. Heavy doses of certain barbiturates produce asphyxiation and brain damage. The tranquilizer thalidomide caused thousands of tragic births in Germany, England, and Canada, where its prenatal use produced babies lacking limbs or with limbs in early stages of embryonic development. When heroin-addicted mothers were admitted to a hospital for childbirth, the heroin was withdrawn from them. Their babies were born with withdrawal symptoms, from which they recovered in two or three days. Their sleep patterns were then studied, revealing sleep that differed significantly from normal newborn sleep patterns. The heroin-affected babies had more rapid eye movements, greater variability in heart rates, and no truly quiet sleep, indicating that their central nervous systems had been affected [49].

Since extremely noxious and dangerous stimuli and agents cannot be used experimentally on human beings, a great deal of research is being carried on with animals to find out exactly how radiation and drugs affect them. It has been shown that the stage at which the agents are administered is important in determining the extent of injury and that within certain ranges of stimuli, the stage is more important than the strength [63]. These findings illustrate the growth principle of *critical periods*, described in Chapter 17.

A positive result from abdominal decompression has been reported [13]. Developed by a South African physician, the technique requires an airtight suit or bubble which is placed on the pregnant mother's abdomen. The air pressure is lowered, allowing the fetus to rise in the body cavity. This technique has been used during the last three months of pregnancy. The babies whose mothers have had this treatment have had Gesell developmental quotients that were significantly higher than average. The babies who had the greater number of prenatal decompression treatments had the higher quotients. The inventor of the technique suggests that babies do not get enough oxygen for optimal development during the last stages of prenatal life and that the decompression improves the oxygen supply.

### Infections and Blood Incompatibility

German measles, or rubella, which is preventable by immunization, is a serious threat to the baby in utero. A review of studies of rubella in the Baltimore–

Washington area shows that over 50 percent of the women who contracted the disease during the first three months of pregnancy had either miscarriages, still-births, or handicapped infants [25]. The handicaps included profound hearing loss, severe mental retardation, cataracts, heart defects, low birth weight, growth failure, and abnormalities of blood, bones, and other organs. In children whose mothers had rubella during the second and third three months, handicaps were less severe and included communications problems, hearing defects, mild mental retardation, and small body size [25]. A program of immunizing all children can wipe out rubella [25]. Immunization against rubella is now possible, but it must be done at least three months *before* the beginning of pregnancy. In the meantime, abortion is an answer for some of the pregnant women who contract rubella. Some other diseases dangerous to the fetus are syphilis, smallpox, chicken pox, measles, mumps, scarlet fever, tuberculosis, and malarial parasites.

About 1 pregnancy in 200 results in some disturbance from incompatibility between the blood of the mother and baby. The Rh factor is a substance that occurs in the red blood cells of about 85 percent of white people, 93 percent of blacks, and 99 percent of Mongolian peoples. The remaining minorities are Rh negative [2]. When the mother's blood is Rh negative and the fetus' blood is Rh positive, there is one chance in ten that the infant will have some of his red blood cells destroyed. The way it happens is that the fetus produces antigens which go through the placenta into the mother's blood. Her blood then makes antibodies which go back through the placenta to the baby's blood stream. Results include miscarriage, stillbirth, death after birth, brain damage, jaundice, and anemia. Adequate prenatal care requires a blood test that will detect negative Rh. The physician discovering it would then determine the husband's blood type and learn the chances of incompatibility arising between fetus and mother. Taking into account the finding that the danger from Rh factors increases with each baby after the first, he would be ready to cope with symptoms likely to arise. Much can be done to alleviate the condition immediately after birth or even before birth. Harm to future babies can be prevented immediately after the birth of an Rh positive baby to an Rh negative mother. She can be given medication that will prevent damage to subsequent babies through blood incompatibility.

### Age and Parity of the Mother

The only time a woman of 35 is considered elderly is when she is having her first baby. In this case, she is called, by the medical profession an "elderly primipara," a logical term in light of the fact that the childbearing period is more than two-thirds over. At age 35 and older, the average length of labor is increased beyond the overall average by an hour and a half, and the risk to mother and baby is increased slightly. Maternal mortality, by age and race, is shown in Figure 1–16. Note that the hazards of age are enormously increased if the woman is black, but only slightly increased if she is white. These figures reflect the depressed economic conditions under which many blacks live.

When risk to the baby is estimated, it makes a difference which portion of the first year of life is considered. Although death rates are stated in terms of the mother's age and parity (number of pregnancies she has had), it must be remembered that both age and parity have different significance in different sociocultural settings. Stillbirths rise with increasing age and fall with parity up to the fourth

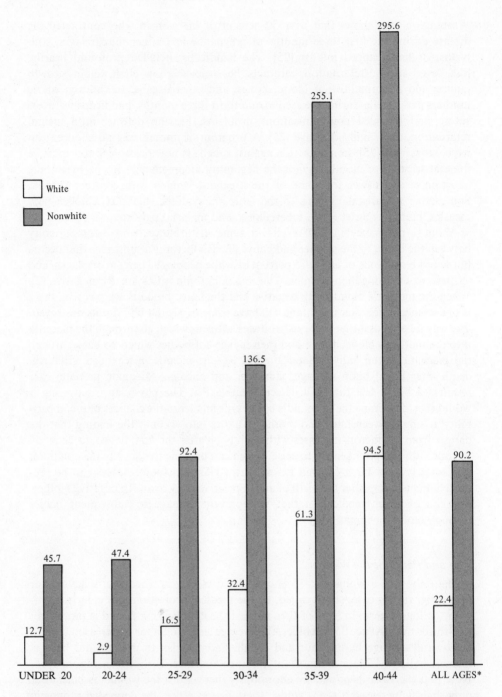

White

Nonwhite

295.6

255.1

136.5

94.5

92.4

90.2

61.3

47.4

45.7

32.4

22.4

16.5

12.7

2.9

UNDER 20    20-24    25-29    30-34    35-39    40-44    ALL AGES*

*Including ages 45 and over.

**Figure 1–16.** Number of maternal deaths for each 100,000 live births, given for nonwhite and white women (United States 1963–65), by age.

Source: Data from *Statistical Bulletin*, Metropolitan Life Insurance Co., December, 1968, p. 2.

pregnancy. The lowest rates are in the 20- to 24-year-age group and the highest in mothers 35 and over. Death within the first month occurs most often with high parity in the youngest age group and next often to mothers of high parity in the oldest age group. The death rate between 1 month and 11 months rises with increasing parity and falls with increasing age. Prematurity rates are highest in 15- to 19-year-old mothers, with the exception of first babies born to mothers over 35, who have the highest prematurity rate of all [30]. Older mothers are also more likely to produce mongoloid children. Before age 30, the risk of having a mongoloid baby is 1 in 1000, while at age 40 it is 1 in 100, and at age 45, 1 in 45 [15]. When defects of all kinds are counted, very young mothers and older mothers produce more impaired infants than do mothers in the ages in between [40].

From all these findings there follows a generalization that the first birth carries an extra risk and that aging and repeated births also add risk. Frequently repeated births carry a risk to the normalcy of the child, as well as to his life. Babies born within one year of a previous gestation were matched with controls born two to five years after the previous gestation. Matching was done for sex, race, hospital of birth, and socioeconomic status [28]. Their gestation ages were equal, but the babies produced in rapid succession averaged significantly smaller birth weights, lower scores on the Bayley tests at 8 months, and lower Stanford–Binet IQs at 4 years. At 1 year of age, the average baby in the experimental group had a smaller head and delayed motor development. A survey of development of 16,000 7-year-old children in Scotland leads the investigator to conclude: "today, in Aberdeen at least, it is clear that the woman who has five or more children—no matter what class she belongs to officially—is likely to have children with IQ scores well below average" [1].

## Teen-Age Mothers

### Adolescent Mothers, A Special Problem

Of all the prosperous countries in the world, the United States has the largest number of adolescent mothers. They account at least in part for our poor showing in regard to infant mortality rates. Before completing their own growth, 197,372 girls produced babies during a recent 12-month period. Among them, 29,000 mothers were 15 years old or under. The baby's growth needs are thus superimposed upon the mother's growth needs. The impact of pregnancy upon the body of a growing mother has not been determined, but the impact on her baby is well known, as has been indicated above.

### Physical Adequacy of the Mother

Studies from several different countries have shown a relationship between height of mother and reproductive performance. Mothers judged poor in physique tended to be short and to have flattening of the pelvic brim. Short mothers are more likely to have complications of pregnancy and delivery, and to produce babies with lower birth weights, greater prematurity, more birth trauma, and more stillbirths. The relationship between stature of mother and physical well-being of baby is not thought to be a direct one, but, rather, both conditions are results of a socioeconomic environment. A poor environment, supplying inadequate food, housing, clothing, sanitation, and education, will stunt the physical and mental growth of children living in it. Short stature is thus associated with low education, early marriage, premarital pregnancy, premature delivery, longer labor, absence of family planning, frequent pregnancies, poor diet, poor housing, and poor use of information, health services, and social services [30].

## The Birth Process

The developments described thus far occur in the course of about nine months. The obstetrician names the delivery date on the pregnant woman's first visit, by adding 280 days to the first day of her last menstrual period. He will warn her, though, that this date is an approximation. Only 4 percent of women deliver on the 280th day; 46 percent deliver within a week of that date; and 74 percent within two weeks of it. Being born and giving birth are physical crises for the two most concerned. The crises are emotional, also, for the two and their family. Thus birth must be understood in various contexts.

### The Processes and Stages of Labor

Labor is the work that the mother does in giving birth. Three distinct stages can be described. *The first stage*, requiring the major portion of the duration of labor, is the opening of the cervix or neck of the uterus. It begins with rhythmic uterine contractions, usually felt as pains. The two types of muscular forces working to enlarge the cervical openings are indicated in Figure 1–17. The uterus resembles a pear-shaped balloon whose walls are made of very strong muscle fibers. The fibers contract, exerting about 30 pounds of pressure on the fluids surrounding the baby. The membranes enclosing the fluids press on the tiny opening in the lower end of the uterus. After the membranes break (the mother cannot feel this), the baby presses on the opening. At the same time another set of muscle fibers, which surround the tiny opening, are relaxing to allow the opening to enlarge. As these muscular processes continue, the tissues of the cervix are pulled back into the general roundish shape of the uterus. When the cervix is completely dilated, the diameter of the opening is about 4 inches.

The muscular processes of the first stage of labor are involuntary. The only way in which a woman can influence them is through relaxation. Although it is still a debatable subject, it is commonly believed that general bodily relaxation, due to absence of fear, plus confidence, hastens relaxation of the muscle fibers surrounding the cervix; fear and tension are thought to increase their resistance to stretching and to result in pain. One of the purposes of education for childbirth is to induce this kind of relaxation.

*The second stage* lasts from the time that the cervix is completely open until the baby emerges from his mother. For a first baby this stage requires an hour and a half on the average; for the second, half as long. The uterus continues to push the baby out. The mother adds a bearing-down action to it, pushing with her diaphragm, but involving her whole body. (See Figure 1–18.) Although she bears down spontaneously, without teaching or conscious thought, a great deal of this activity can be placed under conscious control. Education for childbirth includes teaching the mother to breathe, relax, and bear down in a manner calculated to facilitate the natural labor processes. The confidence factor is just as important in the second stage as in the first in promoting control and either eliminating pain,

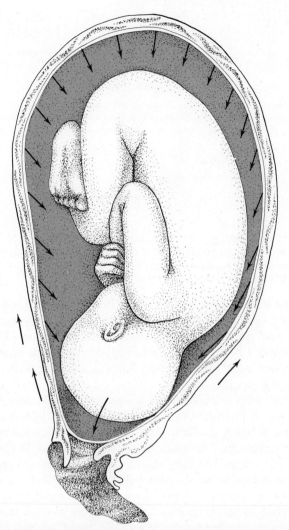

**Figure 1–17.** The baby during the first stages of labor. Uterine contractions push him downward while the muscle fibers surrounding the opening are pulled upward by the upper segment of the uterus, thus enlarging the opening.

SOURCE: Reproduced by permission from J. P. Greenhill, *Obstetrics*, 13th edition. Philadelphia: W. B. Saunders Company, 1965.

reducing it, or making it more bearable. The *third stage* is the expelling of the placenta and membranes. It lasts only a few minutes.

When women discuss the length of labor with each other, they often mark its beginning with the trip to the hospital. Or the beginning may be considered the time when labor contractions become severe. To be accurate, labor length has to be measured from the time of the first contraction to the moment when the placenta and membranes are completely expelled. Therefore, the average figures for length of labor may look formidably long to the woman who takes her neighbor's experience as the norm.

An overall average for length of labor is about 14 hours, divided among the three stages about like this: first stage 12½ hours; second stage 80 minutes; third stage

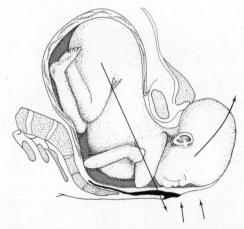

**Figure 1–18.** The baby during the second stage of labor. The mother's bearing-down action, pushing with her diaphragm, adds to the uterine forces pushing the baby out.
SOURCE: Reproduced by permission from J. B. DeLee and J. P. Greenhill, *Principles and Practices of Obstetrics*. Philadelphia: W. B. Saunders Company, 1947.

10 minutes. The second stage requires about 20 contractions for a first baby and 10 or less for subsequent babies. For a first baby, half of the women in a study of nearly 15,000 cases took less than 11 hours; half took more. The commonest length of labor was 7 hours. Women who had already had at least one baby had shorter labors; half under approximately 6 hours, half over, with the commonest length of labor 4 hours [15].

When a normal birth is impossible or dangerous, the baby may be delivered by Caesarian section, a procedure of cutting the mother's abdomen and uterus to remove the baby and then, of course, the placenta. Although this surgical procedure used to be very dangerous, it now carries relatively slight risk. A Caesarian section is much safer for mother and baby than a difficult forceps delivery or a breech birth through a narrowed pelvis. Although there is no limit to the number of Caesarian births one patient can have, each repetition means that the scar in the uterus is stretched by the pregnancy and hence runs a small risk of rupturing. Many physicians recommend sterilizing with the third Caesarian operation.

### Emotional Aspects

The culture in which she has grown up will set the broad outlines of a woman's attitude toward labor. The Judeo-Christian tradition, for example, builds up considerable expectation of pain and tears. According to Mead [59, p. 28],

> in some African tribes, women are expected to shriek, scream, writhe and go through the most terrific expressions of agony, and all the little girl children are brought along to watch, so they will know how to have a baby. In other societies, women are enjoined to the greatest stoicism, and to utter a single cry would be to proclaim yourself not a woman, and again the little girls are brought along to see that they behave like this.

Education and specific experiences are important in setting the mother's expectations of pain and danger and her confidence in her own abilities. The ways in which she handles the fear and pain involved will depend not only on herself, however, but on the support and help she receives during labor. Her husband, the hospital staff and, most of all, the doctor have important emotional functions. Directly connected with the mother's fear or confidence, tension or relaxation, pain or easiness, is the amount and type of anesthetic she will receive. A woman who feels confident and in command of herself and who also feels trust in the help she is receiving will most likely need a minimum of drugs. The terrified patient will seek a maximum, including amnesiacs. (Abnormal physical conditions may require maximum use of drugs too.)

A famous obstetrical event in the animal kingdom pointed up the life-and-death aspects of emotions during labor. A live baby elephant was delivered successfully at the Portland (Oregon) Zoo, after months of anxious waiting and speculation as how to avoid the fiascoes of past elephant reproduction in captivity. One of the innovations which may have spelled success was the presence of several female elephants in the labor pen. These "aunties" were warmly and actively concerned with the mother, even massaging her with their trunks. In contrast to the frantic concern of isolated elephants-in-labor, this mother conducted herself with calm efficiency.

A growing use of psychological means of relieving and controlling pain in labor is probably the result of two trends. First is an increased interest in having childbirth a positive, rewarding experience for the mother and father instead of a trial to be endured. Second is a growing body of evidence that drugs carry more risk to babies than was previously thought to be true. Anesthesia and analgesia during labor and delivery have been shown to have a depressing effect on sensorimotor functioning for at least the first four weeks [4]. Amount of medication was related to muscular, visual, and neural development and to ability to inhibit response to an auditory stimulus. Analgesics have also been found to depress sucking [32] and visual attention [58]. Refined methods of testing for central nervous damage and records kept over long periods of time are yielding indications that analgesics and anesthetics considered normal in America may cause some long-term neurological impairment [9, 33].

There are two well-known methods of preparation for childbirth which have brought pain relief, confidence, and often joy to many women in childbirth. Both methods include teaching of the processes of labor, exercises, and breathing. Neither excludes anesthetics, but uses them moderately when patient and doctor consider them indicated. The Read method, originated by an English obstetrician, stresses emotional education and relief of fear through relaxation and knowledge. The LaMaze (pronounced LaMahz) method, contributed by a French obstetrician, uses conditioning to eliminate or diminish pain. LaMaze courses are available in many if not most parts of the United States and can be located through the International Childbirth Association. Obviously, the approval and cooperation of the physician in charge is a requirement for using any method of education for childbirth. Some skilled and sensitive obstetricians have their own successful ways of giving psychological support and may feel that their patients do not need courses. Many others see childbirth education as a time-consuming operation which can be successfully delegated to specialists trained for that purpose.

*The Baby during Labor*

Being born is a difficult and risky experience that has claimed the attention of philosophers and psychiatrists, as well as physicians and lay people. The great

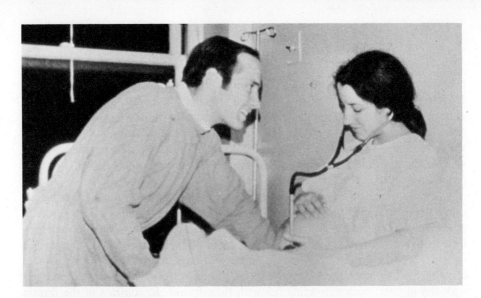

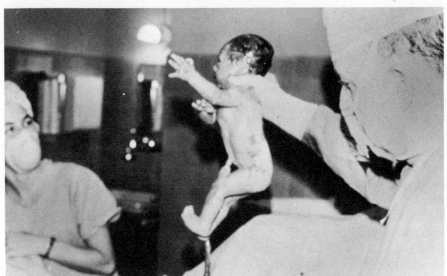

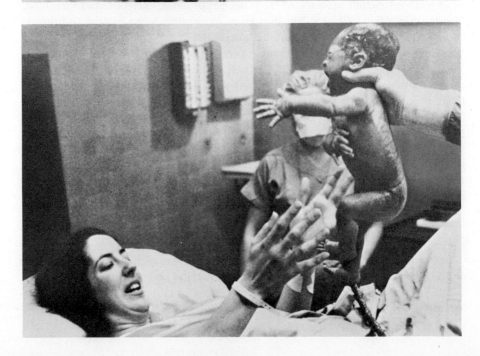

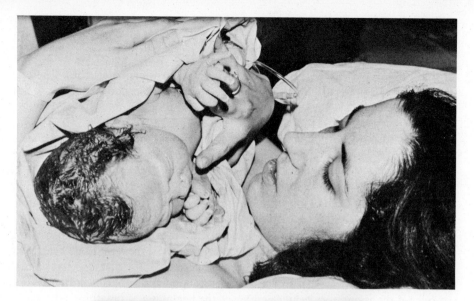

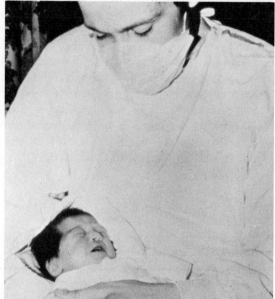

Halvar Loken

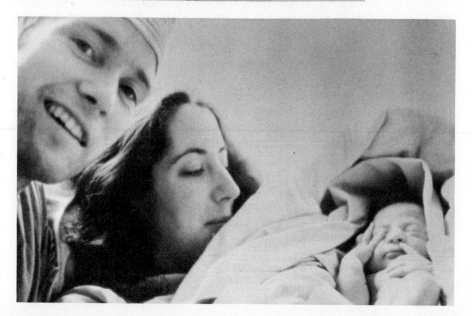

obstetrician DeLee believed that babies suffered pain while being born. The fact that babies give little evidence of a skin pain sense in the early postnatal days is not proof that the global experience of birth is without trauma.

The important bones of the baby's head are separated by the sutures, membranous spaces that feel soft to the touch. Where several sutures meet, the space is called a fontanelle. Figure 1–19 shows the anterior and posterior fontanelles on the top of a baby's head. During labor, the infant's head adapts by becoming narrower as the bones squeeze closer together. They may even overlap. The molding, or squeezing together, may result in a head that looks misshapen at birth, but within a few days, the head resumes a normal shape.

The fetal heartbeat responds to each uterine contraction by speeding up, slowing down, and then speeding up again. As labor progresses, the fetal heart beats very fast, slowly, or irregularly. During a strong uterine contraction, the fetal blood cannot get oxygen from the placenta. The increasing concentration of carbon dioxide stimulates the respiratory center and hence the beginning of breathing after birth. Amniotic fluid and mucus escape from the baby's air passages during expulsion of the baby, due to compression of his chest. The attendant may remove excess mucus from the mouth and throat, using a soft rubber ear syringe. Most babies begin breathing by themselves. If an infant does not breathe, slapping, cold water, and other stimulants are no longer used, but rather a careful resuscitation [15].

The emotional significance of the birth experience is a matter of conjecture. Some schools of thought hold that birth has a lasting psychological influence, while others maintain that the organism is too immature to record experience meaningfully. There is no question but that birth is a critical physical experience and no argument with the fact that the newborn needs adequate physical care if he is to survive.

### Injuries from Abnormal Conditions of Childbearing

The wonderful protective and adaptive resources of both mother and baby result in most infants being born intact. A minority of babies suffer from conditions existing prenatally and during the birth process. Such damage can result in fetal death, stillbirth, death soon after birth, cerebral palsy, epilepsy, mental retardation, behavior disorders, and perhaps speech and reading disorders [40]. The dangerous conditions include complications of pregnancy such as toxemias and bleeding, premature birth, difficult, prolonged, or precipitate labor, malpresentation, general anesthetic, and major illnesses of the mother.

Research is revealing increasingly the milder aspects of birth injury. Follow-up tests of motor, adaptive, and language behavior of babies who suffered stress at birth showed that the effects of stress showed up more in the second six months than during the first six months [31]. A study of infants who had suffered oxygen deprivation during birth, contrasting them with normal babies during the first five days of life, showed the traumatized infants to be significantly less sensitive to pain stimulation and visual stimulation, less integrated in motor behavior patterns, more irritable, and more tense and rigid muscularly [20]. Another study of infants who suffered oxygen deprivation at birth showed them to differ intellectually from normal children at age 3. The oxygen-deprived children averaged 8 points lower in IQ and did less well on tests of concept formation [18]. The longest follow-up study to date is on a group of 16- to 22-year-olds whose breathing had

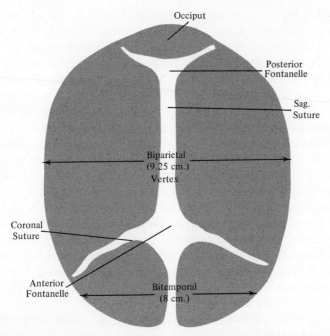

**Figure 1–19.** The fontanelles, or membranous spaces, on the top of a newborn baby's head. (After N. J. Eastman and L. M. Hellman, *Williams Obstetrics.* Appleton-Century-Crofts, 1966. Fig. 5, page 196.)

been delayed for one minute or more after birth [33]. Instead of the normal pattern of having a definite superiority of the preferred hand over nonpreferred in a balancing test, they showed little difference between hands. Oxygen deprivation at birth, then, depressed the score for the preferred hand 16 to 22 years later, showing a permanent effect on the central nervous system.

*Prematurity*

Premature birth is a hazard to life, health, and growth, both physical and mental. A baby is called premature if his gestation period is less than 37 weeks or his weight is under 5½ pounds. Birth weight is not the most accurate indicator of prematurity, as shown by recent studies. A combination of figures for birth weight and gestation period has been found useful for predicting survival and planning care [68]. Low birth weight plus short gestation usually means a more difficult time adapting immediately after birth, requiring a longer stay in the hospital and incubator. After surviving the first few months, however, these babies have a better prognosis than low birth weight babies of longer gestation. The latter had five times as many severe congenital anomalies as did the former.

Head circumference is the best single measurement for estimating gestation age [17]. Since certain abnormalities cause changes in head circumference, probably the most accurate way of estimating maturity is with a combination of head circumference, electroencephalographic data, other neurological data, and motor performance. Many babies with very low birth weights die and among those who survive, about half suffer neurological damage which ranges from minimal to severe mental deficiency [66]. About a third of cerebral palsied children were premature babies. The more premature the child or the lower the birth weight, the greater are his chances of being handicapped and the more severe the handicaps are likely to be [5, 36]. He is likely to suffer more physical illness during the first two years [14]. The premature child tends to score lower on developmental tests in infancy and on intelligence tests in childhood, children of lower socioeconomic status being more depressed in scores than those of higher status [14]. At age 12–13, children of low birth weight showed impaired reading and were below average in grade placement [64]. Prematures are more prone to behavior disorders and social and emotional difficulties. Subtle brain damage, specific reading problems, and hearing losses were suspected when prematures with normal IQs did not do as well as average in school, at age 10 [36]. Abnormal patterns of brain waves have been found in prematures. Physical growth, too, tends to be retarded. Premature infants are likely to be below average in size as children and as adults [36]. Blindness as a result of prematurity is not so frequent now as it was in the 1940s and 50s, when oxygen was routinely given liberally to premature babies. After the discovery that this practice often caused severe damage to the retina, oxygen has been used much more cautiously, but sometimes a choice has to be made between the baby's life and a high risk of injury to his eyes.

The ways in which prematurity is associated with defects are complex. First, the neurological and behavior disorders associated with prematurity may be the results of the same prenatal disorders that caused the baby to be born early. Second, the immature condition of the prematurely born baby makes him less able to stand the stresses and strains of birth and postnatal life. Third, he is treated differently from full-term babies. Kept in an incubator and extra sanitary environment, he is deprived of normal skin contacts and other stimulation. He is probably not breast-fed and may not even be able to seek, find, and suck his food. Later on, the anxiety surrounding his early days may evoke special handling from his family, encouraging dependency.

Since the last two months of intrauterine life is the time when the fat is laid down under the skin, a premature baby looks red and wrinkled, as compared with a full-term baby. His head looks extra big for his tiny body. Depending on how immature he is, he may or may not be able to suck and swallow. Feeding him the right nutriments is a problem, even though mechanical devices can put the food into his stomach. Many hospitals encourage mothers to express their own milk for their prematures, or they may use a human milk bank. Leads on what to feed prematures are being sought through studying marsupials and the secretions that they give to their immature young while in the pouch. The small stature observed in children and adults who were born prematurely may be the result of inadequate nutrition during a critical growth period. All aspects of prematurity are receiving the attention of research scientists, the social as well as the biological. It has been found that parents of damaged prematures respond well to counseling, especially when offered early [66].

After this dreary recital of what can go wrong with a premature child, we want to reassure our readers that some prematures grow up normal. After all, only 40 to 60 percent of infants in the studies surveyed have shown defects. An example of a premature baby who has shown only a slight, temporary problem stemming from it is Laura, to whom this book is dedicated. With a gestation of 36 weeks and a birth weight of 4½ pounds, she could suck and swallow and showed normal neonatal reflexes. As a young child, she had a speech defect that was cured by a few weeks of speech therapy. At age 22, she is a successful businesswoman, a graduate student, a member of Phi Beta Kappa and a happy wife.

Fetology, the new branch of medical science which deals with the fetus, is yielding techniques for diagnosing and treating fetal illnesses and imperfections, thus making it possible to prevent many birth defects. One of the new techniques is amniocentesis, the drawing off of amniotic fluid through a tube put through the mother's abdominal and uterine walls and into the amniotic sac. Analysis of the fluid can show genetic defects, such as Mongolism. The sex of the baby can be determined, and this may be important in a family that is known to have sex-linked defects, such as hemophilia. The fluid can also show if the baby is ill and how ill he is from causes such as blood incompatibility. The baby might be saved by a blood transfusion or a Caesarian delivery. Another diagnostic technique is examination with an amnioscope, an instrument for lighting and viewing the inside of the uterus from the birth canal. It is possible to draw a blood sample from the baby's head through the birth canal. Fetal surgery is performed by making a small opening in the mother's abdomen and uterus, inserting a catheter into the baby or giving other treatment, and then closing the incisions in the mother [2]. Research on animals has demonstrated the possibility of much more complicated fetal surgery [34]. Other techniques that have stimulated advances in diagnosis and treatment include thermography, a way of mapping the pregnant mother through heat waves, ultrasonics, or mapping of the fetus by sound waves and electrocardiograms of the fetus.

*Significance of Socioeconomic Conditions for Childbearing*

Birth control, in the form of both contraception and abortion, is less available to poor, uneducated people, than it is to the middle and upper class. For this reason, among other reasons, more unplanned and unwanted children, in fact, more children, are born to the poor. Thus more pregnancies and more closely spaced pregnancies occur among the women who have the most inadequate diets, the most stressful physical environments, and the most exposure to crises of many kinds. The most careful studies of fetal and infant death, related to socioeconomic status, have been done in Britain [30]. American studies show relationships between mortality and skin color which is highly related to socioeconomic conditions. In Scotland, fetal loss and stillbirths have been higher for semiskilled and unskilled laborers than for professionals and managers ever since statistics have been recorded. When death rates have gone down, the ratio between the classes has been maintained. In the United States, the color differences in perinatal mortality is strongly in favor of whites. The ratio has increased in recent years. Maternal mortality figures reflect the same socioeconomic differences seen in the statistics for infants. Figures 1–15, 1–16, and 1–20 illustrate these differences.

Poor countries show poor performance in childbearing as compared with prosperous countries, just as do the poor in a given country as compared with the well-to-do. Low birth weights occur in 4 percent of Scandinavian births, 7 or 8 percent of British, 7 percent of white American, 10 percent of black American, 18 percent of South African Indians, and 35 percent of Indian births in Madras [45].

The production of children of excellent quality, then, is the outcome of many factors. Poverty is associated with all the factors that work against excellence in

INFANT MORTALITY RATES (BIRTH – 1 YEAR)

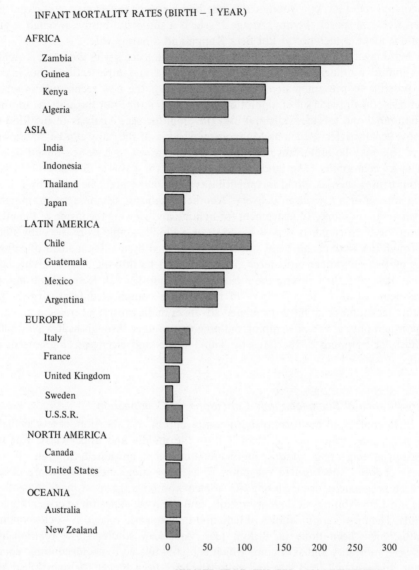

NUMBER OF DEATHS (PER 1,000 LIVE BIRTHS)

**Figure 1–20.** Infant mortality in selected nations.

SOURCE: Data from 1969 World Population Data Sheet, *Obstetrical and Gynecological News*, 1969, 4:10, p. 28. Also from *Demographic Yearbook* 1967, 19th issue; Special topic: Mortality Statistics, Statistical Office of the U.N. Dept. of Economic and Social Affairs, N.Y.: United Nations, 1968.

reproduction. Quantity dilutes quality. A limited number of high-quality babies can be born under certain conditions. Excellent infants require prenatal conditions that assure them of good nutrition, absence of stress and disease, an environment provided by a woman of appropriate age, adequate medical supervision of pregnancy and birth. Since family planning and, when indicated, heredity counseling are now essential for parents who want to give their children the best chance for full development, education is very pertinent to successful childbearing.

## Summary

Fertilization occurs in the middle of a menstrual cycle, when a spermatazoon penetrates a mature ovum. After subdividing for three or four days, the fertilized egg implants itself in the lining of the uterus. Differentiation of the organs and tissues takes place during the first 2 months of life, during which time the organism is called an embryo. Fluid fills the amniotic sac, which encloses and protects the embryo. Having acquired a more human appearance, the embryo's name is changed to *fetus* when he reaches 8 weeks of age. Further differentiation of organs and tissues takes place along the basic form which has been laid down. The organs begin to function. The fetus moves freely and performs many reflex acts. The head end is better developed than the tail end, both physically and functionally.

Pregnancy can be diagnosed through laboratory tests soon after the first missed menstrual period. The mother's awareness of pregnancy may occur even before this time, or it may be delayed until much later, depending upon the symptoms she experiences. The first three months of pregnancy is a time of physiological reorganization which usually involves fatigue. New feelings and emotions go along with the pervasive bodily changes which affect all the systems. Adjustment to pregnancy is affected by physical and psychological preparation for it, by the natural resources of the mother, and by the care and experiences she has during pregnancy. The small, nuclear family tends to place the main burden of emotional support upon the husband. Out-of-wedlock pregnancies show higher rates of physical and psychological disturbances.

Infant and mother are affected by the nutritional state of the mother when the pregnancy is begun, as well as by the adequacy of nutrition throughout the pregnancy. Since mothers vary considerably in their needs, individual nutritional guidance is very desirable. Serious nutritional deficiencies are associated with complications of pregnancy, labor, and delivery, and with defective development of the baby.

Babies respond prenatally to loud sudden sounds by moving, often in sudden movements which are probably similar to the startle response of the newborn. Maternal emotional disturbance, also, is associated with high activity in the fetus. Emotional well-being of the mother probably contributes to the emotional well-being of the baby. Prenatal influence also occurs through physical, chemical, and biological means. X rays, beyond a certain level, are damaging and even lethal. Many drugs, such as quinine, certain barbiturates, and tranquilizers, will damage the unborn baby. Cigaret smoking is associated with premature birth. Many diseases, such as measles, are likely to damage the embryo or fetus. Incompatibility between the mother's blood and the baby's blood will, under certain conditions, harm the baby. Certain risks to mother and baby are increased when the mother is in the later years of childbearing.

Birth is a physical and emotional crisis for the mother, baby, and family. Labor, the work which the mother does in giving birth, consists of three stages. The first stage, the opening of the cervix, is accomplished by muscles which are not under voluntary control. The confident, secure mother can probably help the process by relaxing. The second stage, pushing the baby out, is partially involuntary and partially controllable by the mother. Education for childbirth prepares her to function here. The third stage, a brief process, is the expelling of the placenta. The duration of labor varies considerably, the most common length for a first labor being 7 hours, and for subsequent labors, 4 hours. A Caesarian birth is safer for mother and baby than is a difficult natural delivery.

The mother's emotions and her experience of pain during labor are determined to some extent by what she has been taught to expect. Education for childbirth can be a very positive influence. "Prepared childbirth" uses education, emotional preparation, and support during labor.

The baby is equipped with mechanisms for adapting to the birth process. Some of his responses to this process prepare him for beginning to breathe. A few babies are injured at birth and others are damaged prenatally. Premature birth is associated with neurological disorders. Hereditary defects account for some abnormalities. Most seriously malformed fetuses do not live to full term. Good obstetrical care includes prenatal supervision and education as well as skilled help to the mother and baby during labor and delivery and afterward.

Poverty and lack of education are associated with higher maternal mortality and with greater numbers of children with birth defects, including low birth weights which are associated with below par development. The production of children in excellent condition at birth and with excellent chances of good development is associated both with greater income and greater knowledge and education.

## References

1. Baird, D. Quoted in *San Francisco Chronicle*, January 18, 1969.
2. Berrill, N. J. *The person in the womb.* New York: Dodd, Mead, 1968.
3. Birch, H. Research issues in child health IV: Some philosophic and methodological issues. In E. Grotberg (Ed.), *Critical issues in research related to disadvantaged children.* Princeton, N.J.: Educational Testing Service, 1969.
4. Bowes, W. A., Brackbill, Y., Conway, E., & Steinschneider, A. The effects of obstetrical medication on fetus and infant. *Mono. Soc. Res. Child Devel.*, 1970, **35**:4.
5. Braine, M. D. S., et al. Factors associated with impairment of the early development of prematures. *Mono. Soc. Res. Child Devel.*, 1966, **31**:4.
6. Burke, B. S., Beal, V. A., Kirkwood, S. B., & Stuart, H. C. The influence of nutrition during pregnancy upon the condition of the infant at birth. *J. Nutrition*, 1943, **26**, 569–583.
7. Caldwell, D. F., & Churchill, J. A. Learning ability in the progeny of rats administered a protein-deficient diet during the second half of gestation. *Neurology*, 1967, 17–95.
8. Collis, W. F. R., & Janes, M. Multifactorial causation of malnutrition and retarded growth and development. In N. S. Scrimshaw & J. E. Gordon (Eds.), *Malnutrition, learning and behavior.* Cambridge, Mass.: M.I.T. Press, 1967, pp. 55–80.
9. Conway, E., & Brackbill, Y. Effects of obstetrical medication on the infant's sensorimotor behavior. Paper presented at the meeting of the Society for Research in Child Development, Santa Monica, Calif., March 27, 1969.
10. Cravioto, J. Nutritional deficiencies and mental performance in childhood. In D. C. Glass (Ed.), *Environmental influences.* New York: Rockefeller University Press, 1968, pp. 3–51.
11. Davids, A., DeVault, S., & Talmadge, M. Anxiety, pregnancy, and childbirth abnormalities. *J. Consult. Psychol.*, 1961, **25**, 74–77.

12. Dean, R. F. A. The size of the baby at birth and the yield of breast milk. Studies of undernutrition. Wuppertal, 1946–1949. *Special Report Series, Medical Research Council*, 275. London: Her Majesty's Stationery Office, 1951.

13. Denenberg, V. H. Stimulation in infancy, emotional reactivity, and exploratory behavior. In D. C. Glass (Ed.), *Neurophysiology and emotion*. New York: Rockefeller University Press and Russell Sage Foundation, 1967, pp. 161–190.

14. Drillien, C. M. The growth and development of the prematurely born infant. Baltimore: Williams & Wilkins, 1964.

15. Eastman, N. J., & Hellman, L. M. *Williams obstetrics* (13th ed.). New York: Appleton-Century-Crofts, 1966.

16. Ebbs, J. N., Tisdall, F. F., & Scott, W. A. Influence of prenatal diet on mother and child. *J. Nutrition*, 1941, **22**, 515–526.

17. Eichorn, D. H. Biology of gestation and infancy: Fatherland and frontier. *Merrill-Palmer Quart.*, 1968, **14**, 47–81.

18. Ernhart, C. B., Graham, F. K., & Thurston, D. Relationship of neonatal apnea to development at three years. *Arch. Neurol.*, 1960, **2**, 504–510.

19. Ferreira, A. J. The pregnant woman's emotional attitude and its reflection on the newborn. *Am. J. Orthopsychiat.*, 1960, **30**, 553–561.

20. Graham, F. K., Mantarazzo, R. G., & Caldwell, B. M. Behavioral differences between normal and traumatized newborns. *Psychol. Mono.*, 1956, **70**, 20 & 21, Numbers 427–428.

21. Grimm, E. R. Psychological and social factors in pregnancy, delivery and outcome. In S. A. Richardson & A. F. Guttmacher [45], pp. 1–52.

22. Guttmacher, A. F. Speech at Brown University, Providence, R. I., January 23, 1969.

23. Hall, R. E. His birth without permission. *Sat. Rev.*, December 7, 1968, 78–79.

24. Hamer, J. H. The cultural aspects of infant mortality in Subsaharan Africa. (Ph.D. thesis in Anthropology, Northwestern Univeristy) Ann Arbor, Mich.: University Microfilms, 1962.

25. Hardy, J. B. Rubella and its aftermath. *Children*, 1969, **16**(3), 91–96.

26. Heinstein, M. I. Expressed attitudes and feelings of pregnant women and their relations to physical complications of pregnancy. *Merrill-Palmer Quart.*, 1967, **13**, 217–236.

27. Holden, R. H., Man, E. B., & Jones, W. P. Maternal hypothyroxinemia and developmental consequences during the first year of life. Paper presented at the meeting of the Society for Research in Child Development, Santa Monica, Calif., March 27, 1969.

28. Holley, W. L., Rosenbaum, A. L., & Churchill, J. A. Effects of rapid succession of pregnancy. In *Perinatal factors affecting human development*, Pan American Health Organization, Pan American Sanitary Bureau, Regional Office of World Health Organization, 1969, pp. 41–45.

29. Hurley, L. S. The consequences of fetal impoverishment. *Nutrition Today*, 1968, **3**(4), 2–10.

30. Illsley, R. The sociological study of reproduction and its outcome. In S. A. Richardson & A. F. Guttmacher [45], pp. 75–141.

31. Klatskin, E. H., McGarry, M. E., & Steward, M. S. Variability in developmental test patterns as a sequel to neonatal stress. *Child Devel.*, 1966, **37**, 819–826.

32. Kron, R. E., Stein, M., & Goddard, K. E. Newborn sucking behavior affected by obstetric sedation. *Pediat.*, 1966, **37**, 1012–1016.

33. Leventhal, D. S. Specialized manual skill and personality adjustment 16–22 years after delayed breathing at birth (perinatal apnea): A replication and extension. Paper presented at the meeting of the Society for Research in Child Development, Santa Monica, Calif., March 27, 1969.

34. *Life* magazine. Control of life. September 10, 1965, 55–77.

35. Liley, H. M. I. *Modern motherhood.* New York: Random House, 1967.

36. Lubchenco, L. O., et al. Sequelae of premature birth. *Am. J. Dis. Child.*, 1963, **106**, 101–115.

37. Mead, M., & Newton, N. Cultural patterning of perinatal behavior. In S. A. Richardson & A. F. Guttmacher [45], pp. 142–244.

38. Montagu, M. F. A. *Prenatal influences.* Springfield, Ill.: Charles C Thomas, 1962.

39. *New York Times.* It really may be food for thought. July 28, 1968 (interview with John Churchill).

40. Pasamanick, B., & Knobloch, H. Retrospective studies on the epidemiology of reproductive casualty: Old and new. *Merrill-Palmer Quart.*, 1966, **12**, 7–26.

41. Platt, B. S., Barrett, I. M., & Christie, B. A. The effect of chronic dietary protein-calorie deficiency on reproductive performance of rats: Respiratory metabolism of ova (in press). Cited in *Perspectives on human deprivation.* Washington, D.C.: U.S. Dept. of Health, Education, and Welfare, 1966, p. 244.

42. Plummer, G. Anomalies occurring in children exposed in utero to the atomic bomb in Hiroshima. *Pediat.*, 1952, **10**, 687–693.

43. Pope, H. Negro-white differences in decisions regarding illegitimate children *J. Marr. Fam.*, 1969, **31**, 756–764.

44. Rainwater, L. *And the poor get children.* Chicago: Quadrangle, 1960.

45. Richardson, S. A., & Guttmacher, A. F. (Eds.). *Childbearing—Its social & psychological aspects.* Baltimore: Williams & Wilkins, 1967.

46. Robinson, C. H. *Fundamentals of normal nutrition.* New York: Macmillan, 1968.

47. Rosengren, W. R. Social sources of pregnancy as illness or normality. *Social Forces*, 1961, **39**, 260–267.

48. Salk, L. Mother's heartbeat as an imprinting stimulus. *Trans. N.Y. Acad. Sci.*, Ser. II, 1962, **24**, 753–763.

49. Schulman, C. A. Sleep patterns in newborn infants as a function of suspected neurological impairment of maternal heroin addiction. Paper presented at the meeting of the Society for Research in Child Development. Santa Monica, Calif., March 27, 1969.

50. Scrimshaw, N. S. Malnutrition, learning and behavior. *Am. J. Clinical Nutrition*, 1967, **20**, 493–502.

51. Shank, R. E. A chink in our armor. *Nutrition Today*, 1970, **5**:2.

52. Sherwin, R. W. Perinatal nutrition as a developmental determinant. *Nutrition News*, 1967, **30**(4), 13–14.

53. Smith, C. A. Effects of maternal undernutrition upon the newborn infant in Holland, *J. Pediat.*, 1947, **30**, 229–243.

54. Sontag, L. W. Significance of fetal environmental differences. *Am. J. Obstet. Gynecol.*, 1941, **54**, 994–1003.

55. Sontag, L. W., & Richards, T. W. Studies in fetal behavior. I: Fetal heart rate as a behavior indicator. *Mono. Soc. Res. Child Devel.*, 1938, **3**:4.
56. Spelt, D. K. The conditioning of the human fetus in utero. *J. Exptl. Psychol.*, 1948, **38**, 338–346.
57. Stearns, G. Nutritional state of the mother prior to conception. *J. Am. Med. Assoc.*, 1958, **168**, 1655–1659.
58. Stechler, G. Newborn attention affected by medication during labor. *Sci.*, **144**, 315–317.
59. Tanner, J. M., & Inhelder, B. *Discussions on child development*. Vol. 3. New York: International Universities, 1958.
60. United States Department of Agriculture. *Dietary levels of households in the United States, Spring, 1965, A preliminary report*. Washington, D.C.: U.S. Govt. Printing Office, 1968.
61. Walters, C. E. Prediction of postnatal development from fetal activity. *Child Devel.*, 1965, **36**, 801–808.
62. Watson, E. H., & Lowrey, G. H. *Growth and development of children* (5th ed.). Chicago: Year Book, 1967.
63. Werboff, J. Prenatal factors determining later behavior. In A. J. Schuster (Ed.) *The teaching of infant development*. Detroit: Merrill-Palmer Institute, 1962, 98–105.
64. Wiener, G. Scholastic achievement at age 12–13 of prematurely born infants. *J. Special Educ.*, 1968, **2**, 237–250.
65. Winick, M., & Noble, A. Cellular response with increased feeding in neonatal rats. *J. Nutrition*, 1967, **91**, 179–182.
66. Wortis, H. Social class and premature birth. *Social Casework*, 1963, **45**, 541–543.
67. Yamazaki, J. N., et al. Outcome of pregnancy in women exposed to the atomic bomb in Nagasaki. *Am. J. Dis. Child.*, 1954, **87**, 448–463.
68. Yerushalmy, J. The low-birthweight baby. *Hospital Practice*, 1968, **3**, 62–69.
69. Zamenhof, S., Van Marthens, E., & Margolis, F. L. DNA (cell number) and protein in neonatal brain: Alteration by maternal dietary protein restriction. *Science*, 1968, **160**, 322–323.

# Chapter 2

Halvar Loken

## Early Infancy

Of all the species of infants, the human has farthest to go from birth to adulthood. Born in a very immature condition, he eventually becomes the most complex of creatures. In fact, if his behavior patterns were more biologically preset and determined than they are, he would not have as great possibilities for development as he does have. His brain has almost unlimited potentialities for learning and creating.

Human relationships, as well as human development, owe their variety and complexity partly to the immaturity of the human infant. If children could take off on their own like mice and lions, there would be no brothers and sisters to fight and love, no grandparents, aunts, uncles, cousins, no family at all. This immaturity was and is a necessary condition for humanity. Sometimes it is thought

55

of as a disadvantage for the infant to be able to do so little for himself at birth. Actually the infant can do everything he needs to do in order to survive and grow. Although immature, he is competent to handle the situation in which he first finds himself, provided his mother cooperates with him.

The neonatal period is used here to mean approximately the first month of extrauterine life. It has been defined in various terms, sometimes as the first week, sometimes as the period from birth until the umbilicus is healed. Although the neonatal period is short in time, it is significant because it is the beginning of life as a separate organism. Great are the changes and adaptation which take place in this brief interval.

## Equipment and Functioning

An assessment of the newborn can be made immediately after birth. The usual way of evaluating his functioning is by an Apgar rating, a system of scoring the infant's heart rate, breathing effort, muscle tone, reflexes, irritability, and color. The Apgar test is very useful for predicting survival and for indicating babies who need special care [1]. Apgar scores have been shown to be correlated with intelligence, conceptual, and motor scores at age 4 [18]. More complex examinations, including routine physical examinations and elaborate batteries of tests, are also useful for assessing normality and predicting development [69].

### Appearance

Neonates look strange to most people because new infants are rarely seen. Since they change quickly in looks, the normal appearance at 2 or 3 months is the one that comes to mind when most individuals think of a new baby.

The average newborn baby has a reddish, wrinkled skin which darkens when he cries. The wrinkles smooth out toward the end of the first month, as more and more fat is laid down beneath the skin. Immediately after birth the waxy vernix caseosa covers the skin for about eight hours. The large head is often elongated and bumpy, perhaps with one particularly large lump, the result of molding during birth. The head gradually resumes its normal shape, with possibly the trace of a bump or two remaining. It is quite easy to see some of the six fontanelles, the soft spots in the brain where membranes connect the bony parts of the skull. The flat, broad nose, formed of cartilage, is often pushed out of shape temporarily by the birth process.

His eyelids are puffy, making the eyes look small at first. The eyes, smoky blue for the first month or two, change gradually to their permanent color. They are large in proportion to the rest of the face, since the cranial part of the head is much more fully developed than the rest of the head. Here is an illustration of the principle of development direction: *development proceeds from anterior to posterior*.

Hair may be abundant or scanty, perhaps covering the head and scattered around the body, especially on the back. The body hair disappears and often the scalp hair too. Very often the permanent head hair is a different color from that at birth.

### Size and Proportions

The average birth weight for American babies is $7\frac{1}{2}$ pounds, with the average for boys about 3 ounces more than that for girls [82]. The size of babies varies with many factors, including race, climate, socioeconomic status, age and size of mother, and birth order. American Negro babies have been found to weigh, on the average, 5 ounces less than white babies at birth [49]. Information on birth weights in different socioeconomic groups suggests that the difference in birth weights between white and black is due to socioeconomic factors rather than genetic. The average birth weight for Caucasian babies is 7.50 pounds for boys, 7.44 for girls; Indian averages are 6.48 and 6.35: Indonesian figures are 6.87 and 6.72 [31]. The weight and size of a baby at birth are more strongly related to his mother's size than his father's. The fat-free weight of the newborn correlates 0.50 with the mother's fat-free weight, and 0.04 with the father's [27]. His weight is also related to the quality of environment which the mother has provided. The weight of the placenta and maternal health and nutrition are all related to birth weight [19]. If the baby's birth weight were more strongly related to his father's weight, then there would be great dangers in childbirth for a small woman married to a large man. The hereditary influence of the father makes itself felt during the catch-up period. The catch-up mechanisms allow for growth of a genetically large baby to be slowed down considerably during his last few weeks in utero and then to be speeded up during his first months after birth [31].

Body proportions, compared with those at later ages, show a large head, small trunk, and very short, undeveloped legs. The legs are bowed and drawn up, making them look even smaller than if they were stretched out.

*Physiological Functioning*

**Respiration.** The change from being a water-borne parasite to being an air-breathing, independent individual is a complex one, although one which the new-born is ready to make. An example of his fitness to adapt is that he can stand degrees of oxygen deprivation which an adult could not tolerate. The crucial change is in respiration; and this is begun as he emerges. It may take a day or two for the amniotic fluid and mucus to drain completely from the baby's breathing apparatus. Breathing is irregular, rapid, and shallow, involving the abdomen more than the chest. The neonate is often a noisy breather, wheezing and snuffling in a fashion that can be alarming to first-time parents.

Breathing reflexes are coordinated with and activated by the oxygen-carbon dioxide balance. The amount of air a baby breathes is regulated thus. Coughing, sneezing, and yawning are all reflexes with important survival value. Coughing and sneezing clear the air passages and lungs. Yawning gives a quick gulp of air when needed suddenly.

**Circulation.** The essential change in circulation follows immediately the change in respiration. Only a small quantity of blood goes to the lungs before birth, since it flows to the placenta to exchange products. After birth, blood is forced into the lungs, and the circulation to the placenta is cut off by the closing of the opening that leads from the fetal heart to the placenta. During fetal life, the right and left ventricles of the heart have an opening between them. Within the first week or ten days of postnatal life, the opening gradually closes. Another important change in the circulatory–respiratory combination is that the lungs expand gradually in the first two weeks. During that time, the blood includes almost twice as many blood cells per cubic millimeter as it does immediately after the lungs are fully expanded.

The heart rate decelerates during the birth process and quickly accelerates at birth. A peak heart rate of 174 beats per minute was found at two minutes after birth [81]. The heart then decelerates gradually, showing occasional periods of acceleration. Patterns of response become more stable during the first few months suggesting that important changes in control mechanisms take place during the first month of life [48]. Changes in heart rate are often used by experimenters as a means of measuring the infant's response to stimuli. Respiration is also used thus.

**Digestion.** The newborn changes from taking nutrients in through the placenta to taking food into the mouth and stomach. Hunger contractions and rooting, sucking and swallowing mechanisms, are present at birth. The small lower jaw and the fat pads in the cheeks are equipment for sucking. The mother's breasts supply first colostrum, a highly specialized food adapted to the newborn's needs, not available (as yet) from bottles. The breasts supply milk from the second or third day, regulating its composition and quantity to the maturity of the baby. Thus a delicately balanced nutritive relationship continues to exist between the mother and the baby after birth.

The first material evacuated from the colon is meconium, the material accumulated before birth from cellular breakdown, intestinal secretions, bile, mucus, and material swallowed with amniotic fluid. After three days, the stools assume a character which depends on the type of food, those of breast-fed babies differing noticeably from those of bottle-fed babies in appearance. Breast-fed babies usually have several bowel movements a day during the first few weeks, but after age 1, 2, or 3 months they usually change to a pattern of infrequent movements, one a day or every other day. Bottle-fed babies have one to four, or even six a day at first and later the number decreases to one or two [76]. The kidneys excrete small quantities of urine before birth. Frequency of urination increases after the second day to an average of around 20 times a day, with a wide range of individual differences.

**Metabolism.** The newborn has a higher metabolic rate than the adult, but lower than the preschool child's. Immediately after birth, the temperature drops 2 to 5 degrees and then rises to 98 to 99 degrees after about eight hours. Since mechanisms for maintaining a stable body temperature are immature, the neonate's temperature is unstable. Premature babies' temperatures are even more unstable than those of full-term infants. Heat loss is great through the baby's comparatively large surface, which is poorly insulated because skin and fat layers are thin. The newborn shows little diurnal change in temperature [74]. Thus he gets along best in a controlled temperature, with clothing and bedding carefully regulated to maintain a steady temperature.

**Brain Function.** Although most of the brain cells are present before birth, some of them are not mature enough to function in the newborn. Some studies of the cells have suggested that cortical function is impossible at birth (79). Lower parts of the neonatal brain are much more mature than the upper parts. During the first month, many cells in the motor cortex mature, especially those in the areas controlling the upper trunk, back, and upper arm. By 3 months the level of maturity suggests that simple vision and hearing occur on a cortical level, but that interpretation cannot take place. Some of the research on sensory perception, reported later in this chapter, indicates that the cortex of the newborn does indeed function. In the meantime many of the motor behavior patterns of the newborn, listed below, are witness to the capacities and scope of the neural areas below the cortex.

*Motor Behavior Patterns*

Motor behavior—crying, sleeping, and excreting—can be observed, whereas sensory perception has to be inferred from other behavior. A list of types of neonatal motor behavior follows [16].

Eyes
1. Opens and closes lids both spontaneously and in response to stimuli.
2. Pupils widen and narrow in response to light. Narrow upon going to sleep. Widen upon waking. Widen with stimulation.
3. Following moving stimulus. Also jerky movements.
4. Oscillatory movement.
5. Coordinate, compensatory movements when head is moved quickly.
6. Coordinated movements.
7. Convergence.
8. Eye position in sleep frequently upward and divergent, as in adults.
9. Tear secretion (unusual).

Face and Mouth
1. Opens and closes mouth
2. Lips: licks, compresses, purses in response to touch.
3. Sucks.
4. Smiles.
5. Pushes material from mouth.
6. Yawns.
7. Grimaces, twisting mouth, wrinkling forehead.
8. Retracts lips, opens mouth to touch. Turns lower lip.

Throat
1. Cries. Sometimes sobs.
2. Swallows, gags to noxious stimuli or touch at back of throat.
3. Vomits.
4. Hiccoughs.
5. Coughs, sneezes.
6. Coos. Holds breath.

Head
1. Moves upward and backward when prone, especially to stimuli.
2. Turns face to side in response to touch. Turns from side to side when prone or when hungry or crying.
3. Head shudders to bitter stimuli.
4. Moves arms at random. Arms slash when crying.

Trunk
1. Arches back.

2. Twists, squirms. When head rotates, shoulders and pelvis turn in same direction.
3. Abdominal reflex in response to needle prick as stimulus.

Reproductive Organs
1. Cremasteric reflex (testes raised when inner thigh stroked).
2. Penis erects.

Foot and Leg
1. Knee jerk reflex.
2. Achilles tendon reflex.
3. Leg flexes. Plantar flexion accompanies leg flexion (reverse of adult response).
4. Leg extends in response to gentle push. May support some of weight on first day.
5. Protective reflex (if one foot or leg is stimulated, the other pushes against source of stimulation).
6. Kicking, usually during crying.
7. Stepping movements, when held upright with feet against a surface.
8. Toe usually extends when sole of foot is stroked.

Coordinate Responses
1. Resting and sleeping position: legs flexed, fists closed, upper arms extended.
2. Back arches from head to heels often during crying or when held upside down.
3. Backbone reflex (the side that is stroked or tickled bends in concave direction).
4. Tonic neck reflex or "fencing position" (head turned to the side, facing an extended arm, the other arm bent up near the head).
5. Springing position (when held upright and forward, arms extend forward and legs are brought up).
6. Stretches, shivers, trembles.
7. Startle response (Moro reflex).
8. Crying and mass or general movements.
9. Creeping movements when prone.
10. When held upright and rotated around vertical axis, arms and legs are extended in the direction of the rotation.
11. Body jerks to loud noises.*

This list illustrates the large number and broad range of motor coordinations of which the newborn is capable. Some of these responses are necessary for survival, some have no apparent immediate usefulness, and others may contribute eventually to the infant's organization of his world. As an example of the last point,

* Reprinted by permission from W. Dennis, "A Description and Classification of the Responses of the Newborn Infant," *Psychological Bulletin*, 1934, **31**, 5–22.

the antigravity reflexes might contribute to space concepts [85]. Protective reflexes include blinking to a bright light, withdrawing from painful stimuli, and shivering when cold. Some reflexes such as a startle, or Moro, reflex; the Darwinian, or grasp, reflex, and the Babkin reflex may have been useful in the history of the species, although they serve no clear purpose now. Pressure on the baby's palms produces the Babkin reflex, which consists of opening the mouth wide and turning the head toward the mid line, flexing the forearm, and closing the eyes [36].

### States in Infants

The states of sleeping and waking are obviously different. There are various states of sleeping, and of waking too, all of which have significance for anyone studying the behavior of infants. Several investigators have made classifications of states, resulting in about six items, such as the following [85]: *regular sleep*, breathing smooth and even, little movement of face and body; *irregular sleep*, breathing irregular, movements of body and face, including rapid eye movements (this type of sleep, called REM for rapid eye movements, makes up a higher proportion of sleep, about 50 percent for newborns, than it does at any other age [67]); *drowsiness*, less active than in irregular sleep but more active than in regular, eyes open and close, looking glazed, eyelids heavy; *waking activity*, silent or moaning, grunting, whimpering, spurts of diffuse motor activity, face relaxed or pinched, eyes open but not shiny, skin flushed in activity, breathing irregular; *crying*, vocalizing, grimacing, diffuse motor activity, red face; *alert inactivity*, body inactive, face relaxed, eyes open, bright and shining, respirations faster and more variable than in regular sleep.

The infant's response to stimulation depends upon his state and upon the stimulus. For instance, in both kinds of sleep, infants were insensitive to touch; in alert inactivity, response to touch was increased motility; and in waking activity, touch stimuli resulted in decreased motility [85]. In studying the various sense modalities, investigators usually choose the state of alert inactivity for testing the infant's capabilities. It is in this state that he attends most to particular parts of the environment. The amount of time that 1-month-old boy babies spent in alert inactivity was correlated to length of time spent looking at pictures of faces at 3 months [53].

Babies vary in the amount of alert inactivity they show, from the moment of birth. During the first six hours, some stay awake and show intermittent visual pursuit (looking) for an hour and a half or longer; others fall into a deep sleep as soon as they are cleaned and dressed [84]. All the babies in the study increased from week to week in the amount of time spent in alert inactivity, the weekly average percent of total time being: first week 11, second 17, third 19, and fourth 21.

### Relating to the World through Perception

Although physiological functions occupy most of the newborn's energy, and his first active approach to the world is a foray in search of food, some of his activity is that of taking in sensory stimuli and processing the data. The mysterious question "What is the world like to a baby?" is just as intriguing today as it was to the experimental child psychologists of the twenties and thirties. Although we still cannot tell exactly what he is feeling or experiencing, scientists are breaking

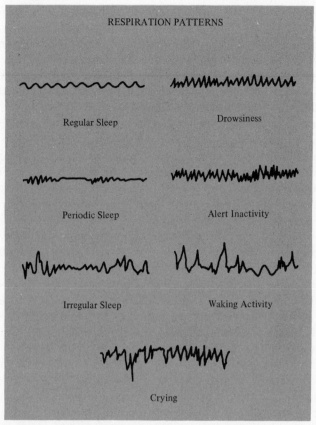

**Figure 2–1.** Respiration patterns in the six states of early infancy.

SOURCE: Reprinted from *Psychological Issues*, 1966, **5**:1, p. 8. By Peter H. Wolff. By permission of International Universities Press, Inc. Copyright © 1966 by International Universities Press, Inc.

through this communication barrier to increased understanding of infants. Using sophisticated equipment, investigators can pinpoint what the infant is looking at and how he looks at it, measure his heart rate, breathing, brain waves, and skin conductivity, and control the conditions of stimulation. The baby emerges from this scrutiny as a creature who follows certain principles of attending, perceiving, seeking, and performing.

**Tactile Senses.** Skin, muscular, and vestibular (inner ear) senses are highly developed before birth, having functioned prenatally longer than the other senses. Sensations from lips, mouth, and other orifices are included in tactile sensations. The skin, being the locus where the individual is in physical contact with his environment, is the place where much interaction occurs. To name the sensations heat, cold, pressure, and pain tells a minimum about tactile experience. Animal experts and clinical experiences with infants have led to the conclusion that tactile stimulation is essential for normal development [14, 15]. Patting, caressing, cuddling, carrying, rocking, changing position, washing, drying—all these activities seem to be soothing and to promote well-being in babies. There is a connection between the skin and sympathetic nervous system [25]. Animal experiments have led to a hypothesis that early sensory stimulation of mammals affects the central nervous system, producing animals that learn better, utilize their food more efficiently, and show less reaction to stress than do average animals.

Frank [25], an inspired theorist in the field of human development, points out that the regular, rhythmic stimulation that the fetus receives from his mother's heartbeat is translated through the amniotic fluid to all of his skin. After birth the baby lying in a crib receives no such stimulation, but a baby carried by a person does, especially so if he is in skin-to-skin contact. Frank goes on to explain how tactile experience is the basis for getting meaning from other sensory experience, for personality development, and for interpersonal relationships. Sounds and sights derive their meaning initially from experiences of touch. The concept of his own body, where it stops and where the rest of the world begins, mother and other people, the objects that make up the rest of the world, are all discovered and understood first through tactile senses, with some help from vestibular senses.

**Hearing.** Although it has long been known that the fetus, and of course the neonate, can hear, it used to be thought that the infant's sensory world was a "buzzing, blooming confusion." Unless he showed a startle reaction—which he did to loud, sudden sounds—a baby gave no indication that one sound or another made any difference to him. Since a baby can neither understand language nor speak, it is difficult for adults to conceive of sounds that could be meaningful to an infant, and of ways in which infants' responses to sound could be observed and measured. Research is showing, however, that the neonate can make fine discriminations and that certain sounds are meaningful in his existence.

Newborn infants can distinguish small differences in pitch. In a Russian experiment [13] on learning, a baby's sucking movements were charted along with sound stimuli on a revolving drum. When a sound occurred, the sucking movements stopped, but when the sound was repeated, the baby gradually shortened the time during which he made no sucking movements. After enough repetitions of sound of one pitch, he continued to suck when it was played. When a sound of different frequency was played, the baby stopped sucking again, thus showing that he could discriminate it from the first sound. Similar experiments have used acceleration of heart rate, rather than cessation of sucking to indicate that the infant discriminates a certain tone. In one of them, a tone was sounded repeatedly until the infant stopped giving any motor response [12]. Then a note of different pitch was sounded. Many babies gave motor responses, and their heart rates increased. Figure 2–2 shows the tracings made by one infant's sucking and by the stimulating tones. On the first presentation, represented by *A*, the up-and-down lines indicate sucking. They stop when a tone is sounded, as shown by the second line. *B* shows the ninth presentation of the same tone, when the sucking lines show no interruption. *C* indicates reactions to a new tone, when the sucking again stops.

Different degrees of loudness of sounds stimulate different reactions. When white noise at 55, 70, 85, and 100 decibels was played to newborns, their heart rates and motor responses increased as the sound level increased [78].

The human heartbeat as a significant sound has been studied by Salk by playing a tape recording in a hospital nursery. The experimental group of newborn babies was exposed continuously to a heartbeat recording. Although there was no significant difference in food intake between these babies and the control group during the first four days of life, they differed significantly in weight gain. The experimental group averaged a gain of 40 grams, and the control group lost an average of 20 grams. Table 2–1 shows both groups' weight change in terms of birth weight.

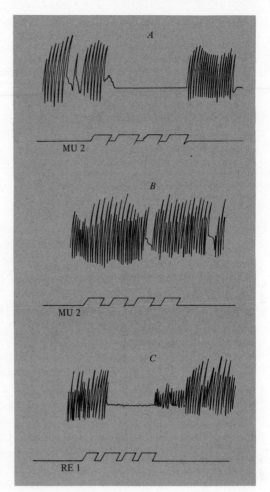

**Figure 2–2.** Differentiation of musical tones by a child 4 hours and 25 minutes after birth. A. Cessation of sucking when a new tone is played. B. Sucking continues during ninth playing of same tone. C. Sucking stops when another new tone is played.

SOURCE: Figure 1A, B, C from A. I. Bronstein and E. P. Petrova, "The Auditory Analyzer in Young Infants." In Y. Brackbill and G. Thompson [Eds.], *Behavior in Infancy and Early Childhood.* Copyright © 1967 by The Free Press Corporation. Reprinted by permission.

They also differed in amount of crying. During the heartbeat sounds, one or more of the nine babies in the nursery cried 38.4 percent of the time, whereas the crying lasted 59.8 percent of the time in the control situation. The author concluded that the heartbeat sound was comforting (anxiety-reducing). Since the publication of Salk's experiments, a heartbeat machine, developed in Japan, has been used in some hospital nurseries to soothe babies [43]. The wisdom of using soothing sound indiscriminately is questioned by Wolff [85], who has studied interrelationships between states and various stimuli and the organization of infant behavior as a whole. After using monotonous stimuli to produce states which looked like regular sleep, he made a provisional recommendation that, "it may be safest to assume that sleep produced or maintained by white noise is not identical with regular sleep, and that artificial devices for putting the baby to sleep may not be entirely innocuous."

Salk's interesting findings have stimulated other experimenters to see whether they could replicate his results. One study [11] showed that newborns reduced their crying when a heartbeat sound was played, but that a metronome and lullabies sung in a foreign language were just as effective as the heartbeat in soothing crying. Another experiment [66] used heartbeat at two levels of loudness

**Table 2–1** Weight Changes in Newborn Babies With and Without Exposure to Heartbeat Sounds

| Group | Gained Weight | | Lost Weight or Did Not Change | |
|---|---|---|---|---|
| | NUMBER | PERCENT | NUMBER | PERCENT |
| 102 babies exposed to heartbeat sound | 71 | 69.6 | 31 | 30.4 |
| 102 babies not exposed to heartbeat sound | 37 | 33.0 | 75 | 67.0 |

SOURCE: L. Salk [70].

(45 and 75 decibels), a regular intermittent tone at the two levels and ambient noise. The heartbeat at 75 decibels was the most effective quietener. Since rhythmic and continuous stimuli of many kinds are soothing to infants [9], it may be that the heartbeat sound owes its pacification powers to these properties. It is still possible, however, that the long prenatal experience in hearing and feeling his mother's heartbeat does indeed make it supreme as a calming rhythmic stimulus.

Another sound that may have significance for the newborn is the cry of another young infant. Although several studies have yielded conflicting evidence on response to crying, a new, carefully controlled investigation indicates that neonates do indeed cry in response to a peer's crying [73]. Tested in cribs with constant temperature and constant visual environment, 75 newborns were divided into groups that were exposed to one of these stimuli: no sound, white noise, and the tape of a 5-day-old baby crying. Crying and heart rate were recorded. Crying occurred in three times as many of the crying-tape group as in the silent control group, as Figure 2–3 shows. There was no difference between the silent control group and white noise group. When duration of crying time was measured, the babies who heard the crying tape cried significantly more than the other infants, but the silent control group did not differ significantly from the white noise group. Heart rate increases in both the white noise group and the crying-tape group exceeded those in the silent-control group. Therefore both sound conditions promoted greater arousal levels, while the crying sound stimulated crying. The experiment shows that the newborn infants responded to the vocal properties of the sound of newborn crying. In a subsequent experiment [72], infants heard recordings of their own crying. Their reactions were compared with those shown when exposed to the crying of another newborn. Their own cry seemed to be a more powerful stimulus, in terms of heart rate increases and duration of crying. It seems likely, then, that as the baby hears himself crying, he is stimulated further to crying.

**Vision.** Although ready to function at birth, the newborn eye has a few immaturities: an incompletely developed fovea (the part of the retina which sees color best), a short eyeball, a relatively large and spherical lens, and an incompletely developed optic nerve [75]. The immaturities result in poor fixation, focusing, and coordination of eye movements. Blinking and tear production are limited. Nevertheless, a newborn baby can fixate a light and shows a pupillary reflex. Within a few days, he follows a moving light. Brightness sensitivity develops rapidly during the first two months [17]. Fixation of objects develops during the first week or two, while following of objects develops throughout the first several weeks. It is impossible to be more specific, since the many studies of infant vision do not yield

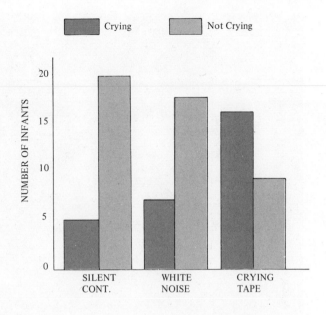

Crying          Not Crying

Figure 2–3. Crying of newborn infants increases when they hear a tape of an infant crying.

SOURCE: M. L. Simner and B. Reilly, "Response of the Newborn Infant to the Cry of Another Infant." Paper presented at the meeting of the Society for Research in Child Development. Santa Monica, March 28, 1969.

identical results. In one intensive study of newborns, 8 pursued a moving bright red ball within two hours of delivery [85]. After 24 hours, all 12 infants made conjugate eye movements, and by the third day all made coordinated head and eye responses. These responses took place only during a state of alert inactivity. Newborns who were sucking on pacifiers reduced their sucking rates when looking at an intermittent moving light [30].

Visual acuity, which depends on accommodation (adjusting the thickness of the lens), is limited during the first month and increases gradually. A baby can focus quite well on objects held at about 7½ inches away from his eyes but cannot accommodate to other distances [32].

Using an apparatus that makes it possible to measure how long an infant looks at either of two visual stimuli, Fantz [22] has shown that infants under two weeks of age can perceive stripes ⅛ inch wide at a distance of 9 inches, a visual angle of

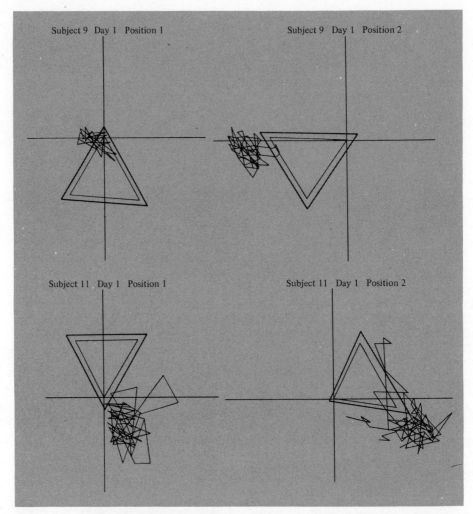

Subject 9  Day 1  Position 1

Subject 9  Day 1  Position 2

Subject 11  Day 1  Position 1

Subject 11  Day 1  Position 2

**Figure 2–4.** Part of the ocular orientation record for one newborn. The outer line represents a solid, black 8-inch equilateral triangle. The irregular lines are a photographic record of where the baby looked.

SOURCE: W. Kessen, "Sucking and Looking: Two Organized Congenital Patterns of Behavior in the Human Newborn." In H. W. Stevenson, E. H. Hess, & H. L. Rheingold [Eds.], *Early Behavior*, New York: John Wiley & Sons, 1967, page 176. By permission.

slightly less than one degree. The infants looked at complex patterns, such as a checkerboard and bull's-eye, more than they looked at simple patterns, such as a square and circle. Using Fantz's method, the visual preferences and abilities of premature and newborns were studied [52]. The prematures, whose gestation age ranged from 32 to 37 weeks, had the same acuity of vision (both discriminated lines subtending a visual angle of 66 degrees). Both groups preferred patterned stimuli to plain. The prematures tended to prefer the simpler stimuli among the patterned ones. The preference for complex patterns is probably due to an unlearned tendency to pay attention to events that involve change or contrast. Newborn babies look more at moving lights than at fixed ones, and at objects with a large amount of black-white contrast than at objects of one shade. Neurological research shows the basis of the infants' tendency to look at events with contrast.

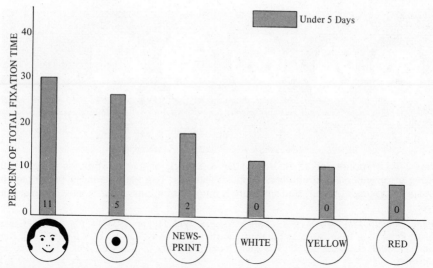

**Figure 2–5.** Relative visual response and number of newborn infants looking longest at representations of face, bull's-eye, newsprint, and white and colored disks.

SOURCE: *Annals of the New York Academy of Sciences*, Vol. 118, pp. 793–814, Fig. 7, R. L. Fantz, "Visual Perception from Birth As Shown by Pattern Selectivity." In H. E. Whipple [Ed.], *New Issues in Infant Development*, © The New York Academy of Sciences, 1965. Reprinted by permission.

Such changes in stimulation of the retina produce excitement in nerve cells which could be the basis for sustained fixation [35]. When a newborn looks at a triangle, his eyes are directed at or near an angle, as can be seen in Figure 2–4. It may be that the area of greatest contrast is most attractive or there may be additional factors influencing the direction of looking [37]. Of all patterns shown, a human face elicited more interest (that is, time spent) than any, especially in the youngest babies. When given a choice between a representation of a face and a bull's-eye or between a face and oval targets with dots, stripes, or blanks, the infants looked longer at the face. It is reasonable to conclude that the newborn infant can pick out from the world a human face, the object which has more significance for his survival and well-being than anything else.

The important result of the infant's having pattern preferences is that he selects from the environment what he will take in through his senses and what he will process. He is not open to every source of stimulation in his surroundings, but exposes himself differentially to his environment. He begins to acquire knowledge from the environment with his first look [23].

**Coordination of Vision and Hearing.** Newborn infants can coordinate vision and hearing to a limited extent. During their first 10 minutes after birth, one baby turned her eyes in the direction of a sound. A toy cricket clicking on one side or the other elicited eye movements half of the time. Most of the eye movements were in the direction of the click [83]. A controlled study done on 64 normal newborn infants confirmed the conclusion that neonates can discriminate location of sound source [42]. Vision and hearing become better coordinated as the child learns through experience.

**Taste.** Taste is functional in the fetus as well as the newborn, although it seems to develop with age. Infants accept sweet solutions and tend to reject those that are salty, bitter, or sour.

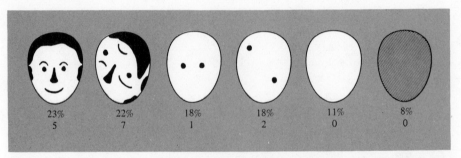

**Figure 2–6.** Responses of 15 infants under one week of age to stimulus targets with varying arrangements and numbers of facial features. Top figure is mean percentage of time spent looking at target. Bottom figure is number of infants looking most often at that target.

SOURCE: *Annals of the New York Academy of Sciences*, Vol. 118, pp. 793–814, Fig. 9, R. L. Fantz, "Visual Perception from Birth As Shown by Pattern Selectivity." In H. E. Whipple [Ed.], *New Issues in Infant Development*, © The New York Academy of Sciences, 1965. Reprinted by permission.

**Smell.** Smell has been investigated, using strong odors and measuring changes in body movements and breathing. During the first few days of life, infants showed sensitivity to chemical nasal stimuli and discrimination between different odors [44]. With repetition of an odor stimulus, the response diminished. A new odor then elicited increased response. The investigators concluded that brain action, as well as sensory organ adaptation, was involved. It would be important to discover what role, if any, smell plays in the life processes of the infant, such as the significance of odors from his mother and other people who care for him. Unfortunately, relevant research has not been done. However, it is known that man has a less developed sense of smell than have most other animals. He therefore receives less information about the environment through this sense modality than he does through sight and hearing, for instance.

**Pain.** Adults would like to know whether a newborn baby feels pain, and if so, what causes pain and how severe it is. Since crying and withdrawal movements are the only indication of pain an infant can give, these reactions have been studied in connection with certain kinds of stimulation. It has long been known that neonates do not cry much when circumcised, especially if given something sweet to suck during the operation. Gastrointestinal upsets, however, result in a great deal of crying. The baby seems to be more sensitive to some kinds of threats than to others and to be able to escape or avoid some more than others [54]. Early research on pain in young infants used pin pricks as stimuli, noting how many were necessary before the baby made some withdrawal response [61]. The more modern method is to use mild electric shock up to a level where a withdrawal action is observed. The stimulus can thus be measured exactly. The experiments show that pain sensitivity increases steadily during the first few days of life. Figure 2–7 shows the decrease in volts required to elicit a reaction of the toe during the first four days. A sex difference was found, as well as an age difference, with girls showing more sensitivity than boys, a result in keeping with the generally greater maturity of girls at birth [46]. Tickling has also been used to explore pain responses, since the two types of stimulation have much in common, and tickling is more acceptable ethically [85]. Newborn babies in all states of rest, responded to tickling with vigorous activity. In states of moderate activity, tickling produced moderate in-

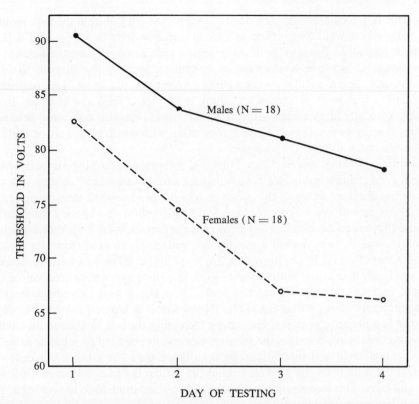

**Figure 2–7.** Responses to electrical stimulation during the first four days of life, showing decrease in volts required to elicit response.

SOURCE: Reproduced by permission from L. P. Lipsitt and N. Levy, "Electro-tactual Threshold in the Neonate," *Child Development*, 1959, **30**. Copyright © 1959, The Society for Research in Child Development, Inc.

creases in activity (51 percent of trials as compared with 94 percent in regular sleep). In the state of crying the infant responded with a reduction in activity as often as he did with an increase.

**Temperature.** Newborn babies increase their muscular activity when the temperature drops [50]. They respond to cold or warm stimuli applied to the skin [62]. While early studies had suggested that babies preferred lukewarm food, a careful investigation [34] of the use of cold formulas has caused a change in the advice given by pediatricians. Comparisons were made between a group of premature infants fed formulas at the usual lukewarm temperature. There were no significant differences in the feeding behavior, food intake, weight gain, vocal behavior, sleep patterns, or regurgitation of the two groups. Thus research indicates no reason for giving babies warm rather than cold feedings. However, there is no proof that infants cannot distinguish between warm and cold formulas.

### Ways of Coping with the World

Through sensory perception, the infant takes in selected information about his environment and processes it. Lois Murphy has studied many children longitudinally (over a period of time). Careful observation has led her to consider control of stimulation a defensive coping device [54, pp. 300–301]. Within the first month, the baby selects what he is going to look at and how long he will regard it [23]. Perhaps he can do the same with other senses, such as controlling the amount of stimulation he gets from his own bodily movement. Murphy also suggests that the child's basic coping orientation takes place very early in life, most likely beginning with early experiences of success or failure in obtaining food and comfort. He is equipped to attend to certain aspects of the world. He also has some behavior patterns, ready to function at birth or soon after, with which he can shape parts of his environment to meet his own needs.

**Tracking, Seeking, and Sucking.** Tracking, seeking, and sucking are part of the repertory of the newborn. This behavior is sometimes called the "rooting reflex": When the cheek is touched, the infant moves his head toward the source of the touch, his mouth open. The newborn is likely to show the rooting reflex after several touches on his cheek rather than after the first stimulus [10]. When touched above the lip, the baby opens his mouth wide and moves his head from side to side. When touched on the lip, he purses his lips or pouts [63]. The first two movements are obviously useful for finding the nipple. The third may cause erection of the nipple, making it easier to grasp and suck. There are at least two components to sucking: expression and suction [37]. Expression is a lapping movement, while suction is a negative pressure, created by increasing the size of the mouth cavity. An orthodontist [6] describes the sucking movements required by a breast as being more complicated and more vigorous than those used for a bottle. In order to express the milk from the pockets behind the areola, the baby advances his lower jaw and bites. This movement, then, would add a third dimension to sucking at the breast, but not to sucking a bottle.

The sucking reflex occurs in response to anything in the mouth and, when the infant is very hungry, to stimuli to other parts of the body. Well-coordinated sucking most likely depends on a pattern of stimuli delivered to the infant's mouth. Although ordinarily the breast provides these stimuli, there are breasts that fail to supply the necessary stimuli due to some of the tissues not being sufficiently protractile [29].* In such a case, the baby is apathetic about sucking. If offered a bottle (which does go farther back in his mouth, thus stimulating the sucking reflex), he is likely to take it more enthusiastically than he does the breast. Infants vary in the strength of their sucking movements and in how well they coordinate sucking, breathing, and swallowing. While the shape of the breast has something to do with this variation, there are individual differences in newborns in efficiency of sucking. These differences were observed during the first few days of life in babies tested with standardized artificial nipples [37].

Strength of sucking varies during a feeding period and changes from one period to another, probably with intensity of hunger. The breast adapts its milk production to the length and strength of sucking on it.

Thus does the infant take an active role in finding and securing food, first by crying, then by turning toward the source of tactile stimulation, preparing the nipple to give milk, and then actively withdrawing the milk from the breast, probably stimulating the breast to give more or less. The roles of the infant and mother are completely complementary, requiring the meshing of two people's activity. The first few days of life are often crucial in establishing successful breast feeding. In

* This condition can be noticed during pregnancy. It is usually possible to correct it then.

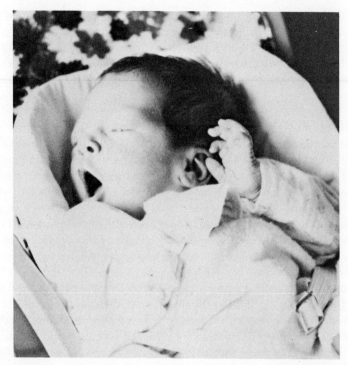

Halvar Loken

addition to failures resulting from inadequate breasts are those which arise because of the baby's having trouble breathing. Sometimes it happens that his upper lip gets pushed over his nostrils, due to the way in which he is placed at the breast. Then he has to fight for air, a frightening experience for him. After only one or two such experiences, he may reject the breast and yet eagerly accept the bottle [29]. For those babies who are in a state of alert inactivity for a period after birth, an opportunity to suck from the breast usually results in well-coordinated sucking [64, pp. 74–75].

As most people know, nonnutritive sucking is soothing to infants. Pacifiers are used widely throughout the world. A study of behavior of 4-day-old infants with pacifiers showed some interesting relationships [86]. They were tested by being tickled with a camel's hair brush during regular sleep, during regular sleep with a pacifier in the mouth but not sucking, during regular sleep while sucking a pacifier. While sucking, infants were less responsive than while not sucking. When a pacifier was in the baby's mouth but he was not sucking, he was likely to respond to the tickling with a new burst of sucking, rather than with increased motility. Apparently sucking blocks other responses.

**Crying.** Diffuse and crying activity are provoked by noxious stimuli from either outside or inside the infant. The state begins with soft whimpering and gentle movements, gradually changing into rhythmic crying and kicking. He enters a state where his own motility makes him more responsive to the unpleasant stimuli. The more sensitive he becomes, the more he moves and the harder he cries [85].

While the young infant cries in response to noxious stimuli such as hunger, pain, and partial body restraint, he does not do so with the intention of influencing an adult to alleviate his discomfort. Adults, however, generally interpret infant crying as meaning that the infant needs something. In the normal course of events, the mother or caretaker offers food or relief from pain or somehow removes noxious stimuli. Thus the newborn baby can effect a beneficial change in his environment through use of a behavior pattern which he had as part of his neonatal equipment.

### Stable Individual Differences in Neonatal Behavior

There are certain obvious differences in babies which are nonetheless important, such as sex, weight, length, color, and hair. Common observation and research [47] show that babies differ from one another in their physiological and psychological reactions during the first days and weeks of life. Frank [26, pp. 63–70] points to the unique structural and functional individuality of every infant as being of prime concern to those who would further his healthy development. The question of basic constitutional differences is of theoretical as well as practical importance, because it is really the problem of what heredity contributes, what environment gives, and how the two interact. How much is given at birth? How fixed is it? Investigations of differences in physiological functioning and behavior, and their constancy, are beginning to fill in the blanks opposite these questions.

The amount of hand-mouth contacting is a measure that shows stable differences from one newborn to another [38]. Finger sucking, hand–face and hand–mouth contacting have been shown to be related to each other and to be significantly different from one infant to another [39]. These movements were highly correlated with total amount of motion. Mouthing (sucking, tongue movements, chewing movements) showed definite individual differences, too, but it was not related to amount of movement. Rather, mouthing was highly related to hunger.

Differences have also been found in heart rate, level of arousal, depth of sleep, tactile sensitivity and strength, oral integration (largely concerned with sucking and rooting), and similarity to fetal position [5, 65]. When 30 neonates were tested systematically with four different stimuli, and rated as to reactions, consistent individual differences were found [7]. A soft tone, a loud tone, a cold disk, and a pacifier were used to stimulate the infants. Some responded vigorously to all situations, some moderately, and others mildly. Not only were the babies different from each other in the vigor of their responses, but they tended to stay in the same position, relative to one another, from the second day of life to the fifth. Stable individual differences have been observed from birth to 4 months in irritability, sensitivity, and tension [8].

## Relationships and Experiences

The meaning of his relationships and the success of his experiences depend upon *what the infant is seeking*. Much of his behavior can be explained in terms of *homeostasis*, the maintaining of physiological equilibrium in the organism. Tension is reduced and balance restored by food-seeking, sucking, and swallowing, through breathing, moving, and having baths and dry diapers. To achieve and maintain successive states of equilibrium also requires a certain level of sensory stimulation—enough but not too much of the various kinds. Equilibrium is continually being disturbed and restored on a new level. In its striving for equilibrium, the organism (either baby or adult) gives preference to some needs over others [77]. For example, a certain degree of fatigue takes precedence over a certain degree of hunger and over a certain level of desire for sensory stimulation. As equilibrium is continually disturbed and created, changes occur in the organism's structure and behavior. These changes are growth and development.

Personality is developing while the newborn is reducing his tensions and maintaining homeostasis. The sense of trust is the crucial aspect of personality growth at this time and for at least the first year of life. Erikson [21, pp. 247–251] writes of the feeling of goodness which comes when the baby is helped to cope with his environment. The world must seem like a good place to be and the people in it trustworthy when he is fed before he is overwhelmed by hunger, when he is kept at a comfortable temperature, and when he receives a satisfactory amount of sensory stimulation. As he is allowed and assisted to use his various competencies in different situations, his trust increases. In the following section, some of his relationships and experiences are examined in the light of personality development.

## Feeding

The feeding of infants can be considered from many angles. The nutritional aspects are crucial to survival and growth. Through feeding, the baby builds feelings about himself, his mother, and the world. The mother, as well as the baby, is affected physically and emotionally. Culture shapes the methods of feeding available. In the United States, women make choices concerning infant feeding which they are often ill-equipped to make. The choice between breast and bottle feeding, which will affect the mother and baby throughout the first several months, must be made immediately after, if not before, birth.

**Physical Aspects.** Most of the world's babies begin their feeding histories at the breast. Only in highly industrialized societies has bottle feeding become a frequently used method. The United States has the dubious distinction of having the lowest breast-feeding rates in the world [56]. Only 18 percent of infants are being completely breast fed on discharge from the hospital [51]. This figure represents a decline of 20 percent in 20 years. Of babies between birth and 3 months, only 11 percent receive any breast feeding [20]. Bottle feeding is successful here because of technological sophistication in regard to making formulas that approximate human milk and presenting it under very sanitary conditions. In underdeveloped parts of the world, breast feeding is closely tied to survival and to growth. Breast feeding can make the difference between life and death or between normal and stunted development. In most of the underdeveloped areas, babies are usually wholly breast fed for at least three or four months, during which time they tend to grow very well and tend to resist disease [80]. The ability of these mothers, many of whom are poorly fed, to produce adequate supplies of good-quality milk is a surprising feature of human reproduction.

Normal lactation periods in mammals correspond to the period of rapid infant growth, when the major part of the growth of the nervous system takes place. Adequate nutrition ordinarily occurs with breast feeding during this important growth period. Animal studies show that babies suffer irreversible growth retardation, including brain deficits, when nursing mothers are seriously malnourished, and this finding suggests that humans may be similarly damaged [71]. Nutritional intake and growth were studied in 215 infants in an impoverished community in Lahore, Pakistan [58]. Fifty percent of the babies were receiving insufficient food

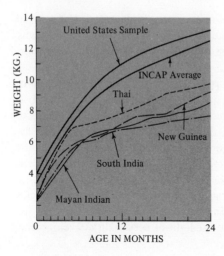

**Figure 2–8.** The weight curves of babies in four underdeveloped countries fall away from the average standard line just at the age when breast feeding is stopped. In two of the countries represented here, breast feeding is stopped at around 3 months. In the other two, about 6 months is the termination date.

Source: M. Béhar, "Prevalence of Malnutrition Among Preschool Children of Developing Countries," in N. S. Scrimshaw and J. E. Gordon [Eds.], *Malnutrition, Learning and Behavior.* Cambridge: M.I.T. Press, 1968. Also from R. L. Jackson and H. G. Kelly, "Growth Charts for Use in Pediatric Practice," *Journal of Pediatrics,* 1945, **27,** 215–229.

during the first month of life, 77 percent by six months, and 87 percent by the end of the first year.

Even when lactating mothers in poor countries live on relatively poor diets, their babies grow better while nursing than they do after weaning, as Figure 2–8 shows. These weight curves, comparing children with an international standard, show a situation that has been demonstrated on many impoverished populations. The baby grows almost normally for the first three to six months. Then the weight curve drops off throughout the preschool years. The beginning of the depression in the weight curve corresponds with the time when breast milk becomes insufficient, and the total food supply and supplementary foods are inadequate. Although breast feeding is often prolonged into the second or third year, it does not provide enough food. Supplementary foods are usually unsuitable, insufficient, and late. Contamination from the unsanitary environment increases, immunity from the mother's milk decreases, and the baby becomes ill more and more often. Poor nutrition and disease interact with each other to depress growth [4].

In the wealthier parts of the world, where an infant's physical survival and health do not depend heavily on breast feeding, a few physical arguments in favor of breast feeding remain. Artificially fed infants differ from breast-fed infants in body composition, physiological reactions, patterns of weight gain, and resistance to disease [3]. Human milk is biochemically suited to human babies and has the added bonus of giving immunity to many diseases. Jaw development is better promoted by the complicated biting and sucking coordinations required by the breast, in contrast to the simple, relatively passive movements instigated by the bottle [6].

Nursing mothers, too, receive physical benefits. In the first few weeks after birth, the baby's sucking stimulates the uterus to contract and hence speeds its return to normal size and structure. There is evidence that nursing a baby reduces a woman's chances of ever having breast cancer [64]. Women whose breasts have too much fatty tissue are likely to find that several months of nursing improves their shape and firmness [64].

**Psychological Aspects.** If rooting, pursing the lips, and grasping results in breast feeding, the chain of results differs from what happens when the result is bottle feeding. The tactile sensations from breast and bottle are different, the breast being warm, more flexible, and responsive to a sucking movement which differs from the sucking required by a bottle. Taste is different, too, not only because of the differences in human and cow's milk, but because the breast gives a low concentration of fats at first and a larger amount of cream at the end. Tactile and olfactory sensations from the mother's body are likely to be more intense in breast feeding because the baby is closer to her skin.

Inability and/or unwillingness to breast-feed is widespread in western culture. Some women do not want to nurse their babies and some do not produce enough milk to sustain their babies. Still others have given up the attempt to nurse because of sore nipples. These mothers may worry about their babies' well-being or they may feel guilty about not being adequate mothers. Research into the psychological results of breast versus bottle feeding has not been definitive. One longitudinal study [33] showed that nursing had to be considered in the child's life context, an important part of which was his mother's personality. The child's sex, the mother's warmth and stability, the length of the nursing period, all had some significance for the personality development of the child. These findings, as well as common sense, raise doubt as to the wisdom of putting pressure on women to nurse their babies when they have strong feelings against it. On the other hand, many women want to nurse and fail because they do not have the right kind of instruction, encouragement, and support for their efforts. Still others would want to do so if they understood more about this elemental process and relationship. A mother's attitudes toward breast feeding and success in it are largely derived from her understanding of and feelings about the whole cycle of reproduction in human beings [56].

A movement to promote breast feeding has met with some success, especially in upper socioeconomic levels.* Many of the people who become interested in prepared childbirth and family-centered hospital care are also convinced of the benefits of breast feeding to both infant and mother. The physical pleasure and psychological well-being of the mother, resulting from breast feeding, are unknown to many women in the western world. In substituting bottles for breasts, it is important to imitate the psychological situation as well as the nutritional. In other words, holding and cuddling during feeding may be as important as getting the formula right.

**Feeding As a Relationship.** When working in harmony, the baby's mouth and the mother's breast together perform an act. Two people contact each other and cooperate. Bottle feeding can also be a cooperative relationship. The baby's feelings of trust and confidence are enhanced by successful use of his abilities for getting food. The mother's parental sense is nurtured and she also grows. (The parental sense or sense of generativity is one of the adult stages of personality development, during which the individual becomes involved in promoting the well-being of the next generation.)

Research on subhuman mammals shows that the development and maintenance of maternal behavior depends upon stimulation from the young. After even a brief period (a few days) of separation from their young, rats, goats, sheep, and other animals lose much of their maternal bonds with the young [68]. One study of human mothers who were separated from their babies for the first few months after birth showed that they often had trouble in establishing maternal feelings [2]. This slight research evidence, along with clinical evidence, raises the question of the effects of separating mothers and babies at birth, a practice in many hospitals.

* La Leche League.

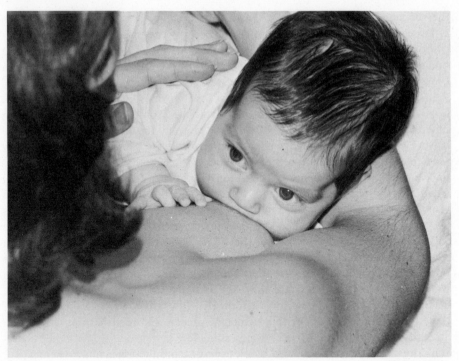

Halvar Loken

While the lying-in period is brief, it may be important for easy development of warm maternal feelings and spontaneous behavior.

**Timing.** If rooting, pursing the lips, grasping, sucking, and swallowing result in ingesting food, then the disequilibrium of hunger is reduced. A state of waking activity or crying changes to a quiet state of sleep or alert inactivity. The accompanying sensory stimulation, especially tactile, not only soothes the baby but promotes growth and mental organization. Such reduction of noxious stimuli occurs promptly in most non-western societies. The practice in most American hospitals is to feed babies on a 4-hour schedule, either taking them to their mothers to be breast-fed or given bottles or feeding them by bottles in the nursery. The 4-hour interval was established long ago from observations that babies' stomachs tended to empty in 4 hours and that, therefore, many babies were ready for food in approximately 4-hour intervals. The custom continues because hospitals run on schedules, and even for those who doubt the value of the 4-hour feeding plan, there is the rationalization that the lying-in period is so short that it does not matter. If homeostasis were the only goal involved, then it really would not matter. The fact that babies live and gain weight would be justification enough. However, the mother–baby relationship is involved. The early experience of the pair may be important in many ways, one of which is in determining whether feeding is by breast or bottle [29].

**Family-Centered Hospital Care.** A growing number of hospitals are offering care that promotes psychological health as well as physical. The 4-hour schedule takes account of neither the baby's competency in seeking and securing food nor of building competency in the mother. Nor is it concerned with the infant's states of hunger and arousal. He may be sleeping when mealtime comes; whereupon he is

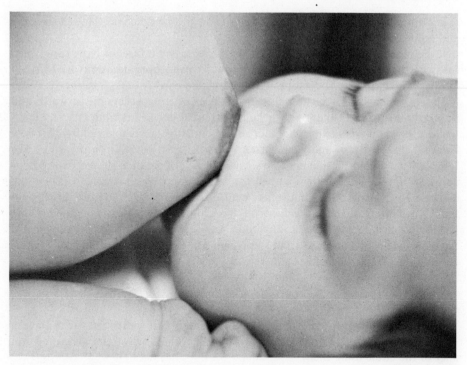

Halvar Loken

wakened and offered food. Or he may have cried, rooted, and sucked for an hour beforehand. In neither situation does he gain confidence in his ability to get food, nor in the world as a place where food is available for the seeking.

The rooming-in plan is a scheme for meeting the physical needs of baby and mother and the psychological needs of the baby, mother, and father. Developed along with prepared childbirth, *rooming-in* is an arrangment whereby the parents get well acquainted with their baby in the hospital. Although there are variations in the procedures, the essentials are thus. The baby stays in the room with his mother for a large portion of the time, in a bassinet beside her bed, or in a container that can be swung over her bed. She can pick him up and care for him if she wishes. The father, the only visitor, carefully washed and gowned, can hold his baby and care for him too. A nurse, or nurse's helper, shows the mother and father the techniques of baby care and does the care when the mother does not feel like doing it herself. When the mother wants to sleep or rest, the baby is taken into another room and cared for by the nurse. The mother is able to get to know her infant as an individual, to begin interacting with him, to find the ways of caring for him which bring most satisfactory results, and to feed him at the times which seem most appropriate. Crying has been found to stimulate a let-down reflex in the breasts of the lactating mother who is relaxed [57]. The breasts then feel heavy and ready for suckling, giving her an urge to feed the baby. The mother is likely to receive interested, informed instruction from a nurse who is skilled at helping newborn babies and their mothers to cooperate in breast feeding. With such assistance, the baby is likely to grasp the nipple in such a way that it will stimulate an adequate sucking reflex and he will avoid the pitfall of getting his nose blocked by his lip. The mother has an excellent chance to feel and be successful from the beginning.

A good beginning with breast feeding can make all the difference between success and failure.

It seems strange that America is having to rediscover a facet of baby care which the underdeveloped countries have never lost. Tribal people almost invariably keep mother and baby together, especially during the early weeks. Visiting in Asian hospitals, we saw bassinets attached to the beds of the mothers in the wards and watched the mothers handling their babies freely. In a private room in a very comfortable hospital we visited a mother in the midst of her whole family. The new baby lay on the lap of an ayah (nursemaid, not nurse) who sat on the floor. The father sat on a chair beside his wife's bed. Two older children played on the floor and held the baby when they wished to. The grandmother sat on a sofa, folding diapers. The warm family atmosphere contrasted sharply with the typical scene in the United States, where advances in the biological sciences, plus an ensuing passion for cleanliness, have sterilized our hospitals physically and psychologically. Some medical staffs are now trying to regain what was lost psychologically, while keeping the physical benefits.

### Additional Aspects of Physical Care

Besides feeding, there are many different infant care practices which have a variety of results. These practices have cultural bases and also reflect the individuality of the adult using them.

**Holding, Cuddling, Rocking, Changing position.** Stimulation to the skin, muscles, and ear senses seems to create quiet states in the young baby, as everyone knows if he has tried these means of soothing crying. The "good feeling" which accompanies tension reduction doubtless occurs here. Crying is probably the only way in which a newborn can indicate this kind of discomfort, unless his state of waking activity also signifies it. Although he may gain some equilibrium on his own through moving his body, he does not have a very handy method of getting someone to hold him. If he cries or if his wriggles result in his being picked up, rocked, and carried, then surely he gets one more assurance that the world is a place where he can find comfort and satisfaction.

An experiment on neonates demonstrates different kinds of behavior resulting from different ways of handling infants [59]. An attempt was made to continue after birth a type of stimulation similar to prenatal stimulation. Mothers were instructed to hold the infant in fetal position, firmly wrapped in a blanket, in close contact with the mother's body. After breast feeding in this position, the mother was to rock the baby very gently. The nurses gave similar care. The control group was on regular hospital routine, with bottle feeding by the mothers. The control group cried about twice as much as the experimental group, especially when no external instigation was present. This experiment demonstrates differences in infant behavior under two different sets of circumstances, which might be characterized as mothering versus hospital routine. One of the specifics in the mothering complex, rocking, has been studied systematically in several subsequent investigations.

The effects of rocking on crying were studied in a hospital nursery [28]. An infant was chosen from the babies who were not crying and was rocked for half an hour and then observed for half an hour, while the other noncrying infants were observed for the same time. Results showed that the rocked infants cried less than the nonrocked. Another study [9] compared the soothing effects of rocking, a

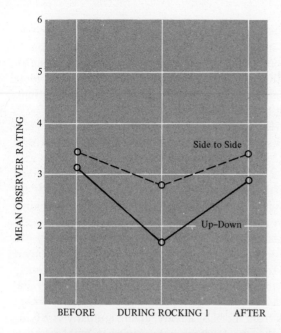

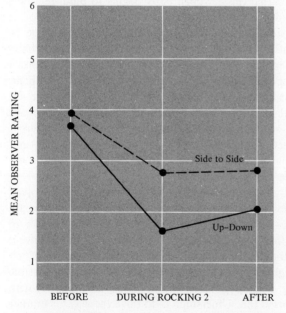

**Figure 2–9.** Amount of activity of young infants before, during, and after one and two sessions of horizontal and vertical rocking.

SOURCE: Reprinted by permission from D. R. Pederson, L. Champagne, and L. L. Pederson, "Relative Soothing Effects of Vertical and Horizontal Rocking." Paper presented at the biennial meeting of the Society for Research in Child Development, Santa Monica, 1969.

sweetened pacifier, a monotonous sound, and warm water. All stimuli had some quieting effect, but rocking had no more than the others. Two types of rocking were compared in a third piece of research [60]. A crib was designed to rock in either a side-to-side motion, like a cradle, or in an up-and-down direction. The infants' activity was measured and rated before, during, and after two sessions of each type of rocking. Figure 2–9 shows the results. The up-and-down rocking was more soothing than the side-to-side. Both types of rocking have a more quieting effect after the second session than after the first.

As every parent and baby-sitter knows, a crying baby can usually be soothed by picking him up and putting him to the shoulder. In studying this phenomenon, it was found that a state of alert inactivity, plus visual scanning, was induced by picking up a crying newborn and putting him to the shoulder [40]. Neither handling nor the upright position alone induced visual alertness. Since handling of young animals and tactile stimulation of human babies have been found to promote growth and development [15], it may be that one of the pathways of early stimulation is visual activation through tactile stimulation.

Touching another person involves two people. It is the simplest and most fundamental kind of relationship. Touching is communication, since two people perceive each other. The communication may well involve emotion, since along with each person's perception may go a feeling tone. By simply being the other person in a touch relationship, the baby profoundly affects his world in the form of his mother and others who care for him. The tender feelings that well up from holding a baby are the energizers of much mature adult work and development.

Although breast feeding is confined to mothers (and wet nurses), anybody can hold and cuddle a baby. A good feeling comes from meeting his needs, restoring his equilibrium, and helping him to grow. What is more, when two people touch, both get tactual stimulation, and the person who holds a baby gets a sensory and emotional satisfaction from the way his arms, chest, neck, and cheeks feel. Perhaps his own heartbeat is reflected back from the baby's body, giving mutually satisfying stimulation. It is in this situation that the newborn baby begins to build relationships with his father, grandparents, brothers, and sisters.

In most, but not all, non-western cultures, babies are frequently held close to their mothers and often sleep with them at night. Americans tend to leave the baby in his crib or playpen unless he indicates a need for care. Each culture has its own way of handling infants and supports it with theories about what is good for them. Some babies are strapped to cradleboards, others swing in hammocks, some are kept vertical, others horizontal. These different methods of handling produce different kinds and degrees of stimulation in the infants. Presumably, different kinds of development would occur in different cultures, and they do. Life and culture are too complex, however, to show a one-to-one relationship between any kind of infant care and a "piece" of adult behavior.

**Bathing and Dressing.** The film *Four Families* [55] shows the activities involved in the physical care of babies in four different cultures. Although the babies are older than newborns, the point is still valid that many different experiences can go under the name of "bath," and that many of those experiences symbolize a cultural attitude toward children. We (the authors) would like to report a personal cross-cultural experience which highlighted for us the different sets of sensations possible in American and Indian bathing. Laura, our 10-year-old, having fallen in love with the nightwatchman's baby, reported that Umersingh didn't like the way his mother bathed him because he always cried and kicked hard when she put him upside down on her legs, splashed water over him and rubbed him with her hand. Laura brought Umersingh home for baths in our washbasin, where he never cried, and moved his legs in the most gentle, relaxed way. "Ummy prefers American baths," she concluded. The uniformly warm temperature of our washbasin, in contrast to splashed water which cooled quickly, was probably one point in our favor. Also, having his whole body submerged must have been a more satisfying tactual stimulus than merely being wet. The buoying quality of the water, too, would give muscular stimulation. Our bath was more prolonged, with much sudsy washing, which must have felt smooth, slippery, and soothing. Even so, Umersingh might have preferred

**Figure 2–10.** An American mother and baby enjoy a bath together. In this family, a social bath is termed "Swedish."

Halvar Loken

the Japanese bath shown in *Four Families* if he could have compared it with American bathing. The Japanese grandmother took the baby into the bath with her, thereby adding all the tactual delights of (and to) her own skin.

Dressing symbolizes and defines attitudes toward the skin and toward activity. The kind and the amount of stimulation and activity possible depend to a large extent on how the baby is clothed. Exposed to the same conditions, a swaddled baby will not get as much stimulation as a naked baby. Swaddling has been shown to promote calmness and drowsiness, but partial swaddling produces excitement, crying, and activity which looks like outrage [85]. When the surrounding temperature is not ideal, tension reduction is achieved by adding or subtracting clothing and coverings in such a way that the infant's temperature is regulated most comfortably.

Other kinds of physical care can be pleasurably stimulating, such as massage and hair brushing, or of doubtful outcome, such as putting black around the eyes and swabbing the nose. Insofar as the baby's actions initiate care that brings tension reduction, his sense of trust probably increases.

## Summary

The newborn baby is usually red, wrinkled, blue-eyed, and bumpy-headed. He has a large head, a small trunk, and very small, bowed legs. His first big adjustment is to establish breathing with his lungs. The next demand upon him is to secure food through his mouth, which he does by using a complex of reflex mechanisms. He is very limited in his ability to regulate his body temperature.

Many different motor coordinations, involving all parts of the body, can be observed in the neonate. Through crying and food-seeking, he effects environmental changes, many of which involve relationships with his mother. Mutual regulation occurs between mother and baby, especially in the realm of breast feeding, where milk supply and strength of sucking become adapted to each other. First experiences in obtaining food and comfort may be influential in patterning the ways in which the infant copes with other problems.

Sleeping and waking are differentiated into six states. External stimulation is most readily received and processed during the state of alert inactivity.

A child probably tries to maintain the level of stimulation which is optimal for him. Tactile and inner ear senses, highly developed before birth, are very important to the infant. Animal experiments show that early tactile experiences promote growth and learning. Human mothers and babies communicate to a great extent through touch. The neonate can hear, even making fine discrimination in pitch. The sound of the human heartbeat probably has significance for him. The newborn responds to visual stimuli, selecting what he regards, and showing preference for a human face and for complex patterns as compared with simple ones. Taste and smell receptors function. Pain sensitivity in the skin increases during the first few days of life. Infants vary considerably in the intensity and selectivity of their responses to stimuli.

Many or most of the neonate's efforts are directed toward maintaining and restoring states of physiological equilibrium. Growth and development occur as new states of equilibrium are achieved. Presumably, comfortable feelings and healthy personality growth accompany optimal maintenance of equilibrium. A sense of trust grows as the baby is fed, comforted, and stimulated satisfactorily and as he plays some part in bringing about these experiences. Flexible, mutually regulated feeding practices contribute to the sense of trust. Mothers and infants can be helped to establish a satisfactory feeding relationship by a rooming-in arrangement in the hospital. This plan includes expert education given by the nurses. Comfortable feelings, stimulation, and relationships are also built through other aspects of physical care, including holding, handling, dressing, and bathing.

## References

1. Apgar, V. Perinatal problems and the central nervous system. In U.S. Dept. of Health, Education, and Welfare, Children's Bureau, *The child with central nervous system deficit*. Washington, D.C.: U.S. Govt. Printing Office, 1965.
2. Appel, G., & David, M. A study of mother-child interaction at thirteen months. In B. M. Foss, *Determinants of infant behavior*. Vol. III. London: Methuen, 1965, 129–147.
3. Bakwin, H. Current feeding practices for infants. *Nutrition News*, 1965, **28** : 3.
4. Béhar, M. Prevalence of malnutrition among preschool children of developing countries. In N. S. Scrimshaw & J. E. Gordon (Eds.), *Malnutrition, learning and behavior*. Cambridge, Mass.: M.I.T. Press, 1967, pp. 30–41.
5. Bell, R. Q. Relations between behavior manifestations in the human neonate. *Child Devel.*, 1960, **31**, 463–478.
6. Berland, T., & Seyler, A. *Your children's teeth*. New York: Meredith, 1968.
7. Birns, B. Individual differences in human neonates' responses to stimulation. *Child Devel.*, 1965, **36**, 249–259.
8. Birns, B., Barton, S., & Bridger, W. H. Individual differences in temperamental characteristics of infants. *Trans. N.Y. Acad. Sci.*, 1969, Ser. II, **31**, 1071–1082.
9. Birns, B., Blank, M., & Bridger, W. H. The effectiveness of various soothing techniques on human neonates. *Psychosomatic Medicine*, 1966, **28**:4, Part 1, 316–322.
10. Blauvelt, H. H. Capacity of a human neonatal reflex to signal future response by present action. *Child Devel.*, 1962, **33**, 21–29.
11. Brackbill, Y., Adams, G., Crowell, D. H., & Gray, M. L. Arousal level in

neonates and older infants under continuous auditory stimulation. *J. Exper. Child Psychol.*, 1966, **4**, 178–188.

12. Bridger, W. H. Sensory habituation and discrimination in the human neonate. *Am. J. Psychiat.*, 1961, **117**, 991–996.

13. Bronstein, A. I., & Petrova, E. P. The auditory analyzer in young infants. In Y. Brackbill & G. G. Thompson (Eds.), *Behavior in infancy and early childhood.* New York: Free Press, 1967, pp. 163–172.

14. Casler, L. Maternal deprivation: A critical review of the literature. *Mono. Soc. Res. Child Devel.*, 1961, **26**:2.

15. Casler, L. The effects of extra tactile stimulation on a group of institutionalized infants. *Genet. Psychol. Mono.*, 1965, **71**, 137–175.

16. Dennis, W. A description and classification of the responses of the newborn infant. *Psychol. Bull.*, 1934, **31**, 5–22.

17. Doris, J., Casper, M., & Poresky, R. Differential brightness thresholds in infancy. *J. Exper. Child Psychol.*, 1967, **5**, 522–535.

18. Edwards, N. The relationship between physical condition immediately after birth and mental and motor performance at age four. *Genet. Psychol. Mono.*, 1968, **78**, 257–289.

19. Eichorn, D. H. Biology of gestation and infancy: Fatherland and frontier. *Merrill-Palmer Quart.*, 1968, **14**, 47–81.

20. Eppright, E. S., et al. The North Central Regional study of diets of preschool children. 3. Frequency of eating. *J. Home Econ.*, 1970, **62**, 407–410.

21. Erikson, E. H. Childhood and society. New York: Norton, 1963.

22. Fantz, R. L. The origin of form perception. *Sci. Am.*, 1961, **204**:5, 66–72.

23. Fantz, R. L. Visual perception from birth as shown by patterned selectivity. *Ann. N.Y. Acad. Sci.*, 1965, **118**, 793–814.

24. Fantz, R. L. Visual preference and experience in early infancy: A look at the hidden side of behavior development. In H. E. Stevenson, E. H. Hess, & H. L. Rheingold (Eds.), *Early behavior.* New York: Wiley, 1967, pp. 181–224.

25. Frank, L. K. Tactile communication. *Genet. Psychol. Mono.*, 1957, **56**, 209–225.

26. Frank, L. K. *The importance of infancy*, New York: Random House, 1966.

27. Garn, S. M. Genetics of normal human growth. In L. Gedda (Ed.), *De genetica medica.* Rome: Gregor Mendel Instit., 1962. Cited in Eichorn [19].

28. Gordon, T., & Foss, B. M. The role of stimulation in the delay of onset of crying in the newborn infant. *Quart. J. Exper. Psychol.*, 1966, **18**, Part 1, 79–81.

29. Gunther, M. Infant behavior at the breast. In B. M. Foss (Ed.), *Determinants of infant behavior.* Vol. I. New York: Wiley, 1961, pp. 37–44.

30. Haith, M. M. The response of the human newborn to visual movement. *J. Exper. Child Psychol.*, 1966, **3**, 235–243.

31. Harrison, G. A., Weiner, J. S., Tanner, J. M., & Barnicot, N. A. *Human biology.* New York: Oxford University Press, 1964.

32. Haynes, H., White, B. L., & Held, R. Visual accommodation in human infants. *Science*, 1965, **148**, 528–530.

33. Heinstein, M. I. Behavioral correlates of breast-bottle regimes under varying parent–infant relationships. *Mono. Soc. Res. Child Devel.*, 1963, **28**:4.

34. Holt, L. E., Jr., Davies, E. A., Hasselmeyer, E. G., & Adams, A. O. A study of premature infants fed cold formulas. *J. Pediat.*, 1962, **61**, 556–561.

35. Kagan, J. Continuity in cognitive development during the first year. *Merrill-Palmer Quart.*, 1969, **15**, 101–119.

36. Kaye, H. The conditioned Babkin reflex in human newborns. *Psychonomic Sci.*, 1965, **2**, 287–288.

37. Kessen, W. Sucking and looking: Two organized congenital patterns of behavior in the human newborn. In H. W. Stevenson, E. H. Hess, & H. L. Rheingold (Eds.), *Early behavior.* New York: Wiley, 1967, pp. 147–179.

38. Kessen, W., et al. Selection and test of response measures in the study of the human newborn. *Child Devel.*, 1961, **32**, 7–24.

39. Korner, A. F., Chuck, B., & Dontchos, S. Organismic determinants of spontaneous oral behavior in neonates. *Child Devel.*, 1968, **39**, 1145–1157.

40. Korner, A. F., & Grobstein, R. Visual alertness as related to soothing in neonates: Implications for maternal stimulation and early deprivation. *Child Devel.*, 1966, **37**, 867–876.

41. Lenard, H. G., Bernuth, H. (von), & Prechtl, H. F. R. Reflexes and their relationship to behavioral states in the newborn. *Acta Pediatrica Scandinavia*, 1968, **57**, 177–185.

42. Leventhal, A. S., & Lipsitt, L. P. Adaptation, pitch discrimination and sound localization in the neonate. *Child Devel.*, 1964, **35**, 759–767.

43. Liley, H. M. I. *Modern motherhood.* New York: Random House, 1966.

44. Lipsitt, L. P. Learning processes of newborns. *Merrill-Palmer Quart.*, 1966, **12**, 45–71.

45. Lipsitt, L. P. Learning in the human infant. In H. W. Stevenson, E. H. Hess, & H. L. Rheingold (Eds.), *Early behavior.* New York: Wiley, 1967.

46. Lipsitt, L. P., & Levy, N. Electrotactual threshold in the neonate. *Child Devel.*, 1959, **30**, 547–554.

47. Lipton, E. L., & Steinschneider, A. Studies on the psychophysiology of infancy. *Merrill-Palmer Quart.*, 1964, **10**, 102–117.

48. Lipton, E. L., Steinschneider, A., & Richmond, J. B. Autonomic function in the neonate. VII: Maturational changes in cardiac control. *Child Devel.*, 1966, **37**, 1–16.

49. Meredith, H. V. North American Negro infants: Size at birth and growth during the first postnatal year. *Human Biol.*, 1952, **24**:290.

50. Mestyan, G., & Varga, F. Chemical thermoregulation of full-term and premature newborn infants. *J. Pediat.*, 1960, **56**, 623–629.

51. Meyer, H. F. Breast feeding in the United States. *Clinical Pediat.*, 1968, **7**, 708–715.

52. Miranda, S. B. Visual-perceptual abilities and preferences of premature infants and full-term newborns. Paper presented at the meeting of the Society for Research in Child Development, Santa Monica, March 27, 1969.

53. Moss, H. A., & Robson, K. S. The relation between the amount of time infants spend at various states and the development of visual behavior. *Child Devel.*, 1970, **41**, 509–517.

54. Murphy, L. B. *The widening world of childhood.* New York: Basic Books, 1962.

55. National Film Board of Canada. *Four families.*

56. Newton, N. Pregnancy, childbirth and outcome: A review of patterns of culture and future research needs. In S. A. Richardson & A. F. Guttmacher (Eds.), Childbearing—Its social and psychological aspects. Baltimore: Williams & Wilkins, 1967.

57. Newton, N., & Newton, M. Psychologic aspects of lactation. *New England J. Medicine*, 1967, **277**, 1179–1188.

58. *New York Times.* Babies in Lahore start out hungry. October 25, 1970.

59. Ourth, L., & Brown, K. B. Inadequate mothering and disturbance in the neonatal period. *Child Devel.*, 1961, **32**, 287–295.
60. Pederson, D. R., Champagne, L., & Pederson, L. L. Relative soothing effects of vertical and horizontal rocking. Paper presented at meetings of the Society for Research in Child Development, Santa Monica, March 29, 1969.
61. Pratt, K. C. The neonate. In L. Carmichael (Ed.), *Manual of child psychology*. New York: Wiley, 1954, pp. 215–291.
62. Pratt, K. C., Nelson, A. K., & Sun, K. H. *The behavior of the newborn infant*. Ohio State University Studies, Contrib. Psychol. No. 10, 1930.
63. Prechtl, H. F. R. The directed head-turning response and allied movements of the human baby. *Behavior*, 1958, **8**, 212–242.
64. Pryor, K. *Nursing your baby*. New York: Harper & Row, 1963.
65. Richmond, J., & Lipton, E, L. Some aspects of the neurophysiology of the newborn and their implications for child development. In L. Jessner & E. Pavenstedt (Eds,), *Dynamic psychopathology in childhood*. New York: Grune & Stratton, 1959.
66. Roberts, B., & Campbell, D. Activity in newborns and the sound of a human heart. *Psychonomic Sci.*, 1967, **9**, 339–340.
67. Roffwarg, H. P., Muzio, J. N., & Dement, W. C. Ontogenetic development of the human sleep-dream cycle. *Science*, 1966, 604–617.
68. Rosenblatt, J. S. Social environmental factors affecting reproduction and offspring in human mammals. In S. A. Richardson & A. F. Guttmacher (Eds.), Childbearing—Its social and psychological aspects. Baltimore: Williams & Wilkins, 1967, 245–301.
69. Rosenblith, J. F. Prognostic value of neonatal assessment. *Child Devel.*, 1966, **37**, 623–631.
70. Salk, L. Mother's heartbeat as an imprinting stimulus. *Trans. N.Y. Acad. Sci.*, Ser. II, 1962, **24**, 753–763.
71. Sherwin, R. W. Perinatal nutrition as a developmental determinant. *Nutrition News*, 1967, **30**(4), 13–14.
72. Simner, M. L. Auditory self-stimulative feedback and reflexive crying in human infants. Paper presented at the meeting of the Eastern Psychological Association, Altantic City, April, 1970.
73. Simner, M. L., & Reilly, B. Response of the newborn infant to the cry of another infant. Paper presented at the meeting of the Society for Research in Child Development, Santa Monica, Calif., March 28, 1969.
74. Smith, C. A. *The physiology of the newborn infant*. Springfield, Ill.: Charles C Thomas, 1959.
75. Spears, W. C., & Hohle, R. H. Sensory and perceptual processes in infants. In Y. Brackbill (Ed.), *Infancy and early childhood*. New York: Free Press, 1967, pp. 49–121.
76. Spock, B. *Baby and child care*. New York: Pocket Books, 1968.
77. Stagner, R. Homeostasis, need reduction and motivation. *Merrill-Palmer Quart.*, 1961, **7**, 49–69.
78. Steinschneider, A., Lipton, E. L., & Richmond, B. Auditory sensitivity in the infant: Effect of intensity on cardiac and motor activity. *Child Devel.*, 1966, **37**, 233–252.
79. Tanner, J. M. *Education and physical growth*. London: University of London, 1961.
80. Thomson, A. M. Historical perspectives of nutrition, reproduction and growth.

In N. S. Scrimshaw & J. E. Gordon (Eds.), *Malnutrition, learning and behavior.* Cambridge, Mass.: M.I.T. Press, 1968, 17–28.

81. Vallbona, C., et al. Cardiodynamic studies in the newborn II. Regulation of heart rate. *Biologia Neonatorum*, 1963, **5**, 159–199.

82. Watson, E. H., & Lowrey, G. H. *Growth and development of children* (5th ed.). Chicago: Yearbook, 1967.

83. Wertheimer, M. Psychomotor coordination of auditory and visual perception at birth. *Science*, 1961, **134**, 1962.

84. Wolff, P. H. The development of attention in young infants. *Ann. N.Y. Acad. Sci.*, 1965, **118**, 815–830.

85. Wolff, P. H. The causes, controls and organization of behavior in the neonate. *Psychol. Issues*, 1966, **5** : 1. New York: International Universities Press.

86. Wolff, P. H., & Simmons, M. A. Nonnutritive sucking and response thresholds in young infants. *Child Devel.*, 1967, **38**, 631–638.

# Chapter 3

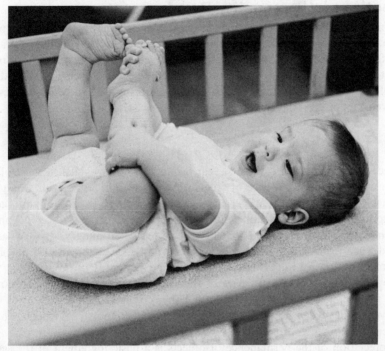

Merrill-Palmer Institute by Donna J. Harris

# Emerging Resources for Coping with the World

The drama of the first two years of life involves the change from horizontal to vertical, from sedentary creature to runner, from crybaby to speaker, from vast dependency to a large measure of autonomy. The changes are comparable to the changes from prenatal to postnatal life, and much more visible and comprehensible. Although the newborn comes equipped for maintaining his body processes, his behavior is largely subcortical, controlled by lower brain centers and not those basic to thinking and consciousness. As the cerebral cortex matures, behavior rapidly becomes more complex and flexible. Reflex activity is suppressed and/or integrated into larger coordinations that have some conscious control. For example, the area of the motor cortex controlling the arms matures before the area that controls the legs. At 3 or 4 weeks, the legs are at their peak of making reflex crawling movements, while the arms, inhibited by cortical control, do not make many reflex movements. The interpretation and use of sensory perception is thought to follow the order of maturing of the cerebral cortex, with vision more advanced

**87**

than hearing during infancy. Active, like all living creatures, and with powers emerging, like all developing creatures, the infant deals more and more effectively with the world, the people in it and himself.

## Directions in Personality Development

Infancy encompasses the first critical period in personality growth and part of the second. The development of the sense of trust comes first, laying the groundwork for a feeling of security throughout life. The development of a sense of autonomy is central to personality growth from about $1\frac{1}{2}$ to $3\frac{1}{2}$ or 4 years of age. Most of the infant's behavior and experiences can be understood in the light of these two achievements in personality development [25, pp. 247–254].

### Trust

Successful growth during the first year results in a well-established sense of trust. Begun with the first experience of securing food and skin stimulation, the growth of trust continues through experiences with things, other people, and the self. The good feelings from tension reduction, repeated consistently in good physical care, make the baby confident that he will be fed when hungry, dried when wet, rocked when restless, and stimulated when bored. He is confident also that he can do something toward initiating these satisfying experiences.

People, largely mother, are part of the good-feeling experiences and come to stand for the whole. Thus the 4-month baby, crying from hunger, stops crying and even smiles when he sees his mother or hears her footsteps, trusting that she will feed him.

Appreciation of the permanence of objects is a basic ingredient of the sense of trust. Through his interactions with the world during his first year and a half, the baby comes to know that things exist even when he is not perceiving them. As will be described in greater detail later in the chapter, the first 18 months is the sensorimotor period, in Piaget's series of stages. The two essential achievements of this period are a realization of the permanence of objects and the organization and control of his movements in space. These two achievements go along together. As the baby controls the movements of his body, he deals with the objects of the world, seeing and feeling them, noticing them as they appear and disappear, understanding that events can take place when he is not watching. He comes to trust the world to have certain kinds of order in it, to be dependable. He also comes to know his own powers and how to use them, a beginning of the sense of autonomy.

Establishing trust also involves learning that mother (and others) exists even when she cannot be seen, and that she will come again and again. The game of peekaboo dramatizes mother's disappearance and reappearance. In playing it, the infant lives and relives the frightening situation which has a happy ending, enjoying it throughout the months when trust is growing as he learns that mother continues to exist apart from him. His sense of self begins perhaps from this knowledge and certainly grows as he explores his own body. Fingering his hand and watching it move yield one complex of sensations; fingering the blanket gives another. Reaching, grasping, securing, releasing, touching, mouthing—all tell him what is himself, what are other things and what he can do, or what he can trust his body to do with the world. As a good feeling goes along with the accumulation of knowledge of his body, his power, the objects outside himself, and other people, then the sense of trust grows. Mistrust arises from discomfort, disappointment, anxiety, inability to explore, discriminate, and cope with the world.*

## Autonomy

In the beginning or early months of the second year, the baby who trusts himself and the world is ready to concentrate on the next stage in personality growth, the development of autonomy. Able to move himself from one place to another, able to pick up, manipulate and reject toys, able to say a few words, able to feed himself some foods, able to "hang on" for a while when he feels the urge to eliminate, he has many choices to make. He feels autonomous as he makes choices freely and wholeheartedly. He gets the feeling "What I do is all right" and a companion feeling, "There are many things that I can either do or not do."

*Me do* is the keynote phrase of the age from 18 months to 2½. Everyone knows how determined 2-year-olds are to do things in their own ways at their own times. The doing and the choosing are the means of growth, for these are the ways in which toddlers test themselves, other people, and the world in order to establish themselves as creatures who function independently and adequately.

Choosing involves taking or leaving, holding on to or letting go. When the child discovers, through active testing, that there are many situations in which he can choose and live comfortably with his choice, then he feels good about himself. He can decide whether to take a proffered hand or not, whether to play with the truck or the bunny, whether to have a second serving of applesauce or not, whether to sit on grandma's lap or stand on his feet. He also needs restrictions that are clear and firm, in order to prevent him from making choices that are beyond him. Frustration and consequent anger are frequent even in older infants who are guided with skill and understanding. Temper outbursts increase in the latter part of infancy, as the child tests himself to find out what he can do and tests his parents and his world to find out what they will let him do. Each successful encounter and choice adds to his sense of autonomy. Shame and doubt arise when disaster follows choice-making and also when the child is not allowed to make enough choices. Shame, doubt, and inadequacy (lack of autonomy) lead to extremes of behavior— rebellion or oversubmissiveness, hurling or hanging on tight.†

In longitudinal studies of children, the beginnings of autonomous behavior have been seen even in early infancy, especially in the ways in which infants defended themselves from unwanted experiences [74, pp. 226–227, 302]. Babies differed in how often and how vigorously they protested over feeding, rejected foods and ended the meal. They differed in ways of rejecting stimulation and being moved. For instance, some babies of 3 or 4 months stiffened their back and legs when adults

---

* The period of development of trust is the *oral stage* in psychoanalytic theory. The mouth is the site of the most important experiences, feeding and the love relationship associated with feeding. Pain from teething is associated with biting and cruel, harsh experiences. In many psychoanalytic writings the skin senses and other senses, too, are greatly overshadowed by the significance of the mouth.

† The period of autonomy is the anal stage in psychoanalytic theory. The central problem is dramatized by the idea of the anal sphincters which open or shut, hanging on or letting go. Depending on the child's experiences with bowel control and control by other people, his personality takes on characteristics like suspicion or confidence, stinginess or generosity, doubt and shame, or autonomy and adequacy.

were performing unwelcome procedures, while others relaxed and went limp. The first reaction resembled taking a stand, even before the child could literally stand up, whereas the second was more like passive resistance. As soon as infants can move around, some will crawl, pull, or stretch to get away from an unpleasant situation, and others will push the adult away, kick, fight, or protest against him.

Infants in the study were shown to differ in how much stimulation they accepted and sought and in how they reduced unwelcome stimulation. Some children were hyperalert to sights and sounds, and others seemed to shut out many of them. Thus while the peak age for concern with autonomy is between 18 months and 3 or 4 years, some attempts at autonomous behavior occur much earlier.

## Physical and Motor Development

Development and change are rapid during the first two years of life. This period, as well as the preschool years, is a time when illness is relatively frequent, and careful physical care is consequently very worthwhile.

After the first month, more or less, a baby really looks like a baby, like babies in ads and photograph albums, like other babies in the neighborhood—chubby, skin pink and white, golden, brown, or whatever it is destined to be, bumps smoothed out, and nose in shape. New coarser hair comes in during infancy, replacing the fine black hair of the newborn (if he had it) and showing more and more the color it is going to be. Compared with an older child, a baby has a large forehead, large eyes, small nose, small chin, and plump cheeks. His hands and feet are chubby and his abdomen round; his delicate skin looks soft and fragile.

Babies differ in appearance, from one to another; the older they are, the more obvious the differences. They differ, of course, in coloring, facial features, amount and type of hair, height, and weight. They feel different, too. Firm muscles and good muscle tone give a solid impression, in contrast to the softness of slacker muscles or abundant fat. The baby's reactions to being held also add to the impression, according to whether the infant holds himself erect, pushes away or yields to the arms which hold him.

### Proportions and Measurements

Changes in shape and proportion continue along the lines charted prenatally, the head regions being most developed, the trunk and legs beginning to catch up, the center of gravity high in the trunk but descending. Birth weight is doubled by 4 or 5 months and tripled at 1 year. Height is doubled by about 4 years. Thus the child starts life as a slender neonate, fills out to a round, plump infant during the first year, and then in the second year, he again becomes more slender, continuing this trend into middle childhood. A ratio useful for diagnosing malnutrition is that of head to thorax. After 6 months of age, the thorax is larger than the head in normal children. The difference in circumference between thorax and head increases with age. When a child is growing inadequately, his weight deficit is related to the difference between head and thorax [21]. Height and weight percentile tables (Tables 3–1 through 3–4) can be used to compare a baby with others the same age and sex. These tables are based on repeated measurements of more than 100 white, normally healthy infants of each sex, living in Boston. Height was measured with the infant lying on his back. This table can be used to tell how many children (of

**Table 3–1**  Height Percentile Table for Boys from Birth through Age 2

| Age | Length in Inches | | | | | | |
|-----|------|------|------|------|------|------|------|
|     | 3%   | 10%  | 25%  | 50%  | 75%  | 90%  | 97%  |
| Birth  | 18¼  | 19    | 19½  | 20    | 20½  | 21    | 21½  |
| 1 mo.  | 19¾  | 20¼  | 20¾  | 21¼  | 22    | 22¼  | 23¾  |
| 2 mo.  | 21    | 21½  | 22    | 22½  | 23    | 23½  | 24    |
| 3 mo.  | 22½  | 22¾  | 24¼  | 23¾  | 24¼  | 24¾  | 25    |
| 4 mo.  | 23½  | 23¾  | 24¼  | 24¾  | 25¼  | 25¾  | 26    |
| 5 mo.  | 24¼  | 24½  | 25    | 25½  | 26    | 26½  | 27    |
| 6 mo.  | 24¾  | 25¼  | 25¾  | 26    | 26¾  | 27¼  | 27¾  |
| 7 mo.  | 25½  | 26    | 26¼  | 26¾  | 27¼  | 28    | 28½  |
| 8 mo.  | 26    | 26½  | 27    | 27½  | 28    | 28¾  | 29¼  |
| 9 mo.  | 26½  | 27    | 27½  | 28    | 28¾  | 29¼  | 30    |
| 10 mo. | 27    | 27½  | 28    | 28½  | 29¼  | 29¾  | 30½  |
| 11 mo. | 27½  | 28    | 28½  | 29    | 29¾  | 30¼  | 31    |
| 12 mo. | 28    | 28½  | 29    | 29½  | 30¼  | 30¾  | 31½  |
| 13 mo. | 28½  | 29    | 29½  | 30    | 30¾  | 31¼  | 32    |
| 14 mo. | 29    | 29½  | 30    | 30½  | 31¼  | 31¾  | 32½  |
| 15 mo. | 29¼  | 29¾  | 30¼  | 31    | 31½  | 32    | 33    |
| 16 mo. | 29¾  | 30¼  | 30¾  | 31½  | 32    | 32½  | 33½  |
| 17 mo. | 30¼  | 30½  | 31¼  | 31¾  | 32½  | 33    | 34    |
| 18 mo. | 30½  | 31    | 31½  | 32¼  | 33    | 33½  | 34½  |
| 19 mo. | 31    | 31½  | 32    | 32¾  | 33¼  | 34    | 35¼  |
| 20 mo. | 31¼  | 31¾  | 32½  | 33    | 33¾  | 34½  | 35½  |
| 21 mo. | 31½  | 32    | 32¾  | 33¼  | 34    | 34¾  | 36    |
| 22 mo. | 32    | 32½  | 33    | 33¾  | 34½  | 35    | 36½  |
| 23 mo. | 32¼  | 32¾  | 33½  | 34    | 34¾  | 35½  | 36¾  |
| 24 mo. | 32½  | 33    | 33¾  | 34½  | 35¼  | 36    | 37¼  |

SOURCE: From *Growth and Development of Children*, 5th edition, by Ernest H. Watson and George H. Lowrey. Copyright © 1967, Year Book Medical Publishers, Inc., Chicago. Used by permission of Year Book Medical Publishers.

the type sampled by this study) out of 100 will be longer or shorter, heavier or lighter than any given baby. For example, Becky, at 6 months, weighs 17 pounds and measures 27¼ inches. The table shows that she is above the 97th percentile in height (length) and slightly below the 75th percentile in weight. Taller than 97 baby girls in 100, she is a very tall girl. In spite of her chubby face and rounded abdomen, the table tells that as to weight, she is average, since 24 in 100 exceed her in weight and no more than 2 exceed her in height.

Height–weight tables which give only averages have little use for the individual, although they are useful for comparing groups. Percentile tables, such as those shown here, give more information than mere averages. However, they take no account of body build nor do they consider heredity. The ideal weight for a short-legged, long-trunked child such as an Aleutian Islander would obviously be greater than for a white American of the same age. The expected height for the child of tall parents is greater than for the child of short parents. For example, for white Ohio sons of short parents, the average length at 1 year was 29 inches, at 2, 33.6; for sons of tall parents, the 1-year length was 30.5 inches and at 2, 35.0 [31].

*Skinfold thickness* is a measurement useful for detecting suboptimal nutrition in large groups of children, as in national surveys [54]. Accurate scales may not be

**Table 3–2** Height percentile Table for Girls from Birth through Age 2

| Age | Length in Inches | | | | | | |
|---|---|---|---|---|---|---|---|
| | 3% | 10% | 25% | 50% | 75% | 90% | 97% |
| Birth | 18½ | 18¾ | 19¼ | 19¾ | 20 | 20½ | 21 |
| 1 mo. | 19¾ | 20¼ | 20½ | 21 | 21½ | 22 | 22½ |
| 2 mo. | 21 | 21½ | 21¾ | 22¼ | 23 | 23¼ | 23¾ |
| 3 mo. | 22 | 22½ | 22¾ | 23½ | 24 | 24¼ | 24¾ |
| 4 mo. | 22¾ | 23¼ | 23¾ | 24¼ | 24¾ | 25¼ | 25¾ |
| 5 mo. | 23½ | 24 | 24½ | 25 | 25½ | 26 | 26½ |
| 6 mo. | 24 | 24½ | 25 | 25¾ | 26¼ | 26¾ | 27 |
| 7 mo. | 24½ | 25¼ | 25¾ | 26¼ | 27 | 27½ | 27¾ |
| 8 mo. | 25¼ | 25¾ | 26¼ | 27 | 27½ | 28 | 28½ |
| 9 mo. | 25¾ | 26½ | 27 | 27½ | 28¼ | 28¾ | 29¼ |
| 10 mo. | 26¼ | 27 | 27½ | 28 | 28¾ | 29¼ | 29¾ |
| 11 mo. | 26¾ | 27¼ | 28 | 28½ | 29¼ | 29¾ | 30½ |
| 12 mo. | 27 | 27¾ | 28½ | 29¼ | 30 | 30¼ | 31 |
| 13 mo. | 27½ | 28¼ | 29 | 29½ | 30¼ | 30¾ | 31½ |
| 14 mo. | 28 | 28½ | 29½ | 30 | 30¾ | 31¼ | 32 |
| 15 mo. | 28¼ | 29 | 29¾ | 30½ | 31¼ | 31¾ | 32½ |
| 16 mo. | 28¾ | 29½ | 30¼ | 31 | 31¾ | 32¼ | 33 |
| 17 mo. | 29 | 29¾ | 30¾ | 31¼ | 32¼ | 32¾ | 33½ |
| 18 mo. | 29½ | 30¼ | 31 | 31¾ | 32½ | 33¼ | 34 |
| 19 mo. | 30 | 30½ | 31½ | 32¼ | 33 | 33¾ | 34½ |
| 20 mo. | 30¼ | 31 | 32 | 32½ | 33½ | 34¼ | 35 |
| 21 mo. | 30½ | 31¼ | 32¼ | 33 | 33¾ | 34¾ | 35½ |
| 22 mo. | 31 | 31¾ | 32¾ | 33¼ | 34¼ | 35¼ | 36 |
| 23 mo. | 31¼ | 32 | 33 | 33¾ | 34½ | 35½ | 36¼ |
| 24 mo. | 31½ | 32¼ | 33¼ | 34 | 35 | 35¾ | 36¾ |

SOURCE: From *Growth and Development of Children*, 5th edition, by Ernest H. Watson and George H. Lowrey. Copyright © 1967, Year Book Medical Publishers, Inc., Chicago. Used by permission of Year Book Medical Publishers.

available for weighing and exact ages may not be known. Exact age is not necessary when skinfold measurements are used between 1 and 5 years of age. Children with protein–calorie malnutrition were usually below the third percentile and almost always below the tenth.

### Illnesses

Respiratory infections are the most frequent type of physical difficulty for American children, with gastrointestinal upsets second in frequency [103]. Figure 3–1 shows the number of occurrences of various kinds of illnesses in a group of 134 American children between birth and 2 years of age. For over half the children in the world, however, the greatest physical threat is from malnutrition, especially protein malnutrition [56]. And while protein malnutrition contributes to the high death rate in underdeveloped countries, the majority of afflicted children survive, impaired physically and often mentally [17]. Growth in height and weight of well-nourished children slows down in the latter half of the first year. At the same time, the rate of muscle growth increases. Also at this age, the baby is getting a smaller proportion of his calories from milk. For each unit of body weight, the 6-months-

**Table 3-3** Weight Percentile Table for Boys from Birth through Age 2

| | Weight in Pounds | | | | | | |
|---|---|---|---|---|---|---|---|
| Age | 3% | 10% | 25% | 50% | 75% | 90% | 97% |
| Birth | 5¾ | 6¼ | 7 | 7½ | 8¼ | 9 | 10 |
| 1 mo. | 7½ | 8½ | 9 | 10 | 10½ | 11½ | 13 |
| 2 mo. | 9 | 10 | 10½ | 11½ | 12 | 13¼ | 14¾ |
| 3 mo. | 10½ | 11 | 11¾ | 12½ | 13½ | 14½ | 16¼ |
| 4 mo. | 11¾ | 12½ | 13¼ | 14 | 15 | 16¼ | 18 |
| 5 mo. | 13 | 13¾ | 14¼ | 15 | 16½ | 17¾ | 19½ |
| 6 mo. | 14 | 14¾ | 15½ | 16¾ | 18 | 19¼ | 20¾ |
| 7 mo. | 15 | 15¾ | 16¾ | 18 | 19 | 20¾ | 22¼ |
| 8 mo. | 15¾ | 16¾ | 17¾ | 19 | 20½ | 22 | 23½ |
| 9 mo. | 16½ | 17¾ | 18¾ | 20 | 21½ | 23 | 24½ |
| 10 mo. | 17¼ | 18¼ | 19½ | 20¾ | 22½ | 23¾ | 25¼ |
| 11 mo. | 18 | 18¾ | 20¼ | 21½ | 23¼ | 24½ | 26¼ |
| 12 mo. | 18½ | 19½ | 20¾ | 22¼ | 23¾ | 25½ | 27¼ |
| 13 mo. | 19 | 20 | 21¼ | 22¾ | 24½ | 26 | 27¾ |
| 14 mo. | 19½ | 20½ | 22 | 23¼ | 25 | 26½ | 28½ |
| 15 mo. | 19¾ | 21 | 22½ | 23¾ | 25½ | 27¼ | 29½ |
| 16 mo. | 20¼ | 21½ | 23 | 24¼ | 26 | 27¾ | 30¼ |
| 17 mo. | 20¾ | 21¾ | 23½ | 24¾ | 26½ | 28½ | 31 |
| 18 mo. | 21 | 22¼ | 23¾ | 25¼ | 27 | 29 | 31½ |
| 19 mo. | 21½ | 22¾ | 24¼ | 25¾ | 27½ | 29½ | 32¼ |
| 20 mo. | 22 | 23¼ | 24¾ | 26 | 28 | 30 | 33 |
| 21 mo. | 22¼ | 23½ | 25 | 26½ | 28½ | 30½ | 33½ |
| 22 mo. | 22½ | 24 | 25½ | 26¾ | 28¾ | 31 | 34 |
| 23 mo. | 23 | 24¼ | 26 | 27¼ | 29¼ | 31½ | 34½ |
| 24 mo. | 23¼ | 24¾ | 26¼ | 27¾ | 29¾ | 32 | 35 |

Source: From *Growth and Development of Children*, 5th edition, by Ernest H. Watson and George H. Lowrey. Copyright © 1967, Year Book Medical Publishers, Inc., Chicago. Used by permission of Year Book Medical Publishers.

old baby needs about twice as many calories and five times as much high quality protein as an adult needs. The 2-year-old needs about 70 percent more calories and three times as much protein as an adult [12]. If the infant is living in poverty, his protein is drastically cut as he is weaned onto inadequate foods. At an international conference on nutrition, one of the leaders [56] said,

> for every small child anywhere in the world, of any race or ethnic heritage, of any social or economic background, it is nutritionally now or never. This is particularly so for each newborn infant in city or farm, in desert or jungle, for every day of his first two years of life. Some will make it. Many will not. "Too little" and "too late" may indeed be forever.

**Nutrition and Disease.** Marasmus and kwashiorkor are two severe diseases due to malnutrition. *Marasmus* is a wasting away of body tissues. When suffering from marasmus, an infant is grossly underweight, with atrophy of muscles and subcutaneous fat but with no clinical edema [49]. Marasmus is caused by undernutrition, resulting from insufficient food or from not utilizing food. A severe emotional disturbance can cause the child not to eat or to be unable to utilize food adequately. A longitudinal study of children with *marasmus* was done in Chile, where a recent decline in breast feeding has produced some severe malnutrition in

**Table 3–4** Weight Percentile Table for Girls from Birth through Age 2

| Age | Weight in Pounds | | | | | | |
|---|---|---|---|---|---|---|---|
| | 3% | 10% | 25% | 50% | 75% | 90% | 97% |
| Birth | 5¾ | 6¼ | 7 | 7½ | 8 | 8½ | 9½ |
| 1 mo. | 7 | 8 | 8½ | 9¾ | 10¼ | 11 | 11¾ |
| 2 mo. | 8¼ | 9½ | 10¼ | 11 | 11¾ | 12½ | 13½ |
| 3 mo. | 9½ | 10¾ | 11½ | 12¼ | 13 | 13¾ | 14¾ |
| 4 mo. | 10¾ | 12 | 12¾ | 13¾ | 14½ | 15½ | 16½ |
| 5 mo. | 11¾ | 13 | 13¾ | 14¾ | 16 | 17 | 18¼ |
| 6 mo. | 12¾ | 14 | 14¾ | 15¾ | 17¼ | 18½ | 19¾ |
| 7 mo. | 13½ | 15 | 16 | 17 | 18½ | 20 | 21¼ |
| 8 mo. | 14¼ | 15¾ | 16¾ | 18 | 19½ | 21¼ | 22½ |
| 9 mo. | 14¾ | 16¼ | 17½ | 18¾ | 20¼ | 22 | 23½ |
| 10 mo. | 15½ | 17 | 18¼ | 19¾ | 21¼ | 23 | 24¾ |
| 11 mo. | 16 | 17½ | 19 | 20½ | 22 | 23¾ | 25¾ |
| 12 mo. | 16½ | 18 | 19½ | 21 | 22½ | 24½ | 26½ |
| 13 mo. | 17 | 18½ | 20¼ | 21¾ | 23¼ | 25¼ | 27½ |
| 14 mo. | 17½ | 19 | 20¾ | 22¼ | 23¾ | 25¾ | 28 |
| 15 mo. | 18 | 19½ | 21¼ | 22¾ | 24½ | 26½ | 28¾ |
| 16 mo. | 18½ | 20 | 21¾ | 23¼ | 25 | 27 | 29½ |
| 17 mo. | 18¾ | 20½ | 22¼ | 23¾ | 25½ | 27½ | 30 |
| 18 mo. | 19¼ | 21 | 22½ | 24¼ | 26 | 28 | 30¾ |
| 19 mo. | 19½ | 21½ | 23 | 25 | 26½ | 28¾ | 31¼ |
| 20 mo. | 20 | 21¾ | 23½ | 25½ | 27 | 29¼ | 32 |
| 21 mo. | 20¼ | 22¼ | 23¾ | 25¾ | 27½ | 29¾ | 32½ |
| 22 mo. | 20¾ | 22¾ | 24¼ | 26¼ | 28 | 30½ | 33 |
| 23 mo. | 21¼ | 23 | 24¾ | 26¾ | 28½ | 31 | 33¾ |
| 24 mo. | 21½ | 23½ | 25¼ | 27 | 29¼ | 31¾ | 34½ |

Source: From *Growth and Development of Children*, 5th edition, by Ernest H. Watson and George H. Lowrey. Copyright © 1967, Year Book Medical Publishers, Inc., Chicago. Used by permission of Year Book Medical Publishers.

early infancy [72]. These babies were admitted to the hospital at ages 3 to 11 months, with acute marasmus which had begun at some time between 1 and 5 months. Most of them weighed little more than they did at birth. They were treated to recovery and sent home with a steady and adequate supply of milk. At ages 3 to 6 years, all were clinically normal, with height far below average (lower than the third percentile) for Chilean children. Legs were short. Weights were all above the third percentile, many close to the fiftieth percentile. Thus weights were above normal for heights and some children looked obese. Head circumferences were below normal.

*Kwashiorkor* occurs most often in 1- to 4-year-olds whose diets are very low in proteins while being not so low in total calories [49]. The biochemical changes in the body are quite different in the two diseases, kwashiorkor having more lasting effects after the acute stage is alleviated. Symptoms of kwashiorkor are swelling of face, legs, and abdomen due to water retention, growth retardation, wasting of muscles with some fat retained, apathy, or whimpering. The hair may be reddish and thin and the skin coarse, spotted, or with a rash or lesions. Liver damage and brain damage are likely to occur [65, pp. 216–223]. Full-blown kwashiorkor and marasmus represent only a small part of the worldwide picture of child malnutri-

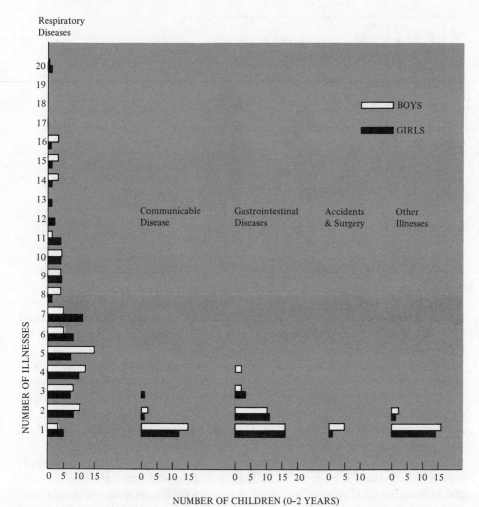

**Figure 3–1.** In 134 children between birth and 2 years, numbers of illnesses and accidents are shown. Respiratory infections are by far the greatest cause of illness in infancy.

SOURCE: I. Valadian, H. C. Stuart, and R. B. Reed, "Studies of Illnesses of Children Followed from Birth to Eighteen Years," *Monographs of The Society for Research in Child Development*, **26**:3.

tion. "Protein–calorie malnutrition is like a huge undersea mountain, a small fraction visible above the surface, while the great bulk is submerged and unseen" [93, p. 42]. All over the world, including the United States of America, poor children are suffering from insufficient protein, often along with insufficient calories. Their physical and mental growth and health are being depressed now and for the future.

A recent nutritional survey of low-income areas in Texas, Louisiana, and parts of New York and Kentucky gives some data on nutrition and disease [88]. The children between 1 year and 3 years old were considerably below the average height of children in the United States. Three times the expected number were below the sixteenth percentile of the Iowa Growth Chart. Figure 3–2 gives an idea of how these children compared with the average in height. The authors reported to a Senate

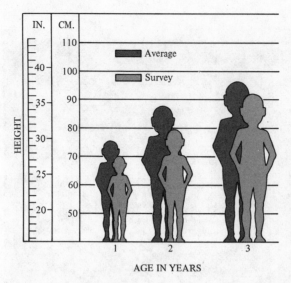

**Figure 3–2.** Average height of boys one-to-three in National Nutrition Survey compared with American averages.

SOURCE: Reprinted by permission from A. E. Schaefer and O. C. Johnson, "Are We Well Fed?" *Nutrition Today*, 4:1, 2–11. Copyright © 1969, Enloe, Stalvey and Associates.

committee; ". . . we found every kind of malnutrition that any of us has seen in similar studies in Central America, Africa and Asia. It is just as prevalent in these areas as it is in many of the remote countries" [88]. The clinical findings included seven cases of severe kwashiorkor and marasmus.

Malnourished children are more likely than well-nourished to suffer all sorts of infections and to have more severe cases. Infections add to the state of malnutrition by depressing the appetite and requiring mobilization of nitrogen and other essential nutrients [92]. After the period of stress is over, during convalescence, the normal course of events is the returning of the nutrients to the tissue from which they were drawn, but this process requires extra proteins and vitamins, the very elements most lacking in the diets of the poor. The baby who started an illness as malnourished, then, is in a worse state of nutrition when the infection subsides and is ready to pick up another infection, for which his resistance is even lower. Malnutrition depresses the body's manufacture of antibodies. Growth is slowed down, since the nutrients it requires are insufficient.

At the time of weaning from the breast, or the time when the mother's milk becomes inadequate, supplementation with poor quality, unsanitary food introduces disease organisms causing infections, diarrhea, and parasite infestations. Widened social contact introduce viral diseases such as measles and other childhood diseases. Pneumonia is a frequent complication of measles.

**Poverty and Disease.** Poverty makes for poor hygiene which spreads disease. In Asia and Africa, drinking boiled water greatly reduces one's chances of contracting amebic dysentery, typhoid, and many more diseases, but the ordinary family does not have facilities for boiling and storing water, nor do they believe it would be worthwhile to do so. The weanling baby receives an inadequate diet not only because the family diet is inadequate but also because his mother believes that a watered gruel is good for him because it looks like milk, that eggs and meat are too strong for him, or that coconut milk will make him stupid. Illiteracy and ignorance of the mother are important influences on the baby's health and growth. Figure 3–3 summarizes the interaction of malnutrition, disease, their causes, and results.

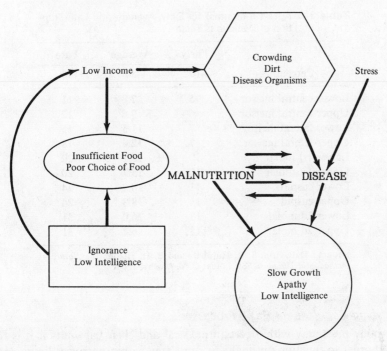

**Figure 3–3.** Interlocking causes and results of malnutrition and disease.

### Injuries

As soon as the baby can creep, he needs increased care in protecting him from accidents. When he walks and climbs, potential danger is much greater. Accidents to toddlers are discussed in Chapter 5, along with accidents at older preschool ages. In Chapters 4 and 5 we shall consider a kind of injury which is taking on new proportions in America: the damage that parents do intentionally to their own children.

### Teething

Almost as obvious as children's increase in height and weight is the appearance of teeth. A baby's toothless grin, the single tooth of a slightly older baby, the gaps left in the row of teeth between the shedding of the first incisors and the coming of the permanent incisors—these are familiar landmarks in development. The timing of tooth eruption differs considerably (more than 10 percent) when Chinese, whites, blacks, Amerinds, East Indians, and Eskimos are compared [32]. The least favored groups seem to have the most advanced eruption times.

Growth studies of American children have shown a low, positive correlation between skeletal development and dental development [32]. The correlation is too small to be useful in predicting maturity.

At birth the crowns of the 20 deciduous (baby) teeth are partially calcified. It will be 7 months or more before one of them appears. Table 3–5 shows average, early, and late timing of eruption of the deciduous teeth.

Genetic factors are important in determining eruption time, size, shape, and discrepancies in number of teeth [105, pp. 386–387]. Environmental influences on health and development of teeth will be discussed later in relation to the school-age child.

**Table 3–5** Ages (in months) for Early, Average, and Late Eruption of Deciduous Teeth

|  | **Early** | **Average** | **Late** |
|---|---|---|---|
| **Percentiles** | 10 | 50 | 90 |
| Lower central incisor | 5 | 7.8 | 11 |
| Upper central incisor | 6 | 9.6 | 12 |
| Lower lateral incisor | 7 | 11.5 | 15 |
| Upper lateral incisor | 7 | 12.4 | 18 |
| Lower 1st molar | 10 | 15.1 | 20 |
| Upper 1st molar | 10 | 15.7 | 20 |
| Lower cuspid | 11 | 18.2 | 24 |
| Upper cuspid | 11 | 18.3 | 24 |
| Lower 2d molar | 13 | 26.0 | 31 |
| Upper 2d molar | 13 | 26.2 | 31 |

SOURCE: Data from S. L. Horowitz and E. H. Hixon, *The Nature of Orthodontic Diagnosis*. St. Louis: C. V. Mosby, 1966.

### Establishing Regularity of Basic Processes

The body must stay within certain physical and chemical limits if it is to stay alive. In order to function optimally, it must stay within narrower limits. Homeostasis, the maintenance of steady states within these limits, is accomplished by integrated control of the nervous and endocrine systems. During the first 3 or 4 months of life, the mechanisms of homeostasis become more and more efficient. The baby settles down to an easier, more automatic supporting of life processes, his energies freed for a wider variety of activities.

Temperature regulation is one of the vital homeostatic processes. A certain constancy has to be kept in spite of heat loss and heat production. The baby regulates his temperature more adequately after the neonatal period than he does in the beginning. For example, the sweat glands become active at about a month of age. Even with temperature regulation improving, infants and young children are still highly susceptible to temperature fluctuation. Bodily temperature is likely to shoot up with active exercise, crying, emotional upset, or rise in surrounding temperature [9, p. 133]. Bodily temperature responds readily to chilling. Infants and young children, when suffering from infections, usually show higher temperatures than do older children. Table 3–6 shows the average temperature throughout infancy and childhood. Note that while the average temperature at 3 months is 99.4, about one third of babies this age have temperatures above 100.2 or below 98.6. At 6 months, two thirds of infants have temperatures between 100.1 and 98.9. The corresponding range at 1 year is 100.2 to 99.2. Thus average temperature and individual variations decrease as the infant grows into childhood. Individual differences continue to exist, though, and it is important to realize that an occasional child may have an unusually high (or low) temperature which is normal for *him* [105].

Heat production increases with age throughout the growth period. The younger the child, the more he is likely to vary from the average and also to vary with himself from time to time [55]. The larger the body, of course, the greater the absolute amount of heat produced. Taken in terms of heat production per unit of body

Table 3–6 Average Body Temperature of Infants and Children

| Age | Temperature | | Standard Deviation | |
|---|---|---|---|---|
| | F. | C. | F. | C. |
| 3 months | 99.4 | 37.5 | 0.8 | 0.4 |
| 6 months | 99.5 | 37.5 | 0.6 | 0.3 |
| 1 year | 99.7 | 37.7 | 0.5 | 0.2 |
| 3 years | 99.0 | 37.2 | 0.5 | 0.2 |
| 5 years | 98.6 | 37.0 | 0.5 | 0.2 |
| 7 years | 98.3 | 36.8 | 0.5 | 0.2 |
| 9 years | 98.1 | 36.7 | 0.5 | 0.2 |
| 11 years | 98.0 | 36.7 | 0.5 | 0.2 |
| 13 years | 97.8 | 36.6 | 0.5 | 0.2 |

SOURCE: From *Growth and Development of Children*, 5th edition, by Ernest H. Watson and George H. Lowrey. Copyright © 1967, Year Book Medical Publishers, Inc., Chicago. Used by permission of Year Book Medical Publishers.

weight, however, the 6-month baby produces more heat than anybody. Heat production builds up from birth to 6 months and then tapers off to adulthood.

Considering what is known about temperature in children, it can be seen that good care includes protection against extremes of temperature and supervision which helps the child to regulate his own temperature. During about the first year a room temperature between 68° and 72° is recommended [9, pp. 133–134]. When the baby can run around, 65° to 68° is a good temperature for him. Adequate clothing helps to keep temperature at an optimal level while also providing flexibility. Since infants and young children produce such large amounts of heat, they are likely to become overheated through active play or when wearing heavy clothing. They will show discomfort by a flushed face, perspiration, and perhaps irritability.

Respiration changes considerably during the first year. The rate slows down to about half what it was at birth. After 1 year, it continues to become slower. Breathing becomes deeper, too. At birth, the diaphragm does practically all of the work in breathing. The chest gradually comes into play during infancy, but thoracic breathing is not well established until the end of the preschool period [105]. A young baby's breathing sounds harsh, irregular, and shallow. Gradually his breathing becomes more regular and less noisy as he changes toward thoracic breathing, as his chest grows, and as the tissues covering his chest thicken and insulate the sounds.

The timing of eating, sleeping, and eliminating becomes regularized. By 3 or 4 months, even the baby who has made his own schedule (fed when hungry, allowed to sleep until he wakens) eats and sleeps at fairly predictable times. The newborn sleeps 16 or 17 hours a day, nearly all of the time when he is not eating and receiving care [76]. From age 1 month to 3 months, the infant stays awake for longer periods, shortening the average number of hours of sleep to 15. From this time until 6 months, he gradually stays awake more in the daytime and sleeps longer at night. During the second year, most babies sleep through the night and take one or two naps during the day. Some time during this year, the second nap tends to drop out, with one nap continued until age 4 or 5 years.

Development takes place in the quality of sleep as well as in the total quantity. Sleep occurs in cycles that include two different kinds of sleep, active and quiet.

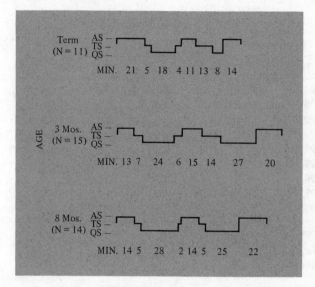

**Figure 3–4.** Changes in length of sleep cycles and changes in relation of active to quiet sleep.

Source: Reprinted by permission from E. Stern, A. H. Parmelee, Y. Akiyama, M. A. Schultz, and W. H. Wenner, "Sleep Cycle Characteristics in Infants," *Pediatrics*, **43**, Figure 1, p. 67, Copyright © 1969 American Academy of Pediatrics.

Active sleep, sometimes called primitive sleep, is characterized by irregular respiration and heart rate, many small body movements, and bursts of eye movements [97]. Primitive sleep is triggered by the reticular system in the midbrain and does not involve the cortex. Quiet sleep, in contrast, is a highly controlled state which involves the cortex as well as lower brain structures. In quiet sleep, breathing and heartbeat are regular, and there are neither body movements nor eye movements. The proportion of a sleep cycle spent in quiet sleep increases as the baby matures. At birth quiet sleep was found to be 37 percent of a cycle, at 3 months 49 percent, and at 8 months 56 percent [97]. This progression indicates the maturation of higher brain structures. Figure 3–4 shows typical sleep cycles at birth, 3 months, and 8 months. Note the lengthening of the quiet phase. The illustration also shows the lengthening of the total sleep cycle. In this study, the total cycle increased from an average of 47.0 minutes at birth to 50.3 at 8 months. (The sleep cycle in adults is about 90 minutes.)

As eating and sleeping become regularized, bowel movements also tend to do so. By 6 months, one or two stools a day are most usual. Wide individual differences occur, however. About half of 2-year-olds have bowel movements at predictable times, and half are unpredictable [87].

*Feeding Behavior*

Feeding is one of the essential ways in which a baby deals with his world. In describing an individual, a family, a culture, or even homo sapiens, it is important to tell what food is used, how it is obtained, and how it is prepared. Foods become endowed with meanings and even become symbols, ways of communicating. (Rice is an almost universal fertility symbol at weddings, coconuts mean good luck in India, wine is a Christian symbol for blood.) The culture into which an infant is born is organized to offer him certain foods in certain ways with certain meanings attached. Within the opportunities and limits he encounters, he develops ways of obtaining food and eating it, as well as ways of thinking and feeling about food. The quantity and quality of food available set limits on the growth of his body, including his nervous system, and this, in turn, sets limits on his intelligence.

Ellen S. Smart

**Figure 3–5.** The sense of autonomy is enhanced as Becky feeds herself.

In *Feeding Behavior of Infants*, Gesell and Ilg [36] devote a section to the history of nursing implements and techniques. They show pictures of artificial baby feeders, including the Roman clay boat, the French cow's horn, the English bubbly pot and pap boat, metal nipples, chamois nipples, and modern glass and rubber equipment. They tell of such practices as pigeon feeding, in which the mother or nurse chewed food before putting it in the baby's mouth, and of soothing teething discomfort with hare's brain or dog's milk. When faced with these historic practices or with some of the customs reported by modern anthropologists, one is struck by the adaptability of infants' feeding behavior.

By the end of the second year, the baby can chew well and can use the basic implements and utensils—cup, spoon, and plate. He can seek and find food and obtain and reject it through the use of words. *All gone, more, drink*, and similar expressions are powerful symbols through which he can control many important events.

**Nursing.** The meshing of roles of mother and infant is a powerful argument for the value of breast feeding. As the previous chapter has shown, the newborn baby's reflex activity is adequate for finding the nipple, stimulating it, and withdrawing milk. The mother's reactions and the baby's can mutually regulate each other, the baby taking what he needs, the mother supplying it. Nevertheless, the majority of American and European babies are fed by bottle. Under conditions of optimal sanitation which are easy for prosperous Westerners to achieve, bottle feeding is safe and convenient, although expensive.

**Weaning.** Emerging resources include new ways of eating. Instead of getting all of his food as liquids which he sucks, the baby learns to bite and chew solids and to drink liquids from a cup. This particular changeover is called weaning. Weaning is also used sometimes to mean any gradual change from immature to mature behavior. In all contexts, weaning usually involves some pushing and encouraging of the child toward more mature behavior. Since an older baby can hold his bottle and carry it with him, he can enjoy his sucking and his autonomy at the same time, whereas with breast feeding, the growing desire for independence may make him accept cup feeding more readily. The timing and techniques of weaning are related to personality development of the child and to cultural prescriptions. Americans are advised by their authorities to wean gradually. The Children's Bureau, The Child Study Association, and Dr. Spock, all recommend gradual substitution of the cup for the bottle or breast. In addition to being gradual, the mother is usually warned that the baby needs extra loving and attention when he is being asked to give up a familiar way of eating. Americans usually wean babies during the first year. The Children's Bureau says, "Take your time with weaning. Breast-fed babies can be weaned directly and gradually to a cup after about 6 months old. Bottle-fed babies usually like to suck the bottle a little longer" [16].

The stress on gradualness and gentleness is consistent with what is known about personality development during the first year. While developing his sense of trust, it is most helpful for the baby to be assured that the world and the people in it can be trusted. Traumatic experiences and major readjustments to life are injurious to the sense of trust and hence to the establishment of the foundations of a healthy personality.

An example of another cultural setting shows how weaning can be crucial to the sense of autonomy, rather than to the sense of trust, when weaning occurs at a time when the sense of autonomy is growing rapidly. A group of Zulu babies were studied before, during, and after weaning, which occurred between 15 and 24 months, at the average age of 19 months [3]. The day of weaning was a serious event, fixed months ahead. Bitter juice of the aloe was put on the mother's breast while the child watched and then the breast was offered to him throughout the day. A charm was put around his neck, to help him in various ways. On the day of weaning, all but one baby refused the breast after the first encounter with the aloe juice. Behavior changes followed a definite pattern of disintegration, followed by integration on a higher level. During the first two hours, the toddlers became more negativistic, aggressive, and fretful. They sucked their fingers and other objects. Some performed stereotyped actions. After the first day, relationships changed with everyone in the home. With their mothers, they first alternated attacking and ignoring, then tried to gain attention by illness, clinging, fretting and crying, and finally paid little attention to their mothers, showing no anger and behaving with increasing independence. Sudden increases in mature behavior included helping with housework, imitating others, using new words, talking more distinctly, leaving home more often, and showing hospitality. Children also became more aggressive and mischievous, spilling water, playing with fire, and wasting food. Eating patterns changed, with preferences for adult food and greatly increased appetite.

These behavior changes can be seen as contributing to a growing sense of autonomy. Normal development during the second year, especially the latter half of the second year, involves establishing oneself as a separate individual. All of these six changes in behavior indicate increased independence, power in decision making, differentiation, and reorganization. The weaning experience apparently precipitated the second stage of personality growth. Thus the method of sudden weaning, conducted differently and timed differently, had a very different result from weaning conducted American-style. Both methods of weaning can be seen to be functional in regard to the stage of personality growth during which they are conducted.

**Self-Regulation of Diet in Infancy.** Of great practical significance is the question of how competent the child is to select the quantity and quality of his food. "Does the baby know how much he ought to eat?" and "Does the baby know what is good for him?" are questions which have long been debated by parents, doctors, nurses, and teachers of young children. The classic experiment of Clara Davis [18, 19] gives information as to choices infants can make under a certain set of conditions. Davis took a group of newly weaned babies and gave them complete freedom to choose their diets from a variety of simple, natural, unmixed, unseasoned foods, including fruits, vegetables, milk, eggs, meat, whole-grain cereals, salt, and cod liver oil. At first a baby tended to sample all of the food on his tray, but later on, he was likely to settle down to a smaller selection of foods. Sometimes an infant would go on a "jag" and eat five eggs at a sitting or drink a large amount of cod liver oil. No child suffered a digestive upset from such a spree. At the end of the experiment, all subjects had grown well, were in good health, and some in better nutritional condition than at the beginning. An analysis of their 36,000 meals showed that the infants had balanced their diets perfectly. Davis [20] paints a vivid word picture of the babies:

> Before meals hands and faces are washed and when the dietitian comes in and says, "The trays are ready," all who can walk join in an eager rush to the dining room, the nurses carrying the others. Bibs are tied on and, as the trays are brought in, the smaller babies often show their eagerness for food by jumping up and down in their chairs, and trying to reach the trays before they are set down on the tables. Yet, once started, they eat with an evident absence of strain, without hurry and without dallying and with poise and complete satisfaction, knowing that they may have all they want of everything. Sometimes they fall asleep while eating as their eyes close like nursing babies. This almost pagan joy of eating reminds one of young animals or the accounts of the eating of primitive peoples. Since they feed themselves with their hands the babies rapidly become independent, and by the time they are fifteen or sixteen months old the nurses' functions are reduced to moving dishes that the child cannot reach and seeing that empty ones are refilled, so that one nurse seated between their tables can attend to two infants. From the age of twenty months on all the babies thus far have been able not only to feed themselves entirely, but to rearrange their dishes on the tray to suit themselves and to hold up empty ones to attract attention when they wish them refilled. These older ones have only waitress service, no nurse sitting beside them. When a baby is through eating, he gets down or is helped down and leaves the dining room whether the others have finished or not.*

Thus research showed that human beings, at least as infants, have the ability to choose a balanced diet from a wide variety of simple, nutritious foods and to eat the amounts they need for adequate growth and maintenance. Even though Davis first reported her research in 1928, it is still misinterpreted quite often. For example, the mother of a crib-chewer declared that it was all right for her baby to eat wood and paint, because Davis had shown that babies could eat whatever they chose! It is impossible and absurd to try to reproduce Davis's experiment at home. What mother can provide cafeteria service while keeping her toddler away from all contact with candy, soft drinks, ice cream, and other snack foods, as well as the dishes she prepares for the other members of the family who like stew, salad, and pie? Davis's contribution was to show that infants of about a year of age can be very autonomous in choosing what to eat, how much to eat, and how to eat it. The possibility that children have good nutrition while being autonomous in the selection of foods requires not only that they be allowed their selections but also

* From C. M. Davis, "Self-Selection of Food by Children," Copyright May 1935, The American Journal of Nursing Company. Reprinted from *American Journal of Nursing*, May 1935.

that all of the choices available to them be foods that are nutritionally valuable in themselves. Chocolate bars and lollipops, pies and doughnuts, were not on Davis's menus.

What happens at mealtime is significant not only for physical growth but for personality development too. Trust grows as the baby learns he can count on satisfying meals turning up as he feels a need for food. Early autonomous activity includes the defensive actions of dribbling, drooling, not accepting, not swallowing, compulsive repetitious acts, using substitute oral comfort, such as sucking fingers, blanket, or pacifier [74, p. 305]. Seeking, finding, and taking in food are positive kinds of autonomous acts.

## Locomotion

The baby's world expands and stimulation increases greatly when he learns to move from one place to another. Much maturation and learning go on before the infant actually creeps, crawls, or hitches.

Growth of the parts of the brain concerned with locomotion is indicated as the baby progresses through the locomotor sequence. The cerebellum, concerned largely with balance and posture, grows slowly during the first few months and rapidly in size and complexity between 6 and 18 months [34]. The sequence of motor development is shown in the silhouettes presented in Figure 3–6. Here is shown progression from fetal position to walking—in 15 months.

The locomotion of the first year is creeping, of the second year, walking. Each of these patterns of moving can be traced from early beginnings. Considering creeping, you can see its beginning in the early attempts to raise the head when the baby is in prone position. Most babies do this momentarily at 1 month or 2 months, gradually lifting their heads higher and for longer periods of time. Although some babies actually make progress by crawling during their first weeks, this reflexlike movement fades out, leaving infants stationary until they develop the more purposive kind of creeping movements. Although maturation plays a major role in the achievement of creeping, anyone who watches a baby go through the final stages before creeping sees a great deal of effort and trial and error. For instance, the *swimming stage* is one in which the baby perches on his abdomen, does a completely ineffectual frog kick, and moves his arms at cross purposes as often as not [94]. Any progress at this point is likely to be backward and slight. Shortly afterward comes a stage when babies try out a variety of methods, such as using the stomach as a pivot, hitching by means of head and feet, shoulders and feet, or buttocks and hand, making a bridge by standing on toes and hands and scooting backward. Although some infants retain idiosyncratic ways of creeping, most do it in the usual style, which is shown in Figure 3–6.

Basic to walking are holding the head and shoulders erect, sitting, making stepping movements, and standing. Even in the first three months, most infants resist with their feet when held in standing position. Gradually more and more of the baby's weight is borne by his feet. Stepping movements (while held) begin in what looks like dancing, standing on the toes, lifting one foot and then the other and putting both feet down in the same place. Later come putting one foot down ahead of the other, and bouncing. Before they can pull themselves up into standing position, most babies can stand onto helping hands or to the rail of a playpen. Some children, however, learn to pull up before they can remain standing [35, p. 39].

**Figure 3–6.** The sequence of motor development, with ages at which the average baby achieves each coordination.

Source: Reprinted by permission from M. M. Shirley, *The First Two Years: A Study of Twenty-Five Babies.* Vol. II: *Intellectual Development*, Copyright © University of Minnesota, Minneapolis, 1933.

Most children learn to walk during the first three months of the second year. Parents often think that their baby really could walk if he would, since he gets around so quickly and easily with one hand held or with just one hand on a piece of furniture. The stage of cruising or walking with help seems to be a period of perfecting walking skills and gaining confidence before setting out independently. Walking is unsteady at first, gradually improving with maturing and practice. Maturation includes a change in proportions and posture, as well as neuromuscular development. The toddler has short legs, a long trunk, large head and abdomen, and consequently a center of gravity high in his trunk. In order to balance himself better, he spreads his feet, walking on a broad base. As his proportions change toward those of childhood, he can afford to place his feet closer together. By the second half of the second year, he can run, covering territory at least twice as fast.

Locomotion includes climbing, too, which looks much like creeping, but begins in the second year, usually in the first three months. Climbing further enlarges the infant's scope of activities, giving him the run of all the floors of his home and access to the sofa, chairs, tabletops, cupboards, drawers.

Because the world expands so enormously with sitting, creeping, walking, running, and climbing, there are a multitude of opportunities for the sense of autonomy to grow. So many choices to make! So many ways in which to test oneself! So many avenues to discovery of powers and limits on powers! It can be very heady or even overwhelming.

**Group Differences in Motor Development.** Whenever motor differences between white and black American infants have been noted in the research literature, the black babies have been advanced in comparison with the whites. A group of black children in New Haven, tested over their first two years of life, showed definite acceleration on the motor section of the Gesell developmental test [57]. Bayley's infant scale of motor development was given to 1409 babies between 1 month and 15 months, in 12 cities representing most of the areas of the United States [5]. Forty-two percent of these babies were black. White and black averages, compared for each month, showed higher values for blacks at every level except 15 months. The differences were highest in the early months, becoming nonsignificant at 1 year. Another investigator [104] divided groups of black and white babies into low, middle, and high socioeconomic groups and tested them at age 12, 24, and 36 weeks on Gesell developmental schedules. She found all black groups superior in motor development at age 12 weeks but at 36 weeks only the black high socio-economic group was superior. Although this author argues against a genetic factor being responsible for the superiority, the genetic explanation is possible. Thirty-six weeks corresponds with the time when Bayley's black and white groups were narrowing the difference between them. The superiority maintained by only the high socioeconomic group could be due to excellent environmental conditions strengthening a genetic superiority which was in the process of leveling out.

African babies have been reported to show extremely advanced motor development. Working under the World Health Organization, Geber [33] tested over 300 babies in Uganda. She found them to be consistently advanced in psychomotor functions, as compared with European and American babies. This finding has been confirmed by other observers of African babies [1, 5, 26]. The acceleration in development is greatest at birth, then gradually decreases. From the first day, the children could hold their heads steady when drawn into sitting position, an achievement of the European child at about 6 weeks. The average Uganda baby sat alone at age 4 months and walked at 10. Some individuals achieved these coordinations earlier. Language, problem solving, and personal–social development were likewise two or three months advanced over European standards. Since the babies were born developmentally accelerated, the reason for their condition must be in something that happened before birth. Geber suggests that the reason for the infant acceleration is the way in which pregnancy is conducted. She describes it thus:

> The arrival of a baby is always looked forward to with great pleasure (sterility is thought to be a calamity) and is not a source of anxiety for the future. The mother is in no way upset by her pregnancy and is active up to the moment of delivery. The unborn child is the chief object of her life, especially as she believes that any other interest may have an adverse affect on him [33, p. 194].

Careful studies of infants in widely separated parts of the world have yielded results similar to Geber's although not as pronounced. Newborn babies in Guatemala were 3 to 5 weeks above American Gesell norms in psychomotor functions and over 1 week ahead in adaptive behavior [17]. The same author reports that in six rural communities in Mexico and Guatemala, infants' superiority on the Gesell test declined from birth until 18 months, when they reached levels below those of European and American babies. Indian research has yielded the same results, using the Bayley infant tests in a longitudinal study of 278 babies [77]. At 1 month of age, the Indian babies were extremely advanced in motor tests and moderately advanced in mental tests. Their superiority declined steadily throughout the first year. A similar report comes from Israel, on groups of home-reared and kibbutz-reared infants who were given Bayley tests throughout the first 27 months [59]. Both groups were superior to American babies from age 1 month to 4 months. Between age 5 months and 15 months, the differences were not significant, although Israeli averages were above the Americans.

The Mexican investigator, searching for an explanation of the superiority of newborns in various parts of the world, suggests that conditions of life in pre-industrial communities may produce fetal environments which result in precocious neonates [17]. He names two possible contributors: the relation of the mother to heavy labor and her high status because of being pregnant. A recent finding with animals suggests an explanation yet to be tested with human beings [42]. Puppies raised on a low protein diet or born from mothers on low protein showed preco-cious development, along with a high tolerance for glucose. Their later development was retarded. It remains to be seen whether human infants show high glucose tolerance plus precocity after having been deprived of adequate protein prenatally and immediately after birth.

## Eye–Hand Coordination and Manipulation

Through the use of his hands, the baby reaches out into the world, finds out about it and changes it. He cannot interact much with his hands until he can sit up, although he does make a beginning in the early weeks. The first three months is a time of contacting objects with eyes more than with hands, following moving objects in several directions. The grasping reflex, present at birth, is strong for the first three months and loses its automatic quality before the first half year. At first the grasping reflex consists of grasping anything that is placed against the palm. Gradually the child becomes able to grasp objects that he touches with his hand, first in a fumbling way and then more and more deftly. At the same time that he is starting to grasp what his hand contacts, around the end of the first three months, he also looks at his hands and glances at the objects he holds [34].

Photographs from Halverson's classic study [41] of the development of reaching and grasping show how grasping changes from a primitive sequence of palm and fingers to a precise coordination of thumb and forefinger. As can be seen in Figure 3–7, coordination of thumb and forefinger occurs when a baby picks up a pellet or a crumb.

In a description of the sequence of development in eye–hand coordination, the principle of differentiation and integration stands out. Early grasping is an all-out event, with both arms active and the whole body straining. On the Gesell test [35], 12 weeks intervene between this kind of approach and a one-handed grasp. Trans-ferring objects from one hand to another comes at the same time as one-handed grasp. Here is the beginning of the differentiation that is basic to human manipula-tion. One hand does one thing while the other does something else, and the two are integrated, working toward one goal. In the course of differentiation and

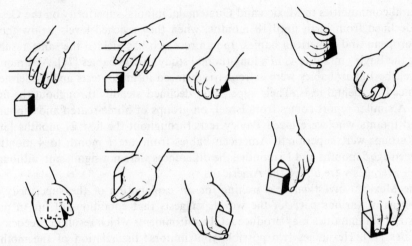

**Figure 3–7.** Stages in the development of grasping.

Source: Reprinted by permission from H. M. Halverson, "An Experimental Study of Prehension in Infants by Means of Systematic Cinema Records," *Genetic Psychology Monograph*, **10**, 107–286. Copyright © 1931, The Journal Press.

integration one hand becomes the preferred hand, to be used as the leader in manipulation. The baby gains in the ability to use objects and to use more than one object at a time. Here are the early stages of man's ability to use tools. You can see him as an infant, hitting a cube against a cup, choosing between bottle and pellet, considering the details of a ball and using a pencil on a paper.

Gesell's normative sequences of eye–hand coordination, like his other sequences of behavioral development, show what the average, middle-class American child does at successive ages. Piaget, too, is interested in the actions of eyes and hands, but in terms of the development of intelligence.

Based on observations of his own infants' interactions with objects, Piaget described sequences of schemas involving eyes and hands. He also pointed out that "the construction of reality" takes place by means of these activities [80]. Through grasping and looking, the infant interacts with the world to develop mental structures or schemas that give rise to new behavior. More is said about Piaget's theories of development in the following section of the book. Many recent studies have been focused on the stages and processes of the development of the concept of object [90]. A study of the development of schemas used in relating to objects [102] is of particular interest here, where we are concerned with eye–hand coordination. Results on 84 infants showed certain clusters of reactions characterizing each level of development. As a baby grew older, his earlier reactions did not disappear, but became less prominent by being integrated into higher-level reactions or used very specifically. The schemas involving eyes and/or hand coordination were holding, mouthing, visual inspection, hitting, shaking, examining, differentiated schemas, and letting go. Their characteristics are

*Holding:* When an object is placed in the hand of an infant over 1 month old, he holds it for 30 seconds or more. He neither looks at it nor brings it to his face, nor does he seem to notice when he drops it. Through the use of this schema, he gets some tactual experience with objects.

*Mouthing:* The infant brings the object in his hand to his mouth or tries to do so, as shown by opening and closing his mouth. All infants in the study showed mouthing at 2 months. This schema is very prominent in early interactions with objects but later tends to drop out, as far as play materials are concerned.

*Visual Inspection:* In the beginning stages of this schema, the baby catches glimpses of objects as he brings them to his mouth. Gradually he holds objects in view for longer periods of time and looks at them intently. All infants did visual inspection at three months. This schema does not drop out but becomes integrated into higher level examining.

*Hitting:* An up-and-down motion of the arm is the basis of several hitting schemas, which most infants showed by age 4 months and all by 7 months. The most frequently seen one was hitting an object on a surface. There is also the schema of waving an object, which is like hitting but the object does not touch a surface. Patting is another variation. If hitting results in sounds, then the schema serves to establish coordination between hand movements and sound perception.

*Shaking:* Moving the arm from side to side is similar to hitting and occurs at about the same time, by age 5 months in most babies, and by age 10 in all observed. At first shaking is indiscriminate but soon is applied mainly to objects that make a noise.

*Examining:* This is a complex schema, including looking, turning, poking, feeling, manipulating. Whereas in earlier stages, the schemas of holding, visual inspection and hitting were used for themselves, the emphasis here is on interaction with the object. Schemas are used according to how they affect the object. Most infants used examining by age 6 months, all by 10.

*Differentiated schemas:* After he begins examining, the baby develops a cluster of new schemas which include tearing, pulling, crumpling, squeezing, rubbing, sliding, and pushing. He applies these schemas appropriately to different objects. Most babies used differentiated schemas by age 7 months, all by 10.

*Letting go:* Dropping becomes possible when the baby can let go at will. He uses dropping for finding out how things fall and what noises they make when they land. At 8 months most infants dropped objects purposefully, at 9 months all did. Throwing develops one to two months after dropping, permitting observation of trajectories, speeds, and perceptual transformations and coordinating this information with muscular sensations of greater and less effort.

A concept of object implies that the child knows that the object continues to exist after it disappears from his view. When he hunts for an object after it has been placed behind a screen, he shows that he has some notion of its permanence. Examining behavior increases during the period just before the child is able to solve the problem of finding the hidden object [90].

## Attention

In the previous chapter, the neonate's attention to certain stimuli was noted. The state of alert inactivity was found to be the condition in which the young infant attends most readily to visual stimuli. Infants select certain stimuli to attend to and pay attention for longer periods to some than to others. Movement and contour, or dark–light contrast, are some of the determinants of visual attention in young infants. Attention has been studied by measuring how long an infant looks at a stimulus and/or monitoring his heart rate, which decelerates as he attends [62].

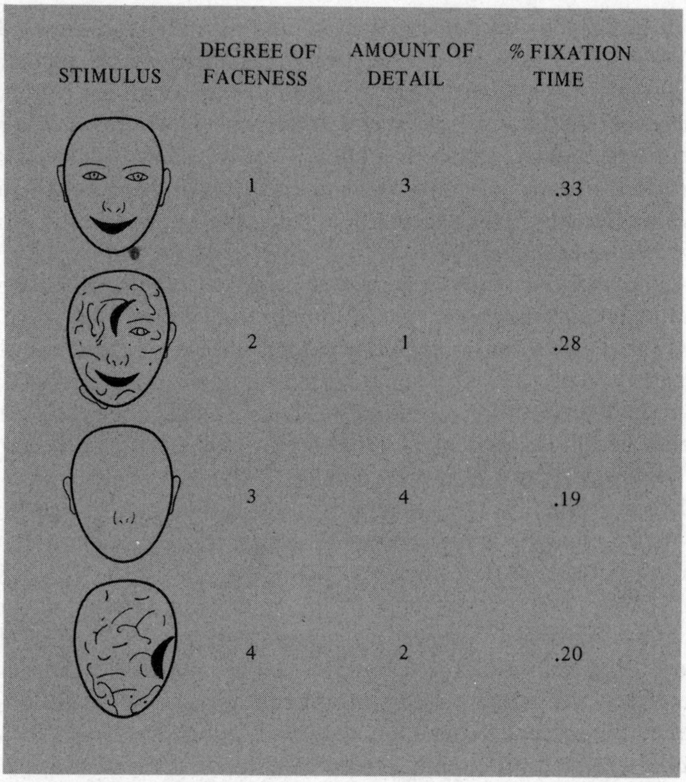

**Figure 3–8.** Stimuli used to test responses to resemblance to the human face and to complexity, with rank orders on the two dimensions and fixation times.

SOURCE: Reprinted by permission from R. A. Haaf and R. Q. Bell, "A Facial Dimension in Visual Discrimination," *Child Development*, **3-8**, Figure 1, p. 895. Copyright © 1967, The Society for Research in Child Development, Inc.

One-year-olds showed preference for complex auditory stimuli by responding for a longer time when lever-pushing resulted in a chime than they did when it resulted in a bell sounding [96].

**Determinants of Visual Attention.** Complex patterns are consistently preferred (as measured by looking time) over plain surfaces by both newborn and older infants [27]. This preference, which seems to be innate, is highly functional for the baby in getting to know and understand the world around him, in learning to recognize objects, places, and people, and in creeping without bumping into things or falling off edges. At the normal time for learning to creep, for instance, the baby stays away from a surface pattern which indicates a dropoff, even though that pattern is only a simulation of an edge. The early preference for the human face may begin from preference for pattern and complexity. However, the face may derive attractiveness by being the first object which the baby experiences as being influenced by his own activities. Infants show excitement and pleasure when they realize that they can make something happen [106].

Response to "faceness" or similarity to a face, was pitted against a dimension of complexity in an ingenious experiment using the drawings shown in Figure 3–8. The drawing at the top, which is the one most like a real face, received the most visual attention from 4-month-old boys [40]. The real face ranks third in amount of detail, or complexity. The most complex stimulus, which is second in faceness, ranks second in amount of regard accorded it, whereas the second most complex drawing ranks last.

The baby's tendency to look at another person's eyes is consistent with a strong preference for the bull's-eye pattern, which is preferred to stripes from the age of 2 months [28]. Infants in the third month looked eight times as long at the bull's-eye as at the stripes. Further preference experiments showed babies choosing bull's-eye and circular patterns over lattice patterns equated to the circular arrays in length of contour, number, and size of elements, area, light reflectance, and contrast.

Faces and facelike stimuli have been explored in many studies with infants. By 2 months of age, a solid object is preferred over a flat one, by 3 months, a textured sphere over a textured disc and a solid head model over an outline form. In order to see whether familiarity had something to do with choosing facelike stimuli, a nursing bottle containing milk was paired with the round and oval objects. The bottle received less attention than the other stimuli from infants 2 to 5 months old, nor did it evoke more response before feeding time than after [28].

Stimuli that are almost like real faces, but not quite, are powerful attractors of attention. This phenomenon has been explored by using drawings or photographs of faces with scrambled features and blanked-out features. At 6 months infants looked longer at the realistic faces, but after that age they showed increasing preference for the distorted faces [51]. The authors theorize that while the infant is developing a schema (an inner representation) of an object, that object is very attractive. After he has a well-developed schema, through which he easily recognizes the objects it represents, he is attracted to novelty, or deviations from his schema.

The effect of changes in stimulation on the attention paid by infants to visually presented objects was investigated in a study that used mobiles that were progressively more different than one of standard design [99]. The babies were between 4 and 5 months old. At home, for three weeks, they were all shown the same mobile for half an hour a day. They were presumed to have developed a schema of the mobile. In the laboratory each of seven groups was shown a mobile which was related to the standard mobile in a controlled way. Those infants who were shown a moderately discrepant mobile in the laboratory looked longer at it than those infants who were shown a minimally or maximally discrepant one. They paid attention to novelty, if the new stimulus was not too different from the one for which they had a schema.

Reasons for a long fixation time are not all the same. By studying other responses which go along with the long fixation, it has been found that normal faces received more smiling and greater cardiac deceleration than did distorted faces, although fixation times did not differ [51]. Thus the infant may look for a long time because he enjoys the sight, as with a familiar face, or because he is trying to reduce the uncertainty (to assimilate or accommodate) in the case of the distorted face, which is close to his face schema but different enough to not fit.

The effect of uncertainty on attending behavior was studied by varying the location of the stimulus rather than the stimulus itself [15]. A game of peekaboo with two groups of infants aged 5 to 10 months and 12 to 19 months was played under three degrees of uncertainty. One third saw the face which played peekaboo always appear in the same spot, one third had the face alternating from side to

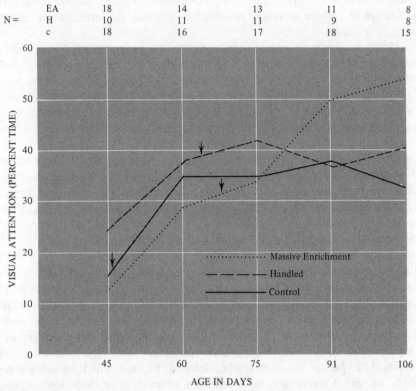

|     |     |     |     |     |     |     |
| --- | --- | --- | --- | --- | --- | --- |
|     | EA  | 18  | 14  | 13  | 11  | 8   |
| N = | H   | 10  | 11  | 11  | 9   | 8   |
|     | c   | 18  | 16  | 17  | 18  | 15  |

**Figure 3–9.** Percent of observation time during which three groups of infants showed visual attention.

SOURCE: B. L. White and R. Held, "Plasticity of Sensorimotor Development in the Human Infant." In J. Hellmuth [Ed.], *Exceptional Infant: The Normal Infant*, Vol. I. 1967, New York, Brunner/Mazel, Inc. By permission.

side, and the remainder had random presentations. The extent to which both age groups persisted in playing the game varied with the amount of uncertainty involved. In other words, the alternating face evoked more persistence than the face in the same place, and the random appearances received more attention than the alternating.

**Individual Differences.** Attentiveness varies between individual babies [40, 61]. The highly attentive infant tends to remain highly attentive, at least throughout the first year, as long as the stimuli given are interesting and relative to his age level [61]. Sex differences in attentiveness have also been found. At 6 and 13 months of age, girls attended longer to visual stimuli and preferred more novel sounds than did boys [52].

One source of individual differences in visual attentiveness has been found in the amount and variety of experience available to the young infant [109]. (Visual attention was defined as a state in which the eyes are more than half open and the direction of gaze shifting at least once every 30 seconds.) The subjects were physically normal institution babies, half of whom were given 20 minutes of extra daily handling. These babies were significantly more visually attentive than the controls. A second experimental group received "massive enrichment" which included 20 minutes of extra handling, placement in prone position, removal of crib bumpers which interfered with seeing ward activities and addition of stabiles, printed sheets and bumpers instead of plain. As Figure 3–9 shows, visual attention was first slower in the enrichment group but at about a month after the experiment started, at age 75 days, the enrichment group increased sharply in visual attention, as compared with the handled and control groups.

## Intellectual Development

The infant experiences people, objects, and himself as he interacts with his environment. He explores through his sensory and motor resources, making some changes in the objects and people he contacts, changing himself as he receives sensory data and processes them. He communicates with people, rapidly improving his techniques for doing so. As he refines his methods of communicating, he is also developing a tool of thinking.

### Cognition

*Cognoscere*, Latin for "to know," gives rise to the term *cognition*, one of man's most human activities. By *cognition* is meant the individual's becoming acquainted with the world and the objects in it, including himself. He comes to understand relationships between objects and between himself and the world, by taking in information through his senses and processing it and acting on it. While cognition is of great practical use from day to day and from moment to moment, man cognizes just for fun in addition to cognizing for necessity. The toddler's flow of "Wazzat?" the curiosity of the preschool child, the drive of the research scientist—all reflect a certain amount of wanting to know for the sake of knowing. Cognition goes on during most of what is called play in infancy. While using all of his resources for dealing with the world, the infant is also cognizing and developing cognitively.

**Sensorimotor Intelligence, According to Piaget.**  Intelligence is a process of organization which extends the biological organization of the body [79, p. 407]. Intelligence includes adaptive thinking and actions. The child constructs his intelligence through his own efforts, beginning with what is genetically given. Piaget calls sensorimotor intelligence practical intelligence, since it has no words at its service for use in thinking and problem solving: ". . . in place of words and concepts it uses percepts and movements organized into 'action schemata'"* [80]. The mental structures, or intellectual abilities, which the child builds during the sensorimotor stage are what he needs for constructing and reconstructing objects.

The achievement of the infancy stage in cognition is to come to know one's immediate environment as permanent objects and background, separate from oneself. *Permanent* means that the object (bottle, mother, rattle, and such) continues to exist even though it is moved, hidden, or placed in a new relationship with other objects (such as mother in a party-going hat). All the parts of an object (such as the nipple on a bottle) must be known to exist even when they cannot be seen.

Understanding some facts about movement is a part of coming to know permanent objects. A child has to find out that when an object is moved, it can be put back again, that when it turns around, it can be turned in the other direction,

---

* In his writings Piaget used *schemata* as the plural of the word *schema*. We follow the practice of most American writers and use *schemas* as the plural.

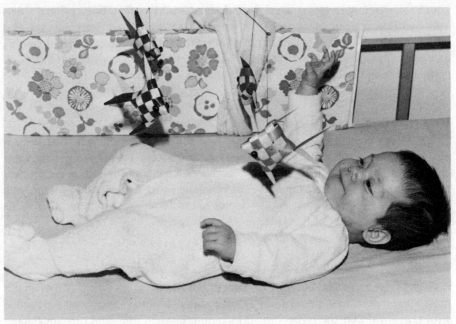

Halvar Loken

that when an object is moved away, he can reach it by a path other than the one taken by the object, in fact by many different paths.

Starting with the resources he has for dealing with the world, the baby uses them to develop new patterns of action. For example, he integrates schemas of mouthing, holding, and looking (see pages 108–109). The result is an examining schema. Using this method of exploration many times with toys, bottles, clothing, and other objects, the infant makes progress toward the conviction that objects are permanent. Other behavior patterns, involving seeing, smelling, tasting, hearing, touching, and manipulating, are used in getting knowledge of the world. Locomotion, moving from place to place, gives the baby chances to map out the space in which he lives, getting to truly cognize it and himself as an object in space.

As experience with reality shows his existing resources to be inadequate or insufficient, the baby develops new schemas through accommodation or improvements in what he has. When the child falls only slightly short of being adequate to cope with an experience, his feeling tone is pleasant and interesting. Growth is stimulated. When he is very inadequate in dealing with the experience, the child is frightened and tries to withdraw [43].

Piaget has described six substages of the period of sensorimotor intelligence,* the period during which the infant establishes basic knowledge of the world. Piaget is not concerned with the exact ages at which children reach the successive stage of intelligence. He is interested in *how* rather than *when*, and in which structures are invariably built before certain other structures. The substages of sensorimotor intelligence are:

I. *Simple Reflexive Action.* The schemas of the neonatal period include the reflex movements described in Chapter 2 and a general mass activity. The perceptual abilities described in Chapter 2 are also schemas of the early sensorimotor period.

* This account follows Flavell [29, pp. 85–121].

During this stage, various abilities, such as the sucking reflexes, improve and consolidate. The baby can neither reach for an object nor search for it. There is no indication that he cognizes objects as separate parts of the environment or as distinct from himself.

II. *Primary Circular Reactions.* Neonatal behavior patterns begin to change through maturation and experience. The baby learns to bring his hand to his mouth and to suck on it, most likely his thumb. He touches his hands together and fingers them, looks at his hands and at objects grasped by his hands. Objects grasped by the hands are carried to the mouth. He looks at an object making a noise. He does not know what he can cause and what takes place independent of his own actions.

III. *Secondary Circular Reactions.* The baby develops ways of prolonging interesting events. When a change in the environment results from his actions, he is likely to repeat those actions. He reaches for the toy suspended from his crib, hits it, watches it move and hits it again.

He still does not search for an object that has disappeared, suggesting that he still does not conceive of it as existing permanently. However, if all but a small part of an object is covered, as when his bottle sticks out from under his blanket, he recognizes it and can recover it. If an object is made to disappear slowly, he follows it with his eyes and continues the movement of his eyes in the direction in which the object went. If, however, it is jerked away, or quickly screened, he does not look for it. One of Piaget's experiments with his son, Laurent, showed that the baby did not even miss the bottle when it was hidden quickly. Just before a feeding time, when Laurent was hungry, Piaget showed him his bottle, whereupon Laurent cried. Piaget quickly hid the bottle and Laurent stopped crying. This sequence was repeated several times. When Laurent could see a small portion of the bottle, he cried harder than ever [78, p. 30].

Another interesting aspect of substage III, evident in Laurent's behavior, was failure to realize the existence of the nipple if it did not show. When he saw a small portion of the bottle but not the nipple, he tried to suck the bottle itself, but when the nipple was visible, he turned the bottle around so that he could suck the nipple. Thus he cognized the bottle as a suckable object, but unless he could see the nipple, he did not deal with the bottle as an object with a specialized suckable portion. Thus in this stage, objects are becoming endowed with permanence, but the process is not complete.

IV. *Coordination of Secondary Schemas.* Secondary circular reactions become coordinated with each other to form more complex schemas. The new schemas are used definitely as means to ends. This is the earliest age at which the baby shows intention in a definite and unmistakable way. For example, hitting is not just for the sake of hitting, but in order to grasp a new object. Piaget tells how Laurent, at $9\frac{1}{2}$ months, pushed his father's hand and at the same time pulled on the toy which Piaget was holding [79, p. 219].

There is true searching for a vanished object, although still not complete appreciation of the object's permanence. Piaget describes how his daughter Jacqueline searched for a toy parrot. First, Piaget covered it with his hand. Jacqueline raised his hand and grasped the parrot. Piaget slowly took the toy away from her, hid it under a rug and put his hand on her lap, on the spot where the parrot had first been. Jacqueline raised his hand and looked under it for the parrot. This process was repeated three times [78, p. 51].

V. *Tertiary Circular Reactions.* Instead of merely prolonging or reproducing interesting events, the baby tries to produce new events. He experiments to see what will happen. He appears definitely curious, looking for new experience.

Now the baby looks for a vanished object in the place where it disappeared instead of in the place where he last found it. He demonstrates increased understanding of movements of objects by following a trajectory and looking at its end and by throwing something in back of himself and turning around in the other direction to look for it.

Throwing and dropping toys are common kinds of play at this age, as the infant examines movements of objects, disappearance, and reappearance, building his understanding of the permanence of objects. Piaget watched Laurent using various methods of letting a tin can fall from his hands and then dropping a chunk of bread first as a whole and then in the form of crumbs. Later Laurent dropped toys from different positions.

VI. *Invention of New Means through Mental Combinations.* Instead of having to go through a series of sensorimotor explorations and trials, the child can find solutions mentally. He begins this stage by representing objects and actions to himself. Probably the first kind of representing is to act it out. Piaget's daughter, Lucienne, illustrated this behavior when she was trying to get a little chain out of a match box. She looked at the small opening, not knowing how to open it wider, then opened and shut her mouth several times, each time opening it wider [78, pp. 337–338]. After a few quiet moments, she used a new technique to open the box with her finger. Lucienne's opening of her own mouth was a symbolic act, representing the opening of the box, which she desired. This stage, in coping with problems, is midway between trying out solutions in action and thinking them out. When problems are solved by thinking, without any action, the child is representing objects and actions to himself by symbols which are entirely within. He thinks of ways of acting and tries them out by thinking. He can think of objects which are not present, of past events, and of events which might happen.

The toddler shows his new powers by imitation and pretending and insightful problem solving. When he imitates a past event, he shows that he has a mental image of it. When he pretends, he uses a mental image of a behavior pattern to act out that pattern in a new situation. Feeding a doll, he uses his mental image of his mother's behavior, acting it out at his little table. The achievement of imitation, pretending, and insightful problem solving marks the completion of the stage of sensorimotor development. As with all the stages outlined by Piaget, the average age for beginning and ending a stage is not placed exactly but approximately. The sensorimotor stage, according to Piaget, ends at around 18 months. Gesell [35, p. 71] places imitation and pretending at 2 years, which is probably closer to the age at which most children achieve these feats.*

Ordering and classifying, cognitive behavior which develops noticeably during the next stage of intellectual development, can be observed in its very beginnings during infancy. Gesell mentions the 1-year-old's sequential play with cubes as being a preliminary to ordering and counting, and his looking at a round hole while holding a matching block as being incipient perception of geometric form [35, p. 65]. Between 12 and 24 months, infants will do some selective ordering and group-

* Piaget's observations on sensorimotor activity were on his own children, who were most likely advanced in development. The importance of Piaget's work lies in his revealing the ways in which intelligence grows. Gesell contributed information on norms.

ing when presented with an array of two different kinds of objects, such as four clay balls with four yellow cubes [86]. Selective ordering and grouping activity increased with age between 12 and 24 months.

**Knowing the Self.** Only a small beginning in self-cognition can be made in infancy, but it is essential. To know reality means to know that you are an object distinct from other objects, including background and people. One of man's unique features is the ability to stand off and look at himself, himself as an individual and himself as related to the rest of the world.

Although one may recognize a human being as an organism-in-a-field, as an individual intimately bound up with and interacting with his environment, the common definition of a baby's or a man's boundary is his skin. For most practical purposes, he stops where his skin stops. When a baby fingers his hands, bites his toes, lets his hand fall on his chest, when he watches these actions with his eyes, feels them with both hands, with mouth and toes, with chest and hand, he is coming to know his body. He is cognizing his body, or building an inner image of it. The sensations which come from within, largely gastrointestinal, add to the image. At first, the baby probably does not make a distinction between his own body and his mother's. Psychoanalysts say that gradually he realizes their separateness as he experiences wanting the breast and not getting it. There are additional experiences of separation from the mother—being alone instead of seeing her, feeling the tactile pleasure of her arms and face and hearing her voice. These separations also define his being from his mother's.

The body image surely grows in clarity as the infant finds out which events in the world are caused by him and which are not. In fact, the two are reciprocal. It is only around 4 months of age that the baby seems to make a dim connection between one of his actions and an event, such as hitting the cradle gym and seeing it swing. He gradually cognizes the interaction of his body with the rest of the world and as he does, he knows his body better.

**Parents' Contribution to Development of Sensorimotor Intelligence.** Parents provide two essential parts of the world of children's learning, the home base and the field to explore. Shortly before he is able to move around on his own, the infant becomes attached to important people, especially his mother. (The process of attachment is described in the following chapter.) When separated from people to whom he is attached, or threatened with separation, the baby makes efforts to regain contact or nearness, crying, reaching, leaning, looking, and if possible, pursuing. These efforts, attachment behavior, preclude exploratory behavior. When, on the other hand, the mother is present or nearby and available, the baby is free to explore. Studies on both monkeys and humans show clearly that the mother's presence facilitates exploration of the environment. Locomotion, manipulation, and visual exploration were studied in an experimental situation involving 56 one-year-old babies and mothers [2]. Figure 3–10 shows the frequency of these three kinds of exploratory behavior in a series of situations. Episode 1, not shown, consisted of the mother carrying the baby into the room, ushered in by a person who then departed. The room contained two adult chairs, a child's chair, and toys. In Episode 2, the mother put the baby down on the floor and sat down on her chair. Babies showed a high degree of locomotion, manipulation, and visual exploration. In Episode 3, a stranger entered, sat quietly, conversed with the mother, gradually approached the baby and showed him a toy. Note the sharp decrease in exploratory behavior with the entrance of the stranger. In Episode 4, the mother

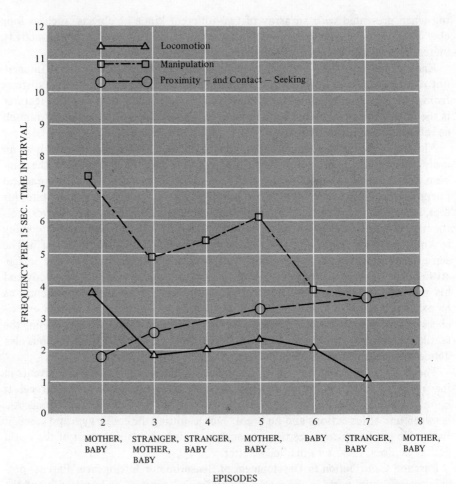

**Figure 3–10.** Babies' exploratory and proximity- and contact-seeking behavior under different conditions of mother presence.

SOURCE: Adapted from Mary D. S. Ainsworth and Silvia M. Bell, "Attachment, Exploration and Separation: Illustrated by the Behavior of One-Year-Olds in a Strange Situation," *Child Development*, 1970, **41**, 49–67.

departs and attachment behavior (crying and searching) increase, while exploratory behavior remains depressed. In Episode 5, the mother returns and tries to get the baby to explore more. Visual and manual exploration do pick up significantly, although locomotion does not. The mother then departs again and Episode 6 shows further decline of exploration. Crying, which is negatively correlated with exploration ($r = -0.67$), increases. The stranger returns, and Episode 7 shows the lowest levels of exploration. Reunion with the mother, in Episode 8, involves heightened proximity-seeking. The experiment demonstrates the supportive function of the mother (or attachment object) in providing a base from which her baby can examine the world by looking, handling, and moving through space. Through these activities, the infant obtains stimulation necessary for his sensorimotor development.

The second type of contribution made by the mother and other caring people is direct stimulation, and an environment offering optimal stimulation. A mother picks up her baby, cuddles, pats, strokes and kisses him, murmurs words of baby talk, and sings a lullaby to him. Giving him a great rich field of perception: touch sensations on the skin of his body and head; muscle sensations as his muscles are pressed by his mother's hands and as he moves himself; inner ear stimulation as his head swings up from a horizontal to vertical orientation and the balance mechanisms operate; a completely different visual world, full of varied objects instead of walls and ceiling; for his hands to feel, his mother's clothing, her firm shoulder, soft neck and hair; against his cheek, her warm cheek and lips; her voice to listen to. His cognition, his knowing of the world, proceeds through sensory experiences, these and others. Picking him up is only one small act among the many educational acts his mother performs. She props him up, too, so that he can see the world from this angle. He looks at his hands, at toys his mother puts in his lap, at his hands contacting the toys. Babies of 3 or 4 months who have had normal opportunities (for American culture) strain to sit up and show by their pleasure in being propped that this is welcome experience. A frequent change of position prevents fatigue and enriches the sensory field. Here is one place where resident grandparents and older brothers and sisters can add to a baby's education, since mothers often have many duties in addition to baby teaching, and many fathers are absent all day.

When sitting and examining schemas are sufficiently developed, the normally experienced infant enthusiastically accepts and examines all objects that come his way. For example, here is part of a half hour's observation of an 11-month-old baby.

> George pulled himself to his feet and stood watching his mother for a few minutes. He moved around the rail of the playpen by putting one foot out to the side and bringing the other up to it. . . . He squealed, tried to hurry and fell down. . . .
>
> Mrs. MacIntyre gave George a cardboard box with a ball in it. George pounced on the ball and dropped it . . . he crept after it and then put it back in the box. He took it out, dropped it, crept after it, and so on, going through the whole process four times. He sat and watched the adults for a minute. Then he picked up a stuffed cat by the tail. His fingers slipped up and down the tail. He squeezed the cat and touched the fur. He poked its eyes and pulled the whiskers. A red ribbon and bell around the cat's neck came in for a share of fingering and pulling. George dropped the cat and pulled himself up.
>
> George sat down and picked a string of brightly colored beads out of his toy basket. He looked at several of the beads and poked at them with his finger. He shook the string and put it round his neck. Then he tried to get it off by pulling down. The beads worked down over his arm. George roared until his mother pulled them off. He put them on again immediately. . . .
>
> George beat on the saucepan and lid with the spoon, gnawed the spoon, put the lid on the saucepan with a bang, removed the lid. He thumped the pan on the lid and the lid on the pan, put the spoon in the pan and the lid on his head. He put the ball in the saucepan [95, pp. 122–123].

Thus a baby sought and found many sensations. Visual sensations were combined with touch, giving varieties of shape, texture, size, and color. Touch sensations came from his hands, lips, gums, tongue, knees, feet, and buttocks. He elicited sounds. Active as George was, he could not have experienced such a wealth of sensations had the toys and play materials not been present in his environment. Due to his mother's planning, management, and constant care, he had the wherewithal to educate himself.

Several studies have demonstrated the importance of sensory stimulation during the sensorimotor period. Both the amount of stimulation and quality of stimulation provided by the mother are related to the baby's motor and mental status [111]. By *quality* is meant the appropriateness of the stimulation to the child as an individual and to his developmental level. A study done in infant welfare clinics in England, where 90 percent of young children are served by such clinics, related babies' sensory and motor development to their mothers' ways of caring for them [8]. The infants who received maximum stimulation were furthest ahead on the tests of sensory and motor achievement.

**Deprivation of Sensorimotor Experience.** A dramatic study of sensorimotor stimulation was done by comparing two groups of infants in Lebanon. The effect of sensorimotor experience on IQ was demonstrated by a comparison between subjects from a well-baby clinic and a group from a creche where babies were kept in cribs with covered sides [23]. The latter could see nobody but the caretakers, and those only rarely. Bottles were propped for feeding. Caretakers picked the babies up only for physical care. Words and caresses were very rare. When tested on the Cattell Infant Scale, the clinic group had an average IQ of 102; the creche group, 68. The institution babies had had practically none of the experiences which would give them a fair chance on the test. The test requires that babies over 2 months be held on an adult's lap for many of the items. The creche babies had not sat on laps, and therefore had not had the sensory perceptions and the consequent cognitive development that stem from lapsitting. Such restricted children would not have a fair chance in real-life situations, either. A study of babies in institutions in Iran is concerned with the development of motor coordination under conditions of deprivation [22]. In Institution I, where the infants lay in cribs with covered sides, they remained in the cribs until they were able to pull themselves to sitting, when they were placed on pieces of linoleum on the stone floor. There were no toys. Bottles were propped in the beds. Baths were given on alternate days. The control group was from Institution III, where babies were held in arms while fed, placed prone, propped to sit, put in playpens on the floor and given plenty of toys. Both groups were tested on five motor items.

Table 3–7 shows their achievements. Children in Institution III were much superior to those in Institution I, although the former did not equal the performance of home-reared children. Although all normal American home-reared children sit alone by 9 months and nearly all walk alone by 2 years, among the children in Institution I less than half could sit alone before age 2 years. Only 8 percent could walk before age 3 years.

Children in Institution I were thus severely retarded in motor development. They also showed differences in mode of locomotion. Almost all who could progress did it by scooting, whereas those in Institution III progressed by creeping. The author reasons that the babies scooted because they had never been placed in positions where creeping and preparation for creeping were possible. They rarely, if ever, rolled from supine to prone in their cribs because the cribs were very small and the mattresses soft. In contrast, a child in Institution III, often prone in bed and on the floor, could raise his head, push with his arms, raise his chest, pull his arms and legs beneath his body and thus practice creeping. Thus delayed walking, as well as delayed creeping, can result from denying a child the prone position. The child who creeps can go to the playpen rail or a piece of furniture and pull himself to his knees. He may walk on his knees. Soon he pulls himself to his feet. He then is

Table 3–7 Motor Achievements of Babies in Two Contrasting
Institutions in Iran

| Institution | Percent of Group Passing Each Test | | | |
|---|---|---|---|---|
| | I | I | III | III |
| N | 50 | 40 | 20 | 31 |
| Age Range | 1.0–1.9 | 2.0–2.9 | 1.0–1.9 | 2.0–2.9 |
| Sit alone | 42 | 95 | 90 | 100 |
| Creep or scoot | 14 | 75 | 75 | 100 |
| Stand holding | 4 | 45 | 70 | 100 |
| Walk holding | 2 | 40 | 60 | 100 |
| Walk alone | 0 | 8 | 15 | 94 |

SOURCE: Reprinted by permission from W. Dennis, "Causes of Retardation Among Institutional Children: Iran," *Journal of Genetic Psychology*,
**96**, 46–60. Copyright © 1960, The Journal Press.

in a position to practice walking while hanging on, and this he does, in the normative
sequence for Americans, for two or three months.

The data assembled by a number of investigators have been summarized to
show that rate of intellectual growth is influenced in infancy by the number of new
objects and events experienced. The more varied the experiences the child has
coped with, the more the child seeks new experiences [44, pp. 148–149]. That is,
the more curious he becomes. Thus children who have had few toys and other
stimulation become apathetic, as do institutional children who have had limited
space and opportunities to explore.

Infants born into a culture of poverty in America and in poor countries all over
the world are likely to have inadequate sensory and motor opportunities, as well
as many other environmental restrictions. Near our home in India was a water
tank where washermen and washerwomen worked. Their babies and young children
sat on the ground nearby with nothing in their hands, perhaps hearing the repeated
whack-whack of the clothes on the rocks. In the center of town, women sat on the
sidewalks selling fruit, baskets, or sticks for cleaning teeth. Babies lay or sat beside
them, hearing the noises of the street, but again, with nothing in their hands and
rarely, if ever, a word directed to them. Once we saw a yearling putting pieces of
broken pottery into one of the clay pots his mother was selling. He had found the
only play materials that would ever come his way on the Delhi sidewalk. What
would happen to his sensorimotor experience after he had exhausted the possibilities of the pots and fragments of pot? Many American infants, too, have few
encounters with objects of varying size, shape, texture, color, and temperature,
few chances to look, hold, squeeze, suck, bite, taste, smell, hear, examine, climb
onto, crawl under, push, pull, drag, ride, swing, jump, float, and splash.

**Compensatory Education for Infants.** Project Head Start was an attempt to
compensate for deficiencies shown by many poor children in the early grades at
school, sensorimotor experience being only one of the areas in which these children
had been deprived. While enriching and compensating at 4 and 5 years of age was
helpful, it was not enough. Head Start was too late. Intervention by 18 months is
recommended for deprived children, both rural and urban [24]. Educational programs for infants are now under way. They will be described more fully in the next
chapter, since relationships with people are very much involved. Rich sensorimotor

experience is basic in all of these programs, however. Whether the babies are cared for in groups, as in the Children's Center in Syracuse, N.Y. [13], or taught by tutors in the home, as in programs at the University of Illinois [75] and the National Institute of Mental Health in Washington [89], or taught by mothers who have received special parent education, as at the University of Florida [38], infants are given a variety of toys, materials, and sensorimotor experiences suited to their level of development. Results reported from infant education studies are positive, in terms of measured cognitive gain. In Syracuse, the mean gain in developmental quotient was 5.6 points after 7.5 months [13]. The Washington project, using measures at intervals from 14 months to 36 months, showed steadily increasing differences in mean scores between the experimental and control groups. Of special interest here are the highly significant differences on a perceptual test at 3 years [101]. The Florida project, using the Griffiths Mental Development Scale on the babies' first birthdays, reported significant superiority of the experimental group in general IQ, hearing, speech, and eye and hand coordination [38]. The Illinois project reported significant gains after one year of home tutoring, in IQ as measured by the Stanford-Binet, and significant differences between experimental and control groups on conceptual tests [75].

*Communication*

Communication gradually takes on a conscious and purposeful quality, overlaid upon the subcortical feeling and tactual experiences and behavior displays of the newborn. The baby cuddles and snuggles in ways that spell love and affection to adults. Perhaps to the baby it means simply a good feeling or a feeling of warmth and closeness. It is a relationship which a baby can choose or reject, since even during the first half of the first year, he will sometimes snuggle close, relaxing and melting his body to conform with the adult's while at other times he will stiffen and push his body upright. During the second year, to cuddle or not to cuddle is a choice that the baby prefers to make. While he wants and needs loving arms and a hospitable lap, it is important to him to take it or leave it according to how he feels at the moment. He cries and shoves the gushing auntie who snatches him up to hug and kiss him at an inappropriate time, communicating to her clearly.

Stroking, patting, and hugging develop out of early cuddling. Kissing probably comes from the pursing reflex of feeding. During his first two years, the baby takes into himself the acts of love he has experienced, the gestures by which his family have symbolized their love for him. He gives them back, and the expression of love becomes more of a true communication.

Children in the second year often communicate purposefully with their hands, pulling another person to show him something, pushing him away, putting a hand over a mouth that is saying what the child does not want to hear, pointing at food, toys, and wet pants. Such language of the hands can be very effective in transferring ideas, even without a single word. Insofar as they achieve what the baby wants, these methods of communicating are, to him, adequate ways of coping with the world.

Vocal communication begins with crying, which has a variety of patterns in the neonate [110]. Spectrograph analysis has shown the basic cry of the newborn to consist of a characteristic rhythm of cry, rest, inspiration, rest. Adults usually interpret the basic cry as meaning hunger, although Wolff says it has no causal relationship with hunger. Variations from the basic rhythm are commonly identified as the "mad" or angry cry, the pain cry, and the frustration cry. There is also a typical cry of a brain-damaged baby, more shrill and piercing than a normal cry. Mothers usually respond differently to cries, especially experienced mothers. They are likely to be tolerantly amused after answering a "mad" cry and disturbed when they hear a pain cry.

Bell and Ainsworth [7] have analyzed the relationship between infants' crying and maternal responsiveness during the first year of life. In general, the more responsive the mother, the less often the baby cried and the shorter his periods of crying. Babies who cried little and whose crying decreased during the year had mothers who were more responsive than did babies who cried a great deal and whose crying increased. Babies who decreased in crying and who had responsive mothers were more likely than their opposites to communicate through channels other than crying.

Not crying at 1 month is a passive reaction to frustration; it is correlated with passivity at 1 year, shown both by crying, at that age, and by apparently waiting to be carried over a barrier [61]. Crying, or the tendency to cry, remains in everyone's repertory of communication as a way of showing distress.

**Language.** The great human invention, spoken language, is of vast significance as a method of communication. "The child may begin as a parrot, imitating what others say, but he will end as a poet, able to say things that have not been said before but which will be grammatical and meaningful in his community" [11]. The human baby, unlike all other babies, has innate capacities for understanding and producing speech. Some investigators suggest that the human brain has a genetically given predisposition to develop a set of special structures which generate language [69]. The language generator must include information-processing procedures which are activated by exposure to speech. The language generator can respond to any language, and of course the language to which the child is exposed determines what he will understand and speak. At birth the infant vocalizes and responds to sounds. He interacts with his environment through his genetically given organs of speech and brain structures to understand and produce language. Language comprehension can be built up without producing speech at the same time. Since deaf and blind children learn to speak, neither hearing nor seeing is essential for language learning. Some sort of interaction with a speech community, however, is necessary. Maturation of the nervous system, the respiratory system, and the organs of eating are also basic to language development. In fact, language is intimately related to all the maturation and learning that take place in the child.

**Beginnings of Speech.** The amount of vocalizing by an infant is influenced by various factors, some of which were investigated in boy and girl babies between 7 days and 14 days of age and again at 85–95 days [50]. As can be seen by Figure 3–11 the amount of vocalization varied considerably with the state of the infant, at both 10 days and 90 days of age. The infants were most vocal in the active awake state, defined as eyes open and sustained movement involving more than one limb. The passive awake and drowsy states included considerably less vocalization, even less than the state of active sleep. There is a sequence in the sounds that all babies make, and considerable regularity in the ages at which they are produced [45, 46, 48]. The first noncrying sounds are vowels. During the first 2 months about four vowel sounds are heard in noncrying vocalization. The earliest vowels are those made in the front part of the mouth. A new vowel sound appears about

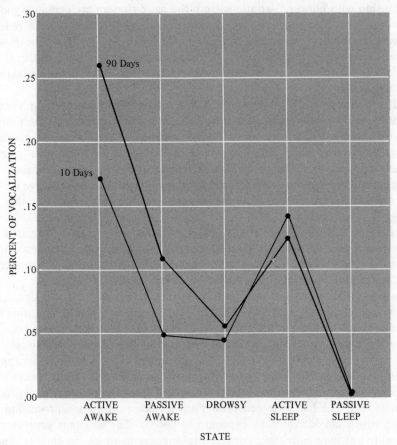

**Figure 3–11.** Age and state associated with amount of infant vocalizations.

SOURCE: Reprinted by permission from S. J. Jones and H. A. Moss, "Age, State and Maternal Behavior Associated with Infant Vocalizations." Paper presented at the meeting of the Society for Research in Child Development, Santa Monica, March 29, 1969.

every two months during the first year. The first consonant, *H*, is associated with gasping and crying. The early consonants are those made in the back of the throat, and the labials and dentals are the last to come.

The sounds made at the earliest stages of development are based on movements similar to those used in sucking and swallowing. It is only after breathing and eating and physiological equilibrium are established that the infant coos and plays vocally. Progress in language seems to be associated with postural development, too. "Talking back," or responding vocally to a human face and/or voice, first occurs at 2 or 3 months, the time when the baby holds his head erect. Since it is well-known that babies will talk more when a person responds to their vocalizing, one study focused on different types of social stimulation, to see which is most effective [91]. Three-months-old babies were compared as to amount of vocalizing after their utterances were reinforced by an adult talking, smiling, or rubbing the baby's abdomen, or by combinations of these adult behaviors. Results showed all reinforcing conditions to be effective for increasing infant vocalizing. A variety of adult action will increase vocalizing in babies.

The early sounds made by infants have been classified into discomfort cries and

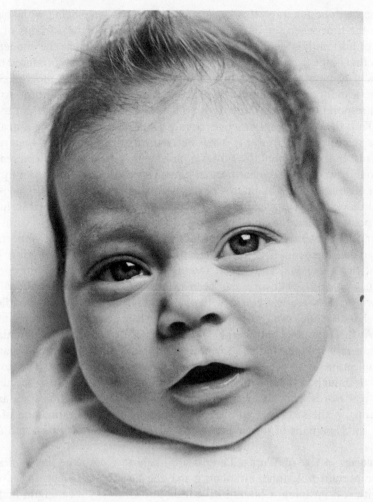

Halvar Loken

comfort sounds, in an attempt to show how language has biological roots [64]. Both types of sounds are, of course, expressive. Discomfort cries, which begin immediately after birth, at first consist of front, narrow vowels, frequently shrill and nasalized, resulting from tension in the whole body including the face. In the second stage of discomfort cries, consonants like *w, l,* and *h* are added. The third stage of discomfort cries includes *m* and *n* sounds. Comfort sounds occur in a relaxed state, starting after discomfort cries have begun. The first stage of comfort sounds are vowel-like and indistinct, developing into *a, o, u.* Back consonants, such as *g, k, r,* are added in the second stage and front consonants, *p, b, m, t, d, n,* in the third stage. The almost-universal use of *mama* or *nana* for mother or nurse might be accounted for by the fact that if the hungry baby makes anticipatory sucking movements while giving a nasalized discomfort cry, the result is mama or nana. *Papa* might be explained as the result of vocalizing in a state of relaxation [64].

Babbling is a series of repetitive sounds, uttered in a state of contentment and relaxation. In contrast to expressive sounds of comfort and discomfort, babbling seems to be done for its own sake. The baby seems to be playing with sounds. It may be the time when the baby practices the phonemes (smallest units of sound) typical of his family's language and when he minimizes or drops the phonemes not used by that language [83]. The greatest number of phonemes are produced between ages 8 and 12 months. The peak for repetition of sounds is at 12 months. Some of the American infant's babbling sounds like words to the adults near him. American parents respond in a special way to *tata* and *dada*, for instance, but not to *geegee* or *lili*. Thus the older infant practices sounds he hears spoken around him and also receives reinforcement (reward) when he chances to utter sounds that resemble real words. In the early months, however, at least the first three, all babies make the same sounds whether they hear normal human speech or not, as shown by a comparison of sounds made by infants of deaf and hearing parents [60]. This is not to say that they cannot tell the differences between different kinds of sounds, however, but to point out that they make a variety of sounds spontaneously.

Other events connected with the mouth are probably of great importance in language development. It is during the time that the teeth are erupting, 6 to 28 months, that the labial and dental sounds are established. The connection with early sucking and swallowing has been mentioned. Spoon and cup feeding and swallowing solids are associated with the babbling period. At 10 months, most infants handle solids well, eating a variety of them and chewing some chopped foods. At this time also, considerable vocalizing occurs in the feeding situation [68].

Expressive jargon, a kind of speech used in the middle of the second year, is not communication in the sense of expressing ideas through words. The youngster sounds as though he were really talking, but none of it makes sense because there are no real words in it, rather like double-talk. There are rhythm rises and falls and feeling in the sounds. Expressive jargon is probably an expression of feeling for the child, perhaps of ideas, and it may be intended as a contact with another person.

**Beginnings in Use of Words.** Parents are likely to record the baby's first word as an important milestone, although it may be hard to tell whether the word is used with real meaning. Children have been known to say meaningful first words as early as 7 months, as did the little girl who commented "buh" each time the hourly bus thundered past her house. The median time for uttering the first word is about 11 months, for children of middle-upper socioeconomic families [66]. Two words are the most common vocabulary at 12 months. The year-old baby covers a lot of territory under his own powers of locomotion, whether it be creeping, or walking with support, or even independent walking. A rush of new experiences stimulates the learning of new words. A single word at this point stands for a whole experience, often an emotionally toned one. "CAR" might mean, "Here we are, going for a ride in the car, seeing the wide world and having such an exciting time together." At 16 months, Becky's word, "Ow" meant, "This particular object is out of place, or inappropriately arranged. I am not going to continue with my play until you make everything right." Single words can also be commands, requests, names, and actions. The one-word sentence is the usual mode of expression from about 12 to 18 months, when the baby begins to combine words [66]. The first combinations may be functionally one-word utterances, such as *allgone* or *whazzat*? While the average vocabulary increases slowly between 12 and 18 months, it picks up quickly during the following six months. Most babies start to combine words during this time when they are adding words rapidly. The early two-word sentence usually consists of a noun and a verb or predicate word, such as *Daddy allgone*. Words are usually put together in the right order, although the sentences are not complete and words are omitted. The words which give the essential meaning are the ones used first. One reason for this may be that those are the words stressed by adults, just as when children try to repeat words that are too long and difficult, they reproduce the stressed syllables, such as '*raffe* for *giraffe*' [10, p. 219].

**Understanding of Language.** Communication is a reciprocal process; language must be understood as well as spoken. The understanding of what other people say occurs before the ability to express oneself in words, as you can see in yourself by the many words which you understand yet never use in speech. The child as a talker has been studied more than the child as a listener because it is more difficult to detect what he hears than what he says. Recent studies have shown, however, that infants under a year of age make fine discriminations in listening to speech. Infants between 20 and 24 weeks of age showed that they perceived a difference between *bah* and *gah* when their heart rates changed upon presentation of *bah* after becoming habituated to *gah* [71]. When tapes of the mother's voice and of distortions of the mother's voice were presented to infants of 3, 6, and 9 months, the infants showed through quieting and crying behavior that they discriminated the difference [100]. Another study [107] found 6-month-olds adapting their production of vowels and consonants to differing numbers of vowels and consonants played to them on tapes. When boys between 11 and 15 months of age were given opportunities to choose which recorded sounds they would hear, these infants showed definite preferences which changed from time to time [30]. Operating a machine attached to the playpen, the infants could choose between the mother's voice, a stranger's voice, music, and between different types of vocalized sounds. The subjects showed that they could tell the difference and they preferred some to others, such as the mother's voice over simple music.

Understanding of words is ordinarily shown between 9 and 12 months when babies respond and adjust to such words as *no* and *bye-bye*. An occasional infant shows comprehension of words earlier, as did the little girl of 6 months who would open her mouth when her mother said *peaches* after keeping it firmly shut on presentation of squash with the word *squash*. *No*, *bye-bye*, and *peaches* are not merely sounds but indicators of situations which have important meaning for the baby.

**Autonomy and Language.** The ability to communicate with language must surely facilitate the sense of autonomy. For instance, saying "drink" can produce water at one's lips or "out" can transform the whole environment from indoors to outdoors. The extension of the child's powers and control is enormous. As it dawns upon him that everything has a name, that verbal symbols exist and that he can use them, he must have a surge of satisfaction over his expanded powers. One can imagine next a push to discover just how much he can do with these symbols, words, in both understanding and controlling the world and the people in it, including himself.

**The End of Infancy.** By the end of the sensorimotor period, the child has gone about as far as a creature can go without true language. Here is where other animals stop in their mental development, but man takes a great leap forward. *Words come to stand for things and actions.* Instead of having to go through sensory and motor acts, words can be manipulated in a twinkling. One doesn't even have to be where the problem is. He can think and talk about things which are remote in time and space. *The world is expanded and differentiated* as words come to stand for parts of experience which were formerly embedded in a larger experience. (Knowing *red*, he can pick out things that are red.) *Words are combined.* Here is what makes man's speech truly different from the utterances of birds and animals. He can combine words in ways which he has not even heard before, to mean something which has the same meaning for his listener. No wonder that, for many students of human nature, this intellectual leap marks the end of infancy, since it transforms the individual into a very different kind or person.

**Parents' Contribution to Language Development.** Language education is another activity which goes on spontaneously for normal infants in normal homes, with the mother taking the lead as teacher. The mother and others ordinarily talk to the baby in affectionate tones while they are feeding, bathing, changing diapers, picking up, cuddling, and otherwise taking care of the baby. There is also the conversation of the household which forms a background and punctuation marks in an infant's experience.

Students of human nature have long pondered on how infants learn to speak. Imitation and reinforcement of meaningful sounds by parents are understandable enough as contributing to the learning of language, but they do not explain why the child tries to imitate. The structure of the organs of speech and spontaneous exercising of them in vocal play are also understandable as part of the process. Research on language and personality disorders has led to an appreciation of the mother's essential role in language development. Slowness in starting to talk, defective articulation, and stuttering are all associated with certain kinds of disturbed parent–child relationships [67, 68].

Several studies shed light on the process of learning to talk, showing how it is related to the infant's experiences in the family. Infants vocalized more when adults smiled at them than when they looked with solemn faces at the babies [85]. A psychologist noted that his 10-weeks-old infant made an average of 4 sounds per 3-minute period under ordinary circumstances. When the father said "Hello" every 10 seconds, the baby averaged 18 sounds per 3-minute period [63]. An experiment on influencing sound production used subjects of lower socioeconomic status between 13 and 30 months of age [47]. Their parents were given picture-story books and encouraged to read to the toddlers. At the end of the experimental period, the stimulated children were producing significantly more sounds than a control group. Several investigations have shown the language development of infants in institutions to be below normal. One such study [81] found speech development the most retarded of the four Gesell areas, which are described on page 129. Production was more retarded than comprehension. Sound production was beginning to be deficient in the second month and no words were spoken at 1 year. Another study [84] conducted in an institution compared the behavior of babies who had many caretakers with that of babies who were cared for by only one person. From 6 to 8 months of age, the experimental infants had the attentive care of one person for seven and a half hours a day. They became more socially responsive than babies on the regular routine. At 18 months of age, after they had settled down in adoptive homes, the infants were tested again. The only significant difference between experimental and control groups was that the former vocalized more. The "quality of stimulation," mentioned before [111] as significant, probably operated here. One caretaker would be more likely than many caretakers to offer stimuli appropriate to the child as an individual.

These studies offer convincing proof that the infant's early experience with people's talking have definite effects on his own language behavior. One theory suggests that sounds become associated with mother and with the experiences of comfort and stimulation which her presence brings. As the baby hears himself make a sound like mother makes, he feels comforted and happy, just as he does in her presence. Thus he stimulates himself to make more noises like mother makes. "Words are reproduced if and only if they are first made to sound good in the context of affectionate care and attention." This theory has been borne out by a study in which the sound production of infants was shown to be related to the warmth and amount of vocalization of their mothers [82]. On visits to the infants' homes, records were made of their sound production, including crying as well as cooing. Correlations between infant vocalization and mother vocalization and between infant vocalization and mother warmth increased with age.

The early stages of learning to talk are deeply emotional as well as intellectual and motor. Language is embedded in the total mass of experience, affected by a multitude of factors. None of the studies mentioned above explains *why* children begin to talk. We shall return to this question in Chapter 6.

### Measuring Infant Intelligence

Many tests of infant behavior are available. Three widely used tests are the Gesell Developmental Test [35], Bayley's Scales of Infant Development [6], and the Cattell Infant Intelligence Scale [14]. Uzgiris and Hunt's ordinal scales, based on Piaget's delineation of stages of sensorimotor development, constitute an instrument which is used for research in infant development [102].

The Gesell tests consist of four categories of items—motor, adaptive, language, and personal–social behavior—arranged at age levels according to where the average child showed the behavior pattern. In testing an infant, his behavior in each area can be matched to a normative level, giving his developmental age in motor, adaptive, language, and personal–social behavior. Conflicting conclusions have been drawn from studies on the predictive value of the Gesell tests. Some studies have shown little or no correlation between Gesell scores and later intelligence test scores [98]. Other investigators have found the Gesell tests to predict later behavior very well, as in a study which found significant correlation with an intelligence test (WISC) at 10 years [4]. The tests are also helpful in detecting and diagnosing neurological abnormalities.

The Bayley Scales of Infant Development consist of a motor scale and a mental scale, derived from repeated examinations of 1409 infants in 12 research centers scattered throughout the United States [70]. Norms are given for each half-month level. The Bayley scales have been used in several different parts of the world, since they provide a method for comparing different populations of infants. Bayley mental scale data from Israeli infants have been factor analyzed into different scales, the names of which suggest the main functions included in them: eye–hand, manipulation, object–relation, imitation–comprehension, vocalization–social contact, and active vocabulary [58]. The items of the first two scales can be classified as belonging to Piaget's third stage of sensorimotor development, the third scale to Piaget's fourth stage. All three first scales are similar to Gesell's Adaptive Behavior.

The Cattell Scale was developed as a downward extension of the Stanford–Binet test of Intelligence, which is described in Chapters 6 and 10 of this book.

Like the Stanford–Binet, it provides a mental age score, which can be converted into an intelligence quotient. The scale, given at 8 months, showed significant low correlations with IQ at 7 years for white and black girls and for white boys, but not for black boys [37]. When the Bayley Scale was given at 20 months to a sample of children drawn from a whole community in Hawaii, it was a good predictor of IQ at age 10 [108]. Combined with a pediatrician's appraisals, the tests served even better. Problems in school achievement could be expected when Cattell IQ and pediatricians' ratings were low. There seems to be little doubt that clinicians can use Gesell and Cattell tests to predict retarded, average, and advanced development.

## Summary

The sense of trust grows as the baby has successful experiences in seeking and finding food, comfort, and stimulation, as he gains more and more control of his body, and as he comes to realize that certain regularities and permanencies exist in the world. He develops trust in his mother and in other key people as they repeatedly interact satisfactorily with him.

The sense of autonomy grows quickly during the second year, as the baby realizes his power as a maker of choices. He knows himself as a person who can decide which action to take, to do or not to do, to hold on or to let go. Healthy personality growth results not only from experiencing himself as choosing, but upon an accompanying conviction that what he does is generally all right and acceptable. The negative feelings typical of this stage are doubt and shame, feelings which occur when the child has too few opportunities for choosing and also when his choices are disastrous.

Physical development is rapid during infancy, with changes occurring in appearance and proportions. The deciduous teeth erupt. The basic physiological processes of respiration and temperature control become regularized, along with the timing of eating, sleeping, and elimination. Feeding behavior matures as the infant learns to hold his food, to sit up, to drink from a cup, to chew, and to control situations by talking. Although no specific technique of feeding has been shown to have definite results, the emotional context of feeding is significant. Weaning, the substitution of cup for breast or bottle, can be conducted and timed in various ways. When offered a wide variety of simple foods, year-old babies choose adequate diets. Many of the infant's autonomous acts occur in feeding situations.

Progress in locomotion takes place in a regular sequence of achievements. Creeping is perfected during the first year, walking during the second. The sense of autonomy grows as the child gains upright position and as he becomes more and more mobile, enlarging the scope of his interactions and his possibilities for choice making. Manipulation also develops through a regular sequence, increasing the baby's competence in exploring his environment, changing it, and understanding it.

Attention is determined by certain properties of stimuli and by the infant's maturity and experience. Movement, contour, and complexity are attractive to young infants. Faces are especially compelling. When objects are becoming familiar (the child is building a schema or inner representation), they are very attractive. When the object *is* familiar (the schema is well developed), novelty, in the form of a variation from the schema, is preferred.

Cognition is the activity of coming to know and understand. Cognitive development takes place in a sequence which stretches throughout infancy, childhood, and adolescence. The infant first interacts with his environment through reflex patterns. Then he adapts and combines these patterns to enlarge his repertory. He comes to realize that objects and people continue to exist even when he cannot see them. He experiments, trying out different kinds of actions in order to see their results. Finally, he imitates and pretends, representing objects and actions to himself mentally. As he cognizes the environment, he also comes to know himself more clearly, as an object which is distinct from the rest of the world. He also realizes his mother as a creature distinct from himself and from everything else. Cognitive development is promoted by a mother and other members of the family who offer the baby a rich variety of experiences.

The acquisition of language extends the child's powers, encouraging growth of the sense of autonomy. The baby discovers that words stand for objects and actions, and that everything has a name. Language learning takes place in the context of family communication, the baby experiencing other people talking to each other as well as direct interaction with his mother and others. The process is deeply emotional as well as cognitive and motor.

The Gesell, the Cattell, and the Bayley tests of infant behavior can be used to distinguish between retarded, average, and advanced development. Combined with other kinds of data they can also be used to predict later intellectual development.

# References

1. Ainsworth, M. D. S. Personal communication to the authors. April, 1963.
2. Ainsworth, M. D. S., & Bell, S. M. Attachment, exploration and separation: Illustrated by the behavior of one-year olds in a strange situation. *Child Devel.*, 1970, **41**, 49–67.
3. Albino, R. C., & Thompson, V. J. The effects of sudden weaning on Zulu children. In W. Dennis (Ed.). *Readings in child psychology*. Englewood Cliffs, N.J.: Prentice-Hall, 1963, pp. 128–148.
4. Ames, L. B. Predictive value of infant behavior examinations. In B. Staub & J. Hellmuth (Eds.), *Exceptional infant*. Vol. I: *The normal infant*. Seattle: Special Child Publications, 1967, pp. 207–239.
5. Bayley, N. Comparisons of mental and motor test scores for ages 1–15 months by sex, birth order, race, geographic location and education of parents. *Child Devel.*, 1965, **36**, 379–411.
6. Bayley, N. *Bayley's scales of infant development*. New York: Psychological Corporation, 1968.
7. Bell, S. M., & Ainsworth, M. D. S. Infant crying and maternal responsiveness: Reinforcement reassessed. Paper presented at the meeting of the Eastern Psychological Association, Atlantic City, June, 1970.
8. Blank, M. Some maternal influences on infants' rates of sensorimotor development. Paper presented at the meeting of the Society for Research in Child Development, Berkeley, April 12, 1963.
9. Breckenridge, M. E., & Murphy, M. N. *Growth and development of the young child* (8th ed.). Philadelphia: Saunders, 1969.
10. Brown, R. *Social psychology*. New York: Free Press, 1965.
11. Brown, R., & Berko, J. Word association and the acquisition of grammar. *Child Devel.*, 1960, **31**, 1–14.

12. Calder, R. Food supplementation for prevention of malnutrition in the pre-school child. In National Research Council, *Preschool child malnutrition: Primary deterrent to human progress.* Washington: National Academy of Sciences, 1966.
13. Caldwell, B. M., & Richmond, J. B. The children's center in Syracuse, New York. In C. A. Chandler et al, *Early child care.* New York: Atherton, 1968, pp. 326–358.
14. Cattell, P. *The measurement of intelligence of infants.* New York: Psychological Corporation, 1940.
15. Charlesworth, W. R. Persistence of orienting and attending behavior in infants as a function of stimulus-locus uncertainty. *Child Devel.,* 1966, **37**, 473–491.
16. Children's Bureau. *Your baby's first year.* Washington, D.C.: U.S. Govt. Printing Office, 1962.
17. Cravioto, J. Nutritional deficiencies and mental performance in childhood. In D. C. Glass (Ed.), *Environmental influences.* New York: Rockefeller University Press and Russell Sage Foundation, 1968.
18. Davis, C. M. Self-selection of diet by newly weaned infants. *Am. J. Dis. Child.,* 1928, **39**, 651–679.
19. Davis, C. M. Self-selection of diets. *The Trained Nurse and Hospital Review,* 1931, **86**:5. Cited in C. A. Aldrich & M. M. Aldrich, *Feeding our old-fashioned children.* New York: Macmillan, 1941.
20. Davis, C. M. Self-selection of food by children. *Am. J. Nursing,* 1935, **35**, 403–410.
21. Dean, R. F. Effects of malnutrition, especially of slight degree, on the growth of young children. *Courrier,* 1965, **15**, 73–83.
22. Dennis, W. Causes of retardation among institutional children: Iran. *J. Genet. Psychol.,* 1960, **96**, 46–60.
23. Dennis, W., & Najarian, P. Infant development under environmental handicap. *Psychol. Mono.,* 1957, **71**, 1–13.
24. Edwards, E. P. Kindergarten is too late. *Sat. Rev.,* 1968, June 15, 68–70, 76–79.
25. Erikson, E. H. *Childhood and society.* New York: Norton, 1963.
26. Falade, S. Le développement psychomotor du jeune *African* originaire du Sénégal au cours de sa première année. Paris: Foulon, 1955. Cited in Geber [33].
27. Fantz, R. L. Visual perception from birth as shown by pattern selectivity. *Ann. N.Y. Acad. Sci.,* 1965, **118**, 793–814.
28. Fantz, R. L., & Nevis, S. Pattern preferences and perceptual-cognitive development in early infancy. *Merrill–Palmer Quart.,* 1967, **13**, 77–108.
29. Flavell, J. H. *The developmental psychology of Jean Piaget.* Princeton, N.J.: Van Nostrand, 1963.
30. Friedlander, B. Z. The effect of speaker identity, voice inflection, vocabulary, and message redundancy on infants' selection of vocal reinforcement. *J. Exper. Child Psychol.,* 1968, **6**, 443–459.
31. Garn, S. M. The applicability of North American growth standards in developing countries. *Canad. Med. Assoc. J.,* 1965, **93**, 914–919.
32. Garn, S. M., Lewis, A. B., & Kerewsky, R. S. Genetic, nutritional and maturational correlates of dental development. *J. Dent. Res.,* 1964, **44**, 228–242.

33. Geber, M. The psychomotor development of African children in the first year and the influence of maternal behavior. *J. Soc. Psychol.*, 1958, **47**, 185–195.

34. Gesell, A., et al. *The first five years of life.* New York: Harper, 1940.

35. Gesell, A., & Amatruda, C. *Developmental diagnosis.* New York: Hoeber, 1951.

36. Gesell, A., & Ilg, F. *Feeding behavior of infants.* Philadelphia: Lippincott, 1937.

37. Goffeney, B., Henderson, N. B., & Butler, B. V. Negro–white, male–female 8-month developmental scores compared with 7-year WISC and Bender Test Scores. *Child Devel.*, 1971 (in press).

38. Gordon, I. J. Stimulation via parent education. *Children*, 1969, **16**, 57–59.

39. Griffiths, R. *The abilities of babies.* New York: McGraw-Hill, 1954.

40. Haaf, R. A., & Bell, R. Q. A facial dimension in visual discrimination by human infants. *Child Devel.*, 1967, **38**, 893–899.

41. Halverson, H. M. An experimental study of prehension in infants by means of systematic cinema records. *Genet. Psychol. Mono.*, 1931, **10**, 107–286.

42. Heard, C. R. C., & Turner, M. R. Glucose tolerance and related factors in dogs fed diets of suboptimal protein value. *Diabetes*, 1967, **16**, 96.

43. Hunt, J. McV. Experience and the development of motivation: Some reinterpretations. *Child Devel.*, 1960, **31**, 498–504.

44. Hunt, J. McV. *Intelligence and experience.* New York: Ronald, 1961.

45. Irwin, O. C. Infant speech: equations for consonant–vowel ratio. *J. Speech Dis.*, 1946, **11**, 177–180.

46. Irwin, O. C. Infant speech: Vowel and consonant frequency. *J. Speech Dis.*, 1946, **11**, 123–125.

47. Irwin, O. C. Infant speech: Effect of systematic reading of stories. *J. Speech Hear. Res.*, 1960, **3**, 187–190.

48. Irwin, O. C., & Chen, H. P. Infant speech: Vowel and consonant types. *J. Speech Dis.*, 1946, **11**, 27–29.

49. Jackson, R. L. Effect of malnutrition on growth of the preschool child. In National Research Council, *Preschool child malnutrition: Primary deterrent to human progress.* Washington: National Academy of Sciences, 1966.

50. Jones, S. J., & Moss, H. A. Age, state and maternal behavior associated with infant vocalizations. Paper presented at the meeting of the Society for Research in Child Development, Santa Monica, Calif., March 29, 1969.

51. Kagan, J., Henker, B. A., Hen-tov, A., Levine, J., & Lewis, M. Infants' differential reactions to familiar and distorted faces. *Child Devel.*, 1966, **37**, 519–532.

52. Kagan, J., & Lewis, M. Studies of attention in the human infant. *Merrill-Palmer Quart.*, 1965, **11**, 95–127.

53. Karelitz, S., Fisichelli, V. R., Costa, J., Karelitz, R., & Rosenfeld, L. Relation of crying activity in early infancy to speech and intellectual development at age three years. *Child Devel.*, 1964, **35**, 769–777.

54. Keet, M. P., Hansen, J. D. L., & Truswell, A. S. Are skinfold measurements of value in the assessment of suboptimal nutrition in young children? *Pediat.*, 1970, **45**, 965–972.

55. Kelley, V. C., & Bosma, J. F. Basal metabolism in infants and children. In I. McQuarrie (Ed.), *Brennemann's practice of pediatrics.* Vol. I. Hagerstown, Md.: W. F. Prior, 1957.

56. Keppel, F. Food for thought. In N. S. Scrimshaw & J. E. Gordon, *Malnutrition, learning and behavior*. Cambridge, Mass.: M.I.T. Press, 1968, pp. 4–9.
57. Knoblock, H., & Pasamanick, B. Further observations on the behavioral development of Negro children. *J. Genet. Psychol.*, 1953, **83**, 137–157.
58. Kohen-Raz, R. Scalogram analysis of some developmental sequences of infant behavior as measured by the Bayley Infant Scale of Mental Development. *Genet. Psychol. Mono.*, 1967, **76**, 3–21.
59. Kohen-Raz, R. Mental and motor development of kibbutz, institutionalized, and home-reared infants in Israel. *Child Devel.*, 1968, **39**, 489–504.
60. Lenneberg, E. H., Rebelsky, F. G., & Nichols, I. A. The vocalizations of infants born to deaf and to hearing parents. *Human Devel.*, 1956, **8**, 23–37.
61. Lewis, M. The meaning of a response, or why researchers in infant behavior should be oriental metaphysicians. *Merrill-Palmer Quart.*, 1967, **13**, 7–18.
62. Lewis, M., Kagan, J., Campbell, H., & Kalafat, J. The cardiac response as a correlate of attention in infants. *Child Devel.*, 1966, **37**, 63–71.
63. Lewis, M. M. *How children learn to speak*. New York: Basic Books, 1959.
64. Lewis, M. M. *Language, thought, and personality in infancy and childhood*. New York: Basic Books, 1963.
65. Lowenberg, M. E., et al. *Food and man*. New York: Wiley, 1968.
66. McCarthy, D. Language development in children. In L. Carmichael (Ed.), *Manual of child psychology* (2nd ed.). New York: Wiley, 1954, pp. 492–630.
67. McCarthy, D. Language disorders and parent–child relationships. *J. Speech Dis.*, 1954, **19**, 514–523.
68. McCarthy, D. Language development. In N. E. Wood (Ed.), Language development and language disorders: A compendium of lectures. *Mono. Soc. Res. Child. Devel.*, 1960, **25**:3, 5–14.
69. McNeill, D. Developmental psycholinguistics. In F. Smith and G. A. Miller (Eds.), *The genesis of language: a psycholinguistic approach*. Cambridge, Mass.: M.I.T. Press, 1966.
70. Mendelson, M. A. Interdisciplinary approach to the study of the exceptional infant: A large scale research project. In B. Staub & J. Hellmuth (Eds.), *Exceptional infant*. Vol. I: *The normal infant*. Seattle: Special Child Publications, 1967, pp. 15–38.
71. Moffitt, A. R. Speech perception by 20–24 week-old infants. Paper presented at the meeting of the Society for Research in Child Development, Santa Monica, Calif., March 29, 1969.
72. Mönckeberg, F. Effect of early marasmic malnutrition on subsequent physical and psychological development. In N. S. Scrimshaw & J. E. Gordon (Eds.), *Malnutrition, learning and behavior*. Cambridge, Mass.: M.I.T. Press, 1968, pp. 269–278.
73. Mowrer, O. H. Hearing and speaking: An analysis of language learning. *J. Speech Dis.*, 1958, **23**, 143–151.
74. Murphy, L. B. *The widening world of childhood*. New York: Basic Books, 1962.
75. Painter, G. The effect of a structured tutorial program on the cognitive and language development of culturally disadvantaged infants. *Merrill-Palmer Quart.*, 1969, **15**, 279–294.
76. Parmelee, A. H., Schultz, H. R., & Disbrow, M. A. Sleep patterns of the newborn. *J. Pediat.*, 1961, **58**, 241–250.

77. Phatak, P., et al. (Eds.) Motor and mental growth of Indian babies of 1 month to 35 months. Unpublished Research Report No. 1. Baroda, India: Department of Child Development, University of Baroda.

78. Piaget, J. *The construction of reality in the child.* New York: Basic Books, 1954.

79. Piaget, J. *The origins of intelligence in children.* New York: Norton, 1963.

80. Piaget, J. *Six psychological studies.* New York: Random House, 1967.

81. Provence, S., & Lipton, R. C. *Infants in institutions.* New York: International Universities Press, 1962.

82. Rebelsky, F. G., Nichols, I. A., & Lenneberg, E. H. A study of infant vocalization. Paper presented at the meeting of the Society for Research in Child Development, April 12, 1963.

83. Rebelsky, F. G., Starr, R. H., & Luria, Z. *Language development: The first four years.* In Y. Brackbill (Ed.), *Infancy and early childhood.* New York: Free Press, 1967.

84. Rheingold, H., & Bayley, N. The later effects of an experimental modification of mothering. *Child Devel.,* 1959, **30**, 363–372.

85. Rheingold, H., Gewirtz, J. L., & Ross, H. W. Social conditioning of vocalizations in the infant. *J. Comp. Physiol. Psychol.,* 1959, **52**, 68–73.

86. Ricciuti, H. N. Object grouping and selective ordering behavior in infants 12 to 24 months old. *Merrill-Palmer Quart.,* 1965, **11**, 129–148.

87. Roberts, K. E., & Schoelkopf, J. A. Eating, sleeping, and elimination: Practices of a group of two and a half year old children. *Am. J. Dis. Child.,* 1951, **82**, 121–152.

88. Schaefer, A. E., & Johnson, O. C. Are we well fed? The search for the answer. *Nutrition Today,* 1969, **41**, 2–11.

89. Schaefer, E. S. A home tutoring program. *Children,* 1969, **16**, 59–61.

90. Schofield, L., & Uzgiris, I. C. Examining behavior and the concept of object. Paper presented at the meeting of the Society for Research in Child Development, Santa Monica, Calif., March 29, 1969.

91. Schwartz, A., Rosenberg, D., & Brackbill, Y. An analysis of the components of social reinforcement of infant vocalization. Paper presented at the meeting of the Society for Research in Child Development, Santa Monica, Calif., March 29, 1969.

92. Scrimshaw, N. S. The effect of the interaction of nutrition and infection on the preschool child. In National Academy of Sciences, *Preschool child malnutrition: Deterrent to human progress.* Washington, D.C.: National Research Council, 1966, pp. 63–73.

93. Scrimshaw, N. S., & Gordon, J. E. *Malnutrition, learning and behavior.* Cambridge, Mass.: M.I.T. Press, 1968.

94. Shirley, M. *The first two years: A study of twenty-five children.* Vol. I: *Postural and locomotor development.* Monograph Series, 7. Minneapolis: University of Minnesota, Institute of Child Welfare, 1933.

95. Smart, M. S., & Smart, R. C. *Living and learning with children.* Boston: Houghton Mifflin, 1961.

96. Smith, S. S. The effect of stimuli of different modalities as reinforcers of lever-pushing by young children. Unpublished Ph.D. thesis. University of Vermont, 1970.

97. Stern, E., et al. Sleep cycle characteristics in infants. *Pediat.,* 1969, **43**, 65–70.

98. Stott, L. H., & Ball, R. S. Infant and preschool mental tests: Review and evaluation. *Mono. Soc. Res. Child Devel.*, 1965, **30**:3.

99. Super, C. M., Kagan, J., Morrison, F. J., Haith, M. M., & Weiffenbach, J. Discrepancy and attention in the 5-month infant. Unpublished manuscript. Harvard University, 1970.

100. Turnure, C. Response to voice of mother and stranger by babies in their first year. Paper presented at the meeting of the Society for Research in Child Development, Santa Monica, Calif., March 29, 1969.

101. U.S. Department of Health, Education, and Welfare. *Infant education research project Washington, D.C.* Superintendent of Documents, U.S. Govt. Printing Office, Washington, D.C., 1969.

102. Uzgiris, I. C. Ordinality in the development of schemas for relating to objects. In B. Staub & J. Hellmuth (Eds.), *Exceptional infant*. Vol. I: *The normal infant*. Seattle: Special Child Publications, 1967, pp. 315–348.

103. Valadian, I., Stuart, H. C., & Reed, R. B. Studies of illnesses of children followed from birth to eighteen years. *Mono. Soc. Res. Child. Devel.*, 1961, **26**:3.

104. Walters, C. E. Comparative development of Negro and white infants. *J. Genet. Psychol.*, 1967, **110**, 243–251.

105. Watson, E. H., & Lowrey, G. H. *Growth and development of children* (5th ed.). Chicago: Year Book, 1967.

106. Watson, J. S., & Ramey, C. T. Reactions to response-contingent stimulation in early infancy. Paper presented at the meeting of the Society for Research in Child Development. Santa Monica, Calif., March, 1969.

107. Webster, R. L. Selective suppression of infants' vocal responses by classes of phonemic stimulation. *Devel. Psychol.*, 1969, **1**, 410–414.

108. Werner, E. E., Honzik, M. P., & Smith, R. S. Prediction of intelligence and achievement at ten years from twenty months pediatric and psychologic examinations. *Child Devel.*, 1968, **39**, 1063–1075.

109. White, B. L., & Held, R. Plasticity of sensorimotor development in the human infant. In B. Staub & J. Hellmuth (Eds.), *Exceptional Infant*. Vol. I. Seattle: Special Child Publications, 1967, pp. 425–442.

110. Wolff, P. H. The natural history of crying and other vocalizations in early infancy. In B. M. Foss (Ed.), *Determinants of infant behavior:* IV. London: Methuen, 1969, pp. 81–109.

111. Yarrow, L. J., Rubenstein, J. L. & Pedersen, F. A. Dimensions of early stimulation: Differential effects on infant development. Paper presented at the meeting of the Society for Research in Child Development. Minneapolis, Minn., April 4, 1971.

# Chapter 4

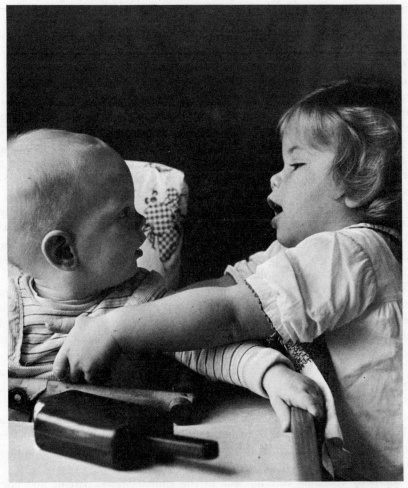

Robert J. Izzo

# Relationships with People

The baby is active in building relationships with people, just as he is active in the world of things. His very arrival causes changes in the world, especially in the people responsible for his care. Their interaction with each other and with him is the basis of social, emotional, and personality development. The baby's family is already anchored in a cultural framework that will direct and limit all of their interactions. The values and attitudes that influence parental behavior are understandable in their cultural context [50]. Before discussing actual parent–child relationships, this chapter will deal with some of the influences on relationships that come from different sources.

## The Social Environment

Three main types of influences are basic to the building of a baby's relationships with people and hence to his social and emotional development. The culture, the family, and the infant himself, all play essential roles in initiating, limiting and guiding interactions.

### *Culture*

Culture influences the infant by drawing the outlines of his parents and structuring his relationships with other people, especially relatives. This function is mentioned first because of the importance of parents to babies. It is only one small aspect of culture, however, and all those other aspects also influence the infant. The language he hears determines what he will speak and to a large extent, how he will think. The food he receives affects not only his preferences but his life and growth. His house, furniture, clothing, grooming equipment, and medicine all bear relation to his health, posture, activity, and attitudes. Toys, art, and music are vital in his cognitive and emotional life. Even the more distant aspects of culture, like government and law, have important effects on infants. For instance, what support does the government give to poor families in the way of nutrition, housing, family planning, and day care of young children? How well do the laws protect children whose parents abuse them?

Ideals of behavior are pictures of how roles *ought* to be performed. What is a good husband? A good wife? A good child? A good employer? Sometimes a culture presents a detailed word picture of an ideal, as did Judaism in Proverbs and Hinduism in the Laws of Manu. Ideals of child-rearing techniques are part of a culture which determine the parental role and the roles of other people concerned with children. These ideals state "right" punishment, rewards, regulations, and other methods of influence. In a simple, stable society most parents treat their children in the ways that they themselves were treated as children, and these ways coincide rather well with the ideals. Ideal patterns are expressed in the folklore and art. To spank or not to spank, to wean early or late, to toilet-train or to let the child train himself—these and similar questions are not really questions to parents who live in an unchanging culture.

In a rapidly changing culture, such as the United States, parents and grandparents often conflict over child care. Parents cannot rely comfortably on custom to give them definite directions on child rearing, since many different and changing directions are available. The same is true of other changing societies, which include a fair share of the world. When actual behavior differs widely from the ideal pattern, then conflict and confusion result.

Ideals for child rearing come in profuse variety in the United States as influenced by social class, ethnicity, region, religion, and other factors. Some attempts have been made to clarify the ideal role through pamphlets, books, and articles giving advice to mothers. Although the publications of the Children's Bureau do not carry religious authority, as do the Book of Proverbs, the Laws of Manu, and the Koran, they do reflect the ideals of the culture. One investigator [88] studied nine editions of the Children's Bureau publication *Infant Care*, spanning about 40 years. She found progressive changes in recommendations for parents, especially in the degree of severity with which the good mother was supposed to cope with various kinds of behavior in her infant. Changes in delineation of the mother's role stemmed from changes in conceptions of baby nature, in fact, of human nature. In 1914 the good mother was urged to be vigilant and relentless in her battle against the child's sinful nature, stamping out thumb-sucking and masturbation. In the thirties the mother must not permit the baby to dominate her. During the forties the mother was advised to be nonchalant in distracting her baby from thumb-sucking and masturbation, since he would be almost equally interested in toys and exploration. Since the fifties there has been no appreciable change in professionals' advice on guidance, as typified by the Children's Bureau and Dr. Spock [40]. Gentleness, gradualism, and a generally permissive attitude toward infants are recommended. An occasional magazine article, however, suggests that parents be more strict. For example, a recent article in *Baby Talk* magazine was titled "Best to start disciplining early" and advocated gently but firmly spanking the 7-months-old baby who cries when he is put to bed [4].

In both Israel and the Soviet Union, social upheaval has led to conscious formulation of child-rearing ideals designed to develop a new culture. In both cases, the child-rearing methods are planned to strengthen devotion to the state and ability to serve it. Since women are workers as well as mothers, they spend considerable time away from their children, and the care provided is planned with certain purposes in mind.

While the *kibbutzim* include only 4 percent of the Israelis, they represent conscious ideals and offer rich opportunities for the study of child development in a planned society. Ideals basic to the child care methods are equality of individuals, including equality between men and women, and deep peer attachment stemming from full participation in the common enterprise [9, p. 25]. Therefore from early infancy, children live apart from their parents in peer groups where they help one another and satisfy one another's emotional needs, learning cooperation rather than competition, and minimizing dependence on parents. Thus they are educated and prepared for the collective way of life [60].

In Moscow 50 percent of children under 2 are enrolled in nurseries, although the figure is only 10 percent for the whole country [18]. The demand for nursery placement far exceeds the supply. The babies are taught by specific methods worked out and described by educational and medical authorities. Children are supposed to develop as fast as possible, to learn at the earliest teachable moment, a value that contrasts with the American notion of letting them grow at their own rate [71]. The Russian teaching methods were carefully designed to promote behavior and values consistent with Communist ideals. Infants are put in groups into large playpens where they are taught to share toys, to help each other, and to play together. Self-reliance and self-control are taught early, since a proper attitude toward work is a major goal. Children learn to supervise one another and to accept supervision. Since the family is subordinate to the state, it is logical that professional educators should know more than parents about what is best for children. Educators work with parents to make sure that they bring up their children correctly and to integrate the child's total education. Bronfenbrenner, a Russian-speaking American psychologist and keen observer of the Russian scene, reports this comment from a Russian who visited in an American day-care center: "I wouldn't have believed it," he said, "if I hadn't seen it with my own eyes. There were four children sitting at a table, just as in our nurseries. But each one was doing something different. What's more, I watched them for a whole ten minutes, and not once did any child help another one. They didn't even talk to each other. Each one was busy in his own activity. You really are a nation of individualists" [18].

### Social Class : A Cultural Influence

Differences between middle-class and working-class behavior have been studied extensively for several decades. More recently, researchers have turned their attention to differences between the very poor and the other socioeconomic levels. Very little research has been done on upper-class behavior [21]. An accumulation of evidence indicates real but often small differences in the way children are brought up in the middle class, as contrasted with the working class. Middle-class parents tend to be warmer, to use more love-oriented discipline, and to be more permissive as to demands for attention from the child, sex behavior, orderliness, aggression, bedtime, and obedience. Working-class parents use more physical punishment, shouting and ridicule, and they tend to be more restrictive [6]. Observations of middle-class and working-class mothers interacting with young children have shown the former being warmer and more stimulating while encouraging the child to be autonomous and to find satisfaction through his own efforts [15]. The working-class mothers were more passive with their children and placed more emphasis on control through rewards and punishments.

The same kinds of differences between middle- and working-class parental behavior have been found in several different cultures. A sample of Greek mothers showed the middle-class group to be more warm and permissive with young children than were the peasant and lower-class urban groups [63]. Similar class differences were found for Italian mothers in a cross-culture study done in Turin and Washington [62]. In a study comparison of the attitudes of German and American mothers, samples in both countries were divided into upper, middle, and lower classes [65]. In both samples, lower-class mothers were most controlling (least permissive), middle-class mothers were next, and upper-class mothers least controlling in regard to their children.

In the United States there is evidence that class differences have changed over time [16]. Before World War II, working-class mothers, in contrast to middle-class mothers, did more breast feeding and more self-demand feeding, weaned children later, and toilet-trained them more leniently. After World War II these trends were reversed, probably due to the middle-class mothers' being in closer touch with the advice of experts and more readily influenced by it. The changes which took place in the concepts of child nature were transmitted faster to middle-class mothers than to working-class mothers by pediatricians, the Children's Bureau, magazine writers, and other parent educators. Middle-class, working-class differences in child training are diminishing [16]. Two sets of observations of mothers with children done 20 years apart show lower-class mothers to be more coercive with their children than middle-class mothers. This research also indicates a progressive change over time in which the general trend is for mothers to be less coercive [84]. Not only do differences between middle- and working-class behaviors tend to be small, but the range of behavior patterns in each class is relatively large [21]. Thus, for example, while more working-class mothers use physical punishment than do middle-class mothers, we might find that Mrs. Carpenter reasons gently with her Danny while Mrs. Lawyer spanks her Jimmy often.

IQ during the first two years of life is not related to socioeconomic level in those studies where birth complications, malnutrition, and poor health are ruled out. Most, but not all, studies indicate that by the end of the third year children from poor families tend to lag behind the average on measures of intelligence [38]. When the 8-month IQs of over 3000 infants were compared with their IQs at 4 years, a downward trend was noted. More dramatic, however, was the status of infants who tested low at 8 months [87]. When tested at 4 years of age, children who had been retarded infants were seven times more likely to have IQs below 79 if they came from poor families than they were if they came from middle-income families. Thus poorly developed infants suffer more damage from a poor environment than do well-developed infants.

*Family*

The infant's family translates the broad culture into a unique specific family culture that the baby experiences directly. The ideals, goals, beliefs, and customs of his family affect the way in which the baby is received and cared for. Suppose he is a fourth child born to a family where every child is a welcome gift from God. In contrast, suppose he is a fourth child born to a family where two children are considered the ideal number. Consider a family that holds that a baby is born wicked and must be trained to be good; that the infant must learn early who is boss; that crying exercises the lungs. Then consider a family that holds that infants have a right to happiness and that children cannot learn anything until they reach the age of reason, at 6 or 7.

Family customs are important in the experience of infants. Many rural Dutch babies ride in boxes on their parents' bicycles, enjoying the stimulation of sun and wind, getting the feel of balancing, watching the Van Gogh-like landscape change before their eyes. Many English babies loll and crawl on the green grass of Kensington Gardens, watching the swans and the fountains, accompanied by parents, brothers, and sisters who play and relax. Indian babies who live in joint families have constant companionship and immediate attention to their cries. Others, who live in small families, are left alone or inadequately tended by small children for long periods when their mothers must carry water.

In these ways, and in other ways, does the family determine the experience of its babies. Cognitive, emotional, and social growth are thus influenced.

The composition and stage of development of the family, of course, affect a baby [27]. For example, it is well known that the first-born carries a different burden from subsequent babies and that, in fact, each order of birth has its own assets and liabilities. The arrangement of sexes affects each child. Being a member of a boy and girl pair is different from being a member of a like-sexed pair. An older boy with a younger girl is different from a younger boy with an older girl. Being a twin is different from being a singleton. It makes a further difference which kind of twin you are, a monozygotic or dyzygotic, like-sex or unlike, and which sex [51].

*Family* to most American readers means parents and children, but even in America millions of children live in families which are otherwise. A parent is absent, a grandparent is present, or other relatives are present. The composition of the family can make a big difference in the amount of stimulation a baby receives. Many people in the house, especially children, make for noise, excitement, handling, play, and variety of contacts. When there are several or many adults present in the household, children are more likely to be continually controlled but less likely to be treated harshly than if parents are the only adults present [27]. The number of children is an important family dimension with meaning for all members. Child-rearing methods of parents of many children are different from those of parents of a few. Every added child complicates the network of human relationships and calls for a redistribution of space, goods, and services. Too many children strain the material and emotional resources of the parents. An excessive number of children for one family may not be the same as too many for another family.

Stages of development refer to a way of looking at family life as cyclic. Each stage has its own characteristics. A typical way of naming the stages is (1) beginning, (2) childbearing, (3) preschool, (4) school-age, (5) teen-age, (6) launching, (7) middle-age, (8) old age, and (9) broken.

It is possible for a baby to be born to a mother when the family is in any one of the stages from (2) to (6) or (7). Infants born in the early stages come to families oriented toward living with babies. Home, furnishings, schedules, menus, and pace are suited to young children. Those who come later are likely to be swept into activities appropriate for older children or teen-agers, such as camping trips and Scout meetings, or perhaps they will be left out frequently as the family goes off to meetings and parties and engages in conversation too mature for the youngest.

*Emotional climate* is a summary term for all the feelings that exist in the home. Love and tenderness are known to be essential ingredients for healthy growth. Affectional interchange in the family has been found to be correlated with test performance of babies at 6 months of age [91]. A longitudinal study at Berkeley yields some correlations between family situations during the first two years of life and intelligence scores in childhood and adolescence [49]. Parental compatibility and lack of conflict over discipline and cultural standards correlated with girls' intelligence throughout childhood and adolescence. Closeness of mother and son during infancy was positively related to the son's test performances between 8 and 18 years. Father's friendliness to the infant daughter was predictive of her intelligence between 7 and 18. Mothers who were energetic, tense, and concerned with their young children, probably responding very carefully to their needs, were more likely than lethargic mothers to have children with high IQs in childhood and adolescence.

The basic factors in emotional climate are the parents' satisfaction with marriage and family living, and their personality maturity in regard to taking on parent roles. Relationships with their own parents also influence the mother and father, since they themselves are children as well as parents. Not only do the parents act in the light of their past experiences as children, but they are affected by present and changing relationships with their own parents. Furthermore, parents react emotionally to such strains as money troubles and inadequate housing. Big crises and joys and small irritations and pleasures all register in the emotional climate of the home, from which the baby receives stimuli.

### Mother's Characteristics

The mother's behavior with the baby is of course a very important set of influences on him, since she controls so much of what happens to him. Some of her responses are determined by what the baby is and does, as will be discussed in the following sections. Other sources for her behavior are wide and varied. Many studies [1, 3, 8, 81, 86, 91, 93] reveal the influence of mother behavior on infant behavior, suggesting that the personal characteristics of mothers have definite consequences in the form of infant development.

The Harvard Preschool Project [86] began studying competence in children who were seen as coping in superior ways with the situations they met from day to day. When the investigators came to realize that competence was well developed in some children by 3 years, they set out to discover how the contributing abilities were built during the first 3 years of life. Although the project is not yet completed, the researchers have tentatively identified different types of mothers who were more or less successful in raising competent children. They are

1. *The competent mother.* She interacts more with the child than does the average mother, initiating some interactions and letting the child initiate some. She is verbal, teaching spontaneously and in terms of cause and effect. Using rational discipline, she often gives choices. She rewards cognitive achievement and mastery while accepting and enjoying the child at his stage of development. She understands his preverbal behavior. She often takes part in role playing with the child.
2. *The mother who almost makes it.* Although she enjoys and accepts the child, she often cannot understand his preverbal cues. She initiates less interaction and less teaching than the competent mother.
3. *The overwhelmed mother.* She often ignores the child. While she gives some evidence of enjoyment, she does little understanding, instructing, or rewarding. Often she is in a low socioeconomic level and has many children. Life is too hard.
4. *The rigid, controlling mother.* A careful household schedule includes placing the child in a play area for certain times. This mother has almost no interaction with the child, as though she does not like him, is not involved, or does not understand his stage of development.
5. *The smothering mother.* She initiates many interactions, responding to every cue and teaching him for hours. She interferes with his activities and rewards him for doing cognitive tasks.

The competent mother, of course, seems to be an important source of competence in her child. The study has so far shown that "confident, competent mothers who are accepting of their role and enjoy and approve of their children seem to produce well-developed children. None of the mothers of poorly developed children could be described in that way." Another finding was that the quality of mother–child interaction is more important than the quantity.

The related functioning of mothers and 1-year-olds was studied at the University of Syracuse [81], using factor analysis of ratings made on the mothers' and infants' behavior and personalities and on the babies' mental and motor development. Since the babies in this study were younger than most of the Harvard subjects, maternal behavior would be expected to differ. However, similarities can be seen in the description of the Harvard competent mother and the Syracuse mother who is high in factor 2, a cluster of behaviors which reads like a description of ideal mother–infant interaction. This type of mother is very loving, shown by frequent happy, affectionate talking, tenderness, sensuousness in handling the baby, play,

**Table 4–1** Mother–Infant Interaction Factor Summary

| | Factor 2 | Factor 1 | Factor 3 | Factor 8 | Factor 7 | Factor 6 | Factor 9 | Factor 4 | Factor 5 |
|---|---|---|---|---|---|---|---|---|---|
| Mother's needs | Emotional, involvement | Warm, supportive, organized, dependent, anxious | Achievement oriented, high drive, good-humored, extroverted, friendly | Exhibitionistic, involved | Anxious | Avoidance of physical contact or stimulation | Self-centered, disorganized, low frustration tolerance | Disorganized, low frustration tolerance, abasive | Permissive, warm, supportive, good-humored, abasive |
| Mother's behavior | Loving, emotionally involved, high vocal and visual contact, skilful care | Involved, high visual contact, high play, exhibitionistic with baby | Exhibitionistic with baby | Vigilant, warm physical contact, overtly maternal | Solicitous, emotionally involved, high rate of response and physical contact | Vigilant, enjoys baby | High play, indifferent to baby's health, overconfident | | Solicitous exhibitionism |
| Baby's needs and behavior | Accelerated development | Lovingness and involvement with mother | Achievement oriented, energetic attempts to dominate mother | Environmentally responsive, sensual | Responsive to comforting, comfortable, attractive, active, low mental age | Good-humored, advanced development, achievement oriented, high drive, fearless, avoidance of physical contact | Impulsive, changeable | Hostile to mother, excitable, self-centered | Good-humored and nurturant toward mother |
| Composite factor description | Involved mothers with accelerated infants | Symbiotic mother-child affective rapport | Parallel active and social achievement orientation | Maternal display behavior with infant sensuality | Slow infants with solicitous and concerned mothers | Mutual maintenance of distance with accelerated infant development and drive | Unwarranted maternal satisfaction with disorganized interaction | Maternal, self-criticism reinforced by demanding and hostile infant behavior | Exhibitionistic indulgence with happy child response |

SOURCE: Reprinted by permission from George G. Stern et al., "A Factor Analytic Study of the Mother–Infant Dyad," *Child Development*, **40**, Table 7, p. 178. Copyright © 1969, The Society for Research in Child Development, Inc.

empathy, attentiveness, enjoyment, and visual contact. The outstanding characteristic of babies belonging to these mothers is accelerated motor and mental development.

The opposite extreme of mother type noted in the Syracuse study was the one characterized by factor 9. This mother was self-centered, disorganized, capricious, overconfident, indifferent, and with low tolerance for frustration. These mothers tend to treat their infants like dolls, playing with them without regard for the baby's needs, feelings, or well-being even though they maintain high visual contact. Infants of such mothers tended to be capricious, lacking in purpose and plan. The interaction between mother and child was disorganized and yet the mother seemed to be satisfied with it. Since space does not permit descriptions of mothers typifying all nine factors plus the resulting interactions, the summary table is reproduced as Table 4–1, for the student who is interested in pursuing this topic.

## Father's Characteristics

Fathers are very important to the development of sex role orientation, especially of boys and particularly during the first four years of life [10, 11]. Fathers may be just as important to baby girls as to baby boys, but because research in this area has focused so largely on boys, the significance of fathers to girls has not been emphasized. The main result of research is proof that the father's presence in the home makes a difference to psychosexual development. Fathers' ways of interacting with infants have not been explored very much, but we know that their interaction is important and that it is different from that of mothers.

Father's verbal interaction was studied in ten father–baby pairs [66]. Twenty-four-hour tape recordings were made every two weeks for three months. One striking result of the analysis was the small amount of time spent by the fathers in interaction with their infants, an average daily frequency of 2.7. The average number of seconds spent each day was 37.7. The father who averaged the most interaction spent only about ten minutes per day talking with his baby. Fathers were different from mothers in their ways of interacting, as shown by comparing results of this study with research on mothers. Fathers talked less often and for shorter periods. Fathers decreased their vocalizations during the first 3 months, while mothers increased theirs. Although the number of cases was very small for comparing sexes, it was noted that fathers of (2-week-old) girl babies talked to them more than fathers of boys that age, but when the infants were 12 weeks old, fathers of boys talked more. This shift is the reverse of what has been observed in mothers of girls compared with mothers of boys. Further studies, dealing with physical interaction, are needed to supplement these findings on verbalization.

## Infant's Characteristics

The baby himself plays a big part in determining the course of relationships with people. Some of his effects are obvious, others subtle. The uniqueness of each infant can be appreciated by considering the interplay of appearance, sex, and temperament, which are only some of the categories under which human beings can be described.

**Appearance.** Looks can make a difference in how a baby is accepted and regarded. Although this statement is more in the realm of common belief than scientific fact, it is important if true. Not only is the matter of beauty or good looks involved here, but of an appearance that suggests something significant to the parents: a family resemblance causing pride or the expectation that the new baby will act like Uncle Joe or like his big brother; fragility, including delicate handling, or sturdiness, inciting rough play; a characteristic thought to predict a personality trait, such as red hair indicating temper or a weak chin indicating weak character.

**Sex.** According to whether the newborn is a boy or a girl, the baby is immediately placed in some categories and removed from others. The infant's sex determines many of the feelings, attitudes, and actions of people. Cultures and families vary widely in the ways in which they interpret and value sex roles. The Shah of Iran divorced a wife he loved (or so the newspapers said) because she bore him no sons, even though she produced daughters. His duty to perpetuate his line, for the good of his country, was a value above and beyond love for his wife. Imagine the welcome a son would receive in such a family and the disappointment that would mount with the birth of each daughter! Followers of religions like Hinduism and Confucianism want sons in order to carry out religious duties toward ancestors and to assure their own religious fulfillment. Therefore the birth of the first son is an occasion of boundless joy and relief from anxiety. Sons are less essential in the West than in Asia. Some Americans prefer daughters. Religion and property are not involved, and daughters are considered easier to bring up. Americans may try not to form a sex preference before a baby is born, realizing that it makes for better relationships to be happy with their offspring no matter which sex it is.

Adults treat boy and girl babies differently. An obvious reason for differential treatment is that adults have different expectations of boys and girls and that they are beginning to teach sex role. Research on both human and monkey infants, however, indicates biological influences also at work, in the form of the infant's own characteristics. Animal research, especially on primates, often gives useful leads for research on humans. Data from several studies at the University of Wisconsin Primate Laboratory have shown differences between interactions of mother monkeys with male infants and mother monkeys with female infants [57]. In the first 3 months of life, males did more mouthing, cuffing, slapping, clasping, and pulling the fur of the mothers, and as they got older, this behavior increased. As the females got older, they decreased in clasping and body contact and increased in cooing and exploration with their eyes, mouth, and hands. The mothers of female infants embraced and restrained them more, withdrew from them less, and groomed them more. Mothers of male infants played with them more and tended to be more aggressive and rejecting. The author concluded that the mothers protected the females more, encouraging them to maintain close attachments, while the males were pushed into independence and wide contacts with the other members of the troop. Thus we see the infant's own characteristics playing a part in development of interactions. Turning to the human scene, boy and girl babies can be seen exerting different influences on their mothers during the first 3 months of life [58]. Boys slept less and cried more and were more irritable than girls. Mothers held boys more than girls, about 27 minutes longer during an 8-hour period at 3 months, for example. As well as being more irritable, males seemed to respond less satisfactorily to mothers' efforts to console them. The data indicated that mothers responded more readily to girls' cries, since they had been more successful in quieting girls.

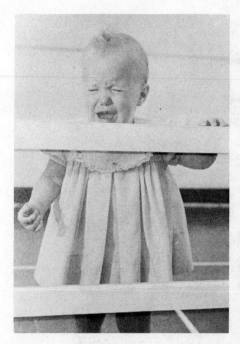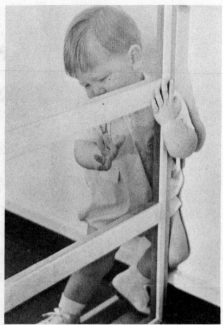

Courtesy Michael Lewis

**Figure 4–1.** Sex differences in response to a frustrating barrier. The baby girl stands and cries; the baby boy tries to get around the barrier.

Two samples of babies examined at 6 and 13 months showed sex differences in their toy preferences, responses to frustration, and interactions with their mothers. At 13 months, each baby was placed in an observation room with toys [37]. The mother, who sat on a chair in the corner of the room, was told to watch the baby's play and to respond as she wished. The floor of the room was divided into 12 squares, permitting recording of the child's position for each 15 seconds of time. When removed from their mothers' laps girls were more reluctant to leave and more often returned immediately. When playing, they stayed closer to their mothers. Girls spent more time touching their mothers, looking at them, and vocalizing to them than did boys. When a barrier was placed between the infant and the mother, with the toys on the mother's side, sex differences in response to stress were seen. Figure 4–1 illustrates the typical difference between boys and girls. Boys were more likely to try to get around the barrier, girls to stand in the middle crying and motioning for help from the mother. Differences in play were seen, also. Girls sat more and spent more time with blocks, pegboard, dog and cat (the only toys with faces). Boys were more active and played more with the mallet, lawnmower, and nontoys, such as the doorknob and electric outlets. Girls used more fine muscle coordination while boys used more large muscles and were more vigorous. Figure 4–2 illustrates typical sex differences in choice of toys and play behavior. Data on mother–infant interaction at 6 months showed the mothers touched girls more than boys. When related to the baby's behavior at 13 months, there was a direct relationship between mothers touching boys at 6 months and boys touching mothers at 13 months. That is, the mothers who did the most touching at 6 months had sons who did the most touching at 13 months. For girls,

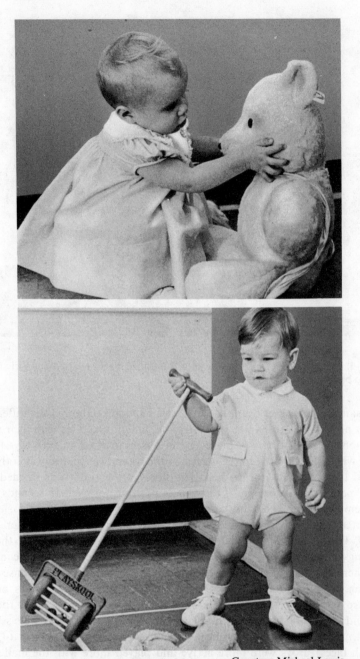

Courtesy Michael Lewis

**Figure 4–2.** Sex differences in choice of toys and play activity. The baby girl sits and plays with the soft, cuddly animal; the baby boy is active with a mechanical toy.

the picture was different. A medium amount of touching by the mother was correlated with a medium amount of touching by the daughter, but mothers who did little or much touching were likely to have daughters who touched them a great deal. Corroboration of mothers' differential treatment is found in observations at beaches, where mothers touched girl babies more than boy babies [28] and in a description of mothers in the feeding situation [59, pp. 346–347]. "Come and get it" typified the attitude toward boys, who were permitted considerable autonomy in establishing their own rhythms and in starting and stopping. "Mother knows best" was the key to the prevalent attitude toward girls, indicating that they were supposed to conform and fit into the mother's way of doing. Mothers tended to hover over girls, to fiddle with their clothing, and to give them a great deal more tactile stimulation than boys received. Given less opportunity to move, to explore and to choose, restricted in expression and yet stimulated, girls must discharge more emotion inward. Here could be a contribution to feminine passivity and masculine activity. From data on infant–mother interaction, it seems that masculine and feminine behavior patterns are built from certain early experiences of the infant which are the results of his own spontaneous behavior shaping the behavior of his parents who are also influenced by cultural and personal notions of sex-appropriate behavior.

**Temperament.** Behavioral style, or temperament, varies from one child to another. Certain qualities have been defined at 2 or 3 months of age and at subsequent ages throughout childhood through observations of 136 children and interviews with their parents [25]. Nine categories of reactivity emerged: *Activity level*, motility during feeding, bathing, handling, play, and proportion of active and inactive states; *rhythmicity*, or biological regularity, in relation to sleep-waking, hunger, and elimination; *approach-withdrawal*, the type of response to new objects or situations; *adaptability*, or ease of modifying behavior in response to changed situations; *intensity of reaction*, level of vigor of response; *threshold of responsiveness*, intensity of stimulation needed to provoke a response; *quality of mood*, the proportion of happy, friendly, pleased behavior to fussing, crying, and unfriendly behavior; *distractability*, readiness to be diverted from ongoing activity by a new stimulus; *attention span* and *persistence*, the time that a child stays with an activity and the strength with which he maintains it in the face of obstacles.

Differing combinations of these categories of reactivity produce children who are different from each other. Although every child is unique, there are recurring types and generalizations about them that can be made. The most usual type shows high rhythmicity, positive approach to new situations, adaptability to change, positive moods, and mild to moderate thresholds of responsiveness. This type is called "the easy child." Such an infant usually fits easily into his family, developing regular sleeping and feeding schedules, accepting new foods, new situations, and strangers. Parents and, later, teachers, are usually very much pleased with an "easy child."

"The difficult child" is his opposite number, being irregular in biological functions, negative and withdrawing from new experiences, having slow adaptability and intense reactions. About 10 percent of the children studied were thus [26]. Mothers find such babies difficult to care for and threatening to their feelings of competence, and families are often upset by their fussing, crying, temper tantrums, and protests. These infants need unusually firm, patient, consistent, tolerant handling. When parents are able to meet these needs, the infants usually learn the rules of social living and function energetically and well. When parents cannot give the needed sort of guidance, behavior problems are likely to develop.

Another type is the "slow-to-warm-up" child, who quietly withdraws from new situations and adapts slowly. This kind of baby needs patience, encouragement, and protection from pressure. The "very persistent" type of child becomes extremely absorbed in an activity and resists efforts to divert him. If adults interfere arbitrarily with what he is doing, he is likely to become very angry.

Behavior of the baby has an immediate and continuing impact [7]. From a study of the first 6 months of life and the relation between the mother's behavior and the infant's, this story illustrates how different temperaments call forth different responses from the family [91]. Two boy babies of the same age were placed in one foster home. Jack was passive and quiet, slept a great deal, showed little initiative and little response to social approaches. George was vigorous and active, showing much initiative and response. By 7 weeks of age, there was a difference in the way the foster mother referred to the babies. George was "George" and Jack was "the other one." By 3 months, the mother complained openly that "the other one" slept too much and did nothing. The whole family wanted to feed George. Nobody wanted to feed Jack. Jack's bottle was propped more often than George's. George was often found in the middle of a family activity, while Jack stayed in the playpen, apart from the general stream of action. With two infants the same age and same sex in the same family at the same time, it is apparent that to an unknown degree the difference in their care and experience was initiated by the babies themselves.

The relationships of the baby with his family depend upon all the people involved and how their personalities fit together. It is conceivable that another mother would have preferred Jack to George, a mother who wanted a quiet baby with little initiative and vigor. Certainly, adults vary in how much they approve of characteristics such as ease and vigor in expression of needs and self-assertion in response to coercion.

### Correlates of Mother Love

Maternal warmth and affection was found to be positively correlated with development in the Cattell Infant Intelligence scale in a longitudinal study of infants in low-income families [21]. The strength of the mother's love was defined, measured, and correlated with infant behavior in a longitudinal study done at the University of California [73]. Using the data from many observations and ratings of maternal behavior, a factor analysis showed the existence of two dimensions of behavior, autonomy–control and love–hostility. Although the first did not show clear relationships to infant behavior, the second did. Tests that tapped the mother's feeling of love and hostility could predict, to a very small degree, the baby's behavior. In other words, small, significant correlations were found between certain maternal measures and certain infant measures. One of the mothers' rating scales which tapped hostility, for example, used these questions: Does she often comment on how much extra work or trouble the child is? Does she tend to overlook the needs of the child? Babies were rated on seven point scales on these characteristics: degree of strangeness, shy to unreserved; activity, inactive to vigorous; speed of movements, slow to rapid; responsiveness to persons, slight to marked; amount of positive behavior; irritability, or tendency to be sensitive to and react to stimulation; emotional tone, unhappy to happy. Mothers' love behavior was found positively related to babies' happiness, positive behavior and calmness, especially between 10 and 36 months. Correlational studies such as this one tell nothing about whether the mother's love caused the babies' happiness or if the babies' being happy and behaving positively caused the mothers to love them.

Although an educated guess would be that the reaction was reciprocal, the results do not permit a definite conclusion.

## Social—Emotional Development

Social behavior is behavior involving interaction with another person. Social development means progressive changes in behavior patterns used in social inter-action. Although all experiences have feeling or affective aspects, some social interactions entail much more affect than others. The affective side of transactions with the environment is basic to social relationships, but so is perception basic. The infant's responses to other people depend upon what he perceives in his environment, how he feels about it, and what he is able to do. As he adapts to his world by changing both the world and himself, he organizes his affective system, as well as his motor and cognitive systems.

Emotional behavior is behavior that shows some sort of change from the characteristic level or mode of response, plus some physiological change and an affective state of pleasure or displeasure [69]. Emotional development refers to progressive changes in emotional behavior. The newborn is generally thought to express only excitement, a general, undifferentiated active state. Bridges' classic study on emotional development of infants resulted in a description of more and more specific emotions being differentiated out of the primary state of excitement. Her theory, represented diagrammatically in Figure 4–3, illustrates one of the principles of development stated in Chapter 17, that development proceeds through differentiation and integration. The diagram shows the emotions of distress and delight, representing all negative and positive affective tones, being differentiated out of general excitement in the early weeks of life. Excitement, distress, and de-light continue in the infant's emotional repertory while the negative emotions of fear, anger, and disgust and the positive ones of elation and affection are added. This rough outline of emotional development has served as a foundation to many of the detailed studies that have been done since then. Of special interest today is the research on attachment: the bond between two people, particularly the attach-ment of infant and mother. Although a great deal is known about infant–mother relationships, information on fathers', siblings', and grandparents' relationships with babies is scarce indeed. Related to attachment, the development and control of fear and the development of curiosity are foci of current research.

### Love and Attachment

Hardest to define, impossible to agree upon, *love*, for our present purposes, means delight in being with, desire to be with, and desire for contact and response from, another person. Perhaps we should add to this list the budding of a desire to give to the other person, not just for the purpose of eliciting a response. Probably this dimension of love is noticeable toward the end of infancy.

Because *love* has so many different meanings, it is fruitful to use more precise terms rather than the word *love* in discussing the love between a baby, his family, and friends. In employing the more exact terminology, we indicate no callousness toward that mysterious emotional relationship, but rather a warm interest in understanding it better.

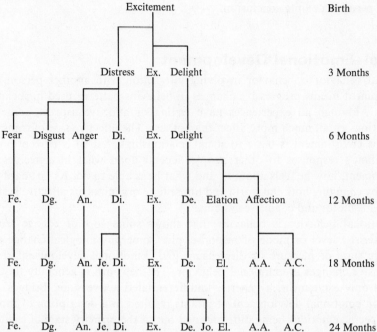

**Figure 4–3.** Bridges' schematic representation of the differentiation of emotion from general excitement in the newborn to 11 types of emotion at 2 years. *Key:* A.A. = Affection for adults, A.C. = Affection for children, An. = Anger, De. = Delight, Dg. = Disgust, Di. = Distress, El. = Elation, Ex. = Excitement, Fe. = Fear, Je. = Jealousy, Jo. = Joy.

SOURCE: Reprinted by permission from K. M. B. Bridges, "Emotional Development in Early Infancy," *Child Development*, 3, 324–341. Copyright © 1932, The Society for Research in Child Development, Inc.

**Attachment.** An attachment is an ongoing condition of an individual through which he seeks proximity to and contact with another person [2]. Human attachment behavior includes approaching, embracing, smiling, and calling. Animal babies, as well as human babies, seek the proximity of certain members of their own species, and each species has characteristic attachment behavior patterns. The bond is created as the baby exercises the behavior patterns basic to attachment and specific to his species. The time required for establishing the attachment differs with the species and the pertinent behaviors. Geese become attached in no more than 2 hours, perhaps a few minutes, through their inborn tendency to follow the first moving, sound-emitting object they see. Herd animals' babies are on their feet a few minutes after birth, following their mothers and forming attachments within the first 2 or 3 days. Primates take a little longer. Clinging seems to be the most important attachment behavior of monkeys, who require 10 days or 2 weeks to form their bonds. Chimpanzees take about 2 months and human babies 5 or 6 months. Human beings, born very helpless and with a long infancy to live through, require extensive and long-continued protection. They are born with the means for instigating the necessary care and for evoking it, not only from the principal caretaker (mother), but from the father, the rest of the family, and other human beings. A long infancy makes possible a long time for adapting and learning, hence the development of very complex behavior and wide individual variations. The genetic code provides for the beginnings and growth of exploratory behavior in coordination with attachment behavior. The child is protected while he learns.

Bowlby [14, pp. 326–327], a pioneer in the study of attachment, points out that in the second quarter of the first year, an infant is ready to make his first attachment to a specific person. After the first 6 months, an infant can still do so, but the older he grows, the more difficult it is to make his first attachment, and if he has not done so by the second year, the difficulties are very great. An established attachment is vulnerable for several years after the first birthday. These facts illustrate the principle of *critical periods in development* which is discussed in Chapter 17.

**Development of Attachment Behavior.** Like many other babies, the human newborn elicits his mother's attention and care when he cries. His crying is a spontaneous expression of distress, and her response is an anxious feeling that she seeks to relieve by stopping his crying. Thus crying fulfills the criterion for attachment behavior in that it brings the pair into proximity or contact. Sucking also brings the two together and causes pleasant sensations in both mother and baby. The human baby also does an approximation of clinging, although he cannot hang on unaided. He grasps what is put into his hands, which means that when he is held to the shoulder, he may grasp the clothing, skin, or hair of the adult. His body snuggles or bends to fit the body on which it rests. These kinds of contact evoke pleasure in the mother—in fact, in most people.

Looking also contributes to attachment. The newborn has a built-in tendency to look at stimuli that move and that have light–dark contrast. Since a face has both attractions, babies look readily at faces, particularly at the eyes, which have a concentration of both contrast and movement. By 3 weeks of age, a live human face elicited more excitement than did a moving drawing of a face [79]. All of the babies in this experiment showed excitement at the human face while actively scanning it, by general limb movements, head movements, and a variety of mouth movements. By 5 to 7 weeks, mouth and head movements declined as part of the excitatory pattern, while smiling and soft cooing increased. Looking and grasping become integrated into nursing behavior, the infant scanning his mother's face and fingering her person while he sucks.

Smiling occurs readily at the sight of a human face by the time the baby is 5 or 6 weeks old. The smile is a very important form of human behavior, having universal meaning of friendliness and cutting across language barriers between adults. Thus, when the infant smiles regularly at his mother and other people, it serves as attachment behavior, bringing people close to him, keeping them with him, and eliciting friendly social behavior in the form of smiles. Cooing and babbling, which often accompany smiling, tie the bonds between baby and others in much the same way that smiling does. Baby babbles. Mother babbles back, nodding and smiling, all quite spontaneously. They scan each other's faces and fixate on each other's eyes.

Familiar objects seem to be pleasurable as the baby recognizes them. He develops schemas or some sort of internal representations with which he can match perceptual experiences. Most likely his mother's face is one of his early schemas. During Piaget's stage of secondary circular reactions, which lasts from about 4 to 8 months, the baby tries to make interesting sights last or to regain perceptual contact with familiar objects. When he succeeds he shows pleasure by smiling, and when he does not he may cry.

Following and approaching are attachment behavior in that they bring the pair closer together or into contact. Until he can crawl or creep, the infant cannot follow bodily, but he can follow with his eyes. The distance receptors, eyes and ears, are also active in the process of making and keeping contact with the object of attachment.

**Signs of Growing Attachment.** A crucial step in the development of social relationships is to distinguish between people and inanimate objects. Observations of infants' responses in home settings indicated that 65 percent of babies made this distinction by 1 month of age. All did by 5 months. Recognition of the mother, indicated by showing excitement and approach movements to her but not to strangers, was exhibited by some infants as early as 1 month, by 81 percent at 3 months, and by all babies at 5 months [92]. By 3 months of age, babies will smile more to reinforcements (saying "Hi, Baby," smiling and lightly touching his chest) offered by the mother than to the same reinforcements offered by a stranger [83]. Even though he apparently perceives a difference between his mother and other people, however, he will smile at strangers and, in fact, smiles at everyone who approaches him until he is around 6 months of age. Then he becomes more selective, smiling at familiar people and most of all to his mother and to other people to whom he is becoming attached. Confidence in the mother, as shown by signs of expecting her to soothe or comfort, was shown in half of babies studied at 3 months and in 75 percent of the babies at 5 months [92].

Continuing to build the bonds of love, the baby vocalizes selectively, "talking" more to his attachment object. Another sign of beginning attachment which occurs as smiling becomes selective, or possibly before, is differential crying. The baby cries when held by someone other than his mother and stops when she takes him. The next step is to watch the object of attachment, as when the baby keeps his mother in view even though he is in someone else's arms. Then comes a definite indication of attachment, crying when the specific person leaves and not crying when other people do. Figure 4–4 shows the intensity with which infants at various ages protested being left by anybody and by attachment objects. The curve for "indiscriminate attachment" shows that babies as young as 2 months may protest when social stimulation is withdrawn but that it takes a maturity of 7 or 8 months to cry for attention from specific individuals. Other indications of attachment include clinging, scrambling over the mother and exploring her person, burying his face in her lap, following the attachment object as soon as he can creep, lifting arms, clapping hands, and crowing in greeting [1]. Attachment behavior is not confined to close physical contacts. Vision and hearing, vocalizing and gestures, are used for keeping and making contact as the infant widens the environment in which he operates. As sensorimotor competency increases, the baby can allow his mother to go farther away, since he is able to contact his attachment objects over a wider area.

**Varieties of Attachments.** Attachment has been studied longitudinally in 60 babies, focusing on the infant's protest at being separated from the objects of attachment [75] and the strength of his crying or whimpering at the ending of a contact between him and the other person. The situations were everyday, ordinary occurrences, such as being left alone in a room, being left in his pram (this was a British study) outside a store, and being put down from arms or lap. Using these criteria, it was found that half of the specific attachments, including attachments to the mother, occurred most often between 25 and 32 weeks. A few occurred earlier and the rest later, between 32 and 78 weeks. Individuals showed variation from time to time in strength of protest over separation. Interesting stimulation made separation much more tolerable, as shown by the frequent acceptance of the mother's

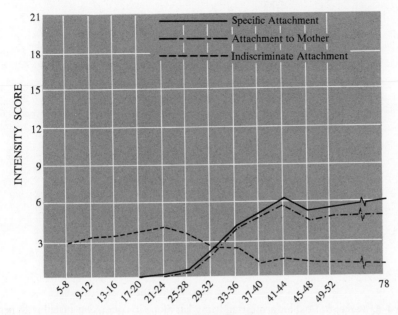

**Figure 4–4.** Development of infants' attachments to the mother, to other persons, and to people-in-general, shown in terms of strength of protest at being left.

Source: Reprinted by permission from H. R. Schaffer and P. E. Emerson, "The Development of Social Attachments in Infancy," *Monographs of The Society for Research in Child Development,* **29**:3. Copyright © 1964, The Society for Research in Child Development, Inc.

absence when she parked the pram outside the shop, on a busy street, in contrast to the protest which occurred on being left alone in bed. Figure 4–5 shows the difference between these two situations. Pain, illness, fatigue, and fear led to intense protest and strong seeking of the mother's presence. When the attachment object returned from an absence, the infant was more demanding of attention, as when the father came in after work. A temporary change in social stimulation, such as the visit of an attentive relative, also brought increased demands on the mother after the period of extra stimulation had ended, but this demand was only temporary.

Often, but not always, the infant becomes attached to one person before he forms attachments to several. Often, but not always, the first person is his mother. Table 4–2 shows the objects of attachment at various ages. It will be noted that the mother soon comes to share the baby's affections with the father, grandparents, siblings, relatives, and friends. The number of attachments depended largely on number of available people. Mere presence was not enough. Babies tended to become attached to people who offered interesting stimulation.

Strongly attached infants were found to have mothers who responded quickly to their indications of need [75]. Subsequent studies have focused on the quality of attachment and behavior of mothers, finding that babies tend to show clear-cut, unambivalent attachment to mothers who are very perceptive, responsive, and eager to gratify them in the feeding situation and socially [8]. The type of attachment which develops under these circumstances is associated with early development of a schema of person permanence, followed by development of a schema of

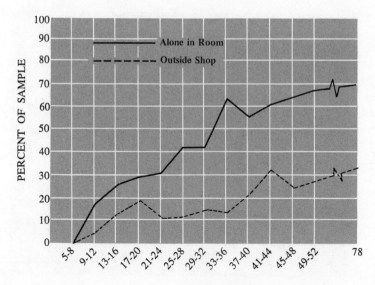

AGE IN WEEKS

**Figure 4–5.** Percent of babies protesting being left alone in room, contrasted with percent protesting being left alone outside a shop. Interesting stimulation makes separation from attachment object much more acceptable.

SOURCE: Adapted from H. R. Schaffer and P. E. Emerson, "The Development of Social Attachments in Infancy," *Monographs of The Society for Research in Child Development*, **29**:3. Copyright © 1964, The Society for Research in Child Development, Inc. Used by permission.

the permanence of objects which is also early [8]. In colloquial terms, a loving, competent mother is likely to have a baby who loves her and whose sensorimotor intelligence progresses rapidly.

**Exploratory Behavior.** As soon as he is able to do so, the baby separates himself briefly from his mother by crawling away to explore and play. The human baby seems to be the only mammalian infant who leaves his mother just as soon as he can move himself, but then he is the only creature who spends 6 or 7 months interacting with the world in a sedentary condition. Separations, however, do not mean detachment. He is still attached, but the bond is elastic and can be maintained through seeing, hearing, calling, and smiling, with only periodic physical contact. When he is playing, he is not looking at or calling to his mother constantly, but only occasionally. The mother or other attachment object serves as a secure base from which the infant can venture forth as an explorer, returning either bodily, visually, or auditorily as he needs reassurance.

The relationship between attachment and exploratory behavior was first studied by Harlow [42] with his baby monkeys who had become attached to wire, cloth-covered mothers. When placed alone in a strange room, the little monkey cowered, crouched, rocked, sucked, and clutched his own body. With the surrogate mother there, the baby clung to her, ventured forth to explore the objects in the room, clung again and explored again, as though he neutralized his fear by contacting her, and derived continued reassurance by seeing her in the room. Later studies on chimpanzees showed a relation between clinging and calming the baby from high levels of arousal resulting from strange situations or separations from companions. After clinging, the little chimp would return to playing and exploring [54].

**Table 4–2** Identity of Attachment Objects : Percentage of Subjects Forming Specific Attachments According to Identity of Object at Successive Age Period

| Identity of Object | Lunar Month Following Age at Onset in First Year | | | | | | 18 Months (CA) |
|---|---|---|---|---|---|---|---|
| | 1ST | 2ND | 3RD | 4TH | 5TH | 6TH | |
| Mother (sole object) | 65 | 53 | 32 | 50 | 47 | 17 | 5 |
| Mother (joint object) | 30 | 35 | 54 | 43 | 50 | 77 | 76 |
| Father (sole object) | 3 | 9 | 7 | 2 | 0 | 5 | 4 |
| Father (joint object) | 27 | 23 | 42 | 29 | 44 | 59 | 71 |
| Grandparent (sole object) | 2 | 0 | 0 | 0 | 0 | 0 | 0 |
| Grandparent (joint object) | 9 | 12 | 14 | 12 | 10 | 29 | 45 |
| Other relative (sole object) | 0 | 0 | 0 | 0 | 0 | 0 | 2 |
| Other relative (joint object) | 5 | 5 | 5 | 14 | 10 | 18 | 16 |
| Friend or neighbor (sole object) | 0 | 0 | 2 | 0 | 0 | 0 | 0 |
| Friend or neighbor (joint object) | 3 | 7 | 7 | 9 | 3 | 12 | 26 |
| Sibling (sole object) | 0 | 0 | 0 | 0 | 0 | 0 | 2 |
| Sibling (joint object) | 2 | 5 | 7 | 7 | 7 | 12 | 22 |
| Other child (sole object) | 0 | 0 | 0 | 0 | 0 | 0 | 0 |
| Other child (joint object) | 3 | 5 | 14 | 7 | 3 | 12 | 14 |

Studies on human babies have shown a similar articulation between attachment and exploratory behavior. The usual plan is for observers, sitting behind a one-way vision screen, to record the actions of babies and mothers in space that is marked off to facilitate accurate measuring of distance. A study of 1-year-old infants was conducted in a setting of seven consecutive 3-minute episodes [3]. The mother entered the room, which had a supply of toys, sat down, put the baby down, and did nothing unless the baby sought her attention. A stranger entered, sat quietly, then approached the baby with a toy. The mother left the room. If the baby was not active with toys, the stranger tried to interest him in them. If he cried, she tried to comfort him. The mother returned, the stranger departed, and as soon as the baby was settled in play, the mother again left. The baby was alone for 3 minutes until the stranger reappeared, behaving as she did before. Then the mother came back. Results showed the largest amount of exploratory behavior, as seen in locomotion, manipulation, and looking, occurring in the beginning of the observation, when the baby was alone with his mother. When the stranger entered, exploration decreased and remained on a low level until the mother returned from her absence. Exploration picked up somewhat, but when the mother left, it dropped again and remained depressed. Proximity- and contact-seeking behaviors increased throughout the experiment. When left alone 37 percent of the babies cried little and searched strongly, 20 percent cried desperately but searched weakly or not at all, and 32 percent both cried and searched. As might be expected, crying and exploration were negatively correlated ($-0.67$ for crying and manipulation). Figure 4–6 shows the amounts of crying and exploratory manipulation throughout the experiment. Other experiments have shown that although infants showed marked distress and almost no locomotion when placed alone in a room, reactions were entirely different when they were permitted to enter an unfamiliar empty room on their own initiative [68]. The latter infants were placed on the floor in front of their mothers in a

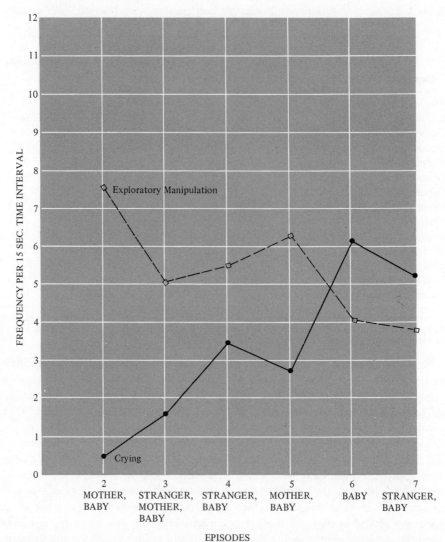

**Figure 4–6.** Amounts of crying and exploratory behavior of 1-year-olds under conditions of mother present and mother absent.

SOURCE: Adapted from M. D. S. Ainsworth and S. M. Bell, "Attachment, Exploration and Separation: Illustrated by the Behavior of One-Year-Olds in a Strange Situation," *Child Development*, **41**, 49–67.

small room adjoining the large room. Whether the large room contained a toy or not, all the infants left their mothers and went into the other room, with no sign of distress. All returned to their mothers and most reentered the large room, some several times. Their behavior illustrates using the mother as a secure base for exploration. These experiments offer strong evidence that attachment behavior and exploratory behavior are in dynamic balance in young children and that both kinds of behavior are related to the mother's presence [3].

Exploratory behavior varies from one infant to another. The quality of temperament called *approach-withdrawal* (see page 149) can be observed as early as 2 or 3 months of age. A tendency to approach new situations rather than to withdraw from them would facilitate exploratory behavior. The baby's social experience in addition to his relations with his mother also affects his exploratory behavior. Since so many research studies have focused on the mother–infant relationship and so few on the infant's additional social life, a study of exploratory behavior of first-born and later born infants is especially interesting [29]. The subjects were a group of 12 first-born babies, and 6 whose next siblings were 6 or more years older and a matched group of 18 whose next siblings were no more than 5 years older. When tested with new, attractive toys, the first-born and widely spaced babies paused much longer before picking up the toy than did the later-borns and showed greater variability in the length of the pause. Later-borns made more responses to the toys, laughed and smiled more, and initiated more play with the examiner. Interviews with the mothers confirmed the expectation that preschool siblings would play often with the baby and that mothers tended to protect first-borns from close contact with others. Most likely the first-borns and widely spaced babies were more fearful and therefore less exploratory than infants who interacted freely with young siblings.

**Separation and Reunion.** The experiments mentioned above have shown that the usual immediate response to involuntary separation from the mother is crying and searching by infants of about 1 year of age. When the mother returns, physical contact usually restores the child's equilibrium. About half of the infants showed angry, resisting behavior when their mothers returned after the second absence [3]. The infants who scored high in contact-resisting behavior tended to be the same ones who scored high in contact-maintaining behavior. This finding suggested that the babies felt much ambivalence, wanting to be close to mother and yet feeling angry at her. The short samples of behavior shown in the experimental situation are consistent with behavior seen in real-life situations involving longer separations of mothers and attached young children.

Bowlby [12, 13, 14] has investigated attachment, separation, and long-term separations in hospitals. When the child between about 8 months and 3 years is first left by his mother, he is likely to cry and protest, showing acute distress and trying to find and regain the mother. The initial phase gives way to despair, when the child is very quiet. Then comes a more active phase when he pays more attention to the environment and interacts with people and things. When children go home after short hospital separations, they often show angry, contact-resisting behavior along with proximity-seeking [46]. Clinging and whining are also very common after hospital separations. It is easy to see how all of these reactions to reunion would be annoying and disturbing to mothers and how they might rebuff or punish the irritating child. A rebuff, however, tends only to intensify the child's attachment behavior [3]. Observations on animal behavior show similar relationships in infant monkeys, who cling all the harder to "heartless mothers" who ignore, reject, or hurt them [44]. When a child persists in clinging, whining and/or angry, aggressive behavior following a separation, recovery is more likely if his mother gives him extra opportunities for the proximity and contacts he is seeking [3].

Separation and reunion are dramatized in the game of peekaboo, which delights children between about 3 months and 4 years of age. It has been suggested that peekaboo symbolizes being and nonbeing, or being alive and being dead [55]. The game is of ancient origin and widespread throughout the world. Some parents have reported that they or their baby invented it. One way of playing it is to put a light cloth over the baby's face, saying "Where's Baby?" He then flails his arms and removes the cloth, revealing wide eyes scanning anxiously until they meet the mother's or father's, whereupon the parent says "Peekaboo" and laughs, and the baby laughs and wriggles with delight. While dramatic play is ordinarily thought of as dominating the years between 3 and 7, peekaboo surely is an instance of playing out a crucial, fearful experience that recurs in the life of the infant. The happy ending of reunion with the loved one is reassuring, suggesting not only that Mother is sure to come back, but that Baby has some control over his fate.

**Peer Relationships.** Since babies in the United States do not often come together in groups, there has not been much American observation of peer interaction in infancy. A few studies have shown that babies did indeed interact with each other, from about 5 months onward. Conflict over toys seemed to be at a peak between 9 and 14 months, with personal aggression increasing with age. Cooperation in play was observed at about 9 months, increased with age and increased considerably at 19 months [41]. Although Americans have not conducted many group care projects with infants, the Soviets and Israelis have had considerable experience with young children in groups. In the yasli-sad of the U.S.S.R., the children are cared for and educated from the age of 2 months to 7 years. Among the objectives of the yasli-sad are fostering friendship and mutual assistance between peers, teaching children to relate good-naturedly to children their own age, to help anyone in need, and to be friendly in work and play [24]. An American observer [18] reports that this teaching is begun in the first year of life when babies are placed in groups in large playpens. The playpens are raised off the floor at heights that permit adults to interact face-to-face with the infants. The youngest babies, who are lying down, are at the highest level. When they can crawl and pull up, the playpens are lowered to maintain face-to-face position with the caretakers. Educators stress making learning situations happy. The teacher is to prevent the types of conflicts which arise among babies if they gather in one place and get in each other's way. The instructress must also watch to see that negative relations do not occur because of one trying to take a toy away from another. During the second year, the children are not expected to play together for long periods, but when together, they imitate and help each other and they are expected not to take toys from each other and not to interfere with each other [24]. Thus do Soviet educators prepare children from the first year of life to live in a collective society.

In another collective society, the kibbutzim of Israel, infants likewise begin early to orient to their peers. Although practices vary somewhat from one kibbutz to another, the descriptions of one observer [9] will give an idea of some of the ways in which infants relate to each other in such settings. The children sleep, eat, and play in the kibbutz, going to their parents' rooms for visits and having their parents visit them. From the first days of life, a baby is in a room with others his age and he sees them more than he sees his parents or siblings. He is never alone. From the time he can crawl, he spends waking time in a large playpen with his age-mates. When the babies can walk, they are together in fenced play yards. Since the caretakers are busy with housework as well as child care, they interfere little with the children's play. In learning to adjust to one another, the babies crawl over each other and push each other down occasionally. They also comfort others in distress and pick up the ones who get pushed over. Helpfulness is much more apparent than any efforts to dominate. "The children are comrades, not competitors" [9, p. 89]. By the time they are toddlers, they have learned much about how to fend for themselves in the group and how to find satisfaction there. They have made a strong beginning in establishing group relations that are their main source of emotional security and orientation.

The long-term results of close peer relationships in infancy have been exposed to careful scientific scrutiny in monkeys [45] but not in man. Harlow had demonstrated that monkeys brought up with surrogate but inanimate mothers grew up to be abnormal. He also found that babies raised with normal mothers but without the company of other babies showed later behavior abnormalities, as far as sex and play were concerned. In order to analyze contributions of mothering and of peer companionship to normal development, he tried raising babies with surrogate mothers, giving them daily time in a playroom with their peers. Although they did not play as much with peers during their first year as did infants with real mothers, these monkeys developed normal play patterns and normal social-sex behavior in their second year.

Nobody knows whether seriously deprived human infants would get a comparable beneficial result from playing together. The same situation could not even occur for humans, even if such experimentation were possible, since they are still immobile at the age (or even at the comparable point in the life span) when little monkeys are racing, chasing, climbing, swinging, scuffling, and playfully biting each other.

It is not feasible to experiment with human beings in such a way as to show a relationship between mother–infant experience and adult sexual behavior. Animal experiments give hints, guides, and suggestions but not blueprints on human behavior mechanisms. Harlow's experiments on monkey infant–infant relationships suggest that the peer relationships of young human beings may be extremely valuable and important in assuring normal growth and in compensating for some deprivation in other areas of life. As for discovering the age at which peer play would have maximum benefits or where its absence would be most serious, the monkey experiments are of little help. Research indicates that preschool social play can help children to recover intellectually from early deprivation [30]. What is more, a "natural experiment" during World War II showed that preschool children could become strongly attached to one another and dependent on one another for emotional satisfaction, in the absence of permanent adults in their world [34]. The group consisted of six children whose parents had been killed or separated by the Nazis during their first year of life (mostly during the first 6 months). They were cared for in a restricted ward in a concentration camp, with changing caretakers, and after liberation, had five or six sets of caretakers. When studied at ages 3 and 4, they were a closely knit, cooperative, affectionate group of children with only tenuous relationships to adults.

*Fear*

Everyone knows how fear feels—stomach turning over, heart racing, mouth dry, skin perspiring, thoughts concentrated on how to get away from the situation in which one is. When infants show distress through crying and apparent attempts to withdraw, adults usually conclude that the children are afraid. When the baby is old enough to cling and to seek proximity to his mother, these behaviors, along with crying and withdrawing, are probably universal indications to adults that young children are afraid.

Fear behavior is neither rigid nor automatic. The physiological basis for fear reactions is inherited, but its expression is an interaction with the environment. Possible reactions are those that facilitate withdrawal from dangers the young are likely to encounter: strangers, heights, excessive stimulation. As the section on attachment behavior has shown, attachment and fear are articulated in ways that promote survival of the infant and that permit exploration and growth. When a strange person, object, or situation causes distress and withdrawal, contact through clinging, touching, or even looking at a loved person restores the baby's equilibrium in such a way that he can approach and explore. Loss of support, pain, loud noises, and other intense stimuli also cause distress reactions which look like fear and which can usually be alleviated by holding the baby close. Individual differences in temperament make for more intense reactions in some infants and less in others. Some can be comforted more easily than others.

A group of infants between 2 and 23 months were examined in a series of fear-provoking situations and other tests, and their mothers were interviewed [72]. Fears of loud noises, masks, a Jack-in-the-box, and a mechanical dog were correlated and showed more intensity in younger and older infants than in those in the middle of the age range. The babies who indicated most fear in these situations of intense stimulation and strange objects tended to be the "cuddliest" babies, or to show highest need for physical contact. This result is consistent with the observation that clinging seems to allay fear. Fear of falling was tested on a visual cliff, a platform of strong glass with a textured pattern under it. Half of the patterned surface is directly under the glass and the other half far below it, giving the visual illusion of a dropoff, halfway across the platform. The fear of crossing the visual cliff increased with age, from 6 months onward. Noncreepers showed different reactions to the two sides of the cliff when placed on its edge, but no fear reactions. Even when pulled across the cliff, they had no fear reactions. Creepers showed some fear, and walkers more fear. Below 10 months of age, the babies did more tactile than visual exploration but after that age, visual exploration increased and tactile decreased. By 5 or 6 months most of the infants could distinguish between the two sides of the cliff, but not between what would support them and what would not. It looked as though experience with space through locomotion was necessary for being able to tell by looking what would offer support for the body. Fear of the cliff was correlated with previous falls, cuddliness, and protest at separation from the mother.

Fear of strangers ordinarily occurs in the second half of the first year and rarely before then. The babies in the study described above showed no fear of strangers until 7 months, moderate fear between 7 and 12, and more fear after 12 months [72]. A certain amount of maturity is necessary before unfamiliar images and expectations must be built up first, in order to have a basis for comparison [19].

Sex differences in fear of strangers were found in another study [70]. The age of onset of fear of strangers was taken as the first month in which the baby showed a clear-cut avoidance response to an unfamiliar adult. For girls, the mean age for this measure was 6.7 months and for boys, 9.1 months. Fear of strangers is also related to the number of social contacts an infant has, both within and outside his family. First-born children showed fear of strangers at younger ages than did later-borns [74].

Fear of strangers becomes meaningful when viewed in the sequence of attachment behavior described on page 154. Positive attachments to the mother and other important human beings are built up, and then discrimination against others

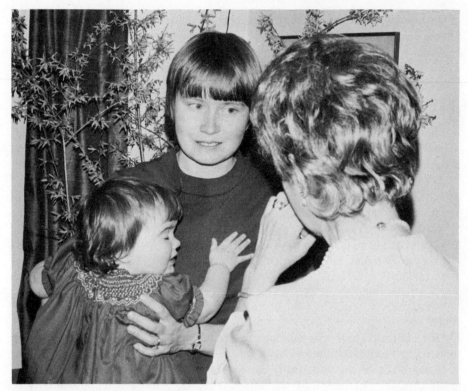

Ellen S. Smart

**Figure 4–7.** Fear of a stranger shown by clinging to mother.

is developed. In the previously mentioned study [75] of attachment in infancy, 77 percent of babies were found to show their first fear of strangers about one month after they showed the beginnings of specific attachments. At 8 to 9½ months, the amount of looking at a stranger has been found negatively related to the infant's fear of strangers [70]. Ainsworth [2], from her observations of infants in Uganda, describes a developmental sequence in response to strangers during the first year of life: (1) No observable discrimination between strange and familiar people. (2) Different responses to mother and strangers, but accepts strangers. (3) The baby stares at strangers but does not show fear reactions. (4) The baby does not approach strangers but allows them to hold him, showing some uneasiness. (5) Fear reactions, ranging from slight apprehension to panic.

Fear of strangers decreases during the second and third years of life, as shown by increasing willingness to accept comfort from a stranger [53]. Fear of being left alone and fear of the dark probably have a large hereditary, maturational basis. It would be very dangerous for a young, wild primate to be left alone, especially in the dark. His fears and protestations would have real survival value. What meaning does this have for human parents? If they think of such fears as natural outcomes of development in infancy, then they will expect to provide comfort and reassurance if such fears are aroused and to be patient until children grow beyond them.

### Applying Knowledge from Research on Fear

1. Avoid separations of the baby from his attachment objects except for brief periods. Since mothers are sometimes necessarily absent, it is wise to encourage

the building of other attachments, which the infant is likely to do with anyone who responds to him and who offers interesting stimulation.

2. Avoid separations and frightening experiences especially at the time when fear of strangers is developing and at its peak. Hospitalization and painful treatments are best postponed if possible. If such experiences are essential, keep the child with a loved person. If the parent is powerless to provide this safeguard to emotional well-being, then provide an object to which the child is attached, such as his blanket, or an object belonging to a person to whom he is attached, such as his mother's purse.
3. Introduce the infant gradually to new situations so as to prevent fears arising from sudden stimulus changes.
4. Provide new situations and gradual changes along with reassurance so as to help the child tolerate novelty and cope with newness.
5. If the baby is afraid of the dark, give him a night light.
6. Use reconditioning, when appropriate. A fear of a specific object or situation may be overcome by experiencing it along with something pleasant and comfortable.

*Anger*

Anger is the distress that accompanies being restrained or blocked in progress toward some sort of fulfillment. Anger involves lashing out rather than withdrawing as in fear. The crying and bodily activity of infants under conditions of bodily tension, such as hunger, look like anger. They seem to be reacting similarly to children and adults who are known to be angry. During the first year, babies learn to use anger for solving some of their problems, to a greater or lesser degree, depending on how successful it is. Some anger expressions seem to be only release of emotional energy.

During the second year, when the desire to establish autonomy is strong, interference with choice making is likely to bring angry resistance, crying, screaming, kicking, perhaps hitting, throwing, and biting. For establishment of a sound sense of autonomy, a baby grows by having many experiences in successful choice making and few in choosing activities where he cannot succeed.

Goodenough's comprehensive and classic study, *Anger in Young Children*, describes and analyzes 1878 anger outbursts of children in the first 8 years of life [39]. Since the observations were recorded by parents, the cases were necessarily selected from families where parents were unusually cooperative and intelligent. As can be seen in Figure 4–8 there was a marked peak in anger outbursts during the second year and then a rapid decline. Little sex difference appeared in infancy, but during the preschool period, boys had significantly more outbursts than girls. At all ages, however, differences between individuals were greater than differences between the sexes.

Anger behavior changed with age. Most of the outbursts during the first 3 years involved display or undirected energy. Such behavior included crying, screaming, stiffening the body, throwing self on floor, stamping, jumping up and down. With age, such primitive bodily responses tended to be replaced with more directed, less violent, more symbolic expressions. The duration of outbursts changed very little, however.

Physical factors were influential. Anger occurred before mealtimes more than at

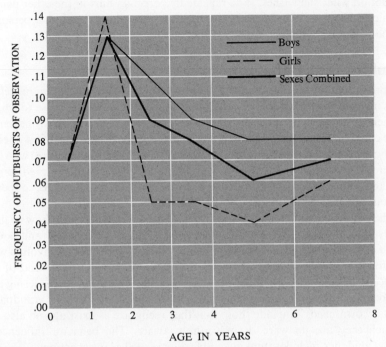

**Figure 4–8.** Number of anger outbursts in ten hours by age and sex.
Source: Adapted from F. L. Goodenough [39].

any other times of day. Children were angry more when ill, even with slight colds or constipation. Outbursts were more frequent among those who had recovered from one or more fairly serious illnesses than among children who had not been ill.

Many psychological factors were shown to be significant. Children who were being toilet-trained showed more anger on days following bedwetting than on days following dry nights. The more adults in the home, the more likely was a child to become angry. When parents shifted from one method of control to another, the child tended to have more outbursts. "Giving the child his own way" was reported more often for children who had many outbursts than for those who had few.

Goodenough comes to this conclusion:

> the control of anger in children is best achieved when the child's be-
> havior is viewed with serenity and tolerance, when the standards are
> adhered to with sufficient consistency to permit the child to learn through
> uniformity of experience, without such mechanical adherence to routine
> that the child's emotional or physical well-being is sacrificed to the de-
> mands of an inflexible schedule. However, when departures from the
> established schedule are made, they should be determined by a recogni-
> tion of the needs of the child and not simply by the convenience or mood
> of the adult in charge. Self-control in the parents is, after all, likely to be
> the best guarantee of self-control in the child.

Hostile aggression is a type of anger expression which will be discussed further in Chapter 8, in relation to the preschool child. The roots of hostile aggression may lie in the infant–mother relationship [77, pp. 221–226]. If it happens that the mother answers the baby's calls after he has become angry through frustration, he may learn to be aggressive with his mother. She thus reinforces his angry behavior because she follows it with satisfactions. He also learns that it hurts her when he does not do what she wishes. If he repeatedly perceives hurt in the other person as he achieves his ends (overcomes his frustrations), then hurting another person may become pleasant to him.

## Regulation of Behavior

Before the end of the first year, the infant who has lived in a harmonious relationship is inclined to cooperate with the important people in his life, those to whom he is attached. The origins of socialization can be seen in the baby's obedience to simple commands and prohibitions given by his parents. Studies on infant obedience show how wrong was the old notion of babies as purely selfish creatures who had to be coerced into social acceptability. The attachment bond seems to predispose the infant to comply with requests signaled by loved people [78]. Thus does cooperation grow out of trust.

In their efforts to regulate what a baby does and when, where, and how he does it, parents are influenced by what they believe to be good for the baby and good for the rest of the family and by their own needs. "Good for the baby" involves what is good for him now and what will help him to grow into the right kind of child, adolescent, and adult. "Good for the rest of the family" means considering all the other people in the home and even some beyond the home, perhaps grandparents. Parents' "own needs" include those that they recognize as existing and also needs of which they are unaware or only dimly aware. The behavior influenced by parental guidance includes thinking and feeling as well as overt action.

Family life has many rhythms. The fitting of small rhythms to one another and into larger wholes is a dynamic process. The ways in which infant and family adapt to one another have important outcomes for both.

### Timing

The term *mutual regulation* is perhaps more apt than *scheduling* to describe what ideally happens in a home with a young baby. Since the newborn baby cannot wait for food and comfort, the family has to adjust pretty much to *his* rhythms if he is to be kept comfortable and helped to feel that the world is worth trusting. After 2 or 3 months, however, a baby can wait briefly for food and attention. With the development of physiological stability, some confidence, and some interest in sensorimotor exploration, he can begin to fit into some of the rhythms of the family. Perhaps he'll sit happily on Daddy's lap for five minutes while Mother finishes her dessert, even though he is hungry. In another month or two, the baby can eat larger meals and can last for longer times between meals. Although he may have some preference as to mealtimes, a mother can fit them into convenient times by gradual change and planning the staying qualities of meals and snacks.

In the matter of sleeping, too, a baby accommodates himself more and more to family rhythms as he matures and as he is guided to do so. In the beginning, sleep follows eating, and waking brings a demand for food. Gradually he stays awake for longer periods and sleeps for a longer time at night, when the rest of the family sleeps. In societies where babies are always with other people, going to bed when the family goes to bed, and sleeping when sleepy during the day, there is no problem of scheduling sleep. American life, especially middle-class American life, is tightly scheduled. Infants have to have naps and go to bed early in order to get enough sleep and also in order for their mothers to get their housework and other jobs done. Parents tend to feel that they need some free, quiet hours without children present, in the evening. Thus getting the baby to go to sleep at certain times often comes to be a problem. It is usually solved by exerting pressure on the baby's own changing rhythms, waking him from previous sleep in time to have him need sleep appropriately, timing meals, arranging baths, play, and outings to induce just enough fatigue.

Babies often come to resist being put to bed, sometimes because they are put to bed when they really are not tired and sleepy. An infant may feel mistrust and lack of confidence in the family who is overeager to get him out of the way. Fears and excitement can prevent and disturb sleep. Sometimes the most careful attention to schedules and emotional security is not enough, and a tired baby cries when put to bed. In such a case, crying is usually brief.

Scheduling includes planning baths, toileting, and dressing at times that fit both the family and baby. Times for play of different kinds and in different places, walks and rides, visiting and receiving guests—all are part of planning for the baby's well-being and for family living. Thus the family, especially the mother, structures the infant's life in time and space, in terms of maintaining his life, stimulating his development, and building relationships with him.

Physical well-being hinges on a schedule that fits the baby. Health and optimal growth require adequate nutrition, rest, and exercise. It takes careful planning and management to see that the baby gets all of these while family living goes on to everyone's benefit. What the baby seems to want at the moment is not always what is best in the overall picture, at least as viewed by the adult. A toddler may want to get into the thick of a game with his kindergartner sister and her friends, not realizing that the results for him would be great excitement, frustration, and fatigue. Or he may be hungry and yet refuse to come in for lunch just because it feels so good to be climbing outdoors.

Cognitive development results from good scheduling, too. For the baby too young to sit up by himself, a frequent change of position and scenery is necessary for giving him mental food (visual and tactual stimulation). When he enlarges his own sphere of operations, first by sitting, then by creeping and walking, his family can still enlarge the scene for him by moving him to different rooms and different furniture and taking him places. Scheduling does not mean that the mother has to pick the baby up at 9 and 11 but rather that she carry on a plan of household activity which includes a change of scene and action for the baby at fairly regular intervals. Her management of his toys has a bearing on mental growth, too. He benefits from some system of rotating toys, so that he gets only a few at a time and frequent changes. Thus a schedule can assure a steady flow of stimulation.

Emotional health is fostered by a suitable schedule. When the infant's physical needs are met before they become overwhelming, he is spared anxiety and frustration. He enjoys the good feeling of trust. Regular holding and cuddling further build up his sense of trust, allaying fears and anxiety and stimulating his senses. Because he trusts, he learns to wait and hope and thus to cooperate as a family member.

*Control and Autonomy*

Parents everywhere set limits on their infants' behavior. If they did not, there would be no more babies, since babies creep and toddle right into danger, whether it be off the platform of a house built on poles over the sea or under a station wagon parked in the driveway. There are always dangers to be kept from exploring fingers and mouths, too—a dung fire in the corner, incense burning before a household god, an electric socket. Little fingers and mouths have to be prevented from destroying precious objects, such as a threaded loom, a clay water pot, or a piece of Steuben glass.

Cultures vary widely in whether babies are expected to learn self-control from the limits placed on their behavior. In some societies, keeping the baby safe is just that and no more. Somebody is expected to look out for him during his early years to see that he does himself no harm. But in many societies, including the American culture, keeping safe is, of course, a prime motive, but a variety of other aims makes for a wide range of practices.

One dimension of parent–child behavior is autonomy-control or permissive-ness-restrictiveness [6]. Parents vary according to how strict or permissive they are with children, or how much autonomy they permit, versus how much they try to control the child. Some parents permit wide autonomy, others a little less; some are very controlling, others somewhat controlling. Parents vary on this dimension within the same culture, and cultures also vary in autonomy-control in adult–child relationships. The teaching manual *Soviet Preschool Education* [24, pp. 24–25] spells out, for example, that the child at 18 months should be taught not to take toys away from others, not to interfere with them, to sit at a table calmly, to obey adults, to feed himself neatly, to wash his hands, to pull up his socks and overalls . . . and more. Probably most Americans would think that this picture presents a great deal of control and not much permissiveness for autonomy.

Ideals in America are probably more diverse than they are in the Soviet Union. Individual freedom and self-expression, however, are high on the lists of many people. The development of a strong sense of autonomy, according to Erikson, requires freedom for a toddler to make choices and planning by adults that will ensure a large proportion of successful choices. Thus the toddler comes to feel, "I can decide" and "What I choose is all right." Some confirmation of the importance of autonomy in infancy for later personality development is offered by longitudinal study on infants and their mothers [59]. During the infancy period, the mothers of the babies were observed and rated on how much autonomy they permitted and how much they tried to control their children. For example, would the mother let the baby decide when he had had enough to eat, or would she try to get him to take more? When the children reached preschool age, they were rated on a number of personality characteristics, and these ratings correlated with the mothers' auton-omy-control behavior. Significant correlations were found, showing that there were relations between the mothers' behavior during infancy and the children's preschool behavior. Table 4–3 shows the size of correlations between mothers' permission for autonomy and characteristics of preschool-age boys. Another study indicates that boy babies and girl babies react differently, in terms of their intellectual development, to opportunities for autonomy and the degree of control given by their mothers [5].

Adaptations in the home which make possible the permission of wide limits include the provision of spaces where little damage can result from play and explora-tion. Fussy, breakable objects can be put away. Furniture can be upholstered or slip-covered in tough, washable fabrics. Floor coverings and draperies can be of relatively indestructible materials. A baby is able to creep in this kind of room

**Table 4–3** Relationship Between Autonomy Permitted by Mother in Infancy and Personality Characteristics of Preschool-Age Boys

| Correlation Coefficient | Personality Characteristic |
|---|---|
| 0.614 | Capacity to maintain internal integration |
| 0.571 | Ability to limit or fend off excessive stimulation |
| 0.511 | Resistance to discouragement |
| 0.610 | Ability to mobilize energy to meet challenge or stress |
| 0.784 | Sense of self worth |
| 0.646 | Clarity in sex role |
| 0.700 | Separation (differentiation of self and others) |

SOURCE: Reprinted by permission from L. V. Murphy, *The Widening World of Childhood* (New York: Basic Books, 1962). Copyright © 1962, Basic Books, Inc.

without hurting himself or anything else. A toddler climbs, explores, runs his cars, and pushes a doll carriage. The bathroom can be arranged so that a toddler can climb steps in front of the washbasin and there enjoy freedom with water play. Some of the cupboards in the kitchen may offer young children freedom to pull out pots and pans and perhaps put them back again.

*Toilet Training*

Here is a kind of restriction that requires the child to bring a reflex activity under conscious control, and which, according to some writers, has far-reaching effects upon personality. Freud, for example, saw toilet training as the important influence on such traits as orderliness, messiness, stinginess, and generosity, but at least one empirical study has failed to show such specific relationships [48].

All societies impose some toilet regulation on children. Toileting is a simple matter for the bare-bottomed babies and toddlers in India and other poor countries with warm climates. Umersingh (whose baths we described in Chapter 2) wore only a shirt until he was about 4 years old. During his first few months, Leela kept a piece of cloth under him in his little bed. When he was in her arms, she held him aside as he started to urinate or defecate. They spent most of their time outdoors and if Umersingh happened to eliminate in the house, it was only on a mud floor, anyway. When children can walk, they squat down to eliminate, perhaps with assistance at first, but also in imitation of their elders, who are often seen squatting by the roadside or in the field. Thus neither clothing nor modesty poses any problem for an Indian toddler in a peasant family. The girls must later learn modesty, but the boys remain free to go as and when they feel moved to do so. .

In the United States and in many other societies, as well, toilet training can cause problems for mothers and babies. The Soviet manual says, in regard to toileting, "It is extremely important to train a child from the very first year of life to be neat" [24]. An investigation of what a group of American mothers said they actually did shows considerable latitude in practice in this country. A few mothers began training when the child was under 5 months, 41 percent began between 5 and 9 months and 30 percent began between 10 and 14 months [77]. Seven months was the average length of time it took to complete bowel training, but there was a range from a few weeks to a year and a half. The later the training was begun, the less time it took. Maturation made learning easier.

Mollie Smart

**Figure 4–9.** A bare bottom makes toileting easy.

Punishment and scolding did not decrease the length of time required but did increase the amount of upset in babies whose mothers were relatively cold and undemonstrative. Severe training had no upsetting effect when mothers were warm in their relationships with the child. The time of beginning training was related to upset, with both early (before 6 months) and late starters (15 to 19 months) more disturbed than those who began between 6 and 10 months. Children trained after 20 months tended to learn quickly and to have little upset. Figure 4–10, taken from an earlier study, shows how much more quickly a child is likely to learn bladder control when his training is started after he has had time for sufficient maturation. Achievement curves for two twins show the slow progress made by Hugh, who began at approximately 7 weeks. By 2 years, Hugh's training was almost complete and Hilton's was begun. Almost immediately, Hilton did as well as Hugh.

The facts in the paragraph above cannot be taken uncritically as a guide to toilet training. At first glance, it would seem logical to say, "Let every mother wait until 20 months to toilet-train her baby." More is involved here than the age of the baby, mainly the personality of the mother. The Sears study of American practices also showed that mothers who were high in sex anxiety tended to begin training early. Perhaps because sex and toileting are connected in the minds of many people, in addition to sheer amount of extra work entailed in laundry, there is a desire to get it over with quickly in those mothers with high sex anxiety. Anxiety cannot be reasoned away. It is a real part of the person. If a mother has strong feelings that

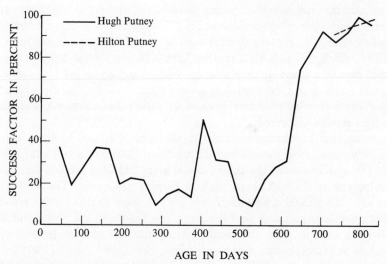

**Figure 4–10.** Records of toilet training of twins, one of whom started early and one late.
SOURCE: McGraw, Myrtle, B.: Neural maturation as exemplified in achievement of bladder control, *J. Pediat.*, **16**:580–590, 1940.

she should begin toilet training early, she may have a healthier relationship with the baby by training him early than by forcing herself to wait. However, when parents are comfortable about allowing the baby a high degree of autonomy, the second half of the second year is the time for easiest learning to use the toilet. By that age most children can perceive signals of imminent elimination, can hang on long enough to get to the toilet, and can release the sphincter muscles at will. The toddler will probably go by himself if his clothing is very easy to manage or if he can be left without pants at appropriate times, and if he has a child's toilet chair nearby. One little girl who had recently learned with such arrangements taught a visiting toddler to go to her toilet chair, after the toddler's mother had met only resistance to her efforts in toilet training.

*Sex Teaching*

Babies learn the names of eyes, nose, mouth, fingers, toes, and many more parts of the body as parents tell them, often playing games such as "This little piggy went to market." A child's concept of self is built as he learns about his physical self in this way. In a happy, affectionate context, he feels good about himself and his body.

When a baby fingers his genitals, as all do, there is probably one chance in ten that the mother who lovingly names his toes will exclaim happily, "There's your penis." More likely, she will say nothing, possibly removing his hands from his penis and distracting him with a toy or something to look at or listen to. Infants are sensitive to sexual stimulation, showing signs of relaxation and pleasure when the genital areas are touched. Newborn boys have erections of the penis. Both boys and girls learn to stimulate their genitals during infancy, through the process of exploring their bodies.

Although some societies permit expression of infant sexuality, Americans and many Europeans take a stern attitude toward it. An exploration of what American mothers said they did with their young children shows ways in which they tried to minimize their children's awareness of sex [77]. They tried to prevent stimulation. Modesty training, to prevent development of sexual interests, began in early infancy in some families. Such a mother kept a diaper on the baby at all times, wrapped him in a towel quickly after his bath, hurrying to get him dressed. Although children might be bathed together when very young, the practice was stopped when they showed any interest in each other's genitals. Parents kept themselves modestly covered.

Assuming that masturbation might result from irritation, mothers kept their babies very clean, using oil and powder regularly. Distraction was a favorite technique. The mother moved the child's hands away from his genitals and gave him something else to do with them, such as playing pat-a-cake. The mother might simply say, "Stop that. It isn't nice," but she was more likely to add a reason that was not quite accurate, such as, "It's dirty." Or she might ask, "Are you itchy?" or "Do you have to go to the toilet?" Many families used no terms for sexual organs and activities; others used vague terms, like "down there"; and still others said baby words, such as "wee-wee." The implication is that if the child has no term for an organ or action, he won't notice it. One mother said, "I think it is very important for them to hardly realize any difference between different parts of their body" [77].

Nobody knows whether minimizing sexual stimulation in the first years of life will suppress sexual activity before marriage. Whatever the rational aspects of the situation may be, it is likely that the restrictive parents act more from what they *feel* to be right than from having thought it out objectively. Sex training differs in an important way from the other kinds of inhibitory training a mother does. When she asks her child to give up his bottle and his diapers, there are more mature forms of behavior to replace babyish ways. With sexual behavior, there is nothing to do but to stop it.

Parent educators have long believed that it was wise to use the names of organs and functions and to permit babies to explore their bodies. Reasons for this point of view include promoting cognition (increased knowledge of the world, a clear body image), building a positive self concept, and laying a foundation for good sexual adjustment as an adult.

## Problems of Deprivation

When a child is deprived, he is not receiving something that he needs or ought to have. The terms *maternal deprivation* and *cultural deprivation* are often used today, but their meanings are not always clear. Maternal deprivation can mean having no mother at all, as in an institution, having a mother whose presence is discontinuous, as when the mother works or the baby is hospitalized, or it can mean having a mother who is with the baby but neglecting or mistreating him. Deprivation can also be thought of in nonpersonal terms, especially sensory, emotional, nutritional, and protectional. *Cultural* deprivation usually implies inadequate experience with objects and language. Often, but not always, a deprived infant is suffering from both maternal and cultural deprivation, since the absence of the mother's care and attention often results in inadequate experience with objects and language. The timing and duration of various kinds of deprivation are important variables. So is the age at which the effects of deprivation are evaluated.

## Stimulus Deprivation

Since children cannot be used in deprivation experiments, the only *experimental* evidence on deprivation comes from animals. This research strongly indicates that stimulation is necessary for the development of basic behavioral capacities [76]. Chimpanzees and cats raised in darkness had varying degrees of visual impairment, depending upon the extent of the deprivation. Puppies raised without their mothers have to have stimulation which approximates licking in order to eliminate, and their feeding behavior is impaired [76].

When children are deprived through unfortunate circumstances, their development can be observed. This has been done in orphanages, and many reports have been made of institutionalized children showing physical, intellectual, language, and emotional retardation [23, 76]. The previous chapter describes an institution in Iran where sensory deprivation was extreme, and the babies showed marked retardation in mental and motor development. When a baby is kept lying in a crib, especially on his back, when the crib sides are covered with plain material, when he has no toys, when people rarely speak to him or touch him, then he is deprived of normal perceptual experiences. This type of deprivation may or may not happen in an institution. It could happen in a home or anywhere. In recent years, child-care institutions have taken note of babies' need for stimulation, and some of them make provisions for it. Groups of institutionalized infants have been studied and found normal in intelligence and behavior [67]. In countries such as the Soviet Union, where institutions for child care are planned to offer personal interaction and rich perceptual experiences, several studies have shown no significant differences between family-reared and institution-reared children [33, p. 12].

Enrichment experiments have been carried on with both humans and animals in the exploration of the effects of stimulation on development. Extra handling, resulting in enriched tactile stimulation, was given to experimental groups in two institutions [22, 85]. In the first study infants were given [22] extra stimulation for 20 minutes a day for 10 weeks. At the end of that time the experimental group scored higher than the control group on the Gesell tests for adaptive, language, and personal-social behavior. In the second study [85], infants were given extra tactile stimulation for 20 minutes a day for 30 days, from the sixth to thirty-sixth day of life. These infants, when compared with their control group, showed significantly more visual attentiveness. Enrichment through stimulation by talking has been shown to promote language production [23]. Massive, carefully planned enrichment of the environment (including tactile, visual, and opportunities for contacting objects with hands) resulted in accelerated visual attention and reaching [85].

There seems to be little doubt that stimulus deprivation and enrichment can have significant short-term effects. The question of how long-lasting such effects might be is an important one. A reviewer of a large number of deprivation studies concludes that unless the deprivation lasts for a long time, there is little evidence that it will have long-term effects [61]. Environmentally deprived children tend to improve when they are placed in normal environments.

## Maternal Deprivation

In studying what happens to the child who does not have enough mothering, the timing and the setting of the separation need to be considered.

**Timing.** The results of separation from the mother vary with the timing of the separation, as to age of child, and duration of separation. Stereotyped rhythmic behavior is frequent in infants reared in institutions, as well as in animals completely deprived of maternal care [19]. Rocking, head-banging, and thumb-sucking are repetitive actions which seem to be soothing to distressed infants and which apparently reduce tensions associated with maternal deprivation. A fear of visual novelty has often been noted in children who use frequent stereotyped rhythms. Autism, a pathological condition in which the baby interacts very little with people, is characterized by all sorts of rhythmic, repetitive actions. Although it is not clear whether the mother or the baby initiates the deprivation, autism is a situation of deprivation for both, since the baby's failure to look at the parents, smile, talk, and reach leads to lack of response on their part. Chimpanzee and monkey infants, as well as humans, use rocking and thumb-sucking as soothing devices when they are deprived of maternal care early in life [19].

Many studies indicate that babies are most likely to be seriously disturbed if they are separated from their mothers after attachment has been established, at about 6 months of age [17]. A study of the impact of maternal environment on children under 6 months showed that when a baby was changed from one foster mother to another, he was likely to show blunted social responses, increased tension, disturbance of routines, physiological disturbances, and developmental regression. The severity and pervasiveness of the disturbance increased with increasing age from 3 to 12 months. At 3 months, only a few showed any disturbance; at 4 months, 50 percent did; at 6 months, 86 percent were disturbed; and at 7 months, all of the infants showed upset upon being moved. When the relationship with the first mother was a close one, the immediate disturbance on separation was more severe; when the relationship between infant and mother was superficial, disturbance was milder [90]. If the disruption of the infant–mother tie is followed by sensory deprivation and lack of a mother substitute, the baby is likely to become depressed and disorganized [15].

When evaluated in adolescence, problems were more severe in children separated from their mothers before 6 months of age than in those separated after 6 months of age [17]. Since this comparison involves two studies, one done in Britain and one in the United States, and since the degree of similarity of the two institutions is not clear, this result should be taken with some caution. Nevertheless, the early-separated children showed greater intellectual deficit and more emotional problems, especially difficulties in forming relationships, inability to concentrate, restlessness, and craving for affection. Both samples of institutionalized children showed more problems at adolescence than did children brought up in foster homes. The institution children exceeded the foster home children in poor school achievement, inability to concentrate, hyperactivity, and craving for affection. These studies indicate that early placement in institutions (separation from the mother with no maternal substitute) is likely to result in intellectual and emotional problems in adolescence, the problems being more severe in those separated before 6 months. The result in adolescence of separation is the reverse of the result in infancy, when the later-separated babies showed most disturbance. The disturbance of the later-separated babies in infancy was probably due to the breaking of the established bond, whereas the adolescent disturbance of the never-attached babies must have been due to not having had experiences essential for development, a situation that might be stimulus deprivation. Or we could think of it in terms of not having had the opportunities to develop attachment behavior and to become attached at the period critical for the growth of attachment.

When effects of separation were evaluated in adulthood, the picture changed again. The small body of research on this topic indicates that harmful effects seem to level out as the child grows up [17]. The authors generally speak of the absence of psychological disorder, which of course is not identical with optimal psychological functioning. One such study [52] involved a follow-up of 20 adults who had been preschool children in London during World War II. Their parents had placed them in residential nurseries. The young adults were studied by means of interviews, projective tests, interviews of their parents, reviews of medical and social agency files, and nursery school records. The subjects were rated on feeling life, inner controls, relationships with people, role performances, and intellectual functioning. The findings showed relatively normal adjustment, with most of the group not significantly different from a normal population. Adjustment varied, however, with the type of nursery, the age at which the child was placed, and his family experiences before and since. Children's villages in Austria and Yugoslavia are institutions where children live in groups with foster parents, from infancy through adolescence [89]. Comparisons at adolescence, with family-reared children, showed no significant differences in intellectual performance, personality development, values, and problems. Nor was there any difference between early and later admissions to the institutions. These studies affirm the plasticity of human personality. They also indicate that institutional care does not necessarily result in disturbed psychological development.

### Multiple Mothering

When an infant's care is shared by two or more women, the situation can be called multiple mothering. Although the infant may be deprived of his own mother for part of the time, he has the care and attention of one or more other women who look after him while he is apart from his mother. Or he may be separated permanently from his own mother and have the joint care of several women. The latter situation was true for children who spent their infancy in home management houses which served as laboratories for colleges of Home Economics throughout the United States. A home management house baby received excellent physical care and rich sensory and social stimulation from many students and several faculty members. The subsequent personality development and academic achievement of some of these children were studied after the children had spent several years as adopted children, living in regular families [35]. The experimental group was compared with a control group of children who had been born into their families and who matched the experimental subjects in age, sex, and intelligence. No difference between the groups was shown in school achievement, anxiety, and social adjustment. A test of personal adjustment favored the control group, suggesting that the children who had had multiple mothering were at a slight disadvantage emotionally.

Children in the Israeli kibbutzim are interesting in regard to multiple mothering, because they see their own mothers only briefly and periodically, while another woman and her assistants take care of them otherwise. A group of kibbutz-reared babies were found to score lower than home-reared on the Griffiths scale, especially in the area of personal-social development. Probably it is more complex for a baby to learn to adjust his motor and social responses to several adults than to one. However, by age 10, the kibbutz-reared children surpassed the home-reared Israeli ones on tests of intelligence and competency [64]. It might be expected here that the children would be slower in forming attachment to their mothers, due to less contact with them. One would also expect the nature of the attachment to be different, less intense, while attachment to nurse, teachers, and peers would also be different from that of home-reared children. Considering the demands of life on a communal farm, it is not surprising that a communally reared child, by age 10, would be better able than a home-reared child to cope with the tasks facing him. Most observers agree that personality development in the kibbutz is different from that in the cities of Israel or in the United States. Bettelheim, a psychiatrist, uses Erikson's model of personality development as a base for describing and speculating on his observations of personality development in kibbutz children. He sees the kibbutz nursery as stimulating less basic trust, since no adult is immediately available at night, and less basic mistrust, since with other infants always present, there is no danger of being left completely alone [9, pp. 304–307]. In each of Erikson's stages of development, Bettelheim finds differences in the kibbutz child, culminating in an adult who escapes despair, but at some cost to personal identity, emotional intimacy, and individual achievement [9, pp. 317–318]. While multiple mothering doubtless contributes heavily to the differences seen in infancy, the whole culture of the kibbutz is basic. The differences between adult kibbutzniks and Americans or other Israelis cannot be considered as due chiefly to multiple mothering, since so many other influences have been at work throughout the various stages of development.

Multiple mothering also occurs in the Soviet Union in the nurseries described in a previous section of this chapter. The teachers in the nurseries carry out carefully constructed, clearly described programs of care and instruction which are consistent with Communist ideals. As in the kibbutz, the child is nurtured and controlled by a complex social order, of which multiple mothering is only a small and integrated part [56].

Multiple mothering can occur at home, as well as in an institution or school. In the joint family of Asia and in some lower- and upper-class families in the West, several or many adults may take care of the baby and have warm relationships with him. Even in large families where a baby is exposed to many people, it takes a certain level of maturity to distinguish between those he knows and those he does not know and a certain amount of progress in attachment behavior in order to care who people are. Mead [82] describes how, in villages she has studied, a baby will be brought up with 30 or 40 people around him all the time and yet at 8 or 9 months, he suddenly rejects all but the 20 or so who have been taking a lot of care of him. A "stranger" from four houses down the street can be very frightening. Mead observes that children cared for by the mother only have more fear of people (and less acceptance) than those cared for by several or many people. She thinks that the adult adjustment of the latter is easier, but points out that the result of one kind of upbringing fits into one culture, the other into another.

Taken all together, the studies on multiple mothering seem to amplify Mead's conclusion. If multiple mothering is a normal part of the culture, then it seems to work well in preparing the child to fit into that culture. If multiple mothering is not, then the child may experience some ill effects from it.

*Maternal Deprivation without Separation*

A different form of deprivation, as compared with separation from the mother, occurs when the mother does not respond to the baby and does not care for him in normal ways. In such cases the child is deprived, even though his mother is physically present.

Evidence of what happens when the mother says she did not want the baby comes from a study done in Brussels [32]. Interviewing mothers within a few days after the birth of their babies, the question was asked, "Did you want to have a baby at the time when your child was born?" Later, from age 4 weeks to 3 years, the 215 unwanted babies were compared with a control group of wanted babies. Significant differences indicated that the desired children had fewer allergies, fewer emotional disturbances, less hostility, and better motor and intellectual development.

Some infants, living in families, fail to gain weight and to grow at normal rates, in spite of no organic pathology. A study of 50 such cases showed inadequate mothering and a disturbed mother–child relationship to be basic to the baby's failure to thrive [20]. There were deficiencies in the ways that the mothers fed, held, and otherwise responded (or did not respond) to the children. Often the mother herself was seriously disturbed, or there was an upset family situation. Sometimes there was something about the infant which made it hard or impossible for the mother to respond nurturantly to him. For example, a very active or hard-to-console baby may be extremely stressful to a mother.

**Battered Babies and Parents.** Since only a small proportion of child abuse cases are reported to legal authorities, the number reported gives little idea of the magnitude of the problem. A Brandeis University survey of adults throughout the United States showed that between $2\frac{1}{2}$ and 4 million people knew of incidents of child abuse during the previous year [36]. Some of these incidents were probably known to more than one person. On the other hand, many attacks on children are known only to the family involved.

Abuse takes two main forms: neglect and attack. Neglect usually results in malnutrition, sometimes in starvation. Diaper rashes, severe skin damage, infestation, and infections also come from neglect. A list of the wounds and fractures inflicted on infants by caretakers makes painful reading for students of child development. The pictures in the book "The Battered Child" [47] are even more heartbreaking than the words. Injuries to infants and toddlers included bruises, burns, abrasions, lacerations, fractures, hemorrhages, and bruises to the brain and internal organs.

There is only a shade of difference between neglect and abuse as threats to physical growth and health. They are also results of disturbed emotional relationships between parents and children. The results of physical abuse, which was diagnosed by skeletal injuries revealed by X ray, were the focus of a follow-up study of 50 children [31]. When the study began, 9 of the children had died from injuries, malnutrition, or at the hands of their mothers. Of the 20 who were eventually studied, 8 were emotionally disturbed, 10 had IQs below 80, and 7 had quite severe physical handicaps stemming from their old injuries. Of the 10 still living in their old homes, 6 were below normal in physical growth.

A hint of what adulthood holds for the battered child is given by studies of parents of battered children. Parents who abused their infants were studied in depth by two psychiatrists [80] who found a pattern of thinking and feeling which was characteristic of such parents. These parents expected and demanded from their babies a kind of behavior that was far beyond the ability of a baby. Such a parent expects maturity and love from the baby, while ignoring the baby's needs, limited abilities, and helplessness. Being immature themselves, and in great need of love, these parents seem to see the babies not as infants, but as parts of themselves, or as the causes of their troubles. An example of such a case is Kathy, mother of 3-weeks-old battered Kenny, who said, "I have never felt really loved in all my life. When the baby was born, I thought he would love me; but when he cried all the time, it meant he didn't love me. So I hit him" [80, p. 110].

Henry, the father of 16-month-old Johnny, whose ear was partially torn from his head, explained it thus, "He knows what I mean and understands it when I say, 'Come here.' If he doesn't come immediately, I go and give him a gentle tug on the ear to remind him of what he's supposed to do" [80, p. 110].

The life histories of the child-attackers show that they themselves were battered children, or at least raised in a similar style. Several had been severely beaten. All had had extremely demanding parents who had early expectations of submissive behavior, prompt obedience, no mistakes, sympathy, approval, and help for parents. Whatever they did, it was never enough, never quite right, it was at the wrong time; it disgraced the parents. These children grew up feeling unloved, disregarded, unfulfilled, and wrong. In some cases the psychiatrists were able to interview and observe the grandmothers of their battered infant patients. They found that the grandparents had experienced as babies the same kind of distorted mothering which they later applied to their own children, who in turn became impossibly demanding, disregarding, and abusing parents [80].

The psychiatrists observed that these abusing parents are not isolated instances, but only extreme instances in the culture in which they live. Many parents in North America and in Europe believe in "Spare the rod and spoil the child," "Children have to be taught to obey," and that children owe it to their parents to do what the parent wants and to be a comfort to the parents. It is just a step to the extreme notion that children exist primarily to satisfy their parents' needs and that children who do not fulfill this obligation should be punished.

Cultural support for the attitude that spawns child abuse has existed in the form of laws that emphasize parents' rights rather than society's rights in regard to control over children. Since the systematic study of the battered child syndrome in the 1960s, laws have been changed in the direction of protecting children more adequately. Before that time, California was the only state in which parental abuse of the child was a crime. Now all states have such laws. Solution of the problem, however, requires more than laws. Parents who abuse children need extensive help. So do children who must be removed from their parents.

A severely deprived infant is likely to grow into a battering adult, not only in the human world, but also among monkeys. Harlow's famous experiments with baby monkeys raised with substitute mothers showed that the infants spent more time with warm, rocking, cloth-covered surrogates than with stationary wire surrogates, even if wire mothers gave milk. Harlow reported that as far as the experimenter could observe, the baby monkey's attachment to a cloth mother was as strong as for a real mother and that the security he gained from a cloth mother was as great as from a real mother [42]. However, when the cloth-mothered babies grew to maturity, neither males nor females were interested in mating. The females who were impregnated and gave birth did not take adequate care of their babies. All showed abnormal behavior ranging from indifference to abuse. They would avoid the infants, knock them down, step on them, beat them, and rub their faces on the floor. They were "helpless, hopeless, heartless mothers devoid, or almost devoid, of any maternal feeling" [43].

The battered child presents a complex social problem. For his physical rehabilitation (if possible) and protection, he needs prompt help in getting hospital treatment and being separated from the person who injured him. Little is known about how successful emotional rehabilitation can be, although there are cases of neglected and damaged children being treated and then adopted by loving parents, whereupon the child seemed to blossom.

## Uniqueness of Individual Development

The genetic endowment of the infant determines how he first interacts with the environment into which he is born. So also does the environment determine how the baby can interact. The baby's successive experiences affect his future interactions. A given external condition has different meaning and significance for different babies. In other words, a given external condition offers differing experiences to different individuals. And it is the *experience,* rather than an external condition, which is significant for development [33, pp. 59–65]. For example, take as the external condition Mother A who handles a baby often and vigorously, speaks and sings to him frequently and loudly, keeps him with her while she works, and maintains contact with him. Baby A is relatively insensitive to perceptual stimulation, showing no reaction to slight stimulation and moderate reactions to what his mother offers. Mother B picks up her baby only when he is in distress or otherwise needs care and leaves him alone when he is quiet. She speaks softly and handles him gently. If Baby A belonged to Mother B, he would be understimulated. Baby B, however, is highly sensitive. Mother A would be much too stimulating for him, keeping him in a state of intense arousal frequently; Mother B gives him the amount and quality of stimulation that he can handle easily. Although their mothers provide widely different external environments, Baby A and Baby B have similar experiences in regard to adequacy of stimulation.

*Roots of Individuality* [33] is the title of a book describing the behavior dimensions and interactions through which an infant elaborates his uniqueness. The study shows relationships between experience and development. One of the important dimensions that bears upon experience is perceptual sensitivity, as seen in the preceding paragraph. Another is activity, "the amount and vigor of body motion typically shown by a given infant in a variety of situations" [33, p. 22]. As has been shown earlier in this chapter, the activity level of an infant can strongly affect his family relationships and hence his experiences. The present study gives some contrasts in behavior of active and relatively inactive infants which are relevant to what is experienced [33, pp. 239–241]. Active infants were more coordinated and complex in their spontaneous behavior, focusing more on the environment including distant stimuli. They vocalized more intensely and in more complex ways. Inactive infants were affected more than active ones by social stimulation and by efforts to interest them in toys. The active ones responded vigorously to people and toys even when little or no effort was made to elicit response. Inactive babies used more sucking and oral activity and were able to soothe themselves through mouth activity. Active babies reacted more strongly to hunger than did inactive ones. As Figure 4–11 shows, crying or screaming in hunger was typical of five of six active babies and of only one out of six inactive infants. It is easy to see how a mother would hurry to assuage the hunger pangs of a screaming baby while the

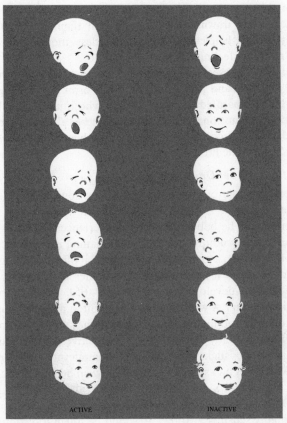

ACTIVE     INACTIVE

**Figure 4–11.** Twelve hungry babies, showing typical behavior for active and inactive infants.

mother of a hungry but silent infant might delay. The ways in which these two groups of babies are dependent on their caretakers show two contrasts: the active babies can find stimulation relatively easily for themselves but need soothing and comfort more; the inactive babies need help in finding interesting things to see and do but can manage quite well in overcoming distress and maintaining equilibrium. This one set of findings explains some of the differences in the ways that individual children react to deprivation situations.

The "roots of individuality" include additional dimensions of infant behavior and further differentiation of parent behavior. Experiences at each age affect subsequent interactions and development.

## Summary

The culture into which a child is born determines the limits of his opportunities for physical, cognitive, and social development. Role prescriptions and ideals for child-rearing, although clear in simple, stable societies, are often confusing in a rapidly changing culture. In the United States methods of child-rearing change relatively fast. A variety of attitudes and methods exist at any one time, varying with such factors as economic level and stage of family development. The infant himself is active in determining how people respond to him. Appearance, sex, and temperament are significant. Sex-linked behavior is influential in shaping mother–infant interactions. An infant's well-being is affected by the fit between his temperament and his family.

Scheduling or timing is basic in the care and guidance of infants. The needs of all family members have to be balanced and adjusted in mutual regulation, taking special account of the baby's immaturity. At the same time that the family takes care of the infant's requirements for food, rest, exercise, and cleanliness, they also build relationships and attitudes. Intellectual development is influenced through all experiences, as well as during play and stimulating interactions. Infant care also includes restrictions, many of which are applied in order to ensure safety and health, others of which exist for the purpose of making life comfortable for other family members. Especially during the stage of development of the sense of autonomy, healthy growth requires clear, firm, minimal restrictions, within which the child can operate freely. Toilet training is accomplished more quickly when begun later, rather than earlier, in infancy. The mother's personality, especially her warmth or coldness, is a factor in success. In toilet training, the mother requires the child to substitute a more mature form of behavior for an immature pattern. In restricting sex activity, however, the mother asks the child to give up an activity without substituting for it.

Emotions become differentiated as the child develops. Love, a term with many implications, has been studied in the context of attachment. An infant shows attachment to another person when he shows desire for the presence, contact, and response of that person. Attachment is shown by selective smiling and vocalizing and by crying at separation from the attachment object. The mother is usually the first attachment object, the father the second. Babies tend to select responsive, stimulating people as objects for their affection. Exploration is facilitated by the presence of an attachment object. The child leaves the mother briefly as attachment bonds become elastic.

Intense infant–mother relationships are frequent in cultures where the mother has little help with the care of her baby. When separated from the mother to whom he is firmly attached, the baby shows disturbance and disorganization. Separation and other love-deprivation experiences have to be interpreted in the life context of the child. Experiments with monkeys suggest that play with peers may compensate somewhat for deprivation in infant–adult affectional relationship. Infant peer relationships are fostered in collective societies.

Infants show fear reactions to intense stimuli, pain, and sudden changes in stimulation. Fear of strangers develops after attachment. The dark is often frightening. Fear of novelty requires having built some schemas which permit discrimination of the familiar and the new. In coping with fear-provoking situations, an infant, like all people, only more so, gains courage and reassurance from the presence of a person to whom he is attached.

Anger involves tension and attack in connection with a blocking situation. Anger outbursts occur most frequently during the second year, when the child is very eager to make choices and yet lacks experience and skills necessary for independent successful action. Parents can minimize young children's anger outbursts by meeting their physical needs before tensions become acute and by maintaining firm, consistent, yet reasonable, control.

Maternal deprivation can take many forms, each of which derives some meaning from the cultural context. Recovery of the child depends upon the form and timing of the deprivation and the form and timing of ameliorative efforts. The battered child is a result of severe parental disturbance in a nonsupportive social setting.

## References

1. Ainsworth, M. D. S. Patterns of attachment behavior shown by the infant in interactions with his mother. *Merrill-Palmer Quart.*, 1964, **10**, 51–58.
2. Ainsworth, M. D. S. *Infancy in Uganda: Infant care and the growth of love.* Baltimore: Johns Hopkins Press, 1967.
3. Ainsworth, M. D. S., & Bell, S. M. Attachment, exploration, and separation: Illustrated by the behavior of one-year-olds in a strange situation. *Child Devel.*, 1970, **41**, 49–67.
4. Applebaum, R. M. Best to start disciplining early. *Baby Talk*, 1969, **34**:11, 10.
5. Bayley, N., & Schaefer, E. S. Correlations of maternal and child behaviors with the development of mental abilities: Data from the Berkeley growth study. *Mono. Soc. Res. Child Devel.*, 1964, **29**:6.
6. Becker, W. C. Consequences of different kinds of parental discipline. In M. L. Hoffman & L. W. Hoffman (Eds.), *Review of child development research.* Vol. 1. New York: Russell Sage Foundation, 1964, pp. 171–208.
7. Bell, R. Q. A reinterpretation of the direction of effects in studies of socialization. *Psychol. Rev.*, 1968, **75**, 81–95.
8. Bell, S. M. The development of the concept of object as related to mother-infant attachment. *Child Devel.*, 1970, **41**, 291–311.
9. Bettelheim, B. *The children of the dream.* New York: Macmillan, 1969.
10. Bigner, J. J. Fathering: Research and practice implications. *Fam. Coord.*, 1970, **19**, 357–362.
11. Biller, H. B. Father absence and the personality development of the male child. *Devel. Psychol.*, 1970, **2**, 181–201.
12. Bowlby, J. *Child care and the growth of love.* London: Penguin, 1953.
13. Bowlby, J. The nature of the child's tie to his mother. *Int. J. Psychoan.*, 1958, **39**, 1–24.
14. Bowlby, J. *Attachment and loss.* Vol. I: *Attachment.* London: Hogarth, 1969.
15. Brody, G. F. Socioeconomic differences in stated child-rearing practices and in observed maternal behavior. *J. Marr. Fam.*, 1968, **30**, 656–660.
16. Bronfenbrenner, U. Socialization and social class through time and space. In E. E. Maccoby, T. M. Newcomb, & E. L. Hartley (Eds.), *Readings in social psychology.* New York: Holt, Rinehart and Winston, 1958, pp. 400–425.
17. Bronfenbrenner, U. Early deprivation in mammals: a cross-species analysis. In G. Newton & S. Levine (Eds.), *Early experience and behavior.* Springfield, Ill.: Charles C Thomas, 1968, pp. 727–764.
18. Bronfenbrenner, U. Introduction. In H. Chauncey (Ed.), *Soviet preschool education.* Vol. 1: *Program of instruction.* New York: Holt, Rinehart and Winston, 1969, p. xiii.
19. Bronson, G. W. The development of fear in man and other animals. *Child Devel.*, 1968, **39**, 407–431.
20. Bullard, D. M., et al. Failure to thrive in the neglected child. *Am. J. Orthopsychiat.*, 1967, **37**, 680–690.
21. Caldwell, B. M., & Richmond, J. B. Social class level and stimulation potential

of the home. In B. Staub & J. Hellmuth (Eds.), *Exceptional infant*. Vol. 1. Seattle: Special Child Publications, 1967.

22. Casler, L. The effects of extra tactile stimulation on a group of institutionalized infants. *Genet. Psychol. Mono.*, 1965, **71**, 137–175.
23. Casler, L. Perceptual deprivation in institutional settings. In G. Newton & S. Levine (Eds.), *Early experience and behavior*. Springfield: Charles C Thomas, 1968, pp. 573–626.
24. Chauncey, H. (Ed.). *Soviet preschool education*. Vol. 1: *Program of instruction*. New York: Holt, Rinehart and Winston, 1969.
25. Chess, S. Temperament in the normal infant. In B. Staub & J. Hellmuth (Eds.), *Exceptional infant*. Vol. 1. Seattle: Special Child Publications, 1967.
26. Chess, S., Thomas, A., & Birch, H. G. Behavior problems revisited: Findings of an anterospective study. In S. Chess & A. Thomas (Eds.), *Annual progress in child psychiatry and child development 1968*. New York: Brunner/Mazel, 1968, pp. 335–344.
27. Clausen, J. A. Family structure, socialization and personality. In M. L. Hoffman & L. W. Hoffman (Eds.), *Review of child development research*. Vol. 2. New York: Russell Sage Foundation, 1966, pp. 1–53.
28. Clay, V. S. The effect of culture on mother-child tactile communication. *Fam. Coord.*, 1968, **17**, 204–210.
29. Collard, R. R. Social and play responses of first-born and later-born infants in an unfamiliar situation. *Child Devel.*, 1968, **39**, 325–334.
30. Dennis, W., & Najarian, P. Infant development under environmental handicap. *Psychol. Mono.*, 1957, **71**:7.
31. Elmer, E., & Gregg, G. S. Developmental characteristics of abused children. *Pediat.*, 1967, **40**, Part I, 596–602.
32. Emery-Hauzeur, C., & Sand, E. A. Enfants désirés et non désirés. *Enfance*, 1962, **2**, 109–126.
33. Escalona, S. K. *The roots of individuality*. Chicago: Aldine, 1968.
34. Freud, A., & Dann, S. An experiment in group upbringing. *Psychoanal. Stud. Child*, 1951, **6**, 127–168.
35. Gardner, D. B., Hawkes, G. R., & Burchinal, L. G. Noncontinuous mothering in infancy and development in later childhood. *Child Devel.*, 1961, **32**, 225–234.
36. Gil, D. G. Incidence of child abuse and demographic characteristics of persons involved. In R. E. Helfer & C. H. Kempe, *The battered child*. Chicago: University of Chicago Press, 1968, pp. 19–40.
37. Goldberg, S., & Lewis, M. Play behavior in the year-old infant: early sex differences. *Child Devel.*, 1969, **40**, 21–31.
38. Golden, M., & Birns, B. Social class differentiation in cognitive development: A longitudinal study. Paper presented at the meeting of the Society for Research in Child Development. Santa Monica, Calif., March 27, 1969.
39. Goodenough, F. L. *Anger in young children*. Minneapolis: University of Minnesota Press, 1931.
40. Gordon, M. Infant care revisited. *J. Marr. Fam.*, 1968, **30**, 578–583.
41. Haas, M. B., & Harms, I. E. Social interaction between infants. *Child Devel.*, 1963, **34**, 79–97.
42. Harlow, H. F. The nature of love. *Am. Psychol.*, 1958, **13**, 673–684.
43. Harlow, H. F. The heterosexual affectional system in monkeys. *Am. Psychol.*, 1962, **17**, 1–9.

44. Harlow, H. F. The maternal affectional system. In B. M. Foss (Ed.), *Determinants of infant behaviour II*. New York: Wiley, 1963, pp. 3–34.

45. Harlow, H. F., & Harlow, M. K. Social deprivation in monkeys. *Sci. Am.*, 1962, **207**:5, 136, 146.

46. Heinicke, C. M., & Westheimer, I. *Brief separations*. New York: International Universities Press, 1965.

47. Helfer, R. E., & Kempe, C. H. *The battered child*. Chicago: University of Chicago Press, 1968.

48. Hetherington, E. M., & Brackbill, Y. Etiology and covariation of obstinacy, orderliness and parsimony in young children. *Child Devel.*, 1963, **34**, 919–944.

49. Honzik, M. P. Environmental correlates of mental growth: Prediction from the family setting at 21 months. *Child Devel.*, 1967, **38**, 337–364.

50. Hunt, R. G., & Winokur, G. Some generalities concerning parental attitudes with special reference to changing them. In J. C. Glidewell (Ed.), *Parental attitudes and child behavior*. Springfield, Ill.: Charles C Thomas, 1961, pp. 174–187.

51. Koch, H. L. *Twins*. Chicago: University of Chicago Press, 1966.

52. Maas, H. S. Long-term effects of early separation and group care. *Vita Humana*, 1963, **6**, 34–56.

53. Maccoby, E. E. Tracing individuality within age-related change. Paper presented at the meeting of the Society for Research in Child Development, Santa Monica, Calif., March 27, 1969.

54. Mason, W. A. Determinants of social behavior in young chimpanzees. In A. M. Schrier, H. F. Harlow, & F. Stolenits (Eds.), *Behavior of non-human primates*. Vol. 2. New York: Academic Press, 1965, pp. 287–334.

55. Maurer, A. The game of peek-a-boo. *Dis. Nervous System*, 1967, **28**, 118–121.

56. Meers, D. R., & Marans, A. E. Group care of infants in other countries. In C. A. Chandler et al. *Early child care*. New York: Atherton, 1968.

57. Mitchell, G. D. Attachment differences in male and female infant monkeys. *Child Devel.*, 1968, **39**, 611–620.

58. Moss, H. A. Sex, age and state as determinants of mother-infant interaction. *Merrill-Palmer Quart.*, 1967, **13**, 19–53.

59. Murphy, L. B. *The widening world of childhood*. New York: Basic Books, 1962.

60. Neubauer, P. (Ed.). *Children in collectives: Child-rearing aims and practices in the kibbutz*. Springfield, Ill.: Charles C Thomas, 1965.

61. O'Connor, N. Children in restricted environments. In G. Newton & S. Levine (Eds.), *Early experience and behavior*. Springfield, Ill.: Charles C Thomas, 1968, pp. 530–572.

62. Pearlin, L. I., & Kohn, M. L. Social class, occupation and parental values: A cross culture study. *Am. Soc. Rev.*, 1966, **31**, 466–479.

63. Prothro, E. T. Socialization and social class in a transitional society. *Child Devel.*, 1966, **37**, 219–228.

64. Rabin, A. I. Behavior research in collective settlements in Israel. *Am. J. Orthopsychiat.*, 1958, **28**, 577–586.

65. Rapp, D. W. Childrearing attitudes of mothers in Germany and the United States. *Child Devel.*, 1961, **32**, 669–678.

66. Rebelsky, F., & Hanks, C. Fathers' verbal interaction with infants in the first 3 months of life. *Child devel.*, 1971, **42**, 63–68.

67. Rheingold, H. L. The effect of environmental stimulation upon social and exploratory behavior in the human infant. In B. M. Foss (Ed.), *Determinants of infant behavior*. Vol. I. New York: Wiley, 1961, pp. 143–177.

68. Rheingold, H. L., & Eckerman, C. O. The infant's free entry into a new environment. *J. Exper. Child Psychol.*, 1969, **8**, 271–283.

69. Ricciuti, H. N. Social and emotional behavior in infancy: Some developmental issues and problems. *Merrill-Palmer Quart.*, 1968, **14**, 82–100.

70. Robson, K. S., Pedersen, F. A., & Moss, H. A. Developmental observations of diadic gazing in relation to the fear of strangers and social approach behavior. *Child Devel.*, 1969, **40**, 619–627.

71. Rosenhan, D. Preface. In H. Chauncey (Ed.), *Soviet preschool education*. Vol. II: *Teacher's commentary*. New York: Holt, Rinehart and Winston, 1969, pp. v–xii.

72. Scarr, S., & Salapatek, P. Patterns of fear development during infancy. *Merrill-Palmer Quart.*, 1970, **16**, 53–90.

73. Schaefer, E. S., & Bayley, N. Maternal behavior, child behavior and their intercorrelations from infancy through adolescence. *Mono. Soc. Res. Child Devel.*, 1963, **28**:3.

74. Schaffer, H. R. The onset of fear of strangers and the incongruity hypothesis. *J. Child Pyschol. Psychiat.*, 1966, **7**, 95–106.

75. Schaffer, H. R., & Emerson, P. E. The development of social attachments in infancy. *Mono. Soc. Res. Child Devel.*, 1964, **29**:3.

76. Scott, J. P. *Early experience and the organization of behavior*. Belmont, Calif.: Brooks/Cole, 1968.

77. Sears, R., Maccoby, E. E., & Levin, H. *Patterns of child rearing*. Evanston, Ill.: Row, Peterson, 1957.

78. Stayton, D. J., Hogan, R., & Ainsworth, M. D. S. Infant obedience and maternal behavior: The origins of socialization reconsidered. Paper presented at the meeting of the Eastern Psychological Association, Atlantic City, 1970.

79. Stechler, G. A., & Carpenter, G. Viewpoint on early affective development. In B. Staub & J. Hellmuth (Eds.), *Exceptional infant*. Vol. 1. Seattle: Special Child Publications, 1967.

80. Steele, B. F., & Pollock, C. B. A psychiatric study of parents who abuse infants and small children. In R. E. Helfer & C. H. Kempe (Eds.), *The battered child*. Chicago: University of Chicago Press, 1968.

81. Stern, G. G., Caldwell, B. M., Hersher, L., Lipton, E. L., & Richmond, J. B. A factor analytic study of the mother-infant dyad. *Child. Devel.*, 1967, **40**, 163–181.

82. Tanner, J. M., & Inhelder, B. *Discussions on child development*. Vol. II. New York: International Universities, 1954.

83. Wahler, R. G. Infant social attachments: A reinforcement theory interpretation and investigation. *Child Devel.*, 1967, **38**, 1079–1088.

84. Waters, E., & Crandall, V. J. Social class and observed maternal behavior from 1940 to 1960. *Child Devel.*, 1964, **35**, 1021–1032.

85. White, B. L., & Held, R. Plasticity of sensorimotor development in the human infant. In B. Staub & J. Hellmuth (Eds.), *Exceptional infant*. Vol. 1. Seattle: Special Child Publications, 1967, pp. 291–313.

86. White, B. L., LaCrosse, E. R., Litman, F., & Ogilvie, D. M. The Harvard preschool project: An etho-ecological study of the development of competence.

Symposium presented at the meeting of the Society for Research in Child Development, Santa Monica, Calif., March 27, 1969.

87. Willerman, L., Broman, S. H., & Fiedler, M. F. Infant development, preschool IQ and social class. *Child Devel.*, 1970, **41**, 69–77.

88. Wolfenstein, M. Trends in infant care. *Am. J. Orthopsychiat.*, 1953, **33**, 12–130.

89. Wolins, M. Young children in institutions: Some additional evidence. *Devel. Psychol.*, 1970, **2**, 99–109.

90. Yarrow, L. J. Maternal deprivation: Toward an empirical and conceptual re-evaluation. *Psychol. Bull.*, 1961, **58**, 459–490.

91. Yarrow, L. J. Research in dimensions of early maternal care. *Merrill-Palmer Quart.*, 1963, **9**, 101–114.

92. Yarrow, L. J. The development of focused relationships during infancy. In B. Staub & J. Hellmuth (Eds.), *Exceptional infant.* Vol. 1. Seattle: Special Child Publications, 1967, pp. 425–442.

93. Yarrow, L. J., Rubenstein, J. L., & Pedersen, F. A. Dimensions of early stimulation: Differential effects on infant development. Paper presented at the meeting of the Society for Research in Child Development, Minneapolis, Minn., April 4, 1971.

# Part II

Robert J. Izzo

# The Preschool Child

# Introduction

Chronological age does not define the exact span of years of this period of life. Our discussion of infancy ended at about 2 years of age, or when the child had completed the growth of sensorimotor intelligence and had begun to use language for communication and thinking, when he had done the major work on establishing his sense of trust and was busy with the problems of establishing a sense of autonomy. With these achievements in intellectual and personality growth, he begins the preschool period. As he progresses through this stage, toward the school age, he works to perfect new coordinations of his maturing body. He builds his mind through coping with certain types of intellectual problems and his personality through further development of the sense of autonomy and then through the development of a sense of initiative and imagination. Interactions with the world of objects and people continue to be the means through which growth takes place and learning is accomplished. The chronological ages at which the various achievements can be noted vary from one child to another. To say, for example, that a certain type of thinking ends at age 7 is not to say that all children under all circumstances achieve a certain mode of thinking but only that the majority of children in a certain culture have done so.

Piaget places the end of one stage of intellectual growth at about 7 years. Erikson places the end of the main concern with the sense of initiative at about 7. Many educational systems throughout the world recognize 7 as a nodal age, a time when the child is appropriately occupied with learning the tools of his culture, whether they be reading, writing, and arithmetic or work such as hunting, fishing, and child care. Therefore, in our consideration of the preschool child, we often include the 6-year-old, even though, strictly speaking, the American 6-year-old is a school-child, required by law to attend school.

Asserting his individuality, testing the limits of himself, his family and his world, pushing out into that world, the preschool child is building his mental structures in complex and wondrous ways. His business is play, a widely varied activity through which he develops his body, personality, intelligence, and emotions. He is the psychologist's darling, because he reveals his inner self so fully. As a baby, he could not tell what he was thinking and feeling. As a school-age child, he won't tell. And as an adolescent, he either won't know or will tell only his friends. Not only does the preschool child *tell* through his words and his behavior, he also delights adults by his mistakes in reasoning and interpretation.

**189**

Preschool thinking has some of the appeal which baby diminutive proportions have. It is "cute." What adult's heart would not be melted by the 2-year-old who, widening her blue eyes at a tug pulling three barges on the river, commented, "Choo-choo going fwimming." Or by this 3-year-old's observation, "Ephalanuts wash with just water; people wash with water, too, and soap for rinsing." Preschool thinking has surprise qualities, too. Think of the jolt received by the six-foot-three father whose nursery school child commented, "Teachers are bigger than mummies and daddies, even bigger than daddies."

A Harvard study has resulted in a list of abilities which make up the essentials of competency in the preschool child. Children vary considerably in acquisition of competencies, so much so that some 3-year-olds are more competent than some 6-year-olds. White's list of competencies indicates important attributes developed during the preschool years, under favorable conditions:[*]

> Non-social abilities
> 1. Linguistic : grammatical capacity, vocabulary, articulation, extensive use of expressed language.
> 2. Intellectual : sensing dissonance, anticipation of consequences, ability to deal with abstractions, such as numbers, letters, rules, taking the perspective of another person, making interesting associations.
> 3. Executive : planning and carrying out multistepped activities, using resources effectively.
> 4. Attentional : maintaining attention to a proximal task while simultaneously monitoring peripheral events.
>
> Social abilities
> 1. Getting and keeping adults' attention in socially acceptable ways.
> 2. Using adults as resources.
> 3. Expressing both affection and hostility to both adults and peers.
> 4. Leading, following, and competing with peers.
> 5. Showing pride in his accomplishments.
> 6. Taking part in adult role behavior or otherwise expressing a desire to grow up.

The first chapter in this section, Chapter 5, deals with personality development, physical maturing, and bodily coordination. The next two chapters are concerned with intellectual growth and its nurture, one chapter dealing with cognitive and language development, the other with imagination and the stimulation of development through education. Since the preschool period is dominated by the development of the sense of initiative and imagination, this aspect of growth is given special emphasis in the present section of the book. As Chapter 7 will show, ongoing research indicates increasingly the importance of the preschool years for basic education. The term *preschool* may not be quite appropriate when schools for young children become more and more available.

* B. L. White, An overview of the project. Paper presented at the meeting of the Society for Research in Child Development, Santa Monica, Calif., March 27, 1969.

# Chapter 5

Merrill-Palmer Institute by Donna J. Harris

## Personality and Body

No longer a baby, the preschool child interacts with an expanding world of people and things. Although physical growth is slower than it was during infancy, he is still growing faster than he will in the years which follow this period. Personality development is dramatic, as he moves from infantile concerns to the stage which gives color and focus to the preschool years.

## Directions in Personality Growth

Two threads dominate the fabric of personality growth during the preschool years: the sense of autonomy and the sense of initiative. If all has gone well during infancy, a firm sense of trust is established by now. Further satisfactory experiences strengthen it, although shreds of mistrust are also present throughout life. Upon the foundation of a sense of trust, the child builds his sense of autonomy, and upon trust and autonomy, his sense of initiative. The success of his preschool interactions determine the adequacy of the sense of initiative and imagination which he builds.

### Autonomy

The sense of autonomy blossoms as the child of 2 or thereabouts experiences the power of doing and deciding that comes with his wealth of budding abilities. Walking freely, although in a jerky trudging style, running a bit stiffly, climbing, bear-walking, knee-walking, galloping, riding a kiddy car, he has many independent modes of locomotion to exploit and choose from. The house and yard are for exploring. His hands easily do his bidding in reaching, grasping, letting go, throwing, turning, pulling, pushing. Toys to manipulate, tools that extend the powers of his hands, milk bottles with clothes pins, Daddy's old hat, Mummy's old purse, crayons and paper, sand and water, mud—all give him choices and successes. "Shall I play with it or not? . . . I'll do what I want with it. . . . What I do is all right."

Talking brings control over both the self and others and a corresponding strengthening of the sense of autonomy. The average increase in vocabulary from 18 months to 2½ years is from 22 to 446 words [66]. Four hundred and forty-six words represent a great many things, ideas, activities, and people brought into the child's orbit of influence. He has made the discovery that everything has a name and that when he can say the name, he can exert some control over the thing.

Even headier is the power to cooperate with people or not. If you ask a 2-year-old, "Do you want to go outdoors?" the chances are that he'll say *no*. Even though he really would like to go out, he gets tremendous momentary satisfaction out of deciding thus. If you say, "We're going out now," he'll most likely trot along happily, the decision having been kept out of his hands. Similarly with helping him finish a job that is too hard, like putting his rubbers on, it is better to do it than to ask, "Shall I help you?" There are many opportunities for choosing and deciding, even when adults limit them. The child decides whether to kiss, hug, and give other endearments, whether to finish his dinner and whether to urinate on the toilet or in his pants. The last decision mentioned, the question of toileting, is the one which, to the psychoanalysts, symbolizes the whole stage of developing autonomy. It is indeed an area where the sternest of parents has a hard time forcing the child and where the child can retain his autonomy under severe pressure. In the normal course of events in Western society, the child exercises autonomy as he brings his sphincters under control and takes on the toileting patterns approved by his family.

Autonomy in a group of nursery school children was measured by ratings of their behavior in separating themselves from their parents and becoming involved with peers and play in the nursery school [52]. Questionnaires answered by their parents showed the degree to which each parent expected autonomous behavior from the child. Significant relationships were found between the parents' expectations of autonomous behavior and the children's actual behavior. Autonomous behavior included practical independent performance which was helpful to the parent and also the child's insistence on doing for himself or acting on his own. For example, "Johnny is two years old. He refuses to eat at mealtime unless he can feed himself."

Autonomous behavior at $2\frac{1}{2}$ predicts nonverbal intelligence and cognitive style at age 6 [55]. Nursery school teachers rated young children on behavior scales which measured their seeking of physical contact and attention, orality (licking, drooling, thumb-sucking, and mouthing), and sustained directed activity. The last includes contentment and absorption in play and following through in play. Performance IQ (solving nonverbal problems) correlated with autonomy at the earlier age as expressed in sustained directed activity and lack of contact-seeking and attention-seeking. It seems reasonable that 2-year-olds who pursue their own play interests independently and persistently would develop better problem-solving abilities than would children who seek contact and help instead of behaving autonomously.

The negative side of a healthy sense of autonomy is a sense of shame and worthlessness. These negative feelings creep in when the youngster cannot choose enough and act independently enough, when the results of his choices and actions are disastrous, and when adults use shaming as a method of control. Because the young child is vulnerable to shaming, adults may use it as a discipline technique, not realizing its dangers for personality development [20]. When a person is shamed, he does not want to be seen or noticed. The use of shaming as a technique of control does not promote good behavior but, rather, defiance and trying to get away with doing what one wants to do. Another unfortunate outcome of poor guidance of autonomy is compulsive repetition of certain acts, a stubborn exerting of power. This type of behavior is probably the source of conforming rigidly to rules as written, in contrast to flexible interpretation of meaning.

> Outer control at this age, therefore, must be firmly reassuring. The infant must come to feel that the basic faith in existence, which is the lasting treasure saved from the rages of the oral stage, will not be jeopardized by this about-face of his, this sudden violent wish to have a choice, to appropriate demandingly, and to eliminate stubbornly. Firmness must protect him against the potential anarchy of his yet untrained sense of discrimination, his inability to hold on and to let go with discretion. As his environment encouraged him to "stand on his own feet," it must protect him against meaningless and arbitrary experiences of shame and of early doubt [20, p. 252].

### Initiative

Just as development of a sense of autonomy dominates the early part of the preschool period, the sense of initiative is the central theme of the latter part. Personality growth is never in a straight line. There is always some backing up and reworking of old problems. Even with a firm sense of trust, there are frights over Mother's being away too long or strangers threatening. Even with a strong sense of autonomy, a child occasionally asserts it in a temper tantrum, a refusal to eat, or a toilet "accident." Little threads of problems run through life as imperfections in trust and autonomy, demanding attention and solutions.

Now at 4 years or so, the sense of initiative claims the center of the stage. The preschool child is an explorer, curious and active. He seeks new experiences for their own sake, the sheer pleasure of sensing and knowing. He also seeks experience in order to fit it in with something he already knows and to make it more understandable. He pushes vigorously out into the world, seeking a wide range of information about it, about people and what they do, about what he himself can do. Grasping a piece of reality, like Mother's high heels and handbag, Daddy's briefcase, or a doctor's kit, he creates the experience he wants, trying on the role of a mother or father or doctor, contemplating what these adults do, imagining how it would be if he himself were doing it. Building a store with cartons, he becomes a storekeeper. He paints a picture. He creates a new world in a stream bed. It is at this stage that children put beans in their ears and stir eye shadow into cold cream. If the child's seeking is successful, then he finds a wide variety of things he can do, make, and create, with the approval of his family and other adults. If he succeeds, he continues as an older child and adult to look for new ideas, solutions, answers, reasons, creative experiences. Imagination will be discussed in greater detail in Chapter 7, where its development will be related to cognitive growth and where both these functions will be seen as integrated in play, which is the business of the preschool child.

Aggression, also, is a function of the sense of initiative, since aggression involves pushing out into the world and attacking. Since aggression is also involved with anger, its discussion will be postponed until Chapter 8, which deals with emotional development and control. Assertive behavior is similar to aggression in being a reaching out and pushing into the environment to explore and manipulate it. Assertion, unlike aggression, does not imply anger. Assertive behavior in 5-year-olds was studied by testing, observations, and teachers' ratings, focusing on the exploration-manipulation sort of behavior and upon destructiveness in the service of learning or exploring [17]. The test of instrumental destructiveness involved telling the child that he could get and keep an attractive top if he would first knock over a pile of plastic glasses that stood in front of the toy. Results showed that this test, as well as teachers' and observers' ratings, was correlated with intelligence as measured by the Stanford–Binet. The measures of assertion were reflections of the child's ability to interact with his environment and to master it. Since intelligence tests measure knowledge and mastery, the child who dealt assertively with his world would be more likely to score high on such tests.

Conscience begins to develop at this time, regulating initiative and imagination. The child takes the voice of his parents into himself, saying what he may do and what he may not do. When he does not obey it, he may feel guilty. Sometimes he even feels guilty for his thoughts and wishes which run counter to the commands of his conscience. His vigorous imagination can easily hit or kill people who oppose him or it can, more deviously, create a bear or a wolf to eat the annoying people. The bear may get out of control and threaten the child himself, especially in a dream. Conscience development will be considered further in the framework of parent–child relationships.

Exploration also involves noticing how other people solve problems and trying their solutions by imitating them. Not only are parents imitated, but peers, older children, and adults may also serve as models. Children select certain models to imitate and they also select certain behavior patterns from the models' repertory, rather than trying to imitate everything that certain models do. Styles of expressing curiosity were noted in a study in a Head Start setting [50]. Some children used mostly verbal methods, some visual, and others manipulative.

Thus do the forces of creativity and social control struggle in the person of a young child, producing dreams of beauty and fright, glimpses of new worlds of achievement, the constriction of guilt. The establishment of a healthy sense of initiative means that the child can interact vigorously under the control of a conscience that is strong enough but not too punishing.

**Activity and Passivity.** While the expression of initiative includes pushing out, exploring, and making beginnings, being active is also an aspect of initiative. Therefore, it is worthwhile to note what has been found about activity and passivity in the early years of life. Individual differences in activity have been observed in infancy, as well as during the preschool and school years [21, 51]. Differences were seen in motor activity and in sensitivity to the environment. Motor differences included those in total amount of activity and those in ways of using the body. For example, some babies were very active with their arms and legs, whereas others turned and rolled more. Some moved quickly, others slowly, some mildly, some forcefully. They varied in the distribution and length of periods of quiet and activity. Some children seemed to keep quiet in order to think [51, p. 5]. At each age, degree of activity and degree of perceptual sensitivity determine certain aspects of interactions with the environment, including people, and thus affect the course of personality development [21, pp. 21–29].

Another approach to the understanding of activity was through a longitudinal study which followed children from birth to maturity [37]. Passivity was defined as the tendency to acquiesce to or withdraw from frustrating situations, instead of dealing with them actively. The opposite of passivity, then, sounds very much like the sense of initiative. Passivity was found to be a highly stable personality characteristic during the first ten years of life. Another characteristic studied was dependence, defined as the child's tendency to seek affection, help, and company of female adults, usually his mother. The opposite of dependency also sounds like an aspect of initiative, since initiative includes independent action. Dependency was found to be a moderately stable personality characteristic during the first ten years of life [37, pp. 50–54].

**Achievement and Competence.** During the preschool years, when the development of the sense of initiative dominates life, it seems more important to get things started than to finish them. Planning, undertaking, exploring, pushing out, and attacking are all of the essence of this period. Achieving (finishing jobs, doing well) becomes much more important during the stage which follows, the period of the development of a sense of industry. Since preparations for each stage of personality development are made during preceding stages, some of the foundations for later achievement can be studied during the preschool years. The young child has experiences that affect his efforts, persistence, and expectations of himself in regard to excellence. As the youngster pushes forward to explore and to try new activities, his parents take certain attitudes toward what he is doing. Some parents hold high standards of excellence for their children; others hold lower standards. Some push children to do well; others let them do more as they will. Some give them a large measure of independence; others control them tightly. There are steps in between each of these pairs of extremes. Research shows that achievement motivation and behavior are affected by experience during the period of development of the sense of initiative and even more in the years which follow [14]. Observations at home and at school showed certain children to be consistently interested in achievement-oriented play. The mothers of these children tended to reward their achievement efforts and their seeking of approval and to ignore requests for help. These children, in contrast to those less interested in achievement, were less dependent upon adults for help and for emotional support [15].

Competence in preschool children is correlated with parental practices which are intellectually stimulating and somewhat tension producing, such as demands for mature behavior and firm discipline [4]. These conclusions came from factor-analytic studies of parent interviews and ratings of children's behavior. Parental techniques which fostered self-reliance, such as demanding self-control and encouraging independent decision making, promoted responsible, independent behavior. In another study [3], a group of preschool children were chosen for being highly socialized and independent, as shown by their self-reliance, exploring, self-assertion, self-control, and affiliation. The parents of these children, as contrasted with the parents of a control group, were consistent, loving, and demanding, respecting the child's decisions, using reason, and maintaining a firm stand when a stand was taken. These parents displayed high nurturance, high control, clear communication, and clear policies of regulation. Thus the parents encouraged initiative in children, but limited the area within which the child could operate. The children were therefore protected from disastrous failure while benefiting from appropriate freedom.

Parent–child interactions in the preschool years are related to achievement behavior at later ages. At age 8 to 10, boys with high achievement needs and high achievement ratings, as contrasted to low achievers, had mothers who had demanded more independence, maturity, and achievement of their sons and who also had rewarded them liberally for fulfilling the demands [80]. In other words, the mothers' demands and rewards during the preschool years were related to the children's achievement during the elementary school years. Figure 5–1 shows the number of demands for mastery and independence made between the ages of 1 and 10 on high-achieving and low-achieving boys. The development of achievement motivation becomes increasingly important during the early school-age period. An extensive body of research on achievement will be reported in Part III, which deals with that age level.

**Sex Differences.** Common observation indicates that boys explore the world more vigorously than do girls. Any teacher of young children will agree that, in general, boys are harder to control than girls. A study of dependency shown by children in the nursery school demonstrated greater dependency behavior in girls than in boys [31]. Boys have been found to be more curious than girls in their reactions to novelty in pictures and toys [46, 67].

Cultural influences in traditional Chinese and Japanese families encourage children to be dependent, obedient, and cautious, and discourage them from exploring, behaving impulsively, and deciding [39]. We have observed the same phenomena in India. Especially when children live in joint families, adults are ever present to supervise, restrain, and protect, preventing an active reaching out and intrusion by young children. Often we have seen young Indian children taken to parties or visiting by their parents. The little child sits beside the mother or close to her, simply looking and listening, or maybe daydreaming, or if given something to play with, quietly playing. An American child his age would most likely explore the room and objects in it, approach some of the people and intrude upon his mother's conversations. Such differences in Asian and American child behavior reflect different cultural values as well as child-rearing methods which support the values.

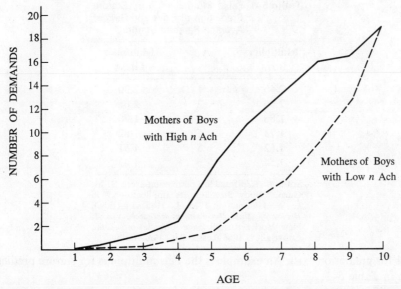

**Figure 5–1.** Demands for mastery and independence made by mothers of boys with high need for achievement and by mothers of boys with low need.

SOURCE: Reprinted by permission from M. R. Winterbottom, "The Relation of Need for Achievement to Learning Experiences in Independence and Mastery," in J. W. Atkinson [Ed.], *Motives in Fantasy, Action and Society*. Princeton, N.J.: Van Nostrand Co., 1958. Copyright © 1958, Van Nostrand Co.

## Physical Characteristics, Experiences, and Their Implications

Although much more independent than infants, preschool children are able to operate independently only within circumscribed areas. The protective and nurturing roles of parents are understood best in the light of the young child's physical characteristics.

### Growth Rates

**Height and Weight.** Growth in height is not so fast as it was during infancy. The growth rate decelerates slowly throughout the preschool period. At 2 years, a child has added 75 percent of his birth length to his height [10, p. 248]. At 4 years, he has added 100 percent to it. Thus the second 2-year period of life sees only one-third as much gain in height as do the first 2 years. A boy's height at 2 is about half of his adult height, a girl's is a little more than half. To estimate her adult height, double the height at 2 and subtract 10 or 12 centimeters [76]. Thus the first doubling of height takes place in 4 years while the doubling which results in the final height takes 16 years. Rate of weight gain follows a slow deceleration from 2 to 3 years and a gradual acceleration from 3 to 5. Birth weight is quadrupled by 2½, showing the rapid rate for weight gain in infancy. Between 2 and 5, the weight gain is less than the amount gained during the first year of life, showing the slower rate at which weight is gained in the preschool period as contrasted with infancy [10, p. 254]. Since the size of a child at any age bears some relation to his size at adulthood, it is possible to predict final height with fair accuracy. Several methods and

Table 5–1 Fels Multipliers for Stature Prediction of Boys and Girls of Average Parental Stature

| Multiplier BOYS | Age | Multiplier GIRLS |
|---|---|---|
| 2.46 | 1 | 2.30 |
| 2.06 | 2 | 2.01 |
| 1.86 | 3 | 1.76 |
| 1.73 | 4 | 1.62 |
| 1.62 | 5 | 1.51 |
| 1.54 | 6 | 1.43 |

SOURCE: Reprinted by permission from S. M. Garn, "Body Size and Its Implications," in L. W. Hoffman and M. L. Hoffman (Eds.), *Review of Child Development Research*, Vol. 2. New York: Russell Sage Foundation, 1966. Copyright © 1966 Russell Sage Foundation.

tables for prediction exist. An example is the Fels multipliers for stature prediction, given in Table 5–1.

Sex differences in height show up in these early years, girls progressing faster toward maturity than boys. The same is true of weight; girls are farther along toward their mature weights than are boys of the same age. However, during the preschool period, boys are slightly heavier and taller than girls, on the average, since their eventual heights and weights are greater.

Slow growth in height and weight has been reported for children in lower socio-economic groups all over the world, including the United States. The bulk of children in underdeveloped countries are retarded in height and weight, the usual average being below the sixteenth percentile for well-nourished children in the United States and Western Europe. In these same countries, the growth of children in the favored socioeconomic groups has been found to be comparable with that of children in the United States and Western Europe [80]. Such studies strongly suggest that nutrition, rather than racial or genetic factors, plays the main role in the growth failure occurring in deprived parts of the world [81, 34].

**Tissues and Proportions.** Rates of growth change for various tissues, as well as for height and weight. The growth of fat and muscle is especially interesting, because of the consequent change from babylike to childlike appearance. Fat increases rapidly during the first 9 months of life, decreases rapidly in thickness from 9 months to 2½ years, and decreases slowly until 5½. At 5½, it is half as thick as at 9 months. Thus does the chubby baby grow into a slender child. Muscle tissue follows a different pattern, growing at a decelerating rate throughout infancy and childhood, lagging behind other types of tissue growth until the puberal growth spurt. (See Figure 5–2.)

Sex differences show up in tissue growth, too. Boys have more muscle and bone than girls; girls have more fat than boys. Of course, there are individual differences, too, in all aspects of growth. Individual differences in amount of fat are greater than sex differences [10, pp. 260–262].

Bodily proportions change due to differential growth rates of various parts of the body. The principle of developmental direction is illustrated here by the growth which takes place in a cephalo-caudal (head to tail) direction. Development is at first more rapid in the head end of the body, with the tail end reaching maturity

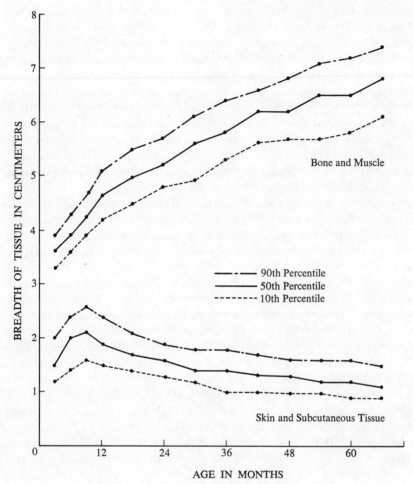

**Figure 5–2.** Rates of growth of bone and muscle tissue and of skin and fat.

Source: Reprinted by permission from M. E. Breckenridge and M. N. Murphy, *Growth and Development of the Young Child*, 8th edition. Copyright © 1969, W. B. Saunders Company.

later. At age 2, the head is still large in relation to the trunk and legs. The abdomen and chest measure about the same but after 2, the chest becomes larger in relation to the abdomen [76, p. 84]. The abdomen sticks out, since a relatively short trunk has to accommodate the internal organs, some of which are closer to adult size than is the trunk. Thus the toddler is top-heavy. The head itself grows according to the same principle, with the upper part closer to completion than the lower part. A large cranium and a small lower jaw give the characteristic baby look to a 2-year-old's face. These proportions, plus fat, result in the diminutive nature of immature creatures which adults find emotionally appealing. Americans call baby humans, puppies, kittens, and other animal infants cute. Germans add *chen* to their names and French *ette*. As the legs, trunk, and jaw grow in relation to the head, the baby loses his "cute" or diminutive look. This is what happens to the human baby between 2 and 5 years of age. By the time he starts to kindergarten or first grade, his proportions more nearly resemble those of the children in the rest of the grades than they resemble his preschool brothers and sisters at home.

Bones of preschool children have their own qualitative characteristics as well as proportional. The younger the child the more cartilage there is in his skeletal system and the less the density of minerals in the bones. The joints are more flexible; the ligaments and muscles are attached more tenuously than in an older child. Thus it is easier to damage young bones, joints, and muscles by pressure and pulling and by infections. The skeletal system is very responsive to changes in environment that produce malnutrition, fatigue, and injury [10, p. 267]. Bone maturation, evaluated by the thickness, number, and shape of small bones showing in X rays of the hand and wrist, has been found to be retarded by two or three years in preschool children of poor, underdeveloped countries [61]. Head circumference was found to be smaller in malnourished preschool children as compared with well-nourished children of the same ethnic origin [61].

The brain is more nearly complete, as to total weight, than the rest of the body. By 3 years, the brain is about 75 percent of its adult weight and by 6 years almost 90 percent. At age 5 the total nervous system is one-twentieth the total weight, in contrast to the adult nervous system, which is one-fiftieth the total weight [76, p. 217].

The fact that there is relatively little increase in brain weight at this time does not mean that brain development is not proceeding rapidly. There is every reason to believe that during the preschool period, there is a continuous increase in the number, size, and complexity of connections between cells in the cortex and in connections between the different levels of the brain [70]. Evidence strongly suggests that Piaget's successive stages of cognitive growth occur as the cortex matures and becomes progressively organized.

The patterning of brain waves shown by electroencephalograms shows characteristic changes during the preschool period [75]. The very slow rhythms prominent in infancy decline, and a faster rhythm reaches its peak of frequency in the preschool period. It has been observed that the time of the rise in frequency of the preschool rhythm is associated with the time of the rise in frequency of temper outbursts. Specific incidents of temper outbursts were associated with immediate, specific increases in this type of brain wave. Another rhythm emerges at about age 5 [76, p. 220].

Of the special senses, *vision* and *taste* are noteworthy in the preschool years. The macula of the retina is not completely developed until about 6 years, and the eyeball does not reach adult size until 12 or 14 [76]. The young child is farsighted because of the shape of the eyeball. Estimates for visual acuity, taken from several studies [19] are: at 2 years, 20/100 to 20/40; at 3, 20/50 to 20/30; at 4, 20/40 to 20/20; at 5, 20/35 to 20/25; at 6, 20/27. Thus even at 6 years of age, the estimated acuity is not yet 20/20. Investigations of the ways in which children use their visual mechanism show that they function in immature ways during the preschool years [24]. Vision screening by trained nonprofessionals has been the means of finding preschool children who need the attention of professionals [29]. An analysis of 109 vision-screening projects shows that 6 percent of the children were referred for professional eye examinations and that 75 percent of those examined had abnormal eye conditions. One to 3 percent of preschool children require glasses [71].

Taste buds are more generously distributed in the young child than in the adult, being scattered on the insides of the cheeks and the throat as well as on the tongue. He probably is highly sensitive to taste. The ear too is significantly different in the young child because of the Eustachian tube which connects the middle ear with the throat. The tube is shorter, more horizontal, and wider in the infant and preschool child than in the older child and adult. Invading organisms find an easy entrance route from the young child's throat to his middle ear. Hence he is more susceptible to ear infections than is the older child.

The internal organs show various immaturities, with implications for child care. For example, the stomach, at 4 to 6 years, has less than half the capacity of the average adult stomach. Calorie requirements at that age, however, are more than half as great as that of an active adult. The shape of the stomach is straighter than in older children and more directly upright than an infant's or older child's. Thus it empties rather readily in either direction. The lining of the digestive tract is easily irritated by seasonings and roughage. The respiratory system matures sufficiently during the preschool years to establish the adult type of breathing, combining abdominal and chest movements. However, air passages are relatively small at this time and the lymphatic system prominent so that tonsils and adenoids are at their maximum size.

### Methods of Assessing Growth

A child can be compared with other children his age or he can be evaluated in terms of his own past growth. As was mentioned in Chapter 3, his heredity can be taken into account by using a mid-parent height table when considering his height. Speed of growth can be calculated at two points in time. An individual's speed of growth can be compared with that of other children.

**Comparisons with Peers.** Height-weight-age tables represent the most common instrument used for making such assessments of growth. Tables 5–2, 5–3, 5–4, and 5–5 give for each age and sex the heights and weights which are at seven points on a percentile scale [76, pp. 89–92]. For example, 4-year-old David is 42¼ inches tall and weighs 34 pounds. Table 5–4 shows that he weighs less than 75 percent of children his age, whereas Table 5–2 indicates his height to be above that of 75 percent of children. These figures suggest that David is slim, but they tell nothing about his body build. Width is taken into account by another type of table [56], combining age, height, weight, and width. This rather complicated table has been little used for practical purposes.

**Comparisons with Self.** Another method of assessing growth is by means of a special record form on which repeated measurements are entered. The Wetzel

**Table 5–2**  Height Percentile Table for Boys from age 2½ through age 5½

| Age | Length in Inches | | | | | | |
|---|---|---|---|---|---|---|---|
| | 3% | 10% | 25% | 50% | 75% | 90% | 97% |
| 2½ yr. | 34¼ | 34¾ | 35½ | 36¼ | 37 | 38 | 39¼ |
| 3  yr. | 35¾ | 36¼ | 37 | 38 | 38¾ | 39½ | 40½ |
| 3½ yr. | 37 | 37¾ | 38½ | 39¼ | 40¼ | 41 | 42 |
| 4  yr. | 38½ | 39 | 39¾ | 40¾ | 42 | 42¾ | 43½ |
| 4½ yr. | 39½ | 40¼ | 41 | 42 | 43¼ | 44¼ | 45 |
| 5  yr. | 40¼ | 41¼ | 42¼ | 43¼ | 44½ | 45½ | 46½ |
| 5½ yr. | 41½ | 42½ | 43¾ | 45 | 46¼ | 47¼ | 48 |

SOURCE: From *Growth and Development of Children*, 5th edition, by Ernest H. Watson and George H. Lowrey. Copyright © 1967, Year Book Medical Publishers, Inc., Chicago. Used by permission of Year Book Medical Publishers.

**Table 5–3** Height Percentile Table for Girls from Age 2½ through Age 5½

| Age | Length in Inches | | | | | | |
|---|---|---|---|---|---|---|---|
| | 3% | 10% | 25% | 50% | 75% | 90% | 97% |
| 2½ yr. | 33¼ | 34 | 35¼ | 36 | 37 | 38 | 39 |
| 3 yr. | 34¾ | 35½ | 36¾ | 37¾ | 38½ | 39¾ | 40¾ |
| 3½ yr. | 36¼ | 37 | 38 | 39¼ | 40¼ | 41½ | 42½ |
| 4 yr. | 37½ | 38½ | 39½ | 40½ | 41½ | 43 | 44¼ |
| 4½ yr. | 38½ | 39¾ | 40¾ | 42 | 43 | 44¾ | 45¾ |
| 5 yr. | 40 | 41 | 42 | 43 | 44¼ | 45½ | 46¾ |
| 5½ yr. | 41¼ | 42½ | 43½ | 44½ | 45¾ | 46¾ | 48 |

SOURCE: From *Growth and Development of Children*, 5th edition, by Ernest H. Watson and George H. Lowrey, Copyright © 1967, Year Book Medical Publishers, Inc., Chicago. Used by permission of Year Book Medical Publishers.

**Table 5–4** Weight Percentile Table for Boys Age 2½ through Age 5½

| Age | Weight in Pounds | | | | | | |
|---|---|---|---|---|---|---|---|
| | 3% | 10% | 25% | 50% | 75% | 90% | 97% |
| 2½ yr. | 25¼ | 26½ | 28½ | 30 | 32¼ | 34½ | 37 |
| 3 yr. | 27 | 28¾ | 30¼ | 32¼ | 34½ | 36¾ | 39¼ |
| 3½ yr. | 28½ | 30½ | 32¼ | 34¼ | 36¾ | 39 | 41½ |
| 4 yr. | 30 | 32 | 34 | 36½ | 39 | 41½ | 44¼ |
| 4½ yr. | 31½ | 33¾ | 35¾ | 38½ | 41½ | 44 | 47½ |
| 5 yr. | 34 | 36 | 38½ | 41½ | 45¼ | 48¼ | 51¾ |
| 5½ yr. | 36¼ | 38¾ | 42 | 45½ | 49¼ | 53 | 56½ |

SOURCE: From *Growth and Development of Children*, 5th edition, by Ernest H. Watson and George H. Lowrey. Copyright © 1967, Year Book Medical Publishers, Inc., Chicago. Used by permission of Year Book Medical Publishers.

**Table 5–5** Weight Percentile Table for Girls Age 2½ through Age 5½

| Age | Weight in Pounds | | | | | | |
|---|---|---|---|---|---|---|---|
| | 3% | 10% | 25% | 50% | 75% | 90% | 97% |
| 2½ yr. | 23½ | 25½ | 27½ | 29½ | 32 | 35½ | 38¼ |
| 3 yr. | 25½ | 27½ | 29½ | 31¾ | 34½ | 37½ | 41¾ |
| 3½ yr. | 27½ | 29½ | 31½ | 34 | 37 | 40½ | 45¼ |
| 4 yr. | 29¼ | 31¼ | 33½ | 36¼ | 39½ | 43½ | 48¼ |
| 4½ yr. | 30¾ | 33 | 35¼ | 38½ | 42 | 46¾ | 51 |
| 5 yr. | 33 | 35½ | 38 | 41 | 44½ | 48¾ | 52¼ |
| 5½ yr. | 35 | 38 | 40¾ | 44 | 47¼ | 51¼ | 55½ |

SOURCE: From *Growth and Development of Children*, 5th edition, by Ernest H. Watson and George H. Lowrey. Copyright © 1967, Year Book Medical Publishers, Inc., Chicago. Used by permission of Year Book Medical Publishers.

Grid [77] is a well-known example of this method. The Grid can be used to indicate the child's body type as obese, stocky, good (average), borderline, fair, or poor and to compare a child with other children in height, width, body volume, and rate of growth. The child can be compared with himself at any time in the past. Growth can be seen as even or uneven. The Wetzel Grid is used by physicians for supervising health and growth.

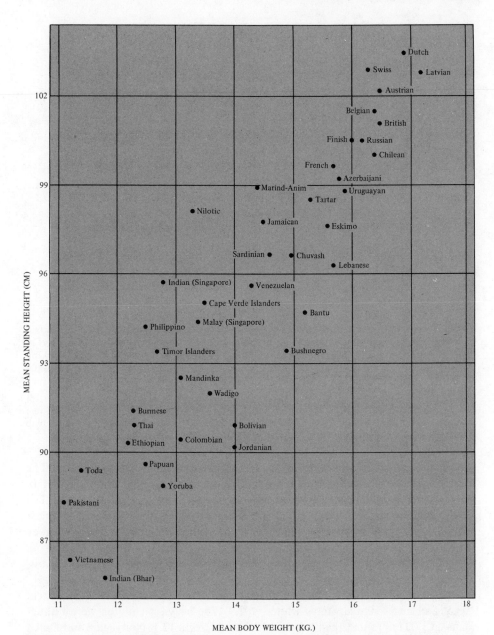

**Figure 5–3.** Mean heights and weights of preschool children in different parts of the world.

SOURCE: Reprinted by permission from H. V. Meredith, "Body Size of Contemporary Groups of Preschool Children Studied in Different Parts of the World," *Child Development*, **39**, Figure 1, p. 359. Copyright © 1968, by the Society for Research in Child Development, Inc.

**Cross-Culture Comparisons.** Body size varies in different parts of the world. Physical measurements on 160 samples of 4-year-old children represent Africa, Asia, Australia, Europe, the Americas, West Indies, and the Malay archipelago [47]. These samples differed as much as 7 inches in average height and 13 pounds in average weight.

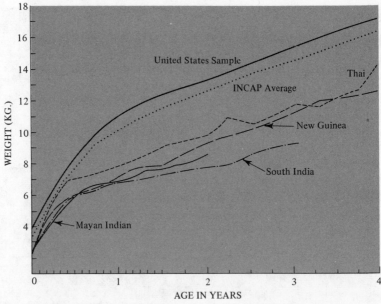

**Figure 5–4.** Average weight-for-age of children in four underdeveloped countries, shown in relation to average weight according to the standards of the Institute for Nutrition in Central America and Panama. The median of the Iowa curves is also indicated, showing that averages for normal Central American children are very close to those for a sample of North American children.

SOURCE: Data from M. Béhar, "Prevalence of Malnutrition Among Preschool Children of Developing Countries," in N. S. Scrimshaw and J. E. Gordon [Eds.], *Malnutrition, Learning and Behavior*. Cambridge: M.I.T. Press, 1968. Also from R. L. Jackson and H. G. Kelly, "Growth Charts for Use in Pediatric Practice," *Journal of Pediatrics*, 1945, **27**, 215–229.

The shortest group was from Bihar, an Indian state known for its famines. The sample of over 3000 children averaged 85.8 centimeters in height. The diet in Bihar is commonly deficient in calories, proteins, calcium, and vitamins. The Bihar children were fifth lightest, at an average weight of 11.8 kg. The lightest sample was from East Pakistan, another area prone to famine and found by a survey team to be deficient in total calories, protein, vitamin A, riboflavin, and iron. The Pakistani 4-year-olds were taller than only three other groups: the Indians, Kwango Negroes, and Vietnamese.

The tallest sample was Czech, at 103.8 centimeters. Next tallest were Dutch, 103.5, and next, United States whites, 102.9. The heaviest children were Lithuanians, at 17.3 kilograms, then Latvian, 17.2, and Czech, 17.1. Norwegian and Dutch were also heavier than United States white children, who averaged 16.7 kilograms.

In the middle of the height ranks were Polynesians, at 96.6 centimeters. Children in the West Indies and Jamaica were midway in weight, averaging 14.5 pounds. Figure 5–3 shows the relation between mean height and mean weight in some of the samples studied.

Growth in weight among preschool children from several underdeveloped countries is shown in Figure 5–4. The children are compared with INCAP standards (Institute of Nutrition of Central America and Panama). The children from Thailand and New Guinea followed an almost normal course of growth for the first 3 months, fell farther and farther below normal for the next year, and then maintained a low level of weight growth. The Guatemalan and Indian children showed a pattern similar to the other two groups in the first 3 months, but after that diverged farther from the INCAP standard. As far as these graphs show, the children do not seem to be dropping farther below the standard line.

*Skeletal Age*

Another way of assessing growth is to measure the maturity of the skeleton, by means of X rays. Early in prenatal life the precursors of most bones appear as cartilage. (The bones of the upper part of the skull develop from membranous tissue.) The cartilage is gradually replaced by bone beginning in the sixth week after fertilization. From this time until the individual is in his twenties bone is being laid down, starting from centers of ossification which appear in highly uniform places in each cartilage. Ossification takes place in the cells through a process of formation of organic salts of calcium and phosphorus. The centers of ossification appear in a fairly uniform order. Bones grow in width or diameter by the addition of bony material on the outer surface of the bone underneath the periosteum (a membrane which surrounds the bone). Long bones grow longer by the addition of ossified materials at their ends. During the growth period, therefore, any given bit of bone is overlaid by later ossified material, not replaced by it.

In long bones another ossification center appears at the end of the cartilage which forms the model of the growing bone. This separate piece of bone is called the epiphysis. The cartilage between the epiphysis and the shaft of the bone (the diaphysis) appears to become thinner and thinner as growth proceeds. Eventually, in normal human beings the epiphysis and diaphysis fuse into one piece of bone, and lengthwise growth in that bone ceases. Just as the timetable of the appearance of centers of ossification is fairly regular for the individual, so the fusion of epiphyses and diaphyses follows a time pattern [57]. As each piece of bone grows, its size and shape changes in a systematic fashion which varies relatively little from one person to another.

All of these changes in bony tissue can be followed in X rays of the bones. The cartilaginous material is transparent to X rays; the ossified material, opaque. Most of the studies of skeletal development have been done using X rays of the left hand and wrist. The developed film is compared with standard illustrations in order to match it as closely as possible to one of them. The skeletal status of a child is expressed in terms of skeletal age, which corresponds to the chronological age at which the children on whom the standards were based usually attained that same degree of skeletal development [26]. Mental age, which is to be discussed in the next chapter, is a similar derived measure of development and is defined in much the same way as skeletal age.

**Bone Growth as a Record of Health.** X rays of the hand yield information about the quality of a child's growth. Lightly mineralized bones may be due to insufficient intake of calcium, or insufficient metabolism of calcium, or both. An X ray film may therefore yield supplemental information concerning the nutritional status of a child. Some kinds of illnesses and other traumatic events in the child's life may result in bands of increased density of the bone at the growing end of the long

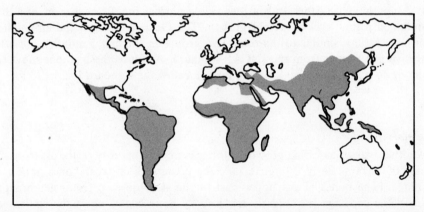

**Figure 5–5.** Geographic distribution of protein-calorie malnutrition shown by shading.

SOURCE: Fig. 8, p. 40, adapted from M. Béhar, "Prevalence of Malnutrition Among Preschool Children of Developing Countries." In N. S. Scrimshaw and J. E. Gordon [Eds.], *Malnutrition, Learning and Behavior*. Cambridge: M.I.T. Press, 1968, pp. 30–42.

bones [26, p. 19]. If they occur, they become permanent records of disturbances in the body's metabolism during that period of the child's life.

The principle of critical periods (Chapter 17) is apparent in the disruption of the orderly sequence of appearance of ossification centers during illness [26, p. 18]. If there is a disturbance in the calcium metabolism, such as occurs during illnesses, at the time when an ossification center is due to appear, its appearance may be delayed until a later time, even until after the appearance of the next scheduled center. When this happens, an X ray film taken subsequently, even perhaps several years later, will show imbalances in the development of individual bones and centers of ossification. Since the age of the bones that are present can be judged from their appearance, it becomes possible to make a judgment as to the time of the crisis and about how severe was the impact on the skeleton (and presumably the total organism). Later X ray examinations can tell at what point the child has made complete recovery.

### Feeding the Young Child

Over 60 percent of the world's preschool children are malnourished [5]. This figure represents 300 million of the 400 million preschool children who live in the underdeveloped areas of the world shown in the shaded portions of the map in Figure 5–5. The figure is conservative, since over 75 percent of these children are underweight. The 60 percent does not include malnourished children in the more prosperous parts of the world; and yet in our own country, a recent nutrition survey found large numbers of children suffering from stunted growth and deficient in many different nutrients [60].

An analysis of the food intake of 121 healthy, middle-class preschool children showed that recommendations for iron were not being met [16]. Although the average child received enough vitamin C, there were a substantial number who had intakes of less than 50 percent of the recommended allowance. While one child may not get enough of a certain nutrient because his mother does not offer it to him, another may refuse to eat any or enough of the food she does give him.

**Nutrients.** Since the majority of the world's children do not have an ample diet

**Figure 5–6.** A two-year-old child with marasmus was photographed on admission to the Nutrition Rehabilitation Unit, Kampala, and again after six weeks on a high protein diet based on local foods.

SOURCE: D. B. Jelliffe, *Child Nutrition in Developing Countries*. Washington, D.C. Agency for International Development, 1969.

from which to select, the most pressing nutritional problem is to make enough good food available to all. The problem is political, economic, agricultural, educational, religious, and social. Even when a fairly good diet is available, young children often do not get full benefit of it. If they are simply expected to eat what they can of the family diet, they may have to contend with peppers and strong seasonings which may damage their gastric systems [11]. A nutritionist [79] who has observed African children for 40 years comments that poor preparation of food, methods of presenting it, and timing of meals are important factors in pre-school malnutrition. The bad effects of emotional disturbances, and excessive bulk, roughage, and spices have not been acknowledged sufficiently. When the culture recognizes that young children need special diets, the food offered is usually high in starch and low in protein. Thus the 4-year-old, who needs 50 percent more protein per pound of body weight than his father, receives bananas, arrowroot, maize, and rice gruel while his father gets meat or beans. The problem of the man getting the best food was mentioned in the discussion of pregnancy. The inequity continues throughout the childhood period, being most serious when growth is most rapid. The Food and Nutrition Board of the National Research Council regularly publishes recommended allowances of food elements for people of all ages. The most recent table of recommended nutrients can be found in Appendix

A. The following guide (Agricultural Research Service) for feeding the preschool child translates the nutrients into foods for each day:

> 3 or more cups of milk and milk products
> 2 or more servings of meat, poultry, fish, and eggs
> 4 or more servings of vegetables and fruits, including a citrus fruit or other fruit or vegetable high in vitamin C, and a dark-green or deep-yellow vegetable for vitamin A at least every other day
> 4 or more servings of bread and cereal of whole grain, enriched or re-stored variety
> Plus other foods as needed to provide additional energy and other food values

Figures are not to be taken completely literally. Individuals vary in the amounts they need and in the amounts they eat from one day to another and from one meal to another. If the foods offered are chosen along the lines of this plan, most preschool children will take what they need from it.

**Timing.** Because a small child's capacity is limited while his needs for growth-promoting and protective foods are great, his nutritional program merits careful planning. Menus and timing are both important. Although feeding a new baby when he cries for food contributes to the early building of a sense of trust, the preschool child benefits from a structured program, including regular mealtimes that fit his stage of maturity. If the child comes to meals hungry but not famished and exercised but not exhausted, he is likely to take in adequate nutrients. For most American children, it works out well to have three meals a day, with a snack in the middle of the morning and another in the middle of the afternoon. The snacks can be planned as to time, quality, and quantity to make the youngster appropriately hungry at family mealtimes. If completely unplanned, snacks are all too prone to be long on carbohydrates and fats and short on proteins, minerals, and vitamins. With his limited capacity for intake and high need for growth-promoting foods, a preschool child cannot afford to eat many empty calories (foods devoid of proteins, minerals, and vitamins). With good planning, eating and sleeping can be tied together in rhythms which assure adequate sleep for the young child. Insufficient sleep leads to fatigue which depresses the appetite.

**Sensory Aspects.** Taste sensitivity varies from one individual to another, in preschool children as well as in older children and adults. An investigation [38] of preschool children's thresholds for the basic tastes—salt, sweet, bitter, and sour—showed degrees of sensitivity to all four tastes to be highly correlated. Preschool children tended to be at the extreme ends of the scale for tasting bitter. That is, they either tasted it or they did not, whereas for sweet, salt, and sour, they could be arranged into groups of high, medium, and low sensitivity. The number of subjects reporting that they were always hungry for meals increased as taste sensitivity decreased. Breakfast was the meal most enjoyed, in contrast to teen-age girls, who have been found to enjoy breakfast least.

Nutritionists recommend variety in the textures of foods which make up a meal. A combination of crisp, chewy, and soft foods is usually enjoyed. Common observation, as well as research [18], shows that preschool children often accept a raw vegetable in preference to the same vegetable cooked. Such a preference may be based on flavor as well as texture. None of the foods liked best by preschool children contained anything gritty or stringy [38].

Taste is not the only sense involved in eating. Sensations of touch come from fingers as well as mouth when young children eat. They often want to feel the slipperiness of gelatin and spaghetti, the crinkliness of lettuce, and the cloudlike softness of a soufflé. Bright colors and color contrasts are thought to be effective in making meals attractive to children as well as to adults. Young children prefer lukewarm food to hot food [10, p. 201]. The sense of smell doubtless plays an important part in enjoyment of eating.

Favorite foods, according to mothers' reports on what preschool children ate, were headed by meats [16]. Next in order came fruits, sweets, and cereals. While some vegetables such as beets and corn were liked and eaten by many children, vegetables were most often mentioned as disliked foods. The most disliked vegetable was lima beans, with spinach, squash, asparagus, and sweet potatoes also unpopular. Fourteen out of 121 children refused all vegetables. Twenty-two specific vegetables were refused by one or more children.

**Emotional Aspects.** Emotional surroundings can enhance or depress appetite. Conversely, hunger disposes the child toward anger outbursts, as seen in Chapter 4. Excitement and upset conditions cause the stomach to stop its movements. To eat with the family may be too stimulating for a young child, or it may add to his happiness and feelings of belonging, depending on what goes on at the family table. Whatever the arrangements, the preschool child has the best chance of eating an adequate diet in an atmosphere that is calm and pleasant.

**Avoiding Problems.**   The year between age 2 and 3 is a time when eating problems often begin. Because the rate of growth has slowed down appetite is likely to be smaller. Parents, remembering the joyous abandon with which their baby waded into his food, may worry when they see that the same child at 2½ toys with his food and fusses over what he will eat and what he will not eat. Urging and forcing at this point often prolong and complicate the problem. Eager to exercise his autonomy, the 2-year-old wants to choose and decide for himself. It is satisfying to decide to eat a small serving and then to ask for more or to refuse it; it can be very annoying to have too large an amount presented, especially if poked at you in spoonfuls. If the child can do it himself, his sense of autonomy is enhanced. He can make progress with a spoon and even more with his fingers if given foods that are easy to pick up. Custard and soup are easier to drink than to spoon up. The young child profits from all arrangements which facilitate self-help and from wide limits within which to do it himself. He does need limits, though, for healthy development of the sense of autonomy. The child suffers, as well as the family, when he is allowed to throw his applesauce on the floor or to grab the food from his neighbor's plate. It is important for him to feel that what he does is all right, and for him to have that feeling, his behavior has to be acceptable to the people around him.

## Planning for Sleep and Rest

Sleep is a protective function which allows for repair and recovery of tissues after activity. Cognition is more adequate and emotional life more positive under conditions of enough sleep.

As children mature, they sleep less. They also change in the proportion of the two types of sleep, as Figure 5–7 shows [59]. Children and adults dream during the rapid eye movement (REM) phase of sleep, which seems to be essential to psychological well-being. REM sleep makes up about 25 percent of sleep at age 2, and nonrapid eye movement (NREM) about 75 percent. Between ages 3 and 5, REM

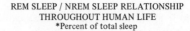

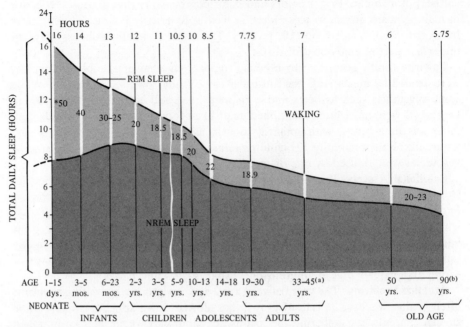

**Figure 5–7.** Ontogenetic development of the human sleep-dream cycle.

SOURCE: Reprinted by permission from H. P. Roffwarg, J. N. Muzio, and W. C. Dement, "Ontogenetic Development of the Human Sleep-Dream Cycle," *Science*, **152**, 604–619, 29 April, 1966. Copyright 1966 by the American Association for the Advancement of Science. Revised since publication in *Science* by Dr. Roffwarg.

constitutes about 20 percent of sleep. The average total hours of sleep at age 2 to 3 is almost 12 and at age 3 to 5, about 11. During the second year a common pattern is two naps a day and an all-night sleep. One nap is more usual between age 2 and 5 and after that, no nap. In some cultures, an afternoon nap is normal for everybody, adults as well as children. Children who had recently given up napping, a group between 4½ and 7 years, were found to take a longer time than children who napped and also a longer time than older children to get into REM sleep [59]. The 4½ to 7 group had a long period of deep NREM sleep before starting REM, suggesting that they were especially fatigued.

Children vary widely, in hours of sleep, consistency of patterns, distribution of sleep between night and day, soundness of sleep, and effects of various influences on sleep. How much sleep is enough? This is a very difficult question to answer with scientific evidence or even to answer in a home situation. A practical way for adults to judge whether children are getting enough sleep is to use as criteria such signs as readiness to get up in the morning, good appetite, emotional relaxation, cheerfulness, warm skin with good color, bright eyes, good posture, activeness in play, curiosity, enthusiasm.

Pediatricians have commented that mothers often find it more difficult to let children establish their own sleep patterns than to let them regulate their own feeding [10, p. 263]. Only 7 percent of parents in an American study [62, p. 269] and 9 percent in an English study [53, p. 246] said that they had no particular bedtime and let the child go to bed when he liked. The majority of parents had a certain bed hour in mind, but they varied considerably as to how strictly they maintained it. Among the English parents variations in strictness were related to class, those in higher occupations reporting more insistence upon prompt bed-going.

While unspecified bed hours may be infrequent, many children manage to post-pone bed-going and sleep, with the result that they sleep for shorter periods of time than children who go to bed promptly. Whether permissively reared children get enough sleep is a difficult question to answer because of the problem of defining *enough* sleep. In countries such as Italy and India, where babies and preschool children go out in the evening with their parents, falling asleep here and there on a friend's sofa or an extra chair at a concert, we have not noticed hyper-activity or signs of fatigue. Young children seemed to sit around more than Americans, but in a relaxed, not tense, way. Extra sitting around might be due to more relaxed adults, fewer toys, less stimulating conditions, and possibly lower available energy due to poor nutrition.

**Avoiding Problems.** Children generally benefit from parental supervision which makes regular sleep and rest a part of their lives. At developmental periods when certain influences disturb sleep, guidance is appropriate. For instance, toward the end of the first year, when strangers are recognized as strange and frightening, it is important for baby-sitters to be well acquainted with the baby, in order to prevent fright when he wakens from sleep. In the latter part of the second year and for some time after that, when motor activities are thrilling and the sense of autonomy is at a crucial stage of growth, a child may find it very hard to accept bed and sleep. Here is where a routine and careful guidance can prevent sleep problems from getting established. It is easiest to go to bed and to sleep after a period when stimulation has been cut down (that is, excitement minimized), and when a regular series of steps toward bed (such as washing, tooth brushing, story, putting teddy bear in bed), and an affectionately firm parent have indicated that sleep is imminent. Dreams are likely to be disturbing, because they are not clearly distinguished from reality. Reassurance after a fright or disturbance is conducive to sleep, as long as it is calm, confident, and given in the child's room. When parents make a big entertainment production out of the incident or take the youngster into their bed, reassurance may come to be a goal in itself.

## Illness and Accidents

**Prevention.** Maintaining life and health in young children is no simple matter for parents, even in the favored environment of western civilization. (In some parts of the world, the odds are against an infant's surviving.) Preventive care means taking a young child regularly to a physician or to a well-baby clinic, where he is immunized against diseases, assessed as to growth and health, and his mother is given advice as to nutrition, physical care, and attention to defects. Dental care is necessary from the preschool period onward. It has been estimated that among American children under 5 years of age, 10 percent have more than eight cavities [7, p. 5]. In areas without fluoridated water, 70 to 80 percent of preschool children have decay requiring treatment, whereas in communities with fluoridation, only 30 to 40 percent suffer such decay [71].

Promotion of health and growth through routines of feeding, sleep, and activity have been discussed. Parents also have the jobs of promoting community health

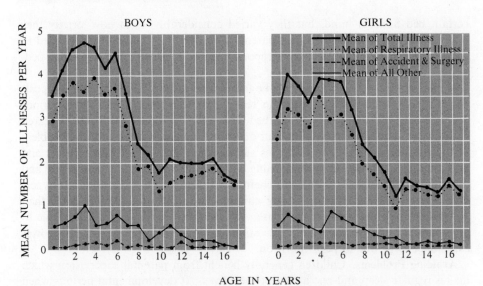

**Figure 5–8.** Incidence of illnesses and certain types of illnesses in boys and girls.
SOURCE: Reprinted by permission from I. Valadian, H. C. Stuart, and R. B. Reed, "Studies of Illnesses of Children Followed from Birth to Eighteen Years," *Monographs of The Society for Research in Child Development*, **26**:3, Figure 13. Copyright © 1961, The Society for Research in Child Development, Inc.

measures, supervising general hygiene in the home, nursing ill children, and keeping children from injury. Although most of the serious childhood diseases are preventable through immunization and many of the lesser illnesses are preventable through home hygiene, many respiratory disturbances and some gastrointestinal illnesses are common even in preschool children living under favorable circumstances. The immaturity of the systems involved makes them prone to infections and disturbances. As shown in Figure 5–8, the peak period for American children's illnesses, with respiratory ailments predominating, is the time from age 2 to 6.

**Accidents.** A young child is more likely to die from an accident than from any of the next five ranking causes of death [49]. Figure 5–9 illustrates this fact, showing that 37 percent of male deaths and 32 percent of female deaths between the ages of 1 and 4 were caused by accidents. These rates are over three and a half times the death rate from pneumonia, the second ranking cause, and nearly four and a half times that from cancer. The accident rates have increased during the past decade largely because of the increase in number of motor vehicle accidents. The other main types of accidents to young children are from traffic, fires, explosions, burns, drowning, poisoning, falls, and inhaling or ingesting food and other objects. Supervision of children outdoors is thus seen to be vital—not only telling them what not to do but watching them and keeping them out of the way of traffic, water, and other hazards. Making and keeping the home safe for young children require constant planning and vigilance. Over two fifths of accidents to young children occur in the home.

Another Metropolitan Life Insurance study [48] showed that about 25 percent of the annual deaths from accidental poisoning in the United States were deaths of children between 2 and 4 years of age. The agents of death were chiefly aspirin and other salicylates, petroleum products, lead, and household pesticides. The obvious implications are that safety of preschool children requires keeping them

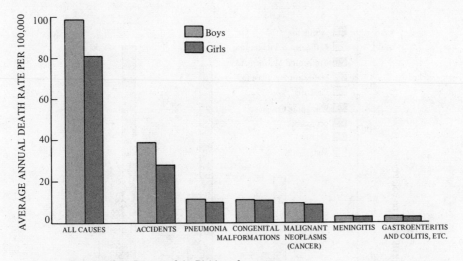

Source:  Basic data from Reports of the Division of
         Vital Statistics, National Center for Health Statistics.

**Figure 5–9.** Accidents and other major causes of death among children between 1 and 4 years of age.

SOURCE: Reprinted by permission from *Statistical Bulletin*, Metropolitan Life Insurance Company, September 1969.

away from many substances of common use in the home. Saying *no* is not enough at this age. Since preschool children tend to be good climbers, the problem of where to keep poisons out of their grasp is an important one to solve.

Studies on children over 6 indicate that accident-proneness is associated with stereotyped patterns of impulsively discharging anxiety through motor activity [43]. Preschool children tend to be impulsive in motor acts, anyway. While the anxiety is the primary place to focus for prevention, it may also be worthwhile to try to help preschool children to act less impulsively.

**International Differences in Threats to Children.** International differences in mortality and illness rates are greatest at the 1-to-4 age-level. Countries with low death rates include the United States, Great Britain, Denmark, Netherlands, Norway, Sweden, and Australia. Death rates in some of the nations with high rates are as much as 40 times the rates in the countries with low rates [63, pp. 206–207]. Figure 5–10 shows the contrast in preschool mortality rates between the United States and three other American countries. Not only are the rates ever so much higher in Colombia, Mexico, and Guatemala, but the leading cause is different. Disturbances of the gastrointestinal tract rank last among principal causes of death in the United States and first in the other countries. Accidents (or violence), the first cause of death in the United States, does not appear as a principal cause in the other countries. The infectious diseases, whooping cough, and measles are still important in Colombia, Mexico, and Guatemala.

A new threat to child health knows no national boundaries. *Air pollution* most likely has adverse effects on health and development, according to a committee of the American Academy of Pediatrics [2]. A review of studies suggests that toxic substances in the air are now contributing to respiratory infections and that they may lead to permanent lung damage. Since pollutants emitted in England fall on Sweden, to cite only one example, the problem is truly international.

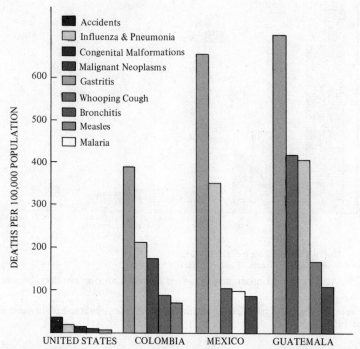

**Figure 5–10.** Five principal causes of death in children 1 to 4 years in United States and three other American countries.

SOURCE: From *Dynamics of Development: Euthenic Pediatrics* by Dorothy V. Whipple, M.D. Copyright © 1966 by McGraw-Hill, Inc. Used with permission of McGraw-Hill Book Company.

**Psychological Care of Ill and Injured Children.** It is frightening to be hurt or sick—frightening to anyone, but especially to a preschool child. Pain itself can be frightening as well as unpleasant. Reduced to a lower level of autonomy, he is disturbed at not being able to control himself and the environment as efficiently as normally. His thinking and his actions are less adequate for coping with the world.

Reassurance from parents makes the pain and fright possible to bear, just as Mother's presence in a disturbingly new situation gives a young child courage to explore. The most reassuring parent is one who combines sympathy with the calm expectation that balance and normalcy will be restored in due time. The ill or injured child is comforted and strengthened by having the limits of his activity redefined appropriately. For instance, "You are going to stay in your bed, but you can move around it all you like. I'll give you this box of toys to play with now. After your nap, you can choose a story for me to read to you." If toys and activities require less effort than his normal top speed, then he can still feel satisfied with what he achieves.

Hospital care for young children has been slowly undergoing a revolution, sparked by the research of Bowlby [8] and Spitz [68, 69] and pushed along by writers such as Robertson [58]. Gradually doctors, nurses, and parents are accepting the evidence that it is damaging for children between 6 months and 3 years to be separated from their mothers, and that even after 3 years of age, separation may be harmful. Some hospitals now permit and even encourage parents to stay with their young children so as to give them the emotional support which they

Courtesy John E. Ball

need every day but all the more when they are ill. Visiting rules have been liber-alized in many places, too. Continuing research efforts confirm the earlier findings on young children's need for closeness to loved people while undergoing traumatic experiences. For example, when 197 British children under 6 years of age under-went surgery for tonsils and/or adenoids, half were admitted to the hospital with their mothers and half were alone. The young patients accompanied by their mothers suffered significantly fewer complications afterwards, both emotional and infective [9]. Interviews with parents of Swiss preschool children showed that emotional reactions after discharge were less frequent among children whose parents had visited them frequently in the hospital and who had had close contact. The differences between frequently visited, closely contacted children and infre-quently visited children were very significant [12]. There is still a big educational job to be done in adapting hospitals to children's emotional needs.* Unfortunately many medical personnel still interpret a young child's stony silence as good adjust-ment, and the flood of tears released by his parents' arrival as evidence that parents are bad for him.

**Parents as Sources of Physical Danger.** Parents are the second most frequent cause of physical injuries to children, ranking second to motor vehicles [28]. The authors of this report strongly suspect that child-beating inflicts many more injuries on children than do even motor vehicles, but that most parental violence is not reported. They estimate that for every child brought to the hospital with positive evidence of parentally inflicted damage, 100 such cases remain undetected. This topic has been discussed more fully in Chapter 4.

* An illuminating film: *A Two-Year-Old Goes to the Hospital* (British National Health Service and World Health Organization).

*Physical Structures and Behaviors*

A child's appearance gives some hints as to how he will behave. Some impressions come from his body build and some from his features. Some research has been done on relationships between physical and behavioral measures.

**Body Build.** Three main types of physique have been described by Sheldon [64]; *endomorph*, round, soft, and plump with more fat and less muscular tissue than other types; *mesomorph*, strong, well-developed muscles and bones; *ectomorph*, tall, thin, delicate-looking. When preschool children were rated by their mothers and teachers and the rating related to physique types, some relationships were established [74]. The adults were likely to see the endomorphic girl as cooperative and cheerful, socially extraverted, and low in tension and anxiety. The mesomorphic girl was often described as energetic. The adults tended to rate the ectomorphic girl as uncooperative, not cheerful, anxious, and aloof. Among boys, relationships were not as clear, but the mesomorphic boy was seen as energetic, aggressive, assertive, cheerful, and social while the ectomorph was depicted as unsocial, shy, reserved, cooperative, and unaggressive, and the endomorph as amiable, and socially outgoing. It is impossible to tell how much the ratings were influenced by what adults expected to see in children of various body types rather than by what the children actually did. However, it does look as though there is some relationship between build and behavior.

**Minor Physical Anomalies.** In order to explore relationships between congenital factors and behavior, a longitudinal study has been done on a group of nursery school children who had been judged normal at birth [72, 73]. Each child was scored for anomalies of hair, eyes, ears, mouth, hands, and feet, such as very fine electric hair, eyelid fold, ears set low, curved fifth finger, third toe longer than second. These anomalies are so slight that they are ordinarily not noticed. Each child's total score was based upon the degree as well as the presence of such anomalies. Behavior measures were obtained at 2½ years by observers who measured time spent in various activities and counted incidences of specific actions, and by teachers' ratings. High scores for anomalies were associated with inability to delay gratification, nomadic play, frenetic play, spilling, throwing, opposing peers, and intractability.

Five years later, a replication of the study [72] showed stable anomaly scores and poor motor control associated with high scores. Such children shifted location more, were less able to delay response, and showed more frenetic behavior than children with low anomaly scores. High-scoring girls were more likely to be fearful and withdrawn, boys to be hyperactive.

The results of this study suggest that the slight physical anomalies and the somewhat disturbed behavior have a common source, rather than that one caused the other. One might reason that very noticeable physical abnormalities cause negative reactions toward children, who then behave poorly. The subjects of this study were normal physically, however, with deviations which could be noticed only through a careful examination. It is very unlikely that they experienced negative reactions due to their appearance. It is possible, however, that hyperactive behavior in infancy elicited hostility from parents which intensified the condition.

# Motor Development

Watch a group of preschool children playing. The first impression is of constant motion. Closer inspection reveals some children sitting looking at books, others squatting in the sandbox, and one or two in dreamy silence beside the record player. The younger the child, the shorter the interval during which he is likely to stay put. Carrying out simple motor acts, he tends to finish quickly. In contrast, the older preschooler weaves simple acts together into more complicated units which take longer to perform. To crawl through a piece of culvert, for instance, takes only a minute and to crawl through several times takes only five, whereas to make that culvert into the Holland Tunnel and to use it as such may take half the morning.

Motor control includes inhibiting actions as well as initiating them and controlling their speed of execution. The ability to perform certain motor acts very slowly was found to be associated with high levels of intelligence in preschool children [42]. In a group ranging from average to very high IQs, the higher IQ children were more likely to do well in tests of drawing a line slowly, walking slowly between two lines, and making a truck move slowly by means of a winch. The experiment also showed that children of higher IQ were just as active in free play as those of average intelligence. It is not certain whether superior ability to inhibit motor acts is the result of superior intelligence or if a common cause, superior development of the nervous system, is responsible for the high scores on both types of tests.

**The Development Sequence.** The chart of motor behavior, Table 5–6, drawn from several sources, shows how development between age 2 and 5 results in a child who moves and manipulates more like an adult than he does like the toddler he used to be. Having worked through stages of using a spoon and fork, holding a glass, and pouring from a pitcher, he can feed himself neatly without having to try very hard. He can even carry on a conversation at meals. He can cut and fold paper. From imitating a circular stroke at 2, drawing a vertical line at 3, and copying a square with some accuracy at 5, he is poised on the brink of learning to write. The 2-year-old, to whom walking steadily, running, and climbing are thrilling achievements, advances through walking tiptoe, hopping, jumping, tricycling, agile climbing, and stunting to the graceful age of 5. Skipping, hopping skillfully, running fast, he looks into an exciting future of skating, swimming, and riding a two-wheeler. Balls, the toys beloved by babies, children, and adults, are used with increasing maturity [27, 36, 41].

**Individual Differences.** One child differs from another in the speed with which he progresses through a sequence of behavior patterns. Individual differences in rate of motor development were apparent in 152 children between 3 and 7 years, who were tested for skill in cutting and tracing a straight line [40]. Although these skills showed fairly high correlations with age (0.63 for cutting and 0.70 for tracing), 2 of the 50 youngest children ranked in the upper third in cutting and 2 in tracing. Four of the 49 oldest children ranked in the bottom third in cutting and 4 in tracing. We have seen 4-year-olds who could swim and ride bicycles and 6-year-olds who spilled their food consistently. Children differ also in speed, power, and accuracy of their muscular coordinations, as witness the "natural athletes" who throw and catch balls efficiently in the preschool years. They differ, too, in balance and grace. When reading a chart that shows average development for various ages, it is important to keep in mind that this is a summary of a group of children and that it does not picture any one child as he is.

**Table 5–6** Some Landmarks in Motor Development During the Years from 2 to 6, from Basic Normative Studies. The Item Is Placed at the Age Where 50 Percent or More of Children Perform the Act. (Initials in parentheses refer to sources. See footnotes.)*

| | Age Two | Age Three | Age Four | Age Five |
|---|---|---|---|---|
| **Eye-Hand** | Builds tower of 6 or 7 blocks (GA) | Builds tower of 9 blocks (GA) | Cuts on line with scissors (GI) | Folds paper into double triangle (TM) |
| | Turns book pages singly (GA) | Makes bridge of 3 blocks (TM) | Makes designs and crude letters (GI) | Copies square (TM) |
| | Spoon into mouth without turning (GA) | Catches ball, arms straight (MW) | Catches small ball, elbows in front of body (MW) | Catches small ball, elbows at sides (MW) |
| | Holds glass in one hand (GA) | Spills little from spoon (GA) | Dresses self (GI) | Throws well (G) |
| | Imitates circular stroke (GA) | Pours from pitcher (GA) | | Fastens buttons he can see (GI) |
| | Puts on simple garment (GA) | Unbuttons, puts shoes on (GA) | | Copies designs, letters, numbers (GI) |
| | | Copies circle (TM) | | |
| | | Draws straight line (TM) | | |
| **Locomotion** | Wide stance, runs well (GA) | Walks tiptoe (GA, B) | Gallops (G) | Narrow stance (GI) |
| | Walks up and down stairs alone (GA) | Jumps from bottom stair (GA, B) | Descends small ladder, alternating feet easily (MW) | Skips (G, MW) |
| | Kicks large ball (GA) | Stands on one foot (GA, B) | Stunts on tricycle (G) | Hops on one foot, 10 or more steps (MW) |
| | Descends large ladder, marking time (MW) | Hops, both feet (MW) | Descends short steps, alternating feet, unsupported (G) | Descends large ladder, alternating feet easily (MW) |
| | Jumps 12″ (MW) | Propels wagon, one foot (J) | | Walks straight line (GI) |
| | | Rides tricycle (GA) | | |
| | | Descends long steps, marking time, unsupported (MW) | | |
| | | Jumps 18″ (MW) | | |

* SOURCES:
B —Bayley, N. "Development of Motor Abilities During the First Three Years." *Mono. Soc. Res. Child Devel.*, 1935, **1**.
GA —Gesell, A., and Amatruda, C. A. *Developmental Diagnosis* (New York: Hoeber, 1951).
GI —Gesell, A., and Ilg, F. L. *Child Development* (New York: Harper, 1949).
G —Gutteridge, M. V. "A Study of Motor Achievements of Young Children." *Arch. Psychol.*, 1939, No. 244.
J —Jones, T. D. *Development of Certain Motor Skills and Play Activities in Young Children*, Child Development Monographs (New York: Teachers College, Columbia University, 1939), No. 26.
MW—McCaskill, C. L., and Wellman, B. L. "A Study of Common Motor Achievements at the Preschool Ages." *Child Devel.*, 1939, **9**, 141–150.
TM —Terman, L. M., and Merrill, M. A. *Stanford-Binet Intelligence Scale* (Boston: Houghton Mifflin, 1960).

**Sex Differences.** At all ages, males tend to do better than females on tests of large muscles coordination, most likely because of their superior strength and muscular development [23]. Girls begin early to show superiority in manual dexterity. Between age 2 and 6, boys have been found to excel in going up and down ladders and steps, throwing, catching and bouncing balls, and jumping from boxes and ladders [41]. Girls performed better than boys in hopping, skipping, and galloping [27]. The latter can be confirmed by observing a kindergarten in the fall, where there are almost sure to be several little boys who merely run or gallop while the other children skip.

Throughout the preschool period, boys continue to show the exploratory, assertive, and vigorous play that has been noted as a sex difference in infancy. Their behavior is also shaped by sex-typing experiences which influence what they have to play with and what restrictions and directions are brought to bear on them. Different cultures have different ways of emphasizing sex-appropriate behavior, some stressing masculine, some feminine, some maximizing sex differences, and some minimizing them.

## Posture

Posture is the way in which the whole body is balanced, not only in sitting and standing, but also in play and rest. Posture is neuromuscular behavior, just as surely as bouncing a ball and drawing a circle are. Parents and teachers rarely make great headway when they try to get children to stand up straight or otherwise consciously improve their posture according to standard ideas of what good posture is. The ways in which a child stands, sits, and moves are the results of a dynamic interplay of forces which cannot be controlled by holding his head up or throwing back his shoulders. This is not to say that good posture is unimportant in its influence on health, growth, and efficiency of movement. It is very important indeed, but it is achieved through good muscle tone and healthy skeletal development, as well as through general physical and mental health. Figure 5–11 illustrates good and poor posture in the preschool child.

Breckenridge and Murphy [10, p. 282] distinguish five important factors when considering body dynamics:

1. *Gravity.* The body is most efficient motorwise if it is arranged symmetrically about a line that passes through the center of gravity (see illustration). The center of gravity drops in the trunk as the child's proportions change, and the lower it is, of course, the easier it is for him to maintain his balance in the upright position. The transverse line in Figure 5–12 shows the location of the center of gravity in the body from birth to adulthood. During the years from two to five, the center of gravity drops from just above the umbilicus to just below it [54, p. 89].
2. *Muscles and bones.* Good tone is important in all muscles. If opposing pairs of muscles are unequal in pull, faulty balance between them results in poor posture.
3. *Stage of development.* We have already mentioned that the young child has flexible joints, due to looser attachment of ligaments and muscles. Also, his center of gravity shifts downward, causing him to adjust gradually to the change. Standing on a wide base at first, in order to maintain his balance, the young child toes out and takes much of his weight on the inner part of his feet.

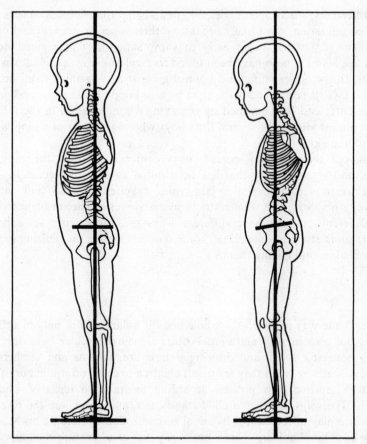

**Figure 5–11.** The child on the left shows good posture, the child on the right, poor posture. The first child's body is arranged symmetrically about a line that passes through his center of gravity. The head and chest are high, chin in, abdomen in, shoulder blades in, curves of back small and knees straight.

SOURCE: Figure 4.3 on page 90 of *Good Posture and the Little Child*, Children's Bureau Publication 219. Washington, D.C.: U.S. Government Printing Office, 1935.

The arch is protected with a fat pad at this point, and it makes him look as though he had flat feet. Knock-knees and lordosis (small of back curving in excessively) are so common in the preschool period as to be considered normal. These conditions usually improve with age.

4. *Individual differences.* There is no one best posture for all, since a child's body dynamics are individual. A stocky child must balance his body in one way, a thin child in another. Varieties of proportions will have their own dynamics.

5. *Environmental influences.* The child's whole regime affects his posture. Obviously, nutrition determines what materials build and maintain his body, and hence is one key to the efficiency with which the body can operate and balance itself. Rest and fatigue, with their intimate connection with nutrition, nerves, and muscles, play a big role in determining posture. Activity is essential, too, for developing coordination, maintaining muscle tissue and promoting its growth. A variety of equipment and opportunities for large-muscle play is hygienic. Shoes, clothing, and furniture all have roles to play in promoting or hampering the dynamic coordination which is ideal for a given child.

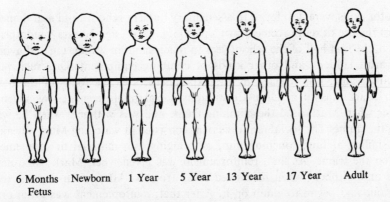

6 Months   Newborn   1 Year   5 Year   13 Year   17 Year   Adult
Fetus

**Figure 5–12.** The horizontal line shows the center of gravity which changes its location in the trunk as body proportions change.

Source: Reprinted by permission from C. E. Palmer, "Studies of the Center of Gravity in the Human Body," *Child Development*, **15**, Figure 7. Copyright © 1944, The Society for Research in Child Development, Inc.

The child's own personality is expressed in his posture, both his general attitudes toward himself and the world and his specific ups and downs. Sometimes a sagging, slumping body is the first indication that something is wrong. A handicap, such as blindness or deafness, often leads to a characteristic posture. A beautifully balanced body is one indication of a healthy child.

The influences of culture on posture can be seen as early as the preschool years. Mead [44, p. 40] gives illuminating examples from three different cultures. In Bali, girls of 2 and 3 walk with a "pregnant" posture because there is much teasing about pregnancy. A girl is told that she is probably pregnant and older people will often hit her on the abdomen, asking, "Got a baby in there?" Among the Iatumul, it is almost impossible to tell boys and girls apart, even with moving pictures, because they are dressed like girls, and all move like girls. Among the Manus, Mead could not tell the little girls and boys apart because they were all dressed like boys and moved like boys.

### Physical Fitness

The past decade has seen the arousal of interest on a nationwide basis in the topic of physical fitness of children. Programs to improve the health and fitness of preschool children have paid more attention to nutrition than to exercise, and rightly so. Many authorities on preschool children take the point of view that preschool children will take appropriate exercise in play if they are given a healthy general program which includes opportunities for using outdoor space and wide variety large-muscle play equipment. Tests of physical fitness on nursery school children have shown a wide range of results, however [65]. While some children scored the maximum on tests of muscular strength and flexibility, others could pass none, and most scored between the two extremes. Since these children had rich opportunities for motor play, other factors must have accounted for their differences. In fact, the study indicated relationships between healthiness of personality and muscular strength and flexibility. Further study has confirmed the relationship between body flexibility and personality, as expressed in a test that explores the child's concept of his body [25].

Motor skills were developed in a sedentary nursery school child as a demonstration of the use of reinforcement principles [35]. Mark, age 3 years 8 months, spent most of the first half of the school year in much random wandering and avoidance of boards, ladders, and other kinds of climbing equipment. One such piece, a climbing frame, was selected by the experimenters as the focus of the behavior which Mark was to acquire. Continuous social reinforcement was given by a teacher when Mark used the climbing frame and was withheld when he was not using the frame. The social reinforcement consisted of watching Mark, speaking to him, smiling at him, touching him, or bringing him material to supplement his play on the frame. At first, reinforcement was given when Mark came near the frame and withheld when he moved away from it. After seven days he touched the frame and began to climb on it. After that, reinforcement was given only for climbing on it. By the second day he spent 25 percent of his outdoor time on the frame, and by the ninth day 67 percent. Later phases of the experiment included reinforcement for other vigorous motor activities and a gradual change to intermittent, rather than constant, reinforcement. Mark then used all the climbing equipment in the yard. When he returned to school the next fall, he spent 50 to 60 percent of his time in vigorous activity and used all the climbing equipment. While few children require as much help as Mark did in establishing patterns of motor play, the study has important implications for nursery school teaching. Probably many more young children would benefit from some reinforcement of vigorous motor activities.

## Hand Preference

By age 2 most children show a preference for the right hand, a few for the left, and a few seem to have little preference. During the next three years, the hand preference becomes more firmly established, and established in more children. Thus hand preference is a developmental trait, a trait which increases with increasing maturity. While there are probably genetic foundations to laterality, social learning also influences hand preference. Figure 5–13, based on data from several investigators, shows how right-handedness increases with age. Note that the preschool years are the time when the greatest increase in established preferences occurs.

Studies on hand preference use an index of handedness derived from sampling a variety of activities. The formula for the index of dominance is $\frac{R - L}{R + L}$. (R is right hand, L is left hand.) Thus $+1$ would be complete right dominance and $-1$ left dominance. Figure 5–14 shows the distribution of such handedness indices for 44 nursery school children [32] who took part in experiments to determine hand preference and who were also observed eating and playing. For example, hand preference was noted while the child ate with a spoon, ate with his fingers, threw a ball, and drew with crayons. The lowest indices for hand preference were found while children ate with their fingers. Random observations for spontaneous acts also gave indices close to zero. About 11 percent of the children showed dominant left-handedness.

Sex differences are small but consistent. All studies concerned with such differences show a greater incidence of left-handedness and ambidexterity in boys. The

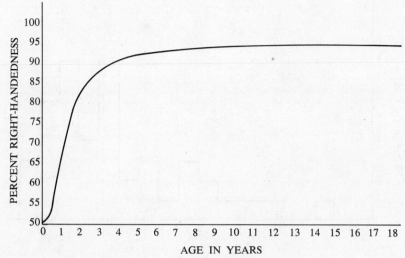

**Figure 5–13.** A steady increase in right-handedness takes place during the preschool years.

SOURCE: Reprinted by permission from G. Hildreth, "The Development and Training of Hand Dominance: II. Developmental Tendencies in Handedness," *Journal of Genetic Psychology*, **75**, 221–254. Copyright © 1949, The Journal Press.

difference may be due somewhat to social conditioning, since girls engage in more hand play than boys, and are more amenable to training.

Stuttering and handedness have long been thought to be associated. Low left dominance or partially converted dominance has been shown to occur in stutterers more than in the general population. Which is cause and which effect, or whether either is cause or effect, is not definitely established. Stuttering tends to occur first at 3 or 4 years, the age when hand preference is being established ordinarily. It has been found that when manual dominance is established, stuttering tends to disappear, at least at this age [32].

The left-handed person incurs many disadvantages in addition to possible speech disturbance. In a world designed for right-handed people, he has to adjust to scissors, golf clubs, classroom chairs, table settings, and countless other arrangements that are awkward for him. There are certain prejudices against left-handers,

**Table 5–7** Incidence of Left-handedness in Schoolchildren over Three Decades

| Author | Year | Percentage of Children Writing with Left Hand |
|---|---|---|
| Hildreth | 1932 | 2.2 |
| Hildreth | 1937 | 4.1 |
| Hildreth | 1941 | 6.2 |
| Carrothers | 1945 | 8.2 |
| Belmont & Birch* | 1963 | 10.0 |

\* In addition to writing as a criterion of handedness, this study also used ball throwing, turning a doorknob, and cutting with scissors.

SOURCE: Data from Belmont and Birch [6], Carrothers [13], and Hildreth [33].

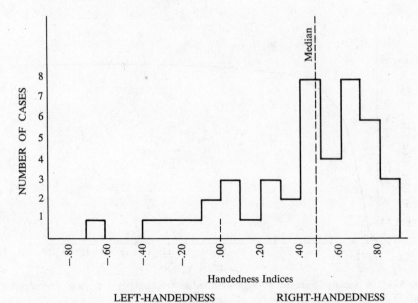

Figure 5–14. Distribution of handedness in nursery school children. Zero indicates no preference, +1 extreme right-dominance, −1 extreme left-dominance.

SOURCE: Reprinted by permission from G. Hildreth, "Manual Dominance in Nursery School Children," *Journal of Genetic Psychology*, **72**, 29–45. Copyright © 1948, The Journal Press.

although feelings against them vary from time to time and from culture to culture. A small percentage of children develop a strong preference for the left hand, in spite of living among right-handed arrangements. It seems wise, for teachers and parents, to respect such a preference and to help the child by giving him left-handed equipment when possible and showing him how to adapt in places where he has to use right-handed tools and arrangements.

Since hand preference is definitely a behavior pattern that becomes established, not one that appears at birth, it is reasonable to expect that experience will influence it. If teaching and learning are important factors in establishing right-handedness, then permissiveness for choosing a preferred hand would increase the incidence of left-handedness. During the years from 1913 to the present, the incidence of left-handedness has indeed gone steadily up [33]. Table 5–7 shows results from studies in different decades.

**Handedness and Eye Preference.** There are preferences in the use of eyes and feet, just as there are for hands, and these preferences are not always consistent. The eye–hand preferences of a large number of black 4-year-old boys and girls were studied in relation to their performances on intelligence tests and perceptual-motor tests [22]. Hand dominance was judged by noting which hand was used in copying geometric forms (part of the perceptual-motor test). Eye dominance was determined by seeing which eye the child used in looking through a hole in a box to see an object at the other end. Eighty-five percent of the children were right-handed, but only 58 percent were right-eyed. Half of the children were right-handed and right-eyed, 31 percent right-handed and left-eyed, 4 percent left-handed and left-eyed, and 11 percent indeterminate. The left-handed, left-eyed group gave the poorest performance of all groups in both perceptual and intelligence tests. The investigators suggest that a neurological deficit underlies both the left dominance and the lower test scores of these children. This explanation fits with the findings of a study reported in Chapter 1 showing disturbed hand dominance in 16- to 22-year-olds who had suffered oxygen deprivation at birth.

The question of laterality is a significant one during the elementary school years, when its reference to writing is obvious. Further discussion of this topic occurs in Chapter 9.

## Summary

Two stages of personality development occur during the preschool period: the development of the sense of autonomy, during the early years, and the development of the sense of initiative, from about 3 years to 6 or 7 years. The sense of autonomy is promoted by clear, firm guidance which permits successful decision making within the limits it imposes. The opposite of sense of autonomy includes feelings of shame and doubt. Initiative and imagination grow as the child explores the world of people and things, as he imagines himself into a variety of roles and activities, and as he successfully seeks reasons, answers, solutions, and new ideas. Conscience develops, along with guilt, requiring a balancing with initiative for adequate personality development. Beginnings of initiative can be seen in infancy, when children differ in activity and passivity. During the preschool years, differences in achievement behavior represent differences in the sense of initiative. Parental encouragement of achievement behavior at this age is likely to have lasting effects. The sense of initiative results from the interaction of a variety of influences, including genetic, constitutional, cultural, and familial.

Physical growth is slower than it is in infancy. The rate of growth in height decelerates slowly during the preschool years. Although boys are slightly larger than girls, girls are closer to maturity than boys. Retarded growth occurs in children in the lower socioeconomic levels in the United States and in the majority of children in underdeveloped countries. Appearance and proportions change from the chubby, babylike configuration to the more slender, childish pattern, due to changes in amount and distribution of fat, as well as growth of muscle and skeletal tissues. Evidence of changes in the nervous system is more in terms of function than of size and structure. The structures of vision are immature. Taste buds are more numerous than in the older child. Characteristic shape, position, and structure make for significant differences, as compared with older children, in the preschool child's middle ear, digestive system, and respiratory system.

Assessment of growth is most often done in terms of a child's height and weight, which are compared with a standard derived from measurements of a large number of children. Or the present status may be evaluated according to a record of past growth. Growth can also be judged from skeletal development. X rays of the bones provide information on the health history of the child, as well as on his present status.

The majority of the world's children are malnourished. Their food is insufficient in quantity and quality. Since fatigue depresses appetite, health care includes careful guidance of rhythms of eating and sleeping. Eating problems are avoided by such guidance plus attention to the physiological, sensory, and emotional aspects of preschool children's eating and by recognition of his eagerness for autonomy. Sleep problems, also, are avoided by appropriate timing, nonstimulating bed-going routines, reassurance in frightening situations, and gentle firmness.

Many illnesses and accidents are preventable by planning, guidance, careful arrangement of the environment, hygiene, immunizations, and medical supervision. Preschool children are especially vulnerable to illness. International differences in preschool illness and death are enormous. Gastrointestinal disturbances rank first as cause of death in many poor countries; accidents rank first in the United States. Parental child abuse contributes heavily to the high "accident" rate. Easily frightened by illness or injury, the young child is reassured by the presence of a loved person, especially if that person is calmly sympathetic.

Physical structure and behavior are related. Body build shows some correlation with personality characteristics. Minor physical abnormalities are related to mild behavior disturbances.

Motor development proceeds through a fairly stable sequence of patterns. Individual children differ in speed of sequential development as well as in quality of performance, as shown in speed, power, and accuracy. In many, but not all, motor performances, boys excel girls. Posture, or body balance, expresses health and influences it. Young children vary in muscular strength and flexibility. Hand preference is established in most children during the first five years of life. Right-handedness increases with age. Left-handedness and ambidexterity occur more often in boys than in girls. Disturbances in lateral dominance are associated with poor perceptual-motor performances, implying an underlying neurological deficit.

## References

1. Agricultural Research Service. *Food for fitness.* Washington, D.C.: United States Department of Agriculture, 1964.
2. Altman, L. K. Pollution danger to children seen. *Wall Street J.,* 1970, November 15.
3. Baumrind, D. Child care practices anteceding three patterns of preschool behavior. *Genet. Psychol. Mono.,* 1967, **75,** 43–88.
4. Baumrind, D., & Black, A. E. Socialization practices associated with dimensions of competence in preschool boys and girls. *Child Devel.,* 1967, **38,** 291–327.
5. Béhar, M. Prevalence of malnutrition among preschool children of developing countries. In N. S. Scrimshaw & J. E. Gordon (Eds.), *Malnutrition, learning and behavior.* Cambridge, Mass.: M.I.T. Press, 1968, pp. 30–41.
6. Belmont, L., & Birch, H. G. Lateral dominance and right-left awareness in normal children. *Child Devel.,* 1963, **34,** 257–270.
7. Berland, T., & Seyler, A. *Your children's teeth.* New York: Meredith, 1968.
8. Bowlby, J. *Child care and the growth of love.* London: Pelican, 1953.
9. Brain, D. J., & Maclay, I. Controlled study of mothers and children in hospital. *Brit. Med. J.,* 1968, **1,** 278–280.
10. Breckenridge, M. E., & Murphy, M. N. *Growth and development of the young child* (8th ed.). Philadelphia: Saunders, 1969.
11. Calder, R. Food supplementation for prevention of malnutrition in the preschool child. In National Research Council, *Preschool child malnutrition: Primary deterrent to human progress.* Washington D. C.: National Academy of Sciences, 1966, pp. 251–257.
12. Cardinaux-Hilfiker, V. Elternbesuche bei hospitalisierten vorschulpflichtigen Kindern. *Heilpädagogische Workblätter,* 1969, **38,** 6–15. (Abstract).

13. Carrothers, G. E. Left-handedness among preschool pupils. *Am. School Board J.*, 1947, **114**, 17–19.

14. Crandall, V. C. Achievement behavior in young children. *Young Children*, 1964, **20**, 77–90.

15. Crandall, V. J., Preston, A., & Rabson, A. Maternal reactions and the development of independence and achievement behavior in young children. *Child Devel.*, 1960, **31**, 243–251.

16. Dierks, E. C., & Morse, L. M. Food habits and nutrient intakes of preschool children. *J. Am. Dietetics Assoc.*, 1965, **47**, 292–296.

17. Dorman, L., & Rebelsky, F. Assertive behavior and cognitive performance in pre-school children. Paper presented at the meeting of the Society for Research in Child Development, Santa Monica, Calif., March 29, 1969.

18. Dudley, D. T. Effects of methods of vegetable preparation on choices and amounts eaten by nursery school children. Unpublished Master's Thesis. Iowa State University. Cited by Korslund [38].

19. Eichorn, D. H. Biological correlates of behavior. In H. W. Stevenson, J. Kagan, & C. Spiker, *Child psychology*. The Sixty-second Yearbook of the National Society for the Study of Education, Part I. Chicago: University of Chicago Press, 1963, pp. 4–61.

20. Erikson, E. H. *Childhood and society*. New York: Norton, 1963.

21. Escalona, S. K. *The roots of individuality*. Chicago: Aldine, 1968.

22. Flick, G. L. Sinistrality revisited: A perceptual-motor approach. *Child Devel.*, 1966, **37**, 613–622.

23. Garai, J. E., & Scheinfeld, A. Sex differences in mental and behavioral traits. *Genet. Psychol. Mono.*, 1968, **77**, 169–299.

24. Gesell, A., Ilg, F. L., & Bullis, G. E. *Vision*. New York: Hoeber, 1949.

25. Gollerkeri, S. B. Relationship between body image and muscular fitness of preschool children. Unpublished Master's thesis. University of Rhode Island, 1963.

26. Greulich, W. W., & Pyle, S. I. *Radiographic atlas of skeletal development of the hand and wrist* (2nd ed.). Stanford, Calif.: Stanford University Press, 1959.

27. Gutteridge, M. V. A study of motor achievements of young children. *Arch. Psychol.*, 1939, **244**.

28. Gwinn, J. L., Lewin, K. W., & Peterson, H. G., Jr. Roentgenographic manifestations of unsuspected trauma in infancy. *J. Am. Med. Assoc.*, 1961, **176**, 926–929.

29. Hatfield, E. M. Progress in preschool vision screening. *Sight-Saving Rev.*, 1967, **37**, 194–201.

30. Hicks, R. A., & Dockstader, S. Cultural deprivation and preschool children's preferences for complex and novel stimuli. *Percept. Motor Skills*, 1968, **27**, 1321–1322.

31. Hicks, S. E. Dependence of children on adults as observed in the nursery school. Unpublished Master's thesis. Pennsylvania State University, 1962.

32. Hildreth, G. Manual dominance in nursery school children. *J. Genet. Psychol.*, 1948, **72**, 29–45.

33. Hildreth, G. The development and training of hand dominance. II: Developmental tendencies in handedness. *J. Genet. Psychol.*, 1949, **75**, 221–254.

34. Jackson, R. L. Effect of malnutrition on growth of a pre-school child. In National Research Council, *Pre-school child malnutrition: Primary deterrent*

*to human progress.* Washington, D.C.: National Academy of Sciences, 1966, pp. 9–21.

35. Johnston, M. K., Kelly, C. S., Harris, F. R., & Wolf, M. M. An application of reinforcement principles to development of motor skills of a young child. *Child Devel.*, 1966, **37**, 379–387.

36. Jones, T. D. The development of certain motor skills and play activities in young children. *Child Devel. Mono.*, New York: Teachers College, Columbia University, 1939.

37. Kagan, J., & Moss. H. A. *Birth to maturity.* New York: Wiley, 1962.

38. Korslund, M. K. Taste sensitivity and eating behavior of nursery school children. Unpublished Master's thesis. Iowa State University, 1962.

39. Kurokawa, M. Acculturation and childhood accidents among Chinese and Japanese Americans. *Genet. Psychol. Mono.*, 1969, **79**, 89–159.

40. Lueck, E. Ability of young children to execute tracing and cutting tasks. Unpublished Master's thesis. Iowa State University, 1962.

41. McCaskill, C. L., & Wellman, B. L. A study of common motor achievements at the preschool ages. *Child Devel.*, 1938, **9**, 141–150.

42. Maccoby, E. E., Dowley, E. M., & Hagen, J. W. Activity level and intellectual functioning in normal preschool children. *Child Devel.*, 1965, **36**, 761–770.

43. Marcus, I. M., et al. An interdisciplinary approach to accident patterns in children. *Mono Soc. Res. Child Devel.*, 1960, **25**:2.

44. Mead, M. In J. M. Tanner & B. Inhelder (Eds.), *Discussions on child development.* Vol. 3. New York: International Universities Press, 1958.

45. Meichenbaum, D., & Goodman, J. Reflection-impulsivity and verbal control of motor behavior. *Child Devel.*, 1969, **40**, 785–797.

46. Mendel, G. Children's preferences for differing degrees of novelty. *Child Devel.*, 1965, **36**, 463–465.

47. Meredith, H. V. Body size of contemporary groups of preschool children studied in different parts of the world. *Child Devel.*, 1968, **39**, 335–377.

48. Metropolitan Life Insurance Company. The frequency of accidental poisoning. *Stat. Bull.*, 1960, **41**:3, 8–10.

49. Metropolitan Life Insurance Company. Accidental deaths high at the preschool ages. *Stat. Bull.*, 1969, **50**:6–8.

50. Minuchin, P. Correlates of curiosity and exploratory behavior. Paper presented at the meeting of the Society for Research in Child Development. Santa Monica, Calif., March 27, 1969.

51. Murphy, L. B. The widening world of childhood. New York: Basic Books, 1962.

52. Nakamura, C. Y., & Rogers, M. M. Parents' expectations of autonomous behavior and children's autonomy. *Devel. Psychol.*, 1969, **1**, 613–617.

53. Newson, J., & Newson, E. *Four years old in an urban community.* Chicago: Aldine, 1968.

54. Olson, W. C. *Child Development.* Boston: Heath, 1959.

55. Pederson, F. A., & Wender, P. H. Early social correlates of cognitive functioning in six-year-old boys. *Child Devel.*, 1968, **39**, 185–193.

56. Pryor, H. B. Width-weight tables (revised). *Am. J. Dis. Child.*, 1941, **61**, 300–304.

57. Pyle, S. I., Stuart, H. C., Cornoni, J., & Reed, R. Onsets, completions and spans of the osseous stage of development in representative bone growth centers of the extremities. *Mono. Soc. Res. Child Devel.*, 1961, **26**:1.

58. Robertson, J. *Young children in hospitals.* New York: Basic Books, 1958.
59. Roffwarg, H. P., Muzio, J. N., & Dement, W. C. Ontogenetic development of the human sleep-dream cycle. *Science,* 1966, **152,** 604–617.
60. Schaefer, A. E., & Johnson, O. C. Are we well fed? The search for an answer. *Nutrition Today,* 1969, **4**(1), 2–11.
61. Scrimshaw, N. S. Malnutrition, learning and behavior. *Am. J. Clinical Nutrition,* 1967, **20,** 493–502.
62. Sears, R. R., Maccoby, E. E., & Levin, H. *Patterns of child rearing.* Evanston, Ill.: Row, Peterson, 1957.
63. Shapiro, S., Schlesinger, E. R., & Nesbitt, E. L. *Infant, perinatal and childhood mortality in the United States.* Cambridge, Mass.: Harvard University, 1968.
64. Sheldon, W. H. *The varieties of human physique.* New York: Harper, 1940.
65. Smart, R. C., & Smart, M. S. Kraus-Weber scores and personality adjustment of nursery school children. *Res. Quart.,* 1963, **3,** 199–205.
66. Smith, M. E. An investigation of the development of the sentence and the extent of vocabulary in young children. *Univer. Iowa Stud. Child Welf.,* 1926, **3**:5.
67. Smock, C. D., & Holt, B. G. Children's reactions to novelty: An experimental study of curiosity motivation. *Child Devel.,* 1962, **33,** 631–642.
68. Spitz, R. A. Hospitalism: An inquiry into the genesis of psychiatric conditions in early childhood. *Psychoan. Stud. Child.,* 1945, **1,** 53–74.
69. Spitz, R. A. Hospitalism: A follow-up report. *Psychoan. Stud. Child.,* 1946, **2,** 113–117.
70. Tanner, J. M. *Education and physical growth.* London: University of London, 1961.
71. U.S. Public Health Service News Release. Quoted by A. F. North, Jr., in Research Issues in Child Health I: An Overview. In E. Grotberg (Ed.), *Critical issues in research related to disadvantaged children.* Princeton, N.J.: Educational Testing Service, 1969.
72. Waldrop, M. F., & Halverson, C. F., Jr. Minor physical abnormalities: Their incidence and their relation to behavior in a normal and deviant sample. Paper presented at the meeting of the Society for Research in Child Development, Santa Monica, Calif., March 29, 1969.
73. Waldrop, M. F., Pedersen, F. A., & Bell, R. Q. Minor physical anomalies and behavior in preschool children. *Child Devel.,* 1968, **39,** 391–400.
74. Walker, R. N. Body build and behavior in young children. *Child Devel.,* 1963, **34,** 1–23.
75. Walter, W. G. Electroencephalographic development of children. In J. M. Tanner & B. Inhelder, *Discussions on child development.* Vol. 1. New York: International Universities Press, 1953, pp. 132–160.
76. Watson, E. H., & Lowrey, G. H. *Growth and development of children* (5th ed.). Chicago: Year Book, 1967.
77. Wetzel, N. C. *Instruction manual in the use of the grid for evaluating physical fitness.* Cleveland: NEA Service, 1941.
78. White, B. L. An overview of the project. Paper presented at the meeting of the Society for Research in Child Development, Santa Monica, Calif., March 27, 1969.
79. Williams, C. D. Malnutrition and mortality in the preschool child. In National Research Council, *Pre-school child malnutrition: Primary deterrent to human progress.* Washington, D.C.: National Academy of Sciences, 1966, pp. 3–8.

80. Winterbottom, M. R. The relation of need for achievement to learning experiences in independence and mastery. In J. W. Atkinson (Ed.) *Motives in fantasy, action and society*. Princeton N.J.: Van Nostrand, 1958, pp. 453–494.
81. Woodruff, C. W. An analysis of the ICNND data on physical growth of the preschool child. In National Research Council, *Preschool child malnutrition: Primary deterrent to human progress*. Washington, D.C.: National Academy of Sciences, 1966, pp. 22–28.

# Chapter 6

Merrill-Palmer Institute by Donna J. Harris

# Intellectual Development

This chapter and the next concern the preschool child's intellectual development, and the measurement and stimulation of that development. Thinking, concept formation, intelligence, and language make up the subject matter of this chapter. Imagination and stimulation of development are the focus of the next. Thought, language, and imagination interweave and overlap as cognitive growth proceeds. Language provides symbols for thinking, and also socializes thought, through interaction with other people. Children talk to others and talk to themselves. Young children talk out loud to themselves. Imagination or fantasy, an unfettered kind of thought or inner life, expresses emotion and complements controlled thought. Fantasy is both inner language and, on occasion, outer language. It is dreams and artistic expressions. Sometimes fantasy is equated with egocentric thought, because both are the means of pleasure seeking rather than truth seeking. Although fantasy is not limited by reality and does not purposefully deal with reality, it sometimes achieves solutions to problems which controlled thought cannot solve. An adult may "sleep on" a problem and awaken with the solution. A child may work through his problems in dramatic play or with dolls. The role of controlled thought is widely appreciated in children's education and development, but fantasy is little understood. Adults tend to dismiss it as a whimsical activity which will pass with time. Some schoolteachers deplore it as a waste of time; others see it as one of the keys to understanding children's thoughts and emotions. [43].

Other keys are available for unlocking the mysteries of children's minds. Tests and experiments are used to investigate cognitive processes and factors which influence them. Observations are made under controlled conditions and the results analyzed. Children are rated by adults who have certain bases for agreeing or disagreeing with statements about their behavior. Results of tests, experiments, observations, and ratings are treated statistically so as to extract generalizations from them and then those generalizations are tested for significance. Knowledge gained from research is then applied, in the case of cognition, by educators. The last part of the following chapter is concerned with some recent developments in preschool education which stem from new knowledge of cognitive development.

## Thought Processes and Conceptual Development

The intellectual landmark of the end of infancy is the completion of the period of sensorimotor intelligence, a phase of cognitive development discussed in Chapter 3. At this point, the child has achieved two major feats, the control of his movements in space and the notion of object constancy. He realizes that an object continues to exist even when he does not perceive it and that it can move in space which also is there when the child is not dealing with it.

Sensorimotor intelligence links successive perceptions and movements, with brief anticipations and memories. It does not take a large, sweeping view: "Sensorimotor intelligence acts like a slow-motion film, in which all pictures are seen in succession but without fusion, and so without the continuous vision necessary for understanding the whole" [63, pp. 120–121].

Representational thought is what makes the period of preoperational thought distinctly different from the sensorimotor period [65]. Instead of confining his interactions to the here and now, the child can think about objects, people, and actions that are not present. He shows that he does this by imitative and imaginative play. Representational thought can be applied to the past, when the youngster acts upon an event that has happened, and to the future in the form of planning which also appears as play. Both actions and objects are used in symbolic ways to serve representational thought. The child begins to use language at about the same time that he starts to use objects and actions in representational thought. Language quickly becomes a powerful tool of thought. Even so, imaginative and symbolic acts continue to be useful throughout life.

The period of *preoperational thought* ordinarily lasts from 18 months or 2 years to 7 or 8. During this time, the child is building mental structures which will eventually result in logical thinking or operations. This he does through his interactions with objects and people. The interaction takes the form of the two complementary processes, assimilation and accommodation [68, pp. 1–6]. The child assimilates by acting on the environment and fitting it into existing schemas. For instance, when first given a wagon or a kiddy car, the young child manipulates the wheels, using an examining schema which is already established. Further examination shows this toy to be different from his other toys and he adapts old schemas and develops new schemas for playing with it, thus accommodating to the wagon as he loads it, pulls and pushes it and unloads it, or as he propels the kiddy car. Through assimilation and accommodation, he learns the properties of toys and other objects, materials such as water, clay, and paint. He also learns ways of manipulating objects through "logico-mathematical experiences" [67]. By arranging, grouping, and counting his blocks, sticks, cars, or anything else, he is *operating* on them. Through repeated actions of this type, he internalizes these logico-mathematical experiences into concrete logical operations. While he is working his way through the period of preoperational thinking, his thought has certain characteristics that distinguished it from concrete logical operations, the period that is to follow.

## Characteristics of Preschool Thinking

1. The young child cannot think from any point of view except his own and he does not realize that he is limited in this fashion. His thought is centered on one perspective, his own. An example of centered thinking in an adult makes this limitation more clear, because it is obviously inappropriate for adults.

**Mrs. A:** My, what a charming accent you have, Mrs. B. I think it is so quaint the way you say "two-dooah Foahd cah" for "two-door Ford car." I'd just love to have an accent like yours.

**Mrs. B:** Your own accent is interesting, Mrs. A. I've never heard anyone say "caow" for "cow," as you do.

**Mrs. A:** Why, *I* don't have an accent. I was born right here in Ohio.

Mrs. A could not consider her own speech from Mrs. B's point of view, nor could she hear Mrs. B's speech from her point of view or from that of anyone but herself. In addition, she could not comprehend that there existed other points of view. She centered in her own and could not move off or decenter.

The preschool child characteristically has but a dim awareness of his psychological self in relation to the rest of reality even though he knows that his body is a separate and distinct object among other objects. He does not know that his thoughts and actions make up part of the situation in which he is. He has little objectivity, or relativism, which means looking from another person's point of view, from another angle in space or time, or imagining how it would be if you were somewhere else. This is not to say that the preschool child cannot step into the role of someone else. He can do it very well indeed, but when he does it, he loses himself. He cannot stand off and view himself from the angle of somebody else, but he can become the other person. He can do through fantasy, in taking the role of another, what he cannot do through controlled thought. Through neither fantasy nor controlled thought, however, can he see both points of view at once and weigh them.

2. Perceptions dominate the young child's thinking. He is greatly influenced by what he sees, hears, or otherwise experiences at a given moment. Literally, seeing is believing. The static picture is what he believes. He does not pay attention to transformations or changes from one state to another. What he perceives at any one time is, however, only part of what a more mature person would perceive. Carolyn, the 2-year-old who remarked, "Choo-choo going fwimming," was beholding on the river a large object, followed by several similar, rectangular objects,

which did in fact resemble a train. The pointed prow of the tug, the decks, the small size, the absence of wheels—all these features did not indicate to her that this object was not an engine, although they would have done so to an older child. If Carolyn saw these aspects of the tug, she ignored past experiences which would have been brought to bear on the situation by a more sophisticated observer. Nobody has seen a train moving itself on anything but a track. Carolyn's thinking was not flexible enough to watch the tug and barges, think of trains and how they run, compare this event with past observations of trains, and then come to a conclusion based on both present and past. Another illustration of the dominance of perception is the ease with which young children can be fooled by a magician. Although the older members of the audience reject the evidences of their senses because they reason on the basis of past experience, the preschool children really believe that the magician found his rabbit in the little boy's coat pocket and that the card flew out of the air into the magician's hand.

One of Piaget's famous experiments is done by pouring beads from one glass container to another glass, taller and thinner than the first. When asked whether there are more or fewer beads in the second glass, the child answers either that there are more, because the level has risen, or that there are fewer, because the glass is narrower. The child centers on *either* height or width, in fact, more often on height, which is more salient [70]. In contrast, a child who had reached the next stage of thought, the period of concrete operations, would reason with respect to both relations and would deduce conservation. His perceptions would be placed in relation instead of giving rise to immediate reactions [63, pp. 130–131].

Perception becomes more flexible, "decentered," with increasing maturity [23]. Children between 4 and 12 were tested with cards containing at least three ambiguous figures apiece. The first cards showed a butterfly with a face in either wing. The score was for number of spontaneous perceptions. The number of perceptions increased with both age and IQ. Four-year-olds typically saw a butterfly but no faces, whereas children 9 and up ordinarily saw the butterfly and both faces. A few of the preschool children with high IQ's gave responses much like those of sixth graders. Thus, with intellectual growth, children became less rigid perceptually, less tied to the first perceptual response made in the given situation.

3. Reasoning at this age is from the particular to the particular rather than from general to particular. Piaget [64, p. 231] tells how Jacqueline, age 34 months, ill with fever, wanted oranges to eat. Her parents explained to her that the oranges were not ripe yet, they had not their yellow color and were not yet good to eat. She accepted the explanation until given some camomile tea, which was yellow. Then she said, "Camomile tea isn't green, its yellow already. . . . Give me some oranges!"

Thus she reasoned that if camomile tea was yellow, the oranges must have become so. She went from one concrete instance to another, influenced by the way she wanted things to be.

4. Preschool thinking is relatively unsocialized. The young child feels no need to justify his conclusions and if he did, he would not be able to reconstruct his thought processes so as to show another person how he arrived at his conclusions. He takes little notice of how other people think, sometimes even ignoring what they say when he is talking. He begins to adjust his thinking to that of other people only as he becomes aware of himself as a thinker and as he grows in power to hold in mind several aspects of a situation at a time. Through years of interaction with

other people, discussing, disagreeing, coming to agreements, the child gradually adopts the ground rules necessary for logical thinking.

### Growth in Conceptualizing

Most 2-year-olds can name pictures or drawings of familiar items, showing that they have inner representations of those objects. The child need not have seen a previous picture of the object in order to recognize what it depicts, thus showing that he has some sort of generalized representation, which might be considered a primitive concept. The Stanford–Binet test shows that the preschool child's typical response to pictures is the naming of figures in them, while the child of 6 or 7 and 11 or 12 tells about actions as well and the child over 12 gives a theme. Thus the conceptualizing of pictures develops from simple and concrete to abstract and complex.

The young child is hard at work organizing his experiences into concepts of classes, time, space, number, and causality. The fact that he does not quite make it until around 4 years is reflected in Piaget's term, *preconceptual thought*, which refers to the first half of the period of preoperational thought. The second half of this period, the stage of *intuitive thought* is characterized by judgments being made on the basis of perceptions rather than on reason. He classifies more and uses more complex representations of thought than he does in the period of preconceptual thought.

**Class Concepts.** Even before the stage of preconceptual thought, children perceive certain similar or identical aspects in objects or in repeated events. One-year-olds will show a primitive kind of grouping behavior when presented with two sets of dissimilar objects, as did the infants who touched several clay balls in succession or several yellow cubes in succession [72]. Preconceptual children will group objects readily on a perceptual basis rather than according to any inclusive and exclusive categories. *Chaining* is a kind of grouping often employed by young children. Given blocks in various shapes, colors, and sizes, a child might put a red triangle next to a red cube, then add a blue cube, a long blue rod, a short blue rod, and a small green rectangle. Each object is related to the one beside it, but there is no overall relationship tying the collection together.

Four-year-old children will group words together in categories when they try to recall them, instead of recalling them more in the order given [74]. For example, a child would be more likely to recall *hat* with *coat* or *dress*, than with *mouth* or *queen*, the words given before and after *hat*. In this grouping we see a conceptualizing of verbal stimuli.

Preoperational children cannot conceive of a given object as belonging simultaneously to two classes, such as a block going with the red things and the wooden things. Nor can they understand a class including a subclass.

The first concepts are concrete, tied to definite objects of events. Through repeated experiences, especially those verbalized by other people in certain ways, the child develops abstract concepts. The concepts he builds will always be affected by the people around him, through the give and take of social living. For example, most children acquire the abstract concepts *red* and *black*. Figure 6–1 shows how a group of American preschool children increased in their successes on tests of matching and naming colors. Living in a culture that uses abstract color names, these children were in the process of acquiring abstract concepts of color, as shown

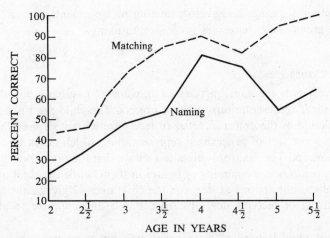

**Figure 6–1.** Age increases in ability to match colors and ability to name colors.

SOURCE: Reprinted by permission from W. M. Cook, "Ability of Children in Color Discrimination," *Child Development*, **2**, Figure 3. Copyright © 1931, The Society for Research in Child Development, Inc.

by naming. How much more difficult, or even impossible, it is for a child to develop an abstract concept of red when *gab*, the word for red, is also the word for blood. Thus *red* and *blood* are forever tied together, as are *black* and *crow* in the word *kott-kott*. Even more concretely tied to perception is the Brazilian Indian word *tu ku eng*, which is used for any and all of these colors: emerald green, cinnabar red, and ultramarine blue. *Tu ku eng* is also a parrot which bears all three colors. Thus green, red, and blue are not only bound up with the parrot but also with each other [100, pp. 234–241].

Sensory, motor, and emotional experiences all enter into the early building of concepts. Young children often group together things that they have experienced together, as did the child who used *quack* to mean duck, water, and all other liquids and the child who used *afta* to mean drinking glass, pane of glass, window, and what was drunk out of the glass [100, p. 226]. The experience of the family group is often used in ordering objects which have no claim to family membership other than belonging in a category. For example, 2-year-old Dickie called two half dollars *daddy* and *mummy*, a quarter *Dickie*, and a dime *Baby*. Children frequently take into account physical qualities such as heaviness, clumsiness, pliability, or prickliness, when naming objects. The name itself is thought to be part of the object, and language can express such qualities. Two children who made up a language used the word *bal* for *place*. The longer the vowel was held, the larger the place. *Bal* therefore meant village, *baal*, town and *baaal*, city. The word *dudu* meant go. The speed with which it was spoken indicated how fast the going was [100, p. 261].

Several experiments have been devised to find out how children will classify (group) objects spontaneously when not given labels to aid in abstraction. The role of perception in concept formation can thus be seen more clearly. In the first experiment [44], children between 3 and 5 years were asked to choose from a group of red triangles and green circles the figures which were the same as another figure. The other figure was either a green triangle or a red circle. (See Figure 6–2.) The younger children chose quickly, without hesitation, usually on the basis of color

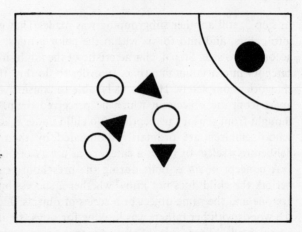

**Figure 6–2.** An ambiguous situation. Matching can be done by either form or color.

Source: Reprinted by permission from H. Werner, *Comparative Psychology of Mental Development*. New York: International Universities Press, Inc., 1957. Copyright © 1957, International Universities Press, Inc.

rather than form. With increasing age, form more often became the basis of choice. Another experimenter [20], using what was essentially the same situation, found that when faced with the choice between form and color as a way of grouping, the older children often showed concern over the ambiguity of the choice. A number of experiments [16, 17, 18, 86] have confirmed the finding that the younger preschool children are likely to classify on the basis of color and older ones on form. It is suggested that contrast effects from color stimuli are dominant and that the young child has a built-in tendency to attend to such contrast. There is evidence to show that there is a hierarchy of stimuli in terms of attention and that the hierarchy changes as the child matures [50]. The salience of the type of stimuli in the child's life is probably a determining factor. These experiments show how the perceptual processes in young children are almost automatic in grouping certain elements. When a grouping is formed, it predominates over other possible groupings, because of the child's inflexibility and lack of control of thought.

Further research dealing with the use of categories shows that the salience of various concepts is related to age during the preschool years [48]. Children between 3½ and 6½ years of age were given systematic choices in how to group a collection of toys. It was possible to classify the toys in terms of color, size, number, form, analytic characteristics (such as having four wheels or two arms), or sex type (for girls or for boys to play with). In general, the children found it easier to use color, number, form, and size for classifying toys than to use analytic concepts or sex type. There were age differences in the use of color, size, and form, the younger children using color and size more easily than form, the older ones using form more easily than color and size. It was suggested that although 6-year-olds are capable of classifying by color and size, form has greater significance for them, because they are learning to read and write, tasks in which form is very important.

When once a preschool child has sorted objects in terms of one particular classification, he finds it difficult or impossible to abandon that classification and sort them into another [46]. The following experiment [34] demonstrates the gradual elaboration of classifying which takes place with growth. Children were given forms of several shapes and colors and told to put them into groups. The first step in ordering is to put the objects into groups of either form or color. The young child (78 percent of 3-year-olds and 33 percent of 4-year-olds) was unable to arrange the objects further even after the examiner set an example. In step 2, most 6-year-olds made subgroups by form after having grouped all the objects by color.

In step 3, still another subgrouping was made. That is, after arranging the objects into colors, and into forms within the color groups, the child then ordered them according to size. Step 4, characteristic of the adult, involves taking more than one category into account at a time. In order to do this, the person has to abstract the categories completely. He has to be able to consider form, color, and size entirely apart from the objects in which he perceived them. This process is a freeing of thought from sensory perception. No child under 8 achieved it unaided. Thus preschool children are ordinarily dominated by their perceptions and unable to deliberately select or reject a category as a way of ordering.

A concept of *all* is built during the preschool years. In the early part of this period, the child does not know whether a succession of objects which look alike are one and the same object or a series of objects. Jacqueline, age $2\frac{1}{2}$, walking in the woods with her father, was looking for slugs (snails). Catching sight of one she commented, "There it is." Seeing another, several yards away, she cried, "There's the slug again." Piaget took her back to see the first one again and asked if the second was the same or another. She answered "yes" to both questions. Jacqueline had no concept of a class of slugs [64, p. 225]. A 2-year-old ordinarily has the concept of "another" when it is a case of wanting a cookie for each hand, or asking for more. The difference between cookies in the hands and slugs on Jacqueline's walk is that the two cookies are present at the same time, whereas the slugs were seen in succession.

A step beyond Jacqueline's dealing with a concept of slugs was shown by Ellen, at $3\frac{1}{2}$. Looking up at the blue Michigan sky surrounding her, she asked, "Is our sky at camp joined onto our sky at home?"

Thus Ellen showed that she realized that the sky in New York State and the sky in Michigan were either the same thing or of the same order of things. By asking, she was trying to develop the appropriate concept.

Adults often wonder why young children accept a succession of streetcorner Santa Clauses as Santa Claus. The reason is seen above, in the child's uncertainty as to whether similar objects constitute an individual or a class. Through experience and discussion, the child builds concepts of *one*, *some*, and *all*. At first, *all* means that he perceives in a given situation. The toddler, listening to his bedtime story about Sleepyboy taking off his clothing, gets up at the mention of Sleepyboy's shoes and points out the shoes of everyone in the family. This early form of generalization is a *plural concept*. It is less mature than the concept of *all shoes*, which begins at around 5. This stage was demonstrated in an experiment where each child was shown two series of trays. The trays in the first series contained a dog and a bird, a dog and a pig, a dog and a cow, a dog and a sheep. Although every child could recognize that this tray had a dog, and that tray, and the other tray, few children under 5 could express the fact that all the trays contained dogs [34].

**Time Concepts.** The earliest experiences of time are most likely those of bodily rhythms, states which recur in regular patterns, such as hunger, eating, fullness. Interactions with the environment impose some patterns on bodily rhythms, calling them by such names as breakfast, nap time, and bath time. Other early experiences which form the basis of time perception include dealing with a succession of objects, such as filling a basket with blocks; taking part in an action which continues and then stops, such as pushing or pulling a wheeled toy; hearing sounds of varying lengths. These experiences, each a seriation of events, are one type of operation which is basic to the notion of time, according to Piaget [69, p. 198],

Events such as these constitute the order of temporal succession. A second type of experience basic to time concepts comes from temporal metrics, the repetitions of stimuli in patterns, such as music and dance, or even rhythms of patting which a parent might do to a child in arms. A third notion, that of duration, is necessary for mature time concepts. Duration involves appreciation of the intervals between events. In early childhood, time is not "an ever-rolling stream" but simply concrete events, embedded in activity. Time and space are not differentiated from each other. Having no overall, objective structure, time is largely the way that the preschool feels it or wants it. To put it in Piaget's terms, the young child judges duration in terms of content, forgetting speed. Adults can appreciate this quality when they consider how long 10 seconds can be under the dentist's drill and how brief a hit Broadway show can be. Or, looking back at events such as your first formal dance or first trip alone, the vivid scene is as yesterday. Accepting the objective nature of time, the dental patient "knows" that the drilling was really only 10 seconds, the audience admits that the show lasted for $2\frac{1}{2}$ hours and the adult realizes that his solitary trip to Grandpa's was 10 years ago.

Time is structured differently by different cultures, groups, and individuals. A Balinese child must learn to orient himself within several simultaneously running calendars. An Eskimo gets a concept of night and day as varying dramatically from season to season, whereas to an Indonesian, night and day are very stable. Minute-conscious Americans are scheduled throughout the days, weeks, and years, equipped with abundant watches, clocks, timers, and calendars. The ages at which American children replace egocentric time concepts with objective ones are not necessarily those of other children in the world. In fact, in primitive time systems, nobody detaches time concepts from the concrete activities in which they are embedded, such as milking time, apple blossom time, or the year that a certain field was planted with yams. Emotional experiences may divide time into lucky and unlucky periods. While Western civilizations have attained considerable objectification of time, there are still many time structures based on personal, emotional, and spiritual experiences—spring, holy days, vacation, mourning period, anniversaries. A child's concepts will be molded by the time concepts he encounters in other people—his family, friends, and teachers. As he checks his notions with theirs, he gradually changes his private, egocentric (self-referred) ones to generally held concepts.

Time concepts of children between 18 and 48 months were studied by both observation and questioning for two consecutive years in a nursery school [1]. All the children in the school were used both years, and all spontaneous verbalizations involving or implying time were recorded. The results show the trend of development in time concepts throughout the preschool period, although since the subjects ranged from high average to very superior intelligence, the age levels at which concepts occurred must be considered as applying to children of above average intelligence. Note, they do show the trend of development in time concepts from egocentric to objective:

> *18 months :* Some sense of timing, but no words for time.
> *21 months :* Uses *now*. Waits in response to *just a minute*. Sense of timing improved. May rock with another child, or sit and wait at the table.
> *2 years :* Uses *going to* and *in a minute, now, today*. Waits in response to several words. Understands *have clay after juice*. Begins to use past tense of verbs.

*30 months :* Free use of several words implying past, present and future, such as *morning, afternoon, some day, one day, tomorrow, last night.* More future words than past words.

*3 years :* Talks nearly as much about past and future as about the present. Duration : *all the time, all day, for two weeks.* Pretends to tell time. Much use of the word *time : what time ? it's time, lunchtime.* Tells how old he is, what he will do tomorrow, what he will do at Christmas.

*42 months :* Past and future tenses used accurately. Complicated expressions of duration : *for a long time, for years, a whole week, in the meantime, two things at once.* Refinements in the use of time words : *it's almost time, a nice long time, on Fridays.* Some confusion in expressing time of events : "I'm not going to take a nap yesterday."

*4 years :* Broader concepts expressed by use of *month, next summer, last summer.* Seems to have clear understanding of sequence of daily events.*

Another study [82] traces the development of time concepts from egocentric to objective by showing how children learn to use a clock. When asked what time events in their day took place, a quarter of 4-year-olds, a tenth of 5-year-olds, and no 6-year-olds either recited their schedules or used words like *morning* and *early.* Numbers, either unreasonable, approximate or correct, were used by the rest of the children.

## Space Concepts

The young child's concepts of space, like his concepts of time, are derived from bodily experience. He gets sensations from within his body and from his interactions with the rest of the world. During the sensorimotor period, he looks, touches, mouths, and moves to build concepts of his body and other objects. During the period of preoperational thought, space is still egocentric, related to the child's body, his movements, and perceptions. Four-year-old Laura named a certain tree "the resting tree" because she often sat under its cool branches for a few minutes on her way home from kindergarten. The land where the "resting tree" was located was the "resting place," and the family who lived there was "the resting tree people."

Space concepts were studied in nursery school children in the same way in which the time study, reported above, was conducted [2]. The order of appearance of verbalized concepts of space is thus shown. As in the time study, the ages given are for children who measured above average on intelligence tests.

*1 year :* Gestures for *up* and *down.*

*18 months :* Uses *up, down, off, come, go.*

*2 years :* *Big, all gone, here.* Interest in going and coming.

*30 months :* Many space words are rigid, exact ones : *right, right here, right there, right up there.* Words were combined for emphasis and exactness ; *way up, up in, in here, in there, far away.* Space words used most : *in, up in, on, at.*

*36 months :* Words express increased refinements of space perception : *back, corner, over, from, by, up on top, on top of.* A new interest in detail and direction : tells where his daddy's office is and where his own bed is, uses names of cities.

*42 months :* *Next to, under, between.* Interest in appropriate places : *go there, find.* Interest in comparative size : *littlest, bigger, largest.* Expanding interest in location : *way down, way off, far away.* Can put the ball *on, in, under* and *in back of* the chair.

* Reprinted by permission from L. B. Ames, "The Development of the Sense of Time in the Young Child," *J. Genet. Psychol.*, 1946, **68**, 97–125.

*48 months :* More expansive words : *on top of, far away, out in, down to, way up, way up there, way far out, way off.* The word *behind.* Can tell his street and city. Can put a ball in front of a chair. Space words used most : *in, on, up in, at, down.**

Primitive languages contain many space words which refer to the body or its motion and location in space. So does everyday (nonscientific) English in such words and expressions as groundwork, sky-high, eye-level, handy, backside, neck and neck. When asking directions from the man in the street, how often does one get an answer such as, "Follow Elm Street for half a mile and then turn right onto Route 4?" Not very often. It is much more likely to be, "You know where the Mobil gas station is down past the cemetery? No? Well then, go to the second stop light and turn kitty-corner to the Catholic Church. You can't miss it." *You can't miss it* is almost inevitable at the end of a set of directions so firmly rooted in concrete experience. The person giving such directions is doing it so much from an egocentric standpoint that he cannot imagine anyone finding the route less clear than it is in his own mind.

The child's progress toward objective space concepts depends not only upon his bodily experiences, moving through space and perceiving objects, but also upon the concepts which adults offer him. Although it is necessary to have experience and to internalize it, the child also checks his interpretations with those of other people.

* Reprinted by permission from L. B. Ames and J. Learned, "The Development of Verbalized Space in the Young Child," *J. Genet. Psychol.*, 1948, **72**, 63–84.

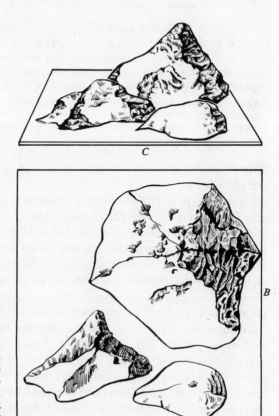

**Figure 6–3.** Model of mountains, as seen from different viewpoints, used in testing children for egocentric concepts.

SOURCE: Adapted from J. Piaget and B. Inhelder, *The Child's Conception of Space.* London: Routledge & Kegan Paul Ltd., 1948. Copyright © 1948, Routledge & Kegan Paul Ltd. Reprinted by permission of the publishers.

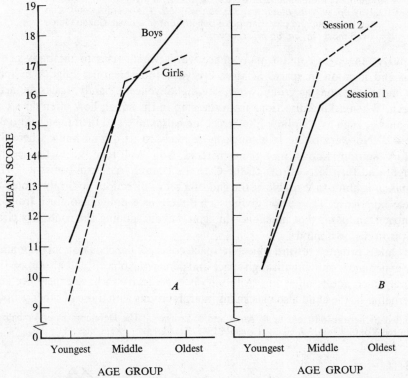

**Figure 6–4.** Scores of children between ages 3 and 6 on a test of ordering in space. The figure on the left shows mean scores of boys and girls on two testing sessions, indicating significant increases with age for ability to order space. The figure on the right shows scores on two tests, two weeks apart, indicating significant increases over a 2-week period.

Source: Reprinted by permission from J. Gottschalk, M. P. Bryden, and M. S. Rabinovitch, "Spatial Organization of Children's Responses to a Pictorial Display," *Child Development*, **35**, Figure 1, p. 813. Copyright © 1964, The Society for Research in Child Development, Inc.

Thus he comes eventually to have an idea of space existing independently of his perception of it.

Piaget [68, p. 211] demonstrates egocentric space concepts by his mountains test. Three mountains are placed on a table, as in Figure 6–3. A doll is placed first at one side of the table, then at another and another. The child is asked to choose from pictures or cutouts what the doll would see in the various positions. A child under 7 or 8 shows no understanding of the problem. He cannot conceive of the mountains as looking different from the way in which he is viewing them, because his space concepts are still tied to his own perceptions. All he can do with the problem is to attribute his own view to the doll.

The ordering of space by preschool children has been studied in terms of their methods of dealing with columns and rows of pictures [30]. Children between 3 years 3 months and 6 years 3 months were tested in two sessions two weeks apart. The child was given a card with rows of pictures of 20 familiar objects and asked to name all the pictures and to report "I don't know" for unfamiliar ones. The order and direction used were noted. Responses were scored for organization, one point being given each time the picture named was adjacent to the one named previously. As Figure 6–4 shows, scores increased very significantly with age and also increased with the same groups over a 2-week period. Therefore, as children grew older, they applied more order to the way in which they dealt with objects in space, as though they realized increasingly that they could be more efficient if they organized their behavior.

The ability to copy the order of the set of objects is first observable between 4 and 5 years of age. It is easier for a child to pile blocks in a certain order than it is for him to make a row which corresponds to a model [40]. In the pile, there is only one way to go, up. In making a row, one can add to the left or to the right. Even when frames were supplied in order that adding to the rows could be done in one direction only, the row constructed was still more difficult. The difference in ease of ordering may be connected with the space orientation of the body itself, up and down being an unchanging dimension, while left and right aspects of the environment change constantly.

**Quantity Concepts.** While a hungry 4-year-old could readily choose the plate with more cookies on it rather than the plate with less, he probably would not be able to understand the words *more* and *less* with complete accuracy. When tested for comprehension of these two words, children between $3\frac{1}{2}$ and 4 reacted about the same to either word [21]. *More* and *less* were undifferentiated from each other, and both were usually taken to mean *more*. This experiment illustrates why a child's use of a certain word cannot be taken as proof that he understands it in its full and accurate meaning. Quantity concepts develop gradually, as do concepts of time, space, and causality.

Like concepts of time and space, number concepts are rooted in early concrete experience. The toddler does not have to count at all in order to choose the plate containing four cookies rather than the plate with two cookies. A configuration of objects, up to 5 or 6, can be grasped perceptually without true number concepts being employed. A larger group may be seen as complete or not because every object is known as an individual. For instance, a 2-year-old (like the others) in a family of eight realizes that eldest brother is absent, not because he has counted and found only seven members present, but because he does not see a certain individual who is often part of the family configuration. The development of perceptual discrimination of numbers of objects was demonstrated in a study of children between 3 and 7 years [51]. The children were asked to discriminate 10 marbles from smaller groups of marbles, to match a group of marbles varying in number from 2 to 10, and to select larger and smaller groups of marbles as compared with a group of 4. Figure 6–5 shows the results of the tests. Perceptual discrimination of number improved steadily, with number discrimination developing first, then number matching, and then group matching. A score of 10 would indicate exact matching, which would involve true counting and comparison. Note that the average scores reached in this period were approximately 8, 7, and 6, suggesting that the discrimination was indeed done on a perceptual, not conceptual, basis. The process by which children learn to match numbers was analyzed from the behavior of children between 3 and 5 years of age [87]. The child was asked to build a row of M & M candies equal in number to one built by the examiner. The youngest children usually aligned the start of the row with the standard and then added candies without regard to density until the rows were approximately equal. The next oldest group placed a candy opposite each end of the model row and then filled in with more candies than the standard contained. The

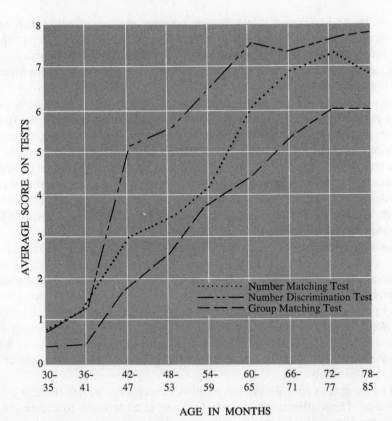

**Figure 6–5.** Improvement between ages 3 and 7 on tests of matching numbers, discriminating numbers, and matching groups.

SOURCE: Adapted from L. Long and L. Welch, "The Development of the Ability to Discriminate and Match Numbers," *Journal of Genetic Psychology*, **59**, 377–387.

oldest group matched the model row in both length and number. Thus the performances of the three age levels demonstrated the development of one-to-one mapping. Even the youngest children showed some notion of a relation between length of line and numerosity.

When a child counts objects and tells accurately that there are 7 apples or 7 blocks, he has a concrete number concept, a more exact way of dealing with numbers of objects than does the child who discriminates on a perceptual basis. An abstract concept, in contrast to a concrete one, is not involved with apples or blocks but with 7. Many experiences with 7 of this and 7 of that occur before 7 becomes free from objects and stands alone. As has been shown with concepts of classes, time, and space, the preconceptual period is a time when thought is quite concretely and specifically tied to personal experience. During this period, however, thought becomes progressively freer.

Certain primitive number concepts illustrate the stage of preconceptual thought. Werner [100, pp. 289–290] tells of cultures where a different type of number name is used for each of seven classes of objects: indefinite and amorphous; long, round, or flat; human being; boats; and measures. He tells of a language where 10 baskets are *bola* and 10 coconuts *koro*. Partially fused, 10 changes as the objects do. A step toward abstraction is shown in the language where *lima*, the word for *hand*, is also the word for *five*. The use of the body as a natural number schema is found in primitive cultures and in children, and alas, in an occasional college student. Number systems based on five or ten obviously have their roots in the human hand. Werner [100, p. 291] says, "At the beginning, no schema is an abstract form purely mathematical in significance; it is a material vessel in which the concrete fullness of objects is poured, as it were, to be measured."

A relationship has been shown, at least in retarded children, between the ability to articulate the fingers and the development of number concepts. Each child was asked to point, with eyes closed, to the finger touched by the examiner. A group showing high ability in number concepts made almost no errors, whereas a group with mathematical disability showed many errors [100, p. 296].

Children who grow up in cultures using abstract number systems must go through the primitive stages of enumeration, but they are offered the abstract concepts to grasp when they are able to do so [11]. (Or, unhappily, they may have the abstract concepts pushed at them before they have built the conceptual bases which underlie them.) Three developmental stages in number conception were described for 72 children between 4 and 7 years: (1) Preconceptual. Number is responded to in purely perceptual terms. When the arrangement of objects changes the perception of number may change. (2) Individual numbers are responded to in conceptual terms. The verbal terms are very helpful here in achieving concepts. (3) Relationship among the individual numbers is understood [101].

Perceptual dominance can be demonstrated in young children's quantification by some of Piaget's tests [61, pp. 49–50]. For example, the child is given a number of flowers and the same number of vases and asked to place a flower in each vase. Then the examiner takes out the flowers and puts them in a bunch. He spreads out the vases and asks, "Are there more flowers or more vases?" The child under 7 or 8 usually says that there are more vases. If the vases are bunched up and flowers spread out, he is likely to say that there are more flowers. He bases his answer on the perception of the amount. The flowers, in a bunch, cover less area than the vases spread out. Therefore he concludes that there are more vases. Instead of recalling his experience of matching flowers to vases, and reasoning that the quantities must be equal, he is so dominated by what he sees that he is not free to use concepts.

Being able to count is no guarantee of being able to cope with a situation similar to the flowers test. Children between 5 and 9, all of whom could count beyond six, were asked to place a rubber doll in each of six little bathtubs, which were placed side by side [41]. Upon questioning, the child agreed that there were the same number of dolls and tubs. Then the experimenter asked him to remove the dolls and place them in a heap. Answers to the questions as to whether there were more dolls or more bathtubs usually brought the answer that there were more bathtubs.

An objective number concept involves knowing that the number of objects is the same, no matter how they are arranged. ...... = ::: = :..: The difference between 5- to 6-year-olds and 7- to 7½-year-olds in regard to this kind of understanding is demonstrated by this experiment [52]. Children were given two groups of four beans to represent eight sweets. Four sweets were to be eaten in midmorning and four more at teatime. Then two more sets of four were presented, and the children were told that these represented sweets to be eaten the following day, when only one was to be eaten in the morning and the remaining three would be eaten with the four teatime sweets. While the children watched, three sweets were taken from the group and added to the other group of four. Thus the children had in front of them two sets, one being 4 + 4 and the other 1 + 7. The experimenter then asked each child if he would eat the same number of sweets on each day. The younger children said "no" that 1 + 7 was either larger or smaller then 4 + 4. The older children gave the correct answer promptly. Questioning showed that they understood the equivalence of the sets and the compensation occurring in the change. The children under 7 demonstrated inability to weigh more than one factor at a time and their centering on what they first perceived. They compared either 1 or 7 with the 4's. The older children, having considerable freedom from perceptual dominance, could consider the several aspects of the situation in relation to one another.

Cardinal number concepts are built from putting objects into groups or classes and then abstracting out the number. Ordinal number concepts come from putting objects in series and then abstracting out the order. Classifying and seriation are therefore both essential activities in building number concepts. Piaget [66, p. 156] maintains that classification and seriation are necessarily learned simultaneously, since the processes are complementary. Below about 5 years a child cannot make a series of objects, as of dolls of increasing size, but between 5 and 6 he does so. At this point, he has great difficulty in finding the correct place for an object which has been omitted from the series, but at around 7 he can do this task easily. At 7 he is sufficiently freed from the perception of the dolls to conceive at the same time of the first doll being smaller than the second and the second smaller than the third.

**Causality Concepts.** The idea of universal laws is absent in primitive and childish thinking. What explanations are given tend to be in concrete and personal terms. Egocentrism in regard to causality occurs at the same time and for the same reasons as egocentrism in concepts of space, time, and number.

The events of the outer world are closely linked with the child's inner world and his needs. During the preschool and school years, causality becomes less subjective. It can be followed through three stages of subjectivity. At first events are explained in terms of the child's own feelings and actions or in terms of people close to him or perhaps in terms of God. Although he does not consider all events to be caused by his own action, as he did in the sensorimotor period, he understands causes as forces resembling personal activity. "The peaches are growing on our tree, getting ready for us to eat." "The moon comes up because we need some light in the night." The next step toward maturity is to see natural events as caused by forces contained in themselves or by vague agents called *they*. "The radish seed knows it is supposed to make a radish." Increasing sophistication of thought decreases egocentrism, and the child begins to see causes as impersonal. For instance, heavy things sink and light things float. Progress in understanding cause is from concrete toward abstract. At first, explanations are merely descriptions of events. QUESTION: "What makes a sailboat move?" PETER: "My daddy takes me out in our sailboat. Mummy goes and Terry goes. Daddy starts the motor and we go chug, chug, chug down the pond."

The idea of universal, impersonal causes is beyond even the stage of childhood thinking and is not achieved by naive adults. The concept of chance is related to the concept of necessity. Both require some logical or formal thought. Young children's explanations tend to be diffuse and inconsistent. Several events are explained by several different causes instead of by a unifying cause. Piaget [61, p. 137] gives these accounts of conversations of an adult with two 5-year-old children, Col and Hei, dealing with the concept of floating:

**Col:** Rowing boats stay on the water because they move.—**Adult:** And the big boats?
—They stay on the water because they are heavy.
**Adult:** Why does the boat (a toy) remain on the water?—**Hei:** It stays on top because
it's heavy. . . . The rowing boats stay on top because they're big.—Fifteen days later
Hei says, on the contrary, that boats stay "because they're not heavy." But comparing
a pebble with a plank, Hei again says: "This pebble will go to the bottom because it
isn't big enough, it's too thin." Finally Hei says that a stone goes to the bottom because
"it's stronger" (than the wood).—And the boats, why do they stay on top? Because the
water is strong.

These children give different, and what look like conflicting, explanations of
events which an adult would unify under universal laws of floating. The children
are showing their inability to consider several factors at one time and their consequent inability to come to general conclusions.

### Achievements in Thinking During the Preoperational Period

In all areas of thinking, the preschool child increases in speed and flexibility.
Strongly dominated by perception and by his wishes in the early years, he moves
toward greater control of his thinking. His earliest concepts of classes, space,
numbers, time, and causes are rooted in concrete, personal experience, gradually
becoming more objective and abstract as he has more experience, especially interactions with other people, who check his thoughts and conclusions.

## Intellectual Development as Revealed by Standardized Tests

Many tests of intelligence have been invented, each according to the concept of
intelligence defined by its creator. Binet, who with Simon, developed the first
standardized intelligence tests, considered three different capacities as consti-
tuting intelligence—the ability to understand directions, to maintain a mental set,
and to correct one's own errors [57, p. 349]. Terman [88], whose revisions of Binet's
tests have had the greatest influence on modern intelligence testing, thought of
intelligence as the ability to think abstractly and use abstract symbols in solving
problems. Thorndike [90], who accepted a concept of intelligence as comprising
problem solving through use of abstract symbols, defined three dimensions of
intelligence: altitude, breadth, and speed. Altitude referred to difficulty of problem,
the more intelligent person being able to solve the more difficult problem; breadth
meant the number of tasks a person could do; speed, of course, referred to how
fast problems were solved. Thorndike considered altitude the most important of
the three attributes of intelligence. Guilford [32, 33] thinks of intelligence as consisting of many different abilities, possibly 120, about 80 of which are already
known. He stresses creativity as a component of intelligence.

### Measurement of Intelligence

Many tests have been designed to measure preschool intelligence, the best known
of which is the Stanford–Binet [89], a derivative of Binet and Simon's original
tests. The Stanford–Binet yields a single mental age score, from which an intelligence quotient, the IQ, is computed. Although the Stanford–Binet can be given to
most 2-year-olds, it is often easier to interest them in tests which have more manipulative materials and which involve more sensory stimulation, such as the Merrill–
Palmer Test [85] or the Gesell Test [27]. Advantages of the latter type include the

adaptability of the scoring to the child's refusing some items and the fact that more than one score can be obtained from each of these tests. The Merrill–Palmer can be scored for verbal and nonverbal items and the Gesell for four areas of development, called motor, adaptive, language, and personal social. Merrill–Palmer scores can be expressed as percentiles, standard deviations, or IQs. Gesell scores are expressed as developmental quotients. The Wechsler Intelligence Scale for Children [97] is favored over the Stanford–Binet by the same examiners for elementary school age children. The Wechsler can also be used for preschool children. Like the Merrill–Palmer, the Wechsler yields verbal and nonverbal scores. The Peabody Picture Vocabulary Test [22] is primarily a screening test which can be given without requiring the child to speak. It has been used widely in Head Start groups. The Peabody test materials consist of 150 plates, each with four pictures. The examiner says a word and the child is asked to point to the picture which best illustrates the word. Quick and easily administered, this test correlates well with other tests of intelligence.

Mental age (MA) is a construct conceived by Binet. A child's MA is found by comparing his test performance with the average performance of a large number of children. Binet gave a large number of tests to a large number of children, found the ages at which most children passed each test, and arranged the tests in order of difficulty. This procedure is essentially the one which has been followed in constructing intelligence tests since then. To show how the MA is found, take, for example, a child who passes the items passed by the average 8-year-old. The child's MA is 8. If his chronological age (CA) is also 8, then he is like the average child of his age. If, however, his CA is 6 he has done more than the average. If his CA is 10, he has done less.

Intelligence quotient (IQ) is a construct originated by Stern, a German psychologist. IQ is a ratio of CA to MA, which has been found to be fairly constant. IQ is found by dividing MA by CA and multiplying by 100. 100MA/CA = IQ.

### IQ as an Expression of Rate of Growth

The intelligence quotient is a measuring of rate of growth in mental age, although the convention of multiplying by 100 obscures this fact. Tom, age 70 months, earns a score of 77 months of mental age. His average rate of mental growth throughout the whole of his 70 months is 1.1. For each month of CA he has achieved 1.1 month of MA. His IQ (MA divided by CA × 100) is 110. Margery, also age 70 months, earns a score of 63 months of mental age. Her mental growth has averaged .9 months for each month of CA. Her IQ is 90. If Tom and Margery continue to grow at their present rates, Tom's IQ will continue to be 110 and Margery's 90. Suppose, however, each grows at the rate of 1 month of MA per month of CA for the coming year. Each will gain 12 months of MA. Tom's MA will be 89, his IQ, 108; Margery's MA will be 75, her IQ 91. The MA changes are large, but the IQ changes are small. At each test the resulting IQ expresses the average mental growth since birth.

### IQ as a Measure of Brightness

The common concept of IQ is as a measure of quality or strength of intelligence. The higher the IQ, the brighter the child and the more capable he is of doing good work at school. Tom, who has been growing at the rate of 1.1 months of mental age for each month of chronological age for 70 months, is brighter than Margery,

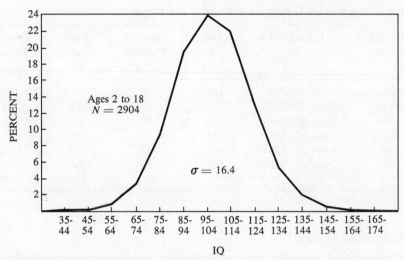

**Figure 6–6.** Distribution of Stanford–Binet IQs in the population on which the test was standardized.

SOURCE: Reprinted by permission from L. M. Terman and M. A. Merrill, *Measuring Intelligence.* Boston: Houghton Mifflin Company, 1937. Copyright © 1937, Houghton Mifflin Company.

who has been growing at an average rate of 0.9 MA months per chronological month. Jean, age 50 months, has been growing at the 1.1 rate and therefore has an IQ of 110. She is just as far above the average 50-month-old child as Tom is above the average child of 70 months. By the time Jean is 70 months old, if her mental growth continues at the same rate, her mental age will be 77 and her IQ will still be 110.

### Distribution of IQs

Figure 6–6 and Table 6–1 show how IQs were distributed in the 1937 Stanford–Binet [89]. *Average* includes 79.1 percent of the population. *Defective*, with 8.23 percent, is a little smaller than *superior*, with 12.63 percent, although the most inferior categories match the most superior in size.

Another way of showing how IQs are distributed is to tell how often a given IQ occurs in 100 cases, or in the case of extreme IQs, how often in 1000 or 10,000. Table 6–2 expresses IQs thus.

**Table 6–1** Distribution of IQs in Children Tested in the Standardization of the Stanford–Binet Test

| Category | IQ range | Percent in category |
|---|---|---|
| Very superior | 140–169 | 1.33 |
| Superior | 120–139 | 11.3 |
| High average | 110–119 | 18.1 |
| Normal or average | 90–109 | 46.5 |
| Low average | 80–89 | 14.5 |
| Borderline defective | 70–79 | 5.6 |
| Mentally defective | 30–69 | 2.63 |

SOURCE: L. M. Terman and M. A. Merrill, Stanford–Binet Intelligence Scale. Boston: Houghton Mifflin, 1960.

**Table 6–2** Frequency of Occurrence of Common and Uncommon IQ Levels

| The Child Whose IQ Is | Is Equalled or Excelled by | Child of IQ: | Equals or Exceeds (%) | Child of IQ: | Equals or Exceeds (%) |
|---|---|---|---|---|---|
| 160 | 1 out of 10,000 | 136 | 99 | 94 | 36 |
| 156 | 3 out of 10,000 | 130 | 97 | 89 | 25 |
| 152 | 8 out of 10,000 | 120 | 89 | 85 | 18 |
| 148 | 2 out of 1,000 | 113 | 79 | 80 | 11 |
| 144 | 4 out of 1,000 | 105 | 62 | 70 | 3 |
| 140 | 7 out of 1,000 | 100 | 50 | 64 | 1 |

SOURCE: R. Pintner, A. Dragositz and R. Kushner. *Supplementary guide for the revised Stanford–Binet Scale*, Form L. Stanford: Stanford University Press, 1944

## Errors of Measurement

Errors are likely to affect any test through less-than-perfect presentation and scoring, through the subject's not performing at top capacity, and through poor conditions of testing, such as noise or discomforts. The standard error of measurement has been calculated for various ages and IQ ranges [89]. For practical purposes, *five* is the standard error. In interpreting any IQ, then, $\pm 5$ should be added to the figure. If Mary's measured IQ is 107, there are 68 chances in 100 that her "real" IQ lies between 102 and 112. There are 95 chances in 100 that Mary's IQ lies between 97 and 117.

The standard error must be used when comparing the IQs of two children and also when comparing two tests on one child. In the first case, the difference between IQs must be at least 10 before a real difference can be said to exist. When tests on the same child are compared, the difference between the two tests must be 10 or more before a real change in growth rate is indicated.

## Predicting Intelligence

Preschool intelligence tests correlate positively with intelligence tests given later. The longer the interval between tests, however, the lower the correlation. At 3 years, intelligence tests have some predictive value, and by age 6, considerable value. The stability and predictive value of intelligence test scores have been explored in a study in which 252 children were tested repeatedly at specified ages between 21 months and 18 years [39]. Figure 6–7 shows how tests given during the preschool years correlated with tests given during the middle school years and during adolescence. A look at what actually does happen to individual IQs is helpful in understanding why statistical prediction has to be done within large ranges. In another study [81] of repeated tests, the greatest gain in an individual case was 58 points, the greatest loss, 32. Figure 6–8 shows records of individual children which illustrate different patterns of changes in IQ. About 25 percent of the cases showed irregular patterns, typified by Case 105. About 20 percent were steady, as shown by Case 112. Other patterns of rising and falling can be seen in the other cases.

In predicting later IQ from preschool IQ, socioeconomic status and initial IQ level are significant. A survey of research on IQ change showed that when children

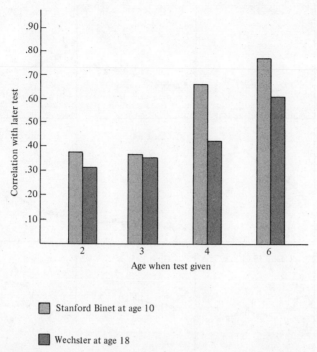

Stanford Binet at age 10

Wechsler at age 18

**Figure 6–7.** Coefficients of correlation between scores of mental tests given to children at ages 2 years through 6 and tests given to the same children at ages 10 and 18. The Stanford–Binet was used at age 10, the Wechsler–Bellevue at 18.

SOURCE: Adapted from M. P. Honzik, J. W. Macfarlane, and L. Allen, "The Stability of Mental Test Performance Between Two and Eighteen Years of Age," *Journal of Experimental Education*, **17**, 309–324.

scored below the median at age 6, changes in IQ were related to socioeconomic status [71]. Children of high SES continued to rise in IQ, while those of low SES continued to drop. This finding is consistent with the results of a study on infants, reported in Chapter 3, showing that babies with low developmental status were likely to improve if they belonged in families of high socioeconomic level but not if they were in families of low socioeconomic level. A low IQ, then, is sensitive to the socioeconomic environment, whether it be favorable or unfavorable, while an above-average IQ is less likely to be affected by SES. While the child was young, socioeconomic status was more strongly related to IQ than when the child was older [71].

Radical changes in the environment are likely to produce radical changes in IQ, especially if the environmental change comes early in the child's life. Compensatory education programs are based on this knowledge. (Such programs will be discussed in the following chapter). The first compensatory education experiments, done at the University of Iowa in the 1930s, illustrate the enormous IQ changes which can result from environmental change [77]. Thirteen mentally retarded children, between 7 and 36 months of age, were transferred from a crowded, unstimulating orphanage to a home for the retarded where each child had a loving substitute mother, attentive aunties, toys, and individualized interaction. At entrance, the retarded children ranged from 35 to 89 IQ with an average of 64. Length of stay

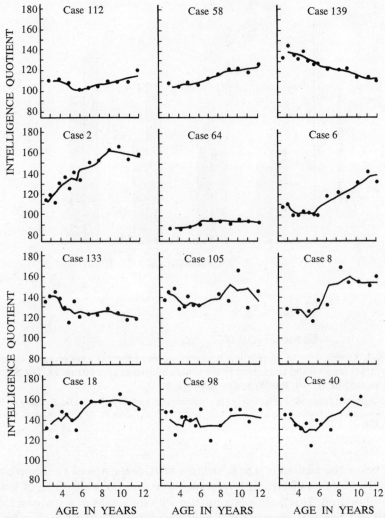

**Figure 6–8.** Examples of individual records of IQs from 2 to 12 years of age, illustrating variation in mental growth patterns.

SOURCE: Reprinted by permission from L. W. Sontag, C. T. Baker, and V. L. Nelson, "Mental Growth and Personality Development: A Longitudinal Study," *Monographs of The Society for Research in Child Development*, **23**, Figure 1. Copyright © 1958, The Society for Research in Child Development, Inc.

was from 6 to 52 months. Every child gained in IQ, all but two more than 15 points. Three gained over 45 points. The highest gain was 58. Over a 2-year period, the experimental group made an average gain of 28 IQ points, while a control group (of the same original average IQ) lost 26 points.

A child's IQ gives a good indication of how well he can do in school now and in the near future. It shows what he is likely to achieve in school in the more distant future. What the IQ tells is in terms of chances and probabilities. It is only a measurement of a limited sample of the child's behavior, telling something about him, but not everything. An IQ should never be thought of as fixed, definite, or final. It should never be used to place a child in a slot from which he cannot move.

## Organization of Measured Intelligence

The abilities which constitute adult intelligence have been studied and delineated by several investigators, using factor analysis. Thurstone [91] identified these factors in intelligence: *space*, the ability to visualize objects; *number*, facility with simple arithmetic; *verbal comprehension*, dealing with verbal concepts and reasoning; *word fluency*, ability to produce appropriate words; *memory*, storing and retrieval of experiences and concepts; *induction*, finding principles; *deduction*, use of principles in problem solving; *flexibility and speed* of thought. Thurstone [92] has devised tests for measuring "primary mental abilities" in children as young as 5, the tests being grouped into motor, verbal, spatial, perceptual, and quantitative categories. Bayley [4] sees intelligence as "a complex of separately timed developing functions . . . with the more advanced . . . functions in the hierarchy depending on the maturing of earlier, simpler ones."

Structure of intellect was compared across race and class for 4-year-olds from black and white, middle- and lower-class groups [76]. Seven factors were found. The largest difference between groups was found in the factor representing verbal comprehension. Here the white middle class was highest, the lower white and middle black equal, and the lower black lowest. There were no group differences for ideational fluency, the free and expansive use of language. The verbal differences between classes and races, then, had to do with functions that use standard English and not with unrestricted production of ideas and language. Nonsignificant differences on the other factors generally showed the middle class exceeding the lower. On black–white comparisons, blacks were superior on some factors and whites on others.

## Class and Ethnic Differences in Response to Tests

Preschool children have recently been studied by many researchers concerned with differences in cognitive structure and function and in reasons for those differences. The widespread interest in preschool education as a way to preventing school problems has led to the search for basic facts on which to build compensatory and preventive programs [37].

Until about the third year of life, social class differences in measured intelligence are not usually found. The time of emergence of these differences is not clear. By kindergarten age or before, disadvantaged children are likely to score lower than other children in general intelligence, language, fine motor coordination, and most cognitive variables on which they are tested [35, 75]. For white children between 2½ and 5, the difference between means of the highest and lowest of seven socioeconomic groups was 22 points [89]. When advantaged and disadvantaged children between 4 and 6 were compared on the Stanford–Binet Test, the difference was 30 points [56]. A longitudinal study of black children showed no difference in intelligence at 18 and 24 months, but at 3 years the difference between the means of the highest and lowest of three socioeconomic levels was 19 points [29]. Of these three groups, the middle-class children obtained the highest IQs, the children from the poor stable families the next, and those from fatherless welfare families, the lowest. Another longitudinal study of black boys showed almost no socioeconomic differences at age 3 years 8 months [58]. Lower- and middle-class boys were compared on the Stanford–Binet IQ, Peabody Picture Vocabulary, Concept Familiarity Index, and a number of perceptual and motor tests. (The lower-class boys were from poor but stable families, not from the lowest class.) Only the picture vocabulary test showed any significant difference. The author suggests that previous studies showing class differences did not include enough precautions for making the lower-class children comfortable in the testing situation. Middle-class children adapt more easily to testing, while lower-class children need extra time and reassurance from the examiner. Since occupation and education are not as highly correlated among blacks as among whites, socioeconomic differences are not likely to follow the same patterns.

Class and race differences were the focus of a comparison of children's cognitive functioning [84], as part of a series of studies which would yield knowledge about the influence of maternal behavior, its effect on children's cognition and implications for desired changes. Disadvantaged mothers and children 4 and 5 years old, both black and white, were tested before the beginning of a Head Start program. There was a lower-class control group which was not going to Head Start and a middle-class group, all white. Tests were selected for measuring skills that might be important in achieving academic success. Many significant social class differences were seen but only a few racial differences. Middle-class children scored higher than lower-class in impulse control, persistence, modeling (imitating an adult in verbal, nonverbal, and prosocial behavior), pointing to colors, and developing strategies of solving pegboard problems. Class differences in maternal behavior were impressive [4]. The middle-class mother most often let her child set his own pace, offered many suggestions on how to find solutions, told her child what he was doing right, and encouraged learning strategies that could generalize to future problems. The lower-class mother often made very specific suggestions, intruded physically into the child's problem solving, and told him what *not* to do. The greater success of the middle-class children in problem solving, self-control, persistence, and imitation seems logical in view of the type of teaching used by their mothers. Only two race differences occurred among the children. The black children had trouble solving the pegboard problems. On level of aspiration, black children pitched their goals higher than either white group, thus aspiring to levels they were very unlikely to reach. The white children, in choosing more feasible goals, were more likely to feel satisfied with the efforts.

The behavioral style of the culture is demonstrated in the family and shown in the child's way of coping with problems. Middle-class American children and working-class children of Puerto Rican origin were compared in responses to the Stanford–Binet test, as part of comprehensive longitudinal research [35]. The Puerto Rican children were tested by a bilingual Puerto Rican psychologist, who chose the language most appropriate for the child. The expected class difference in IQ was found, the average of the middle-class children being 122 and the other group 96.

Each child was observed in his way of responding to the examiner's request for work, whether he started trying right away or delayed his efforts, refused, looked for more, what he said about it. A comparison of the two total groups showed the middle-class children making significantly more work responses. However, the middle-class children made the same proportion (82 and 86 percent) of work responses to verbal and nonverbal items, whereas the Puerto Ricans made only 66 percent responses to verbal items and 85 percent to nonverbal. The groups were the same, then, in responses to nonverbal work demands but significantly different in responses to verbal work demands.

Another difference was in the way a child acted when he did not respond by working. The Puerto Ricans were more likely to be passively unresponsive. When the Puerto Rican child did make a nonwork response, it was likely to be an irrelevant substitution, such as "I want to go to mommy . . . I want a drink." The middle-class children were likely to say *no* and to add some comment explaining that they were not able to do the test. When a comparison was made between the two groups using only children between 90 and 110 IQ, thus equating them for IQ, the same differences in response style appeared. The Puerto Ricans still responded more to nonverbal work demands, while the middle-class children responded equally to verbal and nonverbal tasks. The nonwork responses noted for the total groups also held in the comparison of groups equated for IQ. Therefore the differences between the groups seem to reflect a difference in ethnic style rather than a difference in intellectual competence.

Clinical observations of the examining psychologists amplify the comparisons between the groups. The middle-class children were friendly, interested in the tests, ready to follow instructions, pleased to show what they could do, steady, persistent, likely to tell what they were thinking, and often able to tell whether or not they knew the answer. Although curious about the examiner and the surroundings, their interest did not interfere with their attention to the tasks set for them. The Puerto Rican children were friendly and responsive to the examiner as a person and the situation as social. They were insufficiently task-oriented, as indicated by insisting on playing with toys, being easily distracted, making irrelevant responses or passively failing to respond. The investigators point out the difficulties inherent in the American elementary school for these children whose work style fits better with performance demands than it does with verbal demands.

Recognition, recall and conceptualizing of visual and verbal materials were studied in disadvantaged children between 5 and 7½ years [73]. The main results were consistent with the previously described class differences between middle-class Americans and lower-class children of Puerto Rican origin. That is, the children did better with visually presented materials than with those given auditorily. However, ability to deal with the auditory stimuli increased with age, suggesting, then, that in disadvantaged children processes concerned with visual material develop earlier. When the disadvantaged child enters school, he may be quite adequate in looking at his environment and organizing it visually but quite inadequate in attaching verbal labels, organizing them, and storing them so as to be able to retrieve them easily. He catches up somewhat during the first three years of school and brings his auditory system closer to the level of efficiency of the visual system. In contrast, the middle-class child is likely to start school able to process both kinds of stimuli satisfactorily.

## Language Development

Language supplements the tactile link between the young child and other people and supplants that link in many of the child's relationships with others. Language is a vital tie between past, present, and future, both for the individual and for groups of people. The rapid acquisition of language by the preschool child, shown by increase in vocabulary and development of grammatical structures, is intimately related to the development of autonomy and initiative, to the growth from egocentric thought to objectivity, and to social relationships. And it is also closely related to general intelligence, vocabulary being one of the best single measures. American middle-class culture emphasizes verbal modes, sometimes neglecting other avenues of expression and experience.

## Fusion of Thought and Language

The linking of thought and speech marks the beginning of the period of pre-operational thought. During the sensorimotor period, children think and reason, but they do it slowly and concretely, in terms of the experience of the moment. Higher animals do the same kind of thinking and reasoning that infants do. They also make sounds which have meaning. Baboons use 18 different sounds meaning-fully. Some animals can recognize a few words which stand for people, objects, and actions.

Intellectual development receives a big impetus when thinking and speech come together in the discovery that everything has a name. The average timing of the discovery is between 18 months and 2 years, when the vocabulary increases from around 20 words to almost 300 words. Over 600 words are added annually for the next two years, and then the rate of vocabulary increase drops somewhat [80].

After discovering that everything has a name and that names are very handy in thought and deed, the toddler concentrates on learning as many names as possible. He also invents names, as did a boy of 16 months, who called *yoyo* all portable things with handles and *gogo* all yoyos with lids [96. pp. 34–35]. In a similar vein, a little girl called all drinkable liquid *gaggle-gaggle*. A pair of twins, before using any regular words, said *ee-ee* to each other to call attention to an interesting change in the environment and *aw-aw* when they wanted an exchange of toys. Similarly, a more involved invention of names was noted [34, p. 249] in two boys, 4 and 6, playing with blocks. One did the building while the other handed to him, and to-gether they invented the following names for the blocks: Big thin Window, Little Big Thin Window, Big Stone, Little Stone, Big Knups, Little Knups, Big Pepper-mint, Little Peppermint.

At about the time when children discover that everything has a name, they think that a name is an intrinsic part of the object. Preschool children say that the names come from the objects or that they were made with the things themselves. When Piaget [62, p. 536] asked a young child how people knew that the sun was called the sun, he got this answer, "They saw it was called the sun because they could see it was round and hot."

This notion is strong throughout the period of preconceptual thought and in the thinking of primitive people. To know the name, then, is to have some control over the object. The idea persists beyond the preschool period. The power of names is implied in the cancellation games which schoolchildren play. For instance, Dorothy Levin, contemplating Harry Rogers, wonders if he would make a good husband for her. She puts their names down, one above the other, and cancels the letters. With the remaining letters she recites a stage of courtship for each: like, love, courtship, marriage, like . . . Aha! The magic contained in their names together could get Dot and Harry to the "like" stage only. No marriage! Many if not most adults show some lingering belief in the power of words when they react emotion-ally to a curse.

## Uses of Language

**Verbal Mediation.** One of the important differences between the infant and preschool child is the latter's verbal control of learning. When the child can attach labels to objects and processes, then he can generalize more readily. It is easier to discover principles and act according to them. For example, here is a situation which distinguishes between children in the stage of preverbal learning and those who use verbal mediation in learning [42]. The experimenter hid candy under the smaller of two boxes, presenting the boxes in random arrangement until the child learned to pick up the smaller box. Then a new set of boxes was used in the same way, with the candy under the smaller one. In the second set, the larger box was about the same size as the smaller box in the first pair. The child who had learned to choose according to a specific-sized box would choose the larger from the second set, but the child who had used verbal mediation (saying to himself or aloud something such as "The candy is under the smaller box") would choose the correct one promptly. The third phase of the experiment used two equal-sized boxes, one bearing the picture of a mouse, the other an elephant. The child who had learned the task by verbal mediation immediately knew that the candy was under the mouse, since he had a concept of smallness as indicating location of candy.

Short-term memory, as well as problem solving, is greatly aided by verbal labels. When given labels in connection with remembering colors, preschool children did almost as well as adults [7].

*Reversal-shift problems* are tasks that require a person to respond in the opposite way to that to which he has been successfully responding. For example, a child who has been rewarded for choosing triangles rather than squares is now rewarded for choosing squares rather than triangles. The choice remains in the same dimension, shape. If he had to change from triangles to red or small, that is, from the dimensions of shape to the dimension of color or size, the task would be a nonreversal shift. Reversal shifts are more difficult than nonreversal shifts for most children below 5 years of age. Between 5 and 7, few children make reversal shifts readily, while above 7, the majority do [45]. Verbal mediation is thought to make the difference, the problems being easy if one can say to himself, "Color is what counts. Now the red is right instead of the black." The age-related rise in ability to solve reversal shift problems most likely reflects a rise in ability to use verbal mediation.

There is evidence to show that a preschool child can communicate with himself silently, but that if he verbalizes his message aloud, it will help him to remember the mediator and hence make it more useful [19]. Three-to-five-year-olds were given tasks of matching, naming, and recognizing colors. First the child found a chip "just like this one" from the array of 14 colors. Then the array was covered, one chip shown and the child was asked, "What do you call this color?" Lastly, with the array covered, the child was told that he would be shown a color which would then be hidden while he found one just like it. Most of the children used color names consistently, applying them to a set of colors adjacent in the color circle. In the majority of cases, errors in matching represented choices of colors which the child named with the same term as the stimulus. All children showed this tendency on the matching task, suggesting the use of some sort of covert naming. On the recognition task, however, those who named the stimulus aloud did better. Apparently being able to rehearse internally develops with age, and during the preschool period, saying the mediator aloud helps the child to pay attention to it and to remember it.

The more a child learns through verbal mediation, the more resources he has available to tackle new problems and learn new material. The more words he learns the more readily he stores his experiences as memories. The more memories he stores, the more available is past experience for use in thinking and problem solving. Hence the acquisition of language is an integral part of cognitive growth. The child who does not acquire adequate verbal symbols and who does not use them in thinking is likely to be at a disadvantage in our culture. Problems can, however, be solved without language. Older deaf children [102] and older monkeys [93] can solve reversal shift problems more easily than nonreversal. There are doubtless mediators other than verbal ones.

**Private Speech.** Speech is not always for the purpose of communicating with another person. Sometimes it is for oneself. Some of the speech of preschool children expresses their wishes, needs, intentions, and experiences without regard for any effect that the comments might make on the listeners. The other person's thoughts, feelings, needs, wants, and comments are not taken into account [69, pp. 120–122] Piaget calls this type of speech *egocentric*. By this term, he refers to the fact that the young child is limited to and centered on his own point of view, not that he is selfish. His thought processes are not sufficiently flexible to permit him to consider what the other person is experiencing. Egocentric speech is like a monologue, even when it is broken by remarks from other people. When two people carry on egocentric speech at the same time, it gives a very disjointed result. Stone and Church [83, p. 282] gives this intriguing example of a collective monologue by two 4-year-olds in the Vassar nursery school:

**Jenny:** They wiggle sideways when they kiss.
**Chris:** (*vaguely*) What?
**Jenny:** My bunny slippers. They are brown and red and sort of yellow and white. And they have eyes and ears and these noses that wiggle sideways when they kiss.
**Chris:** I have a piece of sugar in red pieces of paper. I'm gonna eat it and maybe it's for a horse.
**Jenny:** We bought them. My mommy did. We couldn't find the old ones. They were in the trunk.
**Chris:** Can't eat the piece of sugar, not unless you take the paper off.
**Jenny:** And we found Mother Lamb. Oh, she was in Poughkeepsie in the trunk in the house in the woods where Mrs. Tiddywinkle lives.
**Chris:** Do you like sugar? I do, and so do horses.
**Jenny:** I play with my bunnies. They are real. We play in the woods. They have eyes. We *all* go in the woods. My teddy bears and the bunnies and the duck, to visit Mrs. Tiddywinkle. We play and play.
**Chris:** I guess I'll eat my sugar at lunch time. I can get more for the horses. Besides, I don't have no horses now.

Socialized speech, in contrast to egocentric, involves an exchange with others, through asking and answering questions, commenting on what the other person has said, giving him information which has some pertinence. Piaget noted that egocentric speech decreased and socialized speech increased with age, showing a real change in proportion at the end of the period of preoperational thought. At age 4, bright and average children used the same proportion (about 30 percent) of egocentric speech but at age 6, bright children used egocentric speech in only 5 percent of their utterances while average children did so in 18 percent [47].

Vygotsky [95, pp. 16–24], disagreeing with Piaget's contention that egocentric speech simply dropped out with increasing maturity, devised experiments to reveal its function. He put children in what appeared to be quite free situations. Just as the child was getting ready to draw, for instance, he would discover that he had no paper or that his pencil was not the color he needed. In such frustrating situations, the proportion of egocentric speech doubled, in comparison with Piaget's figure for children the same age and also in comparison with Vygotsky's findings for children under nonfrustrating circumstances. (His own figure for egocentric speech in normal circumstances was slightly lower than Piaget's.) The child would say such things as: "Where's the pencil? I need a blue pencil. Never mind, I'll draw with the red one and wet it with water; it will become very dark and look like blue." Vygotsky maintains that egocentric speech is not a mere accompaniment of activity but a means of expression, a release of tension, and a true instrument of thought, in finding the solution to a problem. He showed developmental changes in the use of egocentric speech. In the younger child, it marked the end of an activity, or a turning point. Gradually, it shifted to the middle and then to the beginning of an activity, taking on a planning and directing function. He likens this process to the developmental sequence in naming drawings. First, a little child names what he has drawn; a few months later, he names his drawing when half done; later, he announces what he is going to draw before he does it.

Vygotsky suggests that egocentric speech is a transitional stage between vocal and inner speech, which is a kind of thought. Egocentric speech, he says, "goes underground."

Vygotsky's findings are supported by subsequent studies which show that spontaneous verbal self-expression and self-communication are important means of problem solving for young children [28]. Different levels of cognitive development involve different uses of private speech [47]. A hierarchy of five levels is outlined, as follows:

1. *Presocial self-stimulating language:* words and phrases are repeated for their own sake. The child seems to be playing with words, such as "Pillow pum pum pum, pill, pum."
2. *Outward-directed private speech:* the child speaks to nonhuman objects, such as "Come here, stick." He describes what he is doing but does not add any information to what the other person can easily see for himself, such as "Going up" when he is climbing the stairs.
3. *Inward directed or self-guided private speech:* he asks himself questions and answers them; he guides his own activities by speaking aloud. On this level, comments are goal-directed, whereas in the previous level, they are merely descriptive.
4. *External manifestations of inner speech:* he speaks in such a low voice that nobody can hear what he says.
5. Silent inner speech or thought.

**Private and Communicative Speech: An Example.** The perceptive observations of a linguistically trained mother showed a young child distinguishing between communicative and noncommunicative speech [12]. Richard, at 21 months, when intending to communicate, spoke in a loud voice, made eye contact or bodily contact, and repeated his comments over and over until he got a response from the person addressed. Styles of noncommunicative speech were varied. One was a staccato rhythm; another, beginning by 27 months, a joking tone that was low in pitch, forced, and accompanied by a half smile. Yet another, occurring when he knew he would be forbidden to do what he was asking, included a low, soft voice, fuzzy enunciation, head twisting, and some agrammatical deviation. Between 21

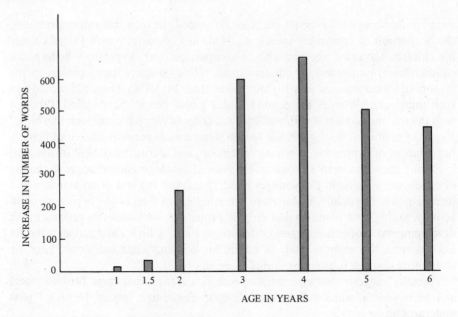

**Figure 6–9.** Number of spoken words added to vocabulary each year from ages 1 to 6. SOURCE: Data from M. E. Smith [80].

and 27 months, about 20 percent of Richard's utterances were communicative in a normal play situation, but while looking at the book with his mother, the percentage was much higher.

### Culture and Language

What could be more obvious than the fact that children speak the language into which they were born, the *mother* tongue? The earliest observable effect of the mother tongue is on the tones produced by the baby. Two Chinese babies, at 6½ months, made sounds very different from those made by Russian and American infants [99]. The Chinese babies made mostly monosyllabic sounds with much tonal variation over individual vowels; the Russian and American infants showed little tonal variation over single vowels but made intonation patterns over several syllables. Other students of infant speech have noticed response to intonation by the fifth month.

The mother tongue also shapes the child's thinking. In Piaget's words, ". . . language conveys to the individual an already prepared system of ideas, classification, relations—in short, an inexhaustible stock of concepts which are reconstructed in each individual after the age-old pattern which previously molded earlier generations" [63, p. 159]. Commenting on Indians who speak English as well as Hindi, a famous Indian author wrote, "English has given them minds which are deeper, wider and more complex in all the mental facilities . . . those who know English well in India constitute a psychological species which is different from those who do not know the language" [14].

### Growth Trends in Acquisition of Language

Figure 6–9 illustrates the spectacular increase in vocabulary during the preschool years. These data are from a classic study of language, in which pictures and

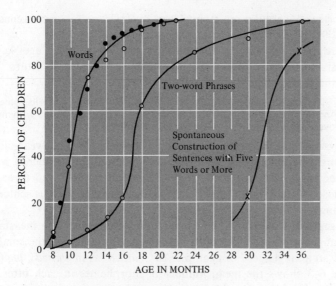

KEY:  ● 49 Austrian children (Buhler, 1931).
      o 114 British children (Morley, 1957).
      X 500 American children (Boston, author's observation).

**Figure 6–10.** Emergence of three levels of language development, words, two-word phrases, and sentences.

SOURCE: Reprinted by permission from E. H. Lenneberg. *Biological Foundations of Language.* New York: John Wiley & Sons, Figure 4.1, p. 133. Copyright © 1967, John Wiley & Sons, Inc.

questions were used to elicit words from children. The number of children represented at each age varied considerably, from 52 at 1 year to 9 at 6 years. The increase from 3 to 272 words during the second year represents a change from nonspeaker to speaker. From 272 words to 896 in the third year also indicates a big change in control of language.

While there are individual differences in the emergence of language, there is also great regularity in this process. Of 486 normal children (free of nervous and mental disease), raised in an adequate environment, less than 7 percent were below the following norms of language development [49, pp. 133–135]. By 39 months, the child names most of the objects in his home, speaks quite intelligibly, understands spoken instructions, makes complex sentences, and communicates spontaneously. Figure 6–10 shows ages at which three major language developmental levels are attained.

**Sentences.** The first type of sentence produced is active, next negative, then question, and last passive [26]. The order for understanding is different from the order for producing. Active comes first, then question, passive, and negative.

One-word sentences of course come first, as discussed in Chapter 3. The second stage, the early sentence, typical of age 2, lasts for a period of four to seven months. The early sentence includes a preponderance of nouns. Lacking articles, it has few auxiliary and copulative verbs and few prepositions and conjunctions. The third stage of sentence formation produces sentences of about four words. Only 1 or 2 sentences out of the 50 are compound or complex. The following story told by a 2-year-old includes second-stage and third-stage sentences:

> Me tell story about angleworm. One time go angleworm. Little girl
> pick up angleworm. Know dat? Angleworm cry. Angleworm lie down

pillows. Angleworm go sleep pillow. Two pillows. Two angleworms. Angleworm wake up.

The fourth stage of sentence formation, appearing at about age 4, yields sentences of six to eight words in length and more complex structure. This story illustrates the fourth stage:

The first Christmas was Jesus' birthday and Santie Claus did come. And I was afraid of him. And after that I was happy that I played with my toys.

An analysis [98] of the presleep utterences of Anthony, a 2½-year-old boy, provides, among other interesting data, information about the number of words in the sentences he used. Anthony used two-word sentences most and three-word sentences almost as often. Figure 6–11 shows percentages of various sentence lengths in his talking.

**Mean Length of Utterance.** The mean length of utterance is a measure which is useful in language studies. The units counted are morphemes, the smallest meaningful units in a language. For example: *cat, eat, ed* (as in *chased*), *ing* (as in *reading*). Table 6–3 shows the mean number of morphemes in each utterance of 13 young children [9]. Mean length of utterance varies from one individual to another. Notice Grace, at 27 months, with an MLU of 3.5, and Betty, at 31½ months, with MLU 2.1. The table also shows whether each child has acquired the use of *be* in the progressive tense (I *am* going rather than I going) and whether he uses *will* or *can*.

**Grammar.** Children can imitate the speech of others before they understand it and they understand more than they can produce independently. The imitation-comprehension-production sequence has been demonstrated for normal children between 2 and 6 years of age and for retarded 6- and 7-year-olds [15, 53]. However, imitation is not the chief mode of language acquisition. If it were so, children would

**Table 6–3** Estimates of Lengths of Utterance and Some of the Grammatical Forms Used by 13 Young Children

| Name of Child | Age in Months | Mean Number Morphemes* | *Be* in Progressive | Modal Auxiliaries *will* or *can* |
|---|---|---|---|---|
| Andy | 26 | 2.0 | no | no |
| Betty | 31½ | 2.1 | no | no |
| Charlie | 22 | 2.2 | no | no |
| Adam | 28½ | 2.5 | no | no |
| Eve | 25½ | 2.6 | no | no |
| Fanny | 31½ | 3.2 | yes | no |
| Grace | 27 | 3.5 | yes | yes |
| Helen | 30 | 3.6 | yes | yes |
| Ian | 31½ | 3.8 | yes | yes |
| June | 35½ | 4.5 | yes | yes |
| Kathy | 30½ | 4.8 | yes | yes |
| Larry | 35½ | 4.8 | yes | yes |
| Jimmy | 32 | 4.9 | yes | yes |

* Mean count from 100 consecutive utterances.

SOURCE: Reprinted from R. Brown and C. Fraser, in U. Bellugi and R. Brown (eds.), "The Acquisition of Language," *Monographs of The Society for Research in Child Development*, **29**:1, Table 13. Copyright © 1964, The Society for Research in Child Development, Inc.

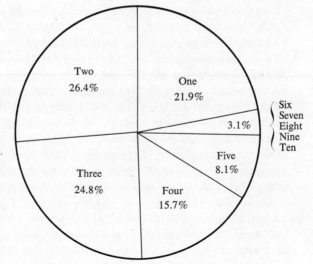

**Figure 6–11.** Presleep utterances of Anthony divided as to number of words in showing relative frequence of use of sentences of various lengths.

SOURCE: Reprinted by permission from R. H. Weir, *Language in the Crib*. The Hague: Mouton & Co. N.V., 1962.

say what they heard others say, instead of generating new statements. After trying to speak a foreign language by using the phrases in the tourist book, the adult knows how impossible it is to communicate with imitated phrases. One has to make the comment to fit the occasion, and this is what children do from the beginning. From their very first attempts to put words together, they do so according to rules. They discover the rules of the mother tongue systematically and apply them as they gain control of them. Research suggests that a child stores fragments of speech which are tagged for meaning and with bits of information concerning context [13]. He gradually analyzes the stored information to produce the rules that govern his speech. The first rules are simple ones. The rules are different from those governing adult speech, approximating them more as the child analyzes the language on more complex levels and as he has new experiences that require revision of the rules he has.

Syntax, the ordering of words, is important from the beginning. Perhaps the first rule is "the subject comes before the verb." Of course we know that the young child does not formulate it like this, but we wonder how he does do it. The first sentences are called *telegraphic speech*, because they include only words carrying essential meaning. In comments such as "See doggie," "Mommy come home," and "Go car," only words carrying necessary information are used. However, these sentences can be understood, because the order of the words is correct. Even though the child reduces sentences to the barest essentials, he usually preserves the word order, an extremely important dimension of English grammar. When passive sentences are first encountered, they are often understood in terms of the order of an active sentence. For instance, 3-year-olds, when asked to show the picture indicating "the cat is chased by the dog," would point to the picture of the cat chasing the dog [5]. This finding indicates that syntax (order) is more important than form to the young child. This finding is not unexpected for speakers of English, a language in which syntax is very important. It is surprising, however, to find that Russian children also order their first two-word sentences strictly, even though Russian is a heavily inflected language, and word order is not so important as it is in English [78]. In fact, it seems to be universal that the subject precedes the object in the dominant actor-action form of a language [31].

Another example of the ways in which children simplify adult grammar is the childish tendency to produce regular inflections. Children and adults were shown a picture of a man swinging something above his head and told: "This is a man who knows how to gling. He glings every day. Today he glings. Yesterday he—?" Adults hesitated and offered *gling, glang, glung* and even *glought;* children confidently replied, "Glinged." [6] There is considerable evidence that the various aspects of grammar are learned in a consistent order [5]. For example, plurals were made by adding *s* before irregular forms were used. Every one of 18 children said *mans* before he used the word *men* [55]. There is also consistency across measures of language acquisition. Turning again to Table 6–3, it can be seen that children whose mean length of utterance was below 3.2 said "I going" and not "I am going." When the MLU was below 3.5, the children omitted *will* or *can* from statements such as "I will go out," saying instead, "I go out." Cross-culture consistencies in language development are also seen. For example, with both Russian and American children, the first negative sentence is a three-word sentence beginning with *no (nyet)*, in spite of the adult Russian form which usually includes two negative words, *nyet* and *ni* [78].

**Learning Language.** Language research indicates that a great deal goes on inside children which is difficult to detect and amazing in its complexity. Sometimes, however, children verbalize revelations of how they learn, and if a knowledgeable person is listening then we can learn from people such as Richard and Anthony.

The young child plays with words in two main ways, sometimes combining these two approaches in the same utterance. He plays with sounds and with the words themselves; he learns to use the language for expressing ideas and communicating. The former function, sometimes called the poetic function, is illustrated by the following quotation from Anthony: "Look at those pineapple . . . in a pretty box . . . and cakes . . . what a sticks for cakes . . . for the click." Learning to use language correctly, Anthony practices and drills himself in sounds, words, and syntax. The records of his bedtime talks show systematic manipulations of language which often resemble the grammars written for the study of a foreign language [98]. The following excerpt is an exercise in noun substitution: what color—what color blanket—what color mop—what color glass. Noun modifiers are explored in this sequence: there's a hat—there's another—there's hat—there's another hat—that's a hat. A verb substitution pattern occurred thus: go get coffee—go buy some coffee. Negatives are practiced: like it—don't like it—like it daddy. He holds a question-and-answer dialogue with himself: There is the light—where is the light—here is the light. Some of Anthony's verbalizations have a large amount of sound play in them, such as: train—Anthony can see the plane—plane—plane—see bubble—bubble's here—bubbles—flowers—bed flowers. Sometimes he comments on his achievements: one two three four—one two—one two three four—one two three—Anthony counting—good boy you—one two three.

One of the important revelations of Anthony's bedtime talks is the self-motivated nature of his language learning. Nobody was responding to him with praise or criticism. Nobody was answering his expressed needs. Nobody was even listening, as far as he knew. Anthony's exploratory combining of words and his persistent drilling must have been for the reward of increased competence. Motives for other aspects of his language activity were probably sensory and expressive pleasure in the sound play and a seeking for understanding of experience.

Since the book on Anthony was published, his two younger brothers have also made their contributions to the study of language development [99]. The private speech of Michael and David showed the same self-motivated aspects seen in Anthony's, the same persistent drilling and creative play, but also individual features.

**Teaching Language.** As long as the normal child is exposed to language, he begins to talk. No special teaching is necessary for the emergence of language [49, pp. 135–137]. However, the way in which language develops is very much influenced by environment. And while a deprived environment leads to poor development, subsequent enrichment instigates improvement. In other words, language potentiality seems not to be injured by environmental deprivation. Research shows that middle-class children usually have larger vocabularies and make more effective use of language than do disadvantaged children. The obvious conclusion is that different experiences at home account for a large part of the difference. But what, exactly, are those experiences?

It was formerly thought that children were helped in learning grammar if the parents expanded their toddler's telegraphic speech. For instance, if Becky said, "Mommy cake," her mother would reply, "Mommy is making a cake," thus showing Becky how to expand her telegraphic statement grammatically. A longitudinal study of children and their mothers does indeed show different language development in Sarah, whose mother made few expansions, and in Eve, whose mother made many [13]. The difference, surprisingly, is in the richness and meaning of what the children said. When compared at the same point in mean length of utterance, although Sarah was older than Eve in months, Sarah's speech had more grammatical words and parts, and Eve's more content words. Sarah said what she said more grammatically, but Eve said more. The implications in this comparison were confirmed by an analysis of 2800 parent utterances in response to child utterances. Sarah's telegraphic comments were followed less frequently by maternal expansions than were Eve's. Apparently, Eve's mother's elaboration of the child's utterances led to more complexity in what the child was trying to express. These findings suggest that richness of ideas and content of speech are more affected by parental teaching than is the acquisition of grammatical forms. There is no indication from research that parental responses of expansion or approval-disapproval have any effect on the child's learning of grammar [8]. It looks as though children learn grammar if exposed to it, but need meaningful interaction in order to elaborate ideas.

The effect of the mother's language and teaching style was examined at the University of Chicago [36]. Black mothers and their preschool children were drawn from four socioeconomic levels, interviewed at home, and then brought to the laboratory for testing and observation. The mothers' patterns of language are of special interest here. The middle-class mothers talked a great deal *more* to their children, in answering questions and instructing them on the tasks set up by the experimenters. The upper-middle-class mothers' verbal output was almost twice as great as that of mothers in the two lowest groups. Quality was different, as well as quantity. Mothers in the highest group were more likely to use abstract words, complex syntactic structures, unusual phrases, and, in general, an elaborate code. Thus these mothers led their children to manipulate the environment symbolically, to recognize subtle differences in language, and to use language in thinking. Through use of language, they encourage children to anticipate what would happen as a result of this or that action, and to delay action while deciding. Contrasting teaching styles can be seen in the following examples of mothers teaching their children to sort toys:

> **Mother I:** All right, Susan, this board is the place where we put the little toys; first of all you're supposed to learn how to place them according to color. Can you do that? The things that are all the same color, you put in the same section; in the second section, put another group of colors, and in the third section, you put the last group of colors. Can you do that? Or would you like to see me do it first?
>
> **Child I:** I want to do it.
>
> **Mother II:** Now, I'll take them all off the board; now you put them all back on the board. What are these?
>
> **Child II:** A truck.
>
> **Mother II:** All right, just put them right here; put the other one right here; all right, put the other one there.
>
> **Mother III:** I've got some chairs and cars, do you want to play the game? (No response) O.K. What's this?
>
> **Child III:** A wagon?
>
> **Mother III:** Hm?
>
> **Child III:** A wagon?
>
> **Mother III:** This is not a wagon. What's this?

The middle-class children performed much better than the working-class children on the sorting tests and also verbalized the bases on which they were sorted. They also reflected more before answering. Planning was much more evident in the middle-class mothers and children, whereas in both verbal and motor behavior, the working-class mothers and children tended to act out of context, without meaning, without anticipation. For instance, a mother would silently watch her child make an error and then punish him. The other mother would anticipate the error, warn the child to be careful, to avoid the mistake, and to consider the important cues before making a decision.

Social class differences in language and teaching style have been confirmed by other studies, showing middle-class mothers using more complex, elaborated speech patterns, more instruction, less physical intrusion, and less negative feedback [4]. Middle-class mothers were more likely to react sensitively to each child as a unique individual.

A class difference in the use of language has been found in a British study of three-year-olds from middle-class and working-class families [94]. The children were matched for IQ and verbal output, but their styles of language use were quite different. The middle-class children talked more about qualitative features of the environment and about cause-and-effect relations and other relations between these features. That is, the children did more analysis and synthesis in their speech than did the children from less educated families. The less favored children were more concrete and personalized in their speech. From a review of studies of children's use of language, Bruner concludes that more highly educated children, as well as adults, use language more analytically, synthetically and without dependence on context, shared percepts and actions [10]. Less educated people speak with more affect and metaphors, more narrative, more ties to places and people, more concreteness ("I said . . . and he said . . .").

These experiments emphasize the interrelatedness of language, thought, and behavior style. Through their use of language, mothers influence their children's development in all these areas.

*Bilingualism in Young Children*

When his family speaks more than one language, a baby begins speaking by using forms from both or all languages [24]. By around age 3, he separates one from another. He may have accents in both languages at first.

As international communication grows more and more important, it becomes more and more desirable for children to speak more than one language. In an earlier era, it was thought to be disadvantageous for a preschool child to learn a second language. Current research suggests the very opposite, that the best time to learn is early and the best way to learn is from a person who speaks that language as his mother tongue, that is, a native speaker. Advantages are in terms of ease of learning sounds, flexibility of brain function, and related cognitive development.

**Learning the Sound Typical of a Language.** Experience during infancy seems to shape the tones produced in babbling, as shown by studies of Chinese, American, and Dutch babies [79, pp. 155–169]. The Chinese baby sounded different to Americans. American listeners could pick out the babbling of an American baby from non-Americans and Dutch listeners a Dutch baby from non-Dutch. However, it seems to be possible throughout the childhood period to produce the sounds of another language quite easily, whereas a person who learns a second language in adolescence rarely sounds like a native speaker and almost always has an "accent."

The learning and production of grammatical and nongrammatical sounds and sequences were investigated in normal, monolingual children between 4 and 9 years of age [54]. For example, *strut*, *drin*, and *stais* are grammatical phonological sequences in English; *Tsut*, *dlin*, and *srais* are not grammatical in English, although they appear in other languages. The children were required to learn, remember, and produce sets of grammatical and nongrammatical sequences of sounds. The youngest children did equally well with learning and remembering both types of material. The oldest could learn and remember the grammatical material more easily than the nongrammatical. All age levels found it easier to reproduce grammatical material rather than nongrammatical. Older children did better than younger in learning, remembering, and producing. While older children learned more efficiently, then, the younger children had less relative difficulty with what was similar to learning a second language.

**Flexibility of Brain Functions.** A brain surgeon [60] reports that the speech area of the cortex can be relocated on the opposite side of the brain if the original area is damaged before about 12 years of age. After that time, the functions of the cortex are quite firmly fixed and the brain cannot build a new speech center. (Age 12 is also the time when the brain reaches maximum weight.) If a second language is learned before age 12, the brain develops a switch mechanism, whereby the child can easily change from one of his languages to another, without confusion, without translating, and without an accent. This switch mechanism works for additional languages, also. The brain specialist recommends beginning a second language in the preschool age, if possible, and says that confusion will not occur if the second language is spoken either by a different adult or by the same adult in a different place. Most important is that both or all languages be learned in childhood, at first from a native speaker, behaving as a mother does with a young child.

**Cognitive Advantages of Bilingualism.** When 4- to 6-year-old Head Start children were tested for their understanding of object constancy, naming objects and using names in sentences, bilingual children were superior on all measures. An analysis of their performances makes clear the advantage that the bilingual child has. Bilinguals did much better in switching labels assigned to objects, such as calling a cup a plate. The subject was asked which object was really a cup and which was called a cup. Bilinguals did better also in using regular labels in sentences and using nonsense labels in sentences. These results suggest greater flexibility in the bilingual and, more specifically, suggest that the bilingual child may be more aware that there are different ways of saying the same thing and that the name is assigned rather than an intrinsic part of the object [25].

## Summary

Thinking, language, and imagination are intimately associated with one another in such a way that each is necessary to mental life. The preschool (or preoperational) stage of thought begins when infant thinking ends, with grasping the idea of the permanence and constancy of objects and also when the child has achieved control of his own movements in space. From this time until about 7 years of age, thinking is dominated by the perceptual experiences of the moment. Thought is centered, since the preschool child finds it extremely difficult to consider how any situation looks to another person. He feels no need to justify his thinking to anyone else. As he moves through the preschool years, his thinking becomes increasingly flexible, less centered, and less dominated by perception. Concepts are at first embedded in concrete experience, becoming more and more abstract as the child has more experiences in grouping objects, dealing with time, space, and numbers, experimenting with processes. The process of abstraction is aided by the abstractions offered by language. Both language and concepts are learned through interactions with people, where the child checks and rechecks his accuracy, eventually achieving socialized thought.

Tests measure certain aspects of intelligence, each test being designed to measure intelligence as defined in a certain theory. Mental age is a score found by matching a child's test performance with that of the average child and noting the age at which the average child succeeded. Intelligence quotient (IQ) is the ratio of mental age to chronological age, a ratio which has some constancy through the years. IQ can be used to express rate of mental development and brightness of quality. Measured intelligence has been analyzed statistically into factors which wax and wane at various ages.

Language develops rapidly in the second year of life, speeding up thought and also making it more precise and flexible. The use of verbal symbols makes problem solving much more efficient. Since the preschool child is centered on his own point of view, his speech reflects this fact. As he gradually increases, through social interaction, in his ability to take into account the viewpoints of other people, he continues to talk to himself as an aid to problem solving and planning and directing his activities. Through social interaction, he also comes to possess and use the concepts with which his culture organizes experience. He also progresses toward the use of adult structure in language, increasing the number of words, refining his use of grammar, and speaking in longer, more complex sentences. The emergence of language behavior is strongly influenced by maturation. The language community determines which sounds shall be retained and which particular language acquired. Parental teaching strongly influences the thinking in which language is involved and which language facilitates.

# References

1. Ames, L. B. The development of the sense of time in the young child. *J. Genet. Psychol.*, 1946, **68**, 97–125.
2. Ames, L. B., & Learned, J. The development of verbalized space in the young child. *J. Genet. Psychol.*, 1948, **72**, 63–84.
3. Bayley, N. On the growth of intelligence. *Am. Psychol.*, 1955, **10**, 805–818.
4. Bee, H. L., et al. Social class differences in maternal teaching strategies and speech patterns. *Devel. Psychol.* 1969, **1**, 726–734.
5. Bellugi-Klima, U. Language acquisition. Paper presented at the symposium on "Cognitive studies and artificial intelligence research," Sponsored by the Wenner-Gren Foundation for Anthropological Research. Chicago: University of Chicago, March 2–8, 1969.
6. Berko, J. The child's learning of English morphology. *Word*, 1958, **14**, 150–177.
7. Bernbach, H. A. The effect of labels on short-term memory for colors with nursery school children. *Psychon. Sci.*, 1967, **7**, 149–150.
8. Brown, R., Cazden, C., & Bellugi-Klima, U. The child's grammar from I to III. In J. P. Hill (Ed.), *Minnesota Symposia on Child Psychology*. Vol. 2. Minneapolis: University of Minnesota Press, 1969, pp. 28–73.
9. Brown R., & Fraser, C. The acquisition of syntax. In U. Bellugi & R. Brown (Eds.) , The acquisition of language. *Mono. Soc. Res. Child Devel.*, 1964, **29**:1, pp. 43–98.
10. Bruner, J. S. *Poverty and Childhood*. Detroit: Merrill-Palmer Institute, 1970.
11. Burn, M. H. Children learning mathematics. *Arithmetic Teacher*, 1963, **10**, 179–182.
12. Carlson, P., & Anisfeld, M. Some observations on the linguistic competence of a two-year-old child. *Child Devel.*, 1969, **40**, 569–575.
13. Cazden, C. B. The acquisition of noun and verb inflections. *Child Devel.*, 1968 **39**, 433–448.
14. Chaudhuri, N. C. The Hindi-English conflict. New Delhi: *Times of India*, October 2, 1967.
15. Cohen M. B. Active and passive language development of grammar. *Conn. College Psychol. J.*, 1967, **4**, 20–24.
16. Corah, N. L., & Gospondinoff, E. J. Color-form and whole-part perception in children. *Child Devel.*, 1966, **37**, 837–842.
17. Corah, N. L., & Gross, J. B. Hue, brightness, and saturation variables in color-form matching. *Child Devel.*, 1967, **38**, 137–142.
18. Cramer, P. The Stroop effect in preschool aged children: A preliminary study. *J. Genet. Psychol.*, **111**, 1967, 9–12.
19. Dale, P. S. Color naming, matching and recognition by preschoolers. *Child Devel.*, 1969, **40**, 1135–1144.
20. Descoeudres, A. Le développement de l'enfant de deux à sept ans. 1921. Cited in Werner [100].
21. Donaldson, M., & Balfour, G. Less is more: A study of language comprehension in children. *Brit. J. Psychol.*, 1968, **59**, 461–471.
22. Dunn, L. M. *Peabody Picture Vocabulary Test*. Minneapolis: American Guidance Service, 1959.
23. Elkind, D., & Scott, L. Studies in Perceptual development. I: The decentering of perception. *Child Devel.*, 1962, **33**, 619–630.

24. Ervin-Tripp, S. Language development. In L. W. Hoffman & M. L. Hoffman (Eds.), *Review of Child Development Research*. Vol. 2. New York: Russell Sage Foundation, 1966, pp. 55–105.

25. Feldman, C., & Shen, M. Some language-related cognitive advantages of bilingual five-year-olds. (Mimeo.) University of Chicago, Chicago Early Education Research Center, 1969.

26. Gaer, E. P. Children's understanding and production of sentences. *J. Verbal Learning & Verbal Behavior*, 1969, **8**, 289–294.

27. Gesell, A., & Amatruda, C. S. *Developmental diagnosis*. New York: Hoeber, 1951.

28. Gever, B. E., & Weisberg, R. W. Spontaneous verbalization of children during problem solving: Effects of task difficulty, age and social class. *Proceedings, 78th Annual Convention, Am. Psychol. Assoc.*, 1970, 297–298.

29. Golden, M., Birns, B., Bridger, W. & Moss, A. Social class differentiation in cognitive development among black preschool children. *Child Devel.*, 1971, **42**, 37–45.

30. Gottschalk, J., Bryden, M. P., & Rabinovitch, M. S. Spatial organization of children's responses to a pictorial display. *Child Devel.*, 1964, **35**, 811–815.

31. Greenberg, J. H. *Universals of language*, 2nd ed. Cambridge, Mass.: M.I.T. Press, 1966.

32. Guilford, J. P. The structure of intellect. *Psychol. Bull.*, 1956, **53**, 267–293.

33. Guilford, J. P. Intelligence: 1965 model. *Am. Psychol.*, 1966, **21**, 20–26.

34. Hazlitt, V. Children's thinking. *Brit. J. Psychol.*, 1929, **30**, 20. Cited in Werner [100].

35. Hertzig, M. E., Birch, H. G., Thomas, A., Mendez, O. A. Class and ethnic differences in the responsiveness of preschool children to cognitive demands. *Mono. Soc. Res. Child Devel.*, 1968, **33**:1.

36. Hess, R. D., & Shipman, V. C. Early experiences and the socialization of cognitive modes in children. *Child Devel.*, 1965, **36**, 869–886.

37. Hodges, W. L. and Spicker, H. H. Effects of preschool experience on culturally deprived children. In W. W. Hartup & N. L. Smothergill (Eds.), *The young child: Reviews of research*, Washington, D.C.: Nat. Assoc. Educ. Young Children, 1967, pp. 262–289.

38. Holtzman, W. H., Diaz-Guerrero, R., Swartz, J. D., & Tapie, L. L. Cross-cultural longitudinal research on child development: Studies of American and Mexican schoolchildren. In J. P. Hill (Ed.), *Minnesota Symposia on Child Psychology. Vol. 2*. Minneapolis: University of Minnesota Press, 1969, pp. 125–158.

39. Honzik, M. P., Macfarlane, J. W., & Allen, L. The stability of mental test performance between two and eighteen years. *J. Exper. Educ.*, 1948, **17**, 309–324.

40. Huttenlocher, J. Children's ability to order and orient objects. *Child Devel.*, 1967, **38**, 1169–1176.

41. Hyde, D. M. An investigation of Piaget's theories of the development of the number concept. Unpublished doctoral dissertation, University of London. Cited in Lovell [52].

42. Jensen, A. R., Learning in the preschool years. In W. W. Hartup & N. L. Smothergill (Eds.), *The young child: Reviews of research*. Washington, D.C.: Nat. Assoc. Educ. Young Children, 1967, pp. 125–135.

43. Jones, R. *Fantasy and feeling in education*. New York: New York University Press, 1968.
44. Katz, D., & Katz, R. *Gespräche mit kindern*. 1928. Cited in Werner [100].
45. Kendler, T. S. Development of mediating responses in children. In J. C. Wright & J. Kagan (Eds.), Basic cognitive processes in children. *Mono. Soc. Res. Child Devel.*, 1963, 33–52.
46. Kofsky, E., & Osler, S. F. Free classification in children. *Child Devel.*, 1967, **38**, 927–937.
47. Kohlberg, L., Yeager, J., & Hjertholm E. Private Speech: Four studies and a review of theories. *Child Devel.*, 1968, **39**, 691–736
48. Lee, L. C. Concept utilization in preschool children. *Child Devel.*, 1965, **36**, 221–227.
49. Lenneberg, E. H. *Biological foundations of language*. New York: Wiley, 1967.
50. Lewis, M., & Harwitz, M. The meaning of an orienting response: A study in the hierarchical order of attending. Princeton, N.J.: Educational Testing Service, 1969.
51. Long, L., & Welch, L. The development of the ability to discriminate and match numbers. *J. Genet. Psychol.*, 1941, **59**, 377–387.
52. Lovell, K. *The growth of basic mathematical and scientific concepts in children*. New York: Philosophical Library, 1961.
53. Lovell, K. Some recent studies in cognitive and language development. *Merrill-Palmer Quart.*, 1968, **14**, 123–138.
54. Menyuk, P. Children's learning and reproduction of grammatical and non-grammatical phonological sequences. *Child Devel.*, 1968, **39**, 849–859.
55. Miller, W., & Ervin, S. The development of grammar in child language. In U. Bellugi & R. Brown (Eds.), The acquisition of language. *Mono. Soc. Res. Child Devel.*, 1960, **31**, 9–34.
56. Mumbauer, C. C., & Miller, J. O. Socioeconomic background and cognitive functioning in preschool children. *Child Devel.*, 1970, **41**, 471–480.
57. Murphy, G. *An historical introduction to modern psychology*. New York: Harcourt, Brace, 1930.
58. Palmer, F. H. Socioeconomic status and intellective performance among Negro preschool boys. *Devel. Psychol.*, 1970, **3**, 1–9.
59. Pedersen, F. A., & Wender, P. H. Early social correlates of cognitive functioning in six-year-old boys. *Child Devel.*, 1968, **39**, 185–193.
60. Penfield, W. The uncommitted cortex, the child's changing brain. *Atlantic*, 1964. **214**, 1:77–81.
61. Piaget, J. *The child's conception of physical causality*. London: Routledge and Kegan Paul, 1930.
62. Piaget, J. Children's philosophies. In C. Murchison, *A handbook of child psychology*. Worcester, Mass.: Clark University, 1933.
63. Piaget, J. *The psychology of intelligence*. London: Routledge and Kegan Paul, 1950.
64. Piaget, J. *Play, dreams and imitation in childhood*. London: Heinemann, 1951.
65. Piaget, J. The attainment of invariants and reversible operations in the development of thinking. *Soc. Res.*, 1963, **30**, 283–299.
66. Piaget, J. *The child's conception of number*. New York: Norton, 1965.
67. Piaget, J. Introduction to M. Almy et al. *Young children's thinking*. New York: Teachers College Press, 1966.

68. Piaget, J., & Inhelder, B. *The child's concept of space*. London: Routledge and Kegan Paul, 1958.

69. Piaget, J., & Inhelder, B. The psychology of the child. New York: Basic Books, 1969.

70. Poteat, B. W., & Hulsebus, R. C. The vertical dimension: A significant cue in the preschool child's concept of "bigger." *Psychon. Sci.*, 1968, **12**, 369–370.

71. Rees, A. H. & Palmer, F. H. Factors related to change in mental test performance. *Devel. Psychol. Mono.*, 1970, 3: 2, Part 2.

72. Ricciuti, H. N. Objects grouping and selective ordering behavior in infants 12 to 24 months old. *Merrill-Palmer Quart.*, 1965, **11**, 129–148.

73. Rifkin, S. H. A developmental study of the effect of auditory and visual language input on the conceptual ability and memory efficiency of culturally disadvantaged children. Paper presented at the Southwestern Psychological Association. February 27, 1969.

74. Rossi, S. I., & Wittrock, M. C. Clustering versus serial ordering in recall by four-year-old children. *Child Devel.*, 1967, **38**, 1139–1142.

75. Ryckman, D. B. A comparison of information processing abilities of middle and lower class Negro kindergarten boys. *Except. Child.*, 1967, **33**, 545–552.

76. Sitkei, E. G., & Meyers, C. B. Comparative structures of intellect in middle- and lower-class four-year-olds of two ethnic groups. *Devel. Psychol.*, 1969, **1**, 592–604.

77. Skeels, H. M. Adult status of children with contrasting early life experiences. *Mono. Soc. Res. Child Devel.*, 1966, **31**, 3.

78. Slobin, D. L. The acquisition of Russian as a native language. In F. Smith & G. A. Miller (Eds.), *The genesis of language*. Cambridge, Mass.: M.I.T. Press, 1966, pp. 129–148.

79. Smith, F., & Miller, G. A. *The genesis of language*. Cambridge, Mass.: M.I.T. Press, 1966.

80. Smith, M. E. An investigation of the development of the sentence and the extent of vocabulary in young children. *Univer. Iowa Stud. Child Welf.*, 1926, 3:5.

81. Sontag, L. W., Baker, C. T., & Nelson, V. L. Mental growth and personality development: A longitudinal study. *Mono. Soc. Res. Child Devel.*, 1958, **23**:2.

82. Springer, D., Development in young children of an understanding of time and the clock. *J. Genet. Psychol.*, 1952, **80**, 83–96.

83. Stone, L. J., & Church, J. *Childhood and adolescence*. New York: Random House, (2nd ed.) 1968.

84. Streissguth, A. P. Social class and racial differences in preschool children's cognitive functioning. Paper presented at the meeting of the Society for Research in Child Development, Santa Monica, Calif., March 28, 1969.

85. Stutsman, R. *Scale of mental tests for preschool children*. New York: World, 1930.

86. Suchman, R. G., & Trabasso, T. Color and form preference in young children. *J. Exper. Child Psychol.*, 1966, **3**, 177–187.

87. Syrdal, A. K., Pufall, P. B., & Shaw, R. E. Development of number in very young children. Paper presented at the meeting of the Society for Research in Child Development. Santa Monica, Calif., March 28, 1969.

88. Terman, L. M. *The measurement of intelligence*. Boston: Houghton Mifflin, 1916.

89. Terman, L. M., & Merrill, M. A. *Measuring Intelligence.* Boston: Houghton Mifflin, 1939.
90. Thorndike, E. L. *The measurement of intelligence.* New York: Teachers College, Columbia University, 1926.
91. Thurstone, L. L. Theories of intelligence. *Sci. Month.,* 1946. **62,** 175–197.
92. Thurstone, L. L., & Thurstone, T. G. *SRA primary abilities for ages 5–7.* Chicago: Science Research Associates, 1950.
93. Tighe, T. J. Reversal and nonreversal shifts in monkeys. *J. Compar. Physiol. Psychol.,* 1964 **58,** 324–326.
94. Tough, J. An interim report of a longitudinal study. Institute of Education, Language and Environment. University of Leeds, 1970. Cited in Bruner [11].
95. Vygotsky, L. S. *Thought and language.* Cambridge, Mass.: M.I.T. Press, 1962.
96. Watts, A. F. *The language and mental development of children.* London: Harrap, 1944.
97. Wechsler, D. *Wechsler intelligence scale for children.* New York: Psychological Corporation, 1949.
98. Weir, R. H. *Language in the crib.* The Hague: Mouton & Company, 1962.
99. Weir, R. H. Some questions on the childs' learning of phonology. In F. Smith & G. A. Miller (Eds.), *The genesis of language.* Cambridge, Mass.: M.I.T. Press, 1966, pp. 153–168.
100. Werner, H. *Comparative psychology of mental development.* New York: International Universities Press, 1957.
101. Wohlwill, J. F. A study of the development of the number concept, by scalogram analysis. *J. Genet. Psychol.,* 1960, **97,** 345–377.
102. Youniss, J. Concept transfer as a function of shifts, age and deafness. *Child Devel.,* 1964, **35,** 659–700.

# Chapter 7

Merrill-Palmer Institute by Donna J. Harris

# The Role of Play in Development

Reporting to the parents of a 3-year-old, the teacher said: "Laura works a great deal with water. She and Cindy have been working in the doll corner most of the time during the past week."

To the uninitiated, the word *work* would seem farfetched in describing anything that Laura, or any 3-year-old, did in the nursery school or at home. Understanding the meaning of play in the child's life, the teacher equated it with work. Play is what the preschool child does when he is not sleeping, eating or complying with other such routines or requests. Although to an adult, play may be just a time filler, to a child play is serious business. Engaging in this serious business, he develops his mind and body, integrating social and emotional functions and the intellectual functions of thinking, reasoning, problem solving, talking, and imagining [1, 52]. Physical environment and guidance are vital influences on the child's development through play. As the last section of this chapter will show, the preschool years are important ones for intellectual growth, even though many people erroneously consider them a time of waiting for education to begin. A more modern mistake is sometimes made by adults who know that enormous cognitive development occurs during the preschool years. They unfortunately jump to the conclusion that preschool children should work on intellectual lessons to the exclusion of growth through play and imagination.

## Play

There are many theories as to the origin, purpose, and function of play. They can be grouped into *psychogenic* and *sociogenic* theories [53]. The former stress the fact that in play, the child uses former experiences and reworks them or assimilates them. The latter focus on the role of novel responses as preparation for future adaptation. Play actually performs both functions and others as well. While promoting and enhancing many kinds of development and relationships, play is its own reward.

### Differentiation and Integration

The developmental principle of differentiation and integration is illustrated by many sequences observable in play. Just as the newborn baby starts with his reflexive patterns to build a new pattern of grasping an object and bringing it to his mouth, so the 2-year-old refines some of his crude coordinations into smaller units which he improves and then combines into complex units. Thus he develops new patterns of thinking and acting which are different from the older, simpler ones and yet include them.

Having only recently progressed from walking to running, the 2-year-old runs just for the fun of it. Stepping high and alternating his feet faster than when he walks, he may add little speed. He climbs for the fun of it, too, on stairs, furniture, jungle gym or inclined boards, going up and down, backward, frontward, on his stomach, on his seat, trying out all possibilities, enjoying the feel of all. Even after walking, running, and climbing have become integrated into more complex motor patterns, they are still used sometimes by themselves and apparently enjoyed for their own sakes. Similarly, tricycle riding, ball throwing and catching, jumping, and cutting with scissors—these are all activities which are used sometimes for themselves and at other times for other ends. As running and climbing become easy and automatic, they are used for other ends, integrated with other actions. The child runs and waves his arms, being a bird; he runs to reach the doll carriage before his sister gets it; he climbs the stairs to get Mommy's knitting for her; he scrambles onto the kitchen counter to find crackers and peanut butter. He modifies walking and running motions to ride a kiddy car and later a tricycle.

By the end of the preschool period, many complex patterns of play have been developed from simple forms of motor play, imagination, manipulation, and perception, but growth is merely off to a good start. Mental development goes on, building more and more involved structures through the interaction between child and environment. The coordinations of ball throwing, catching, running, counting, and others, can be integrated into playing basketball, baseball, and tennis. Counting may be used eventually in playing bridge. Dramatic play can be integrated into acting and writing.

## Sensorimotor Play

Infant play is predominately sensorimotor, since intellectual growth has not progressed beyond the sensorimotor level. Although with increasing maturity play becomes more differentiated and parts of it more complex, the child continues to engage in sensorimotor play. So do the adolescent and the adult. Age is no selector of who lingers beside a tidal pool to bathe his senses in sparkles, clarity, colors, undulating form, chill, salt, and prickles. Anyone can enjoy making a snowball and throwing it. Preschool play has a large sensorimotor component, as anyone who observes young children will notice. Exploration is one facet of the developing sense of initiative. The young child touches objects eagerly, grasps them, runs his fingers lightly over them, even scratches them with his fingernails. Although he has learned, to a large extent, to keep objects out of his mouth, such inhibitions are not complete and he often finishes an examination with his lips and tongue. Color is important, often featured in his comments and greatly enjoyed in toys, art, clothing, and nature. He experiments with sounds, using his voice, musical instruments, and any casual sound makers which come into his grasp.

## Social Play

Infants show interest and pleasure in the company of other infants. During the preschool years, children seek one another and give evidence of enjoying play together. Parents usually recognize some of the benefits of social play. Very often they say, as the reason for sending a child to nursery school: "He needs playmates. We want him to learn to play with other children."

Working with a friend or companion can make a difficult task more acceptable. When 5-year-olds were given a target game, children assigned to work in pairs were more willing to try than those working alone [54]. Those who were least willing to do the task were the ones who were asked to do it alone in front of the class.

The ordinary course of group play as seen in nursery schools or neighborhood is a progression from simple to complex. Two-year-olds watch others, cooperate momentarily, often engage in the same activity as someone else (parallel play), such as shoveling or sliding, but they play in an essentially solitary style. However, even though they may not appear to be interacting, there seems to be a satisfaction in just being near each other. For instance, a rocking boat is a popular plaything in which a group of young children can be together. They tend to be rough with each other, hitting, pushing, poking, grabbing, often seeming to explore each other as *things* rather than as people. Of course, they recognize each other as people, but they are in a process of finding out the basic characteristics of people, especially of children similar to themselves. Will this person fall over when I push him?

What happens when I pull that shiny long hair? How does it feel to hug him? What kind of noise does she make? Egocentric, he seeks information which will eventually help him to grow beyond egocentrism.

At the 2-year level pushing or hitting with the apparent intent to hurt is infrequent. The pushing and hitting that does go on is most often for the purpose of getting a toy that someone else has. Sometimes a child hurts others unintentionally because he does not even recognize them as being there, walking into their play, pushing them aside. Such actions are egocentric, since the child has a limited awareness of himself in relation to the rest of the world and is unable to comprehend the situation as it is to someone else.

Gradually interchange grows more frequent, longer, with more cooperation and more conflict. A nursery school study has shown positive, friendly behavior to be more frequent than negative behavior in social interaction [8]. The former increased with age. With the development of language, more communication takes place. Two children play together, talking about what they are making in the sand, putting dolls to bed, dressing up, pretending a scene that requires two cooperating characters, such as a mother and a baby. Groups of three children playing together are common between 3 and 6 years. While three seems to be the preferred number, groups do increase up to five or six members, especially at the older ages.

In the early stages of group play, children tend to move in and out of the group without changing the content of the play (shifting group play). For instance, Tom, Hal, and Barbie were digging and making dribble castles near the water's edge. Barbie took her periwinkles to visit the hermit crab that Tom and Hal were tending in the pool between their castles. Just as Barbie took off to find another hermit crab, Dulcy settled down beside Barbie's castle to keep the pool from filling in. Later Barbie returned, all four played for a few minutes and then Tom and Hal departed, leaving Barbie and Dulcy with all three castles, pools, and wild life. Play groups are more stable in the older preschool years, as activities become more structured and complex. Conflicts over toys decrease as children learn how to take turns and as their behavior becomes more flexible, with more possibilities for action.

**Friendly Behavior.** Young children have definite preferences in playmates. They can tell which children they like best and least. Observations in nursery schools reveal children playing consistently with liked peers. Degree of popularity can be assessed by sociometric methods adapted to young children. Instead of asking the child the names of his best friends, a useful technique is to show him a board mounted with photographs of all the children in his play group. He can then name or point to the one he likes to play with, the one he doesn't like to play with, one he would like to take home after school, and so on. Popularity scores can be derived from numbers of choices, and characteristics of low, high, and medium scorers can be studied.

High scorers on a picture-board sociometric test were found to be more likely than other children to use positive social reinforcement and to use it with a large number of children [25]. Positive social reinforcers were attention, approval, affection, acceptance, submission, and tokens. Low scorers (rejected children) were likely to give negative social reinforcement, which included noncompliance (refusing to submit or cooperate, ignoring overtures of others), interferences, such as taking property or disrupting activity, ridiculing, blaming, tattling, attacks, threats, and demands. Giving and receiving positive reinforcement were found to be reciprocal activities. That is, those who gave the most got the most. Four-year-olds gave more than 3-year-olds and also spread their reinforcements over a large number of recipients [8]. Boys gave more to boys and girls to girls.

Popular children sometimes use negative reinforcement with their peers. Other children seem to take into consideration the type of aggression used and the situation in which it occurs [39]. Peers are likely to tolerate provoked aggression directed toward an appropriate object, thus considering the intensity of the act and the degree of threat to the recipient.

When 3-year-olds were strongly dependent on their mothers for contact comfort, they were likely to be victims of aggression by other children in the nursery school [35]. That is, children who were immature in their dependent behavior at home elicited aggression at school. More mature dependent behavior, the seeking of help or affection, did not seem to detract from popularity unless it interfered with play [39]. If a young child insists upon sitting on the teacher's lap and monopolizing her attention, then the other children are likely to disapprove. If, however, a child seeks the teacher's help in ways that enhance group play, or if he elicits help and affectionate response from a friend, then he probably gains support and friendship. Some of the conditions which enhance basic sympathetic responses between playmates go back to experiences in the family [27]. Preschool children's consideration for others develops most readily when parents include with their disciplining of children the pointing out the consequences of children's behavior toward other people. (Parent–child relationships are discussed in the following chapter.)

Compliant behavior was studied in 3- to 5-year-olds in a nursery school [10] using time sample observations. *Compliance* was defined as the "frequency and alacrity with which the children acceded to the commands and suggestions of other persons." Degree of compliance with peers was not found to be related to intelligence, nor was there a sex difference. The most compliant children sought more help and more emotional support from other children than did the less compliant children. The most compliant tended to be less aggressive and dominating with their peers than did the least compliant children. The following differences in social behavior between peer-compliant and peer-noncompliant children were found to be statistically significant: opinions are more readily influenced by others; has higher energy level; is more spontaneous and uninhibited; is more distractible; is more suggestible; more often seeks praise and attention from others; is warmer, friendlier; shows more empathic sensitivity to others' feelings; appears more relaxed and easygoing; is less rigid, less inflexible; is less of a perfectionist; exhibits less self-pity; finds it less difficult to make mistakes. In the nursery school, complying with peers seemed to occur in a give-and-take situation rather than in one of dominance and submission. The child who makes many suggestions for play is likely to be a child who frequently agrees with the suggestions of others. It is noteworthy that the children who showed the greatest degree of compliance with peers were also high in the characteristics of mental health.

Sources of friendly behavior are not confined to the child himself. The situation also contributes to how a youngster feels and behaves in relation to another. Experimental proof of the importance of the situation was provided by pairing preschool children in cooperative tasks under three conditions [5]. The picture-board technique was used to find sociometric scores. Children of similar moderate degrees of popularity were paired. The task involved pressing buttons cooperatively.

Reinforcement, in the form of small tokens for cooperative button pressing, was given to experimental groups and not to a control group. Posttesting with the picture board showed an increase in friendship (sociometric) status of the children who had received reinforcement. Therefore, children's social attitudes can be influenced by the conditions under which they interact with each other. The personality characteristics of the participants do not tell the whole story.

Nursery school teachers make use of the knowledge that children's social attitudes and behavior can be changed by the situation in which they interact. Important influences include the planned settings of the nursery school and the teacher's own actions. For example, a 4-year-old boy's antisocial behavior improved greatly when a special teacher consistently reinforced socially acceptable acts and carefully avoided reinforcing antisocial acts [46]. For example, the teacher would say, "Yes, that's right," or smile, nod, and show interest when the little boy helped, showed concern for others, shared ideas or toys, conversed, or otherwise showed friendliness. When he threatened, assaulted, derogated, or disrupted other children, the teacher took action to protect the other children and turned her attention away from the little boy.

Social play becomes more complex as children learn not only more subtle ways of approaching and interacting with each other but also as they develop in motor coordination, language, concepts, and imagination. Play is the arena in which all of these behavior patterns are developed, often simultaneously. The various patterns are analyzed and discussed separately only because the whole picture is too complicated to deal with at once.

## Imagination

Preschool thinking is "cute" in much the same way that infant proportions are "cute"; preschool imagination is beautiful. Imaginative behavior gives the preschool child a special place in the adult's heart. Adults look wistfully at young children's original interpretations of commonplace events, their fresh, bright paintings, poetry, and free-wheeling dramatics. Almost every adult has at least a fleeting memory of being that kind of person himself. "Every child an artist." "The magic years." "The golden years of childhood." What happens to imagination?

### Imagination as Part of the Sense of Initiative

Having developed a firm sense of autonomy and a consequent concept of himself as a person, the child wants to find out what he can *do*. To this end, he explores the world through his senses, through thinking and reasoning, and through imagination. In most situations, of course, these three instruments of exploration are combined. The essential part played by imagination, however, is probably least understood and appreciated. Through imagination, the young child tries on the roles of the important people in his world, the people who do things which he might some day do. Most vital of all are the roles of his parents, and these are the parts he plays first and most often, especially the part of the parent of the same sex. The child imagines being and/or replacing the parent of the same sex. In doing so, he imitates some of the parent's behavior and thinking, including his standards and goals. His own conscience develops through this activity, modeled upon the parent's, encouraged by his desire to be the parent. Gradually, through interaction with both parents, the youngster faces the facts that he can neither be nor replace his parent and that he himself can one day be a parent through growing up and behaving in grown-up ways. He is continually fascinated by the exploration of adult roles, which he does first and foremost through dramatic play, but also through literature and fantasy and even through dancing, painting, and other creative media.

Guilt is a necessary product of the developing sense of initiative, as the child changes from a simple pleasure-seeker to a complex self-regulator. Erikson [17, p. 256] expresses it thus:

> Here the most fateful split and transformation in the emotional power-house occurs, a split between potential human glory and potential total destruction. For here the child becomes forever divided in himself. The instinct fragments which before had enhanced the growth of his infantile body and mind now become divided into an infantile set which perpetuates the exuberance of growth potentials, and a parental set which supports and increases self-observation, self-guidance and self-punishment.

Through imagination, the child appeases and allays some of the conflicts which arise between these two parts of himself, the part which desires and the part which controls (the conscience). When his conscience punishes him too severely with guilt, he can ease the load through imagination. Not only does expression through some creative medium make him feel better; it is a way of solving problems. Imagination is also a powerful means of pushing aggressively out into the world and incorporating some of it into himself.

If life's problems are solved satisfactorily during the years when imagination predominates, then a residue of imaginative activity and a resource of initiative remain, to enliven, sparkle, inspire, and push throughout the rest of life. Such a person will get fresh ideas and will not be afraid to experiment with them. Even though he has attained objectivity, his thinking and feeling will be so flexible that he will be able to take off on flights of imagination. Both creativity and true recreation have their roots in imaginative play.

### Imagination as a Part of Intellectual Development

In its simplest form, imagining consists of representing some part of outer reality by an inner image. Without the ability to use images as representations, man would forever stay in the sensorimotor stage of intellectual development. The first indications of imitative and imaginative play occur in babies during the final period of the sensorimotor stage, when the child imitates his own past actions in very simple, concrete ways. Thus he shows that he has mental images of these actions. For instance, he pretends to go to sleep, curling up in the doll bed or on a pillow, shutting his eyes momentarily. He pretends to eat, perhaps taking a real lick of sand or other make-believe food. He imitates the actions of others, especially his mother. He hugs and loves dolls and soft animals, feeds them, washes them, and puts them to bed. He uses objects imaginatively in order to extend the meaning of newly acquired words, as did 22-months-old Richard [7]. After being told that nodding the head means *yes*, he nodded his own head, saying "Yes, yes, boy." Next he waved his cup up and down, saying, "Yes, yes, cup." Then he did the same with his bowl and fork.

Piaget [43] shows how symbolic games contribute to development during the preconceptual period. The transition from the sensorimotor period to preconceptual is marked by using symbolic patterns with new objects. Jacqueline, having pretended to sleep and pretended to cry, made her toys sleep and cry. Later she pretended to play with a cousin (who was not there) and then to be the cousin. Symbolic play represents experiences the child has had and the meaning that they have for him. It also can be what the child wants life to be. Egocentric, the child becomes submerged in action, loses awareness of himself as separate from the play, and lives in the role that he is dramatizing. The very act of living in that other role, however, leads him away from egocentrism, because it lets him see and feel how it is to be that other person or dog or airplane. As mental growth continues through the preconceptual stage, through symbolic play as well as other experiences, egocentrism gives way to objectivity. Piaget calls imaginative play "the purest form of egocentric and symbolic thought" [42, p. 127]. Symbols, he says, are needed as long as egocentric action prevails, since ready-made language is inadequate for the child's purposes. Language, being the product of society, cannot express all the experience and needs of the individual child, nor can the child master the language enough to serve him very flexibly.

### Types of Imaginative Play

The major forms of imaginative expression in early childhood are discussed in this section. Anyone who works with young children needs to know a great deal about the development and guidance of imagination. The following comments are intended only as an introduction to the topic.

**Fantasy.** Everyone does some thinking which is undirected, free, somewhat symbolic, and difficult or impossible to put into words. Fantasy serves pleasure rather than being directed toward reality or practical issues. Even so, it often produces solutions to problems. Sometimes it is called daydreaming. Fantasy, imaginative thinking, and symbolic thinking all refer essentially to this kind of behavior. Since people engaging in fantasy are not paying attention to the lesson that may be in progress, teachers have traditionally looked upon daydreaming with disfavor. Research in children's thinking shows, however, that fantasy has an essential role to play. Through her studies on imagination in Australian and English children, Griffiths [23] came to see fantasy and symbolic thinking as useful and adaptive ways of coping with life's problems. Instead of being a waste of time, a blank, or a pursuit of pleasure, imagination is a way of dealing with reality which is particularly appropriate for the young child. He can, of course, direct his thoughts to a limited extent, but this free-reining, personal, inner method of symbolic play is his natural medium of action. He makes objective contact with reality and then employs fantasy [23, p. 174].

> Like those simple animalculae that stretch out long pseudopodia into surrounding water in search of food, retiring afterward into a state of apparent passivity while digestion takes place, so does the child seek experience, and, having come into contact with reality in some form, retires within himself to understand and consolidate what he has acquired. He cannot tackle a problem all at once, immediately, even such problems as seem insignificant to us. This is surely the meaning of childhood ; time is needed for adaptation.

Griffiths conducted a series of 20 interviews with each of 50 5-year-olds in situations where the child played freely with drawing materials and was encouraged to say anything he wished. Ink blots and an imagery test were used in addition to the recording of what the child said. For the first few days, comments were controlled and reality-adapted. After three or four days, nearly all children revealed evidence of fantasy. At first, items appeared scattered and chaotic in arrangement, but gradually the elements were linked, themes emerged, and the whole content became complex and closely knit. The whole was not static, but constantly developing in relation to the child's problems and experiences [23, pp. 14–31]. Through fantasy, the child moved from a personal, subjective and egocentric point of view to a more socialized and objective attitude. In order to illustrate this process, there follows a rather long, repetitive account from Griffiths [23, pp. 175–177] of stories told by Dick, reflecting on the subject of possessions and the best ways of coming to own the things that he wants. The repetitive nature of this account demonstrates the ways in which fantasy operates, working over and over ideas, varying them, returning to a theme, adapting it, and moving on to a solution of the problem.

*First phase: Theft*

1. (Third day of the work.) "There was an old man and he had some greengages. And there was a great big giant, and he came and pinched all these greengages, and went away to his house. And this man he went to his house too."

2. (Also on third day.) "And once upon a time there was a lady and she had some eggs. And she was eating these eggs, and an old man came along, and he saw her eating them, so he went up to her and pinched 'em all."

3. (Fifth day.) "Once upon a time there was a burglar and he stole something. And so the copper saw him and this copper took him to prison. He stole a watch and the man was hitting him."

The three stories just given represent what may be called the first phase. At first there is the idea of theft successfully carried out. In the third story two days later he is doubtful already of the advisability of the method, for in spite of extenuating circumstances a thief is punished. He hastens to the next phase.

*Second phase: Goods purchased*

4. (Also on fifth day.) "Once there was a lady and she had some eggs, and a man came down the street, and *he* wanted some. So he went to the stall where the lady bought hers, and he got some and he ate 'em all up."

5. "Some old man had some greengages, and he ate 'em all up, and he said, 'They're good. I think I'll go and buy some more.'"

6. (Sixth day.) "Once upon a time there was a lady running down the street with some apples, and a man wanted some too. And so he asked the lady where she bought 'em. And so *he* went and bought some."

7. (Eighth day.) "Once upon a time there was a lady and a man. So this man he had some apples, and so this lady wanted some. And she asked him where he got his apples so he said out of his garden, and but he didn't. And then the lady found out, and she went to the stall where he bought 'em, and she found out that he was telling lies."

This is the end of the second phase in which the desired article is purchased. In the last story it is interesting to note the emergence of the "garden" idea, anticipating the next phase.

*Third phase: Fruit is grown from seeds*

8. (Ninth day.) "Once upon a time there was a lady, and she was running down the street, and she had some apples and a man saw them, and so he wanted some. So he planted some apple seeds, and some apples grew."

**Creative Language.** Stories and poems are imaginative in both the giving and receiving. Symbolism and beauty can be noted in the form as well as the content. Teachers of young children, and sometimes parents, regard their telling of poems and stories as creative activity. Although there is no definite proof that listening and perhaps writing down the story encourage the child to further expression, adults who work with preschool children generally believe that this is so. Rhythm and imagery are apparent in this moon song, chanted and enjoyed by Ellen at 2½.

> Crescent, crescent, crescent, crescent,
> Crescent goes to sleep, crescent wakes up.
> Ballie, ballie, ballie, ballie,
> Ballie goes to sleep, ballie wakes up.

Sometimes one story will reveal progress in solution of emotional problems. Four-year-old Susan used the following tale with which to struggle symbolically with confusion, fear, good and bad:

> Once Susan was in a theater seeing a grown-up movie. The lady who was giving the movie said, "Our magic fairy who is asleep will have to come out." And so the magic fairy woke up and came out. She chased everybody down the stairs and made everybody dance down the stairs. She chased me down the stairs. When we went out, she spoke to each person as they went out the door and I do not know what she said to the other people, but she said this to me, "You did dance down the stairs but you did not like it." She said that she'd go back in the building and for me to stay there.
>
> She chased me in front of the first car parked outside the theater. Then I started to run up across the bridge as quietly as I could. Then I just had time to sneak into a house and hide. When the good fairy came up, pat-a-pat, pat-a-pat, making a funny pat-a-pat, pat-a-pat, pat-a-pat noise. So I just had time to sneak up into my own house on Giles St. and lock the door when the good fairy came up and went ding-dong, ding-dong on my door bell. I would not open it or Mummy or Daddy or my sister, so the fairy could not get in.
>
> Then the fairy went up and down, flying on top of my roof, for she thought that my house would burn down if she did. But it did not. There was a good fairy inside my house. And she, the good fairy, would not let my house burn down, for she took away the bad fairy's wand, and would not return it. So the bad fairy died, because fairies die when their wands are taken away. And so that was the end of the bad fairy and we all lived happily ever after.

Often the expression of fears and problems helps to minimize them. Adults know how much it helps to talk to a friend about a bad experience, past or anticipated. Young children often do not know exactly what is bothering them, or if they do, they cannot express it straightforwardly. To express it in a story or poem or in another artistic medium can relieve tension, clarify the trouble, and help the youngster to find solutions.

Sometimes hostility shows through the symbols, even when the comment is understood by all to be imaginary and not a real threat. This 5-year-old shows a certain flair for creative imagery, violent as his product is:

I'll push you out the window and you'll make a mess on the pavement
and my Daddy will scrape you up with a knife and spread you on bread
and eat you. Then he'll vomit you up.

A large number of stories, collected from preschool children, contributed to a study of fantasy [19]. Age trends showed increasing length, complexity, and expansion, along with increasing use of fantasy. A 2-year-old boy's story was: "Tractor fall down boom. Fall right down and bust his head off. And he run, run, run" [19, p. 31]. A typical story by 5-year-olds took from half a page to a page.

Sex differences were revealed. Boys seemed to be more intrusive and active and to use more themes of aggression, greater variety of characters, more objects of transportation, objects of nature, and other objects. Girls' stories were more intensive, detailed, involved with feeling, people, the domestic, the here and now. Compare the story of the 2-year-old boy (above) with the following one from a 2-year-old girl: "Once upon a time there was a little girl and she hurt herself. And her mommy came here and she kissed her and made her better" [19, p. 39].

· **Symbolism.** The child's fears and problems are often symbolized by the toys he chooses and by the content of his imaginative games. Discovering an analogy between two objects and situations, he invests one as a symbol for the other. The story of 5-year-old Joyce illustrates this process [23, pp. 141–148]. Joyce and Dorothy were sisters whose father had died two years earlier. More recently, two neighbor children had died, one of them being their playmate, Dorothy L. Joyce sometimes went on errands for Dorothy L.'s mother, who called Joyce "my little girl" and sometimes acted as though Joyce had taken Dorothy's L.'s place. Joyce was rivalrous with her sister Dorothy, a delicate child who received fussing and petting from their parents. Joyce had a china doll which was to her a little girl, and, after Dorothy L.'s death, a dead little girl. When telling the thoughts that came into her mind during a series of play interviews, Joyce disclosed that Dorothy L.'s mother had allowed her to see the dead child in her coffin, where "she was like a china doll." Shortly after this time, sister Dorothy became ill and had to go to the hospital. At this point, her daddy and Dorothy L. disappeared from Joyce's dreams and conversation. She became afraid of her china doll. Instead of taking it to bed with her, she put it on a chair. Waking in the night, she wanted to take the doll into bed, but was afraid that a mouse might get her. "They might get my dolly and get her eyes out with their claws."

Thus Joyce pushed away the reality of her father's death and her sister's frightening disappearance, centering her fears upon an object, the doll, which she used to symbolize all these disturbing occurrences. The doll had formerly been a comforting object. She was still dealing with that object in the daytime, although not at night, when fears were most oppressive. Perhaps she was hanging onto the possibility of getting control of the whole terrifying situation through the doll, which served as such a powerful symbol.

Summarizing the functions of symbolic thinking or fantasy in the life of the child, Griffiths [23, p. 187] makes several points: Fantasy is the normal means of problem solving. Problems are attacked indirectly, often symbolically. The child is only vaguely aware of what he is trying to do. The problem is solved piecemeal, through a series of solutions. The process results in both acquisition of information and a change of attitude. The change of attitude is from personal and egocentric toward socialized and objective.

*Dramatic Play*

Dramatic play, or pretending, is a kind of symbolism. A child can pretend by himself, on a very simple level, as does the toddler who pretends to eat and sleep. Or a child can carry on dramatic play with other children. The make-believe play of children under age 3 is largely personification, such as talking to dolls and other objects, imitative use of objects such as drinking cups, and taking part in such situations as washing clothes. Between 3 and 5, children become more active with materials and engage in more frequent, longer, and more complex imaginative games.

**Sociodramatic Play.** The Israeli effort to educate disadvantaged children has led to research on play. Sara Smilansky's analysis of play clarifies its role in normal development [48]. Sociodramatic play is, as its name implies, both social and dramatic. It serves to promote and integrate young children's social, emotional, and intellectual growth. Smilansky [48, p. 9] gives six essential elements of sociodramatic play:

1. Imitative role play. The child expresses a make-believe role in imitative acts and/or words.
2. Make-believe with objects. Actions or words are substituted for objects.
3. Make-believe in substituting words for acts and situations.
4. Persistence in the episode for at least ten minutes.
5. Interaction of at least two participants.
6. Verbal communication about the play.

The first four elements occur in dramatic play. The addition of the last two are essential for sociodramatic play.

Smilansky has observed that until about 3, a child imitates small pieces of his parents' (and other significant adults') behavior, expressing his identification with them through dramatic play. Thus he irons as Mommy does or drives a tractor like Daddy. After 3, he begins to see that the thoughts, feelings, and actions he has been imitating are not merely single episodes but that they are also reactions to other people. Sociodramatic play is born of the understanding that people react to each other and interact with each other. He needs other children, for now he wants to imitate both actions and reactions. He wants to reproduce the world as he understands it [48, p. 71].

Sociodramatic play was the setting for 65 percent of the positive social reinforcement given by nursery school children to their peers, in the previously mentioned study [8]. Thus they interacted more in dramatic play than they did during involvement with art, music, table games, and such. In response to other children, children gave attention, approval, and submission. They were likely to initiate an exchange by offering affection, personal acceptance, and tokens. Dramatic play also facilitates the use of language, playful expression of anger and hostility, and the trying on of various roles.

By 4½ or 5 years, children who have had rich play experience can make use of a wide range of topics for sociodramatic play. Going beyond home and family, even beyond store and post office, they may explore the moon in an episode that lasts for several days. Astronauts build with large blocks, packing cases, and planks. They store food and drink. They launch, fly, and land. The following half-hour incident illustrates sociodramatic play with a strong adventure theme:

> Bill and Grant were digging with shovels in the dirt in a far corner of the yard. They piled the dirt in a mound against the fence. Both looked ex-

cited. Grant said, "We'll have a pile way up to the sky." Bill asked, "How long will it take to get down to the bottom?" Grant replied, "All night and all day and all night."

Bill accepted the answer without comment. Another boy came over to watch the digging. Bill exclaimed in a high voice, "We smell a *bad* bear and a *good* bear here. So it's very *dangerous*. We're going to find the bears in China. I sleep with the bears at night. I lock them in a cage tight. Then I turn out the light."

Bill and Grant went into the building and came out with a small bottle of water. They poured it on the roots which had been exposed by the digging. "Put the poison on my roots, too" Bill told Grant. "Kill them all."

The teacher told the boys it was time for milk. Sitting on the bench in the coat room, Bill leaned towards Kit and told him earnestly, "The *good* bears and the *bad* bears both know me, but only the good bears know you, cause I've known 'em longer than you have. And do you know what happened one night? A *bad* bear visited me [51].

An incident is rarely a pure example of one kind of play or another. In this bit of play, Bill and Grant practice the coordinations of digging, try on the roles of explorers going to China, and explore the nature of bears and feelings toward bears. Bill seems to be getting the upper hand of a fear of bears, or perhaps of a less specific fear which he has chosen bears to symbolize. The power of imagination makes water into poison, and the little boys can use that poison to kill roots. Probably the roots symbolized a fear or a threat.

## Imaginary Playmates

Imaginary companions of preschool children have long intrigued students of behavior. A frequent production of children in the stage of developing imagination and initiative, imaginary playmates can be human or animal, fleeting or long-enduring, single or multiple, ideals or scapegoats. Studies report a fourth to a third of children as having imaginary companions. The children who create these playmates come in as great a variety as the imaginary creatures themselves, strongly suggesting that the creations serve the needs of the children. Bright children are somewhat more likely to have imaginary companions (or to tell about them) than are children of below average intelligence. Girls are more prone than boys to create their own playmates [28, pp. 394–397]. A study of college students who had had imaginary companions in childhood showed them to have tendencies toward higher than average grades and toward cooperation, friendships, and the experiencing of strong feelings and emotions [16]. Among creative adolescents, producers in literary fields reported more imaginary companions in childhood [25].

## Humor

Humor is an intellectual process which reduces anxiety. Developmentally, the first joke is the game of peek a boo, which dramatizes the baby's anxiety over his mother's disappearance, then presumably reduces his tension. Joking makes psychological pain bearable, expresses fears and wishes which cannot be faced directly, and gratifies forbidden desires. One of man's most creative achievements, humor partakes of both language and gesture, with emphasis on gesture during the preschool period. Humor depends on flexibility of thought, which the preschool child possesses to a very limited extent. The punch line, so important to adult jokes, is beyond his cognitive powers. Therefore, his amusements and his attempts to be funny are not amusing but seem silly to an adult. He may actually be funny in the simplicity of his jokes. Although incongruity and surprise are of the essence of grown-up jokes, a certain subtlety is usually necessary for adults. Furthermore, preschool humor is too far removed from adult problems to be tension-reducing to adults. Incongruity takes precedence over surprise in preschool humor, although surprise can add to the fun.

Falling down is often hilarious, since it includes both aspects of the joke. The person suddenly gets into the wrong position, in the wrong relationship to the floor. A fillip is added by the involvement of the whole body in the situation. Language jokes tend to be in the form of calling objects or events by inappropriate names, especially forbidden words, such as bathroom terms. Long, rambling (pointless to adults) stories may be offered and accepted as jokes, since the surprise element is not essential. These lengthy tales often concern creatures falling down, falling apart and growing together again, getting lost and found, hurt and well, having toilet accidents or performing deliberate excretions. Underlying young children's jokes are their envy of adult size, power, and privileges, worries over the wholeness and safety of their bodies, resentment of adult control in the face of their own autonomy strivings, aggressive impulses which frighten them.

## Music and Dance

Creativity exists both in performance and in enjoying the music and dancing of others. In these areas, as in other parts of the preschool child's experience, exploration is vital. A rich environment offers opportunities to experiment with sound and gesture and with putting them together. Infants enjoy and respond to songs. By age 2, the child who has had some experience with singing will listen to others and will sing spontaneously as he plays. He likes action songs, in which he responds to words with gestures. He joins in with a few words as others sing. His first efforts to sing with a group will probably not be well coordinated, but they soon lead to his being able to follow along with others' singing. Soon he recognizes and asks for certain songs and recognizes various pieces of music [33, pp. 361–365]. Creative expression flows when the few necessary facilities are present—a chance to listen; a chance to sing; the simplest of instruments to play (some can be made from scrap materials [40, p. 13]); a group with whom to play, sing, and dance; experience to play, sing, and dance about. In a simpler society, a child can grow into the music and dance of his parents, watching, imitating, being taken through the motions, and joining in adult dances and music groups when he is sufficiently grown up. In complex western culture, it often takes an adult with special skill and understanding to appreciate and facilitate the young child's creations in music and dance. Such a teacher develops the cognitive processes basic to the child's under-standing and appreciation, as well as the feeling aspects [2, pp. 20–27]. As one student of the dance has said, "A child cheerfully undertakes a multiple career as singer, instrumentalist, actor, and dancer. In what we call 'play', he dramatizes poetry and makes it blood-brother to song" [37, p. 5].

In the machine age many children see little of rhythmic muscular activity which seems to them worth imitating. In contrast, primitive children experience the rhythms of weaving, grinding, and chopping. In a preschool day camp dancing grew out of the small happenings of every day: a Moon Time Dance when the children noticed the moon in the daytime sky, The Sunflower Dance, created by a 4-year-old and 2-year-old who found sunflowers, The Chocolate Sellers, dances of

Mollie Smart

fears, of wonder of God, of cooking [15]. The teacher found that the higher the emotional content in the thought expressed, the more the child seemed to need rhythmic action to express it. With young children, there was rarely dancing without singing or rhythmic language.

With music, as well as dance, young children have potentiality for expression and enjoyment, perhaps even more than that of the average adult. It has been shown that music produces an emotional response in people and a more pronounced response in children than in adults, as measured by the galvanic skin response [57].

## Creative Materials

The same statement could be made of young children's expression through *paint, clay, blocks*, and other materials. These media offer the same types of benefits that the child gets from fantasy, dramatic play, and creative language—increased understanding of the world and his relation to it, expression and understanding of his questions and problems, release of emotional tension, satisfaction from creating beauty and order. In fact, some of the most creative programs for children encourage the use of all forms of artistic expression and enjoyment in relation with one another [50]. Emotionally disturbed children indicate in their artistic expression some of their malaise. Psychology students and professors, with no previous training in understanding children's art, were able to do significantly better than chance in matching paintings to personality descriptions [49]. The judges also separated the paintings of disturbed children from those of normal children. Since the judges could not tell how they did it, the investigators suggest an unidentified intuitive process at work.

A

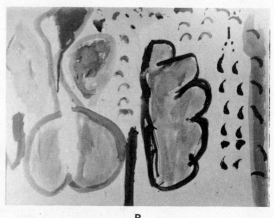

B

D

C

**Figure 7–1.** Development of graphic representation.
A. Scribble
B. Design
C. Pictorial, using circles and rectangles
D. Pictorial

**Figure 7–2 (opposite page).** Development of representation of human form between the ages of three and seven years.

Series by Ellen S. Smart

A

B

C

D

E

When a child first encounters paint, clay, or any other new material, he has to explore it, to find out what it is like and what he can do with it. (Not only children. Watch an African graduate student in the first snowfall of the North American winter!) Set-up and limits are important here—"paint goes on the paper," "blocks are not to throw," "hold the saw this way."

In the graphic arts, a series of stages can be identified. Each child goes through these stages at approximately these ages:

1. *Scribbling, from 1 to 3 years.* During the first quarter of the second year, a baby will make marks with a crayon on a paper, after a demonstration or encouragement to do so. By 18 months, he will scribble spontaneously. Even if paper and crayons are not given, 2-year-olds will make marks in the sand, on a sidewalk, or wall. The young child shows great interest in what he has made. He tries out different types of strokes and placements [32].
2. *Shape and design.* From 2 to 5 years. The child uses the lines that he has developed through his scribbling and makes shapes and designs from them. Even though he cannot write, the average kindergartner can tell printed characters from scribbling [18]. In a kindergarten of high socioeconomic status, 75 percent of the children could distinguish cursive writing from scribbling. When children are making shapes and designs, they do so for the pleasure of making them and not to represent something. A child develops his own style and preferences while discovering how to make more complex designs.
3. *Pictorial, from age 4 onward.* Now the child uses his lines, shapes, and designs to represent reality. Drawings of people are usually the first recognizable pictures. All over the world, children make their early drawings in the same ways. Their pictures of people, houses, trees, suns, boats, trains, and cars give little hint as to whether the young artists were American, Scottish, or Indonesian.

## Enrichment of Preschool Life

The tremendous growth potential of young children demands a rich and varied environment in order to be realized. Supplements to the home, in the form of nursery school, day-care centers, kindergartens, church schools, and play groups provide places where children can reach out to interact with a nurturant world. Although the kibbutzim of Israel and the yasli-sad of the Soviets take over some of the functions that American families reserve for themselves, schools for young children in this country are also based on the idea of adding to the child's life opportunities which his family cannot give him.

Even today, many people still hold the view that the preschool years are a time when the child "just plays," waiting to be old enough to start learning lessons which really count. Even mothers who spontaneously enhance their children's intellectual and personality development are often surprised when they learn of their own vital influence. Although nursery schools have been operating in the United States ever since 1921, the public has neither understood nor promoted their educational potential. Suddenly, however, the problems of poverty and educational deprivation highlighted the growth possibilities that exist in all children during their first years of life. Infancy and preschool years are seen as the time to prevent mental retardation, learning problems, school failure, poor self concept, inadequate language and antisocial tendencies. Special compensatory programs have been developed in attempts to meet the needs of deprived children and their families. First, let us take a look at the traditional nursery school and then at some of the outstanding approaches to compensatory preschool education.

### Traditional Nursery Education

The preschool child is treated as a whole person who grows through differentiation and integration of body, personality, and intellect. Provisions for play, health, and growth are carefully planned and maintained. Social growth is promoted by arrangements which facilitate cooperative play, and guidance which gives insight into motivations and feelings of oneself and others. Equipment and program are attuned to the stages of personality growth which dominate the preschool years.

**Building the Sense of Autonomy.** The miniature world, which strikes the casual visitor as so cute, is child-sized in order that the child can *do the utmost for himself.* He hangs his snowsuit on the hook that is just the right height; his feet touch the floor when he sits on the toilet. The child-sized world is arranged in such a way that its occupants can *make many decisions for themselves*, decisions which turn out to be right. A child selects a puzzle from the puzzle rack and puts it back before he takes another. An easel with fresh paper, paints, and brushes invites him to paint, standing on a floor protector which keeps a spill from being a disaster. The housekeeping corner is full of equipment which children can manage—doll clothes with wide armholes and big buttons, a low bed in which children can snuggle with dolls, a sturdy, stable ironing board with small iron, unbreakable dishes and a place to wash them, grown-up purses, shoes, and hats, for easy dressing up.

The teachers appreciate what it means to young children to be independent successfully, to make decisions that turn out well and to feel worthwhile in what they do. In addition to encouraging and facilitating such behavior, teachers also know what not to do, never to use shaming as a way of controlling behavior, never at any age, but especially at this time of life, since doubt and shame undermine the growth of autonomy. Neither is competition used as an incentive, since it too would threaten the child's growing sense of autonomy.

Discipline in the nursery school is not quite the same as the discipline that many students and parents have known in their lives. It is easier to understand in terms of the sense of autonomy. The teacher sets limits on what the child may decide for himself and what he may do. She makes the limits clear and sticks to them firmly, giving him freedom within them. She does not say, "Wouldn't you like to come indoors now?" She says, "Now it's time to go indoors." She does not say, "Nice little boys don't grab toys from little girls." She says, "Jilly is using the doll carriage now, Tommy. You may have it when she is finished. Could you use the rocking bed now?" Thus a choice really is a choice and a direction is definite. The teacher understands that the children will often test the limits she sets, as part of their growing up. Because the child knows she respects and accepts him as a person, because he trusts her, he can usually accept the limits she sets for him. Because he likes her and wants to be like her, he often wants to do what he perceives she wants. Thus discipline in the nursery school is carefully planned and carried out in such ways that children can grow in autonomy through successful deciding and doing [44, pp. 222–247].

**Building Initiative and Imagination.** Motivational and intellectual aspects of growth are involved here, as this chapter and Chapter 5 have shown. The nursery school's stress on creative activities is one of its most vital ways of contributing to preschool growth. Not only is creativity valuable in itself now and in the future, but imagination is more than a supplement to controlled thought during the preschool years. The young child solves through imaginative processes many problems which he cannot handle by controlled thinking.

Setting him free within comfortable limits, the nursery school invites the child to reach out into his world, to explore it vigorously and curiously, to imagine himself in a multitude of roles, to create a variety of beauty. All of this magic is implicit in the combination of children, raw materials, space, some carefully chosen equipment, and teachers who love children and know a great deal about them. Dramatic play requires only a few simple props, but it needs a push at the right moment and hands off at other moments. The skillful teacher will suggest straightening the corner block before the whole post office tumbles down. She is quick to produce paper that will do for letters for the postman to carry. She suggests that Ronnie could be a customer at the stamp window after he has hung on the fringes unable to get into the game.

Managing paints, clay, paste, and such is so simple that first-time observers often see the teacher doing nothing. It takes real understanding of initiative and imagination, however, to let children create freely, often by keeping quiet and doing nothing. Teachers never "fix up" children's products. They accept them. They never draw models to be copied. They never tell children what to make with materials. They don't say, "What is it?" They listen to what the child spontaneously says about his creations. They show that they realize it meant something to him to do what he did.

Initiative and imagination are stimulated by books, stories, music, trips, pets, plants, and visitors with special messages for children. Such experiences provide ideas which are worked over in dramatic play and creative work with materials.

Perhaps it is in the area of initiative and imagination where the nursery school supplements the home most generously. What home can provide such a constant flow of fingerpaint and play dough? What mother can arrange for a group of peers for daily playmates or be on hand constantly to supervise dramatic play constructively? Or to play the piano for a group of elephants who turn into butterflies? Or to take children to see a hive of bees working behind glass? Or to arrange for her child to find out how a pipe organ works? Or to have his teeth cleaned with a group of his friends, attending the dental hygiene clinic after a child-oriented introduction?

**Facilitating Intellectual Development.** The tremendously rich environment of the nursery school offers never-ending opportunities for building mental structures. The child constantly perceives, integrates his perceptions, and integrates sensory experience with verbal. Toys and materials are readily available for handling in addition to looking, a condition which stimulates richness in thinking about objects [20]. Since most preschool children think preconceptually and intuitively, a nursery school curriculum is designed to give them problems which they are capable of solving. Through building with blocks they learn that two of these equal one of those and that a square can be divided into two triangles. Counting may result from figuring out how many blocks to bring from this shelf and how many from that, when blocks are kept sorted according to size and shape. Counting happens in many situations which have real meaning—two cookies for each child at snack time, time before lunch for singing three songs. How many children go home with

Peggy's mother? The workbench is a place for dealing with linear measure, roughly, of course, in terms of *longer* or *shorter than* or *about the same size as*. The sink is for learning about volume, if you are allowed to pour water back and forth instead of just washing your hands. Useful equipment includes containers graduated as to size and another series of similar size but different shapes. Clay, sand, and mud offer chances to experiment (loosely speaking, not scientifically) with size, shape, and volume. So do many other materials found in nursery schools offer opportunities for development of the schemas of cognition—pegs and pegboards, puzzles, shoes to lace, matching games, color sorting games, musical instruments, records, books.

Language is a vital part of the curriculum. The teacher is a model of clear, pleasantly toned, noncolloquial speech. Skilled in understanding baby talk, she replies in speech which the child comes to imitate. She encourages children to talk, to tell her and other children about their experiences and feelings. New words and concepts come from books, stories, songs, and the many planned new experiences of nursery school. The beautiful books and satisfying storytimes make children look forward eagerly to learning to read to themselves. Here is preparation for reading—good speech, something to talk about, a love of books. Here also is intellectual development taking place through language, when children communicate with others and acquire verbal symbols with which to think.

Concepts of *time* are part of preschool endeavors, even though young children do not handle chronology very objectively. Many of their comments and questions and much of their play shows efforts to straighten out their ideas of time and to understand how life changes. While children make barely a beginning in comprehending the historic past by 8 years of age preschool children are deeply concerned with the sweeping changes in life which have occurred with the passage of time. Before they are interested in or able to tell minutes by the clock, they hear about dinosaurs, horse and buggies, steam locomotives. Through play, conversation, and thought, children arrange these past events and phenomena into a very rough historical concept. In India we found that relatively uneducated people would often tell us, "It happened in ancient times," meaning that it happened before Independence. It could have occurred any time between 3000 B.C. and 1947. "Ancient times" is probably the way children think of the past before they have had the rigors of history lessons brought to bear upon them. The history lessons will be richer in meaning if they come after the past has content for the children, even though it is content without much chronology.

A review of research on teaching in the nursery school [47] yields considerable evidence that nursery school attendance promotes social, language, and intellectual growth. The quality of the nursery school seems to make a difference in whether such growth can be demonstrated. Gains are greatest in the children who start with the greatest room for improvement. Those from homes providing meager stimulation are likely to make the greatest intellectual gains.

*Educational Deprivation*

The culture of poverty includes restrictions which affect every member of the family in every aspect of life and development. By about 2 years of age, the child is missing more and more experiences basic to the type of intellectual growth required for participation in the mainstream of culture. Living in a crowded, noisy home, he learns to ignore sounds, since few of them have any relevance for him. When people speak to him, they speak in single words or in short sentences, often in commands. He may not discover that everything has a name. Lacking this powerful piece of knowledge, he does not seek out names, does not add to his vocabulary, and hence drops farther and farther behind the average child in thinking as well as in talking and understanding language. Nobody corrects his pronunciation, since the adults and older children articulate poorly. Inaccurate phonetically and grammatically, his speech is not easy for the teacher to understand when he goes to school. The child then has trouble understanding the teacher, because she talks in longer, more complicated sentences than he has heard, she sounds her words differently, she uses words he does not know, and she talks about things, places, and events which he has never experienced [29].

Slum homes, in contrast to middle-class homes, offer young children few toys and play materials. Deprived children may never have the visual and tactile stimulation which comes from play with color cones, blocks, nests of cubes, puzzles, paints, clay, crayons, and paper. They lack the emotional satisfactions of cuddly toys and the imaginative and social possibilities of dolls, housekeeping equipment, costumes, and transportation toys. Their motor development is not encouraged, as it would be through the use of climbing apparatus, tricycles, and large building materials. Nature is not seen as orderly, beautiful, and wondrous, since nature is hardly seen at all. Preschool children in slum areas rarely go more than a few blocks from home. A woman who grew up in a slum recalls that as a child, the only beauty she saw was in the sky.

Upon entering first grade, educationally deprived children are at a severe disadvantage in many ways, but most seriously in the main job of the beginner in school, learning to read. In contrast to children from more educated families, they are more personal and concrete, more dependent on action and context, and lacking in the skills of linguistic analysis and synthesis [6]. Disadvantaged children differ from middle-class children in what the teacher's words mean to them, in what they know about themselves. First grade is baffling to those who lack meaningful experiences with language and ideas, toys and places, people and other living things. Unable to cope with reading and other school activities, the educationally deprived child falls farther behind in second grade and still farther as he grows older [12, 13]. His IQ declines. Somewhere around third or fourth grade, he feels hopeless and defeated. Intellectually and educationally retarded, he is a serious problem to the school and to himself.

Many children live under conditions which deprive them of opportunities for normal intellectual development. The culture of poverty, according to various estimates, envelops 15 to 20 percent of the population [26]. While sharing a lack of education and inability to earn an adequate living, these people differ in ethnic subculture. It is estimated that the severely disadvantaged include about 20 million English-speaking Caucasians, 8 million Negroes, 2 million Spanish-Americans, 700,000 Puerto Ricans, and 500,000 American Indians. About 10.7 million children are poor. They are 15 percent of all children under 18 [9].

*Compensatory Programs for Disadvantaged Children*

In the early 1960s, Americans began to develop programs designed to promote normal intellectual growth in children of the very poor. Already the Israelis were tackling such problems with considerable success. The Oriental Jews who had migrated to Israel had a disproportionate number of children with low IQs, as compared with children of European Jews. When reared in the kibbutzim, the Oriental children's IQs equaled those of the Europeans. Americans also had the example of Maria Montessori, who created and directed a highly successful school for poor children in Rome, in 1907. After the United States government created Head Start, in 1965, programs multipled and the public became interested. Many people's hopes were raised too high and they were disappointed when children were not transformed magically, promptly, permanently, and cheaply. Results to date show that good programs can improve the functioning of children and families, that intellectual factors are closely related with physical, social, sociological, and economic factors, and that brief, inexpensive programs are likely to make only temporary changes.

Basically, the nursery schools for deprived children are like the good nursery school described above, dedicated to providing opportunities for full development. Since the disadvantaged child must catch up with what he has missed, in addition to growing in the regular way, his preschool is necessarily adapted to his special needs. Therefore such schools lay particular stress on teaching verbal and perceptual skills, promoting the child's self concept and self-confidence, stimulating curiosity and building a need for achievement. These nursery schools, in contrast to those for normally advantaged children, usually structure their programs more, providing for a great deal of adult–child interaction. Some schools stress the learning of perceptual, conceptual, and verbal skills, paying little or no attention to social and emotional development. The Bereiter and Engelman [3] approach is probably the most famous of such programs. Using tangible rewards and punishments, with verbal drills, learning of rules and application of rules, Bereiter–Engelman programs have produced substantial IQ gains, such as an average gain of 14 points in the first year [30]. Gains tend to continue when the program is continued into the early grades, and academic success is usual. A language tutoring program for 3- and 4-year-olds produced substantial (14.5 in one group, 7 in another) average IQ rises plus enthusiasm for learning and excitement over mastery [4].

Contrasting with programs built on drills, rewards, and punishments is Smilansky's approach to treating deprivation through sociodramatic play [48]. Advantaged Israeli children were found to differ greatly from disadvantaged in terms of their use of play, analyzed by the six criteria presented on page 286. After diagnosing the play level of the children, they were given meaningful experiences which could serve as themes for play; a clinic, a grocery store, and a story. Visits, conversations, observations, toys, and materials were appropriately supplied. Teachers first tried to stimulate sociodramatic play without entering in and then took active part in the play. Children's play improved greatly under these conditions. Meaningful experiences and materials without teacher intervention were not enough, but teacher intervention alone was of some help. Achievement in sociodramatic play was not related to IQ, although minimal normal intelligence seems to be required. Girls made more progress in play than did boys. Although the disadvantaged children remained below the verbal level of the advantaged control group, there was improvement in verbal patterns during the experiment.

Several studies have compared results from two or more types of programs [14, 41, 56]. *Concept training* and *discovery* were used with 2-year-old black boys, half of them lower class and half middle class [41]. In each of the experimental conditions, the child was alone with an instructor for two one-hour periods a week, over eight months. In the concept-training condition, the teacher demonstrated and labeled a concept, such as *on top of, under, rough, smooth, wet, dry.* Then the child performed an act related to the concept and the teacher labeled it, the child demonstrated an instance of the concept and the child used the label correctly. In the discovery condition, the child freely used the same materials that were presented to the concept-training group, and the instructor played with him as though they were in a regular nursery school, letting the child take the initiative. After the eight-month period, both experimental groups were superior to controls on tests. A year later the experimental groups were still superior to controls. Differences between the two experimental groups favored the concept-training group after the eight months' experimental period, but favored the discovery group a year later. Apparently both methods were beneficial, with discovery having more lasting effects. The investigators suggest that the main reasons for success were an early beginning and a systematic, uninterrupted relationship between teacher and child over a period of time.

The more comprehensive programs such as the Early Training Project at Peabody College [22] and the Perry Preschool Project [55] in Ypsilanti have also produced dramatic gains in IQ. There is evidence that any good preschool program produces some rise in IQ. In fact, IQs tend to go up during the first year after school entrance [22]. The important question is whether IQ gains can be *maintained*, and if so, under what circumstances. The Early Training Project report shows that the experimental groups have maintained their superiority over the control groups for three years after the end of the intervention program. Although all groups showed some decline in Stanford–Binet IQ between first and fourth grade, the groups paralleled each other. Therefore, while the school, or perhaps the general culture of poverty, exerted a depressing effect, the gains made by the children in the project were not lost. Tests of school achievement also showed the experimental group to be superior, but the differences between experimental and control groups decreased as the children moved up through the grades. By fourth grade there was a small but nonsignificant difference.

The other results of the Early Training Project are also important, since raising IQs and inducing academic achievement are only fragments of the massive help needed by the very poor. The intervention began as a summer preschool, followed by a year-round program of weekly home visits by a teacher who worked with the child and the mother. The children in this group had three summers of nursery school, and three winters of teacher visits. Another group had two years of summer school and teacher visits for the remainder of the time. By having one control group in the same community and another in a town 60 miles away, the investigators were able to measure the diffusion of the intervention program to relatives and friends of the families in the program. They found solid evidence of diffusion to relatives and friends and also to children in the same family, especially to younger siblings close to the ages of the children in the program. Younger siblings of experimental children tested significantly higher over a two-year period than did younger siblings of control children. It seems reasonable that changes made in the mother benefited the younger siblings as well as the children to whom the program was directed. It is also reasonable that one way of maintaining IQ gains is to involve mothers in the educational process. When mothers learn how to teach their children and when they experience the rewards from it, then they are likely to exert steady and lasting influence on their children's intellectual development. In fact, when children had no nursery school, educated, involved mothers had a greater stimulating effect than similar mothers did on children who were attending preschools [21].

Another important finding from several preschool programs is that greater gains were shown in the programs that started at younger preschool ages. For example, in the Perry Preschool Project study which showed very large gains, the 3-year-olds gained an average of 27.5 to 30.2 IQ points, while the 4-year-olds gained 17.6 to 24.4 [56]. Initial ability is another condition related to gain. The greatest gains tend to be made by children with moderate or slight retardation, whose IQs are in the high 70s and low 80s [21]. The Perry Preschool children were in this IQ range.

Benefits from intervention programs do not always show up immediately. The first group in the Perry Preschool project did not test significantly higher than their control group at the end of kindergarten, but at the end of first grade, they were superior on reading tests and other achievement tests [55]. Likewise, in the Early Training Project, achievement scores of experimental children were more superior to those of controls at the end of the second grade than they were at the end of the first grade.

It is unfortunate that the results of intervention programs are measured so often in terms of IQ points and achievement test scores and so seldom in relation to other important benefits, such as the delight a child shows in mastery of problems, the social adjustment which has been characteristic of the Perry children who gained in IQ, the vision screening, medical and dental examinations and resulting treatments given to 90 percent of Head Start children [36], and the changes in life style among families in the Early Training Project "from the status of environmental victims to people who are beginning to develop environmental mastery." [38].

When it became apparent that an early start and parent participation were important in helping disadvantaged chidren, before-and-after programs were initiated and attempts were made to find new ways of working with children and parents. Parent and Child Centers [31] were started in order to reach children under 3. Follow Through was begun in order to maintain gains made by preschool programs. A television program, "Sesame Street," was designed for disadvantaged preschool children, offering them daily, repeated opportunities to learn language and concepts in a setting of kindness, human dignity, and fun [34]. The potential audience of "Sesame Street" was 12 million children between 3 and 5 years. During the first two weeks of the program, it was estimated that 6 million children watched it. Later, a study of one area found 90 percent of children between 3 and 5, not in day-care centers, watched the program [11]. Viewers have shown substantial gains in learning letters, numbers, sorting, and problem solving. At the beginning of the second year of "Sesame Street," studies showed that children who had watched the program had made greater gains in learning than those who had not watched [24]. The more time they had spent watching the show, the more they had gained. Effects were noted among urban and rural, rich and poor, English-speaking and non English-speaking. Unfortunately, however, many children in poor neighborhoods were not seeing "Sesame Street." Opportunities for viewing "Sesame Street" are to be extended in the United States and offered in at least 50 other countries.

Although the recent increase in day-care centers is motivated by commercial interests as well as by interest in benefiting children, well-run programs can be very valuable to children and families. A good program includes the educational opportunities of a nursery school plus physical care, nutrition, and parent involvement.

## Summary

Play, the main occupation of the young child, is his mode of learning new patterns of thought, feeling and action and of integrating them. While sensorimotor play persists throughout life, social and imaginative play become increasingly influential upon the preschool child's develoment. Play is its own reward. It enhances all of life.

Early social play involves exploration of other children as objects and as persons. Parallel play, typical of 2-year-olds, means engaging in the same activity with little interaction other than watching and imitating. Interactions between young children are temporary and fleeting, increasing as children mature. The earliest group play is loosely structured, permitting children to shift in and out of the activity easily. Sympathetic and cooperative behavior occur in young children. Leadership involves opening possibilities for activities to others and integrating their play. Children vary considerably in the degree to which they can and will fit in with the play of others. Quarrels are common when conflicts occur, but most quarrels are settled rather simply, with little aftermath. As children grow older, they tend to quarrel less frequently but more aggressively. Positive, friendly behavior increases with age, occurring very often in well-liked children. Reinforcement of positive social behavior is effective. Immature children are likely to elicit aggression from children the same age who are more mature.

Imagination, the key to preschool personality development, complements controlled thinking. Through mental images, the child represents experiences and objects to himself. He invents symbols to stand for the images and uses those symbols in his thinking. As he acquires language, he is able to think more and more with the words which his culture gives him as representatives of experiences and objects. In imagination, however, he continues to use some of his own private symbols, and to invent more for his own purposes, in fantasy, symbolic thinking, and dreams. Other forms of imaginative expression include dramatic play, in which human relationships and roles are explored, creative language, which produces stories and poems and humor, which reduces anxiety. Sex differences are apparent in the stories children tell. Young children perform and enjoy in all fields of art, music, dance, painting and sculpture. With all art media, such as paint, clay, and blocks, children develop through an orderly sequence of stages. Children use all forms of imagination in solving problems and in expressing their thoughts and feelings.

Schools for young children supplement homes by providing constructive play opportunities. An excellent nursery school (preschool) offers an environment in which the sense of autonomy and the sense of initiative are nurtured. Guidance and discipline provide limits within which the child can make successful decisions and free choices. Intellectual development is promoted through a rich variety of sensory experiences, available in contexts which lead to conceptualization. The learning of language is encouraged. Preschools have a special contribution to make to culturally disadvantaged children, who are going to school in increasing numbers. Enrichment programs have been successful in raising IQ, improving language, concepts, self concepts, self-confidence, and curiosity, and in preventing progressive retardation in the elementary school. The preschool must work with the family, as well as the child, if the child is to gain maximum benefit from his school.

Federal projects in preschool education, day care, health and family welfare are based on the conviction that the preschool years offer the most promising opportunities for breaking the cycle of poverty. These projects emphasize the promotion of normal, healthy growth before drastic remedial measures become necessary.

## References

1. Almy, M. Spontaneous play: An avenue for intellectual development. *Young Children*, 1967, **22**, 265–277.
2. Aronoff, F. W. *Music and young children.* New York: Holt, Rinehart and Winston, 1969.
3. Bereiter, C., & Engelmann, S. *Teaching disadvantaged children in the preschool.* Englewood Cliffs, N.J.: Prentice-Hall, 1966.
4. Blank, M., & Solomon, F. A tutorial language program to develop abstract thinking in socially disadvantaged preschool children. *Child Devel.*, 1968, **39**, 379–389.
5. Blau, B., & Rafferty, J. Changes in friendship status as a function of reinforcement. *Child Devel.*, 1970, **41**, 113–121.
6. Bruner, J. S. *Poverty and childhood.* Detroit: Merrill-Palmer Institute, 1970.
7. Carlson, P., & Anisfeld, M. Some observations on the linguistic competence of a two-year-old child. *Child Devel.*, 1969, **40**, 569–575.
8. Charlesworth, R., & Hartup, W. W. Positive social reinforcement in the nursery school peer group. *Child Devel.*, 1967, **38**, 993–1002.
9. Committee for Economic Development. Profile of the poor. *Sat. Rev.*, May 23, 1970, p. 23.
10. Crandall, V. J., Orleans, S., Preston, A., & Rabson, A. The development of social compliance in young children. *Child Devel.*, 1958, **29**, 430–443.
11. Culhane, J. Report on Sesame Street. New York Times Magazine, May 24, 1970, pp. 34 ff.
12. Deutsch, M. Facilitating development in the preschool child: Social and psychological perspectives. *Merrill-Palmer Quart.*, 1964, **10**, 249–263.
13. Deutsch, M. The influence of early social environment on school adaptation. In D. Schreiber (Ed.), *The school dropout.* Washington, D.C.: National Education Association, 1964, pp. 89–100.
14. Dickie, J. P. Effectiveness of structured and unstructured (traditional) methods of language training. *Mono. Soc. Res. Child Devel.*, 1968, **33**:8, 62–79.
15. Dixon, C. M. *High, wide and deep.* New York: John Day, 1938.
16. Duckworth, L. H. The relationship of childhood imaginary playmates to some factors of creativity among college freshmen. Unpublished Master's thesis, University of Alabama, 1962.
17. Erikson, E. H. *Childhood and society.* New York: Norton, 1963.
18. Gibson, E. J. The ontogeny of reading. *Am. Psychol.*, 1970, **25**, 136–143.

19. Goodenough, E. G., & Prelinger, E. *Children tell stories*. New York: International Universities Press, 1963.
20. Goodnow, J. J. Effects of active handling, illustrated by uses for objects. *Child Devel.*, 1969, **40**, 202–212.
21. Gray, S. W. *Selected longitudinal studies of compensatory education—A look from the inside*. Nashville, Tenn.: Demonstration and Research Center in Early Education, George Peabody College for Teachers, 1969.
22. Gray, S. W. & Klaus, R. A. The early training project: A seventh-year report. *Child Devel.*, 1970, **41**, 909–924.
23. Griffiths, R. *A study of imagination in early childhood*. London: Routledge & Kegan Paul, 1935.
24. Groseclose, E. Teachers find ABCs are too elementary. *Wall St. J.*, November 15, 1970.
25. Hartup, W. W., Glazer, J. A., & Charlesworth, R. Peer reinforcement and sociometric status. *Child Devel.*, 1967, **38**, 1017–1024.
26. Havighurst, R. J. Minority subcultures and the law of effect. *Am. Psychol.*, 1970, **25**, 313–322.
27. Hoffman, M. L. Parent discipline and the child's consideration for others. *Child Devel.*, 1963, **34**, 573–588.
28. Jersild, A. T. *Child psychology* (6th ed.). Englewood Cliffs, N.J.: Prentice-Hall, 1968.
29. John V. P., & Goldstein, L. S. The social context of language acquisition. *Merrill-Palmer Quart.*, 1964, **10**, 265–275.
30. Karnes, M. B. *Research and development program on disadvantaged children. Final Report, Vol. 1*, May, 1969, University of Illinois, Contract No. OE–6–10–325, U.S. Office of Education.
31. Keliher, A. V. Parent and child centers. *Children*, 1969, **16**, 63–66.
32. Kellogg, R., & O'Dell, S. *The psychology of children's art*. New York: CRM–Random House, 1967.
33. Leeper, S. H., Dales, R. J., Skipper, D. S., & Witherspoon, R. L. *Good schools for young children*, 2nd ed. New York: Macmillan, 1968.
34. Lesser, G. S. Television and the language development of children. Paper presented at the meeting of the New England Psychological Association, Boston, November 8, 1969.
35. Maccoby, E. E. Stability and change in attachment behavior during the third year of life. Paper presented at the meeting of the Western Psychological Association, Vancouver, 1969.
36. McDavid, J. W., et al. Project Head Start: Evaluation and research, 1965–67. A Summary. (Mimeo.) Washington, D.C.: Division of Research and Evaluation, Project Head Start.
37. Maynard, O. *Children and dance and music*. New York: Scribner's, 1968.
38. Miller, J. O. Diffusion effects in disadvantaged families. Urbana, Ill.: *ERIC Clearinghouse on Early Childhood Education*, University of Illinois, 1968.
39. Moore, S. B. Correlates of peer acceptance in nursery school children. *Young Children*, 1967, **22**, 281–297.
40. Office of Economic Opportunity. *Project Head Start Equipment and Supplies*. Washington, D.C.: U.S. Govt. Printing Office, 1965.
41. Palmer, F. H., & Rees, A. H. Concept training in two-year-olds: Procedures

and results. Paper presented at the meeting of the Society for Research in Child Development, Santa Monica, Calif., March 27, 1969.

42. Piaget, J. *The psychology of intelligence*. London: Routledge & Kegan Paul, 1950.

43. Piaget, J. *Play, dreams and imitation in childhood*. London: Heinemann, 1951.

44. Read, K. H. *The nursery school* (4th ed.). Philadelphia: Saunders, 1966.

45. Schaefer, C. E. Imaginary companions and creative adolescents. *Devel. Psychol.*, 1969, **1**, 747–749.

46. Scott, P. M., Burton, R. V., & Yarrow, M. R. Social reinforcement under natural conditions. *Child Devel.*, 1967, **38**, 53–63.

47. Sears, P. S., & Dowley, E. M. Research on teaching in the nursery school. In N. L. Gage (Ed.), *Handbook of research on teaching*. New York: Rand McNally, 1963, pp. 814–864.

48. Smilansky, S. The effects of sociodramatic play on disadvantaged preschool children. New York: Wiley, 1968.

49. Smith, H. P., & Applefeld, S. W. Children's paintings and the projective expression of personality: An experimental investigation. *J. Genet. Psychol.*, 1965, **107**, 289–293.

50. Snow, A. C. *Growing with children through art*. New York: Reinhold, 1968.

51. Student observation. Merrill-Palmer Institute (unpublished).

52. Sutton-Smith, B. The role of play in cognitive development. *Young Children*, 1967, **22**, 361–370.

53. Sutton-Smith, B. Novel responses to toys. *Merrill-Palmer Quart.*, 1968, **14**, 151–158.

54. Torrance, E. P. Peer influences on preschool children's willingness to try difficult tasks. *J. Psychol.*, 1969, **72**, 189–194.

55. Weikart, D. P. (Ed.) *Preschool intervention: Preliminary report of the Perry Preschool Project*. Ann Arbor, Mich.: Campus Publishers, 1967.

56. Weikart, D. P. Comparative study of three preschool curricula. Paper presented at the meeting of the Society for Research in Child Development, Santa Monica, Calif., March 28, 1969.

57. Zimny, G. H., & Weidenfeller, E. W. Effects of music upon GSR of children. *Child Devel.*, 1962, **33**, 891–896.

# Chapter 8

Merrill-Palmer Institute by Donna J. Harris

# Socialization:
# Interaction and Results

An increasing complexity of feelings and emotions accompany the child's growing variety of interactions with people and objects. At the same time, he learns to understand and control his emotions, although not completely, of course. He makes a beginning in the long process of learning to behave and to feel in ways that are acceptable to himself and to society. At the beginning of the preschool period, he has some concept of himself as a physical object in space; by the end of this time, he can think of himself as a person-among-persons. He is affected by the religious–philosophical orientation of his family and his culture.

## Emotional Development

Evidence for emotional differentiation during the preschool years is supplied by a study on awareness of affect concepts in 4-, 5-, and 6-year-olds [34]. With increasing age, children tended to differentiate more between affect concepts, as shown in tests such as sorting pictures with different facial expressions, knowing affect words (happy, sad, mad, angry), inferring subjective state from stick figures, and acknowledging experiences ("a scary dream") and feelings ("Do you sometimes feel lonely?"). Children high in affect awareness were likely to be also emphatic in relations with peers and imaginative in art and in play.

### Love

The discussion of love in infancy pointed out that love, at all ages, involves delight in being with, desire to be with, and desire for contact and response from another person. Early in the course of development, certainly by the time the baby becomes a toddler, love includes another dimension, the desire to give to the other person, expressed in attempts to promote his happiness and well-being. The first dimension, the desire to be with the love object, was explored as *attachment behavior*. Preschool love has been studied in terms of the attitudes of adults in the family, especially *nurturant behavior*, and also in terms of *dependent behavior* in children. The child has a variety of love relationships with the individuals who occupy different family positions. He also has love relationships with peers. This topic was discussed in the previous chapter, in the context of play [20, pp. 204–207].

General emotional atmosphere in the family is ordinarily thought to affect the well-being of the young child. A demonstration of this relationship is offered by a study of parental tensions in relation to child adjustment [11]. Seventy-six preschool children were observed and rated on quality of emotional adjustment. Their parents were interviewed about their relationships to each other. Healthy child adjustment was shown to be related to positive husband–wife adjustment in the areas of sex, consideration for one another, ability to talk over difficulties, and expression of affection. The data gave some indication that girls were more adversely affected by parental tension than were boys. Corroboration of the importance of general emotional atmosphere comes from a study [51] of two groups of preschool children, one from intact families and one from homes broken by divorce. Matched for IQ and age, the children were drawn from community-supported day nurseries. On a projective test of anxiety, the children from broken homes showed more disturbance than did the controls.

**Nurturance.** Probably the most studied component of love, nurturance is a willingness or even eagerness to promote the well-being and development of the loved one. Parents ordinarily have a large feeling of nurturance for their children. Many, perhaps most, adults feel nurturant toward all children. Erikson [30, p. 138] speaks of the sense of generativity, an essential of the mature personality. "Generativity is primarily the concern for establishing and guiding the next generation. . . ." A high degree of nurturance is involved in generativity.

There is a mutuality to nurturance, the other side of the coin being an acceptance of it. The love that a child feels for a parent has a large measure of this acceptance in it. He counts on the parent's nurturance, expecting it and accepting it as a continuing part of life. The development of the baby's sense of trust was due in large part to the nurturance he received or, in Erikson's terms, to the strengths of his parents' sense of generativity. Having learned to trust his family in this way, the child accepts love as the foundation of his world. Even when parental nurture is not very dependable, some of it is much better than none at all. Bowlby has written about the nurturing function of mothers in these words [19, p. 68]:

> In no other human relationship do human beings place themselves so unreservedly and so continuously at the disposal of others. This holds true even of bad parents . . . Except in the worst cases, she is giving him food, shelter, comforting him in his distress, teaching him simple skills and above all providing him with that continuity of human care on which his sense of security rests.

The child's sense of security also requires continuity of the first aspect of love, that his parents will continue to find pleasure in his company. When he acts affectionate, cute, sweet, amusing, and otherwise endearing, part of his motivation is doubtless that of making his parents enjoy him. Although a preschool child's sense of generativity is only in the beginning stages, he does show kindness and generosity to peers and family [76, 77]. Nursery school children have been found willing to share candy, cookies, and money with other children. Generosity, kindness, sympathy, and helping are called *prosocial* behavior. Moral behavior is often understood as including prosocial behavior. This aspect of development will be discussed in greater detail in the chapters dealing with school-age children and adolescents. Jimmy proudly helps Mother to carry the groceries in from the car. Donald tenderly pats Daddy's head on hearing that he has a headache. Polly carries a mug of coffee to Mommy in bed on Sunday morning. All three children promote their parents' comfort in ways that are simple and temporary yet realistic. And while a pat on the head is rather minute when compared to what Daddy did that day for Donald, it is an act of love, recognized and accepted as such by parent and child.

Nurturance in parents is vitally related to the socialization of children. Children are more likely to imitate nurturant models and to identify with them. Parental nurturance is correlated with children's moral development and prosocial behavior. It seems to be literally true that love begets love. Problem solving is also affected by nurturance. Preschool children, when faced with a complex puzzle task, did better under conditions of nurturance from an adult [27]. Highly dependent children were more affected by adult nurturance than were less dependent children.

**Attachment.** Attachment is an ongoing, durable affectional tie of one person to another [1]. It is something inside the person, formed by him through experience with the attachment object. Attachment is what most people understand as love. In Chapter 4, we described the development of ties between the infant and mother and between the infant and other people. Attachment behavior includes clinging, following, smiling, watching, calling, listening, and any other attempts to make and maintain contact, plus crying and protesting at separation. Such behavior continues throughout the second year and most of the third year, in the normal course of development [20, pp. 204–207]. At age 2, the child is likely to cling or climb into his mother's lap when a stranger enters, but at 3, he is more likely to simply stand close to her [58]. At an average age of 2 years and 9 months, attachment behavior changes in such a way that children are much more willing to be separated temporarily from their mothers, more able to feel secure in a strange place and with subordinate attachment-figures [20]. Between 3 and 4, the need for frequent and intense contact decreases, and continues to decrease after 4. However, at 5 and 6 and even older, children like to cuddle occasionally, to hold hands when walking, and to have immediate contact when frightened.

As clinging and proximity-seeking decline, the child increases in making contacts from a distance [58]. He smiles, calls to his mother, talks to her, and shows her things. Another developmental change from 2 to 3 is seen in manipulative play. When left alone and then with a stranger, exploration is more depressed in 1- and 2-year-olds than in 3-year-olds.

**Dependency.** The constructs *dependency* and *attachment* overlap but they are not identical. An attachment is a durable affectional tie to another person. Attachment behavior is oriented to a particular person. Dependency involves seeking help, attention, approval, recognition, contact, and proximity. What is sought is significant, not the person giving it [1]. The same piece of behavior, say, a 3-three-year-old trying to get attention by showing his painting, might be attachment behavior if done in relation to his mother or dependent behavior if done in relation to his baby-sitter. The same piece of behavior also takes on different meanings at different ages and under different circumstances. Normal attachment behavior during the second year includes clinging to the mother when a stranger approaches. The average 4-year-old does not cling to his mother when a stranger approaches. If he does, *dependency* describes it better than *attachment*.

While dependency carries some implication of helplessness and immaturity, there are competent and mature ways of seeking help, contact, and recognition. Dependent behavior is necessary and normal for human beings. Some modes of dependent behavior are immature. The Harvard Preschool Project is concerned with competent behavior of children 3 to 6 years old. Social behavior characteristic of well-developed children was found to include getting and keeping the attention of adults, using adults as sources of information and help, and expressing affection under appropriate circumstances [70]. Less competent children were more likely to seek adults' attention through misbehavior.

As children grow, they change in their ways of seeking help, contact, proximity, attention, and recognition. They are expected to use more mature ways as they get older, ways appropriate to age, stage, and sex. For example, crying is socially acceptable in young children, as long as they do not cry as often as babies do. For school-age children, it is occasionally appropriate for girls, rarely for boys. Adolescent girls and women may properly cry in emotional crises, but adolescent boys and men are not supposed to resort to tears in any but the most extreme situations. Dependent behavior can therefore be classified as to appropriateness of maturity level, as well as according to degree.

Another age change in dependency behavior is in its relation to mutuality. As the person matures he gives more nurturance. Still dependent on others for company and nurturance, he can give as he accepts. The objects of dependency relationships also change. Dependent in the beginning on his mother, the child comes to depend upon other family members, then peers, teachers, other adults, eventually a husband or wife, and, perhaps, finally children.

There are wide cultural differences in parental attitudes toward independence. For example, an observer of another culture commented:

> it appeared that the child in Brazil is fondled, cuddled, hugged more often and to a later age than is general in the United States. There is a strong tendency for parents to be overprotective and indulgent as well,

behavior which is reflected in the cultural conception of the child as "the protected one"—a fragile creature ("his bones are soft") who needs constant warmth, care and protection [75].

North American parents tend to be concerned about dependency in children [29, p. 29]. Often one of their main goals in sending a child to nursery school is to encourage independence.

Many studies have dealt with the effects of mothers' behavior on dependency in children [36]. The availability of the mother has a bearing on the young child's seeking of contact. Two- and 3-year-old boys sought more affectionate contact with their female nursery school teachers when they (the children) came from large families where children were spaced close together [90]. There is some agreement that frustration and punishment in infancy and preschool years are associated with dependency in the preschool period. Evidence comes from studies which correlated mothers' feeding practices and discipline practices with later behavior in their children. The preschool child's dependency tended to be greater if his mother used withdrawal of love to discipline him, showed signs of rejection, punished parent-directed aggression, and was demonstrative with affection [80]. There is agreement in the literature that maternal rejection is associated with dependency in children. Cross-culture research [93] suggests that frustration and punishment in early childhood may affect adult dependency behavior. In cultures where children are punished severely for dependency behavior, adults show greater dependency than adults do in cultures where children's dependency behavior is indulged.

Fathers as well as mothers were included in an extensive study of relations between behavior of children and behavior of parents [13]. Children were observed in a nursery school and in a puzzle task where each child experienced easy success, probable success, and failure. Parent behavior was studied in two 3-hour home visits and in structured interviews with the mother and father. A group of children were identified as highly self-reliant, self-controlled, explorative, and content. Their parents tended to be warm, rational, and receptive to the child's communication, controlling, and demanding. Children who were the least self-reliant, incompetent, and aimless were likely to have permissive-indulgent parents. These parents were warm, encouraged autonomy, and made an effort toward cognitive enrichment. They were low on control, discouraging infantile dependency and rejecting. That is, they accepted dependent behavior and gave little firm direction.

In another study of parents and children, competence and dependent behavior were assessed by observation and interviews [25]. In general, children tended to be most competent and nondependent when parents treated them on their own level of maturity, rather than behaving as though the children were either adults or infants. In this dimension, fathers' behavior had more effect on girls, and mothers' on boys. A study of development from birth to maturity indicated that personality in childhood and adulthood was related to mothers' protective behavior when children were under 3 [46]. The definition of protection was not what many people would think of as an aspect of love or nurturance but was really overprotection. Rather than being a warm, helpful, cherishing pattern, it was rated on "(a) unsolicited and unnecessary nurturance of the child, (b) consistent rewarding of the child's requests for help and assistance, (c) encouraging the child to become dependent on her, (d) overconcern when the child was ill or in danger." A large measure of this kind of "protection" during the first 3 years in girls' lives was

Courtesy Frank Porter Graham, Child Development Center of the University of North Carolina.

associated with a tendency to withdraw from anxiety-arousing situations in adult-hood. In boys' lives, "protection" during the first 3 years was associated with passivity at the 6- to 10-year age.

A certain amount of protection, control, and nurturance are essential for a child's existence and healthy development. Parents are faced with many decisions as to how to give their children enough response, help, contact, proximity, atten-tion, and recognition without forcing or dominating and yet encouraging the child toward independent effort.

**Sibling Love.** Sibling love has a large measure of pleasure in being with the other person, and a less important component of nurturance and dependency. Koch has explored the attitudes existing between 5- and 6-year-olds and their siblings. Since these children are summing up their experiences of the preschool years, and since their younger brothers and sisters are preschoolers, some of the findings are pertinent here. The reasons children gave for wanting to play with their sibs and for not wanting them to leave the family were companionship, protection, general liking for the other child, and appreciation of his services. Older children spoke more of personal qualities such as "cuteness" or "niceness," while second-borns mentioned more the sib's services and protection. Girls reported playing more with younger sibs than did boys. Sibs close in age played together more than those with a greater age difference. Second-borns more often stated a preference for play with the sib and at the same time tended to believe that they played little with the sib. Thus the preschool children did not get all the companionship they sought from their older brothers and sisters.

**Grandparent Love.** Grandparent love relationships between children and grandparents have qualities different from parent–child and sib–sib love. Anthropological studies show that friendly equality between grandparents and children is a product of a certain kind of social structure [86]. Formality between grandparents and children is related to association of grandparents with family authority, through grandparents' either exercising authority or being the parents of the parent who definitely exercises authority over the children. Indulgent, close, and warm relationships are more likely to be built when grandparents have little authority in the family. The age and maturity of the child also influence the relationship [47].

When grandparents (70 grandfathers and 70 grandmothers) were questioned, it became apparent that the role of grandparent is played in a variety of ways [66]. Grandparenthood was comfortable and pleasant to 59 percent of the grandmothers and 61 percent of the grandfathers but difficult and uncomfortable to 36 percent and 29 percent, respectively. According to the style in which roles were played, there emerged three main types of grandparents and a fourth type, the parent surrogate, which applied to grandmothers only. The *fun-seeking* grandparent (29 percent of grandmothers, 24 percent of grandfathers) is probably the type referred to in the study mentioned above. These grandparents are informal and playful, joining the child for the purpose of having fun and mutual satisfaction. Authority lines are unimportant. The dimension of love featured in this relationship, therefore, is the one of delight in the company of the beloved and desire for response from him. The *formal* grandparent (31 percent of grandmothers, 33 percent of grandfathers) probably represents a more old-fashioned type of relationship. The formal grandparent takes an interest in the child, gives treats and indulgences, and occasionally helps the parents, but sees his (or her) role in strict terms. This grandparent does not offer advice and leaves parenting strictly to the parents. Nurturance and pleasure in the child's company are both aspects of the formal grandparent's relationship, with perhaps more emphasis on nurturance, and neither aspect being very strong. The *distant figure* (19 percent of grandmothers, 29 percent of grandfathers) feels remote from the child and acknowledges little effect of the child upon his life. Although this grandparent maintains a benevolent attitude, gives gifts on ritual occasions, and goes through certain motions, there is little feeling or response.

The love which a child experiences with his grandparent will, then, depend on the role his grandparent plays in relationship to him. He will most likely establish a mutually joyous relationship with the fun-seeker, where child and grandparent respond to each other, savoring the pleasures of each other's company. From the formal grandparent, the child will derive a certain satisfaction, knowing that nurturance and some response are forthcoming. The distant figure will probably be the object of indifference to the child, just as the child is to him, although the child will perhaps have some pleasant expectations of material benefits on Christmas and birthdays. The surrogate mother, the role played by some grandmothers, takes on many of the emotional characteristics of the mother–child relationship, although if the mother is also in the picture, the three-way relationship is more complex.

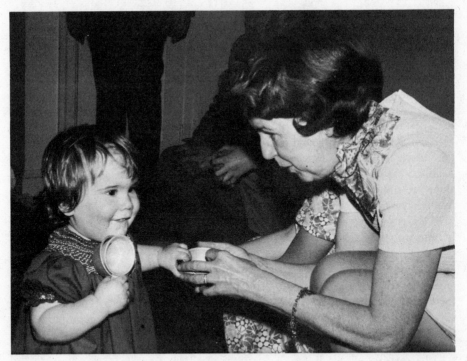

Ellen S. Smart

When grandparents were studied in relation to family structure, differences emerged between paternal and maternal grandparents [48]. Maternal grandmothers were much more positive in their perceptions and reactions than were paternal grandmothers. A majority of the former approved of the parents' child rearing, felt affectionate toward the child, and saw similarities between the child and themselves. Paternal grandparents were different in that it was the grandfather who had very positive responses, much more so than the maternal grandfather, who was quite uninvolved with the grandchild.

Matriarchal families are very common among lower-class black people [74]. Child care is often turned over to the grandmother while the mother earns money. Overburdened by poverty and responsibilities, with no male support, both the mother and grandmother are severe, inconsistent, and inattentive in relation to the child.

### Anger and Aggression

As was pointed out in Chapter 4, anger is the distress which accompanies an attack on a frustrating situation. Diffuse and unproductive expressions of anger, such as crying, kicking, and throwing, are frequent in late infancy and the early part of the preschool period, when the child's desire for autonomy is strong and when he experiences many frustrations. Aggression is sometimes conceived as a controlled and productive attack on problems, resulting in increased knowledge, power, and/or status for the aggressor. In the latter context, the anger which accompanies aggression is a stirred-up, energized feeling which aids in problem solving and contributes to the development of the sense of initiative. Competition between people can involve either hostile aggression or controlled and productive aggression. Many practical dilemmas arise from the dual nature of anger and aggression. While a hostile attack is dangerous and destructive, there is great advantage in being able to fend off an attack and in taking the initiative. Some children use aggression very often in order to cope with frustration; others display little aggression but use dependent behavior in the face of frustration. Aggression can also occur when frustration is not involved.

Experiments by Bandura, Walters, and their associates have shown that children readily imitate aggressive behavior shown to them by live models and by models in films, both human and cartoon [5]. Children reproduced in detail the attacks of an adult model on a large inflated doll. When one group of children saw a model rewarded for aggression and another saw the same model punished, the first group imitated the model and the second did not. Both groups expressed disapproval of the model's behavior, however, calling him mean, wicked, harsh, and bossy. Thus, even though the children considered aggressive behavior undesirable, they imitated what paid off. They made some attempts to justify their choice by calling the victim dumb and selfish. The children who had observed the punished model were then offered rewards for aggressive behavior. They promptly imitated what they had seen the model do, thus showing that they had learned the aggressive behavior, even though they had not performed it when they observed it.

When adults are permissive of aggressive behavior, children tend to act aggressively. Parents vary in how much aggression they permit, against whom they permit it, and how it may be expressed. A group of highly educated parents ranked aggression as high in a list of undesirable behavior. Only avoidance (being aloof, timid, and withdrawn) was less desirable [29]. Middle-class parents usually try to substitute verbal forms of aggression for physical, although they tend to feel that boys should be able to defend themselves by fighting "if necessary." Lower-class parents are more permissive of fighting and may actually encourage it in boys. Most parents discourage aggression against themselves but permitted and encouraged it against other people [8]. In punishing the child physically, parents are effectively demonstrating to the child how to act aggressively. Since they do not permit it toward themselves but encourage it toward others, the child learns how, when, and to whom to behave aggressively.

**Applications of Research on Anger.** Many of the studies mentioned indicate that the results of parental behavior are often unintentional. When one considers that what parents do in the first 3 years of life is likely to be reflected in children's behavior patterns, he is impressed with the complexity of parent–child relationships [74]. Parental action springs from a wide variety of sources other than pure reason and self-control. Even so, there are some steps a parent can take consciously in order to make it easy for a preschool child to do the acceptable thing. Including here the information derived from Goodenough's study of anger, reported in Chapter 4, the following list indicates conditions which discourage physical aggression and encourage the development of self-control:

1. The child is cared for on a flexible routine which provides food, rest, and activity before the child is acutely and painfully in need of these things.
2. Parents and other caretakers answer his calls for help promptly.
3. He is offered many opportunities to achieve and decide in approved ways.
4. Parents disapprove of hostile aggression and stop this behavior firmly.

5. Parents clearly express what behavior is permitted and what is not.
6. Physical punishment is avoided.
7. Avoidance of television programs, films, and books showing aggression and violence.
8. An atmosphere of emotional warmth prevails in the home.

### Jealousy and Rivalry

Jealousy is the angry feeling that results when a person is frustrated in his desire to be loved best; rivalry is the angry feeling that results when a person is frustrated in his desire to do best, to win or to place first. Very often an individual feels jealous and rivalrous toward the same person, although sometimes these emotions can be separated. A child is likely to feel jealous of the baby who displaces him as youngest in the family and to feel rivalrous with the older child, who is stronger and abler than he. Parents and children also feel jealousy and rivalry toward one another. The themes of jealousy and rivalry within the family flame in the most ancient literature. Cain and Oedipus symbolize some of the most disturbing situations which exist in family life.

Jealousy of parents and the resolution of that jealousy make up the psychoanalytic story of the preschool period. The play age, the stage when the sense of initiative is developing, is the phallic stage in *psychoanalytic* terms. Almost every little boy says at least once, "Mummy, I'm going to marry you when I grow up," and every little girl has the equivalent plan for the future with her father. Wanting to be first in the affections of the opposite-sexed parent has as its corollary jealousy of the like-sexed parent. The like-sexed parent represents a powerful, full-blown picture of what the little child hopes to become, even the person who attracts and holds the other parent. As recognition of reality (that he cannot win over the powerful, wonderful parent) helps the boy to give up his attempts to be first with mother, he continues to try to grow more like his father. He identifies with him, feeling less jealous and more affectionate and sympathetic with him. He gains strength by joining with the father. A similar mechanism is thought to work through the girl's attempt to be first with her father.

Jealousy of siblings is usual in western culture, in the typical small family, consisting of parents and children. "Let's send the baby back to the hospital" is the classic suggestion of the preschool child who has just lost his place as youngest in the family.

Two or three decades ago, authorities who advised parents placed great emphasis on the value of preparing the child for a new baby. The hope was that jealousy would be eliminated if the young child understood the reproductive process and the characteristics of neonates and if he realized that such a baby was about to enter the family. He was to "help" get clothes and equipment ready and to learn how to share in the baby's care. Attractive books with such titles as "Your New Baby" were read to the young child as preparation.

Modern experience has not shown any of these actions to be wrong or even useless. On the contrary, the most accepted authorities today still recommend them. While we are not aware of studies definitively proving the worth of "preparing for the new baby," common sense and common experience show that the young child feels more loving and less jealous toward the baby who is introduced thus into his family. The difference today is that some jealousy and rivalry are regarded as inevitable in American culture—in fact, in most cultures. The reason for it is the same reason which the Book of Genesis puts forth in the story of Cain and Abel. Every child wants to be the best loved by his parents. The first child wants it most deeply, since he once was the only child and knew what it was like to have all the attention, company, endearments, and gifts. Interviews with 202 families revealed that the first child was regarded as more selfish and more jealous in families of every size, both white and black [26, pp. 119–131]. In studying two-child families, they found that the second was happier and more generous than the first and that on the average the first child was still reported by mothers as being the more jealous and selfish no matter what type of training he had received, no matter whether he was treated more indulgently than the second child. The authors concluded that no type of training whatever, whether severe, moderate, or indulgent, is likely to eliminate the first child's sense of having been replaced by the second and of having lost some of his parents' love.

The child's interpretation of the new-baby situation is based on reality, as shown by a study of 46 children and their mothers [4]. The behavior of the mother toward the child was rated before, during, and after pregnancy. Substantial and continuing decreases were found in child-centeredness, approval, acceptance, affectionateness, and rapport. Declines occurred in duration of contact, intensity of contact, effectiveness of policy, and babying (an aspect of indulgence). Increases occurred in restrictiveness of policy and severity of penalties. It is possible that some of these changes would have occurred with increasing age of the child, but since they did occur along with the mother's pregnancy and the birth of a baby, it is easy to understand how the young child would hold the new baby responsible for the unhappy turn of events. In addition, he sees the baby enjoying privileges he would like to have or which he is trying to give up, such as sucking a bottle, wetting his diapers, being carried and fondled, crying. One 5-year-old said: "Yes, I would like to change places with my baby brother. Then I could yell my head off and mamma would take care of nobody but me." Another commented, "Sometimes I wish I could tear magazines myself" [50].

Jealous actions include suggestions for getting rid of the baby and attacks on the baby (the most direct) and more devious attacks such as accidents and rough play, acting out aggression with toys, attacking the mother, whining, withdrawing, protesting extreme love and concern for the baby. Later on, jealousy takes such forms as bickering, fighting, teasing, taking toys away. Reasons why parents behave in jealousy-inducing ways are to be found in the culture. In the small American family, there is not enough time and energy to go around after a new baby comes. In contrast, the joint family system provides for several adult women and adolescent girls too who are responsive to all the young children. When a young child's mother is pregnant or busy with a new baby, the child still has the support and attention of women to whom he is attached. The young child's affection and desires for approval are focused less intensively on one person. Therefore one person cannot let him down so severely and even if his mother does disappoint him, aunties and grandmothers are ever ready to care for him and comfort him.

The materialistic and relativistic standards of American society have some bearing on the forms which jealousy and rivalry take. Parents' approval and resulting rewards often depend on how the child compares with his siblings, as well as with children outside the family. To look good and thereby be most approved and loved, he has to be better than someone else, often his brother or sister. If he were loved for himself and if his achievements were measured against some absolute standards, he would have less reason to be jealous of his siblings.

Jealous as siblings are, they normally love each other, too. They often feel ambivalent, pulled in two directions, "Sometimes I love you, sometimes I hate you" is a key to understanding many incidents in behavior of siblings (indeed, of most people) toward each other. When questioned about their relationships, 28 percent of 360 5- and 6-year-olds said that they quarreled constantly with their sibs, 36 percent reported a moderate amount of quarreling, and 36 percent stated that they quarreled rarely [50]. When these children were asked if they would be happier without the sister or brother, about a third of them reported that they would. When the sib was an infant, especially of the same sex, there was less desire to be rid of him than when he was beyond infancy. Apparently infants disrupt their siblings' lives less than do older children. Second-born children, more than first-borns, wanted to be rid of the other children. The wider the age difference between sibs, the more the second-borns wanted to be rid of the first-borns. The second-borns' reasons were largely in terms of the behavior of the sibs themselves, such as, "He always socks me," "She likes to boss me too much," "Sometimes she wishes I were gone." When first-born children wanted younger ones out of the way, their reasons were often in terms of parents' attitudes, especially favoritism toward the other child.

Children often express jealousy and rivalry in play and creative media. The following story by a 4-year-old illustrates imaginative expression of these emotions:

> You see, there was a little pussy and do you know, that the little pussy had to go to the bathroom so badly. He couldn't find a place to go. Finally he found a little girl and she said she'd take him into her house and he could go to the bathroom. The kitty said he'd like to be her pet. Where do you think he went to the toilet? In a pot. That little girl had him for a pet and was so nice to him. One day when the little girl's father came home, he brought a dog for a pet. But that dog was mean to the little kitty and hurt him *so* much. So the little girl didn't like the dog and she just had the kitty for a pet.

This little girl had a sturdy, aggressive toddler brother who knocked down her block buildings and spoiled her doll play. Still in diapers, he was a reminder of her rather recent achievements in toileting and other self-care. It seemed to us that the little girl, represented by the kitty, planned to ignore her little brother, represented by the doggie, as a way of coping with her jealousy and anger at him for intruding in her otherwise satisfactory life.

**Applications of What Is Known About Jealousy and Rivalry.** Jealousy and rivalry are so common in the American family as to be almost inevitable. These feelings can probably be minimized, if not eliminated, by some of the following procedures:

1. Preparing the young child for the birth of a sibling by telling him that the baby is coming, teaching him what babies are like, helping him to understand his own infancy, and assuring him of the parents' continued affection for him.
2. Understanding and accepting imaginative expression of jealousy and rivalry, while firmly limiting direct expression.
3. Acceptance and appreciation of each child as an individual.
4. Avoidance of comparisons between children.
5. Avoidance of the use of competition to motivate siblings.

*Fear*

In infancy, fear has an innate basis in terms of stimuli which induce withdrawal. As the child interacts with his environment, he also learns to be afraid in certain situations. The hereditary basis of fears continues to contribute to emotional development [59, pp. 13–35].

As a child grows up, he goes through age-related stages in regard to what frightens him and how he needs and uses his mother in coping with fears [23]. In early infancy, his mother soothes his fears by relieving distress. After the baby has become attached to his mother, fear of visual novelty occurs, as can be seen in reactions to strangers. Clinging and otherwise contacting the mother alleviates this type of fear and helps him to approach and explore strange objects. Pain and sudden intense stimuli continue to be frightening, as they were in infancy, and to be relieved through the mother or other familiar and nurturant people.

A close friend can have a reassuring and comforting effect on a child who is in a stressful situation, as shown in a study of 4- and 5-year-olds [79]. Beginning in the preschool period and increasingly throughout the rest of childhood, increasing competence enables the child to cope with new situations without help from his mother or other adults.

**Sources of Fear.** Like infants preschool children can acquire fears through *conditioning*. Sometimes one painful experience is sufficient to establish a fear, as when a toddler comes to fear dogs by being pushed over, barked at, or bitten. Or a fear can be acquired from another person in as few occasions as one. For example, a young child can become afraid of thunderstorms through an experience of being in a storm with a person who displays fear of the situation. The fears of parents and children show a correspondence as to both kind and number [35]. In Britain, during World War II, children's reactions to air raids were greatly influenced by whether their parents showed calm attitudes or fearful ones [44].

Television has been found to contribute to fears in 4- and 5-year-old children [71]. Through measures of palmar sweating and through follow-up interviews, children were found to be frightened by violent cartoons and by violent human characters shown on TV. A week later, the children remembered more details from the human violence film than from the cartoon violence or from the two nonviolent shows.

*An overly demanding social situation* puts the child into a position where he has no appropriate response at his command, and hence withdrawal is what he attempts. Johnny comes into the living room suddenly to find several strange adults there. Mother tells him to speak nicely to the ladies, but he is shy and silent. He could have spoken to old friends, or he could have spoken to the new ladies too had he been prepared ahead of time to expect strangers and to say something to them.

*Imagination, initiative,* and *conscience* contribute to fears at this time of life. Eager to explore and to try out new activities, the child tends to push beyond limits set by his parents. When his budding conscience tells him he is doing wrong, or that he wants to do wrong, he may create imaginative satisfactions, only to have those creations frighten him. He is especially likely to imagine animals which have powers he would like to have and to use, such as great strength for attacking other creatures, biting, kicking, or eating them. He may disguise his aggressive wishes quite elaborately, dreaming about such animals instead of telling stories about them or using them in dramatic play. The dream animals sometimes attack their creator, who feels guilty about his destructive wishes and thus suffers punishment.

Table 8-1 Fears Shown by Children Age 2 to 6, in Several Experimental Situations

| Situation | Percentage of Children Showing Fear | | | |
|---|---|---|---|---|
| | 24–35 Months | 36–47 Months | 48–59 Months | 60–71 Months |
| 1. Being left alone | 12.1 | 15.6 | 7.0 | 0 |
| 2. Falling boards | 24.2 | 8.9 | 0 | 0 |
| 3. Dark room | 46.9 | 51.1 | 35.7 | 0 |
| 4. Strange person | 31.3 | 22.2 | 7.1 | 0 |
| 5. High boards | 35.5 | 35.6 | 7.1 | 0 |
| 6. Loud sound | 22.6 | 20.0 | 14.3 | 0 |
| 7. Snake | 34.8 | 55.6 | 42.9 | 30.8 |
| 8. Large dog | 61.9 | 42.9 | 42.9 | |
| Total | 32.0 | 30.2 | 18.1 | 4.5 |

\* Source: Reprinted by permission from Arthur T. Jersild and Frances B. Holmes, "Children's Fears," *Child Development Monographs*, No. 20 (New York: Bureau of Publications, Teachers College, Columbia University, 1935), Table 14, page 237.

Dreams containing animals have been found to make up 61 percent of the dreams of 4-year-olds, whereas at 5 and 6 the figure is only 39 percent [89]. The proportion of animal dreams drops steadily with age, reaching a low of 7.5 percent in adulthood. Fear of the dark may accompany the young child's fears of imaginary animals and bad dreams. When parents were questioned about the fears expressed by their children between birth and 6 years, results showed a progressive decrease in fears which were responses to such tangible stimuli as objects, noises, falling, and strange people and an increase in fears of intangibles, such as imaginary creatures, darkness, being alone or abandoned, threat or danger of injury and harm [42].

The answers of 130 children to the question "What are things to be afraid of?" give information on the fears of children 5 years old and over [61]. Animals were mentioned most often, but less frequently as age increased. Eighty percent of children were afraid of animals at age 5 and 6, 73 percent at 7 and 8. Snakes were mentioned more often than any other animals. Then came lion, tiger, and bear. A third of children under 7 admitted to fear of the dark. Children rarely reported fear of the type which parents try to teach, such as fear of traffic, germs, and kidnapers.

An experimental study of children's fears confirmed the finding that expressed fear of tangible situations decreases with age throughout the preschool period [42, pp. 167–296]. Children were carefully observed when left alone, while walking across inclined boards which fell a distance of 2 inches, entering a dark room, meeting a peculiarly dressed stranger, walking across high boards, hearing a sudden loud sound, picking a toy out of a box containing a live snake, and being asked to pat a dog brought in on a leash. Their actions were judged as indicating fear or not. The percentage of children showing fear at four different age levels between 2 and 6 are shown in Table 8-1.

Fear can be widespread and generalized, in contrast to being focused on a particular object or situation. When fear is widespread, generalized, and unfocused, it is called *anxiety*. The preschool child is likely to experience anxiety when separated for a long time from his mother, father, or main object of attachment. Considerable research has been concerned with what it means to a young child to be separated from his mother and some research has dealt with the question of separation from the father. Maternal deprivation has already been discussed in Chapter 4, where it was shown that deprivation can be either sensory or emotional or both and that the breaking of established bonds between baby and mother has quite a different result from that of separation when attachment is not involved. The effects of partial and complete separation of toddlers from their mothers were explored with children between 16 and 27 months of age [37]. Two groups, carefully equated as to age and sex, were selected, one from each of two nurseries. All subjects were from intact families, without history of separation and with no indications that the children had been rejected. No subject had a sibling in the same nursery. The two nurseries were run identically, with one exception. In the first, the children stayed all day but went home at night; in the second, the children lived 24 hours a day in the nursery. The two groups did not differ in behavior for the first two days, but after that, the residential children showed more intense symptoms of anxiety. They sought relations with adults more intensely, sought affection more, cried more, did more thumb and finger sucking, lost sphincter control more often, and had more colds. The most striking difference was that the residential children showed more and greater hostility. This study indicates that although partial separation from parents is not necessarily destructive, *complete* separation is likely to be so.

Maternal employment is a tempting situation to fasten upon when searching for conditions causing anxiety in young children. Public opinion is often expressed against young mothers who hold jobs outside the home. A thorough review of research on this topic concludes that maternal employment is too global a condition to use as a variable in investigating causes of children's behavior [84]. For example, 26 kindergarten children of fully employed mothers were matched in family factors, age, and sex with 26 kindergarten children whose mothers had never been employed during the lives of these children. No differences were found between the two groups on the nine personality characteristics investigated [82]. Rather than studying such a general condition as employment of the mother, separation might be understood more clearly in terms of the mother's acceptance of her role, the quality of substitute care provided, the age and sex of the child, the relation of the mother's employment to family functioning and its meaning to husband–wife relations [84].

It is sometimes held that when a parent leaves the family through divorce, death, or any other separation, a preschool child is likely to interpret the disruption as due to his own unworthiness. Hence he would suffer a separation anxiety. Since fathers leave households more often than mothers, they are more likely than mothers to cause this kind of fear in preschool children.

**Applications of Research on Fear and Anxiety.** Although some fears are inevitable and even desirable (caution has survival value), children can learn to deal with frightening situations, and adults can help them to do so. Adults can also arrange and plan so as to prevent the development of extreme fears and anxiety. The following procedures are often valuable:

1. When the child is to be separated from the people to whom he is attached, make the transition gradual.
2. At times of crisis, such as illness, keep the child with a person to whom he is attached.
3. Teach the child techniques for coping with situations in which he is inadequate.

4. Prepare the child for dealing constructively with situations which are about to come up. Talking, stories, and dramatic play are useful for this purpose.
5. Use the child's spontaneous expressions of fears, in fantasy, dreams, dramatic play, and artistic productions, to gain insight into what he fears and why he does so, in order to help him deal with the fears.
6. Never force a child into a situation he fears. Rather, minimizing the threat, such as by caging the animal which frightens him, encourage him to approach it in such a way that no harm occurs to him.
7. When a child is frightened by bad dreams, comfort him immediately, make sure that he wakens and agrees that the experience was a dream, not real, and put him back in his own bed, with a light if he wishes.

## Character Development

Both common sense and research show that the American child develops his morality largely through family living. His parents teach him what is right and what is wrong. They push him toward what they consider good behavior and pull him away from the bad. They hold up their ideals for him to see, their inspirations to light the way for him, too. In addition to all this conscious, direct teaching, parents and others exert influences of which they are not aware and which they can turn neither off nor on.

### Definition of Character

"Character is the habitual mode of bringing into harmony the tasks presented by internal demands and by the external world" [72, pp. 1–2]. One function of the personality is to find these modes and to carry through the organizing and integrating required. Another function is to determine what demands from the external world shall be heard. Other demands come from the individual's body and some from unconscious parts of his being. For instance, the child, feeling hungry, searches around to get food in a way he feels to be acceptable, such as asking Mother for a cookie and a glass of milk rather than climbing onto the counter or opening the refrigerator.

### Sequence of Development

The schemas of character, like all the other behavior patterns of the child, undergo changes with experience and age. Although the preschool child is very different from the infant in his moral behavior, he still has a long way to go on the path toward character maturity. The 2-year-old is in the "into-everything" stage. Able to run, climb, manipulate, explore, feed himself, and talk, he can get many gratifications for himself.

Responsive to rewards and punishment, he modifies some of his behavior without thinking or evaluating [3]. For example, in experiments where children are punished for choosing certain toys, they avoid those toys even after the experimenter has left the room. That is, the suppression behavior is internalized in response to punishment.

A parental *no* may function as punishment, especially if said harshly or coldly. Or it may be said in conjunction with some action that prevents behavior, as when the adult removes the pointed scissors from the young child's hand. While the physical world presents some limits to the child, social demands come largely through Mother's voice and hands, supplemented by Father's and other adults. The toddler will pause in what he is doing when someone tells him to stop, or he will do so most of the time. Unless a toy is substituted for the cigarette lighter or the honey pot placed out of reach on the table, the next moment is likely to find the young child once more trying to make fire or to lick and stick.

The next easily observed step in character development occurs when the child obeys rules while watched. Ellen, just under 3, was fascinated by Lucy, a doll that belonged to Susan, age 5. Susan, knowing Ellen's passion for poking Lucy's blue glass eyes fringed with long black lashes, made a strict rule that Ellen was never to touch Lucy. One day Ellen came home from nursery school to behold Lucy sitting on the sofa. She fell on the doll with cries of joy, began to poke Lucy's eyes, and paused when her mother chided her, "Ellen, you know Susie doesn't want you to touch Lucy."

"But Mummy," Ellen said in hurt surprise, "Susie isn't here!"

The voice which commanded Ellen to inhibit impulses toward Lucy was entirely external. When the voice was away at kindergarten, it simply wasn't there, and Ellen felt no restraint.

During the years between 3 and 6, some of the voice of society, via the family, is taken into the child, internalized, made his own, integrated with the rest of his personality. Research shows that internalization takes place most readily when parents are warmly affectionate, firm, and consistent [41, 65, 72]. When the love of the parents has become important to the child, then the winning of their approval is also important. Indeed, the child often takes the role of the parents in talking to himself, either aloud or silently, as did the 2-year-old who wet her pants and then said to her uncle, who was taking care of her: "Naughty girl! You must come and tell Mommy" [57]. The child was playing the mother role, making comments appropriate to the disciplinary function of the mother. This incident, implied many times in many settings, suggests how the child comes to withdraw approval from himself when he does "wrong" and approves himself when he does "right." Warmly affectionate (nurturant) parents who have thus been rewarding to the child will be imitated more and their roles learned better and internalized more into the child. Hoffman [41] shows that children whose internalized moral standards are adaptive and realistic tend to have parents who show disappointment when the child does not live up to their standards. Instead of threatening to withdraw their love or belittling the child, such parents show that they believe the child can live up to the ideal if he would. Thus although the child feels hurt at the time, he too believes that he can do what the parents expect.

Hoffman says, "... we may tentatively conclude that an internalized moral orientation is fostered by an affectionate relationship between the parent and child, in combination with the use of discipline, techniques which utilize this relationship by appealing to the child's personal and social motives."

The mechanisms by which a loving, nurturant parent figure becomes the most effective punisher are analyzed by Unger [88], who argues that strong internal controls cannot grow in a child without an adult who combines the nurturing and punishing functions.* Throughout infancy, the parent's presence is associated with

---

* Some critics challenge this theory by citing what happens to children brought up in communal nurseries. In both Russia and Israel, the children who live in nurseries receive little or no punishment from their parents but from the resident nurses and caretakers. Parents and children have

comfort, pleasant stimulation, relief of hurts and tensions. Absence or unavailability means the opposite, especially during the time when fear of strangers is dominant. The child learns that certain acts on his part result in withdrawal of the parent and consequent anxiety for him. The parent makes it easier for the child to identify these acts and their results by verbalizing it. "That was naughty. You make Mommy angry when you hit the baby." Sending the child to his room or otherwise isolating him has the same effect. Facial cues and tones of voice associated with these situations become sufficient to induce anxiety over the possibility of parental withdrawal. Thus a parent who has never given a spanking or other harsh punishment may be able to control a child by a mere frown or look. This is the foundation of love-oriented discipline. The child regulates his behavior so as not to lose the nurturing presence or approval of a loving adult. The indication that loss of approval is imminent comes first from the parent, either verbally or in gesture, and secondly from the child's own language, aloud in the beginning and silent inner language eventually.

Guilt, according to Unger, is a two-stage process. The first stage is verbal. The child says to himself, "I shouldn't have done that," and the second stage is an autonomic-visceral reaction of fear or anxiety, triggered by the first stage. The second stage is the same reaction which earlier was set off by the withdrawal or threatened withdrawal of the nurturing parent but now is activated by the child's own words to himself. The words to himself are, of course, derived from previous situations where the loving and beloved adult expressed disapproval. Now, in order to end the unpleasant autonomic-visceral reaction of fear or anxiety, he must undo the situation which caused his words to himself. If his past experience with the loving adult taught him that a confession or apology would undo or make up for what he did wrong, then he will confess or apologize and will feel better. If he learned that he must pay for wrongdoing by enduring a spanking or giving up a privilege, then he will attempt to find a punishment that represents these punishments. Or he may have learned that wrongdoing cannot be undone and that he must bear a burden of guilt indefinitely. In the meantime as he continues to grow up, he is having more experiences with parental love and punishment, with doing wrong, and with reinterpretation of moral behavior.

Knowing all this, can parents control their own behavior so as to produce ideal character in children? Some can more than others, but nobody can behave perfectly with his children or elsewhere. Some acts can be direct and intentional while others cannot. Love or rejection, firmness or vacillation, rigidity, or flexibility, emanate from parental personalities with spontaneity. Although much parental behavior springs from unconscious sources and from parts of the personality which cannot be changed at will, there are still parts of parental roles which can be learned and can be consciously controlled. Parents "teach" some of the behavior patterns which constitute character by making their demands clear, consistent,

---

companionship and enjoyment for the brief time that they are together. The nursery caretakers do the punishing. However, the caretakers surely also reward the children with affectionate approval as well as tangible rewards. It is hard to believe that these women would be coldly mechanical disciplinarians, since they choose their jobs and are chosen for them on the basis of having some ability with children and desire to be with children. Why, then, would they not have many of the affectional characteristics of foster parents? It may be that the peer group takes a large part of what Americans think of as the parental role, both the rewarding and punishing aspects. Observations in both Russia [22] and Israel [55] indicate that this may be so.

firm, and suited to the child's abilities, by showing their pleasure in the child's "good" behavior, by giving understandable reasons but not substituting them for firmness, and by avoiding physical punishment.

### Factors in Moral Development

Moral behavior results when a person knows and does what is right and good.

**Cognition.** To know what is right or good involves making a moral judgment. Various cultures give concrete expression to the idea that a certain stage of mental maturity is necessary before the child can exercise either judgment or volition necessary for moral behavior. The Roman Catholic first communion, at age 7, is an example. So is the widespread assumption among tribal people that a child reaches the age of reason and responsibility at about 7. Six or 7 is the common age for starting school in earnest. The transition from preconceptual thought to the stage of concrete operations occurs at about the same time when changes occur in character. What precedes these changes?

The earliest judgments about what is good and bad come from what the parents impose in the way of rules and requirements. As a child comes to know the rules, *good*, to him, means following the rules and *bad* means not following them. Moral realism, according to Piaget [73, p. 106], has these features: (1) Any act which shows obedience to a rule or to an adult is good; a rule is not something thought of by a person, but rather something ready-made, which has been revealed to the adult and is now being imposed by him. (2) The letter rather than the spirit of the law shall be observed. (3) Acts are evaluated according to how well they keep to the rules rather than according to the motives which prompted them. Results, rather than intentions, are what count.

Moral realism is illustrated by 2-year-old Jacqueline Piaget, who had been told what would be the results of a laxative which her mother gave to her [73, pp. 177–191]. She nevertheless came close to tears and looked very distressed when she lost control of her sphincters. To Jacqueline, it was bad not to follow the rule about going to the toilet, even though her mother had explained that she was not responsible for the lapse. Another time, Jacqueline broke a fragile shell which Piaget had given her to play with. She was very upset over the breakage, even though her father tried to persuade her that it was not her fault.

By age 3 or 4, Piaget says, a child shows that he sees a difference between his own intentional breaking of rules and his unintentional breaches. He will plead "Not on purpose" to excuse himself. With the misdeeds of others, however, his attitude differs. Because of his egocentrism, his inability to see anything from someone else's point of view, he does not understand that another person's breaking of rules could be "not on purpose." He judges the other person's acts by the results, since the results are all that he can perceive.

The next stage of moral judgment, that of evaluating an act in terms of right and wrong intentions, is achieved as the child becomes freed from egocentrism. Piaget believes that this comes about not merely through the passage of time but through certain kinds of interactions with the environment, largely interactions with the parents. A child is helped to grow beyond egocentrism as adults cooperate with him by discussing things on an equal footing, encouraging him to find facts and to analyze them. He is hindered when adults behave authoritatively, especially when they give verbal instructions instead of letting children experiment and figure things out. Speaking of the child whose parents take pleasure in wielding authority, Piaget says, "Even when grown up, he will be unable, except in very rare cases, to break loose from the affective schemas acquired in this way, and will be as stupid with his own children as his parents were with him" [73, p. 19].

The question of the timing of Piagetian processes has been of special interest to Americans. For example, some American preschool children have developed faster than Piaget's Swiss subjects in being able to distinguish verbally between intentions and consequences of acts [18]. Maturity of moral judgment was tested in 51 preschool children from two socioeconomic levels; middle class and working class. More than a third of the children were able to judge intentions in one of the stories, although none of Piaget's had done so. Mental age and cultural background seemed to have some influence on the age of attaining the more mature kind of judgment, with a larger proportion of the more mature children in the middle-class and in the Jewish groups. The results of this study are in harmony with Piaget's comments on the role played by parents in helping their children to achieve moral maturity. It is consistent with other studies which indicate that the middle-class families would exceed working-class families in democratic discussion [3, pp. 326–328; 39; 59] and that the Jewish families would similarly exceed the non-Jewish [56]. The changes which Piaget urged in parental use of authority seem actually to have taken place in the trend toward democratic parent practices noted in America [63]. Perhaps the acceleration of a sample of American children in regard to moral judgment can be attributed to such changes in parental practice.

**Volition.** Moral action depends upon willing to do the right and good thing. Moral judgment of itself does not imply action. Everyone has had the experience of judging that an act was wrong and then doing it anyway, or judging that an act was good and failing to do it. Experiments on children's aggression (page 313) showed that children sometimes perform the very acts that they condemn verbally.

The idea of an age or stage of reason and responsibility comes into the topic of moral action, as well as moral judgment. Nobody expects a newborn baby to choose to do right or wrong, but almost everyone considers a 7-year-old to have some freedom of choice. The development of a sense of self gives conviction of freedom of choice. So do the experiences of temptation and guilt. The rightness and wrongness of the child's choices are strongly related to his experiences with parents and other socializing agents. Language is an important tool of volition.

**Language.** The language development which takes place during the preschool period is fundamental to voluntary behavior and hence to moral action. On the basis of his work with Russian children, Luria [54] traced four stages through which speech comes to exercise a regulating influence on behavior. A replication of Luria's study showed the same sequential development in Australian children [45].

1. At 18 months to 2 years, the *initiating function* can be seen. The toddler will clap his hands on command. Instructions will not change an activity that is under way, however. If you tell a child to take off his socks while he is putting them on, or to put rings on a bar while he is taking them off, he cannot change his actions. He only intensifies the efforts he is making.
2. At 3 to 4 years, the child can follow both initiating and inhibiting instructions. He can *wait* for a signal, after being told to do so. However, the initiating part of the instruction is stronger and often the child can inhibit only briefly. If he gets continuous verbal instruction, however, he can inhibit more easily.

3. At about 4 years, when the child's own speech is well developed, he can use it to *start and stop* his own actions. He can follow instructions as to using his own speech for voluntary acts.
4. External regulatory speech becomes internal. The child no longer says it out loud but to himself when he regulates his behavior.

In regard to moral behavior, language has another important function in addition to that of starting and stopping actions. Language is the means by which the child evaluates his actions. "I shouldn't have done that" is the first part of the process of guilt as described by Unger. (See page 322.) There is widespread agreement that signs of guilt in children can be seen first at 4 or 5 years of age, the very time when children reach Luria's third stage in the use of speech to regulate behavior. "I shouldn't do that" is avoidance-mediating, anticipating an anxiety reaction. Talking to oneself is thus involved in feeling guilt and in avoiding guilt by means of controlling one's behavior. Since a certain stage of language development has to be reached before speech can regulate behavior, it follows that intellectual growth plays an essential role in moral behavior. Parents and other family members influence the child enormously in helping him to use language in organizing his mental processes and his behavior. Table 8–2 summarizes moral development in childhood.

## The Self

An adult knows himself as both subject and object. He feels, he knows, he is; he can stand off and look at himself, his feelings, his actions, his relationships. As far as anyone knows, man is the only creature who can look at himself as an object. It is a viewpoint which begins as the infant distinguishes between his body and the rest of reality and which develops gradually, during the preschool period, as the child moves from preconceptual thought toward objectivity. Further elaboration of the self takes place throughout the whole period of development, perhaps throughout all of life.

The development of a sense of autonomy means that the child gets a clearer and clearer concept of himself as a person separate from other objects and other people, distinct in body and distinct in actions. With the growth of the sense of initiative, the child enlarges his concept of self by relating it to the world. Having made

**Table 8–2** Summary of Developmental Changes Basic to Character

| Age | Moral Behavior | Cognitive and Volitional Behavior |
|---|---|---|
| 1 | Obeys commands sometimes | Cooperative with adult who cooperates with him |
| 2 | Obeys more commands | Initiating function of speech. |
| | *Good* means following the rule or instruction. | Verbalizes role of parent. |
| 3 | Obeys when watched. | Inhibiting function of speech. |
| 4 | Begins to internalize demands of parents | Judges other people by acts, not intentions. but sees difference between his own intentions and unintentional breaking of rules. |
| | Some feelings of guilt. | Uses his own speech to initiate. |
| 6 | Conscience fairly internalized. | Uses language to evaluate his actions. |
| | Definitely feels guilt. | |

himself separate and distinct, he integrates his self-concept by trying on different roles (playing fireman, nurse, teacher), exploring, and expressing himself in various media.

Investigations of the development of the self concept have taken two main forms, observing overt actions that have to do with the self and examining evidence from the unconscious. Ames [2] has traced verbalized concepts of self by noting comments made by children of different ages. The 2-year-old's typical remarks are about *me* and *mine*. The 3-year-old says *me too, we, our, let's, I like you, do you like me?* A typical 4-year-old's comment is "I'm bigger than you are." These verbalizations show first a concern with the self, then some thinking of the self along with others, and finally, a comparing of the self with others.

### Problems in Developing Self Concepts

**Deprived Children.** One of the outstanding characteristics of severely deprived children is a negative self concept or even lack of self concept. A child may not even realize that he is a person or that he has a name which distinguishes him from others. The conditions associated with positive self concept or high self-esteem are often found lacking in the families of disadvantaged children [43]. Conditions leading to high self-esteem are acceptance of the child, well-defined limits and values, and respect for the child's decision making within those limits. In very poor families, parents tend to be indecisive, disorganized, apathetic, and rejecting. Low in self-esteem themselves, they do not believe that they can control their own lives, let alone their children's. While they may sometimes be warm and nurturant, they are more likely to try to give children immediate pleasure, through candy, money, toys, and clothes rather than to guide them to develop competency.

In comprehensive compensatory programs, parents are offered help in developing their own competence and self-esteem, as well as effective behavior in relation to their children [38]. Teachers try to show the child that he is a distinct individual, important because he is a person. The child is helped to establish self-confidence and self-esteem as he forms a clear and definite idea of himself. Teachers use many methods for promoting self concepts. They provide mirrors, full length if possible, in places where children can easily look at themselves. They take pictures of the children, show them and discuss them. They may draw pictures or silhouettes of the children. Songs and games are made up to include the children's names. Feelings of autonomy and worthiness are stimulated by opportunities for successful decisions, achievement, and recognition. The teacher's respect for the individual child and her warm response to him are very basic in the development of his self concept.

**Black Children.** Children of any minority group are likely to have some problems with self concepts, but black children in predominantly white societies are especially vulnerable. Studies on racial awareness in preschool children have shown consistently that 3-year-olds can discriminate black–white differences and that negative attitudes are often shown by 5 years [83]. Black children were less likely than white children to choose children of their own race as playmates and guests, and more likely to name their own race as aggressors and less likely to offer aid to a hurt child. Thus black preschool children reflect stereotypes of their own race. Knowing that he is a black child and seeing blacks negatively, a young child develops low self-esteem.

Rising black pride is reflected in the results of a study which compares children's self-identification and preference with findings of an identical study done 11 years ago [28]. More than twice as many in the present-day black preschool group identified the black doll as looking like themselves. While there was an increase in choosing the black doll over the white as a preferred playmate, the difference between eras was not significant, and about half of the black children chose white playmates in preference to black. The white children also showed an increase in those identifying their color correctly and a significant increase in those preferring to play with children the same color.

Some encouraging findings are available. Studies of modification of racial attitudes have shown that white preschool children respond to a reading program that presents black people favorably [87] and to reinforcement procedures designed to encourage positive evaluation of black stimuli by white children [94]. Such programs have good chances of success with young children, since they have had less time than older children for learning unfavorable racial attitudes [49].

## Body Image

An interesting approach to the study of the self is through the study of body image as conducted by Fisher and Cleveland [33]. The common idea of body image is probably the mental picture of one's body. To these authors, however, body image includes the images, attitudes toward and feelings about the body, many of them unconscious, which represent the self and summarize the effects of the child's interaction with the world. The relationships a child has with important people, especially the baby with his mother, are internalized as part of the body image. (This idea is similar to the widespread view that the child sees himself as others see him, that his concept of self grows from the roles he takes with other people and his interpretation of their roles.)

Fisher and Cleveland measured the clarity of body image in terms of the definiteness with which the person perceives the boundary between his body and the rest of the world.* They have found interesting relationships between methods of child rearing and personality characteristics. Comparing nine cultural groups, they concluded that high boundary scores (definite, clear body image) were associated with permissive acceptance of impulse release in young children. The Bhils, an Indian tribe, who made the highest average score, nurse their children until about 3, feed them when they cry, toilet-train them in relaxed style, and express feelings freely. The authors theorize that the more a parent inhibits a child, the more antagonistic their relationship becomes, the harder it is to work out close communication between them, the less easily will the child take the parent as a model, and the less definite will the child's body image be.

Evidence obtained from psychiatric patients suggests that low scorers (indefinite body image) tend to have spent their early years in a family atmosphere of restrictiveness, narrow range of permissible behavior, blocked outlets for relieving tension; they tend to see their parents as threatening, destructive, and disrupting. High scorers tend to come from families where expectations of children are clear and firm, modes of controlling them are open and defined, and the parents represent devotion to a limited number of primary values and lines of living.

---

* Using data from Rorschach tests to give two scores relating to body image.

Whether one starts with the concept of *character* or *self* or *body* or *body image*, the research results converge on the topic of teaching and learning within the family during the early years of life. There is agreement about the importance of clarity, firmness, affection, and commitment to values on the part of parents. However, it is an open question as to how much parents can purposely and voluntarily influence children's personality growth.

## Sex Typing

Sex typing is a process through which a child comes to feel, think, and act in ways considered by his culture to be masculine or feminine. By age 3, a child knows very well whether he is a boy or a girl and has considerable knowledge of and preference for sex-appropriate behavior [32, 78]. Attitudes toward sex role, as shown by tests and observations of dependency, attachment, and imitation, change as the child matures. An investigation of bright and average children showed that sex role attitudes were related to mental age [52]. The same changes occurred in all, but at earlier ages in the brighter children. Thus the child's perception of sex roles and his attitudes toward them are related to the maturity of his cognitive structure.

### Definition of Male and Female Roles

Every culture defines the meaning of male and female, basing it somewhat but not consistently on biological characteristics. The variety of definitions is amazing. In Mead's [62] words:

> Now it is boys who are thought of as infinitely vulnerable and in need of special, cherishing care, now it is girls. In some societies it is girls for whom parents must collect a dowry or make husband-catching magic, in others the parental worry is over the difficulty of marrying off the boys. Some peoples think of women as too weak to work out of doors, others regard women as the appropriate bearers of heavy burdens, "because their heads are stronger than men's" . . . . In some countries the women are regarded as sieves through whom the best-guarded secrets will sift; in others it is the men who are the gossips.

Even though there is wide variety in sex typing, there is a strong tendency for masculinity to be defined in terms of independent, competitive, instrumental coping, and femininity in terms of being loving, attractive, sensitive, and supportive to others. A study of 110 cultures [10] showed widespread trends in sex role teaching. A majority of societies stressed achievement and self-reliance in boys and nurturance and responsibility in girls. In societies where obedience was required, it tended to be of girls more than of boys. Thus, while certain kinds of work or functions can be assigned to either sex, there is considerable consistency in the personality traits which human beings attempt to encourage in one sex or the other. The following list of characteristics was judged by college students and fifth graders to be typical [68]:

| *Masculine* | *Feminine* |
|---|---|
| Never afraid of anything. | Always does what teacher says. |
| Likes to show off. | Likes to act grown up. |
| Likes noisy fun. | Is always polite. |
| Sticks up for own rights. | Likes to do for others. |
| Is bossy. | Is easily embarrassed. |
| Likes to tease others. | Careful not to hurt others' feelings. |

The defining of masculine and feminine behavior is not identical with requiring it. While simple, stable societies tend to have clear definitions and requirements which jibe with them, a complex, fast-changing society tends to vary in requirements, from one ethnic group to another, between social classes, and from family to family.

### Differential Treatment of Boys and Girls

Once we gave a pink sweater before a baby was born. When the baby turned out to be a boy, the mother expressed regrets that she would have to save the sweater until she had a girl. That little boy's color scheme was to leave no doubt in him or in anybody else as to what sex he was! He soon received a wealth of trucks, cars, and erector sets but no dolls. His father played boisterously with him, stimulating vigorous motor play, acting casual about bumps, discouraging tears. And what happened when someone came along to occupy our pink sweater? She received dolls and homemaking toys. She was held tenderly. Her father stroked her curls, tickled her chin, and taught her to bat her long eyelashes at him. Big Brother stroked her curls, tickled her chin, and elicited eye-batting too. The mother applauded when Brother was aggressive, active, and courageous and when Sister was nurturant, beguiling, and sensitive. Often the parents' techniques of influence were subtle—a pat, a shove, a smile, a frown, a tight voice, a song. At other times they were direct—"Don't do that, Brother. Be a big man, like Daddy" or "I was so proud of my girl, acting like a regular little lady."

Reinforcement of sex role behavior by teachers has been observed in nursery schools [31]. After listing all types of play behavior and the proportion of time spent by each sex in each kind of behavior, the investigators concluded that there was a clear sex difference in play preferences. On 27 items, one sex was significantly different from the other. Boys definitely did more of the following: building blocks, playing with transportation toys, riding tricycles, and playing in the sandbox. Girls did more: art activities, playing in kitchen and doll house, doll play, and listening to stories. Girls spent less time in opposite-sex-preferred behavior than did boys. Of the sex-preferred behaviors that were reinforced, 83 percent were feminine. (Reinforcement was recorded when the teacher commented favorably, initiated, or joined in.) That is, teachers who were feminine themselves reinforced both sexes for feminine behavior. Even so, the boys did not become more feminine in their behavior preferences. As mentioned in the previous chapter, boys reinforce boys more, and girls, girls. An analysis of peer reinforcements showed that boys reinforced behavior preferred by boys, and girls reinforced behavior preferred by girls. One boy who had a very high number of feminine choices received ordinary treatment by teachers but much criticism and isolation by peers. These findings suggest that people (both children and adults) reinforce child behavior which is in their own repertoires. While same-sex reinforcement agents are therefore crucial in a child's acquisition and maintenance of sex-appropriate behavior, a variety of agents can serve the purpose. In the children studied here, peer reinforcement, plus interaction at home, were sufficient to assure sex-appropriate play in almost all of the children. An indication that siblings influence sex typing comes from a study of 3- and 4-year-olds making sex-typed discriminations on the *It* test. Children with an opposite-sex sibling scored high in sex-appropriate choices [78]. A child tends to reinforce the characteristics of his own sex in his sibling, no matter which the sex of the sibling. When the sibling doing the reinforcing is also older and consequently has power over the younger one, the reinforcement is likely to be more effective than when the dispenser is younger [85].

### Teaching Biological Sex Differences

The little boy learns that he is a boy before he realizes that the possession of a penis makes a child a boy. Similarly for the girl. The differential treatment of boys and girls makes it clear to them that they belong to one sex or the other. In a clothed society, especially one which prescribes highly distinctive dress for the sexes, children first express the difference between boys and girls in terms of their outfits and hairdos. Parents often avoid labeling the sexual parts of the body, sex feeling, and activities [80, p. 412]. However, when a person knows the name of something, he can discuss it better and reason about it, since labeling is an important aid to learning. Advice to parents from authorities has consistently stated the desirability of telling children the names of their sex organs and of answering their questions directly. Questions during the preschool year are usually first about the names of the sex organs, then about sex differences, such as whether a girl has lost her penis and if not why not. Answers that clarify and reassure are, "A boy has a penis and testicles." "A girl has a vulva and vagina." "Boys grow up to be fathers; girls grow up to be mothers."

Questions about where babies come from are to be expected. "The baby grew inside its mother" is simple and true. The next question, "How did it get out!" is almost inevitable in a preschool child whose questions have been answered in a trust-promoting way. "The vagina stretches to let the baby out. The mother works to push him through." This type of answer is reassuring if it implies that both mothers and babies can cope with the process of birth and if it leaves the way open for more questions. Questions about fertilization and mating rarely come during the preschool period, and if they do, they are simple questions about physiology, not love.

In actual practice, the teaching of sex differences and reproduction rarely takes the simple, straightforward course described above. Because adults have strong feelings about sexual matters, they convey some of them in what they say and leave unsaid and in how they talk and remain silent. The sex education of 4-year-olds in an English city is reported in detail, showing typical behavior of mothers in five social classes [67]. For example, with the question of whether the child knew that babies grow inside their mothers, 20 percent had already told their children, 34 percent said that they would tell if asked, and 46 percent would either evade the question or tell falsehoods [67, p. 377]. The higher the social status of the mother, the more likely she was to tell her child by age 4 and to answer his questions honestly.

Israeli children between 4 and 5½ were questioned about their concepts of sex differences and reproduction [53]. These young subjects proved very willing to discuss the matter and revealed some interesting conceptions and misconceptions which were classified as to the family's ethnic origin (Oriental or Western). About 90 percent of the children knew that there was a relation between the mother's enlarged abdomen and the subsequent birth of the baby. When asked how it is that the baby is inside the mother, the most frequent answer was that he was formed from the food the mother ate. The next most popular explanation was that the baby had always been in his mother's belly and then came the answer that the mother had first swallowed the baby. The notion of the baby entering through the sexual organ was held by only 5 percent of Western boys and 2 percent of Western girls. No Oriental children had this idea. The function of the father was thought of mainly in terms of helping the mother. When asked how the baby came out of the mother, the commonest answer was that the belly was cut open. As for having some notion of birth through the birth canal, 33 percent of Western girls did so, no Oriental girls, 8-percent of Western boys, and 4 percent of Oriental boys.

*Sex Role Preference*

Certain objects and actions are generally considered typical of masculine or feminine involvement. For instance, a lipstick is feminine, a football masculine. Preference for a masculine or feminine role is measured by having the subject choose between objects or activities connoting culturally defined masculine and feminine behavior. Toy preference tests are used to investigate children's sex role preferences. The child is asked to choose the toy he would most like to play with from masculine–feminine pairs, such as a dump truck and a set of doll dishes. Between 3 and 5, children show sex-appropriate preferences [92], boys showing them more consistently than girls [14, 24].

*Sex Role Identification*

The process of learning to feel and behave like a member of one sex or the other is known as sex role identification. As mentioned above, parents define sex roles for their children, reward them for playing the appropriate roles, and punish, or at least withhold rewards, when the children play the wrong sex roles.

Children learn sex-appropriate behavior through *modeling* as well as by reinforcement [9]. That is, the child takes on the motivations and the overt behavior of the model. Children are most likely to imitate a *nurturant* model and will often reproduce even incidental details of behavior [6]. Kindergarten boys who scored high in masculinity were likely to portray their fathers as warm and nurturant and also as giving punishment [64]. The mothers of the high-masculine boys confirmed the warm, nurturant relation between fathers and sons but not the punitive one.

Another salient characteristic of models for children is *power* or *status*. A child is likely to imitate a model whom he sees as controlling resources. The person controlling resources has been shown by experiments to be an even more attractive model than the person giving out rewards [7]. Thus the young child will model both his father and mother, practicing their roles in fantasy and play. Most likely, the mother seems to the toddler to control the most important resources, since she can give or withhold most of what he needs. As the father increases in salience, he becomes a more powerful model. The kindergarten boys who portrayed their fathers as punishing must have perceived the fathers as powerful. In addition to being influenced by the father's warmth, such a boy may take on the feelings and behavior of the father because he also wants the status and power that he sees his father as having.

The importance of father–son interaction for masculinity in the son is shown in studies of boys whose fathers were absent from the home [17]. Five-year-old father-absent boys gave less masculine responses on tests than did father-present boys [15]. When father absence occurred before the fifth year, masculine responses were significantly less than when the father left during the fifth year, suggesting that the young child is more vulnerable to father absence or that the length of time of absence is important, or both.

*Perceptions of Roles of Family Members*

Since parent–child interactions occur in the context of the family, sex typing is related to the family organization, not only to the parents as individuals. For example, the power relationship between husband and wife is pertinent. Sex role preference similarity and imitation in preschool and school-age children was found to be related to dominance in parents [40]. Boys from mother-dominated families were less likely to have masculine preferences than were boys from father-dominated families. With girls differences were not significant. The feminine role preference and orientation of girls was shown, by another study, to be related to the daughter's perceptions of the mother as salient in the family [16]. Salience was not the same as dominance in relation to the father, but depended upon how the girl saw her mother in terms of nurturance, limit setting, and competence, as well as decision making. Girls were likely to be feminine in orientation and preference when they saw their mothers as salient controllers of resources, but they also were likely to regard their fathers positively and as important.

Concepts of sex role are derived to a large extent from concepts of what fathers, mothers, and other family members do. The way in which the child sees the child–father relationship now will also contribute to how he sees it when he plays the father role with his own child. Likewise, his childish observations of the husband–wife roles have implications for his adult life. Tests and anecdotal records of 319 children between 3 and 6 give some indication of preschool children's concepts of fathers and mothers [91]. Since several socioeconomic levels were sampled, the results can be considered representative of a large part of the population. Some of the questions asked were these: What are daddies for? What are mothers for? What are families for? Results showed that concepts of fathers were much more limited than concepts of mothers; mothers were seen as busier than fathers, with many of the mothers' activities focused on children, and fathers being more impersonal; mothers were seen as more supporting and more punishing than fathers; fathers' affections were considered to include mothers and children, with mothers occupying a prominent place, but little indication was given that children realized that they shared the mothers' affection with the fathers.

# Religion

Religion contributes to understanding of self by placing the self in relation to the rest of reality, past, present, and future. While the preschool child is extremely concrete in his concepts of relationships, he does have experiences determined by the religious setting into which he is born.

Parents determine the religious orientation of their child both by uniting him with their religious community, as through circumcision or baptism; by their interpretation of man's relationships to God or gods, to man, to present, past, and future; by the expressed thoughts and feelings about beauty, love and truth, animate and inanimate nature. More indirectly, parents' behavior in general is influenced by their religion.

The religious community may have little or no direct bearing on the young child, depending on how it defines him and how it contacts him. Church nurseries and Sunday school groups can be very important in the child's life. He may enter into them eagerly and actively as his only experience with a peer group. A desirable church school takes account of the child's physical and psychological needs just as a nursery school does, although it stresses religious experiences, such as sacred stories and music, enjoyment of creativity, appreciation of beauty and of nature, worship, and giving. Symbolic and ritualistic performances appeal to children in the stage of developing initiative and also give them concrete experience of their religion.

The sense of trust developed in the beginning of life is the basis for faith in God or gods or the state or whatever one trusts. Since the mother first and then the father and the rest of the family are key figures in the development of the sense of trust, the family is the primary religious agent. They also play the most important roles, with the young child, in the creation of his sense of autonomy, the development of his self, his character, the standards of right and wrong which he makes his own.

The child begins early to muse upon the religious mysteries of which he becomes aware. "What does God look like?" "Why do the angels just come at Christmas time?" "What does *dead* mean?" "When do the seeds start to grow under the earth and how do they know it's time?" "You won't die before I'm grown up, will you?" "Do you think the astronauts will find heaven?" "Why doesn't God give me the toys I've been praying for?" "Don't you hate the people who killed Jesus?"

Answers to questions such as these depend upon the parents' own religion. What they say or do not say affects their child in a religious way, either helping him to build, restricting him to primitive thinking, or leaving him with gaps. Religious practices in the home can have deeply emotional as well as intellectual effects. Grace before meals, family Christmas dramatics, the seder—each of these events is a scene of family unity in which a little child feels a sense of belonging to his group and to something bigger. A memorable religious occasion often touches many of the senses and thus becomes an all-over experience for the child. Consider the variety of experiences during the Hindu celebration of the festival of Ganesh or Gumpati, the god of luck who is a favorite with children. The family brings home a clay model of Gumpati, a fat little boy with an elephant's head and trunk. Placing him on a stand or table in a bare room, they heap flowers, fruit, sweets, and incense at his feet. The child has large muscle experience in the walk home. He sees and touches Gumpati. He smells the flowers and incense. He eats some of the treats. He hears the story of Gumpati's birth and early childhood. After a week or so, there is a parade with music to make and hear. Gumpati in all his glory is transported to the river or lake, where an older boy lets him sink under the waters. The child sees the dramatization of the fact that his Gumpati was only a clay figure and not the real spirit which it represented. He does not *understand* the full meaning of the drama, but he has the picture of it which can later give shape and fullness to the idea.

## Summary

Emotions increase in differentiation during the preschool period, as the child takes part in more interactions and more complex interactions with his parents, siblings, grandparents, and other people. Nurturance offered by adults to children is an expression of their own personality, indicating degrees of development of the sense of generativity. Children's responses to adults include a small measure of nurturance and a large measure of dependence, which varies with the attitudes and behavior of the adults. Siblings are ordinarily ambivalent to each other, showing nurturance, dependence, jealousy, and rivalry, according to the types of experiences they have with one another and to the attitudes and guidance techniques used by adults. Anger, an emotional response to frustration, can be hostile or constructive. Hostile aggression, an angry attack, is often but not always disapproved by parents. The developing imagination of the preschool child contributes to intangible fears, which increase greatly at this time. Concrete fears decrease. As with the infant, the presence of a loved person (attachment object) reassures the frightened child. Research suggests methods of controlling and minimizing anger, jealousy, rivalry, and fear in young children.

Character is the characteristic way in which a person harmonizes his own needs and desires with the demands of the outside world. Considerable development of character takes place during the preschool years, when the child increases in knowledge of rules, in his ability to judge right from wrong, and in his will to do right. Beginning as a person who requires outer control, he grows toward self-control, internalizing the demands of himself. Parental practices and attitudes are extremely significant in determining the type of character built by the child. The child's intellectual growth is part and parcel of his moral growth.

The young child gradually becomes more and more aware of himself as a distinct body and person, separate from other objects and persons. His increasingly complex interactions contribute to his growing concept of self. Through language and dramatic play, he explores, integrates, and expands this concept. His increasing intellectual powers permit greater flexibility of thought, which he eventually uses to view himself as others see him. The establishment and acceptance of his sex role contributes to the concept of self. Male and female roles are outlined by the culture and defined in detail by the family. The family teaches by direct instruction and prohibition, by sex-typing the environment, and by differential treatment of boys and girls. Children respond by identifying with one role or another, by their preference for either role, and by the concepts of family members which they build. Religion contributes broadly to the self concept, by placing the person in a broad orientation to all of existence.

# References

1. Ainsworth, M. D. S. Object relations, dependency and attachment: A theoretical review of the infant-mother relationship. *Child Devel.*, 1969, **40**, 969–1025.
2. Ames, L. B. The sense of self of nursery school children as manifested by their verbal behavior. *J. Genet. Psychol.*, 1952, **81**, 193–232.
3. Aronfreed, J. *Conduct and conscience*. New York: Academic, 1968.
4. Baldwin, A. L. Changes in parent behavior during pregnancy. *Child Devel.*, 1947, **18**, 29–39.
5. Bandura, A. The role of modeling processes in personality development. In W. W. Hartup & N. L. Smothergill (Eds.), *The young child: Reviews of research.* Washington, D. C. National Association for the Education of Young Children, 1967, pp. 42–58.

6. Bandura, A. & Huston, A. C. Identification as a process of incidental learning. *J. Abn. Soc. Psychol.*, 1961, **63**, 311–318.
7. Bandura, A., Ross, D., & Ross, S. A. A comparative test of the status envy, social power and secondary reinforcement theories of identificatory learning. *J. Abn. Soc. Psychol.*, 1963, **67**, 527–534.
8. Bandura, A., & Walters, R. Aggression. In H. W. Stevenson (Ed.), *Child Psychology*. The sixty-second Yearbook of the National Society for the Study of Education. Chicago: University of Chicago Press, 1963, pp. 364–415.
9. Bandura, A., & Walters, R. H. *Social learning and personality development.* New York: Holt, Rinehart and Winston, 1963.
10. Barry, H., Bacon, M. K., & Child, I. L. A cross-cultural survey of some sex differences in socialization. *J. Abn. Soc. Psychol.*, 1957, **55**, 327–332.
11. Baruch, D. W., & Wilcox, J. A. A study of sex differences in preschool children's adjustment coexistent with interparental tensions. *J. Genet. Psychol.*, 1944, **64**, 281–303.
12. Baumrind, D. Child care practices anteceding three patterns of preschool behavior. *Genet. Psychol. Mono.*, 1967, **75**, 43–88.
13. Baumrind, D. Current patterns of parental authority. *Devel. Psychol. Mono.*, 1971, **4**:1, Part 2.
14. Biller, H. B., & Borstelman, L. J. Masculine development: An integrative review. *Merrill-Palmer Quart.*, 1967, **13**, 253–294.
15. Biller, H. B. Father dominance and sex role development in kindergarten-age boys. *Devel. Psychol.*, 1969, **1**, 87–94.
16. Biller, H. B. Maternal salience and feminine development in young girls. *Proc. 77th Annual Convention, Am. Psychol. Assoc.*, Washington, D.C., 1969, **4**, 259–260.
17. Biller, H. B. Father absence and the personality development of the male child. *Devel. Psychol.*, 1970, **2**, 181–201.
18. Boehm, L. The development of conscience of preschool children: A cultural and subcultural comparison. *J. Soc. Psychol.*, 1963, **39**, 355–360.
19. Bowlby, J. *Maternal care and mental health.* Geneva: World Health Organization, 1951.
20. Bowlby, J. *Attachment and loss.* Vol. I: *Attachment.* London: Hogarth, 1969.
21. Breznitz, S., & Kugelmass, S. Intentionality in moral judgment: Developmental stages. *Child Devel.*, 1967, **38**, 469–479.
22. Bronfenbrenner, U. Soviet methods of character education: Some implications for research. *Am. Psychol.*, 1962, **17**, 550–564.
23. Bronson, G. W. The development of fear in man and other animals. *Child Devel.*, 1968, **39**, 409–431.
24. Brown, D. G. Sex-role development in a changing culture. *Psychol. Bull.*, 1958, **55**, 232–242.
25. Clapp, W. F. *Competence and dependence in children: Parental treatment of four-year-old girls.* Washington, D.C.: U.S. Department of Health, Education, and Welfare, 1968.
26. Davis, W. A., & Havighurst, R. J. *Father of the man.* Boston: Houghton Mifflin, 1947.
27. DiBartolo, R., & Vinacke, W. E. Adult nurturance and the preschool child. *Devel. Psychol.*, 1969, **1**, 247–251.

28. Durrett, M. E., & Davy, A. J. Racial awareness in young Mexican-American and Anglo children. *Young Child.*, 1970, **26**, 16–24.
29. Emmerich, W. The parental role: A functional-cognitive approach. *Mono. Soc. Res. Child Devel.*, 1969, **34**:8.
30. Erikson, E. H., *Youth and crisis*. New York: Norton, 1968.
31. Fagot, B. I., & Patterson, G. R. An in vivo analysis of reinforcing contingencies for sex-role behaviors in the preschool child. *Devel. Psychol.*, 1969, **1**, 563–568.
32. Ferguson, L. R. *Personality development*. Belmont, Calif.: Wadsworth, 1970.
33. Fisher, S., & Cleveland, S. E. *Body image and personality*. New York: Van Nostrand, 1958.
34. Gilbert, D. C. The young child's awareness of affect. *Child Devel.*, 1969, **40**, 629–640.
35. Hagman, R. R. A study of the fears of children of preschool age. *J. Exper. Educ.*, 1932, **1**, 110–130.
36. Hartup, W. W. Dependence and independence. In H. W. Stevenson [Ed.], *Child psychology*. The Sixty-second Yearbook of the National Society for the Study of Education. Chicago: University of Chicago, 1963, pp. 333–363.
37. Heinicke, C. M. Some effects of separating two-year-old children from their mothers. *Hum. Relat.*, 1956, **9**, 102–176.
38. Hess, R. D., Gordon, I., & Scheinfeld, D. Intervention in family life. In E. Grotberg (Ed.), *Critical issues in research related to disadvantaged children*. Princeton, N.J.: Educational Testing Service, 1969.
39. Hess, R. D., & Shipman, V. C. Early experience and the socialization of cognitive modes in children. *Child Devel.*, 1965, **36**, 869–886.
40. Hetherington, E. M. A developmental study of the effects of sex of the dominant parent on sex role preference, identification and imitation in children. *J. Pers. Soc. Psychol.*, 1965, **2**, 188–194.
41. Hoffman, M. L. Childrearing practices and moral development: Generalizations from empirical research. *Child Devel.*, 1963, **34**, 295–318.
42. Jersild, A. T., & Holmes, F. B. Children's fears. *Child Devel. Mono.*, No. 20. New York: Teachers College, Columbia University, 1935.
43. Jessor, R., & Richardson, S. Psychosocial deprivation and personality development. In *Perspectives on human deprivation: Biological, psychological and sociological*. Washington, D.C.: U.S. Department of Health, Education, and Welfare, 1968, pp. 1–87.
44. John, E. A study of the effects of evacuation and air raids on children of preschool age. *Brit. J. Educ. Psychol.*, 1941, **11**, 173–182.
45. Joynt, D., & Cambroune, B. Psycholinguistic development and the control of behavior. *Brit. J. Educ. Psychol.*, 1968, **38**, 249–260.
46. Kagan, J., & Moss, H. A. *Birth to maturity*. New York: Wiley, 1962.
47. Kahana, B., & Kahana, E. Grandparenthood from the perspective of the developing child. *Devel. Psychol.*, 1970, **3**, 98–105.
48. Kahana, E., & Rosenblatt, I. E. Grandparenting as a function of family structure. Paper presented at the meeting of the Society for Research in Child Development, Santa Monica, Calif., March 29, 1969.
49. Katz, I. Factors influencing Negro performance in the desegregated school. In M. Deutsch, I. Katz & A. R. Jensen (Eds.) *Social class, race and psychological development*. New York: Holt, Rinehart & Winston, 1968, pp. 254–289.
50. Koch, H. L. The relation of certain formal attributes of siblings to attitudes

held toward each other and toward their parents. *Mono. Soc. Res. Child Devel.*, 1960, **25**:4.

51. Koch, M. B. Anxiety in preschool children from broken homes. *Merrill-Palmer Quart.*, 1961, **7**, 225–232.
52. Kohlberg, L., & Zigler, E. The impact of cognitive maturity on the development of sex-role attitudes in the years 4 to 8. *Genet. Psychol. Mono.*, 1967, **75**, 89–161.
53. Kreitler, H., & Kreitler, S. Children's concepts of sexuality and birth. *Child Devel.*, 1966, **37**, 363–378.
54. Luria, A. R. *The role of speech in the regulation of normal and abnormal behavior.* New York: Pergamon, 1961.
55. Luria, Z., Goldwasser, M., & Goldwasser, A. Response to transgression in stories by Israeli children. *Child Devel.*, 1963, **34**, 271–280.
56. Luria, Z., & Rebelsky, F. Ethnicity: A variable in sex differences in moral behavior. Paper presented at the meeting of the Society for Research in Child Development, Berkeley, April 1963.
57. Maccoby, E. E. Role-taking in childhood and its consequences for social learning. *Child Devel.*, 1959, **30**, 239–252.
58. Maccoby, E. E. Stability and change in attachment behavior during the third year of life. Paper presented at the meeting of the Western Psychological Association, Vancouver, June, 1969.
59. Marks, I. M. *Fears and phobias.* New York: Academic, 1969.
60. Marshall, H. Relations between home experiences and children's use of language in play interactions with peers. *Psychol. Mono.*, 1961, **75**:5.
61. Maurer, A. What children fear. *J. Genet. Psychol.*, 1965, **106**, 265–277.
62. Mead, M. *Male and female.* New York: Morrow, 1949.
63. Miller, D. R., & Swanson, G. E. *The changing American parent.* New York: Wiley, 1958.
64. Mussen, P., & Distler, L. Childrearing antecedents of masculine identification in kindergarten boys. *Child Devel.*, 1960, **31**, 89–100.
65. Mussen, P. H., & Parker, A. L. Mother nurturance and girls' incidental imitative learning. *J. Pers. Soc. Psychol.*, 1965, **2**, 94–97.
66. Neugarten, B. L., & Weinstein, K. K. The changing American grandparent. *J. Marr. Fam.*, 1964, **26**, 199–204.
67. Newson, J., & Newson, E. *Four years old in an urban community.* Chicago: Aldine, 1968.
68. Oetzel, R. M. Sex typing and sex role adoption in relation to differential abilities. Unpublished M.A. thesis, Stanford University, 1962. Cited in Ferguson [32].
69. Office of Economic Opportunity. *Project Head Start Daily Program I.* Washington, D.C.: U.S. Govt. Printing Office, 1965.
70. Ogilvie, D. M. Distinguishing social behaviors of competent and incompetent three- to six-year-old children. Paper presented at the meeting of the Society for Research in Child Development, Santa Monica, Calif., March 27, 1969.
71. Osborn, D. K., & Endsley, R. C. Emotional reactions of young children to TV violence. *Child Devel.*, 1971, **42**, 321–331.
72. Peck, R. F., & Havighurst, R. J. *The psychology of character development.* New York: Wiley, 1960.
73. Piaget, J. *The moral judgment of the child.* Glencoe, Ill.: Free Press, 1960.

74. Proshansky, H., & Newton, P. The nature and meaning of Negro self-identity. In M. Deutsch, I. Katz, & A. R. Jensen (Eds.), *Social class, race and psychological development*. New York: Holt, Rinehart and Winston, 1968, pp. 178–218.

75. Rosen, B. C. Socialization and achievement motivation in Brazil. *Am. Soc. Rev.*, 1962, **27**, 612–624.

76. Rosenhan, D. The kindnesses of children. *Young Children*, 1969, **25**, 30–44.

77. Rutherford, E., & Mussen, P. Generosity in nursery school boys. *Child Devel.*, 1968, **39**, 755–765.

78. Schell, R. E., & Silber, J. W. Sex-role discrimination among young children. *Percept. Motor Skills*, 1968, **27**, 379–389.

79. Schwarz, J. C. Presence of an attached peer and security. Paper presented at the meeting of the Society for Research in Child Development, Santa Monica, Calif., March 27, 1969.

80. Sears, R. R., Maccoby, E. E., & Levin, H. *Patterns of child rearing*. Evanston, Ill.: Row, Peterson, 1957.

81. Seltzer, A., & Beller, E. K. Moral and cognitive development in lower class Negro children. Paper presented at the meeting of the Eastern Psychological Association, Washington, D.C., April 1968.

82. Siegel, A. E., Stolz, L. M., Hitchcock, E. A., & Adamson, J. M. Dependence and independence in the children of working mothers. *Child Devel.*, 1959, **30**, 533–546.

83. Stevenson, H. W. Studies of racial awareness in young children. In W. W. Hartup & N. L. Smothergill (Eds.) *The young child: Reviews of research*. Washington, D.C.: National Association for the Education of Young Children, 1967.

84. Stolz, L. M. Effects of maternal employment on children: Evidence from research. *Child Devel.*, 1960, **31**, 749–782.

85. Sutton-Smith, B., & Rosenberg, B. G. Age changes in the effects of ordinal position on sex-role identification. *J. Genet. Psychol.*, 1965, **107**, 61–73.

86. Sweetser, D. A. The social structure of grandparenthood. In R. F. Winch, R. McGinnis, & H. R. Barringer, *Selected studies in marriage and the family*. New York: Holt, 1962, pp. 388–396.

87. Thompson, K. S., Friedlander, B., & Oskamp, S. Change in racial attitudes of preschool children through an experimental reading program. Paper presented at the meeting of the Western Psychological Association, Vancouver, June 18, 1969.

88. Unger, S. M. A behavior theory approach to the emergence of guilt reactivity in the child. *J. Psychol.*, 1964, **5**, 85–101.

89. Van de Castle, R. L. His, hers and the children's. *Psychol. Today*, 4(1), 37–39.

90. Waldrop, M. F., & Bell, R. Q. Relation of preschool dependency behavior to family size and density. *Child Devel.*, 1964, **35**, 1187–1195.

91. Wann, K. D., Dorn, M. S., & Liddle, E. A. *Fostering intellectual development in young children*. New York: Teachers College, Columbia University, 1962.

92. Ward, W. D. Process of sex-role development. *Devel. Psychol.*, 1969, **1**, 163–168.

93. Whiting, J. W. M., & Child, I. *Child training and personality*. New Haven, Conn.: Yale University Press, 1953.

94. Williams, J. E., & Edwards, C. D. An exploratory study of the modification of color and racial concept attitudes in preschool children. *Child Devel.*, 1969, **40**, 737–750.

# Part III

# The School-Age Child

# Introduction

Almost all cultures take some notice of the child's entering a new phase of life at 6 or 7 years of age. Although, as Piaget has pointed out, there are no general stages which are unique wholes, yet age 6 or 7 marks a shift in important processes of development. The fact that formal education is begun at this time in so many different cultures indicates widespread perception of such a shift. Likewise, writers from Shakespeare to Erikson have made use of this age in dividing life into portions that can be studied. We begin our discussion of this segment of life at 6 or 7 years and end it at the point where the pubescent growth spurt starts, an average age of 10, but a point which occurs within a wide range of years.

The loss of his preschool cuteness is not serious to the schoolchild. While an occasional child may mourn the passing of the days when adults thought him perfectly adorable just because he was a young child, most reports of such feelings of regret are from adults looking far backward toward early childhood. By the time he enters first grade, the healthy child has achieved enough trust, autonomy, and initiative that he wants to become involved with a private world of children, where adults are often unwelcome. Adults are, of course, necessary at times. He loves his parents and cares what they think, but his appetite for sitting on laps and being petted is definitely diminished. Teachers and club leaders are important too, but in limited time and space. It seems as though the child withdraws most into his private sphere of peers and self at the very time (around 10) when he is least attractive to adults—most gangly, least cuddly, restless, dirty, teeth missing, and speaking a language of childhood that is not completely comprehensible to adults.

Building on all that has gone before, the child interacts with a widening world to create new and more complex behavior patterns. Instead of being confined to family, home, and neighborhood, the child is on his own in the school. Warm and acceptant as his teacher may be, he is not special to her, as he is to his mother. He is one of many, and as such, must live with a kind of objectivity which he has not experienced before. Instead of playing with only little boys and girls who are the children of his parents' friends and neighbors, he plays and works with a variety of children. Meeting children from a social class different from his own, he may be surprised to find some of his schoolmates cleaner or dirtier, rougher or gentler, more or less interested in doing well at school than he. Playing in the homes of new friends, he discovers parents, behavior, houses, and yards unlike those he has known. Joining Cubs, Brownies, Bluebirds, or a similar organized group, the child embraces a new culture of symbolic pins, handclasps, and reflecting pools which symbolize his belongingness. His religious connections will expand too. He may make his first communion or begin the study of Hebrew. The public library will enlarge his literary world by conferring the privilege of taking books out. If he lives in a community which sponsors children's concerts, he will be eligible to go to them. Thus he will interact directly with many aspects of the culture which formerly influenced him only through his family.

Privacy is a kind of freedom much enjoyed by the school-age child. Because he is able to take basic physical care of himself and his room, he is often able to keep mother and others out of his room, out of the bathroom, and out of his most secret transactions. Privacy means freedom to take his bath just the way he likes it, to make funny faces in the mirror, to devise messages, signals, codes, club rules, to visit alone with friends. Reading books means freedom to roam in a vast world of thought and imagination. Fast-growing competency in language and thought means greater facility in dealing with all of his private world.

*Industry* is the name Erikson gives to the stage of personality development of the schoolchild. He has also called it *duty and accomplishment*. This is the time when jobs get done, in contrast to the stage of initiative, when they got started but rarely finished. Having explored all sorts of possibilities for action, the child settles down to learn how to do things and to do them well. He becomes involved in the technology of his culture, whether it stresses fishing and making canoes, or reading, writing, and electronics. Withdrawing from home, mother, and the emotional situations involved in them, he turns to the objects, tools, and techniques of the society in which he lives. Most cultures make provisions for this changeover. Literate societies provide schools where teachers begin the long process of teaching reading and writing. Even in simpler cultures, teachers usually help the children learn the appropriate aspects of technology. Often boys learn farming from their fathers and girls homemaking from their mothers. In American culture, an astonishing number of specialists teach such extracurricular subjects as music, dancing, painting, bird watching, star gazing, first aid, camping, and skiing. Recreation workers and youth leaders teach not only these subjects and more but also concern themselves with group dynamics, character, values, leadership, community service, and so on. It is possible for a child to spend all of his hours left over from eating, sleeping, and physical care on lessons of one sort or another.

There are aspects of industry and duty which are better accomplished with other children (in the peer group) and alone, however, than in an onslaught of lessons. Take baseball, for instance. To be a real American boy, you practically have to know how to play it. As a girl, you have to know at least the rules of the game and preferably you can play softball. It takes thousands of practice throws to get to be a good pitcher and as many catches to be a baseman. Where could one do all this except in the neighborhood play lot with his friends? There are many more games whose rules and coordinations must be learned. During the school years children are willing, even eager, to practice and practice and practice—batting a ball, jumping, skating, jumping rope, singing and chanting the ditties of childhood, sewing doll clothes, cutting out cookies, playing cards and other games, identifying specimens and arranging collections. There are social skills to develop too, making and keeping close friendships and being a club member.

Success in the stage of industry results in the child's knowing the pleasure and satisfaction of a job well done. He enjoys being a part of a productive situation.

He knows that he can produce, achieve and accomplish in certain areas, and in those situations, he feels adequate. There are enough of them that he has a general feeling of being an adequate person. There are some places where he does particularly well and others where he just gets by. This knowledge is incorporated into his picture of himself.

A sense of *inferiority and inadequacy* is the result when development does not go well at this time of life. Since time of entrance to school is usually fixed rigidly, the child who is not ready to enter into the stage of industry is at a great disadvantage in personality development. Failure in the beginning work is disastrous to his concept of himself as an adequate person.

# Chapter 9

Merrill-Palmer Institute by Donna J. Harris

# Physical Characteristics and Skills

Slow growth is typical of the period of middle childhood. In both size and proportions, these children change relatively little from year to year. The period of slow growth ends several months before menarche in the girl and a corresponding point of sexual maturity in the boy. Although the period of rapid growth, known as the pubescent growth spurt, is discussed in Chapter 13, in regard to adolescence, it is important to realize that some children in the elementary school are already in the pubescent growth spurt. Growth in height begins to pick up speed, on the average,

345

at about age 9 in girls and 11 in boys. A few girls, however, begin the spurt as early as age 8 and boys at 10. Most girls grow at top speed during their twelfth or thirteenth year, boys during their fourteenth or fifteenth year. A seventh grade classroom is sure to include a wide variety of sizes and stages of maturity. It is safe to generalize that children grow slowly during the early elementary school years.

The middle years are healthier than the preschool period. With growth needs and the burdens of illness claiming less of his energy than they did in an earlier stage of life, the schoolchild has more of himself to invest in relationships, problem solving, and acquiring of skills and knowledge. Now he works to develop and perfect many motor coordinations, enjoying the sense of adequacy which grows from successful performance. His concepts of himself and his body reflect the interactions of his body with the world and also reflect his perceptions of people's reactions to him.

## Physical Growth

Growth can be described in terms of the large, general measurements of height and weight and also in terms of various parts of the body. A third way of considering it has to do with interrelationships of various aspects of growth.

### Growth in Height and Weight

Percentile tables are available for white and black American children from 5 to 18 years of age, in grades 1 through 11 [50]. These tables (9–1 through 9–8) are based on measurements of 8480 children, an 8 percent sample of the children in school in Cincinnati. Age was defined by the student's last birthday. Measurements, recorded to the nearest inch or pound, were made without shoes, outdoor clothing, and sweaters. There are no consistent differences in median height or weight between whites and blacks. Nor do sex differences in height show up clearly in these tables. Evidence from most research indicates, however, that, on the average, males are taller than females excepting during the pubescent growth spurt [16, p. 548]. When physiological maturity rather than chronological age is taken into account, males are considerably taller than females.

**Table 9–1** Percentile Distribution of Height in Inches for White Males (Age Defined at Subject's Last Birthday)

| Age | N (Total = 2973) | Percentile | | | | | | |
|---|---|---|---|---|---|---|---|---|
| | | 3RD | 10TH | 25TH | 50TH | 75TH | 90TH | 97TH |
| 5 | 143 | 41 | 42 | 44 | 45 | 47 | 48 | 51 |
| 6 | 250 | 42 | 44 | 45 | 46 | 48 | 50 | 51 |
| 7 | 268 | 45 | 46 | 47 | 49 | 50 | 52 | 54 |
| 8 | 261 | 47 | 49 | 50 | 51 | 54 | 56 | 58 |
| 9 | 259 | 48 | 50 | 51 | 53 | 55 | 57 | 61 |
| 10 | 221 | 50 | 52 | 53 | 55 | 57 | 59 | 62 |

SOURCE: Reprinted by permission from J. L. Rauh, D. A. Schumsky, and M. T. Witt, "Heights, Weights, and Obesity in Urban School Children," *Child Development*, **38**, 515–530. Copyright © 1967, The Society for Research in Child Development, Inc.

**Table 9–2** Percentile Distribution of Height in Inches for Nonwhite Males (Age Defined at Subject's Last Birthday)

| Age | N (Total = 1208) | Percentile | | | | | | |
|---|---|---|---|---|---|---|---|---|
| | | 3RD | 10TH | 25th | 50TH | 75TH | 90TH | 97TH |
| 5 | 69 | 40 | 42 | 43 | 45 | 47 | 49 | 50 |
| 6 | 110 | 43 | 44 | 46 | 47 | 49 | 51 | 51 |
| 7 | 115 | 45 | 47 | 48 | 49 | 51 | 52 | 56 |
| 8 | 128 | 47 | 49 | 50 | 52 | 54 | 55 | 59 |
| 9 | 121 | 48 | 51 | 52 | 53 | 55 | 56 | 69 |
| 10 | 89 | 50 | 51 | 54 | 55 | 57 | 60 | 63 |

SOURCE: Reprinted by permission from J. L. Rauh, D. A. Schumsky, and M. T. Witt, "Heights, Weights, and Obesity in Urban School Children," *Child Development*, **38**, 515–530. Copyright © 1967, The Society for Research in Child Development, Inc.

**Table 9–3** Percentile Distribution of Height in Inches for White Females (Age Defined at Subject's Last Birthday)

| Age | N (Total = 3010) | Percentile | | | | | | |
|---|---|---|---|---|---|---|---|---|
| | | 3RD | 10TH | 25TH | 50TH | 75TH | 90TH | 97TH |
| 5 | 152 | 38 | 42 | 43 | 44 | 46 | 47 | 49 |
| 6 | 264 | 42 | 43 | 45 | 46 | 48 | 49 | 51 |
| 7 | 251 | 43 | 45 | 47 | 49 | 50 | 52 | 54 |
| 8 | 260 | 45 | 47 | 49 | 50 | 53 | 54 | 57 |
| 9 | 247 | 47 | 49 | 51 | 53 | 54 | 56 | 59 |
| 10 | 268 | 49 | 51 | 53 | 55 | 57 | 59 | 62 |

SOURCE: Reprinted by permission from J. L. Rauh, D. A. Schumsky, and M. T. Witt, "Heights, Weights, and Obesity in Urban School Children," *Child Development*, **38**, 515–530. Copyright © 1967, The Society for Research in Child Development, Inc.

**Table 9–4** Percentile Distribution of Height in Inches for Nonwhite Females (Age Defined at Subject's Last Birthday)

| Age | N (Total = 1289) | Percentile | | | | | | |
|---|---|---|---|---|---|---|---|---|
| | | 3RD | 10TH | 25TH | 50TH | 75TH | 90TH | 97TH |
| 5 | 80 | 41 | 42 | 44 | 45 | 46 | 49 | 50 |
| 6 | 132 | 42 | 44 | 45 | 47 | 48 | 50 | 54 |
| 7 | 132 | 44 | 46 | 48 | 49 | 51 | 53 | 57 |
| 8 | 137 | 46 | 48 | 50 | 51 | 53 | 56 | 59 |
| 9 | 108 | 46 | 50 | 51 | 53 | 55 | 58 | 60 |
| 10 | 88 | 50 | 53 | 55 | 57 | 59 | 61 | 64 |

SOURCE: Reprinted by permission from J. L. Rauh, D. A. Schumsky, and M. T. Witt, "Heights, Weights, and Obesity in Urban School Children," *Child Development*, **38**, 515–530. Copyright © 1967, The Society for Research in Child Development, Inc.

**Table 9–5** Percentile Distribution of Weight in Pounds for White Males (Age Defined at Subject's Last Birthday)

| Age | N (Total = 2973) | Percentile | | | | | | |
|---|---|---|---|---|---|---|---|---|
| | | 3RD | 10TH | 25TH | 50TH | 75TH | 90TH | 97TH |
| 5 | 143 | 37 | 40 | 42 | 46 | 50 | 54 | 59 |
| 6 | 250 | 38 | 41 | 45 | 48 | 52 | 58 | 67 |
| 7 | 268 | 42 | 46 | 50 | 53 | 58 | 63 | 77 |
| 8 | 261 | 44 | 50 | 55 | 61 | 67 | 75 | 83 |
| 9 | 259 | 51 | 54 | 60 | 66 | 74 | 87 | 98 |
| 10 | 221 | 54 | 62 | 66 | 73 | 82 | 96 | 110 |

SOURCE: Reprinted by permission from J. L. Rauh, D. A. Schumsky, and M. T. Witt, "Heights, Weights, and Obesity in Urban School Children," *Child Development*, **38**, 515–530. Copyright © 1967, The Society for Research in Child Development, Inc.

**Table 9–6** Percentile Distribution of Weight in Pounds for Nonwhite Males (Age Defined at Subject's Last Birthday)

| Age | N (Total = 1208) | Percentile | | | | | | |
|---|---|---|---|---|---|---|---|---|
| | | 3RD | 10TH | 25TH | 50TH | 75TH | 90TH | 97TH |
| 5 | 69 | 34 | 36 | 41 | 44 | 49 | 53 | 54 |
| 6 | 110 | 36 | 41 | 44 | 49 | 53 | 59 | 62 |
| 7 | 115 | 43 | 47 | 50 | 55 | 60 | 65 | 69 |
| 8 | 128 | 45 | 51 | 56 | 61 | 68 | 75 | 82 |
| 9 | 121 | 51 | 56 | 59 | 66 | 72 | 81 | 89 |
| 10 | 89 | 52 | 58 | 66 | 72 | 81 | 94 | 110 |

SOURCE: Reprinted by permission from J. L. Rauh, D. A. Schumsky, and M. T. Witt, "Heights, Weights, and Obesity in Urban School Children," *Child Development*, **38**, 515–530. Copyright © 1967, The Society for Research in Child Development, Inc.

**Table 9–7** Percentile Distribution of Weight in Pounds for White Females (Age Defined at Subject's Last Birthday)

| Age | N (Total = 3010) | Percentile | | | | | | |
|---|---|---|---|---|---|---|---|---|
| | | 3RD | 10TH | 25TH | 50TH | 75TH | 90TH | 97TH |
| 5 | 152 | 35 | 37 | 40 | 43 | 48 | 55 | 60 |
| 6 | 264 | 35 | 39 | 43 | 47 | 52 | 56 | 61 |
| 7 | 251 | 37 | 43 | 46 | 52 | 58 | 65 | 72 |
| 8 | 260 | 42 | 47 | 52 | 57 | 65 | 76 | 89 |
| 9 | 247 | 47 | 51 | 57 | 63 | 75 | 87 | 99 |
| 10 | 268 | 51 | 56 | 62 | 70 | 84 | 98 | 116 |

SOURCE: Reprinted by permission from J. L. Rauh, D. A. Schumsky, and M. T. Witt, "Heights, Weights, and Obesity in Urban School Children," *Child Development*, **38**, 515–530. Copyright © 1967, The Society for Research in Child Development, Inc.

**Table 9–8** Percentile Distribution of Weight in Pounds for Nonwhite Females (Age Defined at Subject's Last Birthday)

| | | Percentile | | | | | | |
|---|---|---|---|---|---|---|---|---|
| Age | N (Total = 1289) | 3RD | 10TH | 25TH | 50TH | 75TH | 90TH | 97TH |
| 5 | 80 | 33 | 36 | 37 | 41 | 46 | 51 | 57 |
| 6 | 132 | 34 | 38 | 42 | 46 | 50 | 54 | 67 |
| 7 | 132 | 39 | 44 | 48 | 51 | 58 | 63 | 86 |
| 8 | 137 | 42 | 47 | 52 | 58 | 67 | 76 | 84 |
| 9 | 108 | 46 | 53 | 58 | 65 | 76 | 89 | 104 |
| 10 | 88 | 51 | 58 | 67 | 78 | 89 | 116 | 131 |

SOURCE: Reprinted by permission from J. L. Rauh, D. A. Schumsky, and M. T. Witt, "Heights, Weights, and Obesity in Urban School Children," *Child Development*, **38**, 515–530. Copyright © 1967, The Society for Research in Child Development, Inc.

The weight tables shown here indicate that males are heavier than females between ages 5 and 10 or 11. At 11 for whites and 10 for blacks, the female weights exceeded the male, indicating the earlier pubescent growth spurt in girls. When the sexes are compared at the maturity level, however, males are heavier than females and when fat-free weight is compared, the difference is even greater [16, p. 548].

Girls' earlier entrance into the pubescent growth makes them temporarily taller and heavier. Although the average difference is small (an inch at 12 and 13 years), a fast-maturing girl towers above a slow-growing boy, a discrepancy which causes agony if children between 11 and 15 are pushed into dancing, dating, and other situations where their heights are compared. At all points in the growth cycle, girls are closer to maturity than boys, since they do not have to grow so far to reach it. For instance, 75 percent of adult height is attained by the average 9-year-old boy and by the average 7-year-old girl.

Height increases more steadily than weight, since it is influenced less by environmental changes. Both measurements are, of course, products of the organism's interaction with the environment, but since height depends almost entirely on the linear measure of skeletal growth, and since length of the skeleton is relatively resistant to short-term environmental pressures, progress in height is quite regular. As was mentioned in Chapter 5 the bones do record such traumas as illnesses and malnutrition, but they do it in terms of bone scars, which can be detected only by X ray. Retarded growth and resulting small stature represent a general result of malnutrition, infections, and stress. Weight, in contrast to height, is a sensitive indicator of malnutrition or overnutrition. Weight is related to volume, which is the product of three linear measures. All types of body tissue, skeleton, muscles, fat, blood, and all the rest, contribute to weight. Thus although the skeleton is not shortened by illness or malnutrition, the soft tissues of the body may be reduced.

**Cross-Culture Comparisons.** Eight-year-old children from many regions of the world have been compared in physical measurements in a study using 300 samples [43]. Mean heights of the various groups varied from 106 centimeters in Bihar, India, to 129 centimeters in Norway, a range of about 9 inches. The shortest groups were mainly in Southeast Asia, Oceania, and South America, the tallest mainly in northern and central Europe, eastern Australia, and the United States. Five samples were taller than the United States white group, while only the Norwegian average was greater than that of the black sample from the United States. Weight

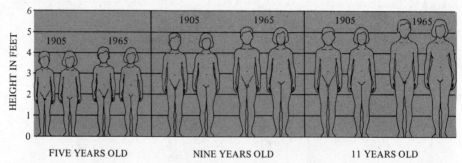

**Figure 9–1.** Increased size of children stems mainly from earlier maturation. A boy and girl aged 5 in 1965, and of average economic circumstances, were taller by about 2 inches than their counterparts of a half-century ago; 9-year-olds of 1965 averaged some 3 inches taller, and 11-year-olds nearly 4 inches taller. The figures are based on measurements made in the United States and Europe.

SOURCE: From "Earlier Maturation in Man," by J. M. Tanner. Copyright © 1968 by Scientific American, Inc. All rights reserved.

averages varied from 17 kilograms to 27 kilograms, a range of about 25 pounds. The average weight of the Norwegians was 50 percent greater than that of the East Pakistanis. The largest children live in parts of the world where nutritious food is abundant and where the infectious diseases are well controlled or largely eliminated.

**Secular Changes.** A growth trend continuing over a long time is evident in the prosperous parts of the world. Children have been growing taller and heavier. For example, between 1880 and 1960 the average North American white 8-year-old increased 9 centimeters in height and 4 kilograms in weight [42]. The trend was noted in France as early as 1835 [16, p. 532]. American, British, and Swedish data indicate that the average gain for 5- to 7-year olds between 1880 and 1950 was about 1.5 centimeters per decade [69, p. 95]. Japanese children have increased greatly in height and weight since the end of World War II, according to a report from the Japanese National Institute of Nutrition [47]. The official linked the gains in growth with changes in the Japanese diet, such as a twentyfold increase in per capita milk consumption over the past 20 years and a doubled intake of animal protein. He commented that if the trend continues as expected, doorways and ceilings will have to be built higher and that, already, clothing and furniture manufacturers have had to revise their specifications. Along with the increase in height and weight there are changes in proportions, with legs growing longer and slimmer and trunks less chunky. The secular increase is now tapering off for the most privileged children, suggesting that some groups are reaching their maximum possible height [28, 64]. Privileged children from different parts of the world have remarkably similar growth patterns [24, 28]. For example, a comparison of heights and weights of high socioeconomic groups in the United States, Guatemala, and Panama showed no significant differences [24].

**Changes in Children of Immigrants.** Children of immigrants to America show great increases in height when compared with children born and reared in the country from which the immigrants came. The children and grandchildren of immigrants duplicate in one or two generations changes that might have taken five or more generations in the mother country [16, p. 533]. The change from Naples to Boston or Tokyo to San Francisco has entailed abrupt improvements in caloric intake, quality of food, disease prevention, and prenatal and infant care.

**Table 9–9** Fels Multipliers for Stature Prediction of Boys and Girls of Average Parental Stature

| Multiplier BOYS | Age | Multiplier GIRLS |
|---|---|---|
| 1.47 | 7 | 1.35 |
| 1.40 | 8 | 1.29 |
| 1.35 | 9 | 1.23 |
| 1.29 | 10 | 1.17 |
| 1.24 | 11 | 1.12 |
| 1.19 | 12 | 1.07 |

SOURCE: Reprinted by permission from S. M. Garn, "Body Size and its Implications," in L. W. Hoffman and M. L. Hoffman (Eds.), *Review of Child Development Research*, Vol. II, pp. 529–561. Copyright © 1966, Russell Sage Foundation.

**Predicting Adult Height.** As stated in Chapter 5, final stature can be predicted fairly well from measurements in childhood. Table 9–9 gives the multipliers to use for boys and girls whose mid-parent height is average or slightly above average, or close to 169–172 centimeters.

Appendix B consists of a height–weight interpretation chart for boys and girls from 4 to 18 years of age, along with directions for using it. In order to reproduce it for this book, the chart had to be reduced in size. While it is still usable, anyone interested in keeping longitudinal records on one or more children is advised to order copies of the chart from the National Education Association or the American Medical Association. The chart in this book can be used for making rough predictions of future height, since children tend to remain in the same channel as they grow.

## Proportions

Compared with preschool children, school-age children are graceful. With a relatively lower center of gravity, longer legs, and slimmer proportions, the older child is steadier on his feet. The photographs on these pages show typical proportions during the elementary school years as well as preschool and adolescent figures with which to compare the figures of middle childhood. (See Figures 9–2, 9–3, and 9–4.) Each new or refined coordination added to the child's motor schemas increases his poise. He fits better into adult furniture, even though it is still too big for him. He has grown out of a crib. Although his feet dangle at the table, he spurns a high chair. His new proportions make for excellent climbing, since longer arms and legs can reach more distant branches and a lower center of gravity steadies him. Similarly with bicycle-riding. Changes in growth rates also show up in facial changes. Relatively large at birth, the brain case is still large at 5. Then the face begins to catch up. The ratio of face to cranium is about 1:3 at 6 and 1:2 at 18 [5].

The changes in body configuration which take place during the years from 4½ to 7½ have been studied in some detail, since this is the period when the child is changing from a preschooler to a schoolchild, from a preconceptual thinker to one who can deal with concrete operations, from one concerned with the sense of imagination to one involved in problems of the sense of industry. In a search for some physical indications of sufficient maturity for assessing school readiness,

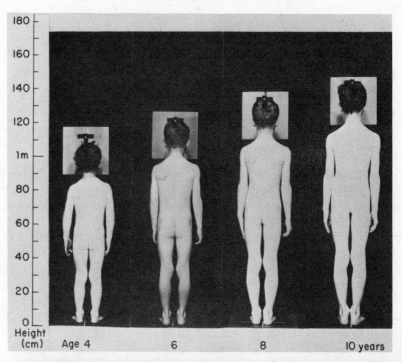

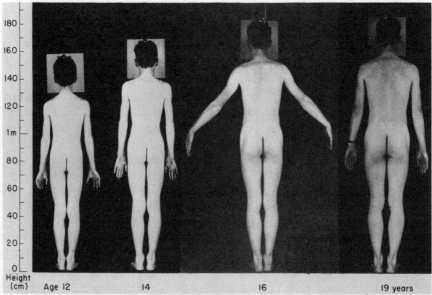

**Figures 9–2** and **9–3.** A typical boy's growth from early childhood to adulthood.

SOURCE: Reprinted from *Growth Diagnosis*, by L. M. Bayer and N. Bayley, by permission of The University of Chicago Press. Copyright © 1959, The University of Chicago Press.

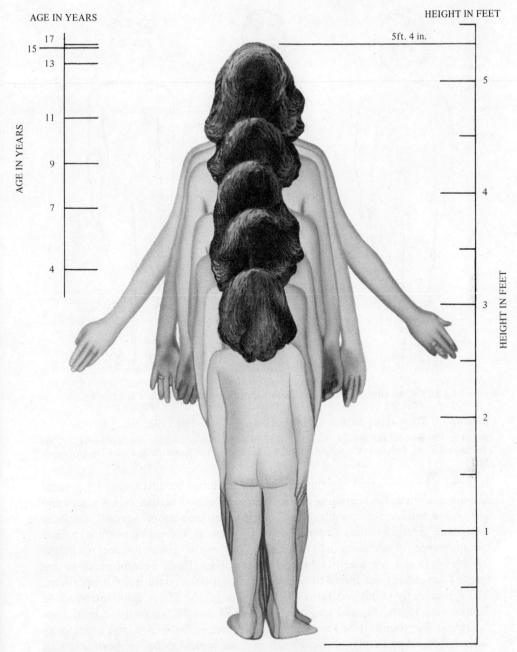

AGE IN YEARS

HEIGHT IN FEET

5ft. 4 in.

AGE IN YEARS

HEIGHT IN FEET

**Figure 9–4.** A typical girl's growth from early childhood to adulthood.

SOURCE: Reprinted from *Growth Diagnosis*, by L. M. Bayer and N. Bayley, by permission of The University of Chicago Press. Copyright © 1959, The University of Chicago Press.

three types of body configuration were distinguished in photographs of boys and girls [58]. Schematic drawings of the figures are shown in Figure 9–5. Judges estimated maturity in terms of both face and body. After the judges of the photographs had agreed on which ones showed the various types of proportions, measurements and relationships between measurements were studied in order to

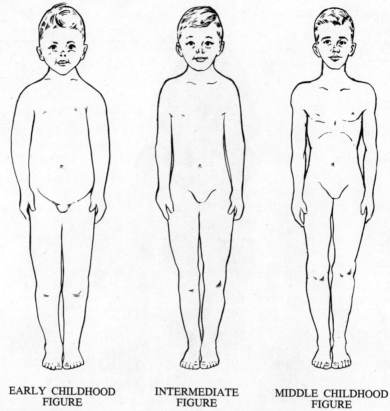

EARLY CHILDHOOD     INTERMEDIATE     MIDDLE CHILDHOOD
FIGURE     FIGURE     FIGURE

**Figure 9–5.** Three types of body configuration seen in middle childhood.

SOURCE: Reprinted from M. D. Simon, "Body Configuration and School Readiness," *Child Development*, **30**, Figure 1. Copyright © 1959, The Society for Research in Child Development, Inc.

find out which indicated the three stages of maturity. Results showed a general slimming down at the beginning of the middle childhood period, making boys and girls quite similar for a while. Then the girls became more typically feminine (rounded). Several indices proved useful in showing increasing maturity: head circumference to standing height (decreasing), waist circumference to height (decreasing), and leg length to height (increasing). Head circumference to leg length (decreasing) was found to be a good indication of maturity of proportions. The typical early childhood ratio was 86 for boys and 85 for girls, intermediate figures were 85 and 81, and middle childhood 81 and 81. Maturity of body configuration was found to be associated with success in first grade, and immaturity with failure. Apparently physical maturity, as indicated by proportions, tells something about the child's readiness for meeting the demands of school. There are, in addition to proportions, other useful physical indicators of maturity as related to success in school. Achievement in fifth grade was found to be correlated with size in relation to age and also with gross and fine motor coordination [40].

### Tissues and Organs

Certain physiological and anatomical characteristics are especially typical of middle childhood. Those mentioned in the following description contribute to the child's appearance or to his behavior or both. *Fat* diminishes gradually and changes in distribution patterns. School-age children look much thinner than preschool children and adolescents. Girls have more fat than boys and it is placed differently, giving them softer contours at all ages after the first year [15]. The *skin* becomes less delicate. *Hair* may darken. While the *muscles* grow in size and in strength of connections with bones, they are still immature in function as compared with an adolescent's muscles. Muscles of school-age children are more readily injured by strain. For example, Little League pitchers are prey to "Little League Elbow," a muscular injury due to overuse. A brief observation in any first grade classroom will demonstrate how difficult it is for 6- and 7-year-olds—especially boys—to immobilize their muscles.

The *digestive* system shows added maturity by having fewer upsets and by retaining food for a longer time. Thus the school-age child does not have to be fed so carefully, so often, and so promptly as the preschool child. Because growth is slow, calorie needs, in relation to the size of the stomach, are not so great as they were earlier and as they will be during the coming growth spurt. The danger at this time is that the child will fill up on empty calories, foods which do not promote growth, such as sugar, starches, and excess fats. With relatively low calorie needs, it is important to eat foods that are high in proteins, minerals, and vitamins. The combination of freedom to move out from his mother's supervision, plus a bit of money in his pockets, may result in an excessive intake of soft drinks and candy.

Children vary widely in *bladder* capacity, boys having less than girls. There are individual differences in frequency of urination, and difference in one individual from one time to another, due to temperature, humidity, time of day, emotional state, fluids ingested, and so on.

Respiration grows slower, deeper, and more regular, changing from 20 to 30 inhalations per minute in the preschool period to 17 to 25 in the school age [68, p. 259]. Infections and disturbances of the respiratory system are fewer and milder than in the early years.

The *heart* grows slowly between 4 and 10 years. During that time it is smaller in relation to the rest of the body than at any other period of life [6]. This fact of growth is one of the reasons why strongly competitive sports are dangerous for school-age children. As the child grows toward maturity, his heartbeat slows down and his blood pressure goes up. Between 6 and 12, he reaches the average adult heart rate of 70–100 per minute. Blood pressure, at an average of 105 mm, is still below the adult norm.

*Ears* are less likely to become infected than they were during the preschool years. With the growth of the lower part of the face, the Eustachian tube, leading from the throat into the middle ear, grows longer, relatively narrower, and slanted. Thus it is harder for disease organisms to invade. With fewer respiratory infections too, there are fewer invading organisms in the child. Although studies on children's hearing have yielded a variety of results, they usually show increasing acuity with age [33]. There is some indication that the average child has greater acuity in the right ear than in the left.

The *eye* changes shape with growth, resulting in farsightedness until about age 6. Studies of visual acuity yield a wide range of results, one showing 20/20 vision to be typical at age 7, another study placing 20/20 vision at age 4 and yet another at 11 to 13 [11]. Thus there is some doubt as to the age when 20/20 vision is normally achieved. It is after 7 when the eyeball gains its full weight and several

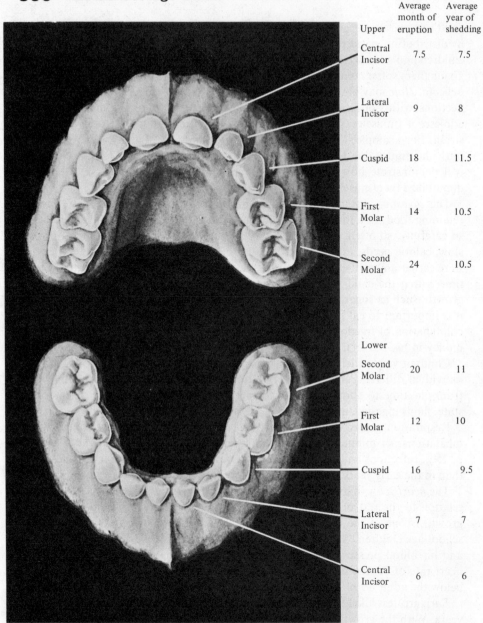

| Upper | Average month of eruption | Average year of shedding |
|---|---|---|
| Central Incisor | 7.5 | 7.5 |
| Lateral Incisor | 9 | 8 |
| Cuspid | 18 | 11.5 |
| First Molar | 14 | 10.5 |
| Second Molar | 24 | 10.5 |
| Lower | | |
| Second Molar | 20 | 11 |
| First Molar | 12 | 10 |
| Cuspid | 16 | 9.5 |
| Lateral Incisor | 7 | 7 |
| Central Incisor | 6 | 6 |

**Figure 9–6a.** The primary (deciduous) teeth.

SOURCE: From "Dental Health Factors for Teachers." Copyright 1966 by the American Dental Association. Reprinted by permission.

years later that full development is completed. Binocular vision is usually well developed at 6 or shortly afterward, although not in all children. Large print is recommended for children throughout the school years [6]. A study of elementary school children showed 59 percent to have visual defects [25]. The defects increased from 17 percent in first grade to 82 percent at the end of the elementary years. Adequate physical care must include attention to signs of visual difficulties and regular eye examinations.

In adults, the right and left hemispheres of the *brain* are specialized for sound

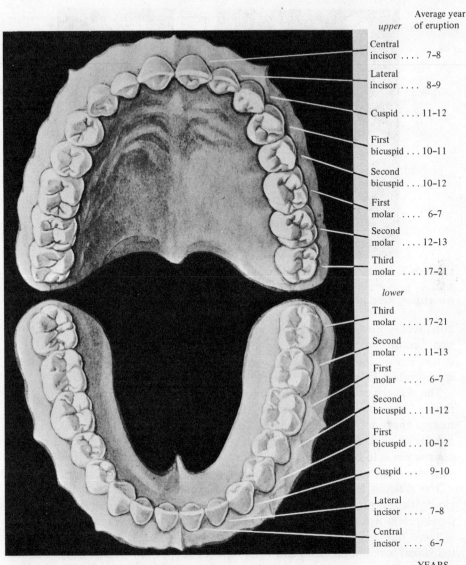

| | upper | Average year of eruption |
|---|---|---|
| | Central incisor | 7–8 |
| | Lateral incisor | 8–9 |
| | Cuspid | 11–12 |
| | First bicuspid | 10–11 |
| | Second bicuspid | 10–12 |
| | First molar | 6–7 |
| | Second molar | 12–13 |
| | Third molar | 17–21 |
| | lower | |
| | Third molar | 17–21 |
| | Second molar | 11–13 |
| | First molar | 6–7 |
| | Second bicuspid | 11–12 |
| | First bicuspid | 10–12 |
| | Cuspid | 9–10 |
| | Lateral incisor | 7–8 |
| | Central incisor | 6–7 |
| | | YEARS |

**Figure 9–6b.** The permanent teeth.

Source: From "Dental Health Factors for Teachers." Copyright 1966 by the American Dental Association. Reprinted by permission.

perception and interpretation. The speech center is normally in the left temporal lobe. Nonverbal sounds are processed primarily by the right hemisphere [34]. By 5 years of age, children show functional differentiation between the hemispheres. Before 10, the speech center can be reestablished on the right side if anything happens to damage the left temporal lobe [49]. If such an accident should occur after 12 years, the speech center cannot be organized on the right side, since the cortex involved has by that time become committed to the interpretation of experience. Thus the school age is a vital time for organization of the brain into laterally specialized functions. Boys do better in perceiving nonverbal sounds (such as dripping water, animal noises, a typewriter) and in spatial perception, whereas

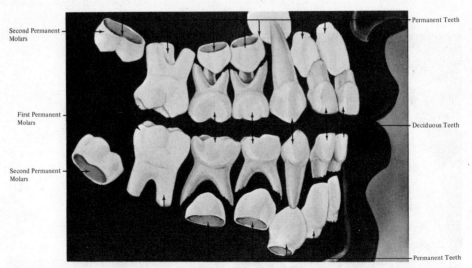

Second Permanent Molars

First Permanent Molars

Second Permanent Molars

Permanent Teeth

Deciduous Teeth

Permanent Teeth

**Figure 9–7.** Dentition of 6-year-old child.

SOURCE: From "Dental Health Factors for Teachers." Copyright 1966 by the American Dental Association. Reprinted by permission.

girls usually do better than boys in language. These findings suggest that boys' right hemispheres mature more rapidly than girls', as far as the lateral organization is concerned, and that probably girls' left hemispheres exceed boys' in lateral specialization [34].

The *skeleton* continues to ossify, replacing cartilage with bone. Since mineralization is not complete, the bones resist pressure and muscle pull less than more mature bones do. Good hygiene includes chairs, desks, and shoes that fit, frequent moving around, and caution in carrying heavy loads. For example, if a pack of newspapers is to be slung from one shoulder, it should be changed often from one shoulder to the other.

The skeleton is a useful maturity indicator, since its level of development is closely tied to progress toward sexual maturity. A child who is advanced in bone development will reach puberty at an earlier age than the average child. Not only is there this general relationship between the two kinds of development, but individual bones in the hand and wrist have a constant time relationship to sexual maturity. For instance, the sesamoid (a smaller round bone at the joint at the base of the thumb) appears within two to two and a half years before menarche [14, p. 107]. In the group of normal girls whose skeletal development was studied during puberty, menarche usually occurred soon after fusion of the epiphyses and shafts of the bones at the tips of the fingers [21, p. 11].

These are important years for *teething*, since most of the changes from deciduous to permanent teeth take place. At almost any time, a child has a gap or two in his jaw, a loose tooth, or one just popping through the gum. Nutrition, including sufficient fluorides, oral hygiene, and dental care are very important in assuring healthy teeth. Speech, nutrition, appearance, and body image are all affected by the soundness of teeth. Figure 9–6 shows the complete set of 20 baby teeth and the complete set of 32 adult teeth, indicating the replacements and additions which transform a young child's jaws into mature jaws. Figure 9–7 shows the two sets of teeth in place, the deciduous ones in the process of losing their roots through resorption, which prepares them to shed, leaving room for permanent teeth, since they exceed the number of baby teeth.

Since first permanent teeth to erupt in most children do not replace deciduous teeth, they are likely not to be recognized as permanent teeth. These teeth are the first molars, which appear just behind the second deciduous molars. As is the case with the deciduous teeth, there are some differences in the times of eruption when corresponding teeth in the two jaws are compared. There are also sex differences. The times of eruption of girls' teeth are earlier than those of boys'. This is in line with the faster rate of maturation of girls, but, comparing tooth for tooth, girls are further ahead in the eruption of some teeth than they are for others [63, p. 70].

## Health and Safety

Fewer American children die than ever before. A recent report on the average annual death rate for children 5 to 14 years of age placed it at less than 6 in 10,000 for boys and less than 4 in 10,000 for girls [45]. A comparison of two decades showed a decline in mortality of about one third for school-age children. In the year when the United States had a death rate of 43.5 per 100,000 for children between 5 and 14, the rate in Denmark was 35.5. Death rates lower than the American were recorded in at least seven countries [57, p. 358]. Between ages 5 and 9, mortality rates in very poor countries are from five to nine times as great as the rates in the most prosperous countries. At 10 to 14 years, the rates in poor countries are three to five times those in wealthy countries. Thus the differential in the mortality rate in children decreases with age, since these figures represent a huge reduction from the situation at ages 1 to 4, when the death rate in poor countries is 20 to 40 times that in prosperous ones [57, p. 206].

Child health needs throughout the world are tremendous. Even in the United States, where health is improving from the standpoint of reduction of accident rates and communicable diseases, there are many areas in which child health could be improved. Malnutrition, disease, injuries, and environmental pollution, including crowding, all continue as threats to children.

### Illnesses

School-age children have fewer illnesses than preschool children do [66]. Respiratory and gastrointestinal upsets decrease considerably, although they continue to be the most frequent types of illness, with respiratory the leading cause. After age 10 there is a further decrease in number of illnesses. The variety of major illnesses is greater during ages 6 to 10 than during all other ages studied, between birth and 18. The list of illnesses at 6 to 10 includes, for example, nephritis, septicemia, meningococcemia, and tuberculosis [66]. Figure 9–8 shows the distribution of the various types of illnesses between ages 5 and 14. According to a national health survey, children in this age group averaged 7.8 days in bed during one year, and 16.4 days of restricted activity, due to illness [37]. Schooldays lost due to illness averaged 5.3 days, with about three fifths of that time due to respiratory diseases [44]. The average number of acute illnesses was three per child. Medical attention was given to children for 54 percent of their illnesses.

The communicable diseases (including measles, chicken pox, mumps, whooping cough, and scarlet fever) are much less threatening to American children than

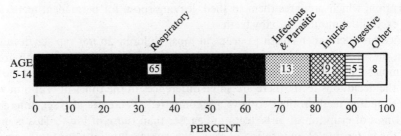

**Figure 9–8.** Frequency of occurrence of various types of illness in childhood.

SOURCE: From Chart B on page 18, "Problems of Youth," Legislative Reference Service, U.S. Government Printing Office, Washington, 1964.

they were in former years. In a longitudinal study of 67 boys and 67 girls, 50 girls and 45 boys had at least one communicable disease and over half of them had two [66]. No child had more than four. Death rates from these diseases declined by 70 percent to 80 percent in one decade, reaching the low figures of between two and seven deaths per million children between 5 and 14 [37].

As pointed out in Chapter 5, most illnesses can be prevented by careful health supervision. Table 9–10a shows diseases that are controlled in the United States by routine immunization. Table 9–10b shows diseases still prevalent in the United States and not yet controlled by immunization. The disease situation is different, of course, in other parts of the world. Constantly increasing travel and communication in the world means that almost any disease might appear in a new location. Therefore, anyone who works with children needs a comprehensive handbook on communicable diseases, not in order to replace the physician who must diagnose and treat, but to be able to observe, refer, and cooperate with medical personnel. Such a handbook [3] is available free from many state health departments. See Appendix D for the vaccination schedule recommended by the American Medical Association and the American Academy of Pediatrics and for a summary of facts about the communicable diseases of childhood.

As Chapter 5 pointed out, many illnesses can be prevented by careful health supervision, carried out under the direction of a physician. Immunizations prevent most of the communicable diseases, as shown in Table 9–10. Optimal nutrition, rest, and exercise help the child to build his body's natural resistance to disease. Protection from extreme stress, both physical and mental, prevents the breakdown of the child's own resources for coping with disease. During middle childhood, one of the competencies to be learned is that of self-care, along with some knowledge of basic physiology and nutrition and of how disease organisms operate. Many children receive inadequate care during convalescence from an illness. Certain effects of an illness linger even after the temperature has returned to normal. And some parents do not even realize that the temperature is usually subnormal for a day or so after being elevated. Under the influence of stress, whether it be from infection, trauma, or psychological causes, the body tends to withdraw amino acids from muscles and other tissues and to use them for mobilization to meet the immediate crisis. After the acute part of an illness is over, therefore, the withdrawn materials must be returned to the raided parts of the body and be incorporated into their tissues [56]. This process requires rest and extra nutrients, especially protein. Muscles are likely to be flabby after an illness. Fatigue and poor posture may result if the convalescent child returns to a normal schedule too soon. Appetite is likely to

Table 9–10

A. Diseases controlled in the United States by routine immunizations, in order of initial usage of immunization

| | | | |
|---|---|---|---|
| Smallpox | 1796 | Polio (Sabin) | 1962 |
| Diphtheria | 1923 | Measles | 1964 |
| Whooping cough | 1933 | Mumps | 1968 |
| Tetanus | 1936 | German measles | 1969 |
| Polio (Salk) | 1954 | | |

B. Diseases still prevalent in the United States

| | |
|---|---|
| Chickenpox | Pinworm disease |
| Cold (common) | Pneumonia |
| Gonorrhea | Staphylococcal disease |
| Hepatitis (viral) | Streptococcal disease |
| Influenza | Syphilis |
| Mononucleosis | Tuberculosis |
| Pediculosis | |

Prepared by Lucile Votta, R.N., from Rhode Island State Department of Health, *Recommendations, 1970,* and Franklin Top (Ed.), *Report of the Committee on Infectious Diseases, 1970,* Evanston, Illinois: American Academy of Pediatrics.

decrease. Lowered emotional control tends to go along with diminished vigor. Therefore, it is wise to arrange a gradual return to normal activity after an illness. Some pediatricians suggest that their patients stay in bed one day after the temperature has returned to normal and that they stay home from school the following day.

**Special Health Problems.** Although certain physical conditions are not considered illnesses, they have harmful long-range effects upon children's health. Dental caries is outstanding as this type of problem. (Many people do not consider it a disease, and since it is not incapacitating, it is rarely accorded the status of illness.) One child in four, at the 5 to 14-year range, has never been to a dentist [44]. A national health survey indicated that about half of the children in this age bracket had had no dental care during the preceding year. When children were divided as to family income, it was found that 5 to 14-year-olds, living in families of less than $4000 income, averaged 0.8 dental visits annually, and those in families of income above $4000 went to the dentist 2.4 times. Some progress toward dental health is being made in fluoridation of water supplies and in treating children's teeth with fluoride.

Long-range problems also include nutrition and fitness. Obesity is becoming more frequent among American children, with its prognosis of increasing obesity in adulthood. Obesity involves psychological problems, as well as physical. Fat children are less accurate than normal or thin children in identifying their own body shapes from photographs [17]. This finding suggests either lack of clarity in body image or denial of fatness, or both [38].

While some children are eating too many calories, others are not getting enough. And even more widespread than the problem of insufficient calories is poor quality of diet. Some children are thin and short because of poor quality and some are obese because of eating poor-quality food while having too many calories. Nutrition problems will be discussed further in regard to adolescents.

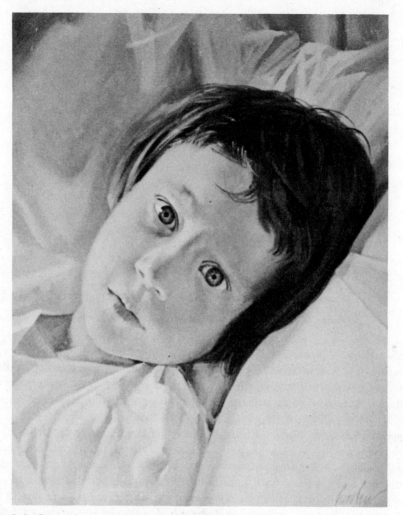

**Figure 9–9.** Stress shows in the face of this ill child.

SOURCE: Reprinted by permission from *Nutrition Today*, 1970, **5**:1.

*Accidents*

Accidental injuries account for about half of the deaths of boys between 5 and 14 and for about one third of the deaths of girls the same age [45]. A comparison of present rates with those of a decade ago shows a substantial decrease in death rate from accidents (about 20 percent). As Table 9–11 shows, motor vehicles are the leading cause of accidental death, killing about twice as many boys as girls. Many of these fatalities occur when children are playing on streets and when they cross streets and highways. Among boys, drowning is second to motor vehicles as a cause of death. About 6700 children die from accidents each year in the United States. The number injured is about 12 million. Nearly one third of the people between 6 and 16 years of age are injured seriously enough to require medical attention or at least one day of restricted activity. About two fifths of the nonfatal injuries occur in or near the home.

As was mentioned in regard to accidents during the preschool years (pages 212–213), certain personality characteristics are typical of children who have many

**Table 9–11** Children's Deaths from Different Types of Accidents

| | Death Rate Per 100,000 | | | | | |
|---|---|---|---|---|---|---|
| | MALES | | | FEMALES | | |
| Type of Accident* | Ages 5–14 | Ages 5–9 | Ages 10–14 | Ages 5–14 | Ages 5–9 | Ages 10–14 |
| All Types | 25.1 | 22.9 | 27.5 | 10.9 | 13.1 | 8.5 |
| Motor vehicle | 10.4 | 10.5 | 10.3 | 5.2 | 6.1 | 4.3 |
| Drowning † | 5.5 | 4.8 | 6.3 | 1.2 | 1.1 | 1.3 |
| Firearm | 1.8 | 0.9 | 2.7 | 0.3 | 0.3 | 0.3 |
| Fire and explosion | 1.7 | 2.2 | 1.1 | 2.3 | 3.5 | 1.0 |
| Falls | 0.8 | 0.8 | 0.9 | 0.3 | 0.3 | 0.2 |

\* According to rank among males.

† Exclusive of deaths in water transportation.

SOURCE: Basic data from Reports of the Division of Vital Statistics, National Center for Health Statistics. Reprinted by permission from *Statistical Bulletin*, Metropolitan Life Insurance Company, September 1964.

accidents. An extensive study [39] on 684 children between 4 and 18 years of age compared groups with high, intermediate, and low accident liability. From school records and interviews with mothers, results showed accident liability to be associated with extraversion, daring, roughhousing, poor discipline, aggressiveness toward peers, impulsivity, carelessness, and unreliability. For girls, attention-seeking was also related to likelihood of accidents.

Oriental (Chinese and Japanese) children in California are injured less frequently than white and black Americans [36]. In traditional Oriental families, children are carefully supervised and sheltered and discouraged from exploration and initiation of activities. It follows logically that Oriental children would be exposed to fewer hazards than would average Americans in the same physical environment. Accident rates depend not only upon the dangers present in the environment but upon the protection offered by adults and also upon the behavior patterns of the child himself.

### Chronic Illnesses and Impairments

Over 2 million children under 14 years of age must live with disabilities which are permanent or of indefinite duration. Figure 9–10 shows how these defects are distributed, with orthopedic defects most frequent, then speech, then hearing and visual defects, in that order [37]. The Children's Bureau, during a year when its crippled children's program gave aid to nearly 340,000 children under 21, reported that congenital malformations accounted for more than a quarter of these patients. About one fifth of the children under care had diseases of the bones and organs of movement. Cerebral palsy accounted for 8 percent, polio 7 percent, eye conditions 6 percent, impaired hearing 7 percent, and impairments from accidents 5 percent [44].

Chronic diseases and long-term disabilities may affect growth adversely. They certainly limit some of the child's activities. Conditions likely to retard growth include chronically infected tonsils and adenoids, intestinal parasites, rheumatic fever, and diabetes [6, pp. 53–56]. Good physical care can alleviate some of these conditions and even in cases where the condition cannot be cured, good care may result in normal growth.

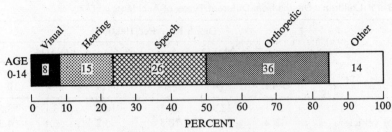

**Figure 9–10.** Frequency of occurrence of various types of impairments and defects in children.

SOURCE: From Chart C on page 19, "Problems of Youth," Legislative Reference Service, U.S. Government Printing Office, Washington, 1964.

## Psychological Effects of Handicaps

The disabled child suffers not only the discomfort of diagnostic and treatment procedures. He also misses out on some of the activities which normal children have as part of everyday life. Requiring more physical care, he actually receives more nurturance from his mother and often from the whole family. He has a narrower social and interpersonal experience. Parents and often teachers give him less work to do, less responsibility to carry [52].

Different types of handicaps, of course, produce different reactions in the children burdened with them and in the social environments in which the children live. For example, when asked to rank five disabilities in order of preference, Jewish children judged confinement to a wheelchair as worse than obesity, and obesity as worse than facial disfigurement [19]. The normative group of children, drawn from a wide selection of environments, ranked obesity as most undesirable, facial disfigurement as next to obesity, and confinement to a wheelchair as the least undesirable of these conditions. Italian children ranked the handicaps in another order. A similar study done on a large number of children in Israel found socio-economic status related to attitude toward disability [7]. Children from poorer neighborhoods considered a physical disability (wheelchair necessary, amputated hand, leg in brace) worse than a cosmetic disability (obesity, facial disfigurement). Children from more prosperous neigborhoods thought the cosmetic handicap was worse than the physical. Thus it can be seen that a child's handicap is interpreted to him according to the particular value system of the people close to him. In studying children's perceptions of other children's handicaps, young children were asked questions about pairs of drawings in which one child was wearing leg braces and the other child was identical except for wearing no braces [30]. Five-year-olds were likely to reject the drawings of the handicapped child, but younger children showed no differences in responses to pictures of handicapped and normal children. While this study does not prove that preschool children are unaware of handicaps in others, it suggests that rejection of handicapped children may be more marked in school-age children than in younger ones.

The specific restrictions required by various handicaps differ from one to another. For example, the dietary requirements for diabetics are very embarrassing to some children, who often try to hide their condition from other children.

Even though there are some specific reactions to handicaps, certain general effects have been found, too. The self concepts of a wide selection of handicapped children were investigated in a summer camp situation, by asking these children and a group of normal children to describe themselves and others [52]. The children's conversations were analyzed into categories, so as to find out which topics were important to them and which, of these topics, were most significant. In general the handicapped children showed realistic facing of life by talking more about "handicap" than did the normal children. The handicapped boys discussed "health" and "physical ability" less, possibly reflecting awareness of the cultural demand that boys should be active and aggressive. "Spatial location" was discussed less by the handicapped, probably because these children had had limited spatial experiences, being unable to move around so freely on their own and not having been taken places by adults as much as normal children are taken. Handicapped girls talked more than normal girls and more than handicapped boys about "giving aid," suggesting the importance to them of receiving aid, as well as the fact that it is easier for girls to accept aid than it is for boys. Comments of the handicapped children indicated that they had fewer interactions with people, with the exception of interactions with mothers. This interpersonal impoverishment probably accounts for their greater use of egocentric comments and expression of self-depreciation and lack of confidence.

As the emotional and developmental situation of the handicapped child becomes understood, it is possible for parents and other adults to help him more effectively. For instance, knowing that handicapped children's spatial experiences are likely to be limited, the adults could plan more carefully to change the child's location and position often and, whenever possible, to take him on expeditions with the rest of the family instead of leaving him home with Mother. Knowing that his feelings of adequacy will be threatened, wise adults will help a handicapped child to develop competencies in the fields where he can operate. The task of broadening his interpersonal contacts is not easy, but constant awareness of it will bring more results than ignoring the matter.

## Motor Coordination

Children's delight in vigorous motor play seems to be universal. Ball games, tag, running, chasing, and jumping games are to be found where children are. The motor skills which a society teaches to its children, however, reflect the values and economic level of that culture.

### The Influence of Cultural Values on Motor Skills

In order to highlight the affluent American culture, consider the Asian society in which many a boy squats at the far end of a loom, assisting a skilled weaver and gradually acquiring his fine coordinations. Other boys do the rough outlining of ivory figures, which men finish and inlay into boxes and tabletops. Little girls struggle to embroider tiny mirrors onto skirts and bags. The aim is excellence in the vocational pursuits of weaving, ivory inlaying, and mirror embroidery. In America, vocational excellence has little place in the motor coordinations which children strive to learn. Their parents' aim is more all-round competence than specialized excellence. In fact, as far as girls are concerned, moderate skill may be preferred to excellence. The bureaucratic, other-directed middle-class society described by social observers of the 1950s [46, 54] would logically try to produce children who could fit into whatever kind of athletic recreation their peers were enjoying. These children would be able to make a fourth at tennis, would know an allemande-left from a right-hand-to-your-partner, and a figure eight from an outside edge, would stick on a horse, and be able to dive neatly from the low board, if not the high board.

Wanting moderate competence in many coordinations, American society offers many organized learning opportunities to children. Rarely do families teach such skills as dancing and swimming. Of 1008 parent–child contacts occurring in the water at two beaches, only 82 were instances of parents instructing children in swimming [60, 61]. (Most of the teaching which did occur was in upper-middle-class rather than lower-middle or lower-class families.) Instead of the informal family instruction of a simpler society, modern arrangements include dancing teachers sponsored by schools, the PTA, or community centers, and swimming teachers hired by the state, community, or club. Standards for teachers are set and controlled by the Red Cross. The water safety manual delineates levels of achievement in swimming and giving children specific goals for various coordinations. By requiring the child to be 12 years old before trying the Junior Lifesaving examination, the Red Cross implies that children under 12 can pass the beginner's, advanced beginner's, and intermediate tests. Thus much of what used to be learned informally, in the way of motor skills, has become formalized, standardized, and, in some instances, commercialized. Children still play, however. And perhaps more self-expression and immediate pleasure is in the trend of the future, with standards of competence in motor performance growing less important to parents. When the youth who have rejected middle-class values become parents of school-age children, we might expect changes in parental hopes and demands.

## Play Activities

The average 6-year-old has acquired the motor skills basic to school-age play. He can throw, bounce, and catch a ball, although he does not do so very smoothly [23]. For many years, he will practice and seek to perfect games which use balls and similar objects for throwing, catching, hitting, bouncing, and carrying. By 6 years of age, a distinct sex difference in ball throwing is easily seen. Boys use a mature pattern of throwing, in which greater power is exerted by changing the weight to the right foot during the preparatory phase and to the left foot during delivery, the left foot having moved forward and the trunk having rotated [12, p. 125]. Girls use a less mature pattern, and some never succeed in pitching overhand.

Able to run and climb well, the child plays games of chase, such as tag and hide-and-seek, his interest in these games increasing steadily from 6 to 9 [62]. Running is basic to skipping, dancing, and skating. Most 6-year-olds can skip and jump rope, and 7-year-olds roller-skate [23]. With these skills, as with ball play, the youngster ventures into new games and coordinations, practicing as he goes in order to achieve competence in a variety of movements. Sometimes he plays follow-the-leader, gaining ideas and courage from a model who knows a little more about the skill than he does. Sometimes he jumps, skates, or bounces by himself, apparently thoroughly enjoying the process of developing motor skills.

The average 9-year-old is interested in a greater variety of play activities than he has been before or will be again [62]. When a group of children between 9 and 10 are asked to check their interests on a large list of activities, everything suggested is

**Table 9–12** Activities Boys Reported Especially Enjoying

| | |
|---|---|
| Bandits | Marbles |
| Bows and arrows | Making model airplanes |
| Boxing | Shooting |
| Building forts | Soldiers |
| Cars | Spacemen |
| Cops and robbers | Throw snowballs |
| Darts | Toy trains |
| Football | Use tools |
| Hunt | Wrestling |

SOURCE: Reprinted by permission from B. G. Rosenberg and B. Sutton-Smith, "A Revised Conception of Masculine-Feminine Differences in Play Activity," *The Journal of Genetic Psychology*, **96**, Table 1, p. 167. Copyright © 1960, The Journal Press.

**Table 9–13** Activities Girls Were Particularly Fond of Playing

| | |
|---|---|
| Blind man's buff | Jacks |
| Building snowmen | Jump rope |
| Cartwheels | Leap frog |
| Clue | London bridges |
| Cooking | Mother, may I |
| Crack the whip | Mulberry bush |
| Dance | Musical chairs |
| Doctors | Name that tune |
| Dolls | Pick up sticks |
| Dressing up | Puzzles |
| Drop the handkerchief | Red rover |
| Farmer in the dell | Ring around the rosy |
| Follow the leader | Scrapbook making |
| Fox and geese | See saw |
| Hide the thimble | Sewing |
| Hopscotch | School |
| Houses | Simon says "thumbs up" |
| Huckle buckle beanstalk | Statues |
| In and out the window | Stoop tag |
| I've got a secret | Store |

SOURCE: Reprinted by permission from B. G. Rosenberg and B. Sutton-Smith, "A Revised Conception of Masculine-Feminine Differences in Play Activity," *The Journal of Genetic Psychology*, **96**, Table 1, p. 167. Copyright © 1960, The Journal Press.

likely to be checked by someone. Tables 9–12, 9–13, and 9–14 represent a partial list of items which 50 percent or more of a group of fourth, fifth, and sixth graders said they liked to do [55]. About 70 percent of these activities are strongly motor, with large muscle coordinations chosen more than four times as often as fine coordinations. Breadth of interest varies from one child to another, some engaging in fewer than ten activities a week and others playing in over 100 different ways [62].

**Table 9–14** Play Activities Enjoyed by Both Boys and Girls

| | | |
|---|---|---|
| Basketball | Tug-o-war | I spy |
| Bowling | Wall dodge ball | Monopoly |
| Cowboys | Clay modeling | Scrabble |
| King of the mountain | Draw or paint | Spin the bottle |
| Racing | Gardening | Tag |
| Soccer | Hide and seek | Tail on the donkey |
| Walk on stilts | Fly kite | Make collections |
| Dominoes | Ghosts | Hiking |
| Shuffleboard | Black magic | Raise pets |
| Baseball | Dodgeball | Stunts in gym |
| Boating | Tiddle di winks | Swimming |
| Fish | Cards | Horses |
| Camping | Checkers | Wood tag |
| Climbing | Pingpong | Kick dodge |
| Ball tag | Horse shoes | Bingo |
| Pool | Tennis | Tic tac toe |
| Post office | Skating | Dog and bone |
| Chess | Horse riding | Volleyball |
| Seven up | Bicycle riding | Roller skating |

SOURCE: Reprinted by permission from B. G. Rosenberg and B. Sutton-Smith, "A Revised Conception of Masculine-Feminine Differences in Play Activity," *The Journal of Genetic Psychology*, 96, Tables 2 and 3, p. 168. Copyright © 1960, The Journal Press.

### Components of Motor Ability

One analysis of the various kinds of motor abilities yields these classes: strength, impulsion, speed, precision coordination, and flexibility [22]. Strength, of course, refers to the amount of force the individual can exert. Impulsion is a measure of the rate at which movements are initiated from stationary positions, whereas speed is the rate of movements which have been begun. Precision is the accuracy with which a position is maintained (static precision) or with which a movement is directed (dynamic precision). Flexibility is freedom to bend and otherwise move the body. These components of motor ability can be studied in relation to different parts of the body, and sometimes in relation to the whole body.

**Strength.** Although strength can be measured in legs, shoulders, and back, or in practically any voluntary muscle, most of the research on increase in strength has been in terms of hand grip. Grip is measured by a dynamometer, an instrument which registers amount of pressure. Measurements of grip strength show a steady increase throughout the school years, boys showing greater strength than girls at each grade level measured (third, sixth, ninth, and twelfth), and Latin American groups being consistently weaker than Anglo American and Afro American. Afro girls were significantly stronger than Latin or Anglo girls at all grade levels [20]. Trunk strength is measured by performance of such exercises as the abdominal pivot (pushing the body around with hands on floor and back arched), push-ups, and leg raising while in sitting position [22]. Limb strength is estimated by dips (squatting and rising), chinning, rope-climbing, and push-ups.

**Impulsion.** Reaction time, or time required to respond to a stimulus, is one measure of impulsion. Reaction time may also be considered a measure of speed. Speed of reaction time increases steadily throughout the school age, with boys reacting slightly faster than girls [18]. Other measures include limb thrust, as shown in jumping, shot-put, short dash, and bar vault. A third measure is tapping, turning small objects, removing, and placing pegs. Girls tend to excel in measures of this type, as shown in a test of making dots alternately in two small circles [9]. Children's speed improved with age between 6 and 9, and at each level, girls were faster than boys.

**Speed.** Speed of movement can be measured for the whole body or for various parts, such as arms, hands, and fingers. Such skills as running and hopping show a steady increase in speed throughout the elementary school years. The gap between the sexes begins to widen at 11 or 12 years of age, after which time boys continue to gain while girls tend to taper off [12, pp. 157–158].

**Precision.** Balance, steadiness, and aiming are all aspects of precision. They are tested by such feats as standing on one foot, walking a line, tracing, threading, jumping and balancing, pursuit aiming, and placing dots in circles. Coordination of the whole body and dexterity of hand and fingers can also be considered as precision.

**Flexibility.** Ease of moving, bending, and stretching contributes to most motor skills. Flexibility is extremely important in dancing and in most sports. Flexibility depends largely on the looseness of the joints and also upon the ease with which the muscles stretch and relax.

### Tests of Motor Ability

Two examples of motor tests will be mentioned here, the Lincoln–Oseretsky Motor Development Scale [59] and the Kraus–Weber Test [35]. Additional tests will be discussed in Chapter 13. The Lincoln–Oseretsky Scale is an individual test for children between 6 and 14 years of age. It consists of 36 items, shown in the sample score sheet reproduced in Table 9–15. The test samples a wide variety of motor skills, including gross bodily coordination, activities of trunk, legs, arms, and hands, finger dexterity, and eye–hand coordination. Although the various components of motor ability, strength, impulsion, speed, precision, and flexibility are all called into play by the various items, no separate scores are given. The child's score is for total or overall level of motor development. By means of percentile tables, the child can be compared with all children his age and with children his age and sex.

The Kraus–Weber Test is concerned with flexibility and strength of large muscles. The test will not delineate the upper limits of strength and flexibility. Rather, it was designed in order "to determine whether or not the individual has sufficient strength and flexibility in parts of the body upon which demands are made in normal daily living." Six simple items make up the Kraus–Weber Test. Each of the six items must be passed in order to pass the test as a whole. No score is given other than passed or failed. The results can, however, be broken down into flexibility and weakness failures.

The Kraus–Weber Test, from which an excerpt is given in Figure 9–11, was given widely throughout Europe and the United States as a measure of physical fitness. Over 4000 American children were compared with Austrian, Italian, and Swiss children. Figure 9–12 shows the incidence of American failures and European failures at all ages from 6 to 16. The European children show up ever so much better than Americans at all ages. What is more, the Americans gave poorer

**Table 9–15** Sample Score Sheet for the Lincoln–Oseretsky Motor Development Scale

| | Description | R-L | Trials Pts. | Notes |
|---|---|---|---|---|
| 1 | Walking backwards, 6 ft. | | 2 | |
| 2 | Crouching on tiptoe | | 2 | |
| 3 | Standing on one foot | R/L | 2/2 | / |
| 4 | Touching nose | | 1 | |
| 5 | Touching fingertips | R/L | 2/2 | / |
| 6 | Tapping rhythmically with feet and fingers | | 1 | |
| 7 | Jumping over a rope | | 1 | |
| 8 | Finger movement | | 3 | |
| 9 | Standing heel to toe | | 2 | |
| 10 | Close and open hands alternately | | 3 | |
| 11 | Making dots | | 2 | |
| 12 | Catching a ball | R/L | 5/5 | / |
| 13 | Making a ball | R/L | 2/2 | / |
| 14 | Winding thread | R/L | 1/1 | / |
| 15 | Balancing a rod crosswise | R/L | 3/3 | / |
| 16 | Describing circles in the air | | 1 | |
| 17 | Tapping (15″) | R/L | 2/2 | / |
| 18 | Placing coins and matchsticks | | 1 | |
| 19 | Jump and turn about | | 1 | |
| 20 | Putting matchsticks in a box | | 1 | |
| 21 | Winding thread while walking | R/L | 1/1 | / |
| 22 | Throwing a ball | R/L | 5/5 | / |
| 23 | Sorting matchsticks | R/L | 1/1 | / |
| 24 | Drawing lines | R/L | 2/2 | / |
| 25 | Cutting a circle | R/L | 1/1 | / |
| 26 | Putting coins in box (15″) | R/L | 1/1 | / |
| 27 | Tracing mazes | R/L | 1/1 | / |
| 28 | Balancing on tiptoe | | 1 | |
| 29 | Tapping with feet and fingers | | 1 | |
| 30 | Jump, touch heels | | 1 | |
| 31 | Tap feet and describe circles | | 1 | |
| 32 | Stand on one foot | R/L | 1/1 | / |
| 33 | Jumping and clapping | | 1 | |
| 34 | Balancing on tiptoe | R/L | 1/1 | / |
| 35 | Opening and closing hands | | 1 | |
| 36 | Balancing a rod vertically | R/L | 3/3 | / |

SOURCE: Reprinted by permission from William Sloan, "The Lincoln–Oseretsky Motor Development Scale," *Genetic Psychology Monographs*, **51**, Table 5, p. 247. Copyright © 1955, The Journal Press.

performances as they advanced in age. The authors attributed the difference in Americans and Europeans to the mechanization of life in America, especially to riding in cars instead of walking. The reports on Kraus–Weber findings stirred up considerable interest in "fitness," even in the White House. Television programs, community recreation and fitness programs, and PTA's rose to the challenge. There has not been complete agreement as to the meaning of "fitness" and as to how serious a matter it was that American children and youth were outclassed by Europeans on the Kraus–Weber Test. Some constructive steps have been taken to improve American youth. These are described in Chapter 13.

## Kraus-Weber Tests for Muscular Fitness
*(There should not be any warm-up prior to taking the tests.)*

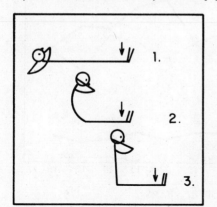

**TEST 1.**

*Purpose:* Tests the strength of the abdominals and psoas.

*Designation:* "Abdominals plus psoas" or A+.

*Position of Person Being Tested:* Lying supine, hands behind neck. The examiner holds his feet down on the table.

*Command:* "Keep your hands behind your neck and *try to roll up* into a sitting position."

*Precaution:* If the person being tested is unable to perform this movement at first try, it may be because he has not understood the directions. Help him a little and then let him try again. Watch for a "stiff back sit-up." This may indicate that either he has not understood you and needs a further explanation with emphasis on "rolling up," or that he has *very* poor abdominals and is doing most of the work with his psoas.

Watch also for a twist of the upper body as he sits up. This may be due to unequal development of the back muscles.

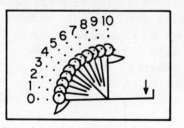

*Marking:* If the person being tested cannot raise his shoulders from the table, the mark is *0*. If unaided, he is able to reach a sitting position, the mark is *10*. If the examiner must help him halfway to the sitting position, the mark would be *5*. The distance from supine to sitting is marked from *0* to *10*.

**TEST 2.**

*Purpose:* Further test for abdominals.

*Designation:* "Abdominals minus psoas" or *A*−.

*Position of Person Being Tested:* Lying supine, hands behind neck and knees bent. Examiner holds his feet down on the table.

*Command:* "Keep your hands behind your neck and *try to roll up* into a sitting position."

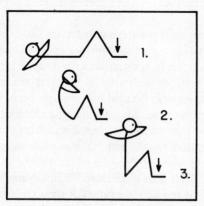

*Precaution:* The precautions are the same as for Test 1.

**Figure 9–11.** Two items from the Kraus–Weber Test are given here to illustrate how the tests for muscle strength and flexibility were conducted.

SOURCE: Reprinted by permission from H. Kraus and R. P. Hirschland, "Minimum Muscular Fitness Tests in School Children," *Research Quarterly*, **25**, 178–185. Copyright © 1954, American Association for Health, Physical Education, and Recreation, Washington, D.C.

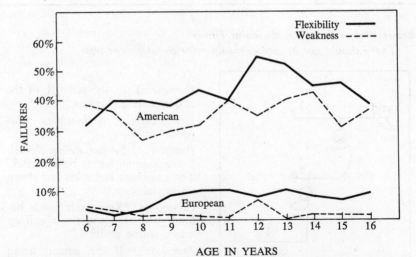

**Figure 9–12.** American children and youth compared with their European age-mates on tests of strength and flexibility, showing many more failures among Americans.

SOURCE: Reprinted by permission from H. Kraus and R. P. Hirschland, "Minimum Muscular Fitness Tests in School Children," *Research Quarterly*, **25**, 178–185. Copyright © 1954, American Association for Health, Physical Education, and Recreation, Washington, D.C.

## Motor Problems

When a child enters school, the ability to sit down and keep still becomes important. From a practical point of view, it is a great help to the teacher if her pupils can inhibit motor activity sufficiently for her to maintain a quiet, orderly classroom, where she can be heard by all. There has been some difference of opinion on how much physical immobility matters for the child's learning his lessons, some teachers maintaining that children can accomplish more while quiet, others believing that bodily activity is an aid to learning, even though inconvenient for the teacher. When normal second grade boys were given tests of impulse control and conceptual thinking, a low correlation was found between impulse control and cognitive level [32].

Relationships between motor inhibition and intellectual behavior have been explored in studies of cognitive style, which will be discussed further in the following chapter. It seems worth mentioning these studies in connection with motor control, also, since a relationship has been found between ability to be still and tendency to form analytic concepts [31]. When children were divided into groups, according to the type of concepts which they formed most readily, the analytic children, as compared with nonanalytic, tended to be less impulsive, less distractible, more able to concentrate, and more able to inhibit motor acts. Observation suggests that more boys than girls show extremes of motor behavior, including impulsive, disorganized outbursts. In another study adult men were rated for involvement in intellectual mastery [31, p. 109]. An analysis (by another rater) of their childhood records showed that inability to inhibit motor activity during the childhood years was predictive of future avoidance of intellectual activities. Further corroboration came from the ratings on attention span of 46 fourth grade children. For boys, but not for girls, an analytic conceptual style was correlated with attention span. Thus childhood motor control was shown to be related to analytic conceptualization in childhood and intellectual involvement in manhood.

It is not certain that motor inhibition is basic to the analytic attitude; it may be that the analytic person inhibits motor activity more easily or that both conditions have a common source. Among kindergarten boys and girls, reflective and impulsive children were compared for their reactions to self-given commands [41]. Tested for inhibiting movement to the self-command "don't push," there was little or no difference between impulsives and reflectives when "don't push" was said aloud. When the self-command was said silently to himself, however, the impulsive child was more likely to push than was the reflective. Thus, at least at kindergarten age, reflective children showed greater inhibition under covert self-direction. Restless, impulsive children are often helped by a routine which gives legitimate opportunities for frequent moving around, combined with calm, firm reminders to reflect before answering. An experiment with hyperactive 9-year-old boys was successful in reducing their distractibility and impulsiveness on maze tests [48]. The boys were trained to give themselves verbal commands, such as *stop, listen, look*, and *think*, before beginning tasks and answering them. A successful physical educator [10] helps hyperactive children by providing a distraction-free setting with learning experiences that are stimulating and interesting, encouraging relative immobility. When normal fifth and sixth graders were given an excellent, broad program in physical education, their *academic* achievement was significantly better than that of controls who had only free play for exercise [27].

**Gestures Inappropriate for Sex Role.** In the previous chapter, it was mentioned that preschool children reinforce each other for sex-appropriate behavior, as shown by taking part in activities and playing with toys preferred by one sex or the other. Physical educators have found that boys who have problems with sex typing often adopt feminine gesture patterns [10, pp. 121–122]. Peers tend to reject such boys, consistent with the facts that boys reinforce boys, and boys reinforce for masculine behavior. Boys with feminine gestures can be taught quite readily to move in masculine ways, thus discarding patterns which irritate their peers and their parents. However, such treatment of symptoms may not be sufficient for coping with the basic problem, which usually lies in the child's relationships with his parents.

**Laterality.** Preference for one hand, foot, eye, or other organ over its opposite, as well as discrimination between right and left sides, all are aspects of laterality or sidedness. Thus laterality is not basically a problem, but it may become one. Left-handedness can be a severe handicap or it may not be. Confusion between left and right can also make trouble for a child.

The topic of hand preference was considered in Chapter 5, in terms of its establishment during the first years of life. During the elementary school years, a practical question concerns the changing of a preference already established. Since research possibilities are greater with older children, more data have been collected on school-age children and more is known about the relation of handedness to other questions concerning right and left. Laterality, or sidedness, includes all of the body, feet and eyes as well as hands. Laterality includes the individual's uses, preferences, and orientations to his own body and to left and right in other people, objects, and situations. Cultures define laterality through language and customs. For example, consider the implications in the Latin words *sinister* and *dexter* for left and right, the French *gauche*, which means awkward, and the fact that both English and German use the word *right* to refer to hand and to being correct. The custom of shaking hands is rigidly prescribed as for the right hand. A child

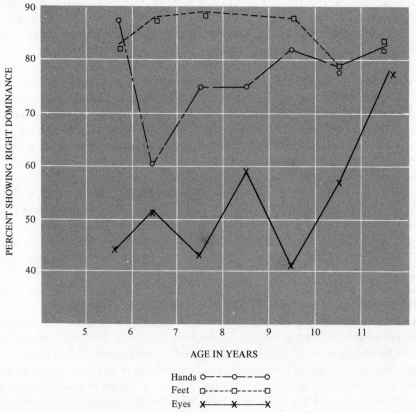

**Figure 9–13.** Percentage of children with established right lateral dominance in hands, eyes, and feet.

SOURCE: L. Belmont and H. G. Birch, "Lateral Dominance, Lateral Awareness and Reading Disability." *Child Development*, 1965, **36**, 57–71.

grows up, therefore, with all sorts of meanings, implications, restrictions, and requirements attached to right and left.

Laterality in schoolchildren has been studied in terms of hands, eyes, and feet [1]. Preferences were determined by asking the child to show how he would throw a ball, turn a doorknob, cut with scissors, and write with a pencil. Eye preference was tested by asking the child to look through a kaleidoscope, sight a rifle, and look at the examiner through a hole in a paper. Foot preference was determined by noting which foot was used for kicking, estimating which foot kicked more skillfully. Figure 9–13 shows lateral preferences for hands, eyes, and feet at each year of age from 5 through 11. In each area, some children made mixed choices, showing that preference was not definitely established. Mixed preferences occurred more often at the younger ages, showing that the development trend toward laterality (mentioned in the discussion of preschool handedness) continues through the elementary school years. The table also shows that lateral preference was stronger for feet than for hands and weakest for eyes. Twenty-six percent of the children showed no clear-cut preference for eyes, whereas 14 percent showed none for hands, and only 4 percent for feet. About half the children were consistent in lateral preferences, and the others showed either crossed or mixed preferences. With increasing age, there was increasing use of the hand and eye on the same side.

Awareness of right and left also increased with age. The children were tested to see when they knew right and left on their own body parts. All questions were answered correctly by 70 percent of 5-year-olds, by 68 percent at 6, 89 percent at 7, 95 percent at 8, 94 percent at 10, and 100 percent at 11. Right–left awareness of own body is achieved about two years before hand preference is established. The authors suggest that the functions of lateral awareness and lateral preference are not closely related to each other.

The ability to make right–left discriminations in regard to the self develops before the ability to do so in regard to other persons and objects. The latter ability begins around 5 years of age and is well developed by 10 [4]. The ability to imitate a model while facing him is more complicated than merely telling right from left, although it includes right–left discrimination. It also involves transposing both the hand and the object acted upon. Success in such a test probably requires taking the other person's point of view and representing to oneself the way objects look and the way the body feels from within the other person. This ability has been found, through a series of tests, to increase with age from 8 to 18 years. Transposition responses increased most markedly between 12 and 14 years of age [67].

Further study on the question of lateral dominance, lateral awareness and reading difficulties has been done with 200 boys selected from the total number of 9- and 10-year-old boys in school in one community [2]. One hundred and fifty of these boys were the poorest readers in the age group, the others serving as a control group. Neither left-handedness nor mixed-handedness was found to be related to poor reading, but a definite relationship was found between left–right awareness and reading. Boys who were confused in identifying their own left and right body parts were more likely to be poor readers than boys who showed normal left–right awareness. Another investigation found a relationship between reading and directional awareness in the first grade but not in the fourth grade [8].

Laterality is also related to electrochemical processes in the body. During childhood, the right hand tends to show a higher galvanic skin response (conducts electricity better) than the left [13]. Boys below 11 years of age showed greater sensitivity to touch in the dominant thumb, as contrasted with the opposite thumb. Another group of children were classified by the number of errors they made in localizing their fingers which had been touched without the subjects being able to see them [51]. At age 10, children with a predominance of errors in locating fingers on the right hand were poorer readers than those who made more errors on the left hand. Six-year-olds showed no relation between reading and finger location errors. Therefore it seems that the source of finger location errors is related to the development or proficiency in reading but not to acquisition or beginning skills in reading.

The effects of forced lateral conversion have been studied by an ingenious method which keeps heredity factors constant while exploring results of differences in experience [70]. In Italy, left-handedness incurs considerable disapproval, and left-handed children are forced to write with the right hand, while in the United States, such coercion is not generally practiced. Left-handed children were selected by testing in Italy and in Italian American populations in Boston. They were compared with right-handed children and with each other. Boston children showed no significant personality differences between right-handed and left-handed groups but Italians were different from one another and from the Boston children. Left-handed

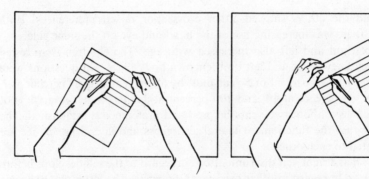

**Figure 9–14.** Recommended writing positions for left-handed and right-handed children.
SOURCE: Reprinted by permission from G. Hildreth, "The Development and Training of Hand Dominance: I. Characteristics of Handedness," *Journal of Genetic Psychology*, **75**, 197–220. Copyright © 1949, The Journal Press.

Italians were more demanding, impatient, subjective, dependent, and hypochondriacal. These characteristics indicate hypersensitivity and heightened self-preoccupation. The results of this research suggest that for healthy personality development it is best not to interfere with a definitely established preference for the left hand.

Left-handed children often need help in arranging the environment. A survey of practices of 19 commercial systems of handwriting gives a summary of present-day techniques for teaching the left-handed children to write [26]. The companies were concerned most with the position of the paper and the position of the arm, hand, and writing instrument. Figure 9–14 shows the recommended positions for left-handed and right-handed children. The left-handed child was thought to profit from help in assuming a certain position at the blackboard and a position while seated. A special kind of pencil has been designed for the purpose of letting the left-handed child see a word as he is writing it. Ordinarily, his hand tends to cover the word as he is writing, thus preventing visual feedback. An experimental group of left-handed children showed significant improvements in spelling when using this pencil, largely due to correcting reversals and omissions [65].

The left-handed child can use adult help in other situations, too, although probably none is so important as that of writing. He can be placed at the dinner table in such a way that his hand preference will not interfere with other people. He will need certain kinds of special equipment, such as left-handed scissors. If adults accept his special laterality casually, he will most likely avoid being embarrassed over it himself and hence will be less inclined to be awkward. Advantages can be appreciated, too, such as those accruing on the baseball diamond and tennis court.

## Summary

Growth is relatively slow during middle childhood. Wide individual differences exist at the end of the elementary school period, however, since the onset of the pubescent growth spurt occurs then in some children and not in others. Boys are, on the average, slightly taller and heavier than girls, except for the years from 11 to 13, when girls are bigger because of being farther along in the pubescent growth spurt. Height increases more steadily than weight, since weight is more responsive to environmental changes.

The largest children in the world live in the most prosperous countries. The largest group is 23 centimeters taller and 10 kilograms heavier than the smallest. In prosperous countries there has been a recent decrease or even termination of the trend for children to grow bigger in each successive generation.

School-age children's bodily proportions contribute to their growing grace and agility. Facial proportions change, too, with the lower portion of the face growing more rapidly than the upper part. Different stages of bodily maturity can be distinguished during the middle years.

Certain aspects of physiological and anatomical maturing are especially significant. Fat decreases and changes somewhat in its distribution pattern. Muscles, although more firmly connected than in the preschool child, are still immature and easily strained. The digestive system is less prone to upsets than in a younger child. In relation to the size of the stomach, calorie needs are small. Bladder capacity varies, girls having a greater average capacity than boys. Respiration becomes slower and deeper. The heart is small in relation to the rest of the body. Growth of the face results in a change in the orientation of the Eustachian tube, which becomes more resistant to invasion by disease organisms. Visual defects increase throughout the school years. The skeleton matures, replacing cartilage with bone. As revealed by X rays, the skeleton is a useful maturity indicator. The baby teeth are replaced by permanent teeth, and additional permanent teeth erupt, the jaw growing to accommodate them.

Although child health has improved in the United States, children continue to face many health problems here and throughout the world. As is true during the preschool years, respiratory disturbances are the most frequent type of illness. The communicable diseases have declined in seriousness and incidence, due largely to immunization. Illness is prevented also by good nutrition, rest, exercise, protection from physical and mental stress, and cleanliness. Health is promoted also by good convalescent care and by teaching children principles and practices of self-care. Special health problems include dental caries and malnutrition, both of which are related to poverty.

Accidents are an important cause of death and injury of children, affecting more boys than girls. Chronic illnesses or impairments affect over 2 million children under 14. Growth is sometimes but not always adversely affected by chronic diseases and long-term disabilities. Certain activities are limited, resulting in handicapped children growing up in environments which differ significantly from those of normal children. Psychological effects of handicaps vary with the type of handicap and with the cultural and family environment of the child.

Many kinds of vigorous motor play, such as ball games, running, chasing, and jumping, are almost universal. Special motor skills reflect the values of the culture in which the child grows up. American parents tend to want their children to be moderately competent in many areas, often turning to experts for instruction for their children. School-age children build upon the basic motor skills learned in preschool years, practicing diligently and achieving a variety of competencies and interests.

The components of motor ability include strength, impulsion, speed, precision coordination, and flexibility. Various tests can be employed to measure these components, either as overall characteristics or as characteristics of certain parts of the body. General motor ability can be measured by a test which places the child in relation to other children his age. A test which measures flexibility and strength, used to compare Americans with Europeans, indicated that American children are inferior in these aspects of motor coordination. The ability to inhibit movement is important for getting along well in school. Impulsive movement is related to style of thinking.

Laterality includes preference for using one hand rather than the other, preference for one eye or for one foot. Cultures define laterality as right or wrong, good or bad, acceptable or not. Certain functions are reserved for one hand or the other. The child who does not fit into such rules and customs is handicapped, both through the attitudes of other people and because tools and arrangements are awkward for him. With some children, the nonpreferred hand can be brought into dominant use, often without noticeable harmful effects. When the child persists in using the unconventional hand, he needs special help in writing and other manual skills. Reading difficulties seem to be associated more with left–right confusion than with lateral dominance.

## References

1. Belmont, L., & Birch, H. G. Lateral dominance and right–left awareness in normal children. *Child Devel.*, 1963, **34**, 257–270.
2. Belmont, L., & Birch, H. G. Lateral dominance, lateral awareness and reading disability. *Child Devel.*, 1965, **36**, 57–71.
3. Benenson, A. S. (Ed.). *Control of communicable diseases in man* (11th ed.), New York: American Public Health Association, 1970.
4. Boone, D., & Prescott, T. Development of left–right discrimination in normal children. *Percept. Motor Skills*, 1968, **26**, 267–274.
5. Breckenridge, M. E., & Murphy, M. N. *Growth and development of the young child* (8th ed.). Philadelphia: Saunders, 1969.
6. Breckenridge, M. E., & Vincent, E. L. *Child development* (5th ed.). Philadelphia: Saunders, 1965.
7. Chigier, E., & Chigier, M. Attitudes to disability of children in the multi-cultural society of Israel. *J. Health Soc. Behavior*, 1968, **9**, 310–317.
8. Cohen, A., & Glass, G. C. Lateral dominance and reading ability. *Reading Teacher*, 1968, **21**, 343–348.
9. Connolly, K., Brown, K., & Bassett, E. Developmental changes in some components of a motor skill. *Brit. J. Psychol.*, 1968, **59**, 305–314.
10. Cratty, B. J. *Perceptual-motor behavior and educational processes*. Springfield, Ill.: Charles C Thomas, 1969.
11. Eichorn, D. H. Biological correlates of behavior. In H. W. Stevenson (Ed.), *Child psychology*. The Sixty-second Yearbook of the National Society for the Study of Education, Part I. Chicago: University of Chicago, 1963, pp. 4–61.
12. Espenschade, A. S., & Eckert, H. M. *Motor development*. Columbus: Charles E. Merrill, 1967.
13. Fisher, S. Developmental sex differences in right–left perceptual directionality. *Child Devel.*, 1962, **33**, 463–468.
14. Flory, C. D. Osseous development in the hand as an index of skeletal development. *Mono. Soc. Res. Child Devel.*, 1936, **1**:3.
15. Garn, S. M. Fat weight and fat placement in the female. *Science*, 1957, **125**, 1091.

16. Garn, S. M. Body size and its implications. In L. W. Hoffman & M. L. Hoffman (Eds.), *Review of child development research. Vol. 2* New York: Russell Sage Foundation, 1966, pp. 529–561.

17. Gellert, E., & Girgus, J. S. Children's awareness of their bodily appearance: A developmental study of factors associated with the body percept. New York: Hunter College 1970. (Mimeo).

18. Goodenough, F. L. The development of the reactive process from early childhood to maturity. *J. Exper. Psychol.*, 1935, **18**, 431–450.

19. Goodman, N., Richardson, S. A., Dornbusch, S. M., & Hastorf, A. H. Variant reactions to physical disabilities. *Am. Sociol. Rev.*, 1963, **28**, 429–435.

20. Goss, A. M. Estimated versus actual physical strength in three ethnic groups. *Child Devel.*, 1968, **39**, 283–291.

21. Greulich, W. W., & Pyle, S. I. *Radiographic atlas of skeletal development of the hand and wrist* (2nd ed.). Stanford, Calif.: Stanford University Press, 1959.

22. Guilford, J. P. A system of the psychomotor abilities. *Am. J. Psychol.*, 1958, **71**, 164–174.

23. Gutteridge, M. V. A study of motor achievements of young children. *Arch. Psychol.* 1939, No. 244.

24. Guzmán, M. A. Impaired growth and maturation in malnourished populations. In N. S. Scrimshaw & J. R. Gordon (Eds.), *Malnutrition, learning and behavior*. Cambridge, Mass.: M.I.T. Press, 1968, pp. 42–54.

25. Harmon, D. B. Some preliminary observations on the developmental problems of 160,000 elementary school children. *Woman's Medic. J.*, 1942, **49**, 75–82. Cited in Breckenridge & Vincent [6].

26. Herrick, V. E. *Comparison of practices in handwriting advocated by nineteen commercial systems of handwriting instruction*. Madison: Committee on Research in Basic Skills, University of Wisconsin, 1960. (Mimeo.)

27. Ismail, A. H., & Gruber, J. J. *Integrated development: Motor aptitude and intellectual performance*. Columbus, Ohio: Merrill, 1967.

28. Jackson, R. L. Effect of malnutrition on growth of the preschool child. In National Research Council. *Pre-school child malnutrition*, Washington, D.C., National Academy of Sciences, 1966, pp. 9–21.

29. Johnson, W., & Fretz, B. Changes in perceptual-motor skills after a children's physical developmental program. *Percept. Motor Skills*, 1967, **24**, 610.

30. Jones, R. L., & Sisk, D. A. Early perception of orthopedic disability. *Exceptional Children*, 1967, **34**, 42–43.

31. Kagan, J., Moss, H. A., & Sigel, I. E. Psychological significance of styles of conceptualization. In J. C. Wright & J. Kagan (Eds.), Basic cognitive processes in children. *Mono. Soc. Res. Child Devel.*, 1963, **28**:2, 73–111.

32. Kahana, B., & Kahana, E. Roles of delay of gratification and motor control in the attainment of conceptual thought. *Proceedings, 78th Annual Convention, Am. Psychol. Assoc.*, 1970, 287–288.

33. Kidd, A. H., & Kidd, R. M. The development of auditory perception in children. In A. H. Kidd & J. L. Rivoire (Eds.), *Perceptual development in children*. New York: International Universities Press, 1966, pp. 113–142.

34. Knox, C., & Kimura, D. Cerebral processing of nonverbal sounds in boys and girls. *Neurophyschologia*, 1970, **8**, 227–237.

35. Kraus, H., & Hirschland, R. P. Minimum muscular fitness tests in school children. *Res. Quart.*, 1954, **25**, 178–185.

36. Kurokawa, M. Acculturation and childhood accidents among Chinese and Japanese Americans. *Genet. Psychol. Mono.*, 1969, **79**, 89–159.

37. Legislative Reference Service. *Problems of youth.* Washington, D.C.: U.S. Govt. Printing Office, 1964.

38. Lerner, R. M., & Gellert, E. Body build identification, preference, and aversion in children. *Devel. Psychol.*, 1969, **1**, 456–462.

39. Manheimer, D. I., & Mellinger, G. D. Personality characteristics of the child accident repeater. *Child Devel.*, 1967, **38**, 491–513.

40. Medinnus, G. R., & Robinson, R. Maturity as a predictor of school achievement. Paper presented at the meeting of the Society for Research in Child Development, Santa Monica, Calif., March 29, 1969.

41. Meichenbaum, D., & Goodman, J. Reflection-impulsivity and verbal control of motor behavior. *Child Devel.*, 1969, **40**, 785–797.

42. Meredith, H. V. Change in the stature and body weight of North American boys during the past 80 years. In L. Lipsitt & C. Spiker (Eds.), *Advances in child development and behavior.* Vol. 1. New York: Academic, 1963, pp. 69–114.

43. Meredith, H. V. Body size of contemporary groups of eight-year-old children studied in different parts of the world. *Mono. Soc. Res. Child Devel.*, 1969, **34**:1.

44. Metropolitan Life Insurance Company. Health of the school-age population. *Stat. Bull.*, 1961, **42**:8, 1–3.

45. Metropolitan Life Insurance Company. Accident hazards of school-age children. *Stat. Bull.*, 1964, **45**:9, 3–5.

46. Miller, D. R., & Swanson, G. E. *The changing American parent.* New York: Wiley, 1958.

47. *New York Times. Japanese taller as diet improves.* May 25, 1969.

48. Palkes, H., Stewart, M., & Kahana, B. Porteus maze performance of hyperactive boys after training in self-directed verbal commands. *Child Devel.*, 1968, **39**, 817–826.

49. Penfield, W. The uncommitted cortex, the child's changing brain. *Atlantic*, 1964, **214**(1), 77–81.

50. Rauh, J. L., Schumsky, D. A., & Witt, M. T. Heights, weights and obesity in urban school children. *Child Devel.*, 1967, **38**, 515–530.

51. Reed, J. C. Lateralized finger agnosia and reading achievement at ages 6 and 10. *Child Devel.*, 1967, **38**, 213–220.

52. Richardson, S. A., Hastorf, A. H., & Dornbusch, S. M. Effects of physical disability on a child's description of himself. *Child Devel.*, 1964, **35**, 893–907.

53. Richardson, S. A., & Royce, J. Race and physical handicap in children's preference for other children. *Child Devel.*, 1968, **39**, 467–480.

54. Riesman, D., Glazer, N., & Denny, R. *The lonely crowd.* New Haven: Yale University Press, 1950.

55. Rosenberg, B. G., & Sutton-Smith, B. A revised conception of masculine–feminine differences in play activities. *J. Genet. Psychol.*, 1960, **96**, 165–170.

56. Scrimshaw, N. S. The effect of the interaction of nutrition and infection on the preschool child. In National Research Council, *Pre-school and malnutrition.* Washington, D.C.: National Academy of Sciences, 1966, pp. 63–73.

57. Shapiro, S., Schlesinger, E. R., & Nesbitt, E. L. *Infant, perinatal and childhood mortality in the United States.* Cambridge, Mass.: Harvard University Press, 1968.

58. Simon, M. D. Body configuration and school readiness. *Child Devel.*, 1959, **30**, 493–512.
59. Sloan, W. The Lincoln–Oseretsky motor development scale. *Genet. Psychol. Mono.*, 1955, **51**, 183–251.
60. Smart, S. S. Personal communication, 1964.
61. Smart, S. S. Social class differences in parent behavior in a natural setting. *J. Marr. Fam.*, 1964, **26**, 223–224.
62. Strang, R. *An introduction to child study* (4th ed.). New York: Macmillan, 1959.
63. Tanner, J. M. *Growth at adolescence* (2nd ed.). Oxford: Blackwell, 1962.
64. Tanner, J. M. Earlier maturation in man. *Sci. Am.*, 1968, **218**(1), 21–27.
65. Ure, D. Spelling performance of left-handed school children as affected by the use of a pencil modified to increase visual feedback. *J. Exper. Child Psychol.*, 1969, **7**, 220–230.
66. Valadian, I., Stuart, H. C., & Reed, R. B. Studies of illnesses of children followed from birth to eighteen years. *Mono. Soc. Res. Child Devel.*, 1961, **26**:3.
67. Wapner, S., & Cirillo, L. Imitation of a model's hand movements: Age changes in transposition of left–right relations. *Child Devel.*, 1968, **39**, 887–894.
68. Watson, E. H., & Lowrey, G. H. *Growth and development of children* (5th ed.). Chicago: Year Book, 1967.
69. Whipple, D. V. *Dynamics of development: Euthenic pediatrics.* New York: McGraw-Hill, 1966.
70. Young, H. B., & Knapp, R. P. Personality characteristics of converted left handers. *Percept. Motor Skills*, 1966, **23**, 35–40.

# Chapter 10

Courtesy Education Development Center

# Intellectual Development

The central problem of the school age, the development of the sense of industry, requires the child to solve intellectual problems and to develop intellectual skills, along with the motor coordinations and social skills which also contribute to his adequacy. As Chapter 6 showed, intellectual development proceeds through growth in three main modes: thinking, imagination, and language. These three activities are intimately related and dependent on one another.

383

## Characteristics of Thinking During Middle Childhood

As was true during the preschool period, an important part of cognition is the taking in of information and processing it into meaningful and useful form. Information and experience are stored as memories, to be tapped when needed. When memories are in the form of words, they are likely to be more easily available. The outstanding cognitive developments during this period are increased freedom and control in thinking and increased understanding of relationships between events and/or symbols. The child takes satisfaction in his feeling that there exists a systematic, productive way of thinking about experience and in his conviction that he can think thus [42, p. 139].

### Flexibility of Thought

While the preschool child reacts rather promptly to his perceptions of the moment, the school-age child can delay his response while he takes several aspects of the situation into account. His thoughts range back and forth in various directions, dealing with more than one perception at a time, comparing them, considering them in relation to past experience and knowledge. Thus he shows more control, as well as flexibility. With his increasing store of memories, his past becomes more and more useful for evaluating and interpreting the present. The preschool child is egocentric or centered in his thinking, limited in such a way that he cannot consider and weigh several pertinent factors at one time; the school-age child is less egocentric or more decentered in his thinking. Another aspect of the immobility of preschool thinking is that the child is centered on his own point of view. With his growing flexibility of thought, the older child can look at situations from the points of view of other people.

The child's increasing mobility of thought enters into everything that he does: his classifying, ordering, and dealing with numbers, his language, his social relationships, and self concepts. His thinking is limited in flexibility, however. He tends to think about concrete things rather than about abstractions.

Reversibility is one aspect of the flexible and controlled thinking which emerges during middle childhood. Reversibility has two meanings, both of which apply. First, the child can think an act and then think it undone. He can think himself partway through a sequence of action, return to the first of it, and then start out in another direction. In contrast to thoughts, motor acts and perceptions are irreversible, since they cannot be undone. Reversibility is one of the most important differences between thought and action. When the child can try out different courses of action mentally, instead of having to touch and see in order to believe, he has the advantage of a quicker and more powerful control over his environment and himself.

The second meaning of reversibility is that any operation can be canceled by an opposite operation. For example, the operation of subtracting 3 from 5 is canceled by the operation of adding 3 to 2. $5 - 3 = 2$ is canceled by $2 + 3 = 5$. Another example is this: all children minus all girls equals all boys; all boys plus all girls equals all children. Also: hemisphere minus torrid zone minus frigid zone equals temperate zone; temperate zone plus frigid zone plus torrid zone equals hemisphere. The child learns that there are certain kinds of things which can be taken apart and put back together again into their original form and that he can do this dissembling and reassembling in his thoughts.

## Concrete Operations

The name that Piaget gives to the stage of cognition which lasts from about 7 to 11 is the period of concrete operations. At this time, the child understands and uses certain principles of relationships between things and ideas. In this understanding and using, he operates on (does something to) objects, ideas, and symbols. As was true in infancy, "to know an object is to act on it" [44, p. 8]. But now the action is interiorized. The child adds and subtracts. He classifies and orders. He applies rules to social situations. Each operation fits into a system, and the systems fit together. The operation two-plus-two-equals-four fits into a system of addition, which is part of a system of arithmetic.

The infant's cognitive behavior is sensorimotor, concerned with simple adjustments to the immediate present, symbolic behavior being completely absent. The preschool child begins to use symbols in some kinds of representational thought. Beginning at around 7 years, children can use symbols consistently to perform acts of cognition which are abstracted and freed from complete dependence on sensory stimulation. In this stage of concrete operations, the child mentally performs acts which he formerly really carried out physically. The adolescent can think in more abstract terms than the child, however. During the years between 7 and 11, the child makes great strides in understanding principles of relationships and in his use of symbols for manipulating or operating on experience. Developing certain logical rules in dealing with his experiences, he performs two important operations: classifying and ordering.

**Classifying.** Although children in the preoperational period are dominated by their immediate perceptions in their grouping of objects, children in the stage of concrete operations can reflect upon and choose the qualities by which they group. From the experience of picking out a group of objects with something in common, the child internalizes (creates a mental structure of) the common quality into a concept of a class. Strolling along the beach, he collects small, hard objects into his pail, squats down and sorts them into a pile of shells and a pile of stones. From these activities, he comes to think of shells and of stones. He builds a concept *shell* and a concept *stone*. From more experiences on the beach, he can build concepts of bivalves and univalves, of clams and scallops, of marine life and terrestrial life. An important aspect of his understanding of classes is that he can also think of subclasses. Suppose our shell collector, in the stage of concrete operations, has his bivalves sorted into a pile of six scallop shells and ten clam shells. Ask him, "Do you have more clam shells or more shells?" He will know that he has more shells. His preschool brother, however, who knows full well the difference between clams and scallops, will most likely answer, "More clam shells." The younger child cannot compare a part with the whole which includes the part; the older child can. When the younger child thinks of the clam shells (the subclass), it seems as though he takes them out of the shells (the class), leaving the scallop shells (the other subclass), with which he then compares the clam shells. It has been found that if a child who is close to the maturity necessary for solving a class inclusion problem is presented with it verbally, he is more likely to succeed than if he has a visual presentation [72]. For example, a verbal presentation was "Suppose I had six jackets and two hats. Would I have more jackets or more things to wear?" The corresponding visual presentation shows six jackets with two hats. The younger child, seeing the pictures, tends to compare hats with jackets instead of jackets with the total number of objects. When the strong influence of perception is removed, it

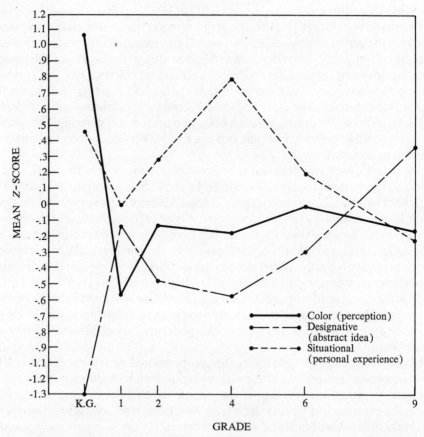

**Figure 10–1.** Age changes in the use of three different bases for classifying objects. Younger children use personal experience and perception more and abstract ideas less than older children.

SOURCE: Adapted from A. E. Goldman and M. Levine, "A Developmental Study of Object Sorting," *Child Development*, **34**, 649–666.

seems, the child on the brink of concrete operations has a better chance with this problem.

A very cherished activity of children in the elementary school years is collecting. Children collect stamps, butterflies, coins, matchbooks, trading cards, evergreen cones, rocks, and so on. Although some of the motivation for collecting may be imitation of peers or receiving a stamp book for Christmas, the main push comes from classifying as an emergent ability. Just as the youngster thrilled to riding his tricycle after he mastered the pedals, he now enjoys collecting for the sake of collecting. And just as he first splashed colors onto his nursery school easel without planning ahead, he starts out as a rather indiscriminate collector. Any stamps— any cones—will do. Crude classifying is satisfying at first. Then finer classifications are made as the child grows in his ability to conceptualize more and more compli- cated classificatory systems. As the child matures, he classifies more and more on the basis of abstract ideas and less on the basis of perception or personal experience. The results from a test of sorting objects, given at several age levels from kinder- garten through college, and also to adult scientists, proves these points [19]. Figure

10–1 shows the prevalence of three different bases for classifying, as they occurred at the various levels of maturity. Classifying on basis of perception is illustrated by the line for color, which drops sharply between kindergarten and first grade and remains fairly constant after second grade. Situation, as a basis for classifying, represents personal experience, as, for example, when the subject explains his selection by saying, "You buy them all in a hardware store." This rationale for sorting is high in the early grades, dropping steadily after fourth grade. Classification in terms of an abstract idea occurs seldom in the kindergarten and frequently in the higher grades.

**Relations and Ordering.** From the experience of arranging things in order, the child internalizes concepts of relations. A little girl arranges her dolls so that they can watch her dance for them, the tallest doll on the bottom step, the next tallest on the second step, and so on up to the shortest doll on top. The child's activities are preparing her to have concepts of decreasing and increasing size, concepts of relations. The place where the term *relations* is commonly used, in regard to family members, is a true example of concepts of relations. Many experiences must go into building the concepts on which family trees hang.

Ordering activities occur often in children's play. Objects collected can be ordered inside their classes—all the coins arranged in order of their minting dates, the evergreen cones according to length. Children may line each other up, using height as a criterion, for the purpose of taking turns. Just as they enjoy using their newly developed ability to classify, so do they enjoy ordering the world in terms of various relations.

Children find the world ordered for them, too. The kindergarten teacher lines them up for going to the bathroom and getting morning milk. Perhaps she helps them to order sounds in terms of high to low or colors from light to dark. Early in the school career, the child meets that remarkable ordering device, the alphabet. An ever-widening collection of symbols called words, he finds, can be ordered in terms of their structure and its relation to the alphabet. He learns that many other kinds of relations and orders exist and that it is his job to learn them. Relations of events in time are called history. Relations of places in space are called geography. (Relate time relations and space relations and you get geology and astronomy, but these come later in school. The child in the stage of concrete operations is aware of them, however.)

Numbers are concepts derived from the operations of classifying and ordering. A cardinal number is a class. *Four* means a group of four apples or four automobiles or four abracadabras. An ordinal number is a relation. Fourth is related to third and fifth in size and position. A real understanding of *four* requires an understanding of *fourth*, and vice versa. Thus classifying and ordering are interlocking and essential processes in the development of number concepts. Understanding of the principle of conservation of quantity is basic to development of the concept of number [45, p. 23].

**Ordering Space.** Previous chapters have discussed early experiences in space. The infant discovers through looking, touching, manipulating, and moving that he is a separate object in space and that he has an inside and an outside. Bodily experience continues to be a source of discovery and of material for building concepts of space. Lateralization is a body-based way of ordering in space which is important in communication and in thinking. The development of laterality has already been considered in the previous chapter, since it related so closely to the

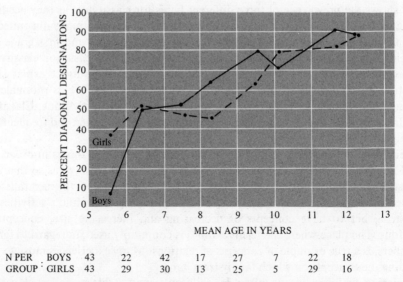

| N PER | BOYS | 43 | 22 | 42 | 17 | 27 | 7 | 22 | 18 |
| GROUP | GIRLS | 43 | 29 | 30 | 13 | 25 | 5 | 29 | 16 |

**Figure 10–2.** Percent diagonal designations in self-drawings by sex and age.

SOURCE: Reprinted by permission from E. Gellert, "Children's Lateralizations of Human Figures: Analysis of a Developmental Transition," *The Journal of Psychology,* **67,** 107–126. Copyright © 1967, The Journal Press.

body. (See pages 373–376.) When children first attribute sidedness to another person, they act as though the other person were a mirror image. Thus the right hand of the other person is the hand directly opposite the child's own right hand. Children between 5 and 13 were asked to make drawings of themselves and then to indicate in the drawing which hand would be used for writing [17]. Transposing orientation, the assigning of right and left to the sides diagonally opposite, increased quite steadily with age, as can be seen in Figure 10–2. The majority of 5-year-olds lateralized mirror-wise, with the girls considerably less likely to do so than boys. By 12 years, about 90 percent transposed. A probable explanation is that transposition occurred as the children grew less egocentric and more able to put themselves into the place of another person.

Measuring of space is done at first with the body and later with an independent measuring tool, when the child discovers that the whole is composed of a number of parts which can be taken apart and added together and that one unit can be substituted for another. Piaget demonstrates the child's understanding of measurement by showing him a tower of blocks on a table and asking him to build another, just like it, on a lower or higher table, of blocks of a different size [43]. The preoperational child builds his tower to the visual level of the model, comparing the two by stepping back and sighting them. A slightly more mature child lays a rod across the tops of the two towers. The next step in appreciation of the problem is to notice that the bases are not the same and to suggest moving his tower to the table where the model is. Since this is not permitted, he then looks for a measuring instrument. He most likely uses his own hands, placing one at the top and the other at the bottom of his tower and moving to the other tower. Then he may line up a point on his own body with the tower. When the idea of a measuring tool, probably a third tower, finally occurs to him, it indicates logical reasoning. He has reasoned that if the measuring instrument is the same as his tower, then it is the same as the model, and the two towers are the same. That is, $B = C$ and $B = A$. Therefore $A = C$. Still later he realizes that he can use a longer rod and mark the point of his tower's height and then later that he can use a shorter rod by counting the number of times he applies it.

**Ordering Time.** When children were asked to reproduce brief intervals of time, they did not show improvement between 6 and 12 years of age [16]. As adults do, they too overestimated time presented aurally more than they did time presented visually. When asked to reproduce rhythms, results were different. Auditory rhythms were reproduced more accurately than visual. Also, errors in both modalities decreased with age. It may be that hearing is more basic than seeing for perception of rhythm.

Age-related improvements occur in estimating and conceiving of long periods of time. For example, a large number of students in elementary school, high school, and college were asked to estimate ages of adults [55]. Sudden increases in accuracy were noted at the fourth grade level and in college. While an appreciation of historical time is still developing throughout the school-age span, and formal thinking about history is impossible until around 16 [35], children profit from learning about past events and earlier cultures. They can eventually order such knowledge in time as they become able to handle more complex time concepts.

## Conservation

As cognitive structures develop, the child builds a more and more permanent, stable, and inclusive picture of the world, the people in it, himself and their inter-relationships. As a baby, he learned about the permanence of objects, that things continued to exist even when he could not perceive them. As a preschool child, he began to form concepts of space, relations, time, and number, but he was dominated by his perceptions. As concepts become more organized the child achieves the idea of constancy. He realizes that certain properties are invariant (remain the same) in spite of transformations (changes) in other properties. Substance, quantity, and number are seen as permanent. Conservation of number, for example, means that the child realizes that 7 is always 7, whether it consists of $3 + 4$, $5 + 2$, :::., ..:.:, ****, or any other arrangement.
***

Conservation of substance means that the child realizes that the amount of material stays the same if nothing is added or taken away, even though the shape and/or position of the material change. One of Piaget's methods of exploring a child's conservation of substance is with two equal balls of clay. After the child has agreed that they contain equal amounts, the examiner rolls one ball into a sauage and asks, "Which has more clay?" The child in the stage of concrete operations will say that they are the same, while the child who has not achieved conservation of substance will reply either that the ball is larger (because it is fatter) or the sausage is larger (because it is longer). A variation on this test is to break one ball into little bits and ask whether the ball or the heap of bits contains more clay. If the child cannot conserve, he will say that the bits contain less (because they are smaller) or that they contain more (because there are more pieces). Conservation of substance can be demonstrated with liquid, starting with the same amounts of lemonade in two identical glasses and then pouring the contents of one glass into a thinner or a fatter glass. Or liquid from one glass can be poured into two and questions asked about whether the amount is the same. When the clay ball and sausage test was

**Table 10–1**   Percentage of Children at Each Year in the Junior School (Ages 7 through 11) in Various Stages of Understanding Conservation of Amount

| No. of Children | Stage 3 Conservation % | Stage 2 Transition % | Stage 1 Non-Conservation % |
|---|---|---|---|
| 1st year (83) | 36 | 33 | 31 |
| 2nd year (65) | 68 | 12 | 20 |
| 3rd year (99) | 74 | 15 | 11 |
| 4th year (75) | 86 | 9 | 5 |

SOURCE: Reprinted by permission from K. Lovell, *Growth of Basic Mathematical and Scientific Concepts in Children* (New York: Philosophical Library, Inc., 1962), Table 1, p. 63.

given to 322 English children between 7 and 12, results showed how conservation ability was distributed [36]. In stage 1, nonconservation, the child denied conservation. In stage 2, he sometimes admitted it, sometimes denied it. In stage 3, he was firmly convinced of conservation.

The idea of conservation is by no means an all-or-none notion which the child either has or does not have. One investigator [76] cautions that conservation should not be thought of as a particular concept but as "an index of a set of semi-inter-related cognitive attitudes." Conservation of number of kindergarten and first grade children was found to be highly related to their success in making differentiations between the magnitudes width versus depth, length versus thickness, height versus width, and age versus height. The mastery of these distinctions occurred before development of conservation of number. As can be seen by Table 10–1, there is a transition stage for the conservation of amount. Research shows that for different situations that have to do with *amount*, conservation is achieved at different times [34]. For example, many children recognized that there was the same amount of rubber in a rubber band before and after stretching before they appreciated conservation in the clay ball and sausage experiment. Furthermore, some of the nonconservers of the ball and sausage situation were able to conserve when liquid was poured into a glass of different shape. Conservation is not achieved at the same time for the different ways of ordering, as, for example, amount and weight. The children who were tested for conservation of amount were tested for conservation of weight also [36]. They were shown two balls of clay, the smaller one weighted so as to make it heavier. After the child had agreed that the smaller ball was heavier than the larger one, the latter was rolled into a sausage and questions asked about the weights of the sausage and ball. Table 10–2 shows the distribution of children at each stage of conservation. Comparing it with Table 10–1, it can be seen that weight conservation, as shown by this experiment, developed more slowly than conservation of amount. Conservation of volume is acquired after conservation of weight. No matter which material was used for testing, conservation of amount, weight, and volume were achieved in that order [62]. However, the times at which the child went through the amount-weight-volume sequence varied from one material to another. On a conservation task involving numbers and length, number conservation was achieved earlier than length conservation [21].

That conservation develops at different times in regard to different situations is an argument for the importance of experience in building mental structures.

**Table 10–2** Percentage of Children at Each Year in the Junior School (ages 7 through 11) in Various Stages of Understanding Conservation of Weight

| Year | Stage 3<br>Conservation<br>% | Stage 2<br>Transition<br>% | Stage 1<br>Non-Conservation<br>% | No. of<br>Children<br>Tested |
|---|---|---|---|---|
| 1st year | 4 | 5 | 91 | 57 |
| 2nd year | 36 | 36 | 29 | 73 |
| 3rd year | 48 | 20 | 32 | 66 |
| 4th year | 74 | 13 | 13 | 168 |
| | | | | 364 |

SOURCE: Reprinted by permission from K. Lovell, *Growth of Basic Mathematical and Scientific Concepts in Children* (New York: Philosophical Library, Inc., 1962), Table 2, p. 71.

As the child interacts with his environment, he learns first here, then there, and finally everywhere, that substance, weight, length, area, and numbers remain the same throughout changes in arrangement and position. The following investigation underlines the role of practical experience in the speed with which weight conservation is learned [34]. Children who were not conservers in regard to amount of sausages and balls of clay were asked, "What would happen to the weight of a piece of butter if it hardened?" and "What would happen to the weight of a lump of clay plasticine if it got harder?" Many more children conserved with the weight of butter than the weight of plasticine. These children had had frequent experience in shopping for butter by weight and in seeing it soften and harden under different conditions at home. They knew from many experiences that the weight of the butter stayed the same under varying conditions of shape and texture. With plasticine, though, the weight had rarely if ever been a matter of any practical importance.

Attempts to teach children conservation have generally met with indifferent success, especially when children were younger than the age at which it is normally learned. Using subjects between 6 years 5 months and 7 years 8 months, with an average age of 6 years 11 months, a successful experiment was carried on [66]. Children who failed tests of conservation were divided into two groups, one of which received instruction and the other of which did not. The instruction was based on the idea that the understanding of reversibility contributes heavily to the appreciation of conservation. Using dolls and doll beds, the experimenter and child went through a standard series of situations in which the child put the dolls into the beds and took them out with, for example, the dolls close together, the dolls closer together and a bed removed, the dolls farther apart, and the dolls farther apart and a bed added. The experimenter would question the child each time in such ways as, "Do you think we can put a doll in every bed now?" Each situation was repeated until the child predicted correctly and confirmed his prediction. All subjects but one succeeded, after training, in demonstrating conservation, and the whole control group showed no change. What is more, the trained children transferred the notion of conservation to a test which used checkers and cards instead of dolls and doll beds.

Another successful experiment in teaching conservation was done with 20 gifted 5-year-olds [49]. The inquiry method, used for nine 20-minute sessions, dealt with classification, multiple classification, seriation, and reversibility. To teach classification, for example, the teacher asked questions which led the children to observe, verbalize, and discuss differences and similarities. Multiple classification was learned by acting out, trying out, and discussing. For instance, with a pile of objects in the center of the table, each child was told to collect items that belonged together. One was to take everything red, another everything that writes. Of course both reached for the red pencil, which led to verbalizing the fact that the pencil belonged in two groups, and to generalizing that an object can be two things at the same time and then to verbalizing other examples of multiple classification. After the experimental group had had these experiences in thinking, they did significantly better than a control group on tests of conservation. The investigators agreed entirely with Piaget's belief that children build their own mental structures through their own activity. "In the area of logico-mathematical structures, children have a real understanding only of that which they invent themselves, and each time that we try to teach them something too quickly we keep them from reinventing it themselves" [46, p. vi]. The experiments with the gifted 5-year-olds were an attempt to let children invent and discover in situations offering maximum opportunities for developing their thought processes.

Conservation is related to many other measures. Transitivity tests might be expected to correlate more highly with conservation tests, and this was indeed the case [53]. (Concrete transitivity was shown when a child, after seeing that stick $A$ was longer than stick $B$ and that stick $B$ was longer than stick $C$, concluded that stick $A$ was longer than stick $C$.) Among children 4 to 10 years of age who were tested for both conservation and transitivity, most of those who showed transitivity also showed conservation, and most of those who did not show transitivity did not show conservation [53]. A child's ability to conserve can be measured by a conservation scale based on a variety of conservation tasks [20]. Performance on the scale is correlated with school grades, high verbal ability, low scores on a lie scale, favorable ratings by teachers and peers, and lack of dominating attitudes in mothers. Among young children who were developing conservation, there was a tendency for those with higher IQs to achieve conservation earlier [2]. The complexity of the task also makes a difference as to whether young children conserve amount. Success in conservation tests was somewhat related to success on a stencil design test, picture vocabulary, reading, and measurement [2]. Thus the development of conservation seems to be influenced by and connected with many aspects of the child's life, both cognitive and emotional.

*Cognitive Style*

Children use their mental structures in a variety of ways. To say that two children have the same IQ or the same mental age is not to imply that they think in the same ways or that they will achieve the same products. Nor does it mean similarity of cognitive behavior if two children develop conservation and transitivity at the same time. To get at some of the differences in the ways in which children behave intellectually, the concept *cognitive style* is useful.

There are different ways of organizing perceptions and classifying and finding solutions to problems. The particular ways preferred by an individual are called his *cognitive style*. Kagan and associates [26] have found that some children analyze the environment much more minutely than do others in forming concepts and producing answers. "Some children are splitters, others are lumpers," they say. The tendency to differentiate the stimulus environment, in contrast to re-

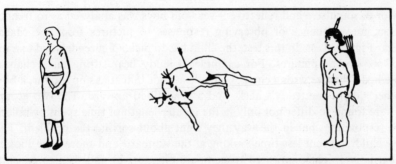

**Figure 10–3.** An example of the stimuli used in the test for conceptual style for children. The child was asked to choose two figures which "were alike or went together in some way."

Source: From J. Kagan, H. A. Moss, and I. E. Sigel, "Psychological Significance of Styles of Conceptualization," *Monographs of The Society for Research in Child Development*, **28**, Figure 2. Copyright © 1963, The Society for Research in Child Development, Inc. Used by permission.

sponding to the stimulus-as-a-whole, they call "an analytic attitude." To test cognitive style in children, they used a set of stimuli, each containing three drawings. The child was asked to select two figures which "were alike or went together in some way." Since the drawings could be grouped in two or three ways, the child's first choice was considered his preference. An analytic response would be choosing the two figures holding knives in Figure 10–3. A relational or thematic response would be choosing the hunter and the dead deer. Other tests used were word association tests, word lists to be learned, and figure sorting tests, all of which gave indications as to the child's preference for conceptualizing by analytical, relational, or inferential concepts. (Inferential concepts involve making an inference about the items grouped together, not on objective description. For instance, the two figures would be chosen not as holding knives but as killers.)

A relational style at age 6 was found more often in children who had, as 2-year-olds, been rated high on seeking contact and high on oral behavior, such as licking, drooling, sucking, and mouthing [41]. The inferential-categorical style was related positively to directed sustained activity (autonomy) at 2 and negatively related to contact-seeking and oral behavior. In this study, analytic style did not show a relation to behavior ratings at 2 years, but other research has found analytic style to be a significant variable.

An analytic style is based on two fundamental tendencies, both of which are quite stable in the individual: the tendency to analyze visual presentations, and reflectivity [28]. Reflectivity refers to one of the characteristics of school-age thought which was discussed in the first part of this chapter, under the heading "Flexibility of Thought," the delaying of a response while considering various aspects of the situation, mentally trying out different solutions before deciding on the answer. Impulsive children answer problems faster and make more errors than do reflective children [27]. Reflectivity does *not* mean the delaying of response because of fear or inability to think of solutions. The opposite of reflectivity is impulsivity which involves responding quickly without first thinking of alternative solutions. Impulsivity-reflectivity seems to be a general and pervasive measure, since an individual's performance was found to be consistent across different tests, given under different conditions [68]. Impulsive and reflective children have been compared in the search strategies they use for solving visual comparison problems [52]. The behavior of impulsive and reflective 9-year-old boys was analyzed as to frequency, duration, and sequence of observing responses to pictures from the Matching Familiar Figures Test. In this test, the child has to pick a figure identical to a model out of six similar pictures. For example, a teddy bear sitting on a chair must be matched. The five wrong choices include a chair that sticks up too far, a bow on the other side of the teddy's neck, and a head tilted upward. The two groups of boys were found to differ not only in the greater length of time spent by reflectives before responding, but in the way they went about solving the problem. The reflective children spent less time looking at the standard and more time looking at the alternatives. They appeared to compare alternatives and then to consult the standard for verification, selection, or rejection. The impulsive children apparently compared the standard globally with one alternative at a time, thus making six decisions in terms of *the same* or *different*. Details were likely to escape them, and while their response was quicker, it was less accurate.

A similar experiment analyzed the scanning behavior of children between 3 and 10 years of age [64]. When required to tell whether two drawings were the same or different, children under 6 tended to look at only a few details of each stimulus and to answer before gathering sufficient information. The majority of children over 6 used an adequate scanning strategy. Thus reflectivity is seen to be age-related; a finding also mentioned by other experimenters [26].

Figure 10–4 shows the increase in analytic responses from Grade 1 through Grade 6. Although there is, on the average, no sex difference in reflectivity, the extremes do show a difference between boys and girls [25]. There are more very reflective boys than girls and more very impulsive boys than girls. Impulsivity is expressed in motor behavior as well as in cognitive behavior. Perhaps the motor impulsivity is basic to the cognitive impulsivity, but in any case, there are more boys than girls who show extreme lack of motor inhibition. The student can easily verify this statement by observing a few times in a kindergarten or grade school, where he will be almost sure to see one or more little boys unable to sit still for more than a few moments. These youngsters wriggle in their chairs, sharpen their pencils often, throw things in the wastebacket, get frequent drinks of water, drop things on the floor, poke their neighbors, and pay attention to all sorts of extraneous stimuli. Understandably, it is likely to be hard for very impulsive children to learn to read. Not only does their motor activity preclude sitting still long enough to concentrate; the beginning reader who responds very quickly is likely to give the wrong answer. Without pausing to look at it long enough or to reflect on whether the letter is *b* or *d* or *p*, for example, the child encounters many sources of error. It has been found that the impulsive child is more likely to make a mistake in the latter part of the word rather than the first part [26].

Now let us examine the other of the two fundamental tendencies which contribute to analytic style the tendency to analyze visual presentations. A significant sex difference is usually found when this area is investigated, with boys and men superior [26, 37, 71]. For example, in Kagan's previously mentioned study, boys would be more likely than girls to group the two figures holding knives, while girls would be more likely than boys to place together the hunter and the deer. There are, of course, girls and women who are analytic in their concept formation, and there are boys and men who prefer relational concepts. Differences exist between individuals, regardless of sex.

The sources of differences in regard to analytic thinking have been sought by

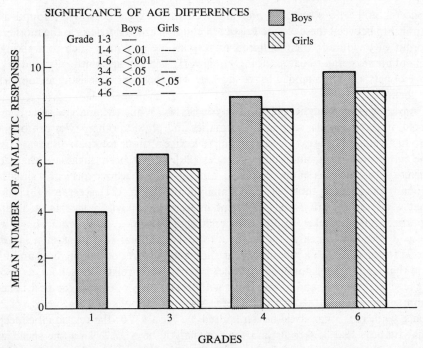

**Figure 10–4.** Analytic responses of boys and girls to conceptual style test, grades 1 through 6.

SOURCE: Reprinted by permission from J. Kagan, H. A. Moss, and I. E. Sigel, "Psychological Significance of Styles of Conceptualization," *Monographs of The Society for Research in Child Development*, **28**:3. Copyright © 1963, The Society for Research in Child Development, Inc.

Maccoby [37], who attributes an important role to the child's assumption of initiative, responsibility, and independence. Since analytic concepts are important for success in mathematics and of less use in language tests, it is pertinent to investigate the child-rearing methods of mothers of analytic and nonanalytic children, and of children with high or low mathematical ability. Overprotected boys, whose mother babied them at age 10 or 11 by taking them to school and helping them to dress, were very poor in math but good in language [32]. Autonomous 2-year-olds had higher nonverbal IQs at age 6 than did children who had shown more dependency at 2 [41].

A comparison of girls who were high in math and low in verbal, with girls whose talents were the opposite, showed that the mothers of the former tended to leave their daughters alone to solve problems. Girls who were high in verbal tests and low in math were likely to have mothers who intruded when their daughters worked on problems, praising, criticizing, and offering suggestions [4]. Further evidence comes from a study in which boys were tested for whether they saw visual presentations as wholes or whether they easily analyzed for details. Interviews with the mothers of these children revealed that the analytic youngsters had been given considerable freedom to explore the environment and to use their initiative, while the nonanalytic children had been kept closely tied to their mothers who were intolerant of self-assertion and who often talked about the dangers of the environment.

More detailed studies of analytic, differentiated children have confirmed earlier findings in regard to the mother's influence on the cognitive development of her child [11]. The investigators were interested in children who had distinct self concepts and who structured and analyzed their experiences. They found a relationship between these characteristics in children and tendencies in the mothers to permit or encourage their children in responsible activities, such as walking to school alone, going to camp, doing homework, keeping appointments, and taking care of pets. Children tended to see mothers with these characteristics as supportive to them.

**Advantages of Analytic and Nonanalytic Styles.** While the analytic style is more useful in certain fields, such as mathematics and physics, other styles can be more productive in other areas. A very strong reflective attitude may be a disadvantage in the humanities, arts, and social sciences [28]. It has been suggested that good memory for faces is more common among people who experience situations globally than among those who react analytically [74, p. 121]. Research [31] shows that while an analytic style is efficient in learning analytic concepts, a different approach gives quicker results with relational concepts. Third grade boys were tested to see how quickly they learned, for example, that *ces* (a nonsense syllable) stood for objects with a missing leg, as shown by pictures of a table, boy, and bird, and that *hib* (another nonsense syllable) meant objects related to school, as shown by teacher, crayons, and globe. Boys with analytic style learned the first concept more quickly. To learn analytic concepts, the analytic boys took an average of 20.3 trials, while the nonanalytic boys required 38.7 trials. For the relational concepts, analytic boys had 35.4 trials and the nonanalytic boys 27.9. Thus the speed with which concepts were learned was related to the cognitive style of the subjects, with each style having an advantage and a disadvantage in the array of tasks presented.

### Cognitive Integration

As the child makes use of his different senses for perceiving, he has the task of putting together the various kinds of information into useful form. He develops more and more effective ways of exploring his environment [13] and of integrating what he finds out about it. When given a choice of attending to information from one sensory modality or another he tends to choose the one most useful for the task [18].

Age-related changes have been shown in the ways in which children examine objects with both eyes and hands [1]. With the task of matching through touching and looking, 3-year-olds made clutching and catching-like movements, using their palms considerably on the objects they were examining. Four-year-olds made the same movements but added more exploration. Five-year-olds used both hands more cooperatively, but not until 6 years did children systematically trace the shape of the figure. By about 9, fingertips were used almost exclusively for exploration, but between 6 and 9, palms and fingertips both were used. Eye movements underwent similar refinement, increasing with age in number and in tendency to sweep across the figure and trace its outlines. Accuracy in matching shapes presented in one modality, such as vision, increases throughout the preschool and school years.

The patterning of intersensory integration can be studied by having children match a pattern of events in one modality with a pattern of events in another. Matching through vision and touch, as described above, is one such type of task. Matching information from listening and looking is another, a type of task which has implications for learning to read. Good readers usually perform better than poor readers in matching auditory and visual patterns [47]. A comparison of normal and learning-disordered children, 8 to 15 years of age, demonstrated a difference in the processes used by the two groups in dealing with auditory and visual material [51]. Stimuli from both modalities were presented simultaneously in the form of a spoken digit and a digit on a card. Three such presentations were made and the subjects asked to report them. Children in the normal group were more likely than the other group to recall the digits in pairs, one seen and one heard, whereas the learning-disordered children were more likely than normals to recall in terms of one modality or in a mixed fashion. Older children recalled in pairs more than younger. Thus the ability to integrate the auditory and visual material was greater in normal children than in learning-disordered, and in older children rather than younger.

Other interrelations between different kinds of sensory modalities have also been found to mature throughout childhood, but at varying times and to varying degrees [9]. For example, visual-touch was better integrated than visual-kinesthetic (muscular sense) or kinesthetic-touch at each age.

The brain functions involved in intersensory integration are depressed by malnutrition [9]. Tests across several sensory modalities were given to Guatemalan village children who had probably suffered early malnutrition and to economically favored urban children. In the village, the taller children did better than shorter ones on tests of intersensory integration, while in the city group, height and intersensory integration were not related. In a malnourished population, short stature indicates the probability of malnutrition during the early months of life, the time when the brain is growing rapidly. Apparently, the function of intersensory integration is depressed by early retardation in brain growth.

The synthesizing of symbolic information includes such tasks as putting together visual symbols, words, and actions. Such integrating involves intersensory systems which probably operate in different ways under different conditions. A task of map-making was used to explore the synthesizing of symbolic information in black and white boys and girls in ghetto, working-class, and middle-class settings [14]. The child made string patterns to match symbols. He was told that a certain pattern was supposed to be a river and others were roads and bridges. He then used the symbols to "Make a bridge going across a river with a road on each side." Both sex and social class were significant factors in success on this test of synthesizing. White middle-class boys scored highest, probably due to their environment rich in mechanical toys and encouragement in their use. Black girls exceeded black boys in working-class and middle-class districts. The author suggests that the girls profited from homemaking responsibilities, such as setting the table, with instruction from their mothers. Black boys in the ghetto excelled over black boys in the working-class districts and middle-class suburbs. These boys were used to taking care of themselves in a dangerous environment. They knew how to use perceptual signals, such as soul-brother signs, and how to run and hide. Thus the success on maplike tasks seemed to result from strengths in different systems for the three groups which excelled.

*Cultural Variations in Intellectual Performance*

When various intellectual abilities are measured, some children are found to vary in their strengths and weaknesses and in their overall ability patterns. Differences

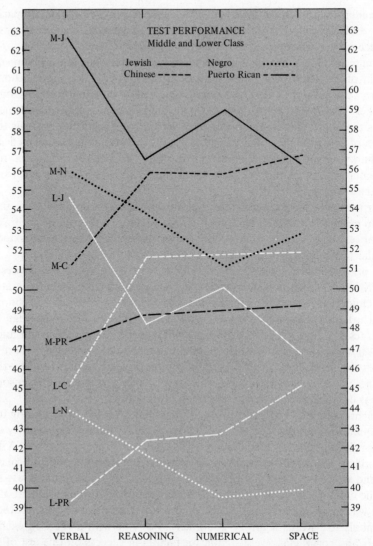

**Figure 10–5.** Mean test profiles of lower- and middle-class first grade children of four ethnic groups. Each profile is the average performance of 20 boys and 20 girls. The tests were specifically constructed to measure these specific abilities at this age level.

SOURCE: Reprinted from G. Fifer, "Social Class and Cultural Group Differences in Diverse Mental Abilities." In *Proceedings of the 1964 Invitational Conference on Testing Problems.* Princeton, N.J.: Educational Testing Service, 1965. Used by permission.

can be seen by comparing children in different countries or in different ethnic or class groups in the same country.

Mexican–American differences were derived from repeated testing of city children from Grades 1 through 12 [23]. The Mexicans were more likely to be passive in coping with tasks and to respond in terms of immediate sensory experience. Americans tended to be more highly differentiated perceptually and cognitively, more venturesome, more willing to risk failure, freer with fantasy, and more direct in approach. Another American–Mexican comparison was concerned with class differences, as well as national [77]. Advantaged and disadvantaged first, second, and third grade children in both countries were given the Matrix Test, which explores classifying activities. Social class differences were observed in both countries but in the United States, the class difference was greater. American children were more successful on the test, the disadvantaged American group being similar to the Mexican advantaged group.

Ethnic group differences are reported in the next two studies, one in the United States and one in Africa. Figure 10–5 shows the results of comparing mental abilities of first grade children from four ethnic groups, each of which was divided by social class. The comparison was made on the basis of scores from tests designed to measure verbal, reasoning, numerical, and spatial abilities. The ethnic groups varied considerably in patterns of abilities. In each group, the lower and middle class showed the same pattern, although they differed in amount of ability [15].

Perceptual discrimination was tested in middle-class African and European children in Kenya, using coeducational, integrated primary schools [5]. Although Europeans did slightly better than Africans, the sex difference was much greater than the ethnic difference, boys being superior to girls.

Class differences in tests of intelligence, achievement, cognition, and language are almost always reported to favor the middle-class over lower socioeconomic groups, as occurred in the study reported above. Critics often question the validity of such tests, however, saying that they are based on the experience of the middle-class child and that they do not measure the strengths of the lower-class child. An object-sorting task was devised to measure how well children could classify objects when no verbal communication was required, in contrast to coding a verbal label [30]. The subjects were 12 middle-class and 12 lower-class boys at four age levels: 6, 8, 10, and 12. (Unfortunately, race differences were not controlled and nearly all of the lower-class boys were black.) As might be expected, the middle-class boys scored higher on making classifications verbally. When objects were classified with no talking required there was no class difference. At 6 years the lower-class boys were below, but by 8 they were above the middle-class boys, and after that, both performances were about the same. These results suggest that middle-class children have developed more efficient conceptual organization before they start to school but that the school experience may stimulate such development in lower-class children. Consistent with these results, another class comparison shows disadvantaged fifth and sixth graders to be ahead on a test of visual fluency [50]. These children produced more visual symbols than an advantaged group and did just as well on tests of esthetic judgment and originality. Thus we see again that when verbal performance is not required, poor children are not always at a disadvantage.

## Cognitive Limitations

During the stage of concrete operations, the child can reason from assumptions and hypotheses, but often he confuses assumptions and hypotheses with factual evidence. That is, he thinks of an explanation and then assumes that it is right. Then he looks for evidence to support it and ignores evidence that contradicts it. This behavior is the *egocentrism* of the concrete operational period. Whereas the preschool child was centered on his own perceptions and viewpoints, the schoolchild is stuck with his own hypotheses. One result of this situation is what Elkind calls *cognitive conceit* [12]. When the child first makes the discovery that adults, usually represented by one of his parents, do not know everything, he assumes that they know very little. If the adult is wrong in one thing, the child figures, then he must be wrong in nearly everything, and if the child is right in one thing, he must be right in nearly everything. Cognitive conceit underlies some of the antipathy that children feel for growing up. It is also basic to the jokes children most enjoy and to many favorite children's stories, such as *Peter Pan* and *Tom Sawyer*, and their fantasies, such as believing that one is adopted and is really the child of royal and/or wealthy parents.

## Language

Intimately associated with cognitive development, language is both a product of intellectual growth and a contributor to it. The school-age child masters more of the mechanics of his language, articulating more clearly, using longer and more complicated sentences, and doubling his vocabulary, both spoken and understood, between first and sixth grade [54]. Vocabulary continues to increase throughout adolescence and into adulthood. Not until the child reaches eighth grade level does his reading vocabulary equal his listening vocabulary [10]. That is, he can understand more words if they are spoken to him than he can by reading them to himself.

*Normative Examples*

Level of abstraction and facility in using *words* can be traced in intelligence tests. To give an idea of the average abilities at each year, the following examples are presented from the Stanford–Binet test [58].

**Year 6.** Defines six words such as *orange, envelope, puddle.*
Opposite analogies. ("A bird flies, a fish . . .)
Describes or interprets a picture.

**Year 7.** Tells what is foolish in an absurd picture.
Tells how two things are alike (an apple and a peach).
Answers questions of comprehension. (What makes a sailboat move ?)
Opposite analogies. (The rabbit's ears are long ; the rat's ears are . . .)

**Year 8.** Defines eight words, such as *gown, roar, eyelash.*
Recalls a story.
Explains verbal absurdities
Gives similarities and differences. (A baseball and an orange.)

**Year 9.** Makes rhymes. (A color that rhymes with head.)

**Year 10.** Defines 11 words, such as *juggler, scorch, lecture.*
Defines two of : pity, curiosity, grief, surprise.
Gives reasons. (Why children should not be too noisy in school.)
Names 28 words in a minute.

**Year 11.** Explains absurdities.
Defines three of : *connection, compare, conquest, obedience, revenge.*
Gives similarities between three things. (Snake, cow, sparrow.)

Socialized speech becomes more frequent as the child grows beyond egocentrism into the stage of concrete operations. More able to look at situations from another person's point of view, he tries to convey meaning, to understand what the other person is telling him, and to give and take through words. (In egocentric speech, the child is not concerned with exchanging meaning with someone else but only with expressing himself.) Through socialized speech, he checks his perceptions and interpretations of reality with other people's. Egocentric speech decreases in observable form (see pages 258–259) as the child learns to speak to himself silently. Egocentric speech thus becomes the tool of thinking, problem solving, and self-regulation. Language continues to be useful as an aid in learning and remembering. Children who showed that they used mediation in problem solving were able to make more use of verbal labeling for learning through observation [63].

Freed from the dominance of moment-by-moment experience, the child can sit back and reflect. He has many more real choices of behavior open to him, since he can delay action while thinking. Having more possibilities for different kinds of action means that he is a more differentiated person, more of an individual. And because of being more truly an individual, there are more ways in which he can relate to other people. Thus the development of speech and thought contribute to the child's development as an individual and a social being.

### Articulation

Normative studies show that most 7-year-olds can articulate all English phonemes satisfactorily. At 5, however, some children do not produce all English sounds adequately. About 75 percent of 1500 children tested after entering kindergarten had at least one misarticulation [56]. Articulation tests and others were given to nearly 500 children in the kindergarten and the tests repeated at six-month intervals for four years [56]. The children with the lowest scores in the kindergarten were also the poorest articulators when they reached second grade. By fourth grade, they still had a number of articulation problems.

Several practical findings resulted from this study. Kindergarten teachers, without using tests, identified the children with the lowest articulation scores, an indication that teachers' reports would be very helpful in identifying the children who will need speech therapy. The most common misarticulations were with s, l, and r, but patterns vary from one child to another.

Well-developed articulation is correlated with ability to apply the rules of morphological change [57]. In addition to articulation tests, the children in kindergarten, first, and second grades were also tested for ability to change words into plurals, possessives, different tenses, and so on. At each age level, children who made the largest number of errors in articulation were also the children who performed poorly on the morphology test, while the best articulators were also superior in morphology.

### Language and Concept Formation

The formation of a concept does not take place by memorizing a word and attaching it to objects. Rather the formation of a concept is a creative process which solves a problem [65, pp. 54–58]. A word is the mediating sign for the concept, helping in its formation, and then coming to stand for it. When a child first uses language, he employs words which stand for concepts, words given him by adults. He communicates with adults using these words which stand for approximations of the concepts for which adults use them. For Bobby, *teacher* means any one of the four ladies who run the four-grade school that he attends. For Bobby's father, *teacher* means any person who stands in an educational relationship to another person, in the past, present, or future, anywhere in the universe. As children progress toward the stage of formal operations, they become capable of forming concepts which are more and more abstract.

The ways in which children learn words through verbal context were examined by Werner and Kaplan in one of the first studies to deal with this process [29, 70]. They show how concepts emerge as products of problem solving, whereas words come to stand for the concepts gradually, during their emergence. The subjects were between 8 and 14 years of age. The task was to find the meaning of 12 artificial words each of which appeared in six different contexts. For example, *lidber* (gather) was presented thus:

1. All the children will lidber at Mary's party.
2. The police did not allow the people to lidber on the street.
3. The people lidbered about the speaker when he finished his talk.
4. People lidber quickly when there is an accident.
5. The more flowers you lidber, the more you will have.
6. Jimmy lidbered stamps from all countries.

Under 10 or 11 years of age, children often indicated that they did not differentiate between the word and its context. Word–sentence fusion was apparent in their answers, as where one little boy said that Jimmy collected stamps from all countries, and then stated, "The police did not permit people to collect stamps on the street." The word *collect* had fused with a word from sentence 6, to make *collect stamps* instead of *collect*.

The younger children's responses often showed a tendency to include more in a word meaning than an older person does and also to perceive a sentence as an undifferentiated whole. For instance, a child of 9 responded to the sentence *People talk about the bordicks* [faults] *of others and don't like to talk about their own.* He said, "People talk about other people and don't talk about themselves, that's what bordick means." Then, when trying to fit his interpretation of bordick into the sentence *People with bordicks are often unhappy*, he said, "People that talk about other people are often unhappy . . . because this lady hears that someone is talking about her and she'll get mad." Thus he took more meaning from the first sentence than an adult would ascribe to *bordick* and tried to fit almost all of the context of the first sentence into the second. He could not isolate the meaning of *bordick* out of the first sentence in order to fit it into the second.

The 9-year-olds gave correct responses to only 6.7 percent of the sets of sentences, whereas the 13-year-olds succeeded with 47.7 percent. The younger children tended not to see the necessity for integrating the cues of all six contexts, but with increasing age, children tried harder and more successfully to integrate. Younger children tended to change the context of sentences to fit with their solutions, whereas older ones showed more respect for the context as given. Throughout the age range studied, there was a growing appreciation of the sentence as a stable grammatical structure. Children between 5 and 14 have been found to increase with age in the ability to abstract and then apply language rules [33]. This process can be facilitated by having children imitate a model and by rewarding correct responses.

Throughout the childhood years the use of compound and complex sentences increases in relationship to the use of simple sentences. Figure 10–6 shows the frequencies of various types of sentences between ages 8 and 14, as calculated from children's written compositions. The language of middle childhood has a

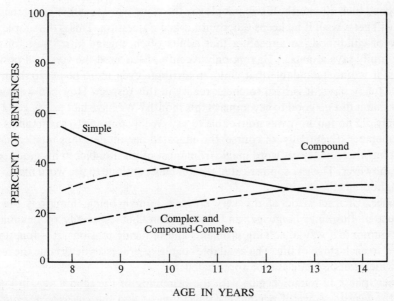

**Figure 10–6.** Frequencies of simple, complex, compound, and complex-compound sentences in written compositions of children ages 8 through 14.

SOURCE: From G. A. Miller, *Language and Communication*, 1951. Used by permission of McGraw-Hill Book Company.

very distinctive flavor. In fact, it has been said that childhood has its own culture, consisting of behavior patterns which are passed from one generation of children to the next, without benefit (or contamination) of adult intervention. An extensive collection [40] of English children's language humor traces jokes and stories historically and geographically, revealing some connections with European and Middle Eastern children's language productions. Children's humor is shown to have broad, deep, and ancient sources, connecting each generation of children with the past. Children apparently teach their rhymes and riddles to one another, initiating the younger ones, leaving the treasure with them and then almost forgetting it.

**Word Magic.** Words give power over reality. The chants of childhood combine names with other magic-making words in order to induce certain feelings or behavior in playmates. For example: Cry, Billy, cry / Stick your finger in your eye / And tell your mother it wasn't I. The name-calling of childhood is half in earnest, half in play. Sometimes it is an imaginative attempt to produce a new verbal pattern, sometimes an effort to control or change reality. Mike, in a burst of annoyance at Chris, shouted "You're a cringing crustacean." The result, a cowed and silent Chris, strengthened Mike's belief in word magic, for had not his words changed his friend?

Word magic, the power of words to change reality, is used more by children than adults, but it is not the exclusive property of children.

<table>
<tr><td>Star light, star bright</td><td>What goes up the chimney?</td></tr>
<tr><td>First star I've seen tonight</td><td>Smoke.</td></tr>
<tr><td>I wish I may, I wish I might</td><td>May your wish and my wish</td></tr>
<tr><td>Have the wish I wish tonight.</td><td>Never be broke.</td></tr>
</table>

If you say RABBITS for your first word on the first morning of the month, you'll have good luck all month. If two people say the same word together spontaneously, each will get a wish if he keeps quiet until asked a question. This is the simple word magic of childhood, so appealing that adults often engage in it "just for fun." (Our family says RABBITS.) Having only recently discovered the very real power of words, it is understandable that children attribute even more power to them than they actually have. It is hard to check reality in this respect. How can we possibly know that it did no good to say RABBITS this month? We have had pretty good luck. It surely did no harm. It was no trouble to say. We'll continue to say RABBITS when we remember. Eventually, of course, the educated person develops intellectually to the point where he rejects word magic from most of his life. Not in his grade school years, however. The less sophisticated person may continue to use word magic often throughout his life.*

**Humor.** Characteristic of the very creative human being, humor is the joint product of thinking, language, and imagination, but especially of imagination. Since humor is a way of solving problems and reducing tensions, it is functionally related to each stage of life. The available cognitive processes determine the level of joke which can be made and/or appreciated.

A new phase in humor begins with the beginning of the school age, in keeping with the *industry* stage of personality development and the *concrete operations* of cognitive development. Long, rambling stories are no longer extremely funny. A joke has to be concise, with a surprise ending or punch line. Jokes are funniest and most enjoyed when they are close to but not beyond the upper level of understanding of the child [75]. Children use ready-made jokes or invent jokes similar to them [73]. With more realistic, objective thinking, the child does not permit himself the free-flowing fantasy of his preschool days, his stage of developing initiative and imagination. Although he still expresses his wishes, fears, aggression, and anxiety, they are further down in his unconscious. They appear in more stylized form, like other people's, as the standard jokes of childhood. The "little moron" jokes are especially appropriate to the school-age child [73]. These children, concerned with industry, duty, and accomplishment, with being smart, with adequacy, find the stupid behavior of the moron tension-relieving. The moron in their jokes is definitely not a child like themselves. He is an older person. The jokes disparage parents, teachers and the silly answers they give children. They reassure children that it is all right not to know the things they do not know and cannot find. Jokes that belittle adults also express cognitive conceit, a result of the egocentrism of the stage of concrete operations [12].

The following selection of typical American jokes comes from a book [22, p. 229]† on middle childhood. Too crude to amuse adults and yet possessing the surprise which a real joke requires, these examples show what is funny and tension-releasing to someone halfway between the preschool age and adulthood.

What is black and white and read all over?
A newspaper.
No. A sunburned zebra.

* A highly sophisticated person, too, may use word magic throughout life if he is a very creative person. Such people have extremely complex and flexible cognitive powers [3, p. 193]. An extremely creative adult can assume a childlike viewpoint temporarily, giving his imagination rein to work naive magic, as did Lewis Carroll.
† From *Behavior and Development from Five to Twelve* by Glen R. Hawkes and Damaris Pease. Copyright © 1962 by Glenn R. Hawkes and Damaris Pease. Reprinted by permission of Harper & Row, Publishers.

What was the president's name 35 years ago?
Franklin Roosevelt.
No. Richard Nixon. His name doesn't change just because he is older.

What do ghosts eat for breakfast?
Ghost toasties and evaporated milk.

What does the mother ghost say to the baby ghost?
Don't spook until spooken to.

Teacher: How would you punctuate this sentence: *I saw a five-dollar bill in the street.*
Jimmy: I would make a dash after it.

Linda: Do you know I don't have all my toes on one foot?
Debbie: No! How did it happen?
Linda: I have five on one foot and five on the other.

What did one eye say to the other?
Just between you and me something smells.

What's twelve and twelve?
Twenty-four.
Shut your mouth and say no more.

What's eight and eight?
Sixteen.
Stick your head in kerosene.
Wipe it off with ice cream.
And show it to the king and queen.

## Imagination

The school-age child can and does use all the modes of imaginative expression in which the preschool child engages—fantasy, dreams, the performing arts, and the producing arts. As it does throughout life, imagination is linked with controlled thinking and language to form the complex system with which human beings think, communicate, solve problems, and create. The balance of these three links is, in middle childhood, a little different from what it was during the preschool years. Controlled thought and language have become more powerful instruments for dealing with the environment.

Some of stored experience is immediately accessible or conscious, some is inaccessible or unconscious, some is preconscious or available but not immediately or perhaps not completely. With increasing control of thought, the older child becomes more and more able to concentrate his attention on a task or on a narrow range of stimuli when he wishes. He can also let his attention wander, daydream, fantasy. In this relaxed attitude of openness to thoughts, memories, ideas, and stimuli, he may be in touch with preconscious material which, with an attitude of strict control, he would not experience. Developing his sense of industry, he feels impelled to learn the accepted practices of his culture, the tried-and-true ways of producing, the techniques of work which adults and older children offer to him. But he is also capable of creative behavior, producing what is new, unique, or original by combining ideas and things in new ways.

**Measuring Creativity.** Some individuals are more creative than others. It is not too difficult to pick out some very creative adults, since they are known, or can be rated and chosen on the basis of original work they have done. Since few children ever produce things or ideas that can be rated in the work world, their creativity has to be assessed in other ways, if it is to be studied. Observation suggests that children vary widely in creativity. Many investigators have tried to distinguish between creativity and intelligence as measured by standardized tests. Success in separating the two processes came through assuming that creativity includes these two elements: abundant production of unique associations; a playful, permissive attitude [67]. Children were tested individually for amount and uniqueness of production in a relaxed atmosphere of playing games, with no pressures of time and few restrictions. Number of unique responses and total number of responses were measured in verbal and visual situations. The three verbal "games" were instances, alternate uses, and similarities. *Instances* included naming all the round things the child could think of, all the things that make a noise, all the square things, and all the things that move on wheels. *Alternate uses* involved telling all the different ways one could use a newspaper, knife, automobile tire, cork, shoe, key, and chair. *Similarities* consisted of telling all the ways in which a potato and a carrot are alike, a cat and a mouse, a train and a tractor, and several other such pairs. Visual tests were giving meanings or interpretations for a number of abstract patterns and lines. Figure 10–7 shows examples of the drawings used.

All the children in a fifth grade class were given the creativity tests and the Wechsler Intelligence Scale for Children, as well as ability tests, achievement tests. Behavior ratings were made. Since creativity and intelligence varied independently, subjects could be placed above or below the mean for each. The investigators were able to divide the subjects into four groups for each sex: high IQ with high creativity, low IQ with high creativity, high IQ with low creativity, and low IQ with low creativity. Many significant differences between various groups were seen.

Girls high in both dimensions were highly self-confident, interested in academic work, and able to concentrate well. Sought after by peers, they also sought and enjoyed companionship. They were also disruptive in the classroom, seeking attention and possibly eager to propose new ideas and activities in order to relieve boredom.

Girls high in creativity but low in intelligence were at the greatest disadvantage of all groups. Cautious, hesitant, lacking in self-confidence, they deprecated their own work, had a hard time concentrating, and disrupted classroom procedures in a protesting fashion. Other girls avoided them and they avoided others.

Girls low in both dimensions apparently compensated for poor academic performance by social activity. Compared with the high creative, low IQ girls, the low-low girls were more self-confident, less subdued, and more outgoing.

The high IQ, low creative girls were self-confident and assured, able to concentrate, fairly hesitant about expressing opinions, and unlikely to be disruptive. While other girls sought her companionship, this type of girl was aloof socially, hesitant to overextend herself or to commit herself.

Only the intelligence and not creativity was pertinent to the behavior ratings for boys in the classroom. The highly intelligent boy was self-confident, interested, and able to cope and to concentrate. The low IQ boys were more likely to be withdrawn, self-deprecating, and self-punishing.

Conceptualizing in boys was related to both creativity and IQ. High IQ, low creativity boys were least likely of all groups to give *thematic* or relational responses (see page 393) when asked to group objects together and tell why they grouped as they did. An example of a thematic response was "getting ready to go out," given by a child who put together a comb, lipstick, watch, pocketbook, and door. Boys high in creativity switched flexibly between the two styles of organizing: thematic and inferential-conceptual. Further testing showed that the high IQ, low

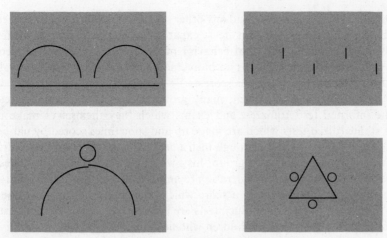

**Figure 10–7.** Stimulus materials for visual part of creativity test.

SOURCE: From *Modes of Thinking in Young Children: A Study of the Creativity-Intelligence Distinction*, by Michael A. Wallach and Nathan Kogan. Copyright © 1965 by Holt, Rinehart and Winston, Inc. Reprinted by permission of Holt, Rinehart and Winston, Inc.

creative boys could use thematic grouping if they were asked to do so. When they were given free choice, however, they did not use themes. These results, along with further evidence on girls' acceptance or rejection of unconventional picture labels, leads to this conclusion: the high IQ, low creativity child is likely to be intolerant of unlikely hypotheses about the world, reluctant to "stick his neck out," afraid of being wrong. Anxiety level is low in this group. It looks as though this type of child is attuned to what succeeds in the ordinary classroom.

Creativity seems to be associated with moderate levels of anxiety. The most creative child is not necessarily the happiest. He may well be sensitive to sadness and pain. High creativity involves not only a playful contemplation of the possible but most likely also requires high persistence and concentration, "an obsessive, task-centered reluctance to put a problem aside" [67].

## Intelligence and Achievement as Revealed through Tests

Most schoolchildren are tested many times as part of academic procedure. Teachers give tests or examinations in order to see how much children have learned and, upon this basis, to give them grades or credits. Intelligence tests, achievement tests, and diagnostic tests are given in various contexts in order to achieve a variety of aims.

Several intelligence tests for children were mentioned in Chapter 6. The Stanford–Binet and the Wechsler Intelligence Test for Children were pointed out as those used most often for individual examinations. Both tests yield IQs. The Wechsler also gives a percentile rating, showing how the child stands in relation to a representative 100 children. Verbal and nonverbal scores are a further advantage of the Wechsler, which is the test most often used with school-age children. When an individual test is administered, a qualified psychologist carries out carefully designated procedures in a room alone with the child. In addition to giving the items in standardized ways, the psychologist pays special attention to the child's comfort, alertness, motivation, and any other such factors which might conceivably contribute to his doing the best he is capable of. The psychologist makes and records observations on the total behavior of the child, in addition to recording passes and failures on tests. Thus an individual intelligence test can yield valuable qualitative information, as well as scores.

For every individual test given, many group tests are administered. Teachers give the informal tests, quizzes, and exams which they themselves make up, as well as standardized tests which are made up and sometimes scored by nationwide test bureaus. A group test is a rough instrument, as compared with an individual test. When a child is one of a group, his own particular feelings, attitudes, and needs cannot be taken into consideration to any degree. No qualitative observation can be made. The result is only a score which is an indication of how one child stands in relation to the group. Such tests are useful for revealing characteristics of the group and for pointing out children who need further study.

### Prediction of Success

Intelligence tests correlate significantly with success in school, as measured by grades. Third and fourth grade children, tested on the Stanford–Binet test and on the California achievement tests, showed these correlations: IQ and arithmetic, 0.59 for girls and 0.50 for boys; IQ and reading, 0.57 for girls and 0.66 for boys [8]. Since the correlations are far from perfect, this table shows that academic success is based upon more than IQ but that IQ is an important factor. The Stanford–Binet and most other intelligence tests are adaptations and refinements of Binet's original procedures, which were devised in order to predict academic success.

There are many different ways of judging success. If the criterion of originality or production of new ideas is considered, then IQ tests are of limited usefulness. Correlations between IQ and some tests of creative thinking are fairly high (from 0.11 to 0.73) if the subjects have a wide range of IQs [48]. For a group of uniformly low, average, or high IQs, however, correlations with tests of creative thinking are generally low (0.00 to 0.45).

Intelligence tests tend to sample the kinds of intellectual processes which produce *the* right answer to each question, whereas creativity tests sample processes which produce unusual, new, original, often multiple answers. The former type of thinking is called convergent, the latter divergent. It is reasonable, then, that if success is being defined in terms of creative production, IQ tests may not be sufficient for predicting it. High IQ is, however, correlated with many other superior characteristics, as will be seen below. British children between 8 and 12, who scored above 140 IQ on the WISC, were studied by means of tests for creativity, logical thinking, mathematics, and personality [35]. These children scored high on mathematics tests, but they had not attained the stage of formal thought to any great degree. Although largely in the stage of concrete thought, as are most children their age, these gifted children were very flexible in thinking and were able to use their schemas in a greater variety of situations than could children of average IQ. A factor analysis revealed that their general intelligence contributed to their success on creativity tests, but that creativity was also dependent on other factors, including logical thinking and abilities measured by verbal and mathematical creativity tests. These children, like American gifted children [69], were generously endowed with desirable personality characteristics and were popular with their peers. A positive relationship was found between creativity and reversibility in operations of classifying when Canadian children were examined with creativity tests and some of Piaget's tests [39].

Success in adult life is more difficult to define than success in school, where grades are easily used as a measure. Many adults can point to at least one former schoolmate who has achieved status and success in business, a profession, or the arts and who used to be a poor student in school. There is, however, some relation beween intelligence at school age and performance as an adult. Children who tested at the low and high ends of the scale and a group of average scorers have been studied as adults. The various criteria of their success include earnings, status, degrees, publications, family behavior, and survival rates. All criteria are shown to have some relation to childhood IQ by the two studies which follow.

Terman and his associates [59] have published four volumes of *Genetic Studies of Genius* in which over 1000 gifted children were studied, between 1921 and 1945. The distribution of Stanford–Binet IQs was between 135 and 200, with a mean of 151. Various criteria of success were used to appraise the subjects 25 years after their selection as gifted children, showing the widespread superiority of these people as adults. Half the men and over half the employed women were in professional occupations. This ratio was nine times the proportion of professional men in the general Californian population. Eighty percent of the men were in the two highest groups, as contrasted with 14 percent in the general professional population. Seventy percent were college graduates, as contrasted with 7 percent for the population of corresponding age. Twenty-five percent of the college graduates were elected to Phi Beta Kappa or Sigma Xi. Twenty-nine percent took graduate degrees. A random selection of people would probably contribute less than 5 percent of the doctors and lawyers produced by the gifted group. The subjects received a proportionately large number of scholarships, assistantships, and fellowships. The gifted group earned significantly more money than the average, even though they were below the age for maximum earning capacity. The group had published 90 books and 1500 articles. Nearly 100 patents had been granted.

Marriage and divorce rates and age at marriage were the same as in the general population, but for the gifted college graduates, as compared with all college graduates, incidence of marriage was higher, age of marriage lower, and the divorce rate lower. The married gifted group showed a slightly higher score on a marital happiness tests than did a group of less gifted subjects. The mean IQ of the 384 offspring tested was 128, with fewer than expected below 80 IQ and those above 150 being 28 times as numerous as in the general population. The death rate was 4.0 percent, significantly lower than that of the general population the same age.

At the other end of the distribution of IQs were 151 adults who had, as schoolchildren, been judged mentally deficient, because of IQs below 70, placement in special classes for a year or more, and teachers' and psychologists' evaluations [6]. The subjects' average age was 42. Only nine of them were institutionalized. All but seven of those not in institutions had at least part-time jobs. About 83 percent were self-supporting part of the time. The range of occupations included all categories from managerial to unskilled labor. The most common occupations were laborer for males, and housekeeper for females. The higher-placed subjects included a business manager and a bookkeeper. The subjects were tested with the Wechsler Intelligence Test, on which scores are expected to be a little higher than on the Stanford–Binet.

The results, however, averaged 23 points higher, an increase greater than the difference in the two tests would explain. IQs ranged from 56 to 104. Improvement in performance scores was greater than in verbal scores.

About a third were entirely self-sufficient, less than half had some assistance from public relief funds, and the remainder lived in institutions or with their parents. Types of dwellings ranged from filthy shacks to costly new houses. Eighty percent of the group were married, with a marriage rate slightly below the general population. Divorce rates were about average. About 80 percent of those married had children, most of whom were making average progress at school. The children's average IQ was 95, with a range from 50 to 138.

Higher than the national average, the death rate was 15 percent, with twice as many males as females deceased. Nearly a third of the deceased had died violently, a much greater percentage than the national average for violent deaths.

In all these measures of success, even in the global one of staying alive, the high IQ group greatly exceeded the low IQs. And while the low IQs did better than might have been expected in several measures, they were below average in most criteria. Overwhelming evidence points to the lifelong advantages of having a high IQ. Table 10–3 summarizes the comparison between the groups.

**Table 10–3** Comparison of High and Low IQ Groups on Criteria of Success in Life

| Success Criterion | Terman's Gifted Group | | | Charles' Retarded Group | | |
|---|---|---|---|---|---|---|
| | ABOVE AVERAGE | SAME | BELOW | ABOVE AVERAGE | SAME | BELOW |
| Occupational status | X | | | | | X |
| Education | X | | | | | |
| Income | X | | | | | X |
| Publications | X | | | | | |
| Marriage rate | | X | | | | X |
| Divorce rate | | X | | | X | |
| Marital happiness | X | | | | | |
| Children's intelligence | X | | | | X | |
| Height & weight | X | | | | | |
| Death rate | | | X | X | | |

Adult outcomes of average childhood IQs are rather surprising. Twenty-five subjects who had tested average (a mean IQ of 100) at age 6 were retested at an average age of 33, when the mean IQ of the group was 107 [7]. At age 6, the range of IQs was 96 to 104; at age 33, IQs ranged from 90 to 132. Changes in IQ ranged from −8 to +29. Thus, a group of children who had tested average at age 6 were scattered all the way from the lower end of the average category to the superior level. In occupational classification, the subjects ranged from unskilled labor to professional, with a wide variety of jobs represented. Educational attainment ranged from eighth grade to graduate school. The results of the study suggest that IQ in the early elementary school years is an inadequate basis on which to predict future achievement and from which to make educational plans for children who test average.

## Estimating Readiness for Educational Experiences

Although IQ accounts in part for academic success, another important influence is the child's readiness to learn from the situation presented. Readiness is a function of the child's stage of maturation and of his "set" or motivation toward the particular kind of learning involved [24, p. 392]. Maturation is tested by physical-motor tests, most of which are appropriate for the infant and preschool child. The Lincoln–Oseretsky test (mentioned in the previous chapter) is an example of a physical-motor test designed for the school-age child. Subject matter-readiness tests are often used upon school entrance and during the early grades, in order to place the child in a class or group where the level and type of work are suited to his maturity and interests. The most frequently used readiness tests are those of reading readiness, which correlate highly (around 0.75) with progress in first grade reading [24, p. 424]. Arithmetic readiness tests are also used. Tests for aptitudes, such as artistic and musical talent, are readiness tests in the sense that they predict whether the child will profit greatly from education in these fields. Aptitude tests do not imply that everyone will eventually reach a state of readiness, however, since specialized talents are distributed quite unevenly throughout the population. Reading tests correlate highly with intelligence tests. It is estimated that a mental age of 6½, as measured by the Stanford–Binet, is necessary for learning to read [24, p. 420]. Reading tests typically explore the following: visual discrimination of differences and similarities in letters, words, phrases, or pictures; auditory discrimination of words, linking them to pictures; motor control in such activities as maze tracing, placing dots in circles, and drawing lines; understanding numbers and relations; remembering and reproducing a story; vocabulary, naming objects, and classifying; reproducing pictures; giving information, by answering questions of common knowledge; laterality, through hand- and eye-preference tests.

## Measuring Achievement Level and Diagnosing Deficiencies

Measures of achievement show what a child has learned and what he can do in the field in question. The ordinary classroom tests and examinations are usually achievement tests, used as a basis for giving marks and grades. Standardized achievement tests are used quite widely, often to reveal how a particular class, school, or area stands in relation to children throughout the country as a whole. The California Achievement Tests [60] are an example of this type of test. Through their use, a child can be compared with a large, carefully selected sample of children. Weaknesses, as well as strengths, can be diagnosed through the use of achievement tests, especially standardized ones. The California Achievement Tests, for example, can serve as a rough diagnostic test, since they consist of a battery. The arithmetic section includes four groups of tests, addition, subtraction, multiplication, and problems. A deficiency in any particular area can point to the need for further diagnostic study and then to definite remedial measures.

## Research

All types of tests are used for research purposes. Sometimes research programs require the giving of tests which are valuable to the individuals involved. Often, however, the investigator has to get information which benefits neither the child nor his parents. The experimenter may be developing his own tests, using the children's performances as the basis of standardizing tests, which will eventually be useful for individual diagnosis. Or he may be testing theories and generating hypotheses. Research can also be done on test data that were originally collected in order to give information about children as individuals.

## Summary

The school-age child feels a necessity to develop intellectual skills as part of a whole network of competencies which contribute to his sense of industry. His thinking increases in both flexibility and control. He can delay his response to the experience of the moment, taking account of several aspects of the situation, weighing them, bringing in past experience, and even considering the future. The points of view of other people are realities which enter into his deliberations and influence his actions. While considering which response to make, the child can think an act and think it undone, thus trying out various courses of action mentally. He also learns that there are certain kinds of processes or operations of thought and of nature which can be done and undone, or reversed.

The child thinks about experiences and symbols in systematic ways. He is not likely to think about pure abstractions, however. In his classifying, he can understand relations between classes and subclasses and between parts and wholes. He relates objects to each other, ordering them in terms of size, age, sound, or some other criterion. Number concepts are built from the combined operations of classifying and ordering. During this period of cognitive development, the child becomes convinced of certain constancies in the environment. He comes to realize that substance, weight, length, area, volume, and numbers remain the same (are conserved) even when changes are made in arrangements and positions. The notion of conservation, like other cognitive achievements, is built through interaction with the environment.

Cognitive style refers to the ways in which an individual characteristically perceives, organizes his perceptions, and seeks solutions to problems. Some children analyze experiences minutely; others respond more to the event-as-a-whole or to the object-in-relation. An analytic style is based on two fairly stable characteristics: the tendency to analyze visual arrays, and the tendency to reflect before responding. At both extremes of reflectivity, very reflective and very impulsive, there are more boys than girls. Analytic thinking seems to be related to child-rearing practices, especially to the promotion of independence, responsibility, and initiative.

Language develops in intimate relationship with thought and with social interaction. The ability to talk silently to oneself increases, contributing to problem solving and self-regulation and opening more avenues of behavior from which to choose. Language development and concept formation contribute to one another. Concepts, and the words attached to them, emerge gradually, as the words become differential from the context in which they appear. As the child matures, he shows increasing understanding of the sentence as a stable grammatical structure.

Imagination continues to be used in problem solving and self-expression, although there is some indication that the school-age child uses imagination less than does the preschool child. A large part of the imaginative expression of middle childhood is through language and humor, which create the distinctive culture of childhood. Language play takes the form of magic-making formulas, verses, and chants which are handed down from one generation of children to another. Jokes and riddles reflect the child's preoccupation with adequacy.

Intelligence, achievement, and special abilities are often tested and measured at this time of life. Most testing is done in groups, at school, in order to assign credit for what the child has learned. The child may be compared with his classmates or with a broader group, even a national sample. Intelligence tests correlate with achievement in school and with success in later life, as measured by many criteria. Although group performance can be predicted fairly well from intelligence tests, such tests tell little about what a given child will achieve. IQ tests and creativity tests tap different intellectual functions. Readiness tests are used to explore various aspects of maturity which are necessary before a child can profit from certain educational experiences. Reading readiness tests are widely used. Diagnostic tests reveal areas where children need remedial help. All types of tests are used for research purposes.

# References

1. Abravanal, E. The development of intersensory patterning with regard to selected spatial dimensions. *Mono. Soc. Res. Child Devel.*, 1968, **33**:2.
2. Almy, M., Chittenden, E., & Miller, P. *Young children's thinking*. New York: Teachers College Press, 1966.
3. Barron, F. *Creativity and psychological health*. Princeton: Van Nostrand, 1963.
4. Bing, E. Effect of childrearing practices on development of differential cognitive abilities. *Child Devel.*, 1963, **34**, 631–648.
5. Bowden, E. A. F. Perceptual abilities of African and European children educated together. *J. Soc. Psychol.*, 1969, **70**, 149–154.
6. Charles, D. C. Ability and accomplishment of persons earlier judged to be mentally defective. *Genet. Psychol. Mono.*, 1953, **47**, 3–71.
7. Charles D. C., & James, S. T. Stability of average intelligence. *J. Genet. Psychol.*, 1964, **105**, 105–111.
8. Crandall, V. J., Dewey, R., Katkovsky, W., & Preston, A. Parents' attitudes and behaviors and grade school children's academic achievements. *J. Genet. Psychol.*, 1964, **104**, 53–66.
9. Cravioto, J., & Licardie, E. R. Intersensory development of school-age children. In N. S. Scrimshaw & J. E. Gordon (Eds.), *Malnutrition, learning and behavior*. Cambridge, Mass.: M.I.T. Press, 1968, p. 252–268.
10. Durrell, D. D. Listening comprehension versus reading comprehension. *J. Reading*, 1969, **12**, 455–460.
11. Dyk, R. B., & Witkin, H. A. Family experiences related to the development of differentiation in children. *Child Devel.*, 1965, **36**, 21–55.
12. Elkind, D. Cognitive structure in latency behavior. Paper presented at the conference on "Origins of Individuality." Madison: University of Wisconsin, Sept. 26–27, 1969.
13. Elkind, D., & Weiss, J. Studies in perceptual development. III: Perceptual exploration. *Child Devel.*, 1967, **38**, 553–561.
14. Farnham-Diggory, S. Cognitive synthesis in Negro and white children. *Mono. Soc. Res. Child Devel.*, 1970, **35**:2.
15. Fifer, G. Social class and cultural group differences in diverse mental abilities. Princeton, N.J.: Educational Testing Service, 1965.

16. Gardner, D. B. Children's perception of time and rhythm: Intersensory determinants. Paper presented at the annual convention of the Rocky Mountain Psychological Association, Denver, May 9, 1968.
17. Gellert, E. Children's lateralization of human figures: Analysis of a developmental transition. *J. Psychol.*, 1967, **67**, 107–126.
18. Gliner, C. R., et al. A developmental investigation of visual and haptic preferences for shape and texture. *Mono. Soc. Res. Child Devel.*, 1969, **34**:6.
19. Goldman, A. E., & Levine, M. A developmental study of object sorting. *Child Devel.*, 1963, **34**, 649–666.
20. Goldschmid, M. L., & Bentler, P. M. The dimensions and measurement of conservation. *Child Devel.*, 1968, **39**, 787–815.
21. Gottfried, N. W. The relationship between concepts of conservation of length and number. *J. Genet. Psychol.*, 1969, **114**, 85–91.
22. Hawkes, G. R., & Pease, D. *Behavior and development from five to twelve.* New York: Harper, 1962.
23. Holtzman, W. H., Diaz Guerrero, R., Swartz, J. D., & Tapia, L. L. Cross-cultural longitudinal research on child development: Studies of American and Mexican schoolchildren. In J. P. Hill (Ed.), *Minnesota symposia on child psychology, Vol. 2.* Minneapolis: University of Minnesota Press, 1969, pp. 125–158.
24. Horrocks, J. E. *Assessment of behavior.* Columbus, Ohio: Merrill, 1964.
25. Kagan, J. Development and personality differences in problem-solving. Paper presented at the Wheelock College Institute for the Exploration of Early Childhood Education. Boston, November 6, 1964.
26. Kagan, J., Moss, H. A., & Sigel, I. E. Psychological significance of styles of conceptualization. In Wright [74], pp. 73–111.
27. Kagan, J., Pearson, L., & Welch, L. Conceptual impulsivity and inductive reasoning. *Child Devel.*, 1966, **37**, 583–594.
28. Kagan, J., Rosman, B. L., Day, D., Albert, J., & Phillips, W. Information-processing in the child: Significance of analytic and reflective attitudes. *Psychol. Mono.*, 1964, **78**:1.
29. Kaplan, E. The acquisition of word meanings: A developmental study. *Mono. Soc. Res. Child Devel.*, 1952, **15**:1.
30. Kaplan, M. L., & Mandel, S. Class differences in the effects of impulsivity, goal orientation, and verbal expression on an object-sorting task. *Child Devel.*, 1969, **40**, 491–502.
31. Lee, L. C., Kagan, J., & Rabson, A. Influence of a preference for analytic categorization upon concept acquisition. *Child Devel.*, 1963, **34**, 433–442.
32. Levy, D. M. *Maternal Overprotection*, New York: Columbia University Press, 1943.
33. Liebert, R. M., Odom, R. D., Hill, J. H., & Huff, R. L. Effects of age and rule familiarity on the production of modeled language constructions. *Devel. Psychol.*, 1969, **1**, 108–112.
34. Lovell, K. *The growth of basic mathematical and scientific concepts in children.* New York: Philosophical Library, 1961.
35. Lovell, K. Some recent studies in cognitive and language development. *Merrill-Palmer Quart.*, 1968, **14**, 123–138.
36. Lovell, K., & Ogilvie, E. A study of the conservation of substance in the junior school child. *Brit. J. Educ. Psychol.*, 1960, **30**, 109–118. Cited in [34].

37. Maccoby, E. E. Woman's intellect. In S. M. Farber & R. H. L. Wilson (Eds.), *The potential of woman*. New York: McGraw-Hill, 1963, pp. 24–39.
38. Neale, J. M. Egocentrism in institutionalized and noninstitutionalized children. *Child Devel.*, 1966, **37**, 97–101.
39. O'Bryan, K. G., & MacArthur, R. S. Reversibility, intelligence, and creativity in nine-year-old boys. *Child Devel.*, 1969, **40**, 33–45.
40. Opie, I., & Opie, P. *The lore and language of school children*. Oxford: Clarendon, 1959.
41. Pedersen, F. A. & Wender, P. H. Early social correlates of cognitive functioning in six-year-old boys. *Child Devel.*, 1968, **39**, 185–193.
42. Piaget, J. *The psychology of intelligence*. London: Routledge & Kegan Paul, 1950.
43. Piaget, J. How children learn mathematical concepts. *Sci. Am.*, 1953, **189**, 74–79.
44. Piaget, J. Cognitive development in children: The Piaget papers. In R. E. Ripple and V. N. Rockcastle (Eds.), *Piaget rediscovered*. Ithaca, N.Y.: School of Education, Cornell University, 1964, pp. 6–48.
45. Piaget, J. *The child's conception of number*. New York: Norton, 1965.
46. Piaget, J. Foreword to M. Almy, E. Chittenden, & P. Miller, *Young children's thinking*. New York: Teachers College Press, 1966.
47. Pick, A. D. Some basic perceptual processes in reading. *Young Children*, 1970, **15**, 162–181.
48. Ripple, R. E., & May, F. B. Caution in comparing creativity and IQ. *Psychol. Reports*, 1962, **10**, 229–230.
49. Roeper, A., & Sigel, I. E. Finding the clue to children's thought processes. In W. W. Hartup and N. L. Smothergill (Eds.), *The young child: Reviews of research*. Washington, D.C.: National Association for the Education of Young Children, 1967.
50. Rogers, D. W. Visual expression: A creative advantage of the disadvantaged. *Gifted Child Quart.*, 1968, **12**, 110–114.
51. Senf, G. M. Development of immediate memory for bisensory stimuli in normal children and children with learning disorders. *Devel. Psychol. Mono.*, 1969, **1**, No. 6, Part 2.
52. Siegelman, E. Reflective and impulsive observing behavior. *Child Devel.*, 1969, **40**, 1213–1222.
53. Smedslund, J. Development of concrete transitivity of length in children. *Child Devel.*, 1963, **34**, 389–405.
54. Smith, M. K. Measurement of the size of general English vocabulary through the elementary grades and high school. *Genet. Psychol. Mono*, 1941, **24**, 311–345.
55. Stevenson, H. W., Miller, L. K., & Hale, G. A. Children's ability to guess the ages of adults. *Psychol. Reports*, 1967, **20**, 1265–1266.
56. Templin, M. C. The study of articulation and language development during the early school years. In F. Smith & G. A. Miller (Eds.), *The genesis of language*. Cambridge, Mass.: M.I.T. Press, 1966, pp. 173–186.
57. Templin, M. C. Longitudinal study of English morphology in children with varying articulation in kindergarten. Paper presented at the meeting of the Society for Research in Child Development, Santa Monica, Calif., March 27, 1969.

58. Terman, L. M., & Merrill, M. A. *Stanford–Binet intelligence scale*. Boston: Houghton Mifflin, 1960.
59. Terman, L. M., & Oden, M. H. *The gifted child grows up*, Vol. IV. Genetic studies of genius series. Stanford, Calif.: Stanford University Press, 1947.
60. Tiegs, E. W., & Clark, W. W. *California achievement tests*. Los Angeles: California Test Bureau, 1934.
61. Torrance, E. P. *Guiding creative talent*. Englewood Cliffs, N.J.: Prentice-Hall, 1962.
62. Uzgiris, I. C. Situational generality of conservation. *Child Devel.*, 1964, **35**, 831–841.
63. van Hekken, S. M. J. The influence of verbalization on observational learning in a group of mediating and a group of non-mediating children. *Human Devel.*, 1969, **12**, 204–213.
64. Vurpillot, E. The development of scanning strategies and their relation to visual differentiation. *J. Exper. Child Psychol.*, 1968, **6**, 632–650.
65. Vygotsky, L. S. *Thought and language*. Cambridge: M.I.T. Press, 1962.
66. Wallach, L., & Sprott, R. L. Inducing number conservation in children. *Child Devel.*, 1964, **35**, 1057–1071.
67. Wallach, M. A. & Kogan, N. *Modes of thinking in young children: A study of the creativity-intelligence distinction*. New York: Holt, Rinehart & Winston, 1965.
68. Ward, W. C. Reflection-impulsivity in kindergarten children. *Child Devel.*, 1968, **39**, 867–874.
69. Werner, E. E., & Bachtold, L. M. Personality factors of gifted boys and girls in middle childhood and adolescence. *Psychol. in Schools*, 1969, **6**, 177–182.
70. Werner, H., & Kaplan, E. Development of word meaning through verbal context: An experimental study. *J. Psychol.*, 1950, **29**, 251–257.
71. Witkin, H. A., Dyk, R. B., Faterson, H. F., Goodenough, D. R., & Karp, S. A. *Psychological differentiation*. New York: Wiley, 1962.
72. Wohlwill, J. F. Responses to class-inclusion questions for verbally and pictorially presented items. *Child Devel.*, 1968, **39**, 449–465.
73. Wolfenstein, M. *Children's humor*. Glencoe, Ill.: Free Press, 1958.
74. Wright, J. C., & Kagan, J. (Eds.), Basic cognitive processes in children. *Mono. Soc. Res. Child Devel.*, 1963, **28**:2.
75. Zigler, E., Levine, J., & Gould, L. Cognitive challenge as a factor in children's humor appreciation. *J. Personal. Soc. Psychol.*, 1967, **7**, 332–336.
76. Zimiles, H. The development of conservation and differentiation of number. *Mono. Soc. Res. Child Devel.*, 1966, **31**:6.
77. Zimiles, H., & Asch, H. A cross-cultural comparison of advantaged and disadvantaged children's ability to classify. Paper presented at the meeting of the Society for Research in Child Development, Santa Monica, Calif., March 27, 1969.

# Chapter 11

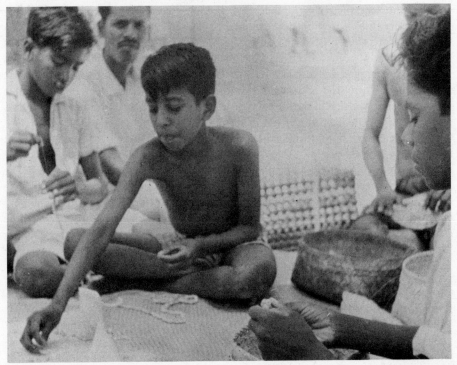

Mollie Smart

# Increasing Competence as a
# Learner and Doer

Ever since birth, or even earlier, the child has been bringing more and more of his environment under control, through his exploration, manipulation, thinking, talking, imagining, and producing changes. Much of the satisfaction he has experienced has been the product of these activities. He has indeed been competent in many ways, including sucking milk, shaking a rattle, creeping, filling a basket with toys, riding a kiddy car, climbing the jungle gym, and playing store. All of these achievements brought joy in the process of mastery. For the most part, these activities were undertaken for themselves because they were intrinsically interesting, not because anyone urged or rewarded the child to explore, learn, and perform [96]. As the child becomes concerned with developing a sense of industry, new dimensions are added to his efforts to explore and control the environment.

## Development of the Sense of Industry

The school-age child becomes interested in doing well and in operating in socially accepted ways. In order to behave thus, it is necessary to learn just what those patterns of thought and action are, to learn the rules of the game. As the previous chapter showed, increasing intellectual maturity results in socialized thinking, whereby the child delays responses while he checks his conclusions and decisions with those of other people, instead of jumping quickly to his own. Some of his satisfaction now comes from measuring up to standards outside himself, from fitting into a bigger and broader world. He is willing to work to learn the basic skills of his culture, the patterns of thinking and doing which mark the difference between being a little child and being a big child on the way to adulthood. He is getting ready to be a producer [28, p. 259].

The child goes about the business of learning his society's skills and rules in style which grows out of his own personality. His performance depends, for example, on how strongly he wants achievement and recognition, how anxious he feels over succeeding, and upon his tendency to reflect before responding. The cultural and social settings within which he interacts will be discussed in the next chapter. In this chapter, the child's development as a learner and producer will be considered in relation to the school, the institution designed especially for teaching him the fundamentals of knowledge.

### Relation of Previous Stages to the Sense of Industry

Each stage of personality development has its roots in the past, being built out of what has gone before. The earlier sense of trust, autonomy, and initiative contribute now to the development of the sense of industry. Time orientation, locus of control, and curiosity can be understood as outcomes of previous stages and as determinants of success in establishing a healthy sense of industry.

**Time Orientation.** In infancy, the sense of trust is derived partly from experiences with time which come from cycles of tension, delay of satisfaction, and satiation [29, p. 181]. As tension builds up during delay, the baby anticipates fulfillment. Signs of approaching satisfaction give hope, and extended delays cause rage. Excess tension, waiting, and rage lead to lack of hope and trust, and in later childhood and adolescence, a disturbed sense of time. The ability to judge intervals of time and the ability to order events in time are related to moral development, as will be seen in a later section of this chapter. Future time orientation is related to achievement behavior which is an important aspect of the sense of industry.

**Locus of Control.** The toddler develops a sense of autonomy through repeated successes in purposefully controlling his environment. As he realizes that he can choose between real alternatives, as he experiences positive outcomes of choices he knows to be his own, he has a sense of autonomy. He feels that he is in charge. Reality includes places where he cannot choose and where he is not in charge. A healthy sense of autonomy grows upon a balance of freedom to choose successfully and limits on choosing. By the time the child reaches the industry stage, he has established convictions about to what extent he is in charge. He believes that he can choose and determine much of what happens to him or he feels that outside forces are largely responsible. Those who locate control outside themselves may believe that fate or luck or other people cause events. The individual with an internal locus of control believes that *he* himself causes events. A child's locus of control may vary from one area of life to another [48].

An internal locus of control is related to achievement behavior [13]. It makes sense to try harder if you believe that your efforts will have the intended results. Success and excellence, so important for development of the sense of industry, are thus dependent on belief in internal locus of control, which is an aspect of the sense of autonomy. The locus of control is established during childhood and changes little during the time between third and twelfth grades [13]. Middle-class children believe more in internal control than do lower-class children, and white children more than black [11]. This finding is logical when one considers the greater power possessed by middle-class people and whites. They really can control their environments more than can people lower on the socioeconomic ladder, and more than blacks. We would expect their children to reflect this bit of reality.

**Curiosity.** The preschool child involves himself with development of the sense of initiative through exploring his environment, the objects and the people in it, the actions of which he is capable. Through play, he tries on different roles and investigates different media as ways of creating and discovering. Among the treasures he gains from successful development of the sense of initiative is curiosity. There are two main forms of curiosity: seeking new experiences, and looking for answers to problems. Seeking new experience includes exploring places, objects, and people, looking for new sensory stimulation, new ideas, and new ways of moving. New experience is rewarding in itself. The second form of curiosity involves reducing uncertainty or dissonance to restore equilibrium. Seeing some differences between what he experiences and what he expects, the child seeks further information in order to resolve the conflict [71]. Insufficient new experience leads to boredom and restlessness; too great an environmental change is either shocking or frightening or both. Curiosity is aroused by appropriate degrees of unusualness and incongruity. Children vary in how much new experience they seek, how many new answers they try to find, and how great an environmental change is satisfying rather than frightening [60]. For boys, but not for girls, early (before 6 months) fear of novelty is associated with shyness and fear of strangeness in childhood [7].

During the preschool years, when the sense of initiative is developing fast, satisfying experiences with exploration lead to a lasting interest in reaching out and discovering. The richer the environment, the more curious the child can become; the more curious he is, the more he can discover in his environment. Curiosity can be both a help and a hindrance in the tasks of middle childhood. In situations where adults demand high conformity, as in schools where routines are sacred, or in homes where privacy, quiet, and order are greatly cherished, a very curious child will be too disruptive. The advantages of curiosity outweigh these small liabilities, however, since it stimulates learning and the development of the sense of industry.

Healthy psychological adjustment is associated with high curiosity in children [68]. Teachers' ratings of overall psychological health correlated positively with scores on tests in which children manipulated objects, examined them freely, and commented on them. Low-anxious children preferred more novelty than high-anxious children [70]. A sex difference was demonstrated in first grade children's and younger children's curiosity and seeking of information and experience. Boys were more curious than girls [70, 88]. Desire for novelty seems to increase with age, at least during the early years [70].

Robert J. Izzo

Intellectual competence is related to curiosity, as might be expected. One piece of evidence comes from a comparison of children whose IQs rose with those whose IQs fell during the years between the ages of 6 and 10 [51]. Responses to a projective test indicated that children with rising IQs were more curious and less passive than those with falling IQs. Another type of evidence is furnished by fifth grade children whose curiosity was judged by ratings of teachers, peers, and selves. A child was called curious to the extent that he moved toward, explored, or manipulated new, strange, or mysterious elements of his environments; showed a need or desire to know about himself and his environment; scanned his surroundings, seeking new experiences; persisted in examining and exploring. A week after hearing a story read, the children were tested for memories of it. The children with high curiosity remembered significantly more than did those with low curiosity [65, 66]. In a third study, tasks were arranged in such a way that some children experienced more curiosity than others during the problem-solving process [72]. The high-curiosity group learned more efficiently (made fewer errors) than the low-curiosity group. Children high in curiosity were found to be more flexible and consistent in thinking and also more creative than children low in curiosity [68].

*Achievement Aspiration*

There are two standpoints from which to consider achievement—the strength of the need or desire for it, and the behavior oriented toward it. Basic to achievement motivation, or the need for achievement, is the child's application of a standard of excellence to the performance he is judging and a feeling tone which goes along with that judgment [59]. In other words, he says, "I did well" or "He did a good job" or "He did a poor job," while having a pleasant or unpleasant feeling about the situation. The goal of achievement behavior is the attainment of approval and avoidance of disapproval, either one's own or somebody else's [15]. Achievement, then, is of the essence of the period of the development of a sense of industry. In order to become a successful learner of the ways of the culture and to become a productive member of society, thus assuring a sense of adequacy, the child must want to achieve and must, in fact, achieve.

**Stability of Achievement Over Time.** Both need for achievement and achievement behavior were studied over a period of 18 years at the Fels foundation. Both types of measurements showed some consistency from one age level to another. Need for achievement was tested at 8 years, by asking children to tell stories in response to pictures (Thematic Apperception Test) and analyzing for achievement themes. Retesting the children at 11 and 14, moderate correlations were found with the need for achievement at 8 years [50]. A similar study on 8 to 10-year-old boys, retested after six years, showed similar results [32]. Achievement behavior, as shown by ratings and interviews at the Fels foundation, showed some consistency from nursery school age to young adulthood. Low but significant correlations were found between ratings during preschool and elementary school years and between elementary school age and early adolescence. Girls' preschool achievement behavior was related to their adult achievement behavior, but boys' was not. By middle childhood, however, achievement striving was related to adult achievement behavior. During early adolescence, intellectual achievement behavior was predictive of adult behavior, but athletic and mechanical achievement efforts were not related to adult behavior.

**Stability of Achievement Across Situations.** During the early elementary school years, a child's expectations of himself tend to be consistent between intellectual, artistic, mechanical, and athletic areas [14]. If he did well in one area, he expected to do well in the others. If he held high standards in one, he was likely to hold high standards in all. However, actual achievement behavior did not show so much consistency across situations. With slightly older children, a relationship was shown between intellectual and mechanical achievement behaviors, but not between intellectual and athletic [73]. A factor analytic study on fifth grade black children, sampling a variety of achievement behaviors, shows that there is a general academic achievement dimension [89]. Achievement showed little or no consistency across situations that were different. The more similar the situations, the more similar the achievement behavior shown by boys, but not by girls. For example, tasks differ in *behavioral* requirements such as that of speaking, writing, listening, manipulating, and observing. *Social* requirements differ as to group versus individual situations, presence of audience, rigidity, and competition. *Cognitive* requirements vary as to convergence or divergence (whether there is only one answer or many), flexibility versus rigidity of thinking, level of abstraction, and receiving or synthesizing information. In addition to the general factor in academic achievement, there were five other factors: behavior in individual work situations, behavior with divergent tasks, recitation, perseverance, and behavior on convergent tasks.

**Sex Differences.** Achievement motivation is not the same for girls as it is for boys. Boys' achievement need and behavior have been studied much more extensively than have girls', perhaps reflecting the general attitude that it is more important for boys to achieve than it is for girls to do so. The difference is, of course, closely related to sex role. Achievement for the sake of achievement seems to motivate boys more than girls, while the seeking of approval and affection is often bound up with the achievement efforts of girls [52]. The boys' achievement behavior was more autonomously motivated, in a sample of early grade schoolboys and girls who were tested for achievement and whose parents were interviewed. For boys, but not for girls, belief in self-responsibility was correlated with scores on academic achievement tests. When academic achievement test scores were correlated with tests of achievement need, a significant relationship was found for boys but not for girls [84]. The girls' achievement was found to relate instead to their desire for affection and approval. In an experimental situation, however, boys and girls responded equally to praise by improving performance on a coding task [90].

The standards of excellence which boys set for themselves tend to be more realistic than those of girls, or at least such was true for 40 day camp children from the first three grades [16]. The boys held standards which corresponded with their performances on intelligence and achievement tests. The opposite was true of girls, whose expectations of success were negatively correlated with their intelligence scores. The sexes also differed in their beliefs about personal responsibility for success. Among the boys but not girls, the more capable ones were strongly convinced that they themselves were responsible for their own achievements. Thus the boys were practical and realistic in their attitudes toward achievement, whereas the girls were more influenced by their wishes and values. Sex role expectations probably account for the differences. Perhaps boys are criticized more than girls when their stated expectations do not fit their performances. It may be that incompetent girls are praised for saying, "I'll try," while very able girls are scolded for being boastful when they predict high success for themselves. At any rate, sex is an important determiner of achievement orientation.

**Some Correlates of Achievement.** High-achieving children are distinguished from average and low achievers by certain characteristics which suggest that in the early years of life, high achievers accept and internalize adult middle-class values. A group of gifted third grade children, studied through tests, observations, and parent-and-teacher interviews, indicated that superior academic achievers are likely to be independent, asking for little help from adults. These children persisted longer at problems, competed more with their peers, expressed less warmth toward their siblings, and had more guilt feelings than average children [20]. Information obtained about the same children, four years later, showed them as persistent, competitive, still mastering and striving, but sometimes aggressive and destructive in order to win, often antagonistic and belittling to adults, more anxious than formerly, and less creative than they used to be [39]. High academic achievement, then, is likely to exact a price, even during middle childhood.

*Competition and Cooperation*

The sense of industry is nurtured by experiences of doing well with the tasks required or encountered. The child finds out whether he has performed adequately

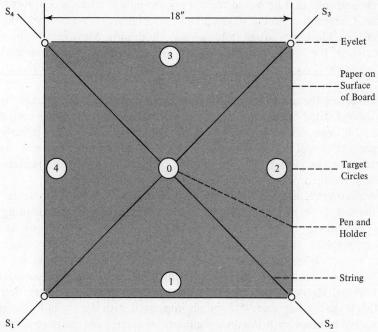

S₄ ——— 18" ——— S₃ — Eyelet

— Paper on Surface of Board

4   0   2 — Target Circles

— Pen and Holder

1 — String

S₁   S₂

**Figure 11–1.** Cooperation board.

SOURCE: Reprinted with permission of author and publisher: Madsen, M. C. Cooperative and competitive motivation of children in three Mexican subcultures. *Psychological Reports*, 1967, 20, 1307–1320.

by measuring himself on the standards provided for him. Middle-class urban society tends to define success and adequacy largely in terms of competition, of doing better than other people. Some children are convinced that they have to be *best* in order to succeed. If only one in a group, or a few in a group, can succeed, then many are doomed to failure, with a resulting sense of inferiority and inadequacy. While highly competitive behavior has served important functions in our society, we are now faced with the need for more cooperative behavior for solving community problems and world problems. Other cultures, some planned and some unplanned, demonstrate different ways of institutionalizing competition and cooperation. We can get insight from research which compares our children with theirs.

Madsen and associates have used a "cooperation board" to elicit cooperative and competitive behavior from children in rural and urban Mexico [62], urban and rural communal Israel [87], and three ethnic urban United States groups [63]. Figure 11–1 is a sketch of the apparatus, a board 18 inches square. A string, fastened to a device holding a pen in the center, is strung through an eyelet fastened to each corner. A sheet of paper is placed on the board. A child sits at each corner and pulls his string. He can pull it only toward himself. If the pen is to be pulled anywhere other than in a straight line from center to corner, children have to cooperate. Circles were placed as shown in the drawing. Children were shown how they could draw lines through the circles. In the cooperative condition, children were told that each would receive a prize if they drew lines through all four circles. All children thus learned how to perform cooperatively. Then the reward conditions were changed, but the task remained the same. Each child was assigned one circle and told that he would receive a prize only if a line was drawn through his circle. Cooperation would pay off, and the children knew how to work the pen cooperatively. However, urban, middle-class children in Mexico were much more competitive in the second condition [62]. When Mexican village children were compared with three urban United States groups, results were dramatic [87]. The Afro-America and Anglo-American groups were aggressively, even wildly, competitive, and the urban Mexican Americans were competitive but less vigorous. In the three United States groups, there was no instance of group cooperation, while the Mexican village group showed no instance of competitive behavior. The experiment in Israel revealed competition in the urban group and complete cooperation in the kibbutzim. The kibbutz children discussed the problem thoroughly and planned procedures, including equal sharing of prizes.

Children compete as groups rather than as individuals in both the Soviet Union and in the kibbutzim of Israel. This arrangement reflects conscious planning on the part of educators, in order to prepare children for cooperative societies. An American psychiatrist observing in Israel found kibbutz life ideally suited to the needs of the school-age child [4, p. 202]. He has easy access to tasks which need doing, which he can do well, and which bring rewards to his age group and to the whole kibbutz. He develops little or no sense of inferiority (page 343). Bettelheim found this stage the happiest: ". . . one is impressed with the joy of living in them, how the day bubbles with interest, stimulation, excitement and satisfaction" [p. 202].

### The Sense of Inferiority

An unfavorable outcome of the development of the sense of industry is too great a sense of inferiority and inadequacy. The child may have too few opportunities to succeed, too great a discrepancy between his opportunities and his resources. His cognitive limitations offer some protection against overwhelming feelings of inferiority. Cognitive conceit (see page 399), the belief that children know more than adults because adults do not know everything, serves a useful function in maintaining feelings of adequacy in the face of actual adult superiority. Damage can result from excessive unsuccessful competition with peers and siblings and from failure in school.

**Anxiety.** Anxiety is a stirred-up, unpleasant, tense feeling, focused only vaguely or generally. Fear indicates the same type of feeling state but with accompanying attention focused on a specific situation or problem. In childhood, according to Erikson [28, p. 408], it is difficult or impossible to distinguish fear from anxiety. Whether fear or anxiety, this unpleasant tension affects the ways in which the child approaches and deals with his job of learning and producing. Some of the tests devised to measure anxiety deal with general situations and others with particular situations, especially school. The type of statements used to test general anxiety are illustrated by the following: "I feel I have to be best in everything." "I notice my heart beats very fast sometimes." "I worry about doing the right things." "It is hard for me to go to sleep at night" [9]. Anxiety over tests is examined by means of questions such as these: "When the teacher wants to find out how much you have learned, do you get a funny feeling in your stomach?" "Do you worry a lot before you take a test?" "While you are taking a test, do you usually think you are not doing well?" [80].

White girls have been found to be higher than white boys in both types of anxiety, general and test anxiety [81]. Since this finding fits in with cultural expectations of boys and girls, it may be that the difference is partly due to youngsters trying to live up to ideal sex roles. Another contributing factor may be girls' tendency to care a great deal about approval and affection and to try to win these prizes through their achievement efforts. Boys, with their more internalized standards of excellence, would understandably worry less about what people thought of them. Black children showed higher levels of anxiety than white children, throughout the second grade population of a large eastern school system [33]. Unlike the white children, black boys were no less anxious than black girls. Their anxiety was strongly related to the mother's educational level. This finding fits with the finding that poor, lower-class parents give few rewards and little encouragement for desirable behavior, especially verbal efforts, that they require obedience and discourage exploration, curiosity, and independent thinking.

Scores on anxiety tests correlate negatively with IQ [82]. These correlations tend to increase with grade level. Probably interaction is reciprocal. Suffering more and more defeats as he goes through school, a child of low intelligence would feel increasingly inferior, anxious, and reluctant to get into the situation of being tested. Learning and achievement show complicated relationships to anxiety. Both the level of anxiety and the difficulty and type of task must be taken into account. While moderate anxiety may help the child in performing fairly easy tasks, anxiety, especially high anxiety, is likely to interfere with success on difficult tasks. To show the significance of type of task, high-anxious and low-anxious children were tested for achievement in reading and arithmetic [12]. The low-anxious group was definitely superior in arithmetic. For reading, there was a slight but insignificant difference in favor of the high-anxious group. Another study, however, a longitudinal one, found anxiety related earlier and more strongly to reading than to arithmetic [82].

The definition of success and failure will vary from one child to another, depending upon what he and others expect of him. To one person a grade of C means success, while to another, anything short of A is a failure. The aspirations of children who achieve on a low level in the class are, on the average, above the level at which they achieve. Therefore, they usually experience failure. In contrast, children who achieve on the highest level tend to pitch their aspirations lower than their achievement level. Therefore, they usually experience success. Success and failure in school are so very public, as compared with success on the job. It is impossible to hide from teachers, classmates, or parents, and even neighbors and grandparents, the exact marks or grades obtained, and just how those grades compare with Betty's, Tommy's, and Jonathan's grades. Contrasting the aspiration level of children who had chronic failure in reading and arithmetic with children who had a history of success, the successful children were seen as aspiring to levels where they succeeded, while the chronically unsuccessful ones set their aspirations with little regard for achievement [3]. Some set extremely high goals which they could never reach, as though a mere gesture would substitute for realistic action.

It seems reasonable that a very mild degree of fear or anxiety would help a child in problem solving, as long as the resulting tense feeling served to focus his attention squarely on the task at hand. A greater degree of fear would immobilize his resources, freezing them instead of energizing them. Repeated experiences with failure would lead to expectation of more failure, a feeling of worthlessness, inferiority, and inadequacy, all of which constitute the negative of a sense of industry.

**Fears.** Specific fears of predominantly white children were studied in Grades 3 through 6 [18]. Girls had more fears than boys, and lower socioeconomic-level children more than higher. The children were asked what they feared now, what fears they had held in the past, and what they expected to fear in the future. The children saw themselves as having been more fearful in the past than at present. They expected to have fewer fears in the future. With the exception of third grade present fears, the present and future fears of all were most often political. In former years, children were more likely to fear supernatural phenomena and animals. Probably modern communications make children aware of world problems at increasingly early ages.

## Areas of Competency

Academic skills figure largely in this picture. Competencies include motor coordinations, skills as a worker at home, knowledge of games and various areas of interest, and knowledge of a religion and of a system of morals and values. In all such areas the child takes over the patterns of his culture, and while making them his own makes himself a functioning member of his society. A positive self concept, as shown by high self-esteem, is related to school achievement, as shown by correlating between self concept and achievement scores in arithmetic and reading [84]. The child benefits greatly from having a wide choice of opportunities for adequacy in order that there will be a goodly number of places in which he really does succeed. A healthy environment therefore includes broad academic areas, a variety of play activities, and chances to work at different jobs and to know many people, places, and objects.

**Reading.** The roots of the skill of reading lie in speech and graphic representation. An earlier chapter showed that speech emerges without direct teaching. So does graphic representation. All toddlers spontaneously make marks, using paper and crayon, if available, and if not, a stick in the sand or charcoal on a rock. Preschool children can separate scribbles from script [35]. A very few children learn to read on their own. A few children learn with minimal help from an older sibling or a parent. Most children learn from teachers, who guide them through the perceptual, conceptual, verbal, and motor performances necessary for success. There are many different methods of teaching reading, and these have been the subject of much research and sometimes heated opinion. There is also controversy as to *when* reading should be taught. Since success in school depends so heavily on reading, naive parents, and sometimes teachers, assume that the earlier formal instruction is begun, the better. A sound foundation for reading is built in the preschool years through development in language, graphic arts, visual and auditory perception, attention, curiosity, motor skills, and esthetic appreciation of books and stories. This vital preparation for reading is much more available to the middle-class child than to the poor child. Compensatory programs attempt to "make it up" to the child. Day-care programs, especially those which take infants and toddlers, are designed to offer opportunities for optimal growth, so as to make compensation unnecessary.

Even with good preparation for learning to read, some children learn faster and more easily than others. The lock-step of the traditional school does disservice to both fast and slow learners. The overwhelming sense of inferiority resulting from reading failure can seriously block a child in his efforts toward competency. The problem, therefore, is threefold: to arrange for each child to learn to read at the time most appropriate for him; to let him proceed at full speed for him; and to have him feel right about himself, whether he learned early or late, quickly or slowly.

The study of reading disorders is a specialized field. Causes of disorders reach into almost every facet of the child's development and relationships, to include basic physical disorders, such as perinatal brain injury, social deprivation in the form of impoverished family background and lack of early stimulation, emotional disruptions, lack of establishment of lateral dominance and preference, motor disturbances, and upsetting educational experiences.

**Writing.** The development of skill in writing involves eye–hand coordination of perceptual and conceptual activity. Aims, values, and practices in teaching handwriting are often rather confused [44]. For instance, if it is important for the child to learn to write in a standard style, then precise coordination is at a premium, and the child who lacks such control must work very hard, with much frustration. When handwriting style is considered an expression of individual personality rather than a standard product, the teacher will help the child to develop his own style within certain limits of legibility. If the main purpose of writing is conceived of as communication, then a high standard of legibility is in order. If writing is done mainly for the individual himself, in order to express his thoughts or take notes for himself, then speed, not legibility, is the prime essential.

Since motor control plays such a large part in learning to write neatly, according to a standard form, and since motor control is not highly correlated with IQ, reading, and other academic achievement, high skill in handwriting may be possible for many children who do not have widespread academic success. This is not to say that a very adequate student might not also write well, but only that chances to be good writers are distributed on a different basis from chances to excel in other subject matter areas. Handwriting, then, might serve some children as a much-needed source of feelings of adequacy and thus aid in development of a sense of industry.

Rarely, if ever, does handwriting express thoughts quickly enough to be efficient and satisfying. The first grader, just learning to write, would be completely frustrated if he wanted to record his thoughts. If an adult will occasionally take dictation from him, he can thus "write" stories and letters which will give him satisfaction and adequacy and which will also develop his ability to communicate through writing. Another effective aid to written expression is the typewriter. After the initial stages of learning to type, which can be done early in this stage of life, or even before, the individual can communicate and record his thoughts ever so much more quickly, efficiently, and legibly by typewriter than by hand.

Writing can be considered in a context quite different from that of making representational marks. Writing is also linguistic expression. In this sense, it shares some characteristics with thought or inner speech and some with socialized speech. A comparison of oral and written language reveals some similarities and differences [40]. The subjects were 320 children, ages 9, 11, 13, and 15, who told and wrote stories. The stories were analyzed for length, type of clauses, and unrelated words used. The findings included these: no tendency for girls to excel boys, except in length of written compositions; more subordinate clauses used in writing than in speaking, increasingly so with advance in age; more adjective and adverb clauses in writing, more noun clauses in speaking; positive correlations between subordinate clauses in writing and age, mental age, IQ, and occupational status of father; no indication that a mature level had been reached in either oral or written stories by age 15. Writing in this sense, then, is an academic skill with its own distinctive characteristics, a skill which shows continuous development throughout the school years.

**Mathematics.** Based on the cognitive activities of classifying, abstracting, ordering, and relating, the learning of number concepts is influenced by the experiences the child has had at home, at nursery school, and at kindergarten. His cognitive style makes a difference, too. The tendency to analyze visual arrays is helpful in abstracting numbers out of groups of objects. Spatial imagery and discrimination are probably quite important to success. Reflectivity, rather than impulsivity, is understandably an aid in problem solving. Thus the intellectual and personality development of the child have a direct bearing on the ease or difficulty he experiences in his first encounters with arithmetic in school. He soon feels adequate or inadequate in regard to mathematics, often reinforced by family or friends. Since mathematical ability is often considered appropriate for men and not for women, many girls inhibit their growth along these lines in order to fit into the sex role which they feel required to assume.

Like the teaching of reading, instruction in mathematics has undergone a revolution since mid-century. The old methods relied heavily upon rote memory and drill. In former times teachers tried to build mathematical concepts by having the child manipulate spoken and written symbols. Most likely, the children who made good progress with these methods were the ones blessed with stimulating environments, in which they had and continued to have rich opportunities for arranging, ordering, grouping, and discriminating. The "new math" incorporates knowledge about concept formation. Number concepts are built with the aid of visual perception and imagery and often other sensory experiences as well. Books and pictures are planned and arranged so as to use visual perception and imagery. Objects such as blocks, rods, beads, and cards are employed not only to provide tactile perception, but to permit the child to arrange, group, and order objects. This type of apparatus has been designed in such a way as to give insight into counting, grouping, addition, subtraction, multiplication, division, measurement, fractions, ratio, decimals, percentage, square measure, and cubic measure. Eventually, of course, the child must free himself of dependence on concrete objects if he is to go very far in mathematics.

The "new math" holds a promise of success for more children. Under the old methods, many children, especially those with limited backgrounds, experienced early failure and discouragement. Now, if a child is allowed to progress at his own rate, the school can offer him materials and experiences with which to build useful concepts. It is theoretically possible for all children (except the severely brain-damaged and ill) to be successful with mathematics in the elementary school. As a child sees himself mastering this important cultural tool, his sense of industry is enhanced, and he enjoys healthy personality growth.

**Maturity As a Predictor of Academic Success.** Physical maturity has been mentioned in the previous chapter as a predictor of success in first grade. A rating scale used by teachers on fifth grade children has shown that social and intellectual ratings, as well as physical, are related to achievement [69]. Significant social items included considerateness of others, cooperativeness in group activities and relationships with peers. Emotional maturity items were attentiveness, self-control, self-confidence, and anxiety. The physical considerations were size and coordination. Intellectual maturity included memory for procedures, eagerness to learn, speed of comprehension, language development.

**Correlates of Academic Incompetence.** A special remedial program for "educationally handicapped" children offered opportunities to find out how nonachieving children differed from children who were doing satisfactory work in school [74]. The subjects, about 2 percent of the school population, had one and a half to two years discrepancy between ability and achievement. The siblings and parents were studied, also, and compared with siblings and parents of matched controls (children of the same sex who were successful at school). Neurological and familial factors indicate some physical basis for the educational handicaps.

Compared with normal controls, the educationally handicapped children were poorer in several tests of hand and finger movements and in right–left discrimination. Medical histories showed the handicapped to have had more colic and irritability in infancy, decreased sound production, poor listening skills, difficulty in communicating with the mother, and more temper tantrums.

The educationally handicapped and their siblings shared impairments in numerical computation, sequencing, fine-perceptual-motor hand–eye coordination, memory, reading, and spelling. Parents had done less well in high school English than had parents of successful children. Fathers were poorer readers. Mothers were poorer mathematicians. The handicapped children, then, may have been influenced by both heredity and environment in their development of unsuccessful academic patterns.

### Performance as a Worker

Development of the sense of industry hinges largely on feeling and being successful as a worker. Some of such feeling and being comes when the child does well in reading, writing, arithmetic, and all the other academic skills. Although school is indeed his job, he knows too that school is not identical with the work world, in which his parents and other adults earn their living. The child needs some success in that world too. Significant work experience adds greatly to his sense of adequacy, contributes to his understanding of adults, his family and society, and gives him experience which can help him in later choice of a vocation. When he does a good job, he wins recognition and respect, giving him a toehold in the work world. Boys and men, in contrast to girls and women, have been found more task-oriented, more concerned about getting the job done and done well [23]. Girls and women showed more interest than boys and men in the social-interaction aspects of the job, the maintaining of happy relations with co-workers.

Whereas simple agricultural or hunting societies offer children easy access to important work, a complex technological society provides severely limited work opportunities. Many of the jobs available both at home and otherwise are in the realm of cleaning and tidying. While necessary and useful, this type of work does not give the child the feeling of being a producer, nor even of being necessary in earning the family living. For instance, after milking the cow, collecting the eggs, and picking the strawberries, the youngster joins with his family in eating the fruits of his labor plus the contributions of other family members. There is no comparable integrating and satisfying experience for the child who straightens up his room, empties the wastebaskets, and carries the empty pop bottles out to the car. Kitchen, basement, garage, and garden do, of course, offer some opportunities for children to contribute constructively to the home. Job possibilities outside the home are probably more curtailed, as compared with those in a simpler society or in a planned society, such as the kibbutz. The young kibbutniks spend part of their time doing exactly the same work that adults do. They raise animals and chickens, cultivate vegetables, clean the house, and may even help with earning the cash income of the kibbutz [4, pp. 161–164].

Even though American children can find few real jobs in the market place (newspaper delivery is almost the only steady one), many children do real work in the organizations for children, such as Boy Scouts, Girl Scouts, 4H, Rainbow, Demolay, Future Farmers of America, Future Homemakers of America, and church clubs. In cooperation with adult leaders and his own peers, the child takes part in service projects and money-making projects, joins in consuming the profits made by the group and thereby enjoys many of the benefits of being a real producer. When leaders and peers judge his performance good, especially when they give unmistakable signs of approval and recognition (badges and pins), the youngster's feelings of adequacy are enhanced and he makes progress in the development of a sense of industry.

*Recreational Activities and Interests*

Children's play activities are the means by which they develop competency on many different levels and in several senses. Already discussed in Chapter 9, motor skills contribute greatly to effectiveness and adequacy. During the school age, many basic motor coordinations are integrated into games which have social meaning as well. Such games—for example, baseball—involve not only the coordinations of hitting, throwing, and running but also knowing a set of rules which tell exactly how to play and also how to feel about the game (being a good sport, competing, team spirit, and such). Performing well in such situations brings recognition, approval, and a sense of mastery over some of the complexities of the social and physical environment. Similarly, intellectual games integrate recently learned skills with social behavior, in a framework of rules. Checkers, Monopoly, and other table games are examples, along with thinking games, such as Twenty Questions and Coffee Pot.

Self-mastery, with little or no reference to other people, is the objective of certain types of games. This type includes the ancient, widespread games which appear spontaneously in the early school years and then disappear just as spontaneously. For example, the game of not stepping on cracks, in which the rule is self-set and is thought to work magic. Through this game, the child controls his own actions and controls the world. In the same way, a child sets himself an obstacle to overcome, such as hopping a certain distance on one foot or holding his breath for a given length of time. Or he seeks a certain form of anxiety in order to master it, as he does in walking on a high place or riding on a roller coaster. Imaginative play is also used in the service of self-mastery. Expressing fears, hostility, or fantasies of grandeur through dramatic play, he gains control through expressing these disturbing feelings and through distinguishing between imagination and reality.

A variety of purposes are served by the individual activities of making collections, reading, watching TV, and creating in art media, all of which the child does for pleasure and recreation. Through these means, he extends his concepts and knowledge. Reading, of course, contributes to competency in almost everything a child does, in addition to giving him enjoyment. Children read a wide range of materials, if they have chances to do so. They especially like stories which get off to a fast start, probably because of the influence of TV and the generally fast pace of modern life [56]. Books of wide appeal include historical stories (because they are full of action), plots with well-sustained suspense, animal stories, humorous tales, informational books, and books in series (because they are collections, as well as books). Although most children enjoy fantasy stories, some children are very particular about the type of fantasy they will accept [56]. Most children read comic books. In a recent year, 30 million of them were sold in this country [56]. It is estimated that each comic is read by three children. The satisfactions from comic books include quick action and adventure, short episodes, very easy reading, availability everywhere, and being an activity which other children share. Many children have nothing else to read. When the reading behavior of 323 seventh grade children was related to other aspects of their behavior, several interesting findings resulted [5]. There was no relationship between reading ability and amount or type of comic books read. Neither school adjustment nor achievement nor intelligence was related to amount and type of comic books read. The children who read comic books read more library books than did children who did not read comics.

Watching television is an important childhood activity (or perhaps it should be called passivity). The average second grade child was found to spend 17 hours a week in front of the TV while by sixth grade, the hours of viewing had increased to 28 [98]. One of the dangers of television is that it crowds out other kinds of activities. The sitting child is not practicing motor skills, which he needs in order to be physically competent; he is not playing games with other children; he is not creating. Some of the effects of television on children have been studied in both England and the United States [46, 83]. In both countries, television had a leveling effect intellectually, stepping up the information obtained by duller children and younger children and reducing the amount of information which older, bright children could have been expected to obtain without television. Comparing children's behavior before and after the families own TV sets, the English investigators found that children went to bed about 20 minutes later on the average when they owned a set. They saw no evidence of harmful physical effects, nor was there any indication that television caused fears or aggression. However, American and Canadian experimental studies have shown children to be more aggressive immediately after viewing films of aggressive models [2, 95]. Effects of viewing aggression have been shown to last for at least six months [45]. Further evidence comes from a study of over 600 third grade children [30]. Classmates' ratings on aggression were correlated with watching television programs that showed a great deal of violence. The evidence presented by these varied studies seems quite conclusive. Television constitutes a threat to children, first of all in stimulating antisocial behavior but also in restricting healthy activity.

Television also extends the child's view of real life through news reports and educational features. The great potential of "Sesame Street," the program designed for preschool children, was mentioned in Chapter 7. The success of "Sesame Street" led to the creation of another program by Children's Television Workshop.

Using new techniques, the program is designed to teach children to read and to help slow readers and those with problems in learning to read.

News reports, especially war scenes, could be expected to have disturbing effects, just as fictional violence does. Or perhaps more. Children know what is going on in the world more than any previous generation of children has known. The dangers of such overexposure are sobering.

### Moral Knowledge and Judgment

The rules governing right and wrong behavior are among the important guides to thought and action which a child seeks to master in his efforts to become a functioning member of his society. He realizes that rules and laws extend beyond his family and that he has obligations and privileges outside the family. In fact, many of the basic rules about how one ought to behave can be stated fairly early in this stage of life, although reasons behind them are not understood. For example, the average 7-year-old can give appropriate answers to these questions: "What's the thing for you to do when you have broken something that belongs to someone else?" and "What's the thing for you to do if another boy hits you without meaning to do it?" [94]. Although they show some relation to conduct, moral knowledge scores are also related to intelligence [97], cultural background, and the desire to make a good impression [55].

**Learning the Rules.** Being able to state the rule governing behavior is only an early stage in a long process of development which continues throughout the age span under discussion. At first, rules are by definition. They cover limited situations, without reasons or explanations. Gradually the child comes to understand the involvement of more and more people and viewpoints. This process was illustrated in a study of children's concepts of money and of the relations between storekeepers, customers, clerks, and manufacturers [92]. The rules which govern buying and selling are based on complicated relationships involving arithmetic, monetary value, profit, ownership, distribution, and the roles which people play. The ways in which children grasped this network of rules and relationships are organized into a sequence of stages of broader and broader understanding. Some of the stages given with the median ages are as follows:

> *Five years eight months:* Rules exist by definition. You need money to buy with. You just can't take goods without paying. In the first of this period, any coins buy any goods. The storekeeper also gives coins. Later, a coin buys objects of certain value, coin and object being matched exactly.
>
> *Six years four months:* Rules cover indirect but imprecise relations. The child knows that a certain amount of money is necessary for a certain purchase and that the amount of change is systematically related to price and amount paid, but he cannot figure out the amounts. He understands that work is worth paying for. He begins to understand that goods cost the storekeeper something and that he pays his helper.
>
> *Seven years ten months:* The value and relations of coins are understood precisely. The children make change exactly.
>
> *Eight years seven months:* He realizes that it does not matter whether the storekeeper gives the goods first or whether the customer pays first.
>
> *Eight years nine months:* He understands more of the impersonal rules which govern buying and selling, that retailers properly charge more than wholesalers, who are too far away to be able to sell directly to the consumer.

*Nine years nine months:* He has impersonal, interconnected concepts of profit, credit, storekeeper, worker, customer, factory owner, and helper.

*Eleven years two months:* He knows that in spite of the impersonal system of profit making, personal, immoral motives sometimes prevail. The existence of a rule does not assure its being obeyed.

**Moral Judgment.** Moral thought and judgment, in contrast to knowledge of the rules, continue to develop throughout the school years. Although the first or second grader knows fairly well what he is supposed to do, his reasons for doing it or not doing it change as he matures. Cognitive growth is basic to the growth of moral thought and judgment. Interaction between people is a fundamental factor in both cognitive and moral development, since the child checks his ideas, beliefs, and interpretations against those of other people, modifies them in accordance with discrepancies he finds, and attempts to justify his thinking to people who disagree with him. In this give and take of social relationships, he shapes his own beliefs within the social and cultural context in which he is growing up. Six aspects of moral judgment have been demonstrated as defining moral development during the elementary school years [55]. Evidence from many different studies is in essential agreement on the development of the following attitudes and viewpoints.

**Intentionality in Judgment.** Young children usually judge an act by its consequences, older children by the intentions which prompted it. This tendency has been tested by Piaget's [76] story of the boy who broke 15 cups while trying to help his mother, in contrast to the boy who broke 1 cup while trying to steal jam. Almost all 4-year-olds say that the boy who broke the large number of cups was worse. About 60 percent of 6-year-olds agree. The majority of 9-year-olds say that the other boy was worse. Although by age 9, most children can apply the principle of intentionality, further cognitive growth and experience contribute to understanding of the principle. The adolescent years see a refinement in understanding and expressing the principle.

**Relativism in Judgment.** There is only one way in which to judge an act, according to the thinking of young children, either right or wrong. If a child and an adult conflict in judging an act, then the adult is right. To illustrate this way of thinking, children were told a story in which a friendly classmate helped a lazy pupil to do his homework, even though the teacher had forbidden the pupil to receive help. The children were asked whether the teacher thought the friendly classmate's behavior right, whether the lazy pupil thought it right, and whether the friendly classmate thought himself right. Most 6-year-olds gave only one judgment, on which all three characters were supposed to agree; most 9-year-olds realized that there were different points of view from which to make this judgment.

**Independence of Sanctions.** An act is bad if it elicits punishment, according to many children of 4 or 5. Between 5 and 7, most children change this point of view to believe that an act is bad because it does harm or breaks a rule. The test story was about a child who obediently watched a young sibling while the mother was away, only to have the mother spank him when she returned. The younger children said that the baby-sitting child must have been bad, because his mother spanked him; most 7-year-olds said that the child was good, because he had done good [54].

**Use of Reciprocity.** Several steps can be distinguished in the process of accepting the idea of doing as you would be done by. Four-year-olds rarely use the concept at all. Between 7 and 10, children usually employ it in a concrete, utilitarian way, avoiding retaliation and courting return of favors. After 10 or 11, children show more feeling about how it would be in someone else's place.

**Use of Punishment As Restitution and Reform.** Younger children believe that retribution should be the main basis for punishment and that severe punishment will reform the wrongdoer. Older children advocate milder punishment, with restitution rather than retribution as the aim [76].

**Naturalistic Views of Misfortune.** At 6 or 7, children are likely to see accidents and misfortunes as punishment for their misdeeds. This confusion diminishes with age, as the child builds more mature concepts of causality.

Further discussion of stages and types of moral judgments occurs in Chapter 17, where some growth trends are traced through childhood and adolescence.

*Moral Behavior*

Since the elementary school child is quite limited in his understanding and application of moral principles, he can hardly be expected to be extensively guided by them in his behavior. Rather, he is guided more by the rules of his family, peers, school, and community. He perceives rules as located outside himself, coming largely from adults. His egocentrism and resulting cognitive conceit (see page 399) makes rule-breaking not so much a moral matter but more a way of proving his cleverness by outwitting adults [27]. Although he has made some beginnings in internalizing rules, a large part of his conscience is still external.

While there seems to be a general factor resulting in individual difference in honesty, a large determiner of whether a child cheats or not is the situation in which he is tempted [8]. When a child cheats in one situation, it does not mean that he will do so in another, since cheating in one context has only a low correlation with cheating in another [41, 85]. In experimental testing of cheating, most children do some, a few a great deal, and a few only a little [41]. In other words, cheating scores were distributed normally. Cheating was also found to depend upon the ease of doing so and upon the risk of detection. No age changes in cheating and stealing have been found experimentally during the school years, although according to parents' reports, stealing and lying decreased after age 6 to 8 [37, 85].

How great a relationship is there between moral knowledge or judgment and moral conduct? Kohlberg has considered this question with the boys whose moral judgment he traced from ages 7 to 16. An experimental measure of cheating showed that those high in moral judgment cheated significantly less than those who were lower. (Also, delinquents scored lower in moral judgment than did normal working-class boys.) When teachers were asked to rate children on conscience and on fairness with peers, the boys' moral judgment correlated .31 with conscience and .51 with fairness [55]. An older study [41] showed a correlation of .43 between moral knowledge and character ratings by teachers and peers, and a correlation of .46 between moral knowledge and tests of honesty. Correlations around .40 between moral judgment and moral behavior were found for lower-class black boys and girls in kindergarten, fourth, and sixth grades [86]. These studies agree, then, that while moral conduct is related to judgment, conduct is not entirely dependent upon judgment.

Several other aspects of behavior have been found related to moral behavior. General intelligence has been shown to contribute to moral conduct [41, 75].

The ability to maintain stable, focused attention also contributes to moral conduct [55]. Probably related to this factor is the ability to control aggressive fantasy [75].

Concepts of time and perception of the passage of time are also related to moral development [86]. Lower-class black children between 5 and 12 were rated by teachers on moral conduct and were given tests of moral judgment, time concepts, and perception of time. The moral judgment tests were based on Piaget's stories. Time concepts were assessed by questions such as "Which meal do you have first, lunch, dinner, or breakfast?" and "What time is it now? What time is it in California?" Time perception was measured by asking the child to reproduce time intervals of 10, 20, and 30 seconds. Similar age-related trends were found for moral judgment, time concepts, and time perception. All three improved steadily from kindergarten to fourth grade and then leveled off. *Concepts* of time and moral *judgment* were highly correlated at all ages. *Perceptions* of time and moral *conduct* were significantly correlated at all ages. *Concepts* of time and moral *conduct* were highly correlated at all ages. Thus time concepts are related to both judgment and conduct, while perception of time is related to conduct only. Another interesting finding is that younger children with the poorest conduct scores tended to overestimate time intervals. Results suggest that regulation of impulse and need gratification, which is essential for moral judgment and conduct, is influenced by the child's ability to order events in time. Moral development, then, is an extremely complex process which can be viewed in different ways and which is inextricably bound up with the child's psychological development and with the various relationships through which he grows.

## Religious Concepts

Children search for meaning in life, for explanations of the great mysteries which puzzle all human beings, for unifying concepts. A sense of adequacy is enhanced by some success in asking questions, being able to discuss them, and finding answers which give some satisfaction. Although religion and philosophy do not occupy the school-age child as much as they do the adolescent, yet the child lays a foundation for his adolescent enquiries.

Religious concepts, like other concepts, are the products of cognitive development and social interaction. Some children receive direct teaching in the form of religious instruction carried on by their church or temple. A series of studies on denominational concepts shows age-related steps in the child's progress toward an adult understanding of his religion [24, 25, 26]. Each child was asked a series of questions about his own denomination: Is your family Protestant (Catholic, Jewish)? Are you a Protestant? Are all boys and girls in the world Protestants? Can a dog or a cat be a Protestant? How can you tell a person is a Protestant? How do you become a Protestant? What is a Protestant? Can you be a Protestant and an American at the same time? After answering *yes* or *no*, the children were asked to explain their answers.

Four aspects of denominational conception could be distinguished: knowledge of characteristics common to all members of the denomination, knowledge of class membership compatible or incompatible with membership in the denomination, knowledge of how membership in the denomination is gained or lost, and knowledge of the signs by which a member of a denomination can be recognized. With Jewish and Catholic children, each of these types of knowledge could be seen developing in three stages. With Protestant children, only the first two types of knowledge developed in three stages. The stages were

1. At about 6 years, the child had a *global, undifferentiated concept*. "What is a Catholic?" JAY: "A person." How is he different from a Protestant? "I don't know." "What is a Jew?" SID: "A person." How is he different from a Catholic? "'Cause some people have black hair and some people have blonde."
2. From 7 to 9, concepts were *differentiated* but *concrete*. "He goes to Mass every Sunday and goes to Catholic School." "He belongs to a Protestant family." Jewishness was understood both as a group of actions and as a family quality, leading to some contradictory answers. Can a dog or a cat be a Jew? STAN: "No." Why not? "They are not human." What difference does that make? "They can't go to the Synagogue or say the prayers . . . but I guess if it belonged to a Jewish family, it could be Jewish."
3. Children between 11 and 14 had a *differentiated* and *abstract* concept of their denomination. The child realizes that his religion is one religion among others. What is a Catholic? BILL: "A person who believes in the truths of the Roman Catholic Church." What is a Protestant? FAITH: "A faithful believer in God and doesn't believe in the Pope." Can a dog or a cat be Jewish? SID: "No . . . because they are not human and would not understand a religion." Gaining membership involves learning and believing. Religion is recognized as a way of categorizing people which is different from other ways, such as by nationality. Can you be an American and a Jew at the same time? "Yes . . . because Jewish is a religion and American is a nationality."

This demonstration of the growth of religious concepts with increasing age is one more illustration of how development is the result of interaction between the child and his environment. In the first stage, cognitive maturity is such that the 5- or 6-year-old can form only a global concept of being a Catholic, Protestant, or Jew. The global concept he forms, however, depends on the religion which is offered to him. Without the religious environment with which to interact, religious concepts would not come into being.

Another aspect of the exploration of the religious institution's impact on children's concepts was concerned with the understanding of causality [31]. The subjects were 153 Protestant, Jewish, and Roman Catholic boys, between 6 and 8 years of age. A rating as to the degree of religious devoutness was obtained through a questionnaire sent to the families and by rating the type of school attended. The solutions given by the subjects to problem situations were classified as animistic, anthropomorphic, and scientific. While there were no differences between the three religions, differences were significant in terms of devoutness. Children from very devout homes gave more animistic and anthropomorphic responses and fewer scientific responses than did children from less devout homes. Similarly, children attending religious schools gave more animistic and anthropomorphic responses and fewer scientific responses than did children attending public schools. Thus it could be concluded that the religious institution tended to retard the development of scientific thinking in 6- to 8-year-old boys. *Some* of the subjects from devout homes and religious schools did give scientific answers. The author pointed out that this could mean that religion and science are not inevitably incompatible. It could also mean that these youngsters, although from devout homes, were not themselves devout, and had, in opposition to their environment, developed modes of scientific thinking.

A philosophical question, fourth graders' interest in living a good life, was examined by having children write about their interests [1]. The 10 schools used were all private ones, probably Catholic. Among nine interest categories, the good life, or living a good life, ranked second. One eighth of all interests listed pertained to it. The order of interests was thus: possession of objects, good life, pets, vocation, travel, relatives, money, school and education. Under interest in good life were items pertaining to living a good life, but an even larger number of items concerned the ultimate purpose of life.

Both research and common sense indicate the importance of curiosity in stimulating intellectual functioning and development. Can curiosity, then, be encouraged and nurtured in grade school children? Experiments using a method called *Inquiry Training* show that children can learn to use curiosity for solving problems [93]. After viewing films of simple physics experiments, fifth and sixth grade children asked questions which could be answered by *yes* or *no*. The children learned to formulate, use, and test hypotheses. The process of discovery through questioning was made more real and functional by a discussion of each session, based on a tape recording of the session.

## The Role of the School

Schools and the sense of industry are made for each other. It is no accident that children are sent to a special institution which imparts the wisdom of the culture at just the age when they become interested in learning it and in becoming producing members of society. What happens to the beginning pupil depends upon the personal resources he brings to school, the values of the culture as transmitted by the school, the makeup of his class, and the behavior of his teacher.

### School Influences

**Values Held by the School.** Since the educational system is a product of the culture, the school prepares the child for the role he is expected to play. In England, the emphasis is on the child as an individual; in India, the child as a family member; in the Israeli kibbutz, the child as a community member; in the USSR, the child as a citizen. The "Open Classroom" [38] epitomizes English efforts to promote the full development of each individual as an autonomous, responsible, thinking, creative person. The child is free to choose what to do from a wealth of opportunities, although if he neglects certain basic parts of work, the teacher will direct him. Research shows that consistent use of the democratic, open style of teaching does indeed promote creativity and flexibility in problem solving [64]. The Russian first grade illustrates successful methods of creating members of collectives: cooperative children who help one another, accept criticism from one another, and put the group ahead of the individual [6]. When the pupil arrives, for example, he is to wipe his feet, greet the teachers and his seat mate by name, obey the teacher, learn all rules and duties of the classroom.

Conflicting values in the United States make the role of the school confused. Should excellence prevail over mediocrity, happiness over duty, or creativity over conformity? These are matters of philosophy or even opinion. And while the

United States Constitution guarantees separation of church and state, many people want character education as part of the curriculum. But what religion or philosophy should guide moral education? What concensus is there on the definition of a good child? Should he be competitive or cooperative, original or obedient? Some school administrators decide that the safest way is to teach academics and leave character education to the home and church. Such a reduction to the lowest common denominator stands in sharp contrast to the Soviets, who seem to know exactly what they want to teach and who do so effectively [6].

One way of getting an overall view of a nation's values is to look at the textbooks prescribed for its schoolchildren. Books and other teaching materials are instruments through which the school affects the competence of its pupils. Textbooks, however, are more than this, since they reflect the values of the whole culture, chosen by the community or even by the state, as compulsory reading for its children. Textbooks hold up the virtues and behavior which adults want children to attain. Because they are chosen by committees and the choice is influenced by additional people, the behavior exalted tends to be conventional and stereotyped. Bronfenbrenner has analyzed values upheld by the Soviets and presents a summary in pictures illustrating "Laws of the Pioneers" [6, pp. 39–48]. An analysis of American textbooks over 60 years is illustrated in Figure 11–2. The themes in stories were classified as to whether they dealt with affiliation (love and friendship), moral teaching, or achievement [19]. Moral teaching decreased steadily, achievement themes decreased from the turn of the century, and affiliation followed an uncertain course.

When Americans began to face the problems of civil rights, poverty, and deprivation, they criticized the textbooks and teaching materials in use at that time. The picture of life presented in readers was often unrealistic. Friendly and helpful behavior was almost always rewarded, for instance, while problems of aggression and greed were handled by pretending that children did not have such problems. Autonomy and initiative were usually discouraged, while skills, enjoyment, optimism, and cooperation were approved. Very conventional sex roles were upheld. Stories showed only white, middle-class children, families, and teachers. A demand for change resulted in books showing children from all ethnic groups, living in a variety of styles. The use of multiethnic readers has led to marked positive changes in the attitudes of white second grade children toward black people, according to the results of a carefully controlled experiment [58]. For older pupils, the way in which history textbooks treat slavery is significant for attitudes toward race relations [43]. Since older textbooks have been criticized as incomplete and distorted, some modern authors are trying to be more realistic and honest [10].

Children may be economically disadvantaged or disadvantaged because they come from a culturally different group. Very often membership in a minority group coexists with low income. The American public schools have been dominated by white, English, Protestant culture. Instead of building upon the knowledge and value system that the child brought with him, educators often assumed that the different child had *no* culture and must be forced into the Anglo-American mold [34]. Recent studies show how wrong such an assumption is. For example, bilingual children in several different situations have been found to do better than monolinguals in several different measures [49]. Bilingual French-Canadian 10-year-olds scored higher than monolinguals in intelligence, concept formation, and flexible thinking. Spanish-speaking first grade children who were taught in both Spanish

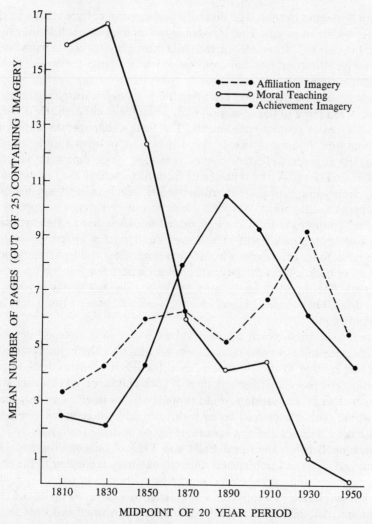

**Figure 11–2.** Values extolled by children's textbooks over a period of a century and a half.

SOURCE: Adapted from R. deCharms and G. H. Moeller, "Content Analysis of Children's Readers," *Journal of Abnormal and Social Psychology*, 1962, **64**, 136–162. Used by permission of the American Psychological Association and Richard deCharms.

and English did better in cognitive growth, communication skills, and social and emotional adjustment than did their peers who were taught only in English. Similar studies have yielded similar results in Mexico and the Philippines. Therefore, instead of ignoring or trying to replace what the child already knows when he enters school, the school system might better accept the child's culture as valuable and then build upon it. Not only would the child retain the cognitive advantages of his own culture but his self-esteem would be enhanced and he would be encouraged to believe that he could control what happened to him. Recent studies on American Indians make these points especially well, when they document the emptiness and despair felt by children (and adults) whose rich culture is ignored or denigrated by the monoethnic system [34, 91].

**Reward System of School.** The diversity in American culture results in children who differ widely in values. That is, what is rewarding to one child may not be to another. In order to learn in school, the child must get satisfaction from his efforts. Concern with disadvantaged children has led to a search for ways in which to motivate their learning.

Havighurst has analyzed the evolution of human reward-punishment system with special reference to the education of disadvantaged children. He distinguishes four main types of reward-punishments. The first, which operates during approximately the first 4 years of life, is the satisfaction or deprivation of physical-physiological appetites. Pleasure comes from food, toys, motor activity, sensory perception, and so on. A new type of satisfaction is added to the first type at about 5 years, praise-disapproval, first from parents, teachers, and age-mates. Then comes approval-disapproval, through the action of conscience or superego. Last is approval-disapproval from the ego or self which is felt to have considerable control over events. Different subcultures develop this system in children at different rates. Some investigators have found lower-class children solving problems just as well as middle-class children when rewards were tangible but not when they were verbal. For instance, one second grade boy did not count beyond 3 when asked to do so, but counted 14 candy hearts, when told that he could have as many as he could count [42].

Different subcultures teach different values and reward systems. For example, many American Indians value cooperation very highly. Their children insist upon helping one another in the classroom, even though the teacher tries to promote competition and individual performance. If such children could be encouraged to teach each other, their learning would probably be more efficient. In general, the school would probably succeed better with culturally different children if teachers could use the children's abilities instead of trying to make them over.

**Relationship Between Individual Child and Type of School Program.** Different programs and styles of teaching suit different children, according to the children's various cognitive and personality characteristics. For example, one child works well by himself, pursuing a topic for a long time, concentrating on it, and resenting interruptions. Another child accomplishes more when small tasks are set for him and when he can change often from one activity to another. Visual aids, teaching machines, and role playing are especially appropriate for children from low socioeconomic backgrounds, since they are likely to do better with visual than with verbal materials [78].

Different methods of teaching reading have been demonstrated to be differentially suited to children according to certain personality characteristics [36]. One system used the phonics method, which provided a maximum of structure, rules, systematic arrangements, and definiteness of directions and expectations. The other used the whole-word method, which gave a minimum of structure, because of its encouragement of intelligent guessing and its lack of rules. The children, all third graders, were rated as to compulsivity (wanting neatness, order and certainty, conforming, perfectionist, rigid, not spontaneous) and anxiety (response to a perceived threat). Compulsive children achieved at a higher level than less compulsive children in the structured classroom, but in the unstructured classroom, there was no significant difference between compulsive and noncompulsive children. The highly anxious children were at a real disadvantage in the unstructured school, where they were excelled by nonanxious children. In the structured school, there was no significant difference between anxious and nonanxious children. Therefore, unless children were assigned to a reading program on the basis of personality tests, some children would be at a disadvantage in either type of program.

### Teachers and Classmates

The child interacts with a specific teacher and a class which constitutes a little social world.

**The Teacher's Role.** Nothing idealizes the teacher's role more beautifully than Erikson's concept of generativity, the seventh stage in personality development. In his words, "Generativity is primarily the interest in establishing and guiding the next generation or whatever in a given case may become the absorbing object of a parental kind of responsibility" [28, p. 231].

The teacher's work is one way of achieving normal adult personality development since everyone who is not to stagnate must have a stake in the next generation. The teacher chooses to nurture intellectual development in growing human beings. Thus she grows at this level while her students grow at theirs.

When the child enters school, his teacher is largely a mother substitute. He may even call her "Mother" by mistake and may do the reverse at home, calling his mother "Mrs. Jones." The attitudes toward authority he learned at home will probably carry over to school. Since nearly all first grade teachers are women, the child will most likely expect his teacher to be like his mother. His trust or mistrust, his hostility or acceptance, his dependency or autonomy will largely reflect what has gone on at home with mother. Gradually he learns the differences between

Courtesy Education Development Center

teacher and mother, both role differences and personality differences. Gradually the teacher differentiates herself more and more from mother. Moving up the grades, teachers become more subject matter-oriented and less concerned with the "whole child" and his adjustment in general. The child comes to see his teacher as the key person in his development of essential competencies.

The teacher's role varies with the sex of the teacher and sex of the child, as well as with age. There is widespread agreement that boys present more problem behavior in school than girls do. Men and women teachers differ somewhat in their interpretations of what is problem behavior and how serious it is.

Not only does the teacher present material to be learned and problems to be solved; she rewards some behavior and punishes other. Through words, smiles, frowns, attention, and ignoring, even more than through marks, displays, or gold stars, the teacher makes it plain, over and over and over again, what kind of behavior she wants from children and what she does not want. She also serves as a model of behavior, especially to those children whose needs she satisfies and who like and love her.

**The Influence of Teachers' Expectations.** Children are known to try to live up to the expectations that salient people hold for them. The power of expectations was found to be even greater than commonly thought, in a series of experiments by Rosenthal and associates [79]. All the children in one school were given an intelligence test. The teachers were told that the test predicted intellectual blooming and were given the names of their pupils (about 20 percent) who could be expected to spurt in academic achievement during the coming year. Each grade consisted of three classrooms, one for above average, one for average, and one for below average achievers. In each classroom, the experimental children had been picked by a table of random numbers. Thus the only difference between the experimental group and the other children was in the minds of the teachers. At the end of the year, the youngest experimental groups had made significant gains in IQ. The first graders had gained 15.4 points more than the other children in their grade. Grades 3 through 6 did not show differences in IQ gains between experimental and control groups. Reasons for the greater effect on younger children are speculative. It may be that they are more malleable. It is also possible that teachers of younger children are special, in being more interested in the whole child and more communicative of feelings, beliefs, and expectations.

**Classroom Influences.** The racial and socioeconomic composition of the class has important effects on the children. The type of education offered to black children has been generally inferior to that available to white children. One example from the South and one from the North will suffice. In Tennessee, black students were found to be a year and a half to two years retarded in grade level when they were transferred to white schools [99]. The same report revealed that only 49 percent of qualified black teachers passed the National Teacher's Examination, while 97 percent of qualified white teachers passed it. In New York City, time sampling of activities in the elementary schools indicated that in classrooms where black children predominated, 50 percent to 80 percent of the time was spent on disciplining and other nonacademic tasks. Where class membership was predominantly white, although of the same socioeconomic level, 30 percent of the time was spent on disciplining and nonacademic tasks [21]. The Coleman report on the nation's schools, based on over 600,000 children, concluded that the characteristics of their classmates constituted the most important influences on children [11]. Disadvantaged children achieved much more in classrooms where most of the children were middle-class. The more middle-class children, the more academic benefit accrued to the poor child in their midst. A subsequent study showed that when white children were in classes with mostly black classmates, they achieved less than when they were in mainly white classes [77]. White children in black schools with close black friends did even more poorly than white children without close black friends. Both segregation and desegregation hold problems for the black child. When the Test Anxiety Scale for Children was given to all second graders in a large eastern school system, black children were found to have significantly higher anxiety scores than white children [33]. In black de facto segregated schools, children had higher anxiety scores than did black children in integrated schools. This result may have been due to the integrated children's having higher socioeconomic status than the segregated blacks. Black children, too, can have problems in an integrated school.

The social threat of hostile, powerful white children can provoke great anxiety, impairing the child's problem solving and learning and even causing him to lower his achievement efforts so as not to compete with the whites [53]. If, however, the black child encounters friendly, acceptant white children and teachers, he is likely to feel encouraged and to raise his achievement efforts. If the academic standards are so high that he sees little chance of success, though, he is likely to become too discouraged to try hard. As probability of failure increases, likelihood of disapproval from parents and teachers also increases. As the child realizes the increasing danger of adult disapproval, he grows more fearful and hostile. Unable and/or afraid to express his hostility against adults, he turns it against himself as self-derogatory attitudes, increased expectation of failure, and desire to escape. These attitudes can be expected to weaken his performance in school [53]. Competence and the sense of industry, then, are likely to be severely handicapped by membership in a subordinate minority group. The combination of participants in every classroom is, of course, unique. Every teacher knows that each class is different and will probably admit that she behaves differently with each. A class develops certain behavior norms, some of which are in line with adult requirements, others of which are deviant. Some classes have a strong group spirit, others have many hostilities and tensions.

The teacher exerts an influence on her pupils' choice of moral standards. A series of Cornell University investigations used a moral dilemmas test to classify children as adult-conforming, peer-conforming, or autonomous, and also to find out whether children would be influenced more by parents or peers or whether they would stick largely to their own convictions [22]. When the moral questions were first presented, children were told that only researchers and computers would see their answers. Later an equivalent set of questions was given and children were told that their answers would be displayed to parents and teachers, at a PTA meeting. A third equivalent set was given and the children told that their classmates, but not teachers and parents, would see their answers. Thus the investigators could measure the amount of shift from the base condition in response to parent or peer pressure. Of special interest here is the difference between classrooms. In predominantly adult-oriented classrooms, teachers were described by their pupils as more supportive and less punitive than were those in peer-oriented classes. Principals described these teachers as less concerned with discipline and book learning than with individuality and creativity.

In peer-oriented classrooms, children reported more time spent with gangs of peers, and more misconduct. These children saw adult standards as being very different from peer standards. Peer-oriented classrooms contained the largest proportion of children who shifted under pressures from either peers or adults. There was little shifting from adult-conformity in adult-oriented classrooms. Autonomous children were somewhat more likely to come from peer-oriented classrooms. Results indicated that the children who achieved autonomy in making moral decisions did so through dealing with cross-pressures from both peers and adults. While autonomy did not result in all children who had these experiences, it is possible that the experience is necessary for development of autonomy. Other contributors to autonomy include, of course, family relationships. The autonomous children were likely to come from homes which gave them high support and moderate discipline and control, whereas the gang-oriented, peer-conformists tended to come from homes of either high punitiveness or high permissiveness. A subsequent study [47] shows that peer-oriented children are likely to have peer-oriented parents. Such parents are, for example, impressed by the argument "All the other kids are doing it."

**The Child's Position in the Classroom.** The child has his own social position, as a member of his school class, a position which is not necessarily the same as the social position held by his family in the community. His own position is both product and cause of his behavior and of how children and teachers feel and behave toward him. Many sociometric studies have shown that each classroom has its own social structure and that each child in it has his own place and relationships. Children in the lower positions have more difficulties than higher-status children. They are less able to cope with frustration; their teachers see them as showing more behavior problems, poorer social adjustment, and more emotional instability; they feel more disliking for other children and this increases as the year goes on; they show more aggressive–assertive or passive–hostile activity, as observed and measured on behavior schedules [57]. The interactions of children and teachers were recorded by observers who did not know the children's sociometric positions. Results yielded these insights into child–teacher interaction: teachers noticed the social behavior of low-status children more than they noticed that of high-status children; low-status boys received more criticism than high-status boys; low-status girls received more affectionate support than did other girls. The teachers were responding to the girls' seeking of affection from them, while being relatively passive in the classroom; they were responding to the boys' typical aggressive, disruptive behavior.

# Summary

The child now feels a need to learn the rules of the game, as they pertain to many aspects of life, as he looks forward to taking his place as a producing member of society. His approaches to learning skills, rules, and various competencies grow out of his motivations and out of the social and cultural settings in which he grows up.

A wide choice of activities assures each child a good chance for success in one or more areas of competency. While academic excellence is out of reach for most children with limited background experience, motor skills and play activities offer them chances to excel. Reading, the key to success in school, is influenced by a multitude of physical, emotional, and experimental factors. Writing, a psycho-motor skill, serves the purpose of communication and self-expression. Mathematics, an area in which many children have experienced inferiority, can be taught on a broad base of experiences with manipulating, grouping, arranging, and ordering.

The sense of industry grows upon success as a worker at home, as well as at school and in the community. Since meaningful jobs are not always easy to find, group leaders and recreation workers often supplement the home in this important area. Play activities also contribute competencies in physical, intellectual, social, and emotional fields.

The learning of society's rules is a long process which begins by being able to state what people are supposed to do and which progresses by grasping more and more of the abstractions involved and by understanding the complicated inter-weaving of social roles. Moral judgment, involving evaluation of actions, matures along with cognitive and social growth. Moral behavior depends upon will and control, in conjunction with moral knowledge and judgment. Religious and philosophical concepts also develop through cognitive and social growth, guided by the type of concepts to which the child is exposed.

Success in development of the sense of industry is strongly influenced by the child's desire for achievement and recognition. Applying standards of excellence to himself, he and others judge his performance. A feeling tone results from that judgment, a happy feeling from approval, or an unpleasant feeling from disapproval. Both the need for achievement and achievement behavior show some consistency over time across situations and in sex differences. Boys apparently have more internalized standards and more realistic goals, whereas girls are more likely to seek approval and affection through their achievement efforts. Characteristics of high-achieving children include independence from adults, persistence, and com-petitiveness.

Anxiety has been studied as general anxiety and as anxiety in the situation of taking tests or examinations. Learning and achievement show complicated relations to level of anxiety. In general, low or moderate anxiety may aid or not deter a child in performing fairly easy tasks, and high anxiety is likely to reduce his competency. Fear of failure is a common type of anxiety of schoolchildren. Failure itself depends upon the relationship of achievement level and aspiration level. Schools often provoke anxiety in children of minority groups.

Curiosity determines the vigor with which a child seeks new experiences. New experiences contribute to further curiosity and to cognitive development. Curiosity can be stimulated by educational techniques.

The American educational system is dedicated to a number of values, some of which conflict with each other. The complexity of the culture requires that the school perform many functions, including the promotion of health and personality development, along with the teaching of traditional academic skills and knowledge. The child's success at school is influenced by his cultural level, which strongly determines his preparation for school, his social position in the classroom, and the fit between his personality and the style and philosophy of his school. Educational materials, especially textbooks, strongly reflect cultural values and concerns.

## References

1. Amatora, M. Expressed interests in later childhood. *J. Genet. Psychol.*, 1960, **96**, 327–342.

2. Bandura, A., Ross, D., & Ross, S. A. Transmission of aggression through imitation of aggressive models. *J. Abn. Soc. Psychol.*, 1961, **63**, 575–582.
3. Barker, R. G. Success and failure in the classroom. *Progressive Educ.*, 1942, **19**, 221–224.
4. Bettelheim, B. The children of the dream. New York: Macmillan, 1969.
5. Blakely, W. P. Study of seventh-grade children's reading of comic books as related to certain other variables. *J. Genet. Psychol.*, 1958, **93**, 291–301.
6. Bronfenbrenner, U. Two worlds of childhood. New York: Russell Sage Foundation, 1970.
7. Bronson, G. W. Fear of visual novelty. *Devel. Psychol.*, 1970, **2**, 33–40.
8. Burton, R. V. The generality of honesty reconsidered. *Psychol. Rev.*, 1963, **70**, 481–500.
9. Castaneda, A., McCandless, B. R., & Palermo, D. S. The children's form of the manifest anxiety scale. *Child Devel.*, 1956, **27**, 315–326.
10. Child, I. L., Potter, E. H., & Levine, E. M. Children's textbooks and personality development: An exploration in the social psychology of education. *Psychol. Mono.*, 1946, **60**, 1–7, 43–53.
11. Coleman, J. S., et al. *Equality of educational opportunity.* Washington, D.C.: U.S. Govt. Printing Office, 1966.
12. Cox, F. N. Test anxiety and achievement behavior systems related to examination performance in children. *Child Devel.*, 1964, **35**, 909–915.
13. Crandall, V. C., Katkovsky, W., & Crandall, V. J. Children's beliefs in their own control of reinforcements in intellectual-academic achievement situations. *Child Devel.*, 1965, **36**, 91–109.
14. Crandall, V. J. Parents' influences on children's achievement behavior. Progress report, NIMH Grant M-2238. Yellow Springs, Ohio: Fels Institute, 1965.
15. Crandall, V. J., Katkovsky, W., & Preston, A. A conceptual formulation for some research on children's achievement development. *Child Devel.*, 1960, **31**, 787–797.
16. Crandall, V. J., Katkovsky, W., & Preston, A. Motivational and ability determinants of young children's intellectual achievement behaviors. *Child Devel.*, 1962, **33**, 643–661.
17. Crandall, V. J. Achievement. In H. W. Stevenson (Ed.), *Child psychology.* The sixty-second yearbook of the National Society for the Study of Education, Part I. Chicago: University of Chicago Press, 1963, pp. 416–459.
18. Croake, J. W. Fears of children. *Human Devel.*, 1969, **12**, 239–247.
19. deCharms, R., & Moeller, G. H. Content analysis of children's readers. *J. Abn. Soc. Psychol.*, 1962, **4**, 136–162.
20. D'Heurle, A., Mellinger, J., & Haggard, E. Personality, intellectual and achievement patterns in gifted children. *Psychol. Mono.*, 1959, Whole No. 483.
21. Deutsch, M. Minority groups and class status as related to social and personality factors in scholastic achievement. *Soc. Appl. Anthropol. Mono. No. 2.* St. Louis, Mo.: Washington University, 1960.
22. Devereux, E. C. The role of peer group experience in moral development: A research progress report. Paper presented at the Fourth Minnesota Symposium on Child Psychology, May, 1969.
23. Distefano, M. K., Jr. Changes in work-related attitudes with age. *J. Genet. Psychol.*, 1969, **114**, 127–134.

24. Elkind, D. The child's conception of his religious denomination. I: The Jewish child, *J. Genet. Psychol.*, 1961, **99**, 209–225.
25. Elkind, D. The child's conception of his religious denomination. II: The Catholic child. *J. Genet. Psychol.*, 1962, **101**, 185–194.
26. Elkind, D. The child's conception of his religious denomination. III: The Protestant child, *J. Genet. Psychol.*, 1963, **103**, 291–304.
27. Elkind, D. Cognitive structure in latency behavior. Paper presented at the conference on "Origins of Individuality." Madison: University of Wisconsin, Sept. 26–27, 1969.
28. Erikson, E. H. *Childhood and society*. New York: Norton, 1963.
29. Erikson, E. H. *Identity, youth and crisis*. New York: Norton, 1968.
30. Eron, L. D. Relationship of TV viewing habits and aggressive behavior in children. *J. Abn. Soc. Psychol.*, 1963, **67**, 193–196.
31. Ezer, M. The effect of religion upon children's responses to questions involving physical causality. In J. Rosenblith & W. Allinsmith (Eds.), *The causes of behavior*. Boston: Allyn and Bacon, 1962, pp. 481–487.
32. Feld, S. C. Longitudinal study of the origins of achievement strivings. *J. Pers. Soc. Psychol.*, 1967, **7**, 408–414.
33. Feld, S. C., & Lewis, J. *The assessment of achievement anxieties in children*. Bethesda, Md.: Mental Health Study Center, National Institute for Mental Health, 1967.
34. Forbes, J. D. *The education of the culturally different*. Washington, D.C.: U.S. Govt. Printing Office, 1969.
35. Gibson, E. J. The ontogeny of reading. *Am. Psychol.*, 1970, **25**, 136–143.
36. Grimes, J. W., & Allinsmith, W. Compulsivity, anxiety and school achievement. *Merrill-Palmer Quart.*, 1961, **7**, 247–271.
37. Grinder, R. E. Relations between behavioral and cognitive dimensions of conscience in middle childhood. *Child Devel.*, 1964, **35**, 881–891.
38. Gross, B., & Gross, R. A little bit of chaos. *Sat. Rev.*, May 16, 1970, 71 ff.
39. Haggard, E. Socialization personality and academic achievement in gifted children. *School Rev.*, 1957, 388–414.
40. Harrell, L. E. A comparison of the development of oral and written language in school-age children. *Mono. Soc. Res. Child Devel.*, 1957, **22**:3.
41. Hartshorne, H., & May, M. A. *Studies in the nature of character*. Vol. I: *Studies in deceit;* Vol. II: *Studies in self-control;* Vol. III: *Studies in the organization of character*. New York: Macmillan, 1928–1930.
42. Havighurst, R. J. Minority subcultures and the law of effect. *Am. Psychol.*, 1970, **25**, 313–322.
43. Hechinger, F. M. History texts take a new look at slavery. *New York Times*, June 14, 1970.
44. Herrick, V. E., & Okada, N. The present scene: Practices in the teaching of handwriting in the United States—1960. In V. E. Herrick (Ed.), *New horizons for research in handwriting*. Madison: University of Wisconsin, 1963.
45. Hicks, D. J. Imitation and retention of film-mediated aggressive peer and adult models. *J. Pers. Soc. Psychol.*, 1965, **2**, 97–100.
46. Himmelweit, H. T., Oppenheim, A. N., & Vince, P. *Television and the child*. London: Oxford, 1958.
47. Hollander, E. P., & Marcia, J. E. Parental determinants of peer-orientation and self-orientation among preadolescents. *Devel. Psychol.*, 1970, **2**, 292–302.

48. Jessor, R., & Richardson, S. Psychosocial deprivation and personality development. In *Perspectives on Human Deprivation*. Washington, D.C. U.S. Dept. of Health, Education, and Welfare, 1968.

49. John, V., Horner, V., & Socolov, J. American voices, *Center Forum*, 1969, **4**:1, 1–3.

50. Kagan, J., & Moss, H. Stability and validity of achievement fantasy. *J. Abn. Soc. Psychol.*, 1959, **58**, 357–364.

51. Kagan, J., Sontag, L. W., Baker, C. T., & Nelson, V. L. Personality and I.Q. change. *J. Abn. Soc. Psychol.*, 1958, **56**, 261–266.

52. Katkovsky, W., Preston, A., & Crandall, V. J. Parents' attitudes toward their personal achievements and toward the achievement behaviors of their children. *J. Genet. Psychol.*, 1964, **104**, 67–82.

53. Katz, I. Review of evidence relating to effects of desegregation on the intellectual performance of Negroes. *Am. Psychol.*, 1964, **19**, 381–399.

54. Kohlberg, L. The development of children's orientations toward a moral order. I: Sequence in the development of moral thought. *Vita Humana*, 1963, **6**, 11–33.

55. Kohlberg, L. Development of moral character and moral ideology. In M. L. Hoffman & L. W. Hoffman (Eds.), *Review of child development research*. Vol. 1. New York: Russell Sage Foundation, 1964, pp. 383–431.

56. Larrick, N. *A parent's guide to children's reading*. New York: Doubleday, 1969.

57. Lippitt, R., & Gold, M. Classroom social structure as a mental health problem. *J. Soc. Issues*, 1959, **15**, 40–49.

58. Litcher, J. H., & Johnson, D. W. Changes in attitudes toward Negroes of white elementary school students after use of multiethnic readers. *J. Educ. Psychol.*, 1969, **60**, 148–152.

59. McClelland, D. C., Atkinson, J. W., Clark, R. A., & Lowell, E. L. *The achievement motive*. New York: Appleton-Century-Crofts, 1953.

60. McReynolds, P., Acker, M., & Pietila, C. Relations of object curiosity to psychological adjustment in children. *Child Devel.*, 1961, **32**, 393–400.

61. Maccoby, E. E. Why do children watch television? *Pub. Opinion Quart.*, 1954, **18**, 239–244.

62. Madsen, M. C. Cooperative and competitive motivation of children in three Mexican subcultures. *Psychol. Rep.*, 1967, **20**, 1307–1320.

63. Madsen, M. C., & Shapira, A. Cooperative and competitive behavior of urban Afro-American, Anglo-American, Mexican-American and Mexican village children. *Devel. Psychol.*, 1970, **3**, 16–20.

64. Malone, P., & Beller, E. K. Effects of different learning environments on creativity of children. Paper presented at the meeting of the Society for Research in Child Development, Santa Monica, Calif., March 27, 1969.

65. Maw, W. H., & Maw, E. W. Establishing criterion groups for evaluating measures of curiosity. *J. Exper. Educ.*, 1961, **29**, 299–306.

66. Maw, W. H., & Maw, E. W. Information recognition by children with high and low curiosity, *Educ. Res. Bull.*, 1961, **40**, 197–201, 223–224.

67. Maw, W. H., & Maw, E. W. Selection of unbalanced and unusual designs by children high in curiosity, *Child Devel.*, 1962, **33**, 917–922.

68. Maw, W. H., & Maw, E. W. Personal and social variables differentiating children with high and low curiosity. Cooperative Research Project No. 1511, Newark, Delaware; University of Delaware, 1965.

69. Medinnus, G. R., & Robinson, R. Maturity as a predictor of school achievement. Paper presented at the meeting of the Society for Research in Child Development, Santa Monica, Calif., March 29, 1969.

70. Mendel, G. Children's preferences for differing degrees of novelty. *Child Devel.*, 1965, **36**, 453–464.

71. Minuchin, P. Correlates of curiosity and exploratory behavior. Paper presented at the meeting of the Society for Research in Child Development, Santa Monica, Calif., March 27, 1969.

72. Mittman, L. R., & Terrell, G. An experimental study of curiosity in children. *Child Devel.*, 1964, **35**, 851–855.

73. Moss, H., & Kagan, J. Stability of achievement and recognition-seeking behaviors from early childhood through adulthood. *J. Abn. Soc. Psychol.*, 1961, **62**, 504–513.

74. Owen, F. W. The Palo Alto study of educationally handicapped children. Paper presented at the meeting of the Society for Research in Child Development, Santa Monica, Calif., March 28, 1969.

75. Peck, R. F., & Havighurst, R. J. *The psychology of character development.* New York: Wiley, 1960.

76. Piaget, J. *The moral judgment of the child.* Glencoe, Ill.: Free Press, 1948.

77. Pettigrew, T. F. Race and equal educational opportunity. Paper presented at the 75th annual convention of the American Psychological Association, 1967.

78. Riessman, F. Low-income culture: The strengths of the poor. *J. Marr. Fam.*, 1964, **26**, 417–429.

79. Rosenthal, R., & Jacobson, L. Self-fulfilling prophecies in the classroom: Teachers' expectations as unintended determinants of pupils' intellectual competence. In M. Deutsch, I. Katz, & A. R. Jensen (Eds.), *Social class, race and psychological development.* New York: Holt, Rinehart and Winston, 1968, pp. 219–253.

80. Sarason, S. B., Davidson, K. S., Lighthall, F. F., & Waite, R. R. A test anxiety scale for children. *Child Devel.*, 1958, **29**, 105–113.

81. Sarason, S. B., Davidson, K. S., Lighthall, F. F., Waite, R. R., & Ruebush, B. K. *Anxiety in elementary school children.* New York: Wiley, 1960.

82. Sarason, S. B., Hill, K. T., & Zimbardo, P. G. A longitudinal study of the relation of test anxiety to performance on intelligence and achievement tests. *Mono. Soc. Res. Child Devel.*, 1964, **29**:7.

83. Schramm, W., Lyle, J., & Parker, E. B. *Television in the lives of our children.* Stanford, Calif.: Stanford University Press, 1961.

84. Sears, P. S. Correlates of need achievement and need affiliation and classroom management, self-concept, achievement and creativity. Unpublished manuscript, Laboratory of Human Development, Stanford University, 1962. Cited in Crandall [17].

85. Sears, R. R., Rau, L., & Alpert, R. *Identification and child-rearing.* Stanford, Calif.: Stanford University Press, 1965.

86. Seltzer, A. R., & Beller, E. K. Judgments of time and moral development in lower class children. Paper presented at the meeting of the Society for Research in Child Development, Santa Monica, Calif., March 27, 1969.

87. Shapira, A., & Madsen, M. C. Cooperative and competitive behavior of kibbutz and urban children in Israel. *Child Devel.*, 1969, **40**, 609–617.

88. Smock, C. D., & Holt, B. G. Children's reactions to novelty: An experimental study of curiosity motivation. *Child Devel.*, 1962, **33**, 631–642.

89. Solomon, D. The generality of children's achievement-related behavior. *J. Genet. Psychol.*, 1969, **114**, 109–125.

90. Stein, A. H. The influence of social reinforcement on the achievement behavior of fourth-grade boys and girls. *Child Devel.*, 1969, **40**, 727–736.

91. Steiner, S. LaRaza: The Mexican-Americans. *Center Forum*, 1969, **4**:1, 4–7.

92. Strauss, A. L. The development of conceptions of rules in children. *Child Devel.*, 1954, **25**, 193–208.

93. Suchman, J. R. Inquiry training: Building skills for autonomous discovery. *Merrill-Palmer Quart.*, 1961, **7**, 147–170.

94. Terman, L. M., & Merrill, M. A. *Stanford–Binet Intelligence Scale.* Boston: Houghton Mifflin, 1960.

95. Walters, R. H., & Willows, D. C. Imitative behavior of disturbed and non-disturbed children following exposure to aggressive and nonaggressive models. *Child Devel.*, 1968, **39**, 79–89.

96. White, R. W. Motivation reconsidered: The concept of competence. *Psychol. Rev.*, 1959, **66**, 297–333.

97. Whiteman, P. H., & Kosier, K. P. Development of children's moralistic judgments: Age, sex, IQ and certain personal-experiential variables. *Child Devel.*, 1964, **35**, 843–850.

98. Witty, P. A., Kinsella, P., & Coomer, A. A summary of yearly studies of televiewing—1949–1963. *Elementary English*, 1963, **40**, 590–597.

99. Wyatt, E. Tennessee. In U.S. Commission on Civil Rights, *Civil rights, U.S.A.—Public schools, southern states.* Washington, D.C.: U.S. Govt. Printing Office, 1962, pp. 105–130.

# Chapter 12

Louise Boyle

# Social Development and Interpersonal Relationships

In his fast-expanding world, the child interacts with a greater and greater variety of teachers and influences. Relationships with peers grow more extensive and complex. While his family continues to be essential for protection, love, and teaching, the school, church, and other institutions play more and more important roles in his life. Through mass media, he contacts thoughts and events originating far from his own neighborhood.

## Social and Cultural Settings

A child is born into a community, a nation, a social class, a racial group, and other such divisions of mankind to which his parents belong. Even before he is aware of these classifications of people, he is affected by his memberships in them.

**451**

As a preschool child, he is influenced largely through his family, but as a school-child, he makes many direct contacts.

## Community

While community is often understood as neighborhood, or town, it can also be taken to mean the whole wide world. It can include all the people of whom one is aware. During the school years, many children do reach out beyond the confines of face-to-face contacts to relate to distant people. The newly acquired skills of reading and writing are keys to expanded relationships. A letter to Grandpa and Grandma may go right across the United States or into another country. Cousins known during vacation visits remain real throughout the year. Through pen pals, many children travel to the other side of the world to build warm friendships. The integrating experience of really helping other children is now a possibility for almost all American children at Halloween. Then they can give up their right to demand treats for themselves in order to collect for the United Nations Children's Fund. Boy Scouts and Girls Scouts spell out ways of learning about the rest of the world and facilitate the making of meaningful contacts and contributions. Schools open up vistas in time and space.

The world is indeed one level of community with which the child interacts. World concern for children is expressed through the United Nations, especially through its health and educational agencies. The federal government is another level of interaction. Here, responsibility for all children is a matter of increasing interest, with more agencies and more money being devoted to child and family welfare. Every state performs some functions for its children, dealing with such matters as health, education, and protection with more or less adequacy. Cities, towns, and sometimes townships have their special areas of responsibility too.

## National

Early in the elementary school years, a child begins to have a feeling of belonging to his own country and a realization that it is different from other countries [41, pp. 30–37]. He develops attitudes toward his own country and others and forms concepts about them.

**Political Attitudes.** Political knowledge is, of course, related to age and cognitive development. Preschool children's political knowledge is very concrete, idiosyncratic, and irrelevant as compared with that of school-age children [74]. For example, when asked what the President does, they made comments such as he has birthdays, he talks funny, he rides horses. Schoolchildren said that he makes laws, passes bills, and makes war.

Nearly 95 percent of 17,000 schoolchildren agreed that "the American flag is the best flag in the world" and "America is the best country in the world." The young child's vague concept of his country develops rapidly during the school years. In the first stage, national symbols, such as the flag and Statue of Liberty, give support and focus for the child's feelings and concepts. The second phase sees the concept of nation acquire more cognitive substance. Ideological components increased—in terms of pride in freedom, the right to vote, and democracy. In the earlier phase, children were more likely to express pride in the President or in our beautiful parks. By fifth grade, children saw the United States and Russia as having different political systems. In the third phase, the United States is seen as a country-among-countries. From third to eighth grade, there was a steady increase in numbers of children believing that the United Nations prevents war—14 percent to 87 percent—and a decrease in those thinking that the United States prevents war—71 percent to 13 percent [41, p. 36].

Schoolchildren reflect the pertinent political issues of the day in the extent of their knowledge of specific topics [74]. When a President has just been elected, they show more knowledge of the presidency. When war is highly salient, children's responses show that they realize it.

**Attitudes Toward People of Other Countries.**   Feelings and knowledge concerning people of other nations become elaborated during the school years. In so doing, a child also adds content to his self concept, as a person belonging to a national group. As such, he sees himself as having certain characteristics and a certain position in the world. Attitudes and ideas about foreign people and fellow countrymen were examined in 3300 children at three age levels in 11 parts of the world [57].

The children were interviewed, first with questions about themselves: "What are you? What else are you?" Then they were asked to name people from other countries who were like them and not like them and a series of questions asked about each group mentioned. Then came questions about seven particular peoples and about people of the child's own country. Finally they were asked which country they would like to belong to if they were not a member of their own. The self concepts revealed by the study showed that most 6-year-olds and 10-year-olds described themselves in terms of sex or age level (I am a boy. I am a girl. I am a child), rather than in terms of nation, religion, or role such as student. Americans, especially, were likely to describe themselves as boys or girls. In contrast, Bantu children were much more likely to describe themselves as members of a race, and Lebanese children gave a high proportion of responses using religion. Most likely the children's answers reflect the ways in which children are defined in their own cultures.

Descriptions of their own national group also reveal something of children's and adults' self concepts. The children varied in how factual and how subjective they were—the Bantu, Brazilian, and Israeli children using the largest number of factual statements, and the Turkish the smallest. Most children tended to stress the good qualities of their own nations, but Lebanese and Israelis made few references to goodness, and Bantu and Japanese hardly ever mentioned good qualities. The following list of descriptive terms shows the words most frequently used by each group for self-description:*

*American:* good, wealthy, free.
*Bantu:* mainly factual statements, similarity references.
*Brazilian:* good, intelligent, cultured, happy, unambitious.
*English-Canadian:* good, wealthy, free, cultured.
*French-Canadian:* good, wealthy, peaceful, patriotic.

---

* Knowing that children's political attitudes and concerns change with relevant political events, we might expect changes in attitudes toward national groups. This study gives information on children's thinking at one particular time. More significant, however, are the developmental trends, shown by age differences, and the differences between cultures which indicate variation in the definitions of people and hence in the self concepts of children.

*French:* good, intelligent, cultured, happy, bad.
*German:* good, ambitious, wealthy, intelligent.
*Israeli:* good, religious, peaceful, intelligent.
*Japanese:* poor, intelligent, bad.
*Lebanese:* similarity references and good.
*Turkish:* good, peaceful, ambitious, religious, patriotic, clean.

Comparisons were made between the children's descriptions of their own group and of the groups they considered desirable. The results suggest something about the children's satisfactions in being what they were. American children tended to choose British, Italian, and Canadian, whom they saw as friendly, good, and similar to themselves. French children, too, indicated satisfaction with their own nation in their choice of nations they considered good, cultured, and intelligent. Japanese, on the other hand, chose other nations whom they held to be good, wealthy, peaceful, cultured, and clean, while they described their own people as poor, intelligent, and bad. This conflict suggests dissatisfaction with their own people and consequently with themselves. Similarly, the Israeli and Brazilian children included wealth as part of their descriptions of desirable nations, but did not describe their own as wealthy.

The questions about how other groups were similar to one's own, and requests to tell about them, brought answers which showed attitudes and knowledge. American children often chose British, Canadians, French, and Italians as similar and Russians, Chinese, Africans, and Japanese as different. Many of the other groups made the same distinction, sometimes placing Americans in the "different" category. Thus a common large category seemed to be Western versus Oriental-African. Expressions of liking and affection toward other nationalities were not dependent on judgments of similarity and difference. National differences in liking of foreign people show American children to be most affectionate while Japanese, Turkish, and Israeli children show least liking of foreign peoples. The 10-year-olds, overall, showed most affection to foreign groups, but among Americans, there was a steady increase in affection from 6 to 14, while Bantu children showed no changes in affection.

Certain age trends could be seen throughout. The youngest children tended to focus on concrete details, such as physical features, clothing, language, and habits, and to give either nonevaluative replies or general responses, such as good and bad. The older children talked more about personality, politics, religion, and wealth and made more evaluative comments. The authors concluded that children come to think about foreign people in increasingly stereotyped ways during the years from 6 to 14. They attributed this trend to several factors, including more complex thinking and language, changes in their self concepts and social relationships, and changes in sources of information. Sources of information were different at different ages. Six-year-olds learned of foreign peoples mainly from their parents, films, and television: 10s and 14s got most of their information from mass media. Probably there is a relation between this increase in stereotyped thinking and the change in sources of information. Perhaps the mass media offer broad generalizations which encourage stereotypes.

Some social class differences were noticed. Middle-class children tended to express more affection toward foreign peoples than did working-class children, with a few exceptions.

*Racial and Ethnic*

As a member of a minority group, the school-age child directly experiences the particular attitudes and actions which other people customarily direct toward his group and which the members of his group direct toward themselves. If he is a member of a group which is easily distinguished by physical characteristics, then his experiences as a member are likely to be more intense and extensive. For many years black Americans, who are fairly distinctive in appearance, have occupied a subordinate social and economic position. Their experience is probably representative of any group so situated.

Parental teaching and expectations are known to vary with race and ethnic group. Children's attitudes toward other ethnic groups are related to their parents' attitudes. When parents were moderately punitive, children's social distance attitudes were found most closely related to the social distance attitudes which the children perceived in their parents [29]. When the child first contacts the attitudes of outsiders toward himself as a minority group member, the parents interpret those attitudes toward him and tell him how he is to think and behave. Parents are faced with the dilemma of explaining hostility, exclusion, or mere condescension while protecting their child's sense of adequacy. Even before he is touched by the world outside the family, the child of a minority group is affected by his parents' attitudes toward themselves and toward him as members of the minority. If they feel angry, resentful, and hopeless, as many poor black people do, then it is hard or perhaps impossible for their child to develop positive feelings about himself [72]. Instead of helping the child to develop competency and feelings of mastery over the environment, the disillusioned, embittered parent teaches the child what he cannot do and about the futility of trying. Although relatively little research has been done on middle- and upper-class Afro Americans, many or most of them obviously provide stable, supportive homes in which children can develop feelings of worthiness. One warm, secure, upper-class mother told of her interpretation to her 9-year-old daughter [102]. Mother and child had watched a television program about the deprivations, trials, and difficulties of being black. They had listened to a description of the unemployment crisis, ghetto living, police brutalities, and inferior schooling. Mrs. Young asked her daughter if she minded being a Negro. She answered, "No, I don't mind."

Her answer to her daughter was, "I'm glad you don't mind. There are many groups of people all over the world who have not been treated fairly. In Germany, it was the Jews; in some parts of Europe, it was the Catholics; in Vietnam, it was the Buddhists. Some people are mistreated because of color or religion and some because they are poor or blind or crippled. You should be especially proud of being Negro because, in your lifetime, you will enjoy a better America, knowing that we are the ones who helped our country to meet her commitment to all of her peoples."

Children are affected by values and hopes, as well as by tensions and hostilities. Attitudes toward achievement and occupations vary from one ethnic group to another. Mothers in six different ethnic groups were interviewed to explore their attitudes and practices in regard to their sons' achievement [79]. The boys were between 8 and 14 years of age. The ethnic groups included were French Canadian, Italian, Greek, Jewish, black and white Protestant. When the mothers were questioned about how they trained their sons for independence and what they demanded in the way of achievement, results showed that Protestants, Jews, and Greeks placed greater emphasis on independence and achievement than did Italians and French Canadians. Blacks often trained children early in independence, but tended to do little achievement training. Differences between Protestants, Jews, and Greeks were not statistically significant. Roman Catholics did significantly less achievement training than did non-Roman Catholic whites. A college education was intended for their sons by 96 percent of the Jewish, 88 percent of the Protestant, 85 percent of the Greek, 83 percent of the blacks, 64 percent of the Italian, and 56 percent of the French Canadian mothers. Vocational aspirations were explored by asking the mothers which occupations (for their sons) would satisfy them. Black mothers obtained the lowest score here, showing that they would make do with less than all the other mothers, probably a realistic reflection of the vocational opportunities which they knew existed. The order of mothers' aspirations, from high to low, was Jewish, Greek and white Protestant, Italian and French Canadian, black. This research points up the influence of ethnic group membership on a child's training in independence and achievement and the values and standards held for him in regard to education and vocation.

### Social Class

Behavior and outlook on life vary considerably with the social position occupied by a family. American middle-class and lower-class behavior has been studied extensively. Less is known about the upper class, since its members are more elusive as subjects for research. Class values and behavior patterns are transmitted from parents to children through their child-rearing practices.

The cognitive behavior patterns transmitted by the lower class have been described elsewhere in this book in sections on educational deprivation. To mention it only briefly here, the lower-class child is relatively reluctant to explore and to ask questions. His mother most likely discourages assertiveness, curiosity, and imagination, encouraging him to wait to be told, to receive, to be acted upon [76].

**Values.** The basic values of the upper class include respect for families and lineage; a belief that money is important, but only as a means to an end; contempt for pretense, striving, status symbols, and conspicuous consumption [5]. The upper-class child enjoys the care, education, and privileges that money will buy, but he has little realization that money is involved. In contrast, the middle-class child is keenly aware of what money will buy and how striving to achieve will bring money. The upper-class child does not learn social striving, nor does he experience social anxiety, since his family is already at the top, relaxed and poised, exercising quiet good taste. The middle-class child learns that he could rise socially by behaving in certain ways.

Middle-class values are achievement and status improvement, respectability and morality, property, money, organizations, self-improvement through the church, school, and civic organizations [23]. Several obervers [20, 21] see traditional middle-class values of competition and self-improvement being tempered by an increased desire for cooperation, conformity, fitting in and popularity. Parents thus affected want their children to be fairly good at everything but not extreme in anything. Lower-class values include security and getting by rather than getting ahead; traditional, patriarchal education; traditional, clearly differentiated sex roles; pragmatism, anti-intellectualism; such excitement as news, gossip, sports, and gadgets; physical expression and power [76]. Middle-class parents value self-direction and self-control for their children more highly than do working-class parents. The latter stress obedience and conformity to external rules [55]. Since middle-class occupations permit and require more initiative and self-direction, while working-class occupations require obedience to rules and directives, it seems that parents are socializing their children for life as they know it. The very poor, also, socialize their children for what they themselves have experienced.

The very poor or the hard-core poor differ from the working class, although they resemble the working class more than they do the middle class. Some tendencies of very poor parents, as compared with parents of higher status, are the use of inconsistent, harsh, physical punishment, fatalism, magical thinking, present-orientation, authoritarianism, strict definition of sex roles, alienation, distrust of society, constricted experience, limited, concrete verbal communication, judging of behavior in terms of immediate results, passivity, low self-esteem, ignorance of sex and reproduction, distrust of opposite sex, little differentiation between children, inconsistent nurturance of children, abrupt granting of independence, marital conflict, family breakdown, little education [18].

These value systems operate not only through parental influence but also through teachers, other children, club leaders, librarians, clergymen, policemen, doctors, and everybody else who contacts children. Although a middle-class child is likely to have predominantly middle-class values held up to him, he will meet few conflicting values. A lower-class child, in contrast, faces a bewildering mixture of value systems when he enters school [53]. His teacher's values conflict with those of his family and friends; verbal achievement versus physical; self-control versus frank expression; self-improvement versus unself-conscious acceptance; equalitarianism versus patriarchy; femininity versus masculinity; tomorrow versus today. It is hard to live up to the teacher's expectations of manners, quiet, orderliness, respect for property, thinking out instead of acting out.

**Interaction of Class and Family in Value Transmission.** Not only do values vary from class to class, but the behavior which transmits the values also varies. Child-training practices and philosophy of the middle and lower classes have been contrasted in many studies. Table 12–1 shows some of the important areas of difference indicated in a summary of this research [20].

The transmission of values and behavior patterns is complicated. A study of boys' acquisition of achievement orientation illustrates the complex ways in which only a few variables interact [80]. Drawn from diverse social strata, 122 boys and their mothers were interviewed. Results showed middle-class mothers and sons to be more similar in values than lower-class mothers and sons. Among lower-class pairs, values were more similar if the mother was older rather than younger. Small- and medium-sized families produced more similarity in mother–son values than did large families.

**Occupational Orientation.** While the concepts of social class and occupational orientation overlap somewhat, certain occupations signifying higher class position than others, there are basic differences in occupation such as agricultural versus industrial or entrepreneurial versus bureaucratic. The latter was taken as the basis of a study of American contrasts in child rearing during the 1950s, when bureaucratic fathers were seen as more affectionate and less authoritarian [60]. Recently a Puerto Rican study has revealed a similar trend [61]. The subjects were boys between 9 and 12 and their parents, divided into three occupational groups:

**Table 12-1** Behavior and Philosophy of Parents of Two Classes

|  | Working Class (Lower Class) | Middle Class |
| --- | --- | --- |
| Behavioral requirements | Specific | Internalized standards |
|  | Obedience, neatness, cleanliness | Honesty, self-control |
|  | Qualities assuring respectability | Boys, curiosity; Girls, considerateness |
| Concept of good parent | Elicits specific behavior | Promotes development, affection, satisfaction |
| Response to misdeed | Focus on immediate consequences of child's actions | Takes into account child's intentions and feelings |
| Discipline techniques | More physical punishment | More reasoning, isolation, appeals to guilt |
| Role differentiation | More rigid. More paternalistic | More flexible, more equalitarian |
| Father as companion to child | Less | More |
| Permissiveness | Less to infant and young child More to older child | More to infant and young child Less to older child |
| Achievement demands | Less | More |

SOURCE: Data from Clausen & Williams [20].

agricultural, industrial-uneducated, and industrial-educated. Parents were interviewed as to their goals and practices. Boys were interviewed and tested. Agricultural mothers, compared with industrial mothers, stressed authority and traditional values and were more restrictive and punitive. The industrial mothers were more permissive and child-centered, sensitive to individual needs. The agricultural fathers maintained the traditional pattern of authoritarian aloofness, demanding obedience and conformity, while industrial fathers were more warm and involved. They encouraged initiative and occasional aggression, trying to strengthen their sons' achievement motivation.

Thus do parents prepare their children for coping with the world as they (the parents) experience it. Conformity, obedience, and cooperation are valuable in agricultural life; individuality, initiative, achievement, competition, and self-expression are functional in industrial life.

## Relationships with Parents

The school-age stage of family life seems to be a difficult one for parents. General satisfaction over the life cycle was studied in 852 couples who were white and predominantly middle class [78]. The low point in satisfaction with family living for husbands and wives came at the time when the oldest child was between 6 and 13. Satisfaction with children was also found to be lowest in the school-age stage [13]. Beyond this rather general assessment of parental and marital satisfaction, little account has been taken of what children do to parents. Hundreds of attempts have been made to find out what parents do to children, or, more accurately, what are the results of certain parent–child interactions upon children.

*The Parental Role*

In a stable, unchanging society, the parental role, as well as other roles, is well-defined. Everybody understands pretty well what a good child is and what a good parent is supposed to do in order to have the child grow up correctly. While parents are not all equally successful, their differences are attributed to variations in capacities and situations, as well as to inborn differences in children. Parents behave as their parents did toward them and when in doubt, mothers turn to grandmothers to be filled in as to proper procedures. Grandmothers may not wait to be asked.

Most modern societies are changing, just as the United States is changing. The faster the changes, the less automatic are parental behaviors. Grandparents are of little help, since their ways are outmoded. Parents must think about the various aspects of their roles, and yet they are offered minimal assistance from the educational system. Using the perceptions of parents whose children were enrolled in a university nursery school, the parental role was analyzed into four main components: goal values, means-ends beliefs, means-ends capacities, and goal achievement [28].

**Goal Values.** What do parents want their children to become? How do they want them to act, feel, and believe? Parents choose both positive and negative goal values. Some goals are problematic in being hard to implement. As we have just seen, the broad social settings of community, nation, and class affect values. Child-rearing authorities, such as Dr. Spock and the United States Children's Bureau, also affect parents' goal values while they reflect social trends. An example of changing goals is that of "breaking the will," held to be desirable a century ago. At present, submissiveness is a negative goal, an undesirable condition.

**Means-Ends Beliefs.** Parents believe that certain methods will be effective in achieving their goals. Child-rearing practices are largely those believed to be means towards the ends that are valued. Five beliefs about child rearing were included in the study of parental role in highly educated fathers and mothers [28]. *Nonintervention,* in which the parent does nothing, is based on the belief that the child will outgrow undesired behavior and will perform desired behavior when he matures enough. *Behavior modification* involves positively reinforcing desirable behavior. That is, rewards and punishments are used. *Motivational modification* is persuasion or reasoning in order to change the child's desire to act or not to act in certain ways. *Situational modification* means changing the setting in the belief that a different environment will elicit desired behavior. *Modeling* is setting an example of desirable behavior in the belief that the child will imitate it.

Of all components of the parental role, means-ends beliefs are probably most responsive to child-rearing authorities. The maturational theory of Gesell (interpreted inaccurately) was very influential a generation ago in justifying nonintervention. Many parents believed that children would automatically grow out of undesirable stages into desirable ones, or that a terrible stage was imminent. Motivational modification receives much support from the popular Haim Ginott. Behavior modification is recommended by the projects of Bereiter and Engleman. Situational modification is upheld by the adherents of Montessori schools. Modeling is often supported in sermons. Bandura has analyzed the dynamics of modeling.

**Means-Ends Capacities.** How well can the parent carry out the child-rearing methods that he believes will implement his goals? Means-ends capacities may or may not be in harmony with means-ends beliefs. When the parent knows what he ought to do but cannot carry it out, then he feels incompetent and he probably is

Courtesy Cornell University

ineffective. For example, a father believes strongly in modeling, but he does not set the good example he wishes his child would follow. Means-ends capacities can be problem areas for parents, who may find help in parent education groups, counseling, psychotherapy, or possibly in books and articles.

**Goal Achievements.** How well does the child meet the parents' standards? The match between parental goal value and child behavior is a measure of success in the parent role.

### Parental Attributes and Parent–Child Relationships

Parent–child interactions are strongly emotional, as well as cognitive. Children's development and behavior can be related to parents' warmth or coldness, love or hostility, restrictiveness and control versus acceptance of the child's autonomy. Researchers have studied a large number of child and parent variables in various combinations and in relation to different constructs. In the remainder of this section, we shall discuss the relation of parental behavior to children's identification, achievement, and cognitive development.

### Identification with Parents

Identification is the process by which one person tries to become like another person in one or more ways. Identification with the parent of the same sex is, according to psychoanalytic theory, an important factor in the personality development of children from 6 to 12. It probably rarely if ever happens that a child identifies only with one parent to the exclusion of the other, nor is it likely to be true that identification goes on only during a limited period of time. Children also react to the expectations which salient people have of them, even though the salient people do not demonstrate the behavior. For instance, Johnny obeys Father because Father expects it, although he himself does not obey Johnny. Each has expectations of the other and each knows what the other expects of him. This sort of learning is the basis of the child's knowing how to play the father's role when he grows up, even though he has until this point played only the role of the child.

How does the child select certain parental behavior on which to model his own, and certain parental expectations with which to cooperate?

An interplay of many factors, at least some of which will not be conscious, will be involved in making such choices. Some research has been done on the influence of sex of child and sex of parent on the child's patterning of identification. For example, boys' reactions to frustration were found to resemble their fathers' reactions to frustration, while girls' were similar to mothers' [87]. The considerably different roles played by mother and father call for different behaviors and learnings in children. One way of systematizing the resulting relationships is by the concepts of *expressive* and *instrumental* roles [70]. Playing an expressive role in a group means being sensitive to the feelings, thoughts, and needs of the other people, aware of their relationships with each other, devoted to promoting their happiness and well-being, understanding them, pleasing them, and enjoying them. Within the family the person having the main responsibility for the care and emotional support of the children is therefore playing the main expressive role. To play an instrumental role is to be responsible for solving the problems facing the group and to assume authority for making decisions. The person playing the instumental role is the final court of appeals, the punisher, the family member with the primary responsibility for the discipline and training of children. The person in the instrumental role settles disputes between members, deciding on the basis of issues involved; the person in the expressive role smooths them over, comforting and consoling the members concerned.

Parental identification of boys and girls can be explained in terms of the instrumental and expressive roles played by parents [49]. A mother plays a family role which is largely expressive, while a father plays both roles, instrumental and expressive, with emphasis on the instrumental role. One piece of evidence for the expressive nature of mothers' roles is that they were more accurate than fathers in perceiving anxiety in their daughters [35]. (Parents were equally perceptive in estimating anxiety levels of sons.) Expressivity and instrumentality are by no means mutually exclusive. Men are both; women are both. On the average, however, men behave instrumentally more often than women, and women expressively more often than men. There are wide ranges of individual differences within each sex, so much so that one finds some men who are more expressive than the average woman and some women who are more instrumental than the average man. However, let us see what happens when the mother is the expressive leader in the family and the father the instrumental.

During infancy and the early preschool years, both boys and girls are more closely attached to their mothers than to their fathers. Thus both sexes first relate to a person playing a largely expressive role. In this relationship boys and girls are exposed to love-oriented discipline and take their basic steps toward internalizing conscience. In this relationship, boys and girls learn to be expressive. The next step toward maturity for both boys and girls is to become attached to the father, outgrowing some of the infantile dependence upon the mother. The father represents the reality of the outside world to his children. The father tends to react expressively with his daughters, enjoying, praising, and appreciating them as feminine creatures, while with sons he is more demanding, exerting pressure and discipline, insisting upon successful interaction with the world. The salience of the father in the family has been shown to have a vital effect on the boy's assumption of his sex role [62]. The more the son interacts with a powerful father, a man who does both punishing and rewarding, the more masculine the boy will be. Sons conformed more to fathers' expectations when fathers were warm and took part in child-rearing [42]. Girls' sex role learning has been found to be enhanced by fathers who encouraged their daughters to take part in feminine activities and by mothers who were warm and self-confident and with whom the daughters had satisfying relationships [63]. Girls' feminine responses were associated with their perceptions of their mothers as salient controllers of family resources [7].

While mothers make little difference in the demands they place on boys and girls, they tend to go along with the fathers in expecting more aggression from boys. Thus according to this theory, it is the father more than the mother who teaches boys and girls to play their sex-appropriate roles. The mother supplements his teaching, especially in defining him to the children as a worthy person, and also in choosing the children's clothing, assigning their jobs, and telling them "boys do this and girls do that." It tends to be the father, however, who has the stronger feelings and reactions about sex-inappropriate activities, especially boys engaging in feminine ones. While mothers sometimes consider it all right for boys to knit or play with dolls, fathers are usually disturbed by such activities. The mother, realizing the father's feelings, sees that the boys do behave appropriately.

## Stimulation of Cognitive Development and Need for Achievement

Families promote intellectual growth in two main ways: by stimulating the child's desire for achievement, and by offering experiences through which the child can grow mentally. The desire for achievement is highlighted during these years, as being an essential in the development of the sense of industry. Normal personality development centers around becoming competent in the basic skills of the culture. Since the academic skills are a vital part of those basic skills, the encouragement of intellectual development is also the encouragement of personality development.

When a parent, especially a father, has a strong desire for intellectual competence for himself, he is likely to stimulate such achievement in his children [52]. The higher the value the father placed on intellectual achievement, the more likely he was to share intellectual activities with his children, to encourage children to engage in such pursuits, and to show great interest in the children's achievements. The mothers behaved similarly, except that they were more likely to show such reactions with daughters than with sons.

At age 10, IQs of both boys and girls were significantly correlated with IQ and education of father and of mother and with socioeconomic status and the educational stimulation and emotional support offered by the home [98]. As compared with IQs of sons, the IQs of daughters had higher correlations with parental ability, educational stimulation, and emotional support.

**Need for Achievement.** The aspirations which hold for their children apparently affect the ways in which parents interact with children, often producing the desired effects. Boys with high-achievement needs tend to have mothers who expected them to be self-reliant at an early age, who gave them freedom to learn, and who rewarded their independent efforts [100]. When observed working together at home, boys with high-achievement aspirations were found to have parents who held high standards for them and who gave them autonomy in working out problems. The mothers of these boys treated them warmly, freely giving both approval and criticism. The fathers showed considerable interest in and involvement with their sons [81]. Subsequent studies have confirmed and extended these findings, showing the negative effects of parental coldness, rejection, and restrictiveness and the positive effects of warmth, involvement, encouragement, and desire to help the child achieve maturity [73].

**Locus of Control.** Not only achievement aspiration, but also the child's belief in his own ability to control what happens, is related to parental behavior. Children between 6 and 13 were more likely to believe in internal control when parents were consistent, warm, supporting, praising, and protective, rather than dominating, rejecting, and critical [24, 51]. There was some suggestion that fathers' attitudes were more influential than mothers' in regard to children's belief in locus of control.

The child's self concept has an influence on his locus of control. Lower-class black children in grades 4 through 7 were studied in terms of self esteem and locus of control, under conditions of success and failure [30]. Failure was attributed to external causes more than success was, suggesting an adaptive mechanism by which the stigmatized child cushions his self concept. Children with higher self esteem were more likely than others to believe themselves responsible for failure and success.

**General Intelligence.** Rising IQs were found to be associated with certain personality characteristics in children and with certain kinds of parental behavior which most likely had been instrumental in producing the personality characteristics [88]. As might be expected from other studies already mentioned, the children whose IQs rose were, on the whole, independent children who ventured forth curiously, explored freely, competed, and showed high need for achievement. The mothers of these children took considerable interest in their children's achievements and encouraged them to master the environment [50].

**Specific Measures.** Several studies deal with particular parental practices and attitudes, relating them to specific aspects of children's intellectual functioning, such as distractibility, flexible thinking, curiosity, and attitudes toward mathematics. Extremes of distractible and nondistractible boys and girls were selected on the basis of a distractibility test [4]. The children were given tasks (puzzle, ring toss, anagrams, and block patterns) to do while their parents, who had been given additional information about solutions, were free to help the children as much or as little as they wished. Rather surprisingly, there was more interaction between nondistractible children and their parents than in the other group, largely due to the nondistractible children initiating it. The quality of interaction differed considerably in the two groups, however. Parents of nondistractible children gave less specific suggestions, more positive encouragement, more evaluative comments, and paid more attention to the child's contributions. Thus while these parents were highly involved, they were also teaching their children to be autonomous.

Flexible thinking in fifth grade black boys from a lower-class community was studied in relation to their fathers' and mothers' behavior [14]. The boys' flexible thinking was evaluated by means of a test designed for that purpose. Parents were observed in teaching specific tasks to their sons and were asked questions selected from the Parental Attitude Research Instrument. Results from the parents' teaching of sons showed a relationship between boys' flexible thinking and parents' manipulating the task materials a moderate amount. Thus the child was most likely to think flexibly if his parents were people who showed him something about a matches-and-squares problem and about a sorting problem, but not too much. Boys' flexible thinking was related negatively to mothers' commanding and positively to fathers' feelings of powerfulness, moderate participation with children and flexible, sympathetic standards. Studies on curiosity [59] also indicate that children are likely to develop effective methods of discovery and learning when parents encourage autonomy while maintaining mutual respect and caring.

**Family Interaction and Cognitive Development.** Extended, rational conversation among family members tends to happen more often at the dinner table than anywhere else [8]. This learning situation is, however, a middle-class custom. In homes of the hard-core poor, there may be no time when the family eats together. When parents and children are together, they usually talk about the most immediate concerns, not about the past and future. Discussions of concepts, causal relationships and logical consequences are almost entirely lacking [93]. Dinnertime conversation is an activity in which either educational enrichment or deprivation may occur.

## Discipline

An important parental function is discipline, which, to most people, includes the regulation of children's behavior, the teaching of self control and the imparting of moral standards. Teachers are also expected to discipline children, the extent of their efforts varying with the culture. Adults often consider it virtuous to be strict disciplinarians, while simultaneously holding the goal of enjoying children and being friends with them [64].

The particular methods of discipline selected by an adult will depend upon his means-ends beliefs and his application of them, upon his means-ends capacities. Probably most people believe in and employ punishment, rewards, reasoning, and modeling. Punishment may be corporal, verbal, deprivation of objects or privileges, or withdrawal of approval and affection. Rewards, too, can be physical, verbal, object-oriented or emotional. Reasoning and explaining help the child to develop the cognitive structure basic to moral judgment. Setting a "good example" offers behavior patterns that the child imitates if he chooses to model his behavior on the adult's.

**Research on Methods of Discipline.** Analyses have been made of the dimensions of punishment and the interactions of punishment with other means of discipline [17, 26, 68, 69]. A typical experiment was one in which seven-year-old boys were tested in conditions of early and late punishment (the sounding of a buzzer when a forbidden toy was touched), intensity of punishment (loudness of buzzer), high and low cognitive structure (much or little explanation of why certain toys should not be touched), and high and low nurturance (much or little attention and approval from the examiner). As expected from previous experiments, response inhibition (not touching forbidden toys) was strengthened by high cognitive structure and high intensity, and somewhat increased by early punishment and nurturance. When cognitive structure was low, high intensity punishment was more effective than low, but when cognitive structure was high, intensity of punishment made no difference. Similarly, when cognitive structure was low, high nurturance strengthened response inhibition but when cognitive structure was high, nurturance made no difference. With low-intensity punishment, early timing was more effective, but when intensity was high, there was no difference between early and late timing. This experiment shows the very complex nature of discipline. While it is clear that cognitive and emotional factors interact, the experiment cannot be taken as a blueprint for parents, since it represents a highly simplified version of what happens in a home.

Studies on the more global interactions of parents and children, done by tests, interviews or observations, also give insights that can be helpful to parents but that will not tell them exactly what to do. The harmful effects of high punishment levels were suggested by the lower IQ's of children whose parents scored high in rejection and punitiveness [46]. The value of a special kind of cognitive structure is suggested by the fact that children tend to show extra concern for human well-being when parents direct their attention to the results of their actions upon the feelings and welfare of others [43]. Children go through stages of moral development as they structure and restructure their schemas underlying moral judgment [54]. As with all kinds of development, moral structures are built from many experiences, of which parent–child interactions are very influential.

## Relationships with Peers

Peers are equals, or in the usual meaning, friends of about the same age. The peer group is an important socializing agent in a child's life. The type of influence exerted by the peer group varies from one culture to another. In the United States and England, the peer group is often sharply differentiated from the world of adults. Children have secrets, codes, and a common culture [67], with which they promote feelings of solidarity in the group and separation from adults. Together they explore ideas, as well as the physical world. Parents often feel that children are entitled to privacy with their friends. Adults expect a certain amount of childhood misbehavior or resistance to adult standards. Much of our research on parent and peer influences is built on the assumption that there will be conflicts between the two. The situation is different in the Soviet Union, where the peer group is systematically manipulated to promote conformity to adult-given standards [10]. Whatever the functions of the peer group, they are related to parent–child relationships, to the school system, and to the culture as a whole.

### Learning of Values, Behavior, and Attitudes

Children expose one another to a variety of sets of values which stem from memberships such as those of family, class, and ethnic origin. The values of a peer group are especially compelling, since a youngster has to accept them in order to be accepted as a member. If the peer values are not too different from those of his family and teachers, a mild conflict between them only serves to differentiate him from adults and to give him a feeling of belonging to the gang. He will suffer if values differ greatly, as when his peers idealize the member who pilfers successfully, while his family requires honesty. Peers reinforce many values which adults approve sincerely but less enthusiastically. Physical bravery in boys is an example. Most parents make some effort to discourage crying and fussing over hurts and dangers, but the group may insist upon bravery, with expulsion the penalty for being a "sissy."

The peer group teaches its members how to act and how to think. Skills are learned through imitation and practice, coordinations, games, the arts, humor, language. Some of the behavior is childhood ritual, which is passed from one generation of schoolchildren to the next and almost forgotten by adults [67]. It includes the chants used with jumping rope and bouncing balls:

> One, two, three O'Leary
> I spy Miss McGary
> Sitting on a huckleberry
> Reading a dictionary.

> Down in the valley where the green grass grows
> There sat Helen as sweet as a rose
> She sang and she sang and she sang so sweet
> Along came her fellow and kissed her on the cheek.

It includes wishing on white horses and "stamping" the first robins of spring (not literally, just touching one thumb to the tongue and pushing it into the other—open—palm).

The group may require certain modes of speech, a secret language such as Pig Latin or simply modified English, tending toward toughness and crudity through dropping G's and mixing up rules about plurals and tenses. Most boys and girls learn vulgar words for sex and elimination processes. It is very exciting and status-defining to use the four-letter words and some swear words, too.

Matters of taste and fashion come strongly under peer influence. It becomes essential to wear woolen knee socks, white ankle socks, or nylon stockings according to what the other girls are wearing, regardless of the weather or of what Mother thinks. One winter everybody slides down the hill on sleds, but the following winter the only vehicle worth sliding on is a tray. The next year, trays are out, but one must buy a gadget which manufacturers have thoughtfully designed to be almost like trays. The group even has strong opinions as to the best kind of candy and gum, opinions which change rapidly.

**Conformity.** The extent and nature of children's conformity to group pressure has been investigated in classroom situations. In one study of lower- and middle-class boys and girls ages 7, 10, and 13, the perceptually-ambiguous task required judging how long a light remained on and how far it moved [36]. The control subjects made judgments privately, while the experimental subjects answered in groups of three, where each could hear the answer of the other two children. Results showed conformity increasing with age, with a greater increase between 7 and 10 than between 10 and 13 years. Girls conformed more than boys. Age changes in boys were greater than those in girls, the 7-year-old boys conforming considerably less than girls their age, but 13-year-old boys conforming on about the same level as girls. A similar study employing unambiguous tasks as well as ambiguous ones showed conformity *decreasing* with age when tasks were unambiguous [45]. Thus it seems that children increase with age in their desire to be correct as well as in their desire to fit in with peers. When the answer is clearly indicated, they tend to choose right, increasing in this tendency with age. When it is difficult to discern, they are influenced by peers, also increasing in this tendency as they grow older. When children were faced with choices in social situations, conformity to parents, as opposed to peers, decreased significantly between Grades 3 and 7 [96].

**Table 12-2** Experiences with Parents and Peers and Responses to Parent and Peer Pressures in Preadolescence

|  | 1<br>Autonomous | 2<br>Adult-<br>Oriented | 3<br>Peer-<br>Oriented | 4<br>Adult- & Peer-<br>Oriented |
|---|---|---|---|---|
| Control, punishment | moderate | low | high or low | low |
| Nurturance | high | high | low | high |
| Contact with mother | high | high | low | |
| Contact with peers | high | low | high | high |
| Peer orientation<br>of parents | | high | | |

SOURCES: E. C. Devereux [27]; also E. P. Hollander & J. E. Marcia, Parental determinants of peer-orientation and self-orientation among preadolescents. *Devel. Psychol.*, 1970, **2**, 292–302.

The Cornell study of conformity to parent and peer pressures described on pages, 443–444, showed some age-level effects for moral judgment [27]. From fifth through eighth grade, children conformed less to adult pressure and more to peer pressure. Conformity to peer pressure was also related to the extent of the child's involvement in and experience with the peer group. Children, especially boys, responded more to peer pressures when they belonged to gangs in which misconduct was frequent. This study confirmed the sex difference found in other studies. Girls responded more than boys to adult pressures. The nature of the dilemmas presented bore some relation to whether children responded more to parents or peers. When issues were seen as serious, children were more likely to conform to adults. Other influences on the children included the nature of the classroom group in which they were, the type of teacher in charge of the class and, as previously described, the parents. There was evidence that autonomous children were likely to have higher IQs than the others.

From cross-culture studies, the Cornell researchers have concluded that peer interaction contributes importantly to the development of moral autonomy [27]. Autonomy seems to develop out of peer experience in the child whose home gives him moderate to high support (nurturance) and moderate levels of discipline and control. Under these circumstances, the child is likely to have the ego strength necessary for making use of adult–peer cross-pressures. Without nurturant, moderately controlling parents, peer-interaction makes for peer-conformity. Without peer-interaction, the nurturant, controlling parents make for parent-conformity. Different combinations of parent-interaction and peer-interaction and of parent–peer cross-pressures were seen in various countries where the study was carried on. Soviet children were most adult-conforming, English most peer-conforming. Americans were second in adult-conformity, Germans third. It was noted that while Soviet children have a great deal of peer-interaction, there is little or no discrepancy between adult and peer values, especially in boarding schools. Hence peer pressures and adult pressures tend to work in the same direction.

**Self Concept.** Every child's concept of himself is built partly through seeing himself as others see him. As a person who belongs to a peer group, liked and accepted by them, he feels himself to be a worthy person. (And, if he is not accepted, he feels unworthy.) If his friends laugh at his jokes and call him amusing, he sees himself as a wit. If they call her "Fatso," she believes that she is *too* fat.

Measuring himself against the standards of peers is another way in which a person's self concept is built. Age-level segregation plus great emphasis on competition make American childhood a very competitive time. It is especially important for a boy to be able to measure up in motor skills. Unless others regard him as adequate in physical coordination, his self concept is likely to suffer. When needed, compensatory physical education can make an important contribution to a boy's self concept [22, p. 135].

Even though peers cooperate in their play, they owe each other nothing in the sense that family members have obligations to each other. Group loyalty is comparatively ephemeral, depending on continuing to meet competitive standards of behavior. The feeling which a youngster gets from successful competition with his age-mates is *adequacy*. Since these years are most critical for development of a sense of adequacy, this aspect of peer influence is a vital one.

Self concept is related to social class, race, and sex. While peer reactions are doubtless influenced by the child's class-related and race-related behavior and appearance, his self concept is shaped by people of all ages, including peers. Development of self concept from first to fifth grade was studied in black and white children whose mothers were on welfare [16]. Not surprisingly, the self concepts of these children from the lowest economic level decreased between first and fifth grades. Girls were more negative than boys in self concept. Black girls were much lower than black boys, and at the first grade level were much lower than white girls. This study is in agreement with other research which indicates that as the child accumulates experience and matures cognitively, he understands more fully what it means to be a member of a racial or ethnic minority [72].

### Position in the Group, Acceptance and Rejection

Children vary in how much they are liked by other children and in how many other children like them. Sociometry is a way of finding out where each child in a group stands in relation to the other children in it: who likes him, who does not like him, and who is indifferent or mild in attitudes toward him. When these data are collected for each child, a picture of relationships within the group can be drawn. By means of sociometry, group relations can be measured and described [66]. Each child is asked to name one or more group members with whom he would like to engage in one or more activities (to sit beside, to go to the movies with, to work with, and so on). The choices are then represented by symbols on a diagram, using arrows to indicate the direction of each choice. Figure 12–1 is a sociogram which shows the friendships of a group of first grade children. Although the majority of choices are between children of the same sex, there are also cross-sex choices. Note the pentagon to the right of the centers which includes a boy chosen by every one of a group of four girls. See the triangle of boys to the lower left of center. One of the boys also chose a girl and one another boy.

The characteristics of children who are accepted or rejected have been assessed by many investigators, using a variety of measuring devices. Friendliness and sociability are, not surprisingly, associated with acceptance, whereas rejection or nonacceptance are associated with hostility, withdrawal, and similar negative social attitudes. Greater intelligence and creativity, if they are not too far above the level of the group, are typical of popular children. Boys are accepted by other boys if they have athletic ability, muscular strength, and are above average size. Socio-

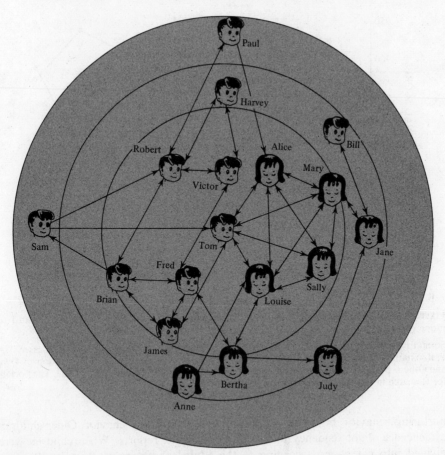

**Figure 12–1.** A sociogram showing friendship choices in a first grade.

SOURCE: Reprinted by permission from Mary L. Northway, *A Primer of Sociometry*, 2nd edition. Copyright © 1967, University of Toronto Press.

economic class also makes a difference, since children tend to choose friends of their own class or a higher one [15]. Older preadolescents fluctuate less than younger ones over a two-week period in their choices of friends [44]. This age trend continues on into adolescence, and is evident from the experience of adults, most of whom recognize that their friendships change slowly over a period of years.

**Personal Characteristics As Seen by Other Children.** An approach to the topic of peer acceptance started with the question "How do children perceive one another?" [101]. The subjects were 267 white and black children, 8 to 13, living in a summer camp. Strangers to each other at the beginning, they lived in groups of eight for two weeks. Each child was asked to choose a child whom he knew most about and to tell all about him. Adults made systematic behavior observations of the camp life. In telling about each other, children showed two strong tendencies: they made broad positive or negative judgments; the judgments were mainly in terms of actions that had direct interpersonal consequences. Individuals showed consistency in the ways in which they described others, whether they described the same child twice or a different child. Within this consistency, there were changes over the two-week period in increasing emphasis on interaction between persons and in giving more organized descriptions. There were some sex differences. Girls emphasized

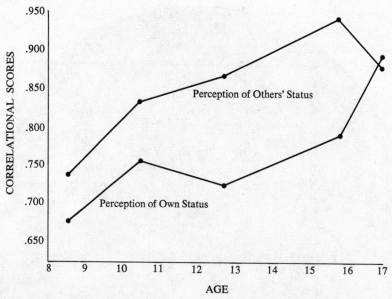

**Figure 12–2.** Age changes in the ability to judge one's own sociometric status and to judge the status of another person.

SOURCE: Reprinted by permission from D. P. Ausubel, H. M. Schiff, and E. B. Gasser, "A Preliminary Study of Developmental Trends in Socioempathy: Accuracy of Perception of Own and Others' Sociometric Status," *Child Development*, **23**, Figure 1. Copyright © 1952, The Society for Research in Child Development, Inc.

nurturing behavior, boys nonconforming and withdrawn behavior. Older children evidenced a slight tendency to give more complex reports. When children were divided into categories according to the adults' observations, these results were found: active and friendly children gave more complex descriptions of peers than did withdrawn or hostile children; active children were more explicit than withdrawn; friendly children made more inferential statements than hostile children; there was a consistent but nonsignificant tendency for friendly children to describe others in a more organized fashion than hostile children. These results suggest that those who take an active part in social relationships perceive other people more sharply than do these who are less active.

Socioempathic ability, the ability to perceive one's own status in a group and the statuses of others, tends to increase with age [1]. Children from Grade 3 through Grade 12 were asked to rate all of their classmates as to acceptability as friends, and to predict how each of the classmates would rate them and be rated by the group. True sociometric status was calculated for each child from the first rating. Accuracy of perception of sociometric status was calculated by correlating the mean predicted statuses with the sociometric statuses. Figure 12–2 shows the correlational scores for accuracy of perception (socioempathic ability) at each age between 8 and 17.

**Personal Characteristics As Reflected by Tests.** The behavior characteristics valued by low- and high-socioeconomic groups of 12-year-olds were studied by using a Guess-Who test [71]. Results showed definite socioeconomic and sex differences in the prestige value of various clusters of behavior patterns. Fighting ability was important to all boys in determining leadership position, but more important to low-socioeconomic boys. Restlessness was less acceptable to High Boys than to Low. An eminent fighter among Low Boys was likely to be also a ladies' man, but among High Boys, the friendly, conforming, "little gentleman" had success with the girls. Among High Boys, the classroom intellectual was not a leader but was not rejected. Such a person among Low Boys would be considered too effeminate and yielding to deserve any recognition. Low Girls were more sharply differentiated as to aggressiveness than were High Girls. Among Low Girls, the fighting tomboy was the one who went out with boys, while among High Girls, the "little lady" was more interested in and successful with boys. The tomboy was unpopular with High Girls, but had considerable prestige with Low Girls. High Boys and Girls value some conformity to adult standards in the classroom and at parties, while low groups did not.

Personalities of very popular, average, and unpopular children were studied with the Rorschach test among other tests [65]. The least popular children showed less emotional control, appeared to be more self-centered, moody, and impulsive, and were often unable to react to a situation even though they desired to participate. The very popular children showed great sensitivity to the social situation, conventional interpretations of social situations, little originality, strong need for affection, and a conscious striving for approval. A more recent study indicates that girls with high need for approval are likely to be popular, while boys with high need for approval are likely to be unpopular [95]. This finding fits with sex role typing which prescribes social responsiveness and pliability for feminine behavior.

Although popular children differed from one another in many ways, all of them had two characteristics in common: they put forth a great deal of energy, and they used their energy for purposes approved by the group [65]. The popular child was likely to be a conformist. He was likely to be conventional rather than creative. He tended to be sympathetic to the needs and wants of others. Some unpopular children were simply unliked, and others actively disliked. They had in common a lack of energy directed to group purposes, but the disliked child used his abounding energy in ways which conflicted with the interests of other children.

Children at both extremes of popularity showed more emotional disturbance than did the average children. Great striving for popularity may be due to feeling a lack of love. The very popular child may pay a severe price in energy expenditure and anxiety. Some children were, of course, both popular and well-adjusted.

Although a person's name is not a personality attribute, still it is a part of him. Research shows that it is an *influential* part of an elementary school child [58]. Popularity was correlated with the group's liking for the first name. Social acceptance within the group was also correlated with ratings for first names derived from outside groups, that is, from children who did not know the bearers of the names involved.

**Leadership.** Comparisons on a large number of physical, sociological, intellectual, and social variables were made between 6- to 11-year-old children [37]. One group of 278 subjects had been frequently chosen as leaders. The contrast group of 416 had rarely or never been chosen as leaders. Leaders, as a group, were significantly healthier, more active, more aggressive, more intelligent, higher achievers, more gifted, more likely to be Caucasian, more socially adept, and better adjusted. The individual leader excelled in at least one of the areas of physical, mental, and social development, but not necessarily in all three.

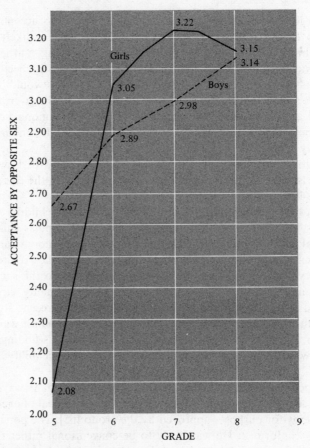

**Figure 12–3.** Acceptance by the opposite sex.
SOURCE: Data from Reese [78].

### Boy–Girl Relationships

Acceptance of members of the opposite sex by boys and girls in Grades 5 through 8 was measured by means of a sociometric test [75]. Since ratings at each level were below neutral, and thus unfavorable, both sexes tended to reject the opposite sex. In the beginning of the year in fifth grade, girls accepted boys significantly more than boys accepted them. However, by the end of the fifth academic year and during the subsequent years through eighth grade, boys accepted girls more than the reverse. Figure 12–3 shows the scores for acceptance of the opposite sex by boys and girls at each level. A child's level of acceptance by the opposite sex was positively related to his score of acceptance by his own sex.

As Figure 12–3 suggests, both boys and girls make progress throughout the grades in becoming more acceptable to the opposite sex. This progress has been analyzed into a series of steps in heterosexual development, steps which occur in a developmental sequence [9]. That is, step A regularly occurs before step B and step C. The steps in the sequence established were wanting to marry some day; having a girl friend or boy friend now; having ever been in love; preferring the opposite sex as a companion for going to the movies; having had a date. This sequence held for suburban boys and girls, urban white boys and girls, urban

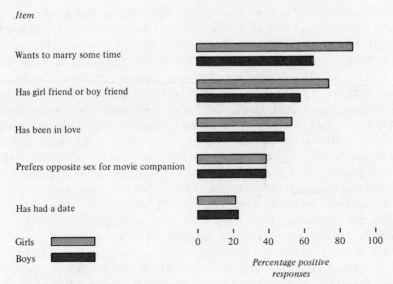

**Figure 12–4.** Heterosexual development scale, showing percentage of positive responses to each item by children 10–12 years old.
SOURCE: Data from Broderick and Rowe [9].

black girls, and rural white boys. Figure 12–4 shows the percentage of positive answers on each item from boys and girls from a Kansas sample, in which rural and urban were represented. The subjects were mostly white, Protestant, and lower class. The first item represents a global concept, that marriage some day would be desirable. Next the child narrows his sights to the idea of having a girl friend or boy friend. Often this relationship is nonreciprocal and exists largely in the mind of one child. The next step, being in love, often refers to the one chosen as boy friend or girl friend, who may still be unaware of his status as love object. Then comes the specific step of appreciating the opposite sex as a companion for going to the movies. Only after this is the child likely to actually go on a date. Thus does the child differentiate dating behavior out of the general desirability of marriage, and a specific girl (or boy) of the opposite sex. In a sample of English 12-year-olds, 90 percent of girls and 57 percent of boys expressed a positive attitude toward marriage [9], figures quite similar to the American ones of 85 percent and 62 percent.

### Sex Role Differentiation

Boys make progress toward thinking, feeling, and acting like men, girls like women. There are great variations in how these processes occur, however, and variations in the end results. In the section on parent–child relations, the influence of each of the parents on sex-role learning was discussed. Children also teach each other sex-appropriate attitudes and behavior. Sex role preferences have been found to be well established by 5 years of age [97]. A longitudinal study indicated that sex role preferences established between 6 and 10 years of age tend to be fairly stable into adulthood [50].

Children's evaluations of sex roles were studied in Grades 1, 2, and 3, in terms of good–bad, happy–sad, strong–weak and big–little [40]. First grade boys were more favorable toward being a boy and girls toward being a girl. The same attitudes were more pronounced in third grade, with boys lowering their evaluations of the opposite sex role more than girls. Boys regarded femininity as both bad and weak, while girls regarded masculinity as bad but not weak.

American girls are allowed greater latitude in sex-appropriate behavior than are boys. Girls incur little or no censure for being tomboys, whereas a boy is severely frowned upon for being effeminate. These statements are borne out by test findings which showed that second, third, and fourth grade girls made many choices of masculine activities, whereas boys showed a strong preference for masculine activities [11]. Girls show a wider range of play preferences than boys, girls taking in many masculine activities along with feminine ones, boys sticking largely to masculine games [82]. Certain playthings are established as appropriate for boys at an earlier age than are corresponding appropriate toys designated for girls [38]. Not only are boys' play roles defined earlier [25], but they are defined more strictly [38]. It seems likely that boys learn their roles as much by avoiding feminine behavior as by acquiring masculine patterns ("Don't be a sissy!"), even when offered a choice between old, dilapidated neutral toys and new, attractive "female" playthings [39]. The same is true of the books which girls and boys choose to read. Boys tend to read boys' books only, while girls read girls' books and boys' books. It is likely that over the years the cultural definition of the girl role has expanded, whereas that of the boy's role has not. Table 12–3 shows the activities which were attributed to girls, boys, and both sexes by children 8 to 11 years old [38]. The percentage of attribution by boys and by girls is shown with each activity listed. For instance, all boys and all girls agree that playing with a doll carriage is a female activity, while 80 percent of girls and 90 percent of boys say that climbing trees and carrying wood into the house are male activities. Concepts of the feminine role, as revealed by this study, seemed to parallel traditional adult female activities to a greater extent than did childhood concepts of the male role parallel adult male activities.

By sixth grade, sex roles begin to have a different look [47]. Girls are not so free after all. At least for the culture of one sixth grade class, there was a real difference in the way sex roles were defined, as determined by using personality and sociometric tests. Boys who were active initiators and organizers enjoyed wide acceptance by classmates, while girls with these qualities were more rejected by classmates and felt more anxious than the other girls. In generalizing about the American middle-class culture this study concludes, "Boys are expected to be somewhat aggressive, direct and analytic, while girls are taught more submissive, conforming, 'ladylike' type of behavior. The girl who identifies with this role gains acceptance and is subjectively aware of fewer discomforts. . . ." In other words, the sixth grade boys were rewarded for playing instrumental roles, and the girls were rewarded for playing expressive roles. The instrumental role requirement for boys was laid down earlier than the requirement for girls.

A study of creativity demonstrated the restriction of sex role by pressures in the classroom [94]. Boys and girls gave ideas and solutions to problems which contributed to the success of the groups for which they were working. Then they were asked to rate themselves and the others on value of contribution. The whole group ranked the boys' contributions ahead of the girls. The objective reality was that boys and girls were equal in contributions. Thus both boys and girls considered that what boys had done was better than what girls had done when both sexes actually had done the same.

**Table 12–3** Percentages of Boys and Girls Seeing Various Activities as Being Either Masculine or Feminine

| Item | Description of Activity | Percentage of Attribution | |
|------|------------------------|:---------------:|:---------:|
| | | Female Sample | Male Sample |
| | *A. Implemented mostly by girls* | | |
| 53 | plays with doll carriage | 100.0* | 100.0* |
| 40 | plays with toy sewing machine | 98.9* | 97.5* |
| 43 | plays with toy dishes | 96.7* | 100.0* |
| 46 | plays with toy carpet sweeper | 95.6* | 92.5* |
| 47 | plays with toy pocketbook | 94.4* | 97.5* |
| 49 | plays with toy electric mixer | 91.0* | 87.5* |
| 29 | helps mother hang clothes | 90.0* | 82.5* |
| 37 | plays with little girl | 88.8* | 90.0* |
| 14 | cares for baby when parents away | 87.8* | 85.0* |
| 35 | dusts table | 86.7* | 72.5† |
| 56 | plays with jump rope | 81.1* | 90.0* |
| 33 | dries dishes | 78.9* | 68.4‡ |
| 23 | washes dishes | 77.8* | 80.0* |
| 25 | clears table | 73.3* | 72.5† |
| 16 | takes dancing lessons | 65.6† | 70.0‡ |
| 51 | plays with jacks | 64.4† | 72.5† |
| | *B. Implemented mostly by boys* | | |
| 38 | plays with toy air-rifle | 94.4* | 95.0* |
| 32 | hitches ride on back of truck | 91.1* | 82.5* |
| 52 | plays with toy trucks | 91.1* | 90.0* |
| 55 | plays with fort and soldiers | 90.0* | 97.4* |
| 21 | helps man fix ceiling | 86.5* | 92.5* |
| 45 | plays with ball and bat | 81.1* | 92.3* |
| 13 | carries wood into house | 80.0* | 90.0* |
| 27 | climbs trees | 80.0* | 90.0* |
| 54 | plays with toy tool bench | 80.0* | 92.5* |
| 24 | plays with little boy | 79.5* | 77.5* |
| 50 | plays with drums | 78.9* | 77.5* |
| 57 | plays with jack-knife | 78.7* | 95.0* |
| 39 | plays with erector set | 76.7* | 82.5* |
| 15 | goes with man to ballgame | 76.4* | 70.0‡ |
| 10 | plays in messy empty lot | 75.6* | 72.5† |
| 8 | plays in street | 74.7* | 77.5* |
| 42 | plays with electric train | 73.3* | 85.0* |
| 17 | shovels snow off walk | 66.7† | 75.0† |
| 44 | plays with marbles | 66.7† | 72.5† |
| 2 | plays on roofs | 63.3‡ | 70.0‡ |
| | *C. Implemented by both sexes* | | |
| 5 | plays at beach | 84.4* | 94.5* |
| 12 | plays in country fields | 72.2* | 72.5† |
| 1 | plays on playground | 69.2* | 75.0† |
| 48 | owns and takes care of puppy | 65.2† | 56.4‡ |
| 7 | plays in park | 63.7† | 72.5‡ |

\* Probability is beyond the .001 level.
† Probability lies between the .01 and the .001 levels.
‡ Probability lies between the .05 and the .01 levels.

SOURCE: Reprinted by permission from R. E. Hartley and F. P. Hardesty, "Children's Perceptions of Sex Roles in Childhood," *Journal of Genetic Psychology*, **105**, Table 2, p. 48. Copyright © 1964, The Journal Press.

A child also restricts his own achievement in accordance with sex role expectations. Sixth grade boys and girls were given tasks which were actually neutral but were presented as appropriate to boys, girls, or both [92]. Boys did their best on the "masculine" tests, worst on the "feminine," and in between on the "tests for both." Girls did equally well on the "feminine" and "tests for both" but worse on the "masculine." Thus expectations of self and others, as well as achievement behavior are affected by the child's evaluation of sex role and of behavior appropriate to it.

## Development of Understanding and Caring

As the young human being grows to maturity in his relationships with other human beings, he sees more and more clearly that other people have thoughts, feelings, and perceptions which relate them to him and to others. As an infant, he treated his peers more as objects than as persons, but as a schoolchild, he realizes that peers are persons much like himself and that even older and younger individuals share many human characteristics with him. As he comes to understand what life is like from the standpoint of another person, he also comes to care about it and he tries to make good things happen to other people. Altruism, or prosocial behavior, is linked thus with the development of role-taking ability and understanding. The development of prosocial behavior has other antecedents, some of which have been identified in recent research.

### Understanding, Role Taking, and Communication

The child's self concept is basic to his conceptions of other people's roles and their relation to his. As he achieves conceptual thought, he can keep his own point of view in mind while trying on the role of another. This is *empathy:* he can think himself into another person, imagine how it is to be that person and still remember that he is himself, with his own thoughts, feelings, and perceptions. Deeper friendships can thus grow. Empathy increases throughout the school years as shown by studies of children's understanding, role taking, and communication.

Children of 6, 9, and 12 years were shown films offering a rich representation of person-to-person interaction [32]. Analyses of spontaneous comments and answers to questions showed age-related trends. Children apparently infer thoughts and/or intentions before feelings and feelings before interpersonal perceptions. Three major categories were, in order: reporting-describing, explaining, and interpreting. Younger children were likely to report objective situation-action and dialogues before they tried to explain behavior. The 6-year-olds answered questions literally and often gave details that seemed irrelevant to adults. The earliest explanations were in terms of situation, later ones in psychological terms, and still later, in terms of interpersonal perceptions. Six-year-olds more often described characters as reacting with feelings, while older ones described them more as thinking, having intentions, and communicating, as well as feeling. Although the greatest increase in understanding personal interaction took place between 6 and 9, there were also increases between 9 and 12. Another study of empathy [86] showed that empathy tended to increase with age, but that there were wide individual differences within each age level. Although there were no sex differences in general, the spurts in growth of empathy came at different times for boys and girls. Empathy

**Table 12–4** Related and Unrelated Contribution to Class Discussions in Elementary Grades

| Contribution | Grade 2 (62 Pupils) | Grade 4 (54 Pupils) | Grade 6 (45 Pupils) |
|---|---|---|---|
| New Topic, not obviously related to what earlier speaker had said | 87% | 33% | 23% |
| New Topic, but apparently suggested by something said by a previous contributor | 8 | 24 | 33 |
| Logical Continuation of a topic previously introduced | 4 | 43 | 44 |

SOURCE: Table adapted by A. T. Jersild, *Child Psychology*, Sixth edition (Englewood Cliffs, N.J.: Prentice-Hall, 1968), p. 455, from H. V. Baker, *Children's Contributions in Elementary School General Discussion*. Child Development Monographs No. 29, pp. 32–33. Copyright Teachers College, Columbia University, 1942. Reprinted by permission.

related to general intelligence and to cognitive awareness of the social and emotional environment. Empathy varied inversely with the size of the child's family and depended somewhat on his ordinal position.

As the child grows more adept at shifting back and forth between his own position and those of others, he can sustain conversations more adequately. When a child talks egocentrically, he expresses himself, but he does not develop a topic. Now he takes on more responsibility of trying to understand what others are communicating to him and of speaking in such a way that they will understand him. This is not to say that all talking is going to be true conversation when once a child can appreciate another viewpoint. Far from it. Even adults are known to engage in egocentric speech. Table 12–4 shows how gradual is children's increase in ability to sustain a discussion. Note that even in Grade 6, 23 percent of the comments made in the discussion period were not related to the topic which had been introduced and developed [2].

Verbal communication skills have been investigated in terms of the child's ability to understand the other person's role and capacities, and the child's ability to use that understanding as a tool in communicating with other persons [33, 56]. In one of these studies [33], Adult A taught the child to play a parchesilike game. Then the child was asked to teach the game to blindfolded Adult B. As might be expected, children increased in communicating ability as they increased in age from Grade 2 through 12. Some of the youngest children were almost entirely indifferent to the blindfold, making comments such as "Pick up this and put it in there." None of the oldest group failed to take some account of the blindfold. This experiment illustrates the child's gradually increasing capacity to put himself in the place of the other person and to use his mobility of thought for improved interpersonal communication, sending messages which are meaningful to the other person. Maturity of the listener plays a complementary part in communication. When children from kindergarten through eighth grade were given a task of verbally communicating graphic designs, success was seen to hinge upon the age of the listener as well as the age of the speaker [56]. Such tasks depend upon at least two abilities in the speaker: his ability to use language and concepts which describe the object or action, and his ability to judge what would be meaningful to the other person. The latter involves role taking.

The development of role-taking ability is likely enhanced by experience with a breadth and variety of social experiences and relationships, with peers, older people, and younger children. Parents contribute by communicating to the child the effects of his actions upon them and by encouraging the child to imagine how he would feel if he were experiencing what another person is now undergoing [48]. An experiment in training second graders to focus on intentions rather than results met with some success [34]. Sociodramatic play, which is so important for the social and cognitive integration of the preschool child, is also useful in stimulating role-taking ability during the early elementary school years.

Through play with peers and its resultant social insights, children gain increasing understanding of social organization. The nature of rules and moral order is clarified gradually through playing games with peers (in addition to experiences with parents and others). The following example shows two boys experimenting with lawmaking.

During a quiet hour at camp, a counselor noticed an 8- and a 9-year-old playing checkers. After some moments of orderly play, Jake made an extremely irregular move. Steve, watching intently, said nothing. A little later, when Steve broke the rules flagrantly, Jake was silent. "Don't you know you can't do that, Steve?" the counselor broke in. "And, Jake, you made a mistake, too."

"That was no mistake," Jake explained. "We made a rule that each person can cheat once during each game. I cheated and Steve cheated. Now we have to finish without cheating."

Although Steve and Jake were in the stage of cognitive development where they generally considered rules as *given* by a vague authority, their cooperative play was the means by which they found that man, even middle-sized boys, can make rules. They learned that by coming to an agreement with each other, they could play satisfactorily within limits which they created.

### Prosocial Behavior

Being kind to other people is called prosocial behavior, or altruism. It may take the form of trying to make the other person feel happy or it may be an attempt to relieve him of pain or threats. Some norms of behavior prescribe altruism as parts of certain roles, such as the parent's nurturant behavior toward the child. Prosocial behavior is expected between people who love each other (who are attached). People also do kindnesses for others whom they do not know or who are casual friends or acquaintances. Again, the giving may be normative, as when Christians contribute to the collection plate or Hindus give to beggars. Or the kindness may be autonomous, when the altruist expects neither rewards, recognition, nor punishment for his actions. Erikson holds that the sense of generativity is necessary for full human development [31, pp. 266–268]. Generativity involves true caring, primarily for the development of the next generation but also for other kinds of development and creativity. As in all of Erikson's senses, there are forerunners in earlier stages, before the stage of crisis. The altruism of the child may well be the shadow of generativity to come, when the adult cares, gives, and comforts without thought of what he will get in return or of what people will think of him.

**Concepts of Kindness.** Adults hold a number of generally accepted criteria of kindness. A person is considered kind when he intentionally benefits another person. The degree of kindness is judged by the strength of the actor's desire to benefit the other person. Other kinds of motivation, particularly self-interest, modify the degree of kindness.

A picture of judgments of kindness was given to samples of age levels from kindergarten through graduate school and economic levels of wide variety [3]. For example, one choice was between a nursery school child who gave another child a block he was not using and a child who gave a block that he needed. The second child was judged kinder, because he sacrificed himself. In addition to self-sacrifice, the story themes included intentionality, choice, obedience, obligation to a guest, trade, bribe, returning a favor, equalizing benefits, and the importance of the benefit. Judgments for each picture-story showed age trends and these varied between stories. By finding the age after which there was no significant increase in understanding, the authors found when each particular kindness concept was understood. By second grade, children understood intentionality and the role of self-interest in a trade. By fourth grade, they appreciated the difference between having and not having a choice, and the roles of choice, obedience, self-sacrifice, obligation, and bribe. Returning a favor was not fully understood until eighth grade and even then, equalizing benefits was not comprehended in adult style. The young child seems to understand kindness in a global way and to differentiate it as he matures. No sex differences were found. Children in Catholic parochial schools, both middle- and lower-class, developed kindness concepts somewhat earlier than children in lower-class public schools.

**Experiments on Giving.** Children are likely to give (to make charitable donations) after watching other people give. One demonstration of this phenomenon was done with fourth and fifth grade children, who played a bowling game with an adult model [85]. When the model won, he took two gift certificates from the large supply provided and placed one in a box labeled "Trenton Orphans' Fund." When the child won, the model looked the other way, so as to show no reaction to whether the child donated or not. Sixty-three percent of the children donated. The model then left the child alone, ostensibly in complete privacy, to play the game and to do as he pleased with the pile of gift certificates. Under these circumstances, about half of the group that had observed a donating model gave, while among a group not exposed to a model, none gave. Among those who had been exposed and who had given in the presence of the model, two thirds gave and one third did not. Among those who had not given in the model's presence, only 6 out of 44 gave. These results suggest that rehearsal of charitable behavior in the presence of a model facilitates internalized or autonomous giving. Thus normative giving is likely to facilitate autonomous giving. The child who, with his parent, contributes to the collection plate or to the beggar has an experience which disposes him toward later giving on his own. Further studies on the role of rehearsal have shown that when rehearsal is voluntary, rather than enforced, its effects last longer and generalize to more situations [83]. Children who had voluntarily rehearsed in the model's presence and who had then given to the Trenton Orphan's Fund were subsequently more likely to give to UNICEF. Excitement or pleasant emotional arousal during observation and rehearsal is likely to facilitate internalization of altruism [83].

Children hear many exhortations to be good, kind, and generous. The effect of preaching on giving has been investigated. When children were told that they should donate, more of them immediately gave than did children who had observed a model and who had observed and rehearsed [99]. When the groups were again compared, a week later, there was no difference in numbers giving, because the number giving in response to verbal exhortation had decreased, while the other groups remained more stable. Inconsistency in practice and preaching affects child behavior predictably. Children tended to imitate the model's *actions*, whether he practiced charity and preached greed, or practiced greed and preached charity [12]. What the child says, however, is affected by what the model says. The child is likely to put verbal emphasis on the norm preached by the model. Children had difficulty in recalling the model's words and deeds when they were contradictory.

Age trends and sex differences in altruism have been found [84]. Normative altruism, as shown by giving when observed, increased with age, but internalized or autonomous altruism, indicated by private giving, had little relationship to age. More girls than boys showed internalized altruism. Teachers' ratings of obedience were positively related to both types of altruism at age 8. Helpfulness was related to internalized altruism throughout the age range 6 through 10 [84].

**Experiments on Helping.** As the child increases in role-taking and communication skills, and consequently in empathy, he might be expected to take more care of others. Feeling their distress or pain, he would try to relieve it, and as he gains in general competence, he would be more able to offer effective help. The influence of age on attempts to help was investigated, along with the influence of a companion versus being alone [90]. Children from kindergarten through sixth grade were tested alone or in pairs. The experimenter left the room, leaving the child playing. Then the noise of a chair falling and the crying and moaning of a 7-year-old girl was played on a tape recorder in the next room, while the experimenter observed through a one-way mirror. If the child went into the adjoining room, the experimenter also went and explained that it was a tape and asked him how he felt about it. All older children were told about the tape. Younger children who went to look for the experimenter were told that the other child was all right and had gone back to her classroom. They and the children who did not attempt to help were encouraged to tell what they thought and felt when they heard the distress sounds. Of the children alone, 32 percent tried to help. Sixty-one percent of the pairs did. The smallest percentages of numbers helping were in the kindergarten and sixth grade, the youngest and oldest. The scores for helping behavior were curvilinear, increasing up to second grade and decreasing after that.

A subsequent experiment sought to explain why the older children gave less help than those in the middle of the age range. Seventh graders were tested as individuals in a situation similar to the one described [90]. To half of these subjects, the experimenter gave permission to leave the room if they wished and to the other half, nothing was said about leaving. Results showed a significant difference in attempts to help. Half of those who had permission to leave tried to help, while only a sixth of the others tried. The percentage helping was as great as the percentage of individual second graders helping in the previous experiment. Thus it seems that the older children's reluctance to help a child in distress was due not to callousness or lack of empathy but to being unwilling to risk doing wrong. In another variation on this experiment, kindergarten and first grade children were given the responsibility of helping if "anything happens" [91]. These children did indeed help more than children who heard distress sounds without having received permission or instructions. The author suggests that our society overemphasizes "thou shalt not" and does not pay enough attention to teaching prosocial behavior.

## Summary

The elementary school years bring a great expansion of environment and resulting experiences for the child. His experiences are determined and limited by the different social and cultural settings into which he is born. His nation affects his values, especially in regard to the value placed upon the individual in contrast to the group and also in regard to materialism and standards of excellence. Racial and ethnic memberships determine many of the prejudices and hostilities which the child encounters, as well as the attitudes, practices, and aspirations of his parents. Social class membership is related to values, parental behavior, and resulting cognitive stimulation for children.

A modern trend in parental behavior seems to be a change away from paternalistic authoritarianism toward cooperative families where both parents are affectionate and nurturant. The parental role can be studied in terms of goal values, means-ends beliefs, means-ends capacities and goal achievements. Children learn to play adult roles by identifying with their parents. Mothers and fathers demonstrate different roles, both of which contribute to the development of boys and girls. Discipline, an important parental function, includes the regulation of behavior, the teaching of self-control, and the imparting of moral standards. Parents vary in their disciplinary methods, using various combinations of corporal and verbal punishment, withdrawal of privileges, acceptance of the child's behavior and feelings, understanding, trust, and rewards. Experimental research on methods of discipline reveals complex interactions between timing and intensity of punishment, cognitive structure, and nurturance. Studies of parent and child behavior support the idea that many dimensions of discipline are important, with cognitive structure of particular significance in moral development. Parents promote intellectual growth in their children by holding aspirations for them, by caring for them in ways which promote independence and the building of desire for achievement, and by giving them experiences which are stimulating, especially conversations.

Children gain much from friends in the way of knowledge, experience, and satisfaction. Values learned in the family are modified through peer interaction. New behavior patterns, learned from peers, promote growth in various areas, especially a conviction of competence. Children often bow to group pressures, even when exerted against their standards and beliefs. A youngster's concept of himself is strongly influenced by the ways in which his peers regard him. Popularity and social position in the group can be tested and measured. The ability to perceive one's own status and the statuses of others increases with age. While different characteristics may be appealing in different groups, in general, popular children tend to be those with abundant energy, who use their energy for group-approved purposes. The very popular child may pay a price, psychologically, for his extended efforts to adjust to the needs and wishes of others.

Boy–girl relationships, like parent–child relationships, have changed over the decades. A friendlier, more cooperative spirit seems to have arisen between boys and girls, in contrast to the extreme antipathy which used to exist during part of the elementary school years. Girls' attitudes toward the opposite sex change more during this period than boys' do.

Peers grow in understanding of each other through this period. Increased cognitive growth is both cause and result. With increased flexibility of thought, the child can take and hold the point of view of another person. Thus he can understand, accept, communicate, and cooperate increasingly. Through these interactions with peers, he deepens his understanding of the whole social group to which he belongs.

## References

1. Ausubel, D. P., Schiff, H. M., & Gasser, E. B. A preliminary study of developmental trends in socioempathy: Accuracy of perception of own and others sociometric status. *Child Devel.*, 1952, **23**, 111–128.
2. Baker, H. V. Children's contributions in elementary school discussion. *Child Devel. Mono.* No. 29. New York: Teachers College, Columbia University, 1942.
3. Baldwin, C. P. & Baldwin, A. L. Children's judgments of kindness. *Child Devel.*, 1970, **41**, 29–47.
4. Bee, H. L. Parent–child interaction and distractibility in 9-year-old children. *Merrill-Palmer Quart.*, 1967, **13**, 175–190.
5. Bell, R. R. *Marriage and family interaction*. Homewood, Ill.: Dorsey, 1963.
6. Bettelheim, B. The children of the dream. New York: Macmillan, 1969.
7. Biller, H. B. Maternal salience and feminine development in young girls. *Proc. 77th Annual Convention of the American Psychological Association*, Washington, D.C., 1969, **4**, 259–260.
8. Bossard, J. H. *The sociology of child development* (3rd ed.). New York: Harper, 1960.
9. Broderick, C. B., & Rowe, G. P. A scale of preadolescent heterosexual development. *J. Marr. Fam.*, 1968, **30**, 97–101.
10. Bronfenbrenner, U. *Two worlds of childhood*. New York: Russell Sage Foundation, 1970.
11. Brown, D. G. Sex-role development in a changing culture. *Psychol. Bull.*, 1958, **55**, 232–242.
12. Bryan, J. H., & Walbek, N. H. Preaching and practicing generosity: Children's actions and reactions. *Child Devel.*, 1970, **41**, 329–364.
13. Burr, W. T. Satisfaction with various aspects of marriage over the life cycle: A random middle class sample. *J. Marr. Fam.*, 1970, **32**, 29–37.
14. Busse, T. V. Child-rearing antecedents of flexible thinking. *Devel. Psychol.*, 1969, **1**, 585–591.
15. Campbell, J. D. Peer relations in childhood. In M. L. Hoffman & L. W. Hoffman (Eds.), *Review of child development research*. Vol. 1. New York: Russell Sage Foundation, 1964.
16. Carpenter, R., & Busse, T. Development of self concept in Negro and white welfare children. *Child Devel.*, 1969, **40**, 935–939.
17. Cheyne, J., & Walters, R. H. Intensity of punishment, timing of punishment, and cognitive structure as determinants of response inhibition. *J. Exper. Child Psychol.*, 1969, **7**, 231–244.
18. Chilman, C. Poor families and their patterns of child care: Some implications for service programs. In Chandler [19], pp. 217–236.
19. Chandler, C. A. et al. (Eds.), *Early child care: The new perspectives*. New York: Atherton, 1968.
20. Clausen, J. A., & Williams, J. R. Sociological correlates of child behavior. In H. W. Stevenson (Ed.), *Child psychology*. The Sixty-second Yearbook

of the National Society for the Study of Education, Part II. Chicago: University of Chicago, 1963, pp. 62–107.

21. Coleman, J. S. *The adolescent society*. Glencoe, Ill.: Free Press, 1961.
22. Cratty, B. J. *Perceptual-motor behavior and educational processes*. Springfield, Ill.: Charles C. Thomas, 1969.
23. Davis, A. *Psychology of the child in the middle class*. Pittsburgh: University of Pittsburgh, 1960.
24. Davis, W. L., & Phares, E. J. Parental antecedents of internal-external control of reinforcement. *Psychol. Rep.*, 1969, **24**, 427–436.
25. DeLucia, L. A. The toy preference test: A measure of sex-role identification. *Child Devel.*, 1963, **34**, 99–106.
26. Deur, J. L., & Parke, R. D. The effects of inconsistent punishment on aggression in children. *Devel. Psychol.*, 1970, **1**, 403–411.
27. Devereux, E. C. The role of peer group experience in moral development: A research progress report. Paper presented at the Fourth Minnesota Symposium on Child Psychology, May, 1969.
28. Emmerich, W. The parental role: A functional-cognitive approach. *Mono. Soc. Res. Child Devel.*, 1969, **34**:8.
29. Epstein, R., & Komorita, S. S. Childhood prejudice as a function of parental ethnocentrism, punitiveness, and out-group characteristics. *J. Per. Soc. Psychol.* 1966, **3**, 259–264.
30. Epstein, R. & Komorita, S. S. Self-esteem, success-failure and locus of control in Negro children. *Devel. Psychol.*, 1971, **4**, 2–8.
31. Erikson, E. *Childhood and society* (2nd ed.). New York: Norton, 1963.
32. Flapan, D. *Children's understanding of social interaction*. New York: Teachers College Press, 1968.
33. Flavell, J. H. Role-taking and communication skills in children. *Young Children*, 1966, **21**, 164–177.
34. Glassco, J. A., Milgram, N. A., & Youniss, J. Stability of training effects on intentionality in moral judgment in children. *J. Pers. Soc. Psychol.*, 1970, **14**, 360–365.
35. Grams, A. Child anxiety: Self-estimates, parent reports and teacher ratings. *Merrill-Palmer Quart.*, 1965, **11**, 261–266.
36. Hamm, N. H., & Hoving, K. L. Conformity of children in an ambiguous perceptual situation. *Child Devel.*, 1969, **40**, 773–784.
37. Harrison, C. W., Rawls, J. R., & Rawls, D. J. Differences between leaders and non-leaders in six- to eleven-year-old children. *J. Soc. Psychol.*, 1971 (in press).
38. Hartley, R. E., & Hardesty, F. P. Children's perceptions of sex roles in childhood, *J. Genet. Psychol.*, 1964, **105**, 43–51.
39. Hartup, W. W., Moore, S. G., & Sager, G. Avoidance of inappropriate sex-typing by young children. *J. Consult. Psychol.*, 1963, **27**, 467–473.
40. Helper, M. M. Comparison of pictorial and verbal semantic scales as used by children. *J. Genet. Psychol.*, 1970 **117**, 149–156.
41. Hess, R. D. & Torney, J. V. *The development of political attitudes in children*. Chicago: Aldine, 1967.
42. Hill, J. P. Similarity and accordance between parents and sons in attitudes toward mathematics. *Child Devel.*, 1967, **38**, 777–791.
43. Hoffman, M. L. & Salzstein, H. D. Parent discipline and the child's moral development. *J. Pers. Soc. Psychol.*, 1967, **5**, 45–57.

44. Horrocks, J. E., & Buker, M. E. A study of the friendship fluctuations of preadolescents, *J. Genet Psychol.*, 1951, **78**, 131–144.

45. Hoving, K. L., Hamm, N., & Galvin, P. Social influence as a function of stimulus ambiguity at three age levels. *Devel. Psychol.*, 1969, **1**, 631–636.

46. Hurley, J. R. Parental malevolence and children's intelligence. *J. Consult. Psychol.*, 1967, **31**, 199–204.

47. Iscoe, I., & Carden, J. A. Field dependence, manifest anxiety and sociometric status in children. *J. Consult. Psychol.*, 1961, **25**:184.

48. Jessor, R., & Richardson, S. Psychosocial deprivation and personality development. In *Perspectives on Human Deprivation.* Washington, D.C.: U.S. Department of Health, Education, and Welfare, 1968.

49. Johnson, M. M. Sex-role learning in the nuclear family, *Child Devel.*, 1963, **34**, 319–333.

50. Kagan, J., & Moss, H. A. *Birth to maturity.* New York: Wiley, 1962.

51. Katkovsky, W., Crandall, V. C., & Good, S. Parental antecedents of children's beliefs in internal-external control of reinforcements in intellectual achievement situations. *Child Devel.*, 1967, **38**, 765–776.

52. Katkovsky, W., Preston, A., & Crandall, V. J. Parents' attitudes toward their personal achievements and toward the achievement behaviors of their children. *J. Genet. Psychol.*, 1964, **104**, 76–82.

53. Katz, I. Factors influencing Negro performance in the desegregated school. In M. Deutsch, I. Katz, & A. R. Jensen (Eds.), *Social class, race and psychological development.* New York: Holt, Rinehart and Winston, 1968, pp. 254–289.

54. Kohlberg, L. *Stages in the development of moral thought and action.* New York: Holt, Rinehart and Winston, 1969.

55. Kohn, M. L., & Schooler, C. Class, occupation and orientation. *Am. Soc. Rev.*, 1969, **34**, 659–678.

56. Krauss, R. M., & Glucksberg, S. Some characteristics of children's messages. Paper presented at the meeting of the Society for Research in Child Development, Santa Monica, Calif., March 27, 1969.

57. Lambert, W. E., & Klineberg, O. *Children's views of foreign people.* New York: Appleton-Century-Crofts, 1967.

58. McDavid, J. W., & Harari, H. Stereotyping of names and popularity in grade-school children. *Child Devel.*, 1966, **37**, 453–459.

59. Maw, W. H., & Maw, E. W. Children's curiosity and parental attitudes. *J. Marr. Fam.*, 1966, **28**, 343–345.

60. Miller, D. R., & Swanson, G. E. *The changing American parent.* New York: Wiley, 1958.

61. Mussen, P., & Beytagh, L. Industrialization, child-rearing practices, and children's personality. *J. Genet. Psychol.*, 1969, **115**, 195–216.

62. Mussen, P., & Distler, L. Child-rearing antecedents of masculine identification in kindergarten boys. *Child Devel.*, 1960, **31**, 89–100.

63. Mussen, P., & Rutherford, E. Parent-child relations and parental personality in relation to young children's sex-role preferences. *Child Devel.*, 1963, **34**, 589–607.

64. Newson, J., & Newson, E. *Four years old in an urban community.* Chicago: Aldine, 1968.

65. Northway, M. L. *What is popularity?* Chicago: Science Research Associates, 1955.

66. Northway, M. L. *A primer of sociometry* (2nd ed.). Toronto: University of Toronto Press, 1967.

67. Opie, I., & Opie, P. *The lore and language of school children.* Oxford: Clarendon, 1959.

68. Parke, R. D. Effectiveness of punishment as an interaction of intensity, timing, age, nurturance, and cognitive structuring. *Child Devel.*, 1969, **40**, 213–235.

69. Parke, R. D., & Walters, R. H. Some factors influencing the efficacy of punishment training for inducing response inhibition. *Mono. Soc. Res. Child Devel.*, 1967, **32**:1.

70. Parsons, R., & Bales, R. F. *Family, socialization and interaction process.* Glencoe, Ill.: Free Press, 1955.

71. Pope, B. Socioeconomic contrasts in children's peer culture prestige values. *Genet. Psychol. Mono.*, 1953, **48**, 157–220.

72. Proshansky, H., & Newton, P. The nature and meaning of Negro self-identity. In M. Deutsch, I. Katz, & A. R. Jensen (Eds.), *Social class, race and psychological development.* New York: Holt, Rinehart and Winston, 1968, pp. 178–218.

73. Rau, L., Mlodnosky, L. B., & Anastasiow, N. Child-rearing antecedents of achievement behaviors in second-grade boys. Final Report of U.S.O.E. Cooperative Research Project No. 1838. Palo Alto: Stanford University, 1964.

74. Rebelsky, F., Conover, C., & Chafetz, P. The development of political attitudes in young children. *J. Psychol.*, 1969, **73**, 141–146.

75. Reese, H. W. Attitudes toward the opposite sex in late childhood. *Merrill-Palmer Quart.*, 1966, **12**, 157–163.

76. Riessman, F. *The culturally deprived child.* New York: Harper, 1962.

77. Riessman, F. Low-income culture: The strengths of the poor. *J. Marr. Fam.*, 1964, **26**, 417–429.

78. Rollins, B. C., & Feldman, H. Marital satisfaction over the family life cycle. *J. Marr. Fam.*, 1970, **32**, 20–28.

79. Rosen, B. C. Race, ethnicity and the achievement syndrome. *Am. Soc. Rev.*, 1959, **24**, 49–60.

80. Rosen, B. C. Family structure and value transmission. *Merrill-Palmer Quart.*, 1964, **10**, 25–38.

81. Rosen, B. C., & D'Andrade, R. The psychosocial origins of achievement motivation. *Sociometry*, 1959, **22**, 185–218.

82. Rosenberg, B. G., & Sutton-Smith, B. A revised conception of masculine-feminine differences in play activities. *J. Genet. Psychol.*, 1960, **96**, 165–170.

83. Rosenhan, D. L. Some origins of concern for others. In P. Mussen, J. Langer, & M. Covington (Eds.), *Trends and issues in developmental psychology.* New York: Holt, Rinehart and Winston, 1969, pp. 134–153.

84. Rosenhan, D. L. Studies in altruistic behavior: Developmental and naturalistic variables associated with charitability. Paper presented at the meeting of the Society for Research in Child Development, Santa Monica, Calif., March 29, 1969.

85. Rosenhan, D. L., & White, G. M. Observation and rehearsal as determinants of prosocial behavior. *J. Pers. Soc. Psychol.*, 1967, **5**, 424–431.

86. Ruderman, L. An exploration of empathic ability in children and its relationship to several variables. Unpublished doctoral dissertation, Teachers College, Columbia University, 1961.

87. Sethi, R. R. The relation between parental consistency in response to frustration and children's imitation of parental responses. Unpublished Ph.D. thesis, Oregon State University, 1969.

88. Sontag, L. W., Baker, C. T., & Nelson, V. L. Mental growth and personality development: A longitudinal study. *Mono. Soc. Res. Child Devel.*, 1958, **23**:2.

89. Staub, E. Effects of variation in permissibility of movement on children helping another child in distress. Proc. 77th Annual Convention, *American Psychological Association*, 1969, **4**, 385–386.

90. Staub, E. A child in distress: The influence of age and number of witnesses on children's attempts to help. *J. Pers. Soc. Psychol.*, 1970 (in press).

91. Staub, E. A child in distress: The effect of focusing responsibility on children on their attempts to help. *Devel. Psychol.*, 1970, **2**, 152–153.

92. Stein, A. H., Pohly, S. R., & Mueller, E. The influence of masculine, feminine, and neutral tasks, on children's achievement behavior, expectancies of success and attainment values. *Child Devel.*, 1971, **32**, 195–207.

93. Taba, H. Cultural deprivation as a factor in school learning. *Merrill-Palmer Quart.*, 1964, **10**, 147–159.

94. Torrance, E. P. Changing reactions of preadolescent girls to tasks requiring creative scientific thinking. *J. Genet. Psychol.*, 1963, **102**, 217–223.

95. Tulkin, R., Muller, J. P., & Conn, L. K. Need for approval and popularity: Sex differences in elementary school students. *J. Consult. Clin. Psychol.*, 1969, **33**, 35–39.

96. Utech, D. A., & Hoving, K. L. Parents and peers as competing influences in the decisions of children of differing ages. *J. Soc. Psychol.*, 1969, **78**, 267–274.

97. Ward, W. D. Process of sex-role development. *Devel. Psychol.*, 1969, **1**, 163–168.

98. Werner, E. E. Sex differences in correlations between children's IQs and measurements of parental ability and environmental ratings. *Devel. Psychol.*, 1969, **1**, 280–285.

99. White, G. M. *The elicitation and durability of altruistic behavior in children.* Unpublished Ph.D. dissertation, Princeton University, 1967.

100. Winterbottom, M. The relation of need for achievement in learning experiences in independence and mastery. In J. Atkinson (Ed.), *Motives in fantasy, action and society.* Princeton: Van Nostrand, 1958, pp. 453–478.

101. Yarrow, M. R., & Campbell, J. D. Person perception in children. *Merrill-Palmer Quart.*, 1963, **9**, 57–72.

102. Young, M. B. A Negro mother speaks. *Parents'*, 1964, **39**:7, 50–51, 78.

# Part IV

# The Adolescent

# Introduction

Pubescence, the period surrounding the peak of velocity in physical growth, is only the beginning of a long critical period in personality growth. Here the problem is posed, "Who am I?" All of adolescence involves finding the answers. As is true of trust, autonomy, initiative, and industry (which have their growth periods earlier), the sense of identity is built throughout life, but it too has a special time of growth. The personality with which the child begins pubescence is the product of all his past interactions with the world.

The more slowly maturing children in Grades 7, 8, and 9 are still in the stage of developing a sense of industry, busy with basic school subjects, perfecting motor skills, earning merit badges, active in like-sexed peer groups. Nearing the completion of this particular stage of development, the successful ones are good at many activities. The unsuccessful ones have a proportionate sense of failure and inferiority by now. Many feel inferior because of poor performance and poor grades at school. Some have found themselves awkward and outclassed in games and sports. Others are unwanted as friends. Some suffer tragically from all kinds of inferiority. Thus, some junior high school youngsters are unready to deal with the crucial question of identity simply because they have not lived through the previous stage, while others are unready because they have not been adequate in the previous stage. Eventually, ready or not, questions of identity will be forced upon them, but the junior high, in its ideal form, is a flexible place where children in different stages of development can find what they need to help them along.

Even though a new critical phase is entered upon, the sense of industry continues to be strained and tested. Further development is required of it, in intimate association with the sense of identity. The adolescent must *do well* in many new areas. He has to develop new competencies—intellectual, social, and moral—and competency in school and on the job. The way in which his childhood sense of industry comes into play is in making him feel that he is adequate or inadequate, likely to be successful or unsuccessful. Erikson underlines the importance of the sense of industry throughout life by repeating Freud's answer to the question "What should a normal person be able to do well?" Freud said, "Lieben und arbeiten." ("To love and to work.") He meant productiveness balanced and integrated with the capacity to be a sexual and a loving being [1, p. 96].

As a time of rebirth into an almost-new body and rapidly expanding mind and world, adolescence is a period of shakeup and testing of all that has gone before. The

489

adolescent's psychological structure is fluid. The stages of developing trust, autonomy, and initiative, as well as the most recent stage of industry, all come in for questioning and reorganization. Problems of trust and mistrust come to the fore in religious upheavals and in disturbed time orientation. Questions of autonomy versus shame and doubt most likely enter into parent–adolescent struggles. The relationship of initiative and guilt is pertinent to the moral development of adolescence.

"The sense of ego identity, then, is the accrued confidence that one's ability to maintain inner sameness and continuity ... is matched by the sameness and continuity of one's meaning for others" [1, p. 89]. Thus does Erikson summarize the role of other people in the growth of an individual's sense of identity. The "other people" include the whole culture, since the person's concept of himself has to be one which is acceptable in his culture. The most important people, as far as "one's meaning for others" is concerned, are those individuals who play important parts in his life: family, friends, sweethearts, teachers, employers. The adolescent sees himself partly through reflections mirrored by all the significant people in his life (the old concept of "the looking-glass self"). He also models his self concept on the ways in which he sees other people, identifying with some pictures, rejecting others. Part of his problem is to hang onto a feeling of being the same person, a person who is changing but who is still continuous and identifiable as the person he has always been and always will be.

Adolescence brings greater differentiation between boys and girls than has existed before. Sex factors elaborate physical, physiological, and personality differences. Social roles become more clearly delineated along sex lines. The establishment of the sense of identity is understandably different for boys and girls. Research [2] indicates that a woman achieves sex identity through intimacy in a close relationship with a man, whereas a man attains sex identity through satisfactory work performance, after which he is ready to establish intimacy with a woman.

Adolescence is only one stage of development. Its end does not mark the end of development, of even physical growth. Growth in height stops, but developmental changes continue to take place in the muscular system and in the face, to point out some obvious ones. *Youth* as a distinct stage has recently emerged. Formerly, youth and adolescence were often lumped together, the term used interchangeably. Keniston, who has made extensive studies of both alienated and committed youth, says that youth is an achievement of postindustrial society, just as adolescence is an achievement of industrial society [3, p. 264]. Before the industrial revolution children graduated into adulthood without benefit of adolescence; they still do in underdeveloped segments of today's world. Industrial society was affluent enough to support its older children while they learned more of the skills and knowledge which society needed. The privilege of adolescence was extended to more and more children until schooling until age 16 became the norm. Postindustrial society is even more affluent and thus needs members with more complex skills and knowledge. Over 40 percent of youth go to college and an increasing number prolong their education into the middle and late twenties.

The first chapter in this section deals with the rapid physical growth and genital maturity, which launch the adolescent into questioning his sameness and continuity. The second chapter is concerned with intellectual maturing, which facilitates deeper thinking and questioning. Caused by his new body and new questions, disturbances in the sense of identity are resolved through successful peer relationships, maturing of relationships with parents, satisfactory vocational, moral, and religious development. The final chapters examine these avenues to a firm sense of identity concluding with a section on youth.

## References

1. Erikson, E. H. *Identity and the life cycle*. New York: International Universities, 1959.
2. Garai, J. E. Sex differences in mental health. *Genet. Psychol. Mono.*, 1970, **81**, 123–142.
3. Keniston, K. *Young radicals*. New York: Harcourt, Brace & World, 1968.

# Chapter 13

Robert J. Izzo

# Physical Growth, Health, and Coordination

A child changes into an adult during *adolescence*, a period lasting from about 11 to about 18 years of age. The changes which take place during adolescence include not only physical events but also psychological and social ones.

# Growth

The child's body changes into an adult's through an almost invariable sequence of events. A person familiar with pubescent growth could tell from a physical examination what change could be expected next and how far the youngster had progressed toward puberty.

### Bodily Changes During Pubescence

*Puberty* is the time when sexual maturity is reached. *Pubescence* is the period of time encompassing the physical changes which lead to puberty. Two years is the average length of time for pubescence, although the span is shorter in fast-maturing adolescents and longer in slow-maturers.

The following list of changes in boys and girls shows the normal sequences for development during pubescence [4, p. 94]. Note that the age of most rapid growth comes not at the very end of pubescence but before menarche (first menstruation) for girls and before certain adult characteristics in boys.

| Girls | Boys |
|---|---|
| Initial enlargement of breasts. | Beginning growth of testes. |
| Straight, pigmented pubic hair. | Straight, pigmented pubic hair. |
| | Early voice changes. |
| | First ejaculation of semen. |
| Kinky pubic hair. | Kinky pubic hair. |
| Age of maximum growth. | Age of maximum growth. |
| Menarche. | |
| Growth of axillary hair. | Growth of axillary hair. |
| | Marked voice changes. |
| | Development of the beard. |

A criterion of puberty which has been found useful for both boys and girls is that of maximum yearly increment in height. Shuttleworth [53], in his classic research on adolescent growth, found the average for boys to be 14.8 and for girls 12.6. The normal range for age at puberty is large, however—10 to 16 in girls and 12 to 18 in boys [4, p. 92].

It is difficult to pinpoint the achievement of sexual maturity, the capacity for reproduction. Menarche is often assumed to be the time when a girl becomes able to have babies, but a sterile period of a year or more probably occurs in most girls after menstruation [39]. Menarche is usually considered the point of sexual maturity, however, since it is a definite event which is easy to remember. There is no corresponding definite event for boys, although a criterion sometimes used is the production of spermatozoa. In research studies on growth in adolescence, the various growth events in the sequence of pubescence are often used, rather than one point such as menarche.

Median ages for menarche in a variety of populations throughout the world are shown in Table 13–1 [21]. The range is large, from 12.4 to 18.8. The table gives no evidence that menarche is directly affected by warmth of climate. Both early maturers and late maturers live in hot climates. No clear genetic differences are seen. While the five African populations sampled are late in reaching menarche, Cuban Negroes are the earliest. The three earliest median menarches are shown by a Negro, a white, and a Chinese group. Genetic influences on menarche can be seen, however, by noting the degrees of similarity in menarcheal age between women of varying degrees of relationship. The average differences in menarcheal age

Table 13-1   Median Age at Menarche in Several Populations

| Population or Location | Median Age in Years* |
|---|---|
| Cuba: | |
| Negro | 12.4 |
| White | 12.4 |
| Mulatto | 12.6 |
| Cuba: | |
| Negro | 12.9† |
| White | 13.0† |
| Mulatto | 13.0† |
| Hong Kong (wealthy Chinese) | 12.5 |
| Florence, Italy | 12.5 |
| Wroclaw, Poland | 12.6 |
| Budapest, Hungary | 12.8 |
| California, U.S.A. | 12.8 |
| Colombo, Ceylon | 12.8 |
| Moscow, U.S.S.R. | 13.0 |
| Tel Aviv, Israel | 13.0‡ |
| London, U.K. | 13.1 |
| Assam, India (city dwellers) | 13.2 |
| Burma (city dwellers) | 13.2 |
| Uganda (wealthy Kampala) | 13.4 |
| Oslo, Norway | 13.5 |
| France | 13.5 |
| Nigeria (wealthy Ibo) | 14.1 |
| U.S.S.R. (rural Buriats) | 15.0 |
| South Africa (Transkei Bantu) | 15.0 |
| Rwanda: | |
| Tutsi | 16.5§ |
| Huru | 17.1§ |
| New Guinea (Bundi) | 18.8 |

* Data from Tanner (1966) unless otherwise indicated.
† Pospisilova-Zuzakova, Stukovsky, and Valšíg (1965).
‡ Ber and Brociner (1964).
§ Hiernaux (1965).

SOURCE: Reprinted by permission from Jean Hiernaux, "Ethnic Differences in Growth and Development," *Eugenics Quarterly*, **15**, 12–21. Copyright © 1968 American Eugenics Society.

between identical twins is 2.8 months, between fraternal twins 12.0, sisters 12.9, and unrelated women 18.6 [21]. Socioeconomic status, expressed through nutrition and other influences on growth, is definitely related to menarche, as will be shown in connection with nutrition (page 510).

The average menarche for white American girls was between 12.5 and 13.0 [57, p. 154]. About two thirds of all girls achieved menarche within the time span a year before to a year after the average. Almost all menstruated within the period of three years before to three years after the average. A very few menstruated before 10, and very few did not reach menarche until after 16.

**Secular Trend in Puberty.** Size increases over time were discussed on pages 350–351. Not only are children growing bigger, but they are maturing earlier in the more

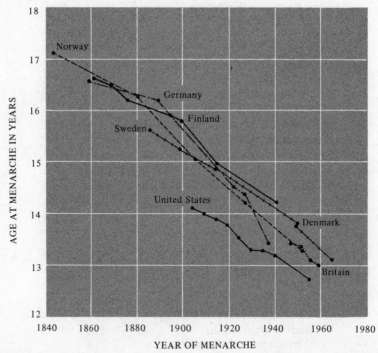

**Figure 13–1.** Age at menarche, or first menstrual period, has declined in the U.S., Britain, and Europe. Girls are estimated to begin menstruation between 2.5 and 3.3 years earlier on the average than a century ago. The age of menarche is an index of the rate of physical maturation.

SOURCE: From "Earlier Maturation in Man," by J. M. Tanner. Copyright © 1968 by Scientific American, Inc. All rights reserved.

prosperous parts of the world [58]. Around 1900 men reached their full height at about 26, but now Europeans and Americans are full grown at 18 or 19 [58]. Puberty is occurring earlier in children living in the most favorable circumstances, as can be seen in records of age of menarche from several countries. In a recent American sample of white mothers and daughters, mean age at menarche for daughters was 12.88, for mothers 14.38 [14]. This difference is greater than the advance in menarcheal age usually seen in one generation. Figure 13–1 shows the declining menarcheal age in western Europe and the United States over more than a century. During the past century, girls in the countries represented have been reaching menarche earlier at the rate of three to four months per decade. Thus puberty takes place two and a half to three and a half years earlier today than it did a century ago [58].

### Growth in Height

Growth speeds up during pubescence, becoming faster as the child moves through the sequence of events which leads to puberty. As was noted above, the period of fastest growth comes before menarche, about six months before. Figure 13–2 shows height increment curves for boys and girls who reached the peak velocity of growth at the average times, the girls between 12 and 13, the boys

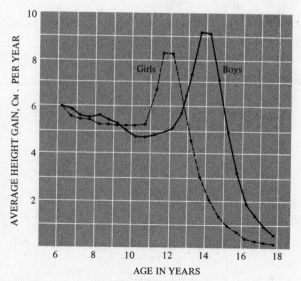

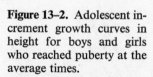

**Figure 13–2.** Adolescent increment growth curves in height for boys and girls who reached puberty at the average times.

SOURCE: Reprinted by permission from J. M. Tanner, *Growth at Adolescence*, 2nd edition. Oxford: Blackwell Scientific Publications Ltd., 1962. Copyright © 1962, Blackwell Scientific Publications Ltd.

between 14 and 15. When increment curves are plotted for early or late maturers, the curves show essentially the same shape, with a rise and then a sharp drop which starts just before puberty.

While everybody expects a youngster to spurt in height, the spurt is still an amazing and often mysterious phenomenon to family, friends, and most of all the person experiencing it. It is amazing because the middle years of childhood are so stable and uneventful from the standpoint of growth. Then suddenly, velocity picks up and the child seems to grow overnight. (The average boy grows 8 inches between ages 13 and 15½; the average girl, 3¼ inches between 11 and 13½.) Families often discuss and wonder about the spurting child's eventual height, how long he will grow so fast and when he will stop. The factors behind each child's peculiar style of growth are so complex and interwoven that parents have little success in prediction.

The taller the child, the taller he can expect to be as an adult. At each age from infancy to the onset of pubescence, height correlates increasingly with adult height. Mary Jane, at age 7, is tall for her age, while Phyllis, at 7, is short. The chances are that Mary Jane will grow to above average height for women, while Phyllis will be petite.

The wide normal range in the age at which puberty is reached means that children vary widely in when they begin the growth spurt, when they reach the peak, and when they finish. John and Bill, the same height at age 13, will be inches apart as adults because John has been rapidly increasing in height for the past year while Bill has not grown noticeably. John will soon shoot ahead of Bill, but Bill will eventually overtake him.

The velocity and duration of the growth spurt vary from one individual to another. When the spurt occurs early, it tends to be more intense but to last over a shorter period than when it occurs at a later age. Early maturers tend to be shorter than late maturers because the longer duration of the growth period in late maturers more than makes up for the brief advantage which more intense velocity gives to the early maturers. This factor accounts for most of the difference in height between men and women. Men have a longer time in which to grow.

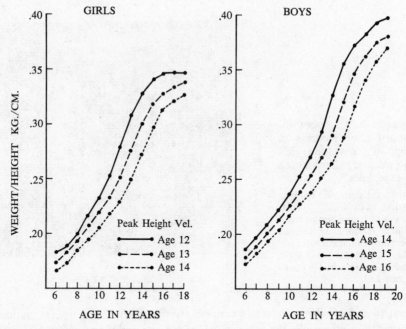

**Figure 13–3.** Weight per centimeter of height for boys and girls who mature early, late, and at the average time.

SOURCE: Reprinted by permission from J. M. Tanner, *Growth at Adolescence*, 2nd edition. Oxford: Blackwell Scientific Publications Ltd., 1962. Copyright © 1962, Blackwell Scientific Publications Ltd.

Linear people, as contrasted with people of rounded shape, tend to be late maturers. Only a small part of their linearity is due to their late maturing, which allows a greater time for growth of the legs than the early maturer has. From the age of 2, people who will mature late weigh less for their height than do those who who will mature early. Figure 13–3 shows the weight per centimeter of height for early, average, and late maturing boys and girls.

Because of the wide variation in both height and weight during adolescence, percentile tables are not so useful at this time as they are earlier for assessing an individual child's status. However, for their value in showing how height and weight are distributed during the teen years, height and weight percentiles (Tables 13–2 through 13–9) are included here, as they are in the other sections of the book which have to do with physical growth. These tables were assembled from measurements of Cincinnati school children, as described on pages 346–349.

*Endocrinology of Growth**

Besides stature and weight, other dimensions of the human body have been studied in similar ways. These include sitting height, and dimensions of the chest and head. Even diameters of the head show increments which follow the same kind of pattern of increments, although the curve for each dimension is unique in some way. The spurt in growth that occurs around pubescence is the result of the complicated but interrelated ebb and flow of endocrine substances in the bloodstream.

* This account follows Tanner [57, pp. 30–31].

**Table 13–2** Percentile Distribution of Height in Inches for White Males
(Age Defined at Subject's Last Birthday)

| Age | N (Total = 2973) | Percentile | | | | | | |
|---|---|---|---|---|---|---|---|---|
| | | 3RD | 10TH | 25TH | 50TH | 75TH | 90TH | 97TH |
| 11 | 228 | 51 | 53 | 55 | 57 | 59 | 61 | 66 |
| 12 | 222 | 54 | 56 | 57 | 59 | 62 | 64 | 66 |
| 13 | 296 | 55 | 58 | 60 | 63 | 65 | 67 | 70 |
| 14 | 268 | 58 | 61 | 63 | 66 | 68 | 70 | 73 |
| 15 | 243 | 58 | 62 | 65 | 67 | 69 | 72 | 74 |
| 16 | 233 | 62 | 65 | 66 | 69 | 71 | 72 | 76 |
| 17 | 70 | — | — | — | 68 | — | — | — |
| 18 | 11 | — | — | — | 68 | — | — | — |

SOURCE: Reprinted by permission from J. L. Rauh, D. A. Schumsky, and M. T. Witt, "Heights, Weights, and Obesity in Urban School Children," *Child Development*, **38**, 515–530. Copyright © 1967, The Society for Research in Child Development, Inc.

**Table 13–3** Percentile Distribution of Height in Inches for Nonwhite Males
(Age Defined at Subject's Last Birthday)

| Age | N (Total = 1208) | Percentile | | | | | | |
|---|---|---|---|---|---|---|---|---|
| | | 3RD | 10TH | 25TH | 50TH | 75TH | 90TH | 97TH |
| 11 | 101 | 51 | 54 | 55 | 58 | 59 | 61 | 64 |
| 12 | 101 | 55 | 57 | 58 | 60 | 62 | 64 | 68 |
| 13 | 86 | 55 | 58 | 60 | 62 | 65 | 67 | 70 |
| 14 | 110 | 58 | 60 | 62 | 66 | 67 | 71 | 76 |
| 15 | 71 | 59 | 63 | 65 | 67 | 70 | 73 | 76 |
| 16 | 56 | 63 | 65 | 67 | 68 | 70 | 72 | 73 |
| 17 | 38 | — | — | — | 69 | — | — | — |
| 18 | 13 | — | — | — | 71 | — | — | — |

SOURCE: Reprinted by permission from J. L. Rauh, D. A. Schumsky, and M. T. Witt, "Heights, Weights, and Obesity in Urban School Children," *Child Development*, **38**, 515–530. Copyright © 1967, The Society for Research in Child Development, Inc.

**Table 13–4** Percentile Distribution of Height in Inches for White Females
(Age Defined at Subject's Last Birthday)

| Age | N (Total = 3010) | Percentile | | | | | | |
|---|---|---|---|---|---|---|---|---|
| | | 3RD | 10TH | 25TH | 50TH | 75TH | 90TH | 97TH |
| 11 | 252 | 52 | 54 | 56 | 58 | 60 | 62 | 66 |
| 12 | 259 | 54 | 56 | 58 | 60 | 62 | 64 | 66 |
| 13 | 272 | 56 | 59 | 61 | 62 | 64 | 65 | 69 |
| 14 | 259 | 58 | 60 | 62 | 63 | 65 | 66 | 70 |
| 15 | 222 | 58 | 61 | 62 | 64 | 65 | 67 | 71 |
| 16 | 227 | 60 | 61 | 62 | 64 | 66 | 67 | 69 |
| 17 | 71 | — | — | — | 64 | — | — | — |
| 18 | 6 | — | — | — | 64 | — | — | — |

SOURCE: Reprinted by permission from J. L. Rauh, D. A. Schumsky, and M. T. Witt, "Heights, Weights, and Obesity in Urban School Children," *Child Development*, **38**, 515–530. Copyright © 1967, The Society for Research in Child Development, Inc.

**Table 13–5** Percentile Distribution of Height in Inches for Nonwhite Females (Age Defined at Subject's Last Birthday)

| Age | N (Total = 1289) | Percentile | | | | | | |
|-----|---|-----|------|------|------|------|------|------|
| | | 3RD | 10TH | 25TH | 50TH | 75TH | 90TH | 97TH |
| 11 | 104 | 52 | 55 | 58 | 59 | 61 | 63 | 64 |
| 12 | 103 | 56 | 58 | 59 | 61 | 63 | 65 | 68 |
| 13 | 123 | 57 | 59 | 61 | 63 | 65 | 66 | 68 |
| 14 | 100 | 59 | 60 | 61 | 63 | 65 | 67 | 71 |
| 15 | 89 | 57 | 61 | 63 | 64 | 66 | 68 | 70 |
| 16 | 57 | 52 | 61 | 62 | 64 | 65 | 68 | 69 |
| 17 | 23 | — | — | — | 65 | — | — | — |
| 18 | 13 | — | — | — | 64 | — | — | — |

SOURCE: Reprinted by permission from J. L. Rauh, D. A. Schumsky, and M. T. Witt, "Heights, Weights, and Obesity in Urban School Children," *Child Development*, **38**, 515–530. Copyright © 1967, The Society for Research in Child Development, Inc.

**Table 13–6** Percentile Distribution of Weight in Pounds for White Males (Age Defined at Subject's Last Birthday)

| Age | N (Total = 2973) | Percentile | | | | | | |
|-----|---|-----|------|------|------|------|------|------|
| | | 3RD | 10TH | 25TH | 50TH | 75TH | 90TH | 97TH |
| 11 | 228 | 59 | 64 | 70 | 81 | 96 | 111 | 131 |
| 12 | 222 | 68 | 74 | 80 | 91 | 104 | 125 | 141 |
| 13 | 296 | 71 | 80 | 94 | 109 | 125 | 147 | 174 |
| 14 | 268 | 81 | 91 | 108 | 123 | 138 | 154 | 172 |
| 15 | 243 | 88 | 103 | 118 | 134 | 152 | 170 | 189 |
| 16 | 233 | 100 | 116 | 130 | 144 | 161 | 184 | 210 |
| 17 | 70 | — | — | — | 143 | — | — | — |
| 18 | 11 | — | — | — | 142 | — | — | — |

SOURCE: Reprinted by permission from J. L. Rauh, D. A. Schumsky, and M. T. Witt, "Heights, Weights, and Obesity in Urban School Children," *Child Development*, **38**, 515–530. Copyright © 1967, The Society for Research in Child Development, Inc.

**Table 13–7** Percentile Distribution of Weight in Pounds for Nonwhite Males (Age Defined at Subject's Last Birthday)

| Age | N (Total = 1208) | Percentile | | | | | | |
|-----|---|-----|------|------|------|------|------|------|
| | | 3RD | 10TH | 25TH | 50TH | 75TH | 90TH | 97TH |
| 11 | 101 | 65 | 69 | 74 | 80 | 88 | 97 | 106 |
| 12 | 101 | 71 | 74 | 83 | 93 | 104 | 117 | 142 |
| 13 | 86 | 72 | 78 | 87 | 98 | 121 | 141 | 163 |
| 14 | 110 | 80 | 91 | 102 | 118 | 137 | 160 | 178 |
| 15 | 71 | 85 | 103 | 118 | 140 | 153 | 170 | 192 |
| 16 | 56 | 105 | 112 | 122 | 140 | 150 | 165 | 171 |
| 17 | 38 | — | — | — | 142 | — | — | — |
| 18 | 13 | — | — | — | 146 | — | — | — |

SOURCE: Reprinted by permission from J. L. Rauh, D. A. Schumsky, and M. T. Witt, "Heights, Weights, and Obesity in Urban School Children," *Child Development*, **38**, 515–530. Copyright © 1967, The Society for Research in Child Development, Inc.

**Table 13–8** Percentile Distribution of Weight in Pounds for White Females (Age Defined at Subject's Last Birthday)

| Age | N (Total = 3010) | 3RD | 10TH | 25TH | 50TH | 75TH | 90TH | 97TH |
|-----|------------------|-----|------|------|------|------|------|------|
| 11 | 252 | 57 | 63 | 73 | 87 | 99 | 113 | 124 |
| 12 | 259 | 64 | 72 | 82 | 95 | 110 | 120 | 133 |
| 13 | 272 | 73 | 87 | 95 | 109 | 121 | 136 | 151 |
| 14 | 259 | 86 | 94 | 103 | 115 | 128 | 143 | 155 |
| 15 | 222 | 90 | 100 | 109 | 119 | 132 | 144 | 162 |
| 16 | 227 | 95 | 102 | 111 | 120 | 132 | 145 | 156 |
| 17 | 71 | — | — | — | 124 | — | — | — |
| 18 | 6 | — | — | — | 112 | — | — | — |

SOURCE: Reprinted by permission from J. L. Rauh, D. A. Schumsky and M. T. Witt, "Heights, Weights, and Obesity in Urban School Children," *Child Development*, **38**, 515–530. Copyright © 1967, The Society for Research in Child Development, Inc.

**Table 13–9** Percentile Distribution of Weight in Pounds for Nonwhite Females (Age Defined at Subject's Last Birthday)

| Age | N (Total = 1289) | 3RD | 10TH | 25TH | 50TH | 75TH | 90TH | 97TH |
|-----|------------------|-----|------|------|------|------|------|------|
| 11 | 104 | 62 | 67 | 80 | 90 | 105 | 118 | 134 |
| 12 | 103 | 67 | 77 | 86 | 99 | 113 | 127 | 144 |
| 13 | 123 | 73 | 88 | 100 | 109 | 123 | 138 | 161 |
| 14 | 100 | 82 | 97 | 107 | 117 | 128 | 149 | 191 |
| 15 | 89 | 91 | 97 | 107 | 118 | 131 | 155 | 182 |
| 16 | 57 | 88 | 102 | 109 | 123 | 131 | 161 | 169 |
| 17 | 23 | — | — | — | 126 | — | — | — |
| 18 | 13 | — | — | — | 114 | — | — | — |

SOURCE: Reprinted by permission from J. L. Rauh, D. A. Schumsky, and M. T. Witt, "Heights, Weights, and Obesity in Urban School Children," *Child Development*, **38**, 515–530. Copyright © 1967, The Society for Research in Child Development, Inc.

During the childhood years before pubescence, growth is stimulated and controlled by phyone, a hormone secreted by the pituitary gland, which lies in the center of the head. From birth to pubescence, the velocity of growth decreases steadily. The pubescent phase of growth is initiated by the hypothalamus, a small area in the base of the brain. When the hypothalamus reaches a certain stage of maturity, its anterior portion releases its restraint on the posterior portion, which then secretes a certain chemical. This chemical acts upon the pituitary gland, triggering its release of trophic hormones. The trophic hormones stimulate the ovaries, testes, and adrenal glands to produce their hormones. Androgens, secreted by the adrenals, of both boys and girls, and by the testes in boys, are the agents that cause pubescent growth.

The different timings of the adolescent growth spurts of the various organs and tissues can be explained by differential sensitivity to the androgens. For instance, the sequence of appearance of pubic, axillary, and facial hair is probably due to different thresholds to stimulation and reactivity to either adrenal or testicular androgens [57, p. 130]. The skin of the pubis thus responds to the smallest increase of androgen, growing hair in early pubescence. The skin of the axilla requires a larger amount of androgen before it produces hair, and the skin of the face an even larger amount.

The differences between early and late maturers are in part differences in the timing of the beginning of the adolescent growth spurt. These are probably genetic in origin since the spurt is related to the age of sexual maturity, which is known to be strongly hereditary. Environmental factors also influence pubescent growth, as will be shown in the section on nutrition at adolescence.

### Growth in Weight

The curve of increments of weight begins to rise earlier than does the curve of increments of height. This difference can be accounted for in part by the earlier increase in the width and depth measurements of the chest and hips. The pre-adolescent increase of subcutaneous fat and muscle also contributes to the earlier increase in weight.

Unlike muscle and bone, *fat* has periods of decreasing as well as of increasing during the growth span. Fat thickness increases from birth to 9 months, decreases to about 6 years, increases slowly until about a year before the height spurts start. In boys, fat has a growth spurt lasting about two years. Then, when the height spurt has been going for about a year, fat decreases until the height spurt ends. Fat then increases until it reaches a level at least as great as the preadolescent level. Girls increase more steadily than boys in growth of fat [57, pp. 19–25].

Fat thickness throughout childhood is closely related to weight at maturity [18]. By measuring fat thickness semiannually, it was shown that between 1.5 and 12.5 years of age, children in the top 14 percent in fat were advanced by about half a year's growth. Fat thickness was associated with skeletal maturity. The authors suggest that overnutrition or supernutrition results in speeded maturation, and general dimensional growth, in addition to subcutaneous fat. A series of studies on obesity in adolescents [9, 26, 54,] revealed activity level as a crucial difference between obese adolescents and normal ones who ate about the same number of calories. The level of activity affects metabolic rate and hence the rate at which calories are used. These results raise the question of whether inactivity is related to early maturity, as well as to fat.

### Changes in Proportions

The changes in average proportions can be seen in Figure 13–4, which uses the Sitting Height/Stature Ratio and the Trunk–Breadth Index. The former is the percentage of total height that is contributed by sitting height. According to the diagram (see Figure 13–4) at 1 year sitting height is about 64 percent of total height for boys and about 62 percent for girls. From ages 5 to 12 the girls' and boys' ratios are the same (on the average), but the ratios decrease throughout the age range up to 12 since the legs are growing faster than the trunk, neck, and head. From 12 to 15 for girls and from 14 to 18 for boys the ratio increases slightly as the trunk grows more rapidly than the legs.

The Trunk–Breadth Index is the ratio of hip width to shoulder width. Hip width is the distance between the crests of the pelvis. Shoulder width is the distance between the outer ends of the acromium, at the ends of the clavicles. The higher

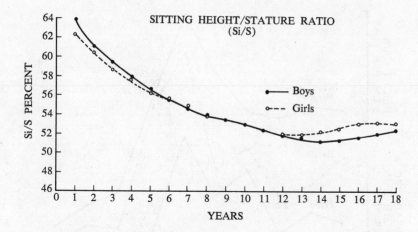

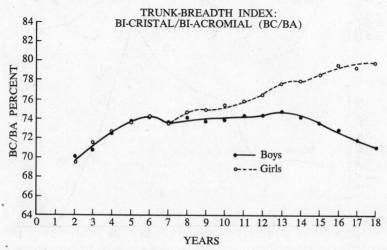

**Figure 13–4.** These ratios, the ratio of sitting height to total height (above) and the ratio of hip width to shoulder width (below), are shown for each year from birth to 18, indicating average changes in proportions as children mature.

SOURCE: Reprinted from *Growth Diagnosis*, by L. M. Bayer and N. Bayley, by permission of The University of Chicago Press. Copyright © 1959, The University of Chicago Press, Chicago.

the Index, the wider the hips are in relation to the width of the shoulders. Up to about the age of 8, on the average, the Index for boys and girls is the same. From 8 to 18, girls' average Index increases steadily, as the hips increase faster in width than do the shoulders. The average Index for boys stays at the same amount from 7 to 13, then drops as boys' shoulders increase faster than do their hips. Pubescent changes can be seen in almost every part of the body. The growth spurts of the various parts of the body do not coincide exactly with one another but are spread throughout the pubescent period. Figure 13–5 shows the timing of the spurts of several different body measurements. Notice that the peaks for growth in weight and head circumference come after the peaks for growth in height and hand length.

If a child grew in the way that a balloon blows up, he would keep the same proportions all the way along, but he does not. Spurting now in one measurement,

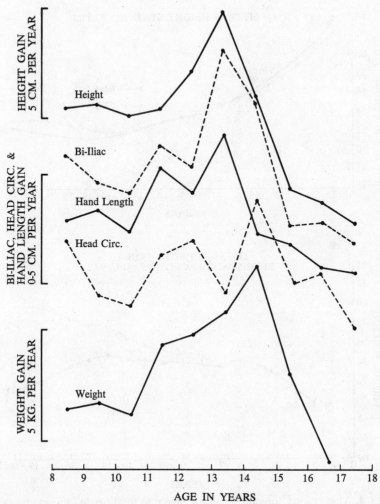

**Figure 13–5.** Adolescent increment growth curves, showing spurts and peaks for various body measurements.

SOURCE: Reprinted by permission from J. M. Tanner, *Growth at Adolescence*, 2nd edition. Oxford: Blackwell Scientific Publications Ltd., 1962. Copyright © 1962, Blackwell Scientific Publications Ltd.

now in another, he often looks different from the way he looked just a short time before. Spurts in head length and breadth make the eyes look smaller. The nose and lower jaw grow more than other parts of the face, changing its proportions from childish toward adult. The ways in which a boy grows out of his suits are predictable, since the spurts of the various parts of the body follow a sequence. First the trouser legs become too short. If his mother can lengthen them, they will last for another four months until his hip growth makes the trousers too tight. Since chest breadth increases at the same time as hip width, a new suit is in order. It is a good idea to buy it wide in the shoulders, since the spurt in shoulder breadth comes just a few months after the spurts in chest and hip width. This suit will become too short in the jacket with the peak of growth in trunk length which comes about a year after the peak of growth in leg length. A filling-out process will make the jacket too tight just after it becomes too short, since the peak in muscle growth comes soon after the peak in trunk length. (Although boys' suits illustrate these changes better than girls' clothing, the same sequence of changes takes place in girls.)

Both boys and girls tend to worry as their feet spurt in growth. This spurt happens when the height spurt gets under way or before it [36]. The earlier it happens, of course, the larger the youngster's feet seem to him and to his family, who tend to be concerned about the frequent need for new shoes as well as about what looks like awkwardness.

### Changes in Organs

The *viscera* undergo pubescent growth spurts [57, p. 18]. Most data on visceral growth are cross-sectional, and therefore the nature of their spurts has not been so clearly demonstrated as with outer body measurements. The cardiovascular system has been studied in terms of blood pressure, pulse rate, capacity for athletic and work effort, and recovery from work. Since the heart is relatively small during childhood, undergoing a growth spurt in pubescence, there is always the question for an individual as to how mature his heart is in relation to the rest of his body. Therefore, children and young adolescents should be protected from physical over-exertion [7, p. 223]. A rise in blood pressure and a drop in pulse rate begin with puberty, with boys exceeding girls in both [62, pp. 230–231]. Chest cavity and lungs increase, while rate of breathing decreases. In addition to the size of the body, however, pubescence brings a steady decrease in volume of air taken in. The sex difference grows in favor of boys, who develop a much larger lung capacity than girls.

The *nervous system* matures during the adolescent period, but the exact nature of the changes has not been mapped in much detail. The intellectual changes at adolescence must have their counterparts in the nervous system. There is evidence for a small growth spurt in the brain at adolescence [57, p. 15]. Physical measurements of heads indicate that there may be some brain growth along with growth in bone and membranes. An adult type of brain wave pattern becomes established during adolescence [61, p. 134].

### Development of the Primary and Secondary Sex Characteristics

The organs of reproduction grow enormously. Although only cross-sectional data are available for the growth of the uterus and ovaries, they show these organs as increasing in weight between ages 10 and 20. The male primary reproductive organs have been studied longitudinally. The stages of genital development are numbered according to the advancement of the primary and secondary sex characteristics. Stages of pubic hair growth, for example, are:

1. Prepubescent. About the same as in early childhood.
2. Sparse, long, slightly pigmented, downy hair.
3. Darker, coarser, curlier, spread over small area, but larger area than in 2.
4. Hair resembles adult hair but covers small area.
5. Adult quantity, quality, and distribution.

The average time to go from stage 2 to stage 5 is four years, but it may be done in as short a time as two years or as long as six.

Axillary hair usually appears when pubic hair is reaching stage 4, but it may come earlier. Circumanal hair appears just before axillary. Boys' facial hair comes at about the same time as axillary hair, developing through a sequence, as does pubic and axillary hair. Body hair develops for some time after puberty, with hair on the chest appearing last.

The voice change takes place throughout pubescence, sometimes continuing for years afterward. The spurt in growth of the larynx takes place at about the same time as the spurt in the trunk growth. Nine low notes are added to the average boy's voice between age 10 and adulthood, and only three low ones to the girl's. The boy loses four high notes, and the girl gains one [25].

The apocrine sweat glands of the axillary and genital regions enlarge and secrete sweat, which has a strong odor. The sebaceous glands enlarge and secrete more oil. Their ducts, which do not enlarge correspondingly, are likely to become plugged with the secretion, causing or contributing largely to the skin difficulties so frequent at this age.

Breast changes occur in boys as well as in girls. About a half of boys have some enlargement of the breasts at about stage 4 of genital development and lasting from a year to 18 months. Breast development in girls has been outlined in five stages:

1. Prepubescent. Elevation of papilla only.
2. Breast bud. Small mound of papilla and breast. Enlargement of areola.
3. Breast and areola enlarge further.
4. Areola and papilla project to form mound above level of breast.
5. Mature stage. Areola recedes to general contour of breast. Papilla projects. The breast bud tends to appear about a year and a half before the menarche. Breast bud and pubic hair usually occur within a year of each other.

The growth spurt of the ovaries probably begins about a year before the breast bud, the uterus and vagina, at about the time the breast bud appears. Early menstrual cycles tend to be irregular. Ovulation probably does not occur often. Full fertility is probably not reached until the early or middle twenties.

### Sex Feelings and Desires

The dramatic development of the reproductive system, culminating in sexual maturity, implies sexual activity or at least the desire for it. While some children are capable of true sexual response [31, p. 103], sexuality is heightened at puberty, especially for boys. Boys frequently experience sexual arousal and tension which they urgently desire to discharge through orgasm. By counting frequency of sexual "outlets," which include masturbation and nocturnal emissions, Kinsey [32] concludes that males are most active sexually during their teens and that the mid-teens are the most sexually active years of life. While there is some question as to whether sex desire is adequately measured by frequency of outlets [6, pp. 67–68], Kinsey has shown that in regard to number of orgasms of all kinds, adolescent boys greatly exceed adolescent girls. The 15-year-old boys reported an average of five orgasms per two-week interval, while only 23 percent of girls that age had experienced orgasm, and of those, the average frequency was less than one in two weeks. When sexual feeling or arousal is taken into account, adolescent girls appear more sexually responsive than when orgasm is the criterion. By age 13, 34 percent of girls, by 15, 53 percent, and by 20, 89 percent experienced sexual arousal [31, pp. 512–513].

These figures are given only to show that the average adolescent has had sex feelings and desires, the boy more frequently and acutely than the girl. There are wide individual differences in frequency and intensity of desire and in how it is satisfied. In Chapter 15 we shall discuss the role of sex in the development of personality and in interpersonal relationships.

## Physical Care and Health

Since any period of rapid growth is a time of vulnerability to certain deprivations or noxious influences, adolescence, especially pubescence, must imply important physical needs. Extra food and rest for fast growth stand out as important. Because the adolescent is declaring his independence, *how to* meet his physical needs is often as problematic as knowing what he needs. Health is important at any age, but at this time, when a youngster has such a confusion of problems to cope with, it is especially helpful for him to feel well and to have maximum energy.

### Illnesses

Adolescents are more free from illness than children are. A study of children from birth to 18 [60], where illness scores included both frequency and severity, showed lowest scores in the 14–18 bracket, with scores almost as low in 10–14. Greater than in any other period of childhood were the numbers of children who suffered no illness other than respiratory. The number of communicable diseases dropped sharply in early adolescence and continued to decrease in the later period. Most of the cases of communicable disease were of moderate severity.

**Venereal Disease.** Venereal disease is a serious threat to adolescents. The incidence of gonorrhea diminished during the 1950s but increased by 50 percent during the 1960s [38]. Syphilis has increased among minors [45]. Since many cases of venereal disease are not reported to public health authorities, even though physicians are required to do so, reported rates represent a minimum. It has been estimated that from 10.8 to 16.9 cases per 100 treated patients are reported. The recent reported rate of gonorrhea for 15- to 19-year-olds was 531 per 100,000 population. The popularity of oral contraceptives is a factor in the increase of venereal disease. Pills offer no protection, while the more old-fashioned condom is indeed a disease preventive as well as a contraceptive.

**Sex Differences in Illnesses.** Boys exceeded girls in number of total illnesses. Boys had about three times as many gastrointestinal upsets as girls. Accidents and surgery were much alike for the sexes. Figure 13–6 shows the number of illnesses in each category for boys and girls. The differences between categories are much greater than the sex differences. Note the high frequency of respiratory difficulties as contrasted with the other types of illness. Male rates for gonorrhea are higher than female, and nonwhite rates are higher than white. The rates per 100,000, as recently reported, were male white, 178.4; female white, 141.8; male nonwhite, 4016.0; female nonwhite, 1821.6 [38].

The study quoted above dealt with illnesses. While the investigator recorded health problems not classified as illnesses, such as eye difficulties or teeth requiring

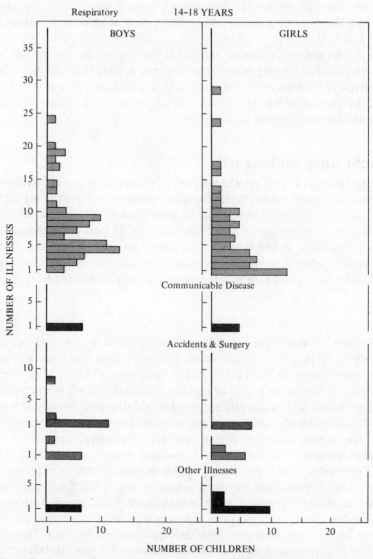

**Figure 13–6.** Frequency of various types of illnesses suffered by adolescents.

Source: I. Valadian, H. C. Stuart, and R. B. Reed, "Studies of Illnesses of Children Followed from Birth to Eighteen Years," *Monographs of The Society for Research in Child Development*, **26**:3.

dental care, those conditions are not included in the report. Certain physical conditions threaten the young person's self concept. Acne, for example, the skin ailment so typical of the teen years, has vast psychological significance. The young person trying to build an acceptable body image suffers acutely when he beholds his pimply reflection in the mirror and when he imagines how he looks to other people. Adolescents so afflicted often spend many hours fussing and agonizing and many dollars in the search for a cure. Figure 13–7 shows the relatively enormous incidence of skin difficulties occurring in the second decade of life. Diseased teeth and tonsils, while not actually illnesses, can cause lowered resistance to disease, fatigue, and possibly emotional upset.

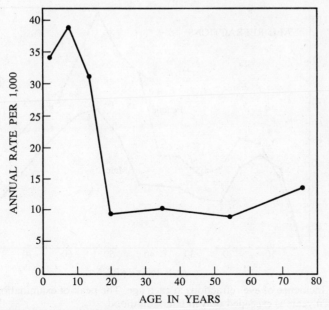

**Figure 13–7.** Frequency of diseases and defects of the skin.

SOURCE: Adapted from F. K. Shuttleworth, "The Adolescent Period," *Monographs of The Society for Research in Child Development*, 3:3.

*Sensory Handicaps*

The incidence of eye difficulties rises in the teens, as shown in Figure 13–8, which shows the number of eye examinations given in 9000 families. You can see that there is a peak of eye trouble in adolescence which is not exceeded until the decade of the forties. While adolescents may not have worse vision than younger children and adults, their need for accurate eyesight is probably greater since good vision is important in academic success. Eye defects have their psychological impact, just as acne does. Many people feel that glasses spoil their appearance, and adolescents feel it most keenly since their appearance is so significant. Contact lenses are a happy solution for some youngsters, but not for others, since some individuals cannot adjust to them, some cannot afford them, and some deficiencies cannot be corrected by them.

*Accidents*

Accidents are the greatest single cause of death in the second decade. The years from 15 to 24 are the most vulnerable period, according to the Metropolitan Life Insurance Company [37]. During this age period 61 percent of deaths of boys and 39 percent of deaths of girls were caused by accidents. Motor vehicle accidents were responsible for 39 percent of the deaths of 15- to 24-year-old males and of 22 percent of deaths of females that age. Here, then, are some of the figures behind the fact so unpopular with young men, that they must pay higher insurance rates on their cars than do girls the same age.

Other kinds of accidents and injuries are also of concern in the adolescent years. We have already mentioned that in the early part of this period, the heart may be

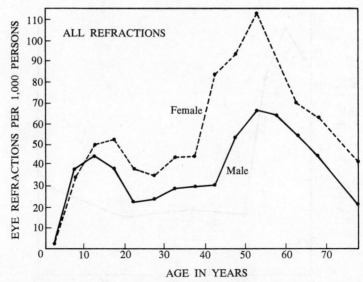

**Figure 13–8.** Incidence of eye refractions at each age. The peak of examinations required during the teen years is exceeded only in later adulthood.

SOURCE: Reprinted by permission from F. K. Shuttleworth, "The Adolescent Period," *Monographs of The Society for Research in Child Development*, 3, Figure 217. Copyright © 1938, The Society for Research in Child Development, Inc.

relatively small and therefore inadequate for a strain imposed by highly competitive athletics. Rapid growth in bones, muscles, joints, and tendons makes them especially vulnerable to unusual strain. The increase of strength and vigor in adolescents, especially in boys, may tempt them to overexertion, especially if their teammates and coach egg them on and their girl friends admire from the sidelines.

### Nutrition

Studies on the effects of wartime famine have shown that malnutrition in childhood delays the onset of the pubescent growth spurt [57, pp. 83–87]. The body has great recuperative powers, which result in a speed-up of growth when nutrition returns to the higher level. There is, however, a point of no return, beyond which growth failure cannot be erased by improved conditions. This point is illustrated by the Chilean children, previously described who recovered from kwashiorkor. Even though they received adequate diets, their heights continued to be abnormally small, while their weights became extreme for their heights, giving them an obese appearance [49].

Indications of the delaying effect of malnutrition on menarche come from Guatemala, where urban girls of high socioeconomic status were compared with poor rural girls. Figure 13–9 shows the percentage of girls menstruating at each year of age between 11 and 17. The median age for menarche in the high group is about 13, for the low, 14.5.

Evidence from the Harvard–Florence research project also shows the influence of socioeconomic factors on age of menarche. In Florence, Italy, girls whose families had moved up in socioeconomic status reached menarche a year earlier than their mothers did. Girls whose families had moved down were a year later

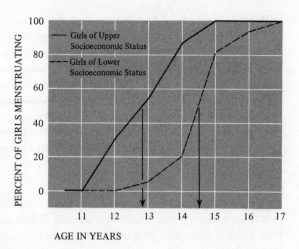

**Figure 13–9.** Percentage of Girls Menstruating at Different Age Levels in the Two Groups. ——— Urban group; ———— Rural group.

SOURCE: Reprinted from *Human Biology*, **38**:2, 1966, by Kamla P. Sabharwal, Silvia Morales, and José Méndez by permission of the Wayne State University Press. Copyright 1965 by Wayne State University.

than their mothers in reaching menarche [64]. Further evidence for the importance of environmental factors is that the decline in age of menarche over the past century has occurred only in countries where technological advances have occurred, along with improvement in nutrition [65].

Deficiencies in any of the elements required for growth—vitamins, minerals, and proteins—can have adverse effects on energy level, resistance to disease, behavior, emotions, and appearance. Adolescents are all too likely to eat empty calories, foods which contain mostly sugar, starch, and flavorings, and perhaps fats, such as soft drinks, pastries, potato chips, and candy. If the empty-calorie foods are added to the wholesome diet, the result is too many calories and a fat adolescent. If they are substituted for it, the result is dietary deficiency. This is not to say that some empty-calorie foods cannot be eaten with impunity during the teen years. At the peak of the pubescent growth spurt, calorie needs are enormous. The average boy between 16 and 19 needs 3600 calories, more than he has ever needed before or will again. The average girl between 13 and 15 needs 2600 calories, an amount exceeded only by the lactating mother. These figures do not accurately indicate the caloric needs at the peak of the growth spurt, since they are derived from age groups rather than from groups based on physiological maturity. The actual number of calories needed is greater than these figures. A fast-growing boy may literally never get filled up. His stomach may be too small to hold as many calories as his body can use unless he eats at very frequent intervals, or what seems like all the time to his mother. The calories used for energy can, of course, be empty ones, since sugar and starch are converted into fuel.

**Obesity.** The problem of overweight is an increasing one in affluent countries, an ironic situation when the majority of the world's children are malnourished. Obese adolescents suffer anguish as well as threats to health. Estimates of the prevalence of obesity in childhood and adolescence range from 10 percent to 30 percent [42]. Ten percent obesity was found among the Cincinnati school children whose measurements were used to make the tables on pages 499–501 [44]. At age 16, obese black girls outnumbered obese white girls, two to one. Among the boys, the difference was in the other direction. There were more obese white boys than black. Genetic factors are also involved, since certain body types (mesomorphic-endomorphic) are associated with obesity and since overweight in parents is correlated with overweight in children. Environmental factors, as well as genetic, are involved in the parent–child similarity [42]. Many other factors may contribute to obesity including psychological and metabolic. By nutrition education of mothers, it may be possible to prevent obesity in infancy and childhood. The obese adolescent needs medical help which will include attention to the complexity and multiple nature of causes of the problem. A study of teen-age girls whose heights and weights placed them in the obese channel of the Wetzel grid (see page 202) showed that they ate poorer diets and fewer calories than did the other girls in the same school [20]. These results are confirmed by other studies of obese girls [26] and boys [4].

*Rest*

For many youngsters, pubescence ushers in the desire to sleep on Saturday mornings and on other mornings, as well. Their rapid growth requires more rest than did the quiescent growth of the elementary school years. Adolescents tend to stay up later at night than they did as children. They are busy with schoolwork, visiting with friends, especially over the telephone, paying attention to appearance. Parental control is resisted. When growth slows down, they can and do get along with less sleep than they needed as children.

*Drugs*

Americans use a very large number of chemical substances in order to make changes in their bodies and minds. The use of certain of these substances by adolescents constitutes health problems, both physical and mental. Only a brief comment can be made here, since a thorough treatment of the subject requires a book in itself. We shall discuss the drugs commonly used by adolescents and their effects on bodies and minds.

**Drinking.** Alcohol is a depressant, affecting the nervous system selectively. Since it first acts upon the part of the brain involved with critical thinking, the relaxing of inhibitions may be interpreted as stimulation. The next higher level of alcohol concentration depresses the function of the brain areas that control motor acts. Then, in order, come emotional unbalance, perceptual disturbances, coma, and death. While few teen-agers are alcoholics, drinking and acceptance of drinking increases with grade level throughout high school and from high school to college [50]. Eventually, one out of every 14 drinkers becomes an alcoholic [27, p. 101].

Although direct harm to bodily tissues is unlikely to be a serious problem during adolescence, young people often experience other difficulties resulting from the use of alcohol. Removal of inhibitions leads to problems such as quarreling, unplanned sex, and pregnancy. Accidents and injuries result from impaired motor coordination. Frequent and habitual drinking will most likely restrict experiences and growth opportunities and may lead to academic failure.

**Smoking.** It is now well known that smoking causes heart and lung diseases and yet children continue to start smoking and smokers continue to smoke. Since there is no generally successful method of breaking the habit of smoking [48], recent research has concentrated on finding out why children start to smoke and how to prevent it [34]. At the time when the Surgeon General of the United States received a report from his committee on smoking, it was estimated that at age 12 about 5 percent of boys and one percent of girls smoked, but that by 17, 40 to 55 percent of youth were smoking [59]. While smoking rates have gone down among adults, they have increased among teenagers [22]. In Grades 5 through 12 in the whole school system in Indiana, 35 percent of boys and 21 percent of girls smoked [34]. A youngster who had a smoking best friend and who belonged to a smoking peer group was very much more likely to be a smoker himself. The relation between smoking and having parents who smoke was relatively slight. Older brothers and sisters have been found to be influential [22]. Awareness of health hazards showed no relation to smoking, smokers and nonsmokers being similarly knowledgeable about the dangers. Attitudes toward television commercials about cigarets also showed no relation to smoking [34].

Youngsters may start to smoke because of peer pressure and/or because smoking represents adult status and independence to them. Over 5000 British boys between 11 and 15 were questioned as to how they perceived smoking in regard to themselves, their ideals, and peers [35]. The boys associated toughness and precocity with smoking. Smokers were influenced by these perceptions to continue smoking. Nonsmokers were attracted by the notion of toughness which gave them some incentive to start smoking. Both groups associated educational success with non-smoking and both valued educational success. Evidence from another study [55] shows that smokers are more rebellious than nonsmokers during the elementary and junior high school years. Furthermore, adult smokers showed more rebellious-ness than nonsmokers. The authors of this study point out the futility of trying to prevent adolescents from beginning and continuing smoking by making authoritative pronouncements.

**Hallucinogens.** Drugs which cause sensory distortions without greatly disturbing consciousness are called hallucinogens [27, p. 50]. Marijuana and LSD are probably best known. The cannabis plant produces a chemical used in several different forms and called by many different names throughout the world. Americans smoke the leaves, as pot or grass. Or they smoke the much stronger resin, as hash (hash-eesh). Physical reactions include rapid heartbeat, twitching of muscles, pupil dilation, reddish eyes, lowered body temperature, lowered blood sugar, dehydra-tion. Hunger and drowsiness are likely. The mind-altering effects, showing action on the brain, are of course, the reason for using the drug. Most young American users of marijuana are looking for new experiences and these they find in the form of mood changes, perceptual distortions, and changes in conceptualizing. Driving while high on pot is therefore dangerous. The psychological reactions are very variable, depending on the social environment, the mood the user is already in, the strength of the drug, and past experience with the drug. Marijuana is thought not to be physically addicting, which means that withdrawal does not cause physi-cal symptoms such as cramps and vomiting. Users can and often do become psychologically addicted or dependent on marijuana, however. Because adolescents hear that it is not physically addicting, they often think that it cannot become a habit. False reassurance also comes from the mildness of the drug and the ease of taking a small amount at a time. Many individuals do try it briefly and use it in-frequently, running into no obvious harm beyond the legal risk (which is indeed serious). Some try it briefly and give it up because it induces feelings of anxiety or passivity and lethargy. Still others adopt it as a way of life, withdrawing from the demands of studies, athletics, creative pursuits, and regular social life, finding satisfaction in the group that shares the drug experience. A psychiatrist [1] says that it is often difficult to determine just when addiction starts and that it can only be diagnosed when the person has trouble giving up the drug. The World Health Organization calls marijuana and other forms of the cannabis plant chemical the most abused drug in the world [66]. Extended use of it causes lethargy, dissociation, and withdrawal from human contact.

A fair number of pot smokers go on to something stronger, something which will give more exciting "expanded" experiences and release them more from the bounds of reality [66]. They use LSD, LTP, peyote, mescaline, or morning glory seeds, but most likely LSD. Physical side effects of LSD include nausea, vomiting, aches and pains, and possible chromosomal damage and damage to unborn children [27]. Action of LSD upon the brain is indicated by dilated pupils, increased blood pressure, and stronger reflexes. Sensory areas of the brain are stimulated, and inhibiting mechanisms are blocked. Thus visual hallucinations are produced and often intensification or diminishing of senses of hearing, touch, temperature, and pain. Senses may become fused or scrambled and the individual hears colors or smells music. He may be euphoric and feel that he has great mental clarity or comprehension, possibly the result of the combination of brain arousal and disturbed sensory activity leading to heightened awareness of previously stored information [27, p. 51]. This information becomes available as preconscious material. (An aspect of the normal creative process is the receiving and using of preconscious material.) A shared LSD trip often produces attachment between members of the group.

Dangers of LSD include the very real possibilities of injury or death while on a trip, due to falling out of a window, thinking one can fly, or ignoring traffic dangers because of feeling immune to injury. A "bad trip," where anxiety and panic occur instead of euphoria, may lead to suicide attempts. Recurrence of symptoms can happen even weeks or months after taking LSD, even after only once. Long-lasting mental illness can also result. While it is difficult to get information on the extent of use of hallucinogens by adolescents, it is known that these drugs are in common use not only in colleges but in the high schools throughout the United States [50, p. 469].

**Amphetamines.** Providing stimulation to the brain and sympathetic nervous system, these psychic energizers produce an increased heart rate, increased blood pressure, constriction of certain blood vessels, pupil dilation, faster breathing, sweating, and a dry mouth [27]. Bodily activity increases and the user feels more confident, happy, fearless, and less tired. He becomes more talkative and impulsive. Appetite decreases. Amphetamines are taken in pills for reducing and for staying awake and alert for working, playing, or studying longer than the person normally could. They are also used for kicks, sometimes combined with alcohol or barbiturates. *Speeding*, injecting a huge amount of amphetamine into a vein, gives an euphoric high called a *rush*. Repeated injections keep the speed freak awake and active for days until he is completely exhausted.

Excessive and prolonged use of amphetamines causes physical and mental damage. The student who uses it to stay awake for long periods becomes exhausted. He may become dependent, feeling depressed and sluggish without the drug. Liver damage may result. Prolonged use and increasing doses can cause sleeplessness for long times, mood changes, and severe mental disorder, with feelings of superiority, suspiciousness, hallucinations, and excitement [27]. Speeding may transmit hepatitis, since contaminated needles are often used. Drivers under the influence of amphetamines are extremely dangerous.

**Volatile Solvents.** Glue sniffing is done by younger adolescents and even by grade school children, probably because airplane glue is easily available. Solvents are depressants but the first psychological effect is a feeling of pleasantness, cheerfulness, euphoria, and excitement, very similar to the first stages of drinking alcohol [27]. Then the glue sniffer acts drunk and disoriented. His speech is slurred. Next comes drowsiness, stupor, and unconsciousness, which may last for an hour. Toxic effects include irritation of the skin, mucous membranes, and respiratory tract and injury to heart, liver, kidneys, blood, bones, and brain. Insomnia, nausea, increased salivation, and weight loss occur. Solvents produce strong psychological dependence and strong tolerance, which means that the dosage has to be increased in order to get the desired effects. Repeated daily use of solvents has caused many deaths.

**Heroin.** Teen-age heroin addicts have become a serious medical problem. Heroin is a depressant, blocking out experience of the world. Addiction occurs rapidly and often irreversibly. An overdose is likely to kill. The use of heroin often leads to tetanus, hepatitis, skin ulcers, damaged veins, heart disease, and allergic reactions. Addicts come from a wide variety of family backgrounds and socioeconomic levels. They tend to be passive, avoiding conflicts instead of trying to solve them [15].

*Supervision of Adolescent Health*

It takes the combined efforts of home, school, and community to see that adolescents get even a minimum of health protection. Schools and other community agencies usually offer something in the way of screening for sensory defects and certain gross physical defects. Immunizations may be given on a community basis. The school lunch program is effective in raising the nutritional level of some youngsters, but is not generally appreciated for its potentially great contribution. A good physical education program can contribute enormously to sound health and growth. Many responsibilities are left to the home—providing regular medical and dental care, giving an adequate diet, planning for rest, seeing that clothing is not only warm enough but that it protects growth, such as bras and shoes that fit. Here, as in other areas, the adolescent's search for independence often collides with parents' duties as protectors.

Chapter 1 stressed the importance of beginning a pregnancy with a well-nourished, physically fit body. The health and development of both mother and baby are affected by the pregnancy. The high school years are a good time for girls to learn how to prepare themselves to be adequate mothers physically and to develop an interest in doing so. High school programs in nutrition, health, and human development could make great contributions to the next generation.

# Motor Development

"One mark of childhood is a strong desire to be active. One sign of maturity is a strong inclination to sit down" [24]. Jersild's observation sums up the course of motor activity in many American adolescents. Jersild goes on to say that if maturity consists of sitting down, then girls achieve it earlier than boys. The quality and quantity of motor activity during adolescence, however, is a complex story which, even though it ends in relative quiet, adds to one's understanding of human development.

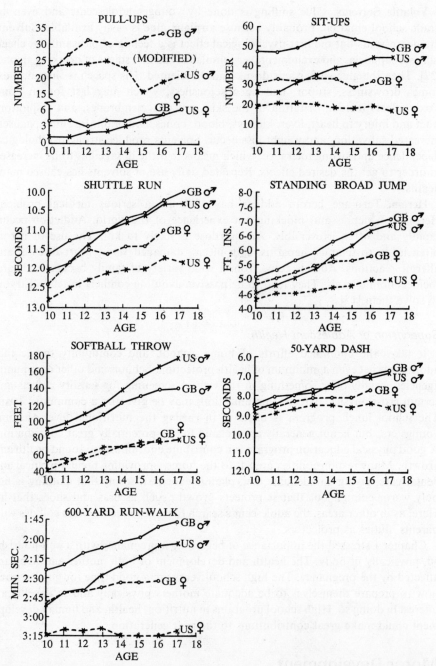

**Figure 13–10.** Comparisons between American and British youth on several athletic events.

SOURCE: Data from W. R. Campbell and R. H. Pohndorf, "Physical Fitness of British and United States Children," in *Report of Conference on Health and Fitness in the Modern World* (Chicago: Athletic Institute, 1961), pp. 8–16. Reprinted by permission from T. K. Cureton, "Improving the Physical Fitness of Youth," *Monographs of The Society for Research in Child Development*, **29**, Figure 1. Copyright © 1964, The Society for Research in Child Development, Inc.

Body build and rates of growth, factors strongly dependent on heredity, are important determinants of who shall be successful. Boy athletes on interscholastic teams in both elementary and high schools are definitely superior to other boys in maturity, body size, muscular strength, endurance, and power [11]. Social and cultural influences play a part in the degree and type of motor coordinations developed. Physical care and opportunities for learning are also factors in the development of motor skills.

### American Youth Compared with Others

In Chapter 9, we mentioned the Kraus–Weber test of minimum muscular fitness, by which American children and adolescents were demonstrated to be inferior to their age-mates in Europe. Four years later, over 8000 American youngsters between 10 and 17 were examined for physical fitness on a much more thorough battery of tests and compared with over 10,000 British boys and girls [10]. Figure 13–10 shows some of the results of this comparison. British boys were consistently superior to American boys and British girls to American girls. What is more, British girls made some improvements during the teen years, while American girls made almost none. Similar results came from a Japanese study [43], which showed Japanese youth to be superior to American in endurance, strength, and flexibility. Swedish children were found to have a higher work capacity (demonstrated by oxygen-intake capacity) than American children [3, 46].

Since these discoveries were made public, efforts to improve the physical condition of Americans have been considerable and have met with some success. The few American children who attended excellent fitness programs scored just as high as Europeans [13, p. 139]. Physical education research centers and laboratories have demonstrated methods of improving physical structure and function. Some of this work is reported in a monograph based on research done in the Sports-Fitness School of the University of Illinois [13]. The research proves that physical education can improve boys in physique and in specific skills, as well as in balance, flexibility, agility, strength, power, and endurance. American physical education, according to the director of this research, has been particularly deficient in training for endurance, since the emphasis has been largely on play and games, with little attention to sustained exercise. Nor has there been much systematic development of strength in various sets of muscles, through exercises designed for the purpose.

### Strength

Longitudinal studies on increase of strength have shown boys making gains throughout adolescence, while girls tend to taper off after pubescence. Figure 13–11 shows four measures of strength for boys and girls. Tanner points out that in all four of the boy's curves a marked spurt can be seen between ages 13 and 16 and a less definite spurt in the girls' hand grip curves between 12 and 13½. An ethnic difference in girls' grip strength has already been mentioned on page 368. The superiority of Afro-American girls over Latin and Anglo occurs throughout the elementary grades but becomes very pronounced by Grade 12 level [19]. A sex difference in strength of arm thrust arises at puberty, and the small difference in arm pull increases then. Boys also show spurts in strength of back and legs and in strength per pound of body weight [13]. The pubescent growth spurt in boys is closely associated with the spurt in strength, while in girls it is not. It is probably

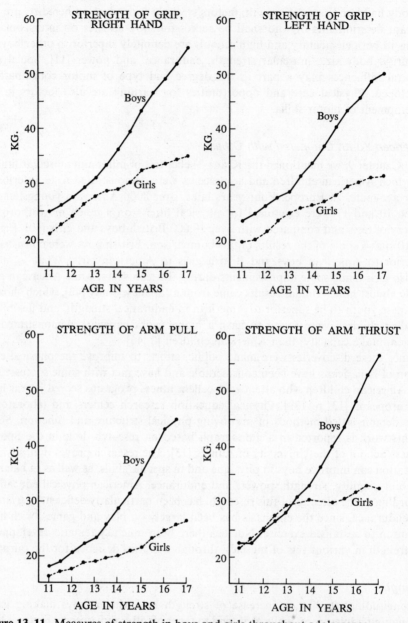

**Figure 13–11.** Measures of strength in boys and girls throughout adolescence.

SOURCE: Reprinted by permission from J. M. Tanner, *Growth at Adolescence*, 2nd edition. Oxford: Blackwell Scientific Publications Ltd., 1962. Copyright © 1962, Blackwell Scientific Publications Ltd.

pertinent that the increase in vital capacity which occurs in boys at this time is not matched by such an increase in girls [57, pp. 133–135]. These very real differences in strength are basic to the fact that boys excel girls in athletics during late adolescence. However, the girl's lack of increase in strength cannot be dismissed as genetic when we have the contrast of girls in other countries who do improve in strength throughout their adolescence.

## Coordination

Several investigators have studied motor coordination by means of the Brace test, which may tap basic, generalized motor factors. It consists of a series of tests of agility and balance, such as jumping up, clapping feet together, and landing with feet apart [16]. The Brace test was used along with other basic athletic performances on 165 boys and girls, repeating them on the same subjects over a period of four years. Boys increased steadily in all measures throughout the whole period. After 14 years, girls showed a gradual decline in dash and broad jump, little if any change in distance throw and Brace test, and an increase in jump and reach scores. While sex differences existed at all ages, boys gained marked superiority from 14 onward. Figure 13–12 shows the results from these tests.

**Adolescent Awkwardness—Fact or Fancy?** Ever since it was found that boys steadily improve in the Brace test and that girls do not change for the worse, students of adolescence have thought that adolescent awkwardness might be just a myth. If the average trend is steadily toward greater balance and agility, or no less of either, how, then, can the adolescent be more awkward than the child? The answer may be that adolescents show increased self-awareness and frequent uncertainty as to how to play the new roles required of them. Indecision and lack of self-confidence rather than neuromuscular inability are reflected in jerky or obvious movements. Realizing that they are expected to be awkward, perhaps they play the role somewhat on purpose. There is still the fact that different parts of the body grow at different rates, especially the reality of feet growing long before full height is reached. Do adolescent boys trip over their feet more often than younger boys or men? The Brace test might not reveal it. (It does not.) Observations in natural settings may be the only way to reach a definite answer to such a problem!

## Speed

Between the years of 7 and 13, the average boy cuts 2.4 seconds off his time for the 60-yard dash and 8.2 seconds off his time for the 600-yard run [13, pp. 19–22]. In speed involving large muscles, boys improve throughout the teen years. Girls show little or no gain in speed, when judged thus. When speed of manual tasks is measured, differences tend to be in favor of boys, but not always. Reaction time, measured by the time it takes to respond to a sound, probably reaches a maximum at 13 or 14, with little sex difference. Tests of simple eye–hand coordination usually show little improvement after 14 or 15, with boys somewhat superior. The development of these abilities is charted in Figure 13–13.

## Endurance

Endurance, or stamina, refers to being able to keep up an activity for a considerable length of time. Endurance is developed by muscles and also by the circulatory system. For example, hopping tests the endurance of feet and leg muscles, while running a mile requires considerable endurance from the circulatory and respiratory systems, as well as from feet and leg muscles and other muscles [13, p. 90]. Analysis of cardiovascular endurance has shown that at least eight measurable factors are involved, including such conditions as velocity and force of heart ejection stroke, vagus tone, pulse rate in the quiet state and after moderate exercise, and blood pressure adjustment to hard work. Thus stamina and its improvement

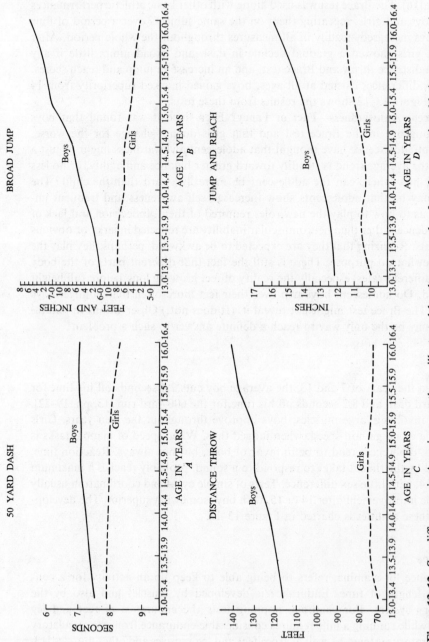

**Figure 13–12.** Sex differences in American youth are illustrated by these records of performance in athletic events during the years from 13 through 16.

SOURCE: Reprinted by permission from A. Espenschade, "Motor Performance in Adolescence," *Monographs of The Society for Research in Child Development*, **5**, Figure 8. Copyright © 1940, The Society for Research in Child Development, Inc.

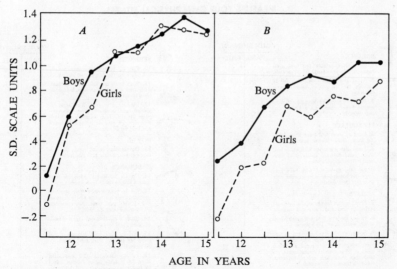

**Figure 13–13.**  *A:* Reaction time to sound, by age and sex. *B:* Speed of eye–hand coordination.

SOURCE: From R. H. Seashore and H. E. Jones, "Development of Fine Motor and Mechanical Abilities," *Yearbook of the National Society for the Study of Education*, Forty-third Yearbook, Part I, p. 127. Used by permission of the National Society for the Study of Education.

can be measured not only by noting how long a boy can keep at a given activity but by making a large number of laboratory measurements.

The following methods of developing endurance have been proved successful at the University of Illinois Sports-Fitness School [13, pp. 92–93]:

1. Adjustment to the full program is expected to take several weeks, even up to eight.
2. Activities are cycled and paced to permit continuous activity over a long period, such as by alternating walking and running, by cross-country running, long cycling trips, canoe trips, long hikes, and by gradually working at a faster pace.
3. Rest intervals are planned also, with provision for a midday rest and for a longer night sleep than boys usually take.
4. Deep breathing is taught and emphasized.
5. Careful attention to motivation includes participation and demonstration by instructors, use of standards and records and inspirational stories of athletes.
6. Nutrition is planned and supervised and moderation required. Emphasis is placed on the use of vegetables, fruits, lean meats, and whole grain cereals. Skim milk is preferred to whole milk and real fruit juices to imitation. Animal fats, chocolate, soda, and fried foods are curtailed.
7. The best activities for developing circulatory-respiratory endurance include steeplechase running, continuous muscular exercise for 30 minutes, interval training (cycles of fast and slow) in running, skating, swimming, cycling, rowing, and taking tests in endurance runs.

*Influence of Training on Physical Fitness and Physique*

Youngsters who have had good physical education show up consistently as superior to those who have had poor programs or none [13, pp. 142–145]. The

## MEASURE YOUR OWN PHYSICAL FITNESS

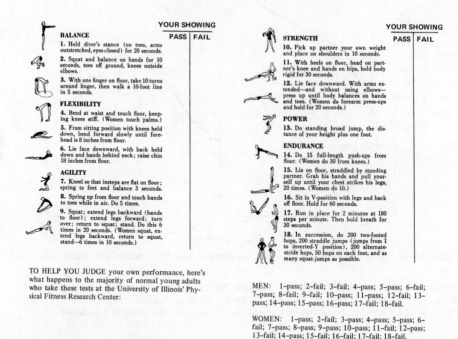

TO HELP YOU JUDGE your own performance, here's what happens to the majority of normal young adults who take these tests at the University of Illinois' Physical Fitness Research Center:

MEN: 1–pass; 2–fail; 3–fail; 4–pass; 5–pass; 6–fail; 7–pass; 8–fail; 9–fail; 10–pass; 11–pass; 12–fail; 13–pass; 14–pass; 15–pass; 16–pass; 17–fail; 18–fail.

WOMEN: 1–pass; 2–fail; 3–pass; 4–pass; 5–pass; 6–fail; 7–pass; 8–pass; 9–pass; 10–pass; 11–fail; 12–pass; 13–fail; 14–pass; 15–fail; 16–fail; 17–fail; 18–fail.

**Figure 13–14.** Test of motor fitness devised by T. K. Cureton.

SOURCE: Reprinted by permission from T. K. Cureton, "How to Keep Your Family Young," *Redbook*, April 1955. Copyright © 1955, McCall Corporation, New York.

Cureton Test of Motor Fitness, shown in Figure 13–14, measures balance, flexibility, agility, strength, and endurance, thus sampling fitness more broadly than do the Kraus–Weber and Brace tests. Table 13–10 shows the average improvement from year to year on the Cureton Test. Improvements after training have been demonstrated in many different motor activities, including balancing, flexibility tests, agility tests, strength, power and endurance tests, and also in such specific performances as hopping, dipping, rope skipping, and chinning [13].

Fat, muscles and even bones change during the course of a good fitness program. A special program for boys with underdeveloped upper bodies resulted in significant increases in biceps, chest, abdomen, and shoulders [2]. Both structural and functional improvement occurred in the feet of boys who had foot defects [13]. Well-functioning feet, of course, are basic to good posture.

**Table 13–10** Performance on Cureton Motor Fitness Test

| Age in Years | Range of Scores | Average Score |
| --- | --- | --- |
| 10 | 2–13 | 7.05 |
| 11 | 3–14 | 8.43 |
| 12 | 1–16 | 9.21 |
| 13 | 3–17 | 10.00 |
| 14 | 2–17 | 11.22 |
| 15 | 5–17 | 11.79 |

SOURCE: T. K. Cureton, "Improving the physical fitness of youth," *Monographs of the Society for Research in Child Development*, **29**:4.

*Relation Between Motor Coordination, Physique and Maturity*

The Medford, Oregon, Boy's Growth Study included cross-sectional and longitudinal studies of hundreds of boys between 7 and 18 years of age [11]. One set of results from the study shows relations between body structure and motor ability. Sheldon's [51] categories of body types were used: *mesomorph*, in which strong muscles and bones predominate, with large head, broad shoulders and chest, large heart muscle, and minimal fat; *endomorph*, who has a round head, large abdomen and internal organs, weakly muscled arms and legs with much fat, but slender wrists and ankles, much subcutaneous fat; *ectomorph*, possessing a thin, narrow face and body, spindly arms and legs, a narrow heart, relatively large skin area and nervous system. Endomorphy and mesomorphy were associated with gross strength and ectomorphy with low strength. Mesomorphs were superior on measures of muscular endurance and in physical fitness, an index which relates strength measures to norms based on age and weight.

Boys' spurts in strength of grip, arm pull, and arm thrust occur as part of the sequence of pubescence, in connection with the growth of the shoulder, back, and pectoral muscles [57, pp. 133–137]. Other motor spurts can be similarly related to bodily growth. Early maturing boys spurt early in strength, late maturing boys are late in strength spurts. The peak of the strength spurt occurs about a year and a half after the peak height velocity and a year after the peak weight velocity. The menarche marks approximately the end of the girls' spurt in strength. There is evidence to show that male hormones are involved in development of male strength.

"To him that hath shall be given" holds true for the physical endowments of boys. The slow maturing, childish-looking boy is also weak and poor in athletics, as compared with the fast maturer, who looks like a man and can throw strength as well as bulk into a competition. Even so, the boy who will put forth enough effort can improve his appearance and physical status, provided he has access to good physical education.

*Significance of Motor Coordination to Adolescents*

Athletic prowess is a social asset to boys, as well as a source of experiences of physical mastery and adequacy. Boys, girls, and adults admire the athlete, the strong, able, masculine-looking male. While girls may get direct satisfaction from motor adequacy, they lack the added fillip of widespread social acclaim for athletic performance. There may indeed be mild approval for winning the girls' badminton tournament, but in most American high schools, such approval is mild indeed. It might work up to a higher pitch in a private girls' school, where the athletic tradition is stronger than in the public schools. In other cultures, even in such closely related ones as Canadian and English, the ideal woman is more athletic than she is in America, and the adolescent girl receives much more recognition for athletic achievement than she does here.

Even in the area of male athletics the American emphasis has been largely on the doings of a few experts whom other people watch. The newer trend in physical education is, however, to encourage adolescents to learn coordinations which they will use throughout life for recreational, social, and health purposes. Swimming, tennis, and dancing are therefore more valuable than basketball, football, and track. When a motor pattern has meaning for the person and when it fits into the cultural role, it becomes worthwhile to learn it well. Witness girls dancing! They dance as well as boys, if not better.

## Some Relationships Between Physical Development and Psychological Development

Like the change from tadpole to frog or from caterpillar to butterfly, the change from child to adolescent brings an essentially new body into existence. The person has to come to terms with his new body in many ways. Updating his body image, he includes in it the revised notions of where he stops and the rest of the world begins, what his body can do, how to control it, whether it looks beautiful or ugly, good or bad to him, and how it appears to everyone else in the world. A strong sense of identity requires that the adolescent see himself as the same person who used to have a childish body.

Physical appearance is a matter of real concern to most adolescents, to younger ones more than older ones. A teen-ager is likely to look into a mirror and wish for something different from what he sees. Applying tape measure to bust, waist, and hips, she sadly notes discrepancies from the measurements of the reigning Miss America. In the process of getting used to his new face and physique, he compares them with those of his peers and also with currently popular movie stars, TV personalities, and models. Nobody wants to be too different from the peer group, an understandable attitude when identity is still shaky. During the flapper era, a full-bosomed girl often felt impelled to slouch, while in the age of the padded bra she could more easily hold herself proudly. Beauty is defined variously in different ages. So are masculine and feminine appearance. But whatever the current definition of a beautiful girl, that's what a girl wants to be. Likewise for a handsome, masculine man, with more emphasis on the *masculine* than on the *handsome*.

While some desired physical features can be achieved through art and science, such as blond hair and straight teeth, height and body build are stubbornly resistant to willful interference. Since a common ideal for femininity is a small, dainty body and for masculinity, a large, strong body, many girls would like to be smaller, while many boys wish they were larger [12]. As any TV fan or reader of magazine ads knows, the ideal American male figure is athletic-looking, with strong muscles and bones, a mesomorph, in Sheldon's classic description of body types. Endomorphs and ectomorphs rarely play hero roles or model the latest clothes. Some associations between body build and behavior have been found and some could be logically expected, such as mesomorphs being good athletes. *Expectations* of behavior are strongly related to body build in males. Boys between 10 and 20 years of age rated pictures of the three types of male figures on 30 items in terms of choosing the man who would assume leadership, have many friends, not smoke at all, endure pain the best, and so on [33]. Of the 30 items, there was only one (put his own interests before others) in which the mesomorph did not receive the most favorable choices, most of which were highly significant. Therefore, the mesomorph is associated with a socially positive stereotype, while the stereotypes of endomorphs and ectomorphs are generally negative.

Because the timing of the pubescent growth spurt plays such an important part in determining a young adolescent's size, it is evident that early maturers differ from the late maturers in what influences their personality growth.

## Early and Late Maturity

The relationship between physical maturity and personality development has been considered in several studies. One approach [29] was to contrast the experiences, behavior, and attitudes of early maturers with those of late maturers. Physically accelerated boys at 17 years were found to receive general acceptance and to be treated as older, able people. They were rated as above average in physical attractiveness, grooming, matter-of-factness, and relaxation. Often successful as student leaders and athletes, they showed little striving for status. The contrasting boys, maturing late, were treated more as little boys than as men. They were rated as significantly less attractive than the early maturers, but exceeded the first group in eagerness, initiative, and sociability. Disadvantaged by small physical size, they apparently tried to compensate by striving for attention and status. Further study of the personalities of early and late maturers yielded a picture of the former as self-confident, independent, and socially capable while the latter often had negative concepts of themselves, feelings of inadequacy, rejection, and dependency, and felt rebellious toward their parents [40]. When the same boys were studied in adulthood, the early maturers were seen as continuing in the same pattern of success [28]. They were poised, responsible, achieving, and at ease with what was expected of them in their social roles. The late maturers, as adults, were exploratory, insightful, independent, and impulsive. Thus each pattern of growth to maturity has certain advantages in adulthood. Another study of the relationship between physical maturity and personality compared early, late, and average maturers [63]. The comparisons between early and late maturers agreed with the earlier research, but average maturing boys were much more similar to early maturers than to late maturers. Thus while it is disadvantageous to mature late, it makes little or no difference, in terms of favorable personality characteristics, whether a boy matures early or at the average time.

Considering the question of effects of the timing of maturity on girls' personalities, it was surprising to find results similar to those of the study on boys [30]. Early maturing 17-year-old girls too had more favorable concepts than did late maturing girls, even though they must have been bigger than their classmates during early adolescence. The late maturers showed a greater need for recognition, somewhat more dependency, and slightly poorer relationships with parents than did the early maturers. Apparently being closer to adulthood had outweighed the supposed disadvantage of being big in a culture where attractive females are supposed to be small. The study mentioned above, in which early, average, and late maturers were compared, yielded results for girls which were similar to findings for boys, but less pronounced. The investigators concluded that while there is some evidence that late maturing has some adverse effects on girls, rate of physical maturation is less salient in the personality development of girls than of boys [30].

Another approach was from the point of view of peers [17]. Girls in Grades 6 through 9 were tested to determine the effect of physical maturity on prestige. Sixth graders received high prestige ratings more frequently when they were in the same developmental phase as their classmates. That is, they had not reached menarche. In the following three grades, however, physical acceleration was an advantage in receiving prestige ratings. Here, then, is some explanation of the results of the study mentioned above, where physically accelerated 17-year-old girls had favorable self concepts. Their peers likewise held favorable concepts of such girls.

## Physical Characteristics

Relationships have been found between physical characteristics and various kinds of mental functions, although usually no causal relationship between the two is made clear. For example, height and weight are correlated with intelligence [5, 53, 57]. Examples of relationships between fitness and coordination measures come from the Medford Boy's Growth Study [11]. Boys who scored high on physical fitness measures at age 13 tended to be outgoing, enterprising, competitive, and successful at school while those rated high in motor ability were also active, ambitious, confident, alert, successful in schoolwork, and popular with teachers and peers. When boys of 12 and 15 years were divided into high and low groups on the basis of physical fitness but equated as to IQ, the high fitness group was superior on scholastic achievement tests and grades in school. Physical development, measured on the Wetzel Grid, was related to reading achievement [23].

One aspect of cognitive style seems to be related to physical development in college men and high school boys [8]. The aspect of cognitive style investigated was *automatization*, the ability to perform well on simple repetitive tasks. Various body dimensions were taken and the men rated for amount of body hair. The thickset, hairy, masculine-looking boys and men tended to do better than their opposites in tests of automatization. The strong automatizers must have had higher androgen levels than the men whose bodies were farther away from the extreme of masculinity, since androgens stimulate the development of male characteristics. This research gives no indication of whether the strong male physical characteristics cause strong automatizing or whether a more basic condition (such as a large androgen supply) is responsible for both the physical and mental characteristics.

These studies deal with only a few of the ways in which physical development can and might affect and be affected by an adolescent's attitudes toward himself and the world. The developmental factors, of course, interact with other events and conditions. For example, very creative people often have a history of a long illness during childhood. They also have such background factors as educated mothers who pursue interests of their own, leaving children free to think their own thoughts. A child socially isolated by physical illness, surrounded by cultural opportunities, mentally and emotionally free, would understandably experiment intellectually and imaginatively. Other examples can be drawn from the area of motor coordination. The social success of a football player is legendary, while the awkward boy shrinks from the dance floor to find solace as a ham radio operator.

## Summary

Adolescence, the period of changing from child to adult, is physical, psychological, and social. The sequence of physical changes which result in puberty (sexual maturity) takes place during pubescence. The timing and duration of pubescence varies between individuals and between the sexes, with girls, on the average, two years ahead of boys. Growth speeds up during pubescence, the peak in height velocity occurring about six months before puberty. Early maturers have a shorter, faster growth spurt than late maturers. Linear people tend to be late maturers, rounded people early maturers. The pubescent growth spurt and the developmental sequence of sexual characteristics are triggered and controlled by hormones from the pituitary, hypothalamus, and gonads. The timing of puberty and its antecedent changes seems to be largely genetic, although somewhat influenced by environmental factors.

Changes in proportions occur in the predictable sequence, since different parts of the body, including the viscera, reach their peak velocities at varying times during the pubescent growth spurt. Various sex differences increase, such as that of lung capacity. The primary and secondary sex characteristics develop in a sequence. Definite stages have been outlined for both sexes. Sexual feelings, especially those of boys, are heightened at puberty.

Physical needs include large amounts of food and rest, since this period is a time of rapid growth. The meeting of such needs is often inadequate because of the adolescent's insistence upon making his own decisions. Adolescents are relatively free from illness, although they may suffer from many health problems, such as acne, eye troubles, and diseased teeth. Accidents, especially motor vehicle accidents, cause a large proportion of the deaths and injuries during this time of life. Calorie needs are very large during adolescence. Nutritional problems include dietary deficiencies and obesity.

American children and adolescents were, and probably still are, inferior to European and Japanese in almost all tests of physical fitness. An outstanding lack in American physical education is in the area of endurance training. Good physical education has brought some youngsters up to the level of Europeans and has demonstrated methods of meeting the needs of Americans.

During the adolescent years, strength increases in the average boy but tapers off in the average American girl. A general test of motor development showed steady increases in boys and little change in girls. While boys are superior in speed of large muscle movements, such as running, a sex difference is not clear in manual speed. Athletic prowess is a great social asset to the boy and of minor importance to the girl.

Physical and psychological growth are interrelated in many ways. Physical phenomena interact with social, intellectual, and personality development. Physical appearance and adequacy are of great concern to the adolescent, since he is involved in building a sense of identity. Early maturers differ from late maturers in personality characteristics, as rated by others and as reported by boys and girls themselves. The former are more likely to have favorable self concepts.

## References

1. Angel, K. No marijuana for teenagers. New York: *New York Times Magazine*, November 30, 1969.
2. Araki, C. T. The effects of medicine ball activity on the upper body development of young boys. Unpublished Master's thesis, University of Illinois, 1960. Cited in Cureton [13].
3. Astrand, P. O. Experimental studies of physical working capacity in relation to sex and age. Copenhagen: Munksgard, 1952. Cited in Cureton [13].
4. Ausubel, D. P. *Theory and problems of adolescent development*. New York: Grune & Stratton, 1954.
5. Bayley, N. Individual patterns of development. *Child Devel.*, 1956, **27**, 45–74.
6. Blos, P. *On adolescence*. Glencoe, Ill.: Free Press, 1962.
7. Breckenridge, M. E., & Vincent, E. L. *Child development* (5th ed.). Philadelphia: Saunders, 1965.

8. Broverman, D. M., Broverman, I. K., Vogel, W., & Palmer, R. D. The automatization cognitive style and physical development. *Child Devel.*, 1964, **35**, 1343–1359.

9. Bullen, B. A., Monello, L. F., Cohen, H., & Mayer, J. Attitudes toward physical activity, food and family in obese and nonobese adolescent girls. *Am. J. Clin. Nutr.*, 1963, **12**, 1–11.

10. Campbell, W. R., & Pohndorf, R. H. Physical fitness of British and United States children. In *Report of conference on health and fitness in the modern world.* Chicago: Athletic Institute, 1961, pp. 8–16. Cited in Cureton [13].

11. Clarke, H. H. Contributions and implications of the Medford, Oregon, Boys' Growth Study. Unpublished manuscript. Eugene: University of Oregon, 1968.

12. Cobb, H. V. Role-wishes and general wishes of children and adolescents. *Child Devel.*, 1954, **25**, 161–171.

13. Cureton, T. K. Improving the physical fitness of youth. *Mono. Soc. Res. Child Devel.*, 1964, **29**:4.

14. Damon, A., Damon, S. T., Reed, R. B., & Valadian, I. Age at menarche of mothers and daughters, with a note on accuracy of recall. *Human Biol.*, 1969, **41**, 161–175.

15. Edson, L. $C_{21}$, $H_{23}$, $NO_5$—A primer for parents and children. *New York Times Magazine*, May 24, 1970, 92–95.

16. Espenschade, A. Motor performance in adolescence. *Mono. Soc. Res. Child Devel.*, 1940, **5**:1.

17. Faust, M. S. Developmental maturity as a determinant in prestige of adolescent girls. *Child Devel.*, 1960, **31**, 173–184.

18. Garn, S. M., & Haskell, J. A. Fat thickness and developmental status in childhood and adolescence. *Am. J. Dis. Child.*, 1960, **99**, 746–751.

19. Goss, A. M. Estimated versus actual physical strength in three ethnic groups. *Child Devel.*, 1968, **39**, 283–291.

20. Hampton, M. C., Shapiro, L. R., & Huenemann, R. L. Helping teen-age girls improve their diets. *J. Home Econ.*, 1961, **53**, 835–838.

21. Hiernaux, J. Ethnic differences in growth and development. *Eugenics Quart.*, 1968, **15**, 12–21.

22. Horn, D. Quoted in *Providence Evening Bulletin*, June 8, 1970.

23. Hurster, M., & Archer, M. Selected parameters of school achievement among urban adolescents: A study in four New York City junior high schools. *J. School Health*, 1967, **37**(10), 511–518.

24. Jersild, A. T. *The psychology of adolescence.* New York: Macmillan, 1957.

25. Jersild, A. T., & Bienstock, S. F. A study of the development of children's ability to sing. *J. Educ. Psychol.*, 1935, **25**, 481–503.

26. Johnson, M. L., Burke, B. S., & Mayer, J. Relative importance of inactivity and overeating in the energy balance of obese high school girls. *Am. J. Clin. Nutr.*, 1956, **4**, 37–44.

27. Jones, K. L., Shainberg, L. W., & Beyer, C. O. *Drugs and alcohol.* New York: Harper & Row, 1969.

28. Jones, M. C. Psychological correlates of somatic development. *Child Devel.*, 1965, **36**, 899–911.

29. Jones, M. C., & Bayley, N. Physical maturing among boys as related to behavior. *J. Educ. Psychol.*, 1950, **41**, 129–148.

30. Jones, M. C., & Mussen, P. H. Self-conceptions, motivations and interper-

sonal attitudes of early- and late-maturing girls. *Child Devel.*, 1958, **29**, 491–501.

31. Kinsey, A. C., Pomeroy, W. B., Martin, C. E., & Gebhard, P. H. *Sexual behavior in the human male*. Philadelphia: Saunders, 1948.

32. Kinsey, A. C., Pomeroy, W. B., Martin, C. E., & Gebhard, P. H. *Sexual behavior in the human female*. Philadelphia: Saunders, 1953.

33. Lerner, R. M. The development of stereotyped expectancies of body build-behavior relations. *Child Devel.*, 1969, **40**, 137–141.

34. Levitt, E. E., & Edwards, J. A. A multivariate study of correlative factors in youthful cigaret smoking. *Devel. Psychol.*, 1970, **2**, 5–11.

35. McKennell, A. C., & Bynner, J. M. Self images and smoking behavior among school boys. *Brit. J. Educ. Psychol.*, 1969, **39**, 27–39.

36. Meredith, H. V. Human foot length from embryo to adult. *Human Biol.*, 1944, **16**, 207–282.

37. Metropolitan Life Insurance Company. The causes of premature death. *Stat. Bull.*, 1961, **42**:5, 9–11.

38. Metropolitan Life Insurance Company. Patterns of venereal disease morbidity in recent years. *Stat. Bull.*, 1969, **50**, 5–7.

39. Montagu, M. F. A. *Adolescent sterility*. Springfield, Ill.: Charles C Thomas, 1946.

40. Mussen, P. H., & Jones, M. C. Self-conceptions, motivations and interpersonal attitudes of late- and early-maturing boys. *Child Devel.*, 1957, **28**, 243–256.

41. National Academy of Sciences, National Research Council. *Pre-school child malnutrition*, 1966. Washington, D.C.

42. National Dairy Council. Natural history of obesity: Infancy through adolescence. *Dairy Council. Dig.*, 1968, **39**:1, 1–4.

43. Noguchi, Y. A comparative study of motor fitness between Japanese and American youth. Tokyo: Ministry of Education, 1960. Cited in Cureton [13].

44. Rauh, J. L., Schumsky, D. A., & Witt, M. T. Heights, weights and obesity in urban school children. *Child Devel.*, 1967, **38**, 515–530.

45. Rhode Island State Department of Health. R. I. showing an increase in syphilis. *Providence Evening Bulletin*, June 24, 1970.

46. Rodahl, K., Astrand, P. O., Birkhead, N. C., Hettinger, T., Issekutz, B., Jones, D. M., & Weaver, R. Physical work capacity. *Arch. Environ. Health*, 1961, **2**, 499–510. Cited in Cureton [13].

47. Sabharwal, K. P., Morales, S., & Mendes, J. Body measurement and creatinine excretion among upper and lower socio-economic groups of girls in Guatemala. *Human Biol.*, 1966, **38**, 131–140.

48. Schwartz, J. L. A critical review and evaluation of smoking control methods. *Pub. Health Rep.*, 1969, **84**, 483–506.

49. Scrimshaw, N. S., & Gordon, J. E. (Eds.). *Malnutrition, learning and behavior*. Cambridge, Mass.: M.I.T. Press, 1968.

50. Sebald, H. *Adolescence: A sociological analysis*. New York: Appleton-Century-Crofts, 1968.

51. Sheldon, W. H., & Tucker, W. B. *The varieties of human physique*. New York: Harper, 1940.

52. Shilo, I. Seker al hathalat haveset ben benot batey hasefer birushalayim. [Survey on the age of menarche in school pupils in Jerusalem.] *Harefual*, 1960, **59**, 305–307. *Psychol. Abs.*, **37**:952.

53. Shuttleworth, F. K. The physical and mental growth of girls and boys age six to nineteen in relation to age at maximum growth. *Mono. Soc. Res. Child Devel.*, 1939, **4**:3.

54. Stefanik, P. A., Heald, P. F., & Mayer, J. Calorie intake in relation to energy output of obese and nonobese adolescent boys. *Am. J. Clin. Nutr.*, 1959, **7**:55.

55. Stewart, L., & Livson, N. Smoking and rebelliousness: A longitudinal study from childhood to maturity. *J. Consult. Psychol.*, 1966, **30**, 225–229.

56. Tanner, J. M. *Education and physical growth*. London: University of London, 1961.

57. Tanner, J. M. *Growth at adolescence* (2nd ed.). Oxford: Blackwell, 1962.

58. Tanner, J. M. Earlier maturation in man. *Sci. Am.*, 1968, **218**, 21–27.

59. United States Public Health Service. *Smoking and Health*. Washington, D.C.: Public Health Service Publication No. 1103, 1964.

60. Valadian, I., Stuart, H. C., & Reed, R. B. Studies of illnesses of children followed from birth to eighteen years. *Mono. Soc. Res. Child Devel.*, 1961, **26**:3.

61. Walter, W. G. Electroencephalographic development of children. In J. M. Tanner & B. Inhelder (Eds.), *Discussions on child development*. Vol. I. New York: International Universities, 1953.

62. Watson, E. H., & Lowrey, G. H. *Growth and development of children* (5th ed.). Chicago: Year book, 1967.

63. Weatherley, D. Self-perceived rate of physical maturation and personality in late adolescence. *Child Devel.*, 1964, **35**, 1197–1210.

64. Young, H. B. Biological and chronological age. Paper presented at the meeting of the Society for Research in Child Development, April 12, 1963.

65. Zacharias, L., & Wurtman, R. J. Age at menarche. *New England J. Med.*, 1969, **280**, 868–875.

66. Zinberg, N. E. Facts and fantasies about drug addiction. In R. E. Grinder (Ed.). *Studies in adolescents*. New York: Macmillan, 1969.

# Chapter 14

Robert J. Izzo

# Intellectual Development

Psychological growth is just as dramatic as physical growth at the beginning of adolescence. Between 12 and 14 years, on the average, thought processes are reorganized on a higher level, making the adolescent as different from the school-age child as the school-age child is different from the preschool child. The new level of thinking, formal thought, is not the automatic result of accumulated years any more than the transition from sensorimotor to preoperational intelligence is automatic. New schemas result from the child's using what he has already to interact with the environment. His achievements depend upon his own resources and what the environment offers. Some adolescents, therefore, go further than others in building and using the structures of formal thought. Some individuals never achieve formal thought.

## The Stage of Formal Thought or Logical Operations

Each new stage in thinking brings greater freedom and stronger control in intellectual operations. The stage of formal thinking carries the greatest mobility of all the stages. The infant is confined to his own sensory perceptions and motor acts of the immediate present. The preschool child uses words and symbols to represent actions and perceptions, thus speeding up his dealings with the world, but he is still confined largely to individual objects and events. Egocentric in that he is tied to one perception or another, his thought is not free and mobile enough to weigh and balance various aspects of an experience with each other and with other knowledge. The school-age child's thought is free in that he can delay response while considering and judging much information. He can also think an act and then think it undone, since thought is reversible at this age. The adolescent excels him, however, in freedom, control, elaboration, and completeness of thought.

### Characteristics of Adolescent Thinking

The distinctive characteristics of thinking in the stage of formal operations, as compared with previous stages, can be summarized under the following headings:

**Freedom, Mobility, and Flexibility.** The adolescent can think in terms of abstract symbols, instead of having to base his thought on concrete things and events. He is thus freed from restraints of time and space, able to range throughout the universe, entertaining concepts with which he has had no real experience, such as the notion of infinity. Thus he is free to move in his thoughts and he is flexible, free to move in any direction. He does not get stuck with his perceptions, as does the preschool child, or stuck with his conclusions, as does the school-age child. A child–adolescent difference in flexibility of thought is demonstrated by a concept–production task [8]. Fourth grade and ninth grade subjects were asked to tell how a shoehorn, a table knife, and a pair of scissors were alike. Half of each group saw real objects and half were given the names verbally. The older group produced significantly more concepts than the younger (4.71 versus 2.88). For the adolescents, it made little difference whether the stimuli were given in concrete or verbal form but for the fourth grade children it made a large difference. The younger subjects gave over twice as many similarities when the objects were presented as they did when the verbal labels were given. Thus the younger children's thinking was more dependent upon perception than was the adolescents'. Further study [9] showed that adolescents could shift more readily than could children in their mode of conceptualizing.

**Control.** Formal thinking requires strict control of thought. Similar to the child's achievement of considering more than one perception before acting, but much more complex, the adolescent's achievement includes keeping himself from being distracted by irrelevant thoughts, taking account of all premises or pertinent information, holding all aspects in mind while considering one, organizing information, relating it and reflecting on all aspects of the situation before concluding.

One particular facet of the abstract attitude which distinguishes the stage of concrete operations from formal operations is this: the adolescent can think about his own thinking; the child cannot. Here, then, is another step away from ego-centrism and toward mobility of thought, to be able to stand off and reflect upon one's own intellectual activity. This is to be truly self-conscious, a complex, differentiated being.

Logical thought involves starting with the premises or what is given, neither adding to it nor subtracting from it, and reasoning with that information. For example:

Blonde hair turns green on St. Patrick's Day.
Bertha has colored her hair blonde.
It will turn green on St. Patrick's Day.

When asked if the last statement is true, the person employing formal thought would say *yes*. The person not thinking formally would probably say, "Blonde hair does not turn green on St. Patrick's Day. I've never seen it happen," or perhaps, "Bertha's wouldn't turn green, anyway, because it isn't really blonde." Piaget [29] places the change to formal thinking at around 11 or 12. Below 12, he says, children rarely solve this problem:

Edith is fairer than Susan.
Edith is darker than Lily.
Who is the darkest of the three?

Until then, they give such answers as, "Edith and Susan are fair, Edith and Lily are dark; therefore Lily is darkest, Susan is fairest and Edith in between."

In her study of children's thinking, Donaldson [6] found that between 12 and 14, children increased sharply in being able and willing to accept the given conditions and to reason within them, but even the sharp increase did not mean that a child *always* reasoned formally. She tells of Robin, when faced with this problem:

Five boys, Jack, Dick, James, Bob and Tom go to five different schools
in the same town. The schools are called North School, South School,
East School, West School and Central School.
Jack does not go to North, South or Central School.
Dick goes to West School.
Bob does not go to North or Central School.
Tom has never been inside Central School.
What school does Jack go to? What school does Bob go to?
What school does James go to?
What school does Tom go to?

Robin eliminated North, South, and Central to deduce that Jack went to East or West. He then apparently could not see how to combine the negative information about Jack with the positive statement about Dick. "You would have to find out the district he was in," Robin suggested. Unable to deal with the problem as stated, he added his own experience. He knew that children usually went to schools near their own homes and so pulled in this information with disregard for the premises as given. Donaldson says that difficulty in solving a problem increases the tendency to ignore premises.

Flexibility and control of intellectual operations increased between ages 12 and 14 in an experiment on concept formation [47]. Each problem, consisting of a series of slides, required an answer of a single attribute, such as *black* or *cross*. It was possible to get the right answer after the first four slides. Each successive cycle of three slides gave enough information for solution. Results showed significant differences between the 12-year-olds and 14-year-olds, but not between the 14-year-olds and 16-year-olds. The 12-year-olds gave answers not in accord with the im-mediately previous slide, showing that they were less efficient than the older subjects in dealing with information given directly. The younger subjects were less able to remember their previous guesses in order to check them with current information. They were less able to maintain their guesses when current information confirmed them and less able to change their guesses when current information did not confirm them. The older subjects, both 14-year-olds and 16-year-olds, more readily held or changed their guesses in the light of all previous information.

**Explanation of Phenomena.** While the school-age child feels satisfied after he has *described* something, an adolescent explains it [28]. Description means relating the parts of a phenomenon with each other; explanation means relating the phenomenon and its parts to other phenomena. For example, take the physics experiment of boiling water in a tin, sealing, and cooling the tin. The child will describe the collapse of the tin. The adolescent is more likely to try to explain what he saw, relating it to a vacuum being produced and atmospheric pressure acting on the tin. He will attempt to make as complete an explanation as he can, possibly invoking concepts of boiling, gaseous state, condensation, vacuum, pressure, and strength.

**Consideration of What Is Possible.** "The adolescent is the person who commits himself to possibilities . . . who begins to build 'systems' or 'theories' in the largest sense of the term" [16, p. 339]. The child is concerned with *what is*, the adolescent with *what is plus what could be*. The relationship between the real and the possible is new in adolescent thinking, as compared with childish thinking. In formal thinking, the individual uses a system to discover all possible combinations or relationships and to make sure that he *has* found them all. He uses a system to establish a rule, from which he can make predictions. By 14 or 15, according to Inhelder and Piaget, the adolescent can use the combinatorial system. That is, he varies one factor at a time, keeping all other things equal, and determines the effect of one factor. This method, of course, is the essence of research.

The following account of one of Piaget's experiments [11] demonstrates the difference between a 7-year-old and a 13-year-old in tackling a problem in chemistry. The younger child's approach was relatively unsystematized. He took the perceptually salient element and combined it successively with each of the other elements. The older child set about systematically to try all possible combinations of elements.*

> In experiment I, the child is given four similar flasks containing colorless, odorless liquids which are perceptually identical. We number them: (1) diluted sulphuric acid; (2) water; (3) oxygenated water; (4) thiosulphate; we add a bottle (with a dropper) which we call *g*; it contains potassium iodide. It is known that oxygenated water oxidizes potassium iodide in an acid medium. Thus mixture (1 + 3 + *g*) will yield a yellow color. The water (2) is neutral, so that adding it will not change the color, whereas the thiosulphate (4) will bleach the mixture (1 + 3 + *g*). The experimenter presents to the subject two glasses, one containing 1 + 3, the other containing 2. In front of the subject, he pours several drops of *g* in each of the two glasses and notes the different reactions. Then the subject is asked simply to reproduce the color yellow, using flasks 1, 2, 3, 4 and *g* as he wishes [Inhelder and Piaget, 1958, pp. 108–109].

The two behavior protocols which follow illustrate the kinds of concrete-formal differences we have been discussing:

> **Ren** (7;1) tries 4 × *g*, then 2 × *g*, and 3 × *g*: *"I think I did everything . . . I tried them all."*—"What else could you have done?"—*"I*

---

* From Flavell's *The Developmental Psychology of Jean Piaget*, Copyright 1963, D. Van Nostrand Company, Inc., Princeton, N.J. Reprinted by permission.

*don't know."* We give him the glasses again: he repeats 1 × *g*, etc.—
"You took each bottle separately. What else could you have done?"—
*"Take two bottles at the same time"* [he tries 1 × 4 × *g*, then 2 × 3 × *g*,
thus failing to cross over between the two sets (of bottles), for example,
1 × 2, 1 × 3, 2 × 4, and 3 × 4].—When we suggest that he add
others, he puts 1 × *g* in the glass already containing 2 × 3 which results
in the appearance of the color: "Try to make the color again."—*"Do I
put in two or three?* [he tries with 2 × 4 × *g*, then adds 3, then tries it
with 1 × 4 × 2 × *g*]. *No, I don't remember any more,"* etc. [*ibid.*,
p. 111].

      **Cha** (13;0): *"You have to try with all the bottles. I'll begin with the
one at the end.* [from 1 to 4 with *g*]. *It doesn't work any more. Maybe you
have to mix them* [he tries 1 × 2 × *g*, then 1 × 3 × *g*]. *It turned yellow.
But are there other solutions? I'll try* [1 × 4 × *g*; 2 × 3 × *g*; 2 × 4 × *g*;
3 × 4 × *g*; with the two preceding combinations this gives the six
two-by-two combinations systematically.] *It doesn't work. It only
works with"* [1 × 3 × *g*].—"Yes, and what about 2 and 4?"—*"2 and 4
don't make any color together. They are negative. Perhaps you could
add 4 in 1 × 3 × g to see if it would cancel out the color* [he does this].
*Liquid 4 cancels it all. You'd have to see if 2 has the same influence* [he
tries it]. *No, so 2 and 4 are not alike, for 4 acts on 1 × 3 and 2 does not."*
—"What is there in 2 and 4?"—*"In 4 certainly water. No, the opposite,
in 2 certainly water since it doesn't act on the liquids; that makes things
clearer."*—"And if I were to tell you that 4 is water?"—*"If this liquid 4 is
water, when you put it with 1 × 3 it wouldn't completely prevent the
yellow from forming. It isn't water, it's something harmful"* [*ibid.*,
p. 117].

Between 11 or 12 years and 14 or 15 years, adolescents progress in being able to
set up tests for their hypotheses and to discard those hypotheses which do not fit
the facts [28]. In addition to being able to try out all possible combinations systematically, the formal thinker realizes that hypotheses are arbitrary. He can think of
a possible explanation and then think of another, discarding one as it is found
wanting. The child, in contrast, is likely to get trapped by his own hypotheses
because when he thinks of an explanation, he tends to think that he has settled the
matter. Thinking it has made it a reality to him. The adolescent hangs onto the
fact that it was a thought and therefore reversible and replaceable. He can entertain
the idea that an hypothesis is possibly right or probably right, seek new evidence,
weigh it and change the degree of probability of correctness, hang on again and
look for further information. Because he can control his thought processes, he can
delay conclusions while considering possibilities. Because he is mobile and flexible
in thought, he can discover the possibilities to weigh.

### Time Orientation

The ability to delay before responding to a problem is correlated with success in
solving certain kinds of problems. Being able to delay immediate gratification in
order to achieve more gain and pleasure in the future is an aspect of *future orientation*. While different cultures vary in time orientation, Americans generally esteem
future orientation as an attitude necessary for achievement. American children
become more future-oriented as they mature, as shown by an analysis of stories
written in response to pictures [20]. Subjects included five age groups: school
children, adolescents, college students, businessmen, and senior citizens. There was
an age trend up to college age, adolescents being more future-oriented than children, and college students more than adolescents. The adults were less future-
oriented than the adolescents and college students. Future orientation is correlated

with certain personality dimensions. Indices of adjustment are related to future time orientation in adolescence [17].

Future orientation of Dutch students changed with increasing age between 14 and 21 [24]. The younger ones were mostly concerned with themselves in the future, while the oldest subjects were involved with the general future as well as the personal. The investigator was surprised at how realistic all these students were and also noted their self-confidence. Boys were concerned with a greater number of areas of future life than were girls. High achievers, also, had a characteristically broad range of future involvements. Apprehension about the future increased with age and with range of future interests.

**Disturbances in Time Orientation**. During adolescence a mild diffusion of time perspective is common, according to Erikson [10, p. 169]. The young person feels a sense of urgency and yet acts as though time were of no importance. He finds it hard to start and stop activities, to go to bed, to get up, to get his work done. Eventual coming to terms with time is essential for the development of a sense of integrity, which means accepting one's place in time and space, one's own particular life cycle [10, p. 139]. Perhaps problems of time are more significant today than they ever have been before, because of the ever-present possibility of annihilation of mankind. Enabled by his cognitive growth to consider a new time perspective, the adolescent may become intrigued with the overwhelming importance of the present moment or the mysterious joys of merging with an eternal entity. Leary [19] the prophet of the psychedelic way of life, urges young people to bend time to their own immediate pleasure, slowing their perception of it through chemical control of their brains.

### Prevalence of Formal or Abstract Thinking

Nobody performs constantly at his highest level. An adolescent who is capable of formal thought does not apply it at all times and in all places.

Even though a person can think logically, there is no guarantee that he will do so. Grandparents notoriously stray from the facts when describing their grandchildren. An overweight person is all too likely to draw unwarranted conclusions about why his diet did not work. A study of thinking in adults [44] demonstrated flights from logic among a group of people who might be expected to respect premises more than the average person. The subjects were professors and other highly educated men. They were asked to draw conclusions from a set of statements and to discuss the compatibility of the statements. The answers revealed many instances of men telling what they thought about the statements themselves. The tendency to stray from the premises increased in men over 35 years of age, suggesting that this aspect of logical thinking is not stable after being established.

When children are in the process of moving from the stage of concrete operations into the stage of formal thought, their achievements differ from one area to another. Transition into the higher level is not a sudden, all-or-none event, but a gradual working through, in the various subject matter areas. Seventh grade and tenth grade students were tested on acquisition and application of concepts from science, social studies, and literature [36]. The two grades were similar on acquisition, which represents a lower level type of understanding, probably including rote learning. The tenth grade was definitely superior on application, which requires more abstract understanding. Intercorrelations between tests of application in the three areas were significantly higher for tenth grade students. That is, seventh graders were unevenly developed across subject matter areas, in regard to formal thinking, but tenth graders had achieved some consistency as to formal thinking in the three areas. This finding has educational implications for the junior high school, where a student is likely to be able to do abstract thinking in one area but not in another.

**Use of Different Types of Concepts in Classifying.** The development of concept usage was explored in children and adolescents, using a series of classifying tasks [3]. Each choice was from five categories: color, shape, relational function (e.g., bat and ball), homogeneous function (e.g., bat and hammer), and abstract function (e.g., bat and deck of cards). The first two represent perceptual bases of classifying; the last three, logical. Adolescents used all five categories of concepts. The use of relational concepts increased steadily up to age 11 and then leveled off. Use of homogeneous and abstract concepts increased throughout childhood and adolescence.

**Formal Thought and IQ.** Both chronological age and mental age are related to acquisition of abstract thinking. Boys of average intelligence made significant gains in formal thinking between 12 and 14 years, while those below average made their greatest gains between 14 and 16 [46]. The group superior in intelligence were already using logical operations at age 12 and made increases between 12 and 16.

**Rural–Urban Contrasts.** As a child is growing up, he builds his cognitive structures in response to the demands and opportunities offered by his culture. A peasant village and an industrialized setting in Mexico were the sites of an investigation in which rural and urban children were compared in cognitive style [21]. In order to see what type of concepts 12- and 13-year-olds would form, this array of items was used: banana, orange, bean, meat, milk, air, fire, and stone. The first two items were presented and the child was asked, "How are a banana and an orange similar?" Then, "How is a bean different from an orange and a banana?" Next, "How are a bean, a banana, and an orange alike?" Then another item was added and the two questions asked and so on to the last item, the stone, where only the difference was asked. The response style most typical of the village children was one concerned with concrete reality. This peasant type tells differences accurately but is likely to fail at explaining similarities, not because he cannot do so but because he does not choose to do so. Similarity to him means almost exact likeness, such as between two oranges. An example of the *concrete* style of thinking is this response to the first four items, "All of them can be eaten but they are not alike because meat is not round nor is it like a banana or a bean." This type of child is not interested in similarities but in the uniqueness of things. The type most characteristic of urban children, although it by no means included all of them, was called *abstract*. In telling how things were similar, they classified them abstractly, either by name or by function. An intermediate type, *concrete–abstract*, included both village and city children but more of the latter. This type was likely to use functions and names for telling similarities, moving from concrete to abstract as the tasks became more difficult. They tended to use concrete, perceptual terms when the problem could be answered adequately by such methods.

The cognitive style of children is thus consistent with the demands of the culture. Peasant children, like peasant societies, are concerned with concrete reality and perceptible attributes and with differentiation and not equivalence. Urban children, like industrialized societies, can easily move away from their perceptions to organize their experiences into abstract classifications. The differences noted here are probably significant in understanding the difficulties peasants have in moving into an industrialized society.

### Thinking about Thinking

The adolescent develops the ability to think about his own thinking and about the thinking of other people.

**The Thoughts of Others.** "I wonder what he is thinking of me. I wonder what he thinks I am thinking about him. I wonder what he thinks I think he is thinking about me." This kind of thinking develops in adolescence, with slight beginnings in childhood and an upswing around 11 and 12 years of age [23]. More of the children tested were capable of the first thought than the second. The third statement implies even more complex thinking.

The ability to think about the thoughts of others enables the adolescent to construct an imaginary audience for himself [7]. He gets the feeling of being the focus of attention, being on-stage. When he is critical of himself, he imagines his audience as critical, also. When he is self-admiring, his audience admires him. He often imagines other people as having thoughts which they do not have and which are, in reality, his own. Herein lies the basis of egocentrism in adolescence: failing to distinguish between his own thoughts, feelings, and wishes and those of others. The loud, show-off, faddish behavior of an adolescent group is easier to understand when one realizes that every member is both actor and audience. The ability to imagine the thoughts of others is also the basis for the sense of intimacy, which develops in late adolescence. As the adolescent differentiates more and more between other people's thoughts and his own, he interprets theirs more realistically.

Another result of confusing his own thoughts with those of other people is that he develops magnificent ideas about how society can and should be improved. He assumes that his fellow citizens want these improvements and makes vague plans for his own future which encompass the changes. Thus he does not distinguish between his own point of view as a person organizing his future and the point of view of the social group to which he belongs [16, pp. 343–345].

The mobility of thought achieved in the formal period is what empowers the adolescent to think of many possibilities for his own future and for transforming society. Instead of being tied to the concrete aspects of reality, to *what is*, he can soar out into the realm of the possible. Thus an adolescent is able to fuse (or confuse) two viewpoints *because* a new level of thinking has been achieved. This kind of egocentrism disappears gradually as the young person assumes adult roles, especially the work role in a real job. When he meets the realities of dealing with the society which he has considered reforming, he learns the difference between what he can actually do, what he wishes could happen, and what society wants.

This special kind of adolescent thinking is very enduring in Western culture. Adults expect young people to be idealistic and impractical in their dreams of remaking the world. There is general belief that this type of thought has value for both the adolescent and society, in opening up possibilities for his future development and for social innovations.

**His Own Thoughts.** The young adolescent, in the early stages of awareness of himself as a thinking being, often regards himself, particularly his feelings, as very special and unique [7]. His imaginary audience probably contributes to this notion. Sometimes the conviction of personal uniqueness results in a "personal fable," expressed in a very private diary, a personal relationship with God, a belief that one cannot die or that one cannot become pregnant. The personal fable, along with grandiose schemes for improving society, is gradually transformed into more manageable proportions. As the adolescent differentiates the thoughts of others from his own, he also becomes able to regard his own thinking more objectively. As thought grows more mobile and flexible, he can stand off and look at himself as a person. He can consider himself as a physical specimen, as a person-among-persons, as an intellectual being or as a person in any one of the numerous roles he plays—son, friend, sweetheart, student, and so on. He sees himself as a person-in-relation.

Discovery of oneself, as a person to be thought about objectively, is sometimes experienced as coming rather suddenly. A psychiatrist's study of Vassar girls [25] showed a crisis of self-discovery to be common between the years of 15 and 18. A crisis of independence was often closely related to the crisis of self-discovery. The former had to do with emancipation from parents and getting established in adult roles, the latter with revelations about identity. Often involved were feelings about parents, siblings, peers, self, and sexuality. One girl likened her self-discovery to the appearance of a third eye, with which she could see herself. Another could remember not thinking about herself in this way and then becoming able to do so when she was in junior high school. The girls showed an urgency to grow psychologically and made rapid progress in solving their problems.

Self-cognition makes it possible for the adolescent to see himself as continuous with the child he once was, how he differs and how he is the same. He can see his continuity with the adult that he is becoming. He can look at himself in the ways in which other people and the community see him. Integrating all of this information and all of these points of view, he strengthens his sense of identity. At the same time, he begins to grow beyond the limits of adolescent thinking as he differentiates between his own plans and hopes and those of his social group.

## Language Development

Used for both communication and thinking, language power expands with growth of vocabulary, facility in expression and understanding, elaboration of concepts, and adoption of the symbolic organization which the culture offers.

### Increase in Vocabulary

The number of words understood far exceeds the number used in speech. When children were given a recognition vocabulary test, the average number of words understood in Grade 1 was 23,700, with a range from 6000 to 48,000, and in Grade 12, 80,300, with a range from 36,700 to 136,500. Figure 14–1 shows results of this study for Grades 2 through 11, indicating the steady rise in number of words understood. In a study which dealt with university students, their recognition vocabulary was estimated at an average of 156,000 words [35]. Vocabulary continues to grow throughout the life span [31].

To figure out how many words an adolescent actually uses is an almost impossible task. An estimate of the average English child's vocabulary at age 14 is between 8000 and 10,000 words, a number similar to estimates made for American

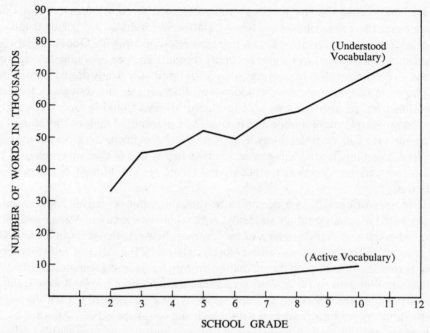

**Figure 14–1.** Average sizes of understood vocabulary and active vocabulary (estimated) at various ages.
SOURCES: M. K. Smith [35] and A. F. Watts [43].

children [43]. Between 7 and 14, the English child is judged to increase his vocabulary by about 700 words a year. The increase from 14 to 20 averages about 10,000 words, resulting in an adult vocabulary of 18,000 to 20,000 words.

A particular kind of vocabulary develops during adolescence, especially in subcultures of crime and delinquency. *Argot* is the term for the special words devised and used by participants in these cultures and, to a certain extent, by other adolescents as well. Knowledge of argot increases during adolescence. This is one vocabulary test on which boys score higher than girls.

## Elaboration of Concepts

Many words have fuller and more abstract meanings for adolescents than for younger children. When asked to define words, the more complete definitions of adolescents indicate the more complex thought processes at work. Formal thought tries to take account of all possibilities inherent in the situation. Hence a word definition must encompass all meanings of the word. A child might say "Poverty means you're hungry"; an adolescent might say, "Poverty is a state of being without desirable goods and/or qualities." Interpretations of pictures, like definitions of words, show a progression from concrete to abstract and from limited to complete as the child progresses through the stages of thinking. The preschool child names objects ("Dog, mommy, basket"), the school-age child describes the picture by relating some of the elements ("The lady is chasing the dog. The dog has a shirt in his mouth.") The adolescent interprets the picture ("It's washday. The lady's cross at the dog for running off with the clean clothes. The dog is only playing.")

*Relation of Language to Thinking*

Through language, experience is put into symbolic form, in which it can be manipulated and processed by methods which other people use. The individual gets from his social group these methods of dealing with his experience. He gets them through the use of language, and he uses language to check back on his experiences, their results and meanings. While most people are capable of taking methods of thinking from their culture, few contribute new methods to their fellow men. For example, many students are capable of understanding and using calculus, but few will invent a comparable method of organizing data.

The relationship between thought and speech which adolescents achieve includes three functions: external speech, inner speech, and thought, according to Vygotsky, the Russian authority on thought and language. External speech is usually interwoven with thought, although it can occur without thought. Inner speech, derived from both external speech and thought, can be simply silent reciting, but rarely is just that. It can be largely thinking in pure meanings, but is not just that. "It is a dynamic, shifting, unstable thing, fluttering between word and thought ..." [41, p. 149].

Thought itself does not have to be put into words. Sometimes a thought cannot be put into words. There are no units of thought, unlike speech, which has words as units. A thought is global, present at one time, but to be expressed in speech, it has to be developed in a succession of words. Vygotsky has likened a thought to a cloud shedding words. Words rarely express the whole thought, since a thought has a feeling and willing part to it. These subtle aspects are communicated somewhat through words, but largely through gesture, intonation, and context.

*Written Language*

Style of writing is in part a product of choice of language. It is also an expression of personality characteristics. An analysis of stories written by high school junior girls and girls of 19 and 20 years of age shows definite age-level differences [38]. The high school girls were more flamboyant in their writing, showing melodramatic, personal self-expression. "She seems to enjoy letting herself go, using many 'exclamation point' statements and naive clichés." The older girls wrote much more objectively, in controlled or constricted style. "She tends to an Olympian of dispassionate stance and often sounds like a rather condescending bluestocking." The age-level difference held across social class and education. The more abstract thinking of the older adolescent is thus reflected in her writing.

# Creativity

Just as inner speech flutters between word and thought, so does thought itself shift between controlled thinking and fantasy or imaginative thinking. Adolescence sees a resurgency of imagination in many forms. Having greater control over his intellectual processes, the adolescent can move more rapidly and easily between purposeful thinking and fantasy. Unlike the preschool child who loses himself in a dramatic role, the adolescent can imagine himself into a role and then stand off to observe himself in it.

While creativity is the breath of life to the preschool child, the school-age child is concerned with industry, duty, and accomplishment, with matters of fact, with learning what reality is and how to cope with it. The adolescent, thinking about what is possible, not just what is, creates new situations and original solutions in his imagination.

### Creative Thinking

There are many definitions and concepts of creative thinking. It can be discussed in terms of process or product. For example, considering flexibility of thought is focusing on process while evaluating the uniqueness or usefulness of a solution is judging in terms of product. Creativity can also be studied in terms of the individuals who have made products recognized as creative works.

One well-known approach to understanding creative thinking is that of Guilford [14], who categorizes abilities underlying creative thinking. He distinguishes between divergent thinking and convergent thinking. The first produces new answers, selecting them from an indefinite number of answers which might fit; the second finds the one right answer. Although much of creative thinking is divergent, some convergent thinking is necessary, too. Sometimes in the course of producing an original solution, one has to ask and answer a question that has only one right answer. Factors in divergent verbal thinking include fluency, flexibility, and elaboration. Fluency includes easy recall of information, words that fit certain classes, words or phrases that make certain relationships (such as opposites) and producing connected discourse in phrases or sentences. One type of flexibility, called adaptive flexibility, involves turning old interpretations into new ones, such as thinking up a number of clever titles. For example, a clever title for "The Fox and the Grapes" was "The Fox Griped About the Grapes." Elaboration means building up or rounding out what is given. The flexibility, fluency, and elaboration factors just mentioned had to do with verbal information. Other parallel factors, according to Guilford, pertain to visual and symbolic information. Some people are creative verbally, others artistically, and still others mathematically.

Other tests of creativity have been devised by Torrance [39], who has done extensive testing for creativity from kindergarten through college. He has used verbal and nonverbal tasks to measure fluency, flexibility, and originality. Chapter 10 reported a study in which different levels of creativity and IQ were compared [42]. Similar studies have been conducted on adolescents, although they reported on limited types of combinations of IQ and creativity scores [13]. When a large range of IQ is studied, as from 62 to 150, it has been found that with a low IQ, scores on creative tests are also low, but when IQ is high, there is a wide range of performance on creative tests [15]. The most gifted people, the greatest producers and contributors, are usually those who are high in both intelligence and creativity.

### Characteristics of Creative Individuals

Studies on creative people usually show them to be high in flexibility, fluency, drive, involvement, openness, curiosity, autonomy, independence of judgment, self-confidence, self-acceptance, humor, empathy, desire for complexity, and easy tolerance of ambiguity. Characteristics related to low creativity rather than high include rigidity, premature judgment, defensiveness, contentedness, gentleness, conservatism, patience, virtuousness, and concern for others [1, 30].

Cognitive behavior was explored in two very different groups of 16-year-old

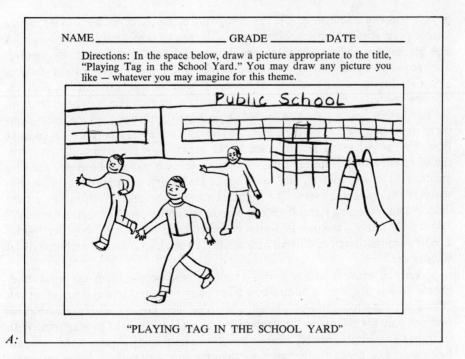

"PLAYING TAG IN THE SCHOOL YARD"

A:

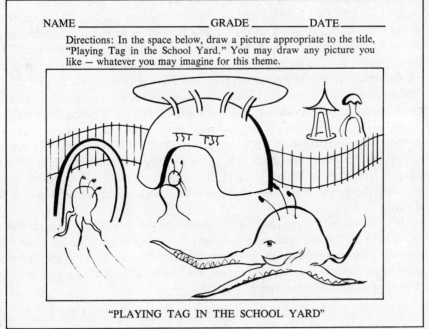

"PLAYING TAG IN THE SCHOOL YARD"

B:

**Figure 14–2.** *A:* Drawing by a High-IQ student. *B:* The same topic, drawn by a High Creative student.

SOURCE: Redrawn by permission from J. W. Getzels and P. W. Jackson, *Creativity and Intelligence.* New York: John Wiley & Sons, Inc. 1962. Copyright © 1962, John Wiley & Sons, Inc.

boys of superior intelligence [5]. The first group consisted of students in a summer science program for high school students in the top 10 percent of their classes, with high grades in mathematics and science. These boys, then, were potentially creative. The second group was made up of a summer remedial program for bright students who were failing in high school. The subjects were shown two series of pictures. The first started with a boy and changed slightly with each successive picture until the last, which was a girl. The second series began with one showing ambiguous parts and ended with a complete picture. The high achievers changed their concept from boy to girl at an earlier point in the series, showing greater flexibility of thought. They took a longer time to respond to each picture, however, showing greater reflectivity, control, and tolerance of ambiguity, as opposed to the impulsivity of the underachievers. The high achievers elaborated much more in their descriptions, changing terms from one picture to another, such as saying "athlete," "dancer," "queer," in contrast to the underachievers repeating, "boy" or "girl." The two groups therefore differed in flexibility, control, tolerance of ambiguity, and elaboration.

A study of creative artists points out that these people often see what other people do not observe, in addition to what people ordinarily see. They often call attention vividly to unnoticed phenomena, using their powers of accurate observation not only for their own satisfaction but also for the benefit of mankind. With their greater mental capacity, creative people can hold many ideas at once, compare more ideas and hence synthesize more than the ordinary person. Often extremely vigorous, both mentally and physically, they lead complex lives, in touch with a complex universe. They contact and use the unconscious life liberally, with broad and flexible self-awareness. They can easily regress to primitive fantasies, naive ideas, and tabooed impulses and then return to rationality and self-criticism. "The creative person is both more primitive and more cultured, more destructive and more constructive, crazier and saner, than the average person" [1, p. 159].

Self concepts of adolescents, as shown by responses on an adjective checklist, showed a distinctive picture of creative adolescents [34]. Chosen for creativity through testing and rating of productions, these high school students showed awareness and acceptance of opposing forces in their personalities. More often than controls, they saw themselves as imaginative, original, uninhibited, outspoken, rebellious, complex, reflective, cynical, idealistic, and aloof. The control group more often described themselves as dependable, cooperative, conventional, quiet, and silent.

Field of work bore a relationship to characteristics revealed in biographies of creative boys [33]. Those who were especially creative in science tended to be more masculine, serious-minded, and persistent. The artistic creative boys showed more wide-ranging interests, preferred complex, asymmetrical stimuli to a greater extent and were more spontaneous and gregarious.

### Family Backgrounds of Creative Adolescents

The family experiences of highly creative individuals have shown some characteristics that differ from the ordinary [4, 12, 22, 32]. Mothers were more highly educated, more highly trained, and more likely to have careers outside the home. Their homes were less child-centered; the children were granted autonomy earlier, trusted to do the right thing without a great deal of supervision. Homes differed from their neighbors' as to conventional standards of cultural, artistic, and intellectual matters. Thus the children felt a certain sense of aloneness because of estrangement from the people near them. Some of the families moved often, an experience that reinforced children's feelings of being alone. Mothers were concerned with children's internal qualities, such as values, rather than with externals and specific behavior. Reports of highly creative high school students, in contrast to their less creative classmates, indicated that their parents provided consistent discipline, that fathers engaged in many activities and hobbies with daughters, and that mothers were very involved in activities with sons, showing much interest in boys' achievement [4].

## Sex Role and Creativity

Nobody needs research studies to prove that the great creative achievements in science and the arts have been made chiefly by men, not by women. In Chapter 10, evidence was quoted to show that boys are given more experiences that promote independent thinking and that creative behavior is probably related to this kind of thinking. Overemphasis on conforming to sex role depresses creativity in both sexes [40, pp. 111–114]. Creative behavior requires both sensitivity and independence. Sensitivity is feminine and independence masculine, according to cultural definitions of sex role. Therefore, the creative boy is likely to seem feminine and the creative girl masculine.

Some insight into feminine role and creativity is provided by a study of children and adolescents. Gifted, creative boys, as defined by both IQ measures and measures of creative behavior, were high in dominance, venturesomeness, individualism, self-assurance, self-discipline, and independence of group opinion [45]. Gifted, creative adolescent girls were more enthusiastic, individualistic, and non-conforming than their peers. However, they differed less from peers than did gifted, creative girls in middle childhood, and they also differed less from peers than their male counterparts did. In contrast to the boys, the gifted girls differed from peers in sociability, dominance, self-assurance, self-discipline, and self-sufficiency. Also, they were less accepted by classmates [18]. Most likely, the girls are caught in society's ambiguous attitudes toward gifted women. While they themselves and their parents and teachers want them to achieve and realize their potentialities, they fear for their feminine image and popularity with boys. As they grow from childhood into adolescence, they become more aware of the problem of conflicting roles. Hence the gap widens between gifted boys and girls in freedom to express creative potentiality.

The childhood of highly creative college girls was part of an intensive study at Mills College, a place where opportunities are ample for development of individuality and creative expression [1, pp. 105–113]. Parents of the more creative girls were likely to have intense artistic and intellectual interests and high moral principles. They were effective and successful. Children and parents had felt close to each other. As children, the highly creative girls had had more intellectual interests and higher aspirations, described as a preference for "complex, unstereotyped symbolic activity." Comparing them with their classmates in college, they showed more interest in writing, painting, drawing, working with clay, acting, play-making, and reading. Comparing them with creative men, little difference was found in personality traits. The creative women expected to marry and to combine a career with marriage. Follow-up studies after graduation showed the highly creative women continuing to grow in complexity of outlook while their less creative classmates did not change.

### Application of Knowledge about Creativity

Both parents and teachers may wonder if they can purposefully promote creativity in children. Research on family background and relationships has shown that the parents' personalities and background are significant. The likelihood of producing a creative child is increased when parents are active in intellectual, cultural matters; when parents guide the child while recognizing him as an active, able, trustworthy person; if parents do not mind being unconventional and different from their neighbors. This is hardly a blueprint for parental procedure, since nobody can turn on such global conditions at will.

Many authorities have given advice to teachers on nurturing creativity in their students. There is a question as to how great a factor is the teacher's own personality. How creative must a teacher be in order to perceive and promote creativity in students? Research indicates that highly creative teachers stimulate more originality in their students than do less creative teachers. Since teachers are less globally involved with their pupils than are parents with offspring, the former can often control their interactions more objectively and hence use "methods" more effectively than can parents.

Consider the findings on creativity together with what is known about adolescence. Intellectually, adolescents are able to think more freely and flexibly than are children. Although originality is related to firmness in sticking to one's judgments, adolescents often need the support of their peers in order to feel a sense of identity. Being different from the group involves some disapproval from both peers and teachers. The most creative adolescents, however, seem to care relatively little about approval. Their values differ from those of more ordinary peers and teachers. Inner satisfaction seems to matter more than marks, prizes, money, and praise. Perhaps adults can do some deliberate promotion of creativity by encouraging youngsters to think and act independently. If unusual ideas and products are valued, then perhaps approval-dependent adolescents will feel freer to create.

Psychologists and educators are working on various ways of promoting creativity. The method of "inquiry training" has already been described in Chapter 11, where curiosity of elementary school children was considered. Courses in creative problem solving have been developed by several people in various institutions. An example is the course taught by Parnes [26] at the University of Buffalo. Here students are helped to overcome various kinds of blocks to thinking, such as overemphasis on competition and fear of failure. They learn to defer judgment (not to criticize) while they are producing ideas—to wait until later, when the ideas are formed. (This method of thinking is also called *brainstorming*.) Different ways of finding and solving problems are taught. Social settings are relaxing and confidence-promoting. Students who had taken such a course produced significantly better ideas and more ideas than other students [27]. In general, results from various kinds of creativity training have been encouraging. When teachers appreciate the creative process and when they direct students' interest toward being original and clever, their students tend to produce more ideas and unusual work [14]. It is generally held that creativity will be encouraged when the student is regarded as a unique individual whose perceptions and productions are respected, when he is encouraged to gather information and organize it, when techniques of domination, force, shame, and guilt are avoided, when a spirit of play, adventure, or exploration is maintained.

## Summary

A reorganization of thought processes results in a new level of intellectual activity, formal thought, which is logical and abstract. Thinking becomes more mobile and flexible, less egocentric. Contrasted with the child in the stage of concrete operations, the adolescent can consider and make use of a greater amount of information, delaying his conclusions and responses while weighing and judging. The adolescent can think without using concrete objects or events, while concrete thinking is the essence of the intellectual operations of childhood. The adolescent uses and builds systems of thought, by which he searches for possible combinations and relationships and by which he determines whether he has found all combinations and relationships. Formal reasoning means accepting the conditions given and keeping to those conditions while solving the problem. Formal thought requires a high degree of control. Another characteristic of this stage of intellectual development is the ability to think about one's own thinking, an achievement which results in a highly complex person.

Individuals vary in the degree to which they think formally. An individual may achieve abstract concepts in one area and not in another. Logical thinking depends upon the young person's opportunities for developing it, upon the demands made upon him, and upon the roles he wishes to play in life.

Concerned about how society could and should be improved, the adolescent is likely to make grand plans for his own role in transforming society. He grows more realistic as he becomes an adult, especially as he works at an adult job. Thus he comes to differentiate more accurately between what might be and what is, between his own needs and those of his society, further differentiating himself as a person. He can then reflect upon his own thinking, and he can see himself as a person-in-relation.

Language development includes not only increases in vocabulary, but increased processing of experience into symbolic form. The forms thus used are taken from the culture, socializing the individual's thinking according to reality as interpreted by his fellow men.

Due to his increased intellectual complexity, the adolescent can control his thinking in order to consider his imaginative and creative behavior. Creative thinking results in new ideas, products, and solutions. Although conventional intelligence tests do not measure original thinking, tests for creativity have been devised. Such tests include measures of verbal fluency, flexibility of thought, elaboration of ideas, and independence of judgment. Men have created more in art and science than have women. Boys are given more experiences in independent, analytic thinking, to which creative behavior is probably related. Restrictive sex role training is likely to curtail creativity in both sexes. When adolescents scoring high on IQ tests are compared with those scoring high on creativity tests, the former are found to be more socially interactive and the latter more solitary and independent in their thinking. Background differences between such groups are distinguishable, especially differences promoting autonomy and independence in the highly creative people. Psychologists and educators are trying to promote creative behavior by approving independent thinking, by courses in creative problem solving, and by setting up courses in ways which require children to seek and find answers for themselves.

## References

1. Barron, F. The needs for order and for disorder as motives in creative activity. In C. W. Tyler & F. Barron (Eds.), *Scientific curiosity: Its recognition and development*. New York: Wiley, 1963.
2. Barron, F. *Creative person and creative process*. New York: Holt, Rinehart and Winston, 1969.
3. Crager, R. L., & Spriggs, A. J. Development of concept utilization. *Devel. Psychol.*, 1969, **1**, 415–424.
4. Dauw, D. C. Life experiences of original thinkers and good elaborators. *Except. Child.*, 1966, **32**, 433–440.
5. Davids, A. Cognitive styles in potential scientists and underachieving high school students. *J. Special Educ.*, 1968, **2**, 197–201.
6. Donaldson, M. *A study of children's thinking*. London: Tavistock, 1963.
7. Elkind, D. Egocentrism in adolescence. *Child Devel.*, 1967, **38**, 1025–1034.
8. Elkind, D., Barocas, R., & Johnsen, P. Concept production in children and adolescents. *Human Devel.*, 1969, **12**, 10–21.
9. Elkind, D., Medvene, L., & Rockway, A. S. Representational level and concept production in children and adolescents. *Devel. Psychol.*, 1970, **2**, 85–89.
10. Erikson, E. H. *Identity, youth and crisis*. New York: Norton, 1968.
11. Flavell, J. H. *The developmental psychology of Jean Piaget*. Princeton: Van Nostrand, 1963.
12. Getzels, J. W., & Jackson, P. W. Family environment and cognitive style. *Am. Soc. Rev.*, 1961, **26**, 351–359.
13. Getzels, J. W., & Jackson, P. W. *Creativity and intelligence*. New York: Wiley, 1962.
14. Guilford, J. P. Creativity: its measurement and development. In S. J. Parnes & H. F. Harding (Eds.), *A source book for creative thinking*. New York: Scribner's, 1962, pp. 151–168.
15. Guilford, J. P. Creativity; yesterday, today and tomorrow. *J. Creative Behavior*, 1967, **1**, 3–14.
16. Inhelder, B., & Piaget, J. *The growth of logical thinking*. New York: Basic Books, 1958.
17. Klineberg, S. L. Changes in outlook on the future between childhood and adolescence. *J. Pers. Soc. Psychol.*, 1967, **7**, 185–193.
18. Kurtzman, K. A. A study of school attitudes, peer acceptance and personality of creative adolescents. *Except. Child.*, 1967, **34**, 157–162.
19. Leary, T. Speech at Kingston, Rhode Island, March 11, 1969.
20. LeBlanc, A. F. Time orientation and time estimation: A function of age. *J. Genet. Psychol.*, 1969, **115**, 187–194.
21. Maccoby, M., & Modiano, N. Cognitive style in rural and urban Mexico. *Human Devel.*, 1969, **12**, 22–23.
22. MacKinnon, D. W. The nature and nurture of creative talent. *Am. Psychol.*, 1962, **17**, 484–495.

23. Miller, P. H., Kessel, F. S., & Flavell, J. H. Thinking about people thinking about people thinking about . . . : A study of social-cognitive development. *Child Devel.*, 1970, **41**, 613–623.

24. Mönks, F. Future time perspective in adolescents. *Human Devel.*, 1968, **11**, 107–123.

25. Nixon, R. E. An approach to the dynamics of growth in adolescence. *Psychiatry*, 1961, **24**, 18–31.

26. Parnes, S. J. The creative problem-solving course and institute at the University of Buffalo. In S. J. Parnes & H. F. Harding (Eds.), *A source book for creative thinking*. New York: Scribner's, 1962, pp. 307–323.

27. Parnes, S. J., & Meadow, A. Effects of "brainstorming" instructions on creative problem-solving by trained and untrained subjects. *J. Educ. Psychol.*, 1959, **50**, 171–176.

28. Peel, E. A. Intellectual growth during adolescence. *Educ. Rev.*, 1965, **17**, 169–180.

29. Piaget, J. *The psychology of intelligence*. London: Routledge & Kegan Paul, 1950.

30. Piers, E. V. Adolescent creativity. In J. F. Adams (Ed.), *Understanding adolescence*. Boston: Allyn & Bacon, 1968, pp. 159–182.

31. Riegel, K. F. Speed of verbal performance as a function of age and set: A review of issues and data. In A. T. Welford & J. E. Birren (Eds.), *Behavior, aging and the nervous system*. Springfield, Ill.: Charles C Thomas, 1965, pp. 150–190.

32. Roe, A. *The making of a scientist*. New York: Dodd, Mead, 1952.

33. Schaefer, C. E. Biographical inventory correlates in scientific and artistic creativity in adolescents. New York: Unpublished Ph.D. thesis, Fordham University, 1967.

34. Schaefer, C. E. The self-concept of creative adolescents. *J. Psychol.*, 1969, **72**, 233–242.

35. Smith, M. K. Measurement of the size of general English vocabulary through the elementary grades and high school. *Genet. Psychol. Mono.*, 1941, **24**, 311–345.

36. Stone, M. A., & Ausubel, D. P. The intersituational generality of formal thought. *J. Genet. Psychol.*, 1969, **115**, 169–180.

37. Thorndike, R. L. Some methodological issues in the study of creativity. *Proceedings of the 1962 Invitational Conference on Testing Problems*. New Jersey: Educational Testing Service, 1963, pp. 40–54.

38. Tooley, K. Expressive style as a developmental index in late adolescence. *J. Project. Techniques Personal. Assess.*, 1967, **31**:6, 51–59.

39. Torrance, E. P. Factors affecting creative thinking in children: an interim report. *Merrill-Palmer Quart.*, 1961, **7**, 171–180.

40. Torrance, E. P. *Guiding creative talent*. Englewood Cliffs, N.J.: Prentice-Hall, 1962.

41. Vygotsky, L. S. *Thought and language*. Cambridge, Mass.: M.I.T. Press, 1962.

42. Wallach, M. A., & Kogan, M. N. *Modes of thinking in young children*. New York: Holt, Rinehart and Winston, 1965.

43. Watts, A. F. *The language and mental development of children*. London: Harrap, 1944.

44. Welford, A. T. *Ageing and human skill*. London: Oxford University, 1958.

45. Werner, E. E., & Bachtold, L. M. Personality factors of gifted boys and girls in middle childhood and adolescence. *Psychol. Schools*, 1969, **6**, 177–182.

46. Yudin, L. W. Formal thought in adolescence as a function of intelligence. *Child Devel.*, 1966, **37**, 697–708.

47. Yudin, L., & Kates, S. L. Concept attainment and adolescent development. *J. Educ. Psychol.*, 1963, **54**, 177–182.

# Chapter 15

Ellen S. Smart

# Parents, Peers, and the Quest for Identity

Parent–child relationships change during adolescence from protection–dependence to affectionate equality, or so they do in the ideal American situation. The change involves turmoil in parent and child, as they learn to play new roles and feel new feelings as the child establishes a mature sense of identity.

Much of social and emotional growth in adolescence takes place with contemporaries of both sexes. The sense of identity includes a firm concept of where one fits with other people, especially people of his own generation. The young person's image of himself is built partly on his interpretations of the ways in which others

551

regard him. Is he seen as bold or timid, witty or tongue-tied, handsome or funny-looking? Is she considered artistic or all thumbs, steady or flighty, intelligent or stupid? The reputation will influence behavior as well as self concept. Friendships and love relationships enhance self concepts and promote constructive behavior and personality growth. Failure to find friendship and love can be threatening.

The peer group is made up of members of both sexes, and under it is included friendship and popularity. Relationships with the opposite sex are considered as those which progress toward and include love, sex, and marriage.

## Cultural Perspective

The forms of adolescence vary with cultural forms throughout the world and within the United States. For instance, urban, suburban, and rural adolescents differ significantly in this country [24]. Douvan and Adelson found suburban adolescents to be more privileged than the others in range and diversity of leisure activities, dating, group membership, and joint family activity. Rural adolescents were much more restricted in most types of opportunities for development, while city youngsters were also restricted in breadth, and were propelled rapidly toward adulthood.

Since we have already discussed other cultural differences, such as social class, in earlier chapters, we shall go on to features of American culture which have special meaning for parent–adolescent relationships. Many observers have noted that American parents and children have conflicts or disagreements with each other. Sometimes this situation is called a *generation gap*. Some contributors to this situation are:

**American Ideals.** Where every individual has a right to life, liberty, and the pursuit of happiness, the attempt to establish a distinct identity is going to be pretty vigorous. Not only does the individual have the right to be himself, but he has a heritage of go-getters—explorers, colonists, pioneers, inventors—young people, full of initiative, not doing what their parents told them, but out on their own, improving on what their parents did. These ideals result in continual social changes, making parents and adolescents unsure of their roles in regard to each other.

**The Nuclear Family.** Father, mother, and children make up the typical American family. The two-generation family is the norm, even though in actual practice many families have additional members living with them, and many also are minus a parent. Children are expected to grow up, move out and start their own two-generation families. A rupture in parent–child relationships is implicit in this expectation where parents and children intend to be quite independent of each other after the children reach adulthood.

In contrast, in some cultural settings in the United States and in other cultures, the joint family or the stem family may be typical. Both types see generations as connected intimately, expect no break between children and parents. As parents grow old, children take more and more responsibility for them instead of pushing off on their own. Children are not encouraged to develop distinct identities as individuals, but to feel a family identity. An adolescent does not have to work so hard to achieve a sense of identity because it is already partly built for him. Therefore, he stays *with* his family psychologically as well as physically. Even if he goes away for a while to be educated, as many Indian youths do, he still belongs deeply to his whole family and returns to them when he can. This is not to say that Indian adolescents live in complete harmony with their parents but only that they conflict less than do Americans.

Americans usually believe that you have only one life to live. It's not so with over half of the world's people. A belief in reincarnation usually exists in cultures which have joint family, stem family, or any kind of extended family. An individual's sense of identity is thus part of an identity which extends into the infinite past and future. His religion most likely involves ancestor worship, or at least a duty toward ancestors, with the assurance that his descendants will be obligated to him in the same way. Thus a person is not alone, to find himself. He *belongs*, in time and space. He therefore feels no necessity to cut himself off from his parents or from the other people who are part of his identity.

**A Fast-Changing Society.** The rapid pace of science and technology tears an ever-widening gap between generations. From the time when technology produced the automobile, America has seen continuing changes in behavior patterns and values, especially regarding sex. Society is becoming less work-oriented, more leisure-oriented. Although less socialistic than many countries, the United States continues to legislate for social welfare, while rugged individualism is favored less than it used to be. Bureaucratic businesses and government have replaced many small, independent operations.

Children are insisting upon honesty, scorning hypocrisy as the sin of sins, while parents may have made peace with materialism and the concrete fruits of their labors. Adolescents feel that parents are hopelessly old-fashioned. Parents know that they are. Parents are often not sure what is right and what standards to insist upon. Here is one of the sources of the loss of moral authority suffered by parents, their uncertainty due to a youth which differed from their children's experience of today.

**Mass Media and the Shrinking World.** It used to be that learning to read opened a child's eyes to the existence of standards and authorities which differed widely from those of his parents. Now television assaults him in infancy. Children as well as parents are at the mercy of the advertising octopus which exploits childish fears and fantasies, and the entertainment industry, which reduces man to the lowest common denominator. Insofar as parents' values and standards differ from those promoted by mass media, conflict with adolescents is generated. Easy communication and travel bring youngsters into contact with different worlds of discourse. Middle-class Christian parents seem small-town and narrow-minded to Jane who wants to bring a dark-skinned friend home for vacation, to Ken who is dating a Jewish girl, and to Walter, who is living in a commune.

## Conflict

### Different Interpretations of Parent–Adolescent Conflict

The psychoanalytic point of view is that conflict is a necessary part of growing up. If an adolescent does not battle his parents in one area, he will in another.

"I take it that it is normal for an adolescent to behave for a considerable length of time in an inconsistent and unpredictable manner; to fight his impulses and accept them; to ward them off successfully and to be overrun by them; to love his parents and to hate them; to revolt against them and to be dependent on them; to be deeply ashamed to acknowledge his mother before others and, unexpectedly, to desire heart-to-heart talks with her; to thrive on imitation of and identification with others while searching unceasingly for his own identity; to be more idealistic, artistic, generous and unselfish than he will ever be again, but also the opposite: self-centered, egotistic, calculating" [33]. These are the words of Anna Freud. She goes on to say, "There are few situations in life which are more difficult to cope with than an adolescent son or daughter during the attempt to liberate themselves." Levy and Munroe [57] also extend sympathy: "I wish I could offer a pain-dispelling drug to mothers during this second birth, this delivery of children into the adult world." They hold that an adolescent has to fight his parents in order to grow up. Not only does he reject his parents, but also his baby-self, with whom parents are intimately associated. While rejecting childhood and parents, in order to strive toward identity as a distinct and independent being, he still wants the love, comfort, and protection which parents gave him. Thus parents are wrong no matter what they do, and children have to pick fights. This point of view is often comforting to bewildered parents, since it helps to allay their guilt and feelings of inadequacy. If adolescents have to go through a difficult stage, then parents simply have to wait patiently, confidently, and lovingly until the young people grow out of it into civilized adulthood!

Another point of view is this: While conflict often occurs, it is neither essential nor inevitable. Recent studies show amiable relations between parents and adolescents to be the usual situation [2]. Adolescents mature most easily when parents place reasonable limits on their behavior and when they are affectionate, interested, and active with their children [44, 69]. Research gives considerable evidence to show that this is so. For example, when college students were asked to recall how they felt toward their parents before they were 15 years old, approximately half of them reported that they had felt very close to both parents [54]. Compared with a group who had not been close to both parents, these students had more positive ratings on several personal and family characteristics. They were more likely to be virgins, to have received sex information from parents and from it to have developed healthy attitudes toward sex in marriage, giving family training as their reason for refraining from premarital sex relations. They tended to evaluate themselves more highly on personal attractiveness, to be satisfied with their sex, to have little trouble making friends with the opposite sex, and to have confidence in their chances for successful marriage.

When high school students discussed their expectations of adults, they indicated that parents' primary role is the provision of a happy home life [86]. The parental behavior that they most disliked included constant scolding or punishing, overly strict rules, indifference, neglect, distrust, being unreasonable, not showing love, and not explaining.

According to reports of adolescent boys and girls about tension and conflict in their families, greater education of parents and higher socioeconomic status are associated with more harmonious family life [65]. Researchers generally agree that parents are very important to adolescents, but the degree to which parents are problems seems to vary from one study to another, depending somewhat on the question posed. A study of over 200 teen-agers in church groups found parents to be the most significant figures in the lives of the children and to represent over 65 percent of the concerns expressed by the children [76]. When a broader cross

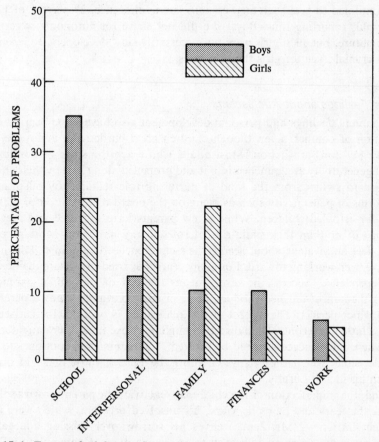

**Figure 15–1.** Extent of adolescents' concern with various types of problems, by sex.

SOURCE: Adapted from J. F. Adams, "Adolescent Personal Problems as a Function of Age and Sex," *Journal of Genetic Psychology*, **104**, 207–214.

section, over 4000 adolescents, were asked to report the biggest personal problem causing difficulty, school problems ranked first [1]. As Figure 15–1 shows, personal problems (usually relationships with peers) were equally troublesome with parent problems, and for boys, financial concerns also ranked equal with parental and personal. Other difficulties plagued the subjects of this inquiry, also. Family problems made up only 10 per cent of the most pressing difficulties reported by boys and 22 percent of those of girls. Family problems tended to decrease with age, while school problems did not but even increased somewhat for boys. Boys' financial problems also increased. These facts put adolescent–parent conflicts into perspective as real aspects of adolescent life, but not dominant. (See Figure 15–1.)

## Sex Differences in Conflict

Boys are much more active than girls in seeking independence from parents. In their large national survey of boys and girls, Douvan and Adelson included the question "Have you ever broken a rule?" [24, p. 150]. Only 10 percent of 14- to 16-year-old boys said they had not, while 26 percent of girls said they had not.

Girls continued to give such answers into late adolescence, 27 percent of 17- and 18-year-olds reporting thus. Boys who did not strive for autonomy were judged very immature, but such girls were not necessarily slow developers. Independence is a less crucial issue for girls than for boys.

### Parents' Feelings about Adolescents

The parents' feelings and personal development also have some bearing on the production of conflict. Even though children are a burden and annoyance, they also give joy and satisfaction. Most adults who reach the stage of developing a sense of generativity are launched into it and propelled along in it by their children. It is hard to switch from the kind of nurturing role required by offspring into other forms of generativity such as being on the board of education or collecting money for crippled children. While a few parents have nurtured and created in situations other than their child-raising roles, many have not. Most parents, if not all, feel ambivalent about seeing their children become adults. This is what they have been working toward. For many years they tried to prepare their children for independence. Success, however, means the end of the job of parenthood. Viewing the almost-finished product, at 18 or so, it occurs to many a parent that the job is not perfect. The impact of this realization is twofold. First it seems as though a little more control and direction might improve the son or daughter to the point where future success would be assured. The parent then continues to try to make decisions which the youngster knows he himself must make in order to establish his identity firmly.

Second, the imperfection of the child may reactivate the parent's own adolescent feelings, the fears and pains he knew, his unsolved problems which were almost forgotten until now. Mr. Jenks relives his sorrow over missing college when Freddie gets a low score on college entrance examinations. Contemplating Glady's generous proportions, Mrs. Kaufman plumbs the despair she felt over her own bulk at 16. The shame and guilt which accompanied youthful sex behavior generate the parental explosion which greets Helen's appearance in a new bathing suit which leaves practically nothing to the imagination. In all these situations, parents seem to their children to be overreacting. To themselves, they are simply trying to protect their children from dangers they know to be much more serious than the children realize.

The real essence of the sense of generativity is wanting the child (or creature or project) to grow in the way that is best for him. Not only does the parent have to let him go on his own at the right point, but the parent also has the problem of knowing what way *is* best, and where to compromise with reality while aiming toward perfection. Sometimes only the threat of disaster will move a parent from a rigid insistence upon making decisions for the adolescent whose growth depends upon making his own. Larry's parents permitted him to drop out of college for a year only when a psychiatrist told them that he was in danger of an emotional breakdown. Janet's parents stopped criticizing her boy friend when they realized that, if she married him, the breach they were creating would probably be permanent.

It is also possible for parents to be too laissez-faire with adolescents. A hands-off policy can give too little guidance and support to the youngster who needs and wants to stand on his own and yet at the same time needs and wants the security of being held to standards of behavior in which his parents truly believe. Parents who have read about adolescents' need for independence may grant more freedom than their children can profitably use. Some parents are so uncertain about their own beliefs and standards that they cannot be firm in setting limits for adolescents. And some parents don't care enough. They may give up the struggle from fatigue, pressures from other areas of life, or a feeling of hopelessness, as did one divorced mother who moved away, leaving two teen-age girls at home with plenty of money, one to go to high school, the other to college. Perhaps the most sophisticated parents of all, appreciating the need for a delicate balance between freedom and control, will agonize over achieving that balance.

Quite aside from the annoyance of adolescent ambivalence, negative parental feelings are engendered from the financial burden which adolescents place upon parents. Probably this feeling is confined to middle-class parents. While middle-class children often earn money, they are still expensive to keep. Costing more than adults to feed and clothe, adolescents represent a large cash outlay even before they go to college, that fabulously costly place where expenses grow every year. Upper-middle-class parents find that scholarship aid is unavailable or present in such minute quantities as to make little difference in the great drain which education represents. As adolescent children go about their business of athletics, cheerleading, dating, fraternities, telephoning, joyriding, beach parties, and shopping, hardworking parents sometimes resent these noncontributing consumers.

In lower socioeconomic levels, the picture is different. Children are expected to earn money as soon as they can and perhaps contribute to family support. Among black families of the lowest socioeconomic stratum, the mother is often the central, powerful figure. She cares for her own children and takes responsibility for her grandchildren who are born to her own adolescent girls [73]. Rainwater sketches a typical family, in which men and boys are constantly demeaned and each member exposes the emptiness of the other members' claims to competence. Human nature is conceived of as bad, destructive, and immoral. The mother therefore expects her adolescent to be a bad person unless she is very, very lucky.

When we turn to particular problems and parents' feelings about adolescents' disturbed behavior, the example of running away is pertinent. In one county in Maryland during a 12-month period, the county police dealt with 1026 reports of missing children [77]. Their median age between 15 and 16, the runaways were distributed among all economic and educational levels. Families often asked for help and welcomed chances to talk about their problems. The Beatles show their remarkable understanding of the troubled adolescent world in their interpretation of the parents' point of view, when the parents discover that their daughter has run away. They have given her everything money could buy and have sacrificed for her for so many years. The mother breaks down and cries to the father that their baby is gone. They ask each other how she could be so thoughtless, hurt them so much, when all they did was to struggle to do their best. And now they wonder what they did that was wrong.

## Parents' Marital Situation

The way in which parents relate to each other is full of meaning for their children. Not only are they affected as individual persons but as future husbands, wives, fathers, and mothers.

Attitudes toward love were studied in white, middle-class high school seniors [51]. The marriage relationship of the parents was found to be most strongly related to the attitudes held by the young people. When parents were living together, the children were more likely to have realistic attitudes toward love, while more romantic attitudes were held by adolescents whose parents were separated by either divorce or death.

Effects on children of certain kinds of family situations have been investigated. Of these, authority patterns and father absence are of special interest.

### Authority Patterns

The traditional pattern of authority in the American family, as in families in most of the world's cultures, was for the father to be considered the head of the household by all the members. All important decisions and all decisions basic to the countless choices that have to be made from day to day were made by the husband and father. In colloquial terms, the man of the household was the boss. Recent studies reveal a different picture in modern family life.

When wives were asked to tell whether they or their husbands usually made decisions in each of eight areas of family living, they were given five alternative answers, ranging from "Husband Always" through "Wife Always." Differential weights were given the answers at each point, and the scores summed across the eight areas. The scores at the ends of the resulting scale were called "Husband Dominant" and "Wife Dominant." Two out of eight of the families fell into the "Wife Dominant" group; another two out of eight were "Husband Dominant"; the remaining four were equal or showed "Balance of Power" [11, p. 45].

When three alternatives were permitted to the question as to power, 40 percent of children between 7 and 15 said that their parents were equal [42]. The opinion that power was shared equally was held more often by older youngsters than younger ones and more often by girls than by boys. Perhaps children's reports reflect an actual decline in the father's power as the family gets older. The highest paternal power was reported by 8-year-olds [29]. Children's views in this respect agree with findings from interviews with wives, where fathers of oldest children were seen as less powerful than fathers of youngest children [11].

Perhaps the most significant generalization to be drawn from this wealth of data is that about half of American families carry on a democratic form of life in the home. Or so it appears to their children. Authority is shared and decisions made jointly by husband and wife in 50 percent or more of families studied. It is possible that the figure is greater, since children are more likely to make all-or-none choices than to see and describe relationships in all their subtleties. Another indication that a balance-of-power, or cooperative partnerships, may exceed dominated families is that older children, more than younger children, see their fathers as having less absolute authority and sharing more with their wives. Older children would be more likely to perceive the complex relationship which cooperation involves.

Black adolescents' perceptions of family power structure have been studied recently [50]. Over 500 ninth grade boys and girls were queried as to how their parents made decisions about work, expenditures, and child rearing. White-collar, blue-collar, and unskilled occupational levels were sampled. Syncratic (shared, democratic) decision making was the most frequent pattern reported. Power structure was to be more often syncratic than father- or mother-dominated, at all occupational levels. Males reported more father participation than did females, and females reported more mother participation than did males. The black father was seen as more salient and more participating in family life than he has appeared to be in former studies. The study suggests that black men are becoming more important figures in family life.

**Authority Patterns, Modeling, and Cognitive Structure.** The importance of reasoning or cognitive structure had already been mentioned as mediating the effects of punishment (page 464). The power level or authority pattern of the parents interacts with parental reasoning in influencing the extent to which children want to be like their parents [28]. The subjects for this investigation were almost 10,000 students, drawn from grades 7 through 12, who answered questions about how much they would like to be the kinds of persons their mothers and fathers were and about how decisions were made in their homes. Three levels of parent power were distinguished—autocratic, where the parent just tells the child what to do; democratic, where the child has many chances to make decisions but the parent has the last word; and permissive, where the child makes his own decision either with or without the interest and suggestions of the parent. Another aspect considered was how much the parent explained rules, policies, decisions, and suggestions to the child. Results showed that at all three power levels, frequent explanations were associated with the child wanting to be like the parent. Taking power level into consideration, the democratic parents were most attractive as models to their children, permissive parents next, and autocratic parents least attractive as models. Figure 15–2 shows the extent to which boys and girls wanted to be like parents at the three power levels, with amount of explaining or cognitive structure taken into account.

### Father Absence

One-parent families make up 13 percent of American families [75]. Most one-parent families are those in which the father is absent, and it is the children of these families, especially boys, who have been studied most. Most research has been focused on personality development. However, cognitive development, also, has been found to be depressed in both boys and girls in father-absent homes [83].

The mother's interpretation of the father, whether he is present or absent, is an influence on the personality development of children, especially of boys [8]. For healthy masculine development, it is important that the mother give positive descriptions of the father's masculinity, in terms of characteristics such as competence, strength, and physical prowess. The mother's feelings about masculinity, men, and the father are significant in her relationships with her son.

As noted in Chapter 12, fathers are likely to differentiate between boys and girls more than mothers do, thus playing the more salient part in sex typing. When the father is absent, it is up to the mother to be more active in sex typing, if it is going to be done by a parent. Other family members can make some contributions in this area [83]. Brothers, grandfathers, and uncles often do so. For example, the Kennedy brothers purposefully took over the responsibility of providing a masculine influence for children who had lost their fathers. Psychologically healthy mothers are more likely to be able to counteract the effects of father absence in their sons' personality development [70]. The bereaved mother's ego strength, as shown in ability to take on some of the father's functions and to use all possible

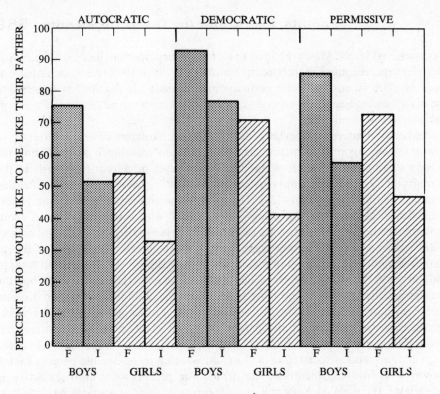

F = Frequent parental explaining
I = Infrequent parental explaining

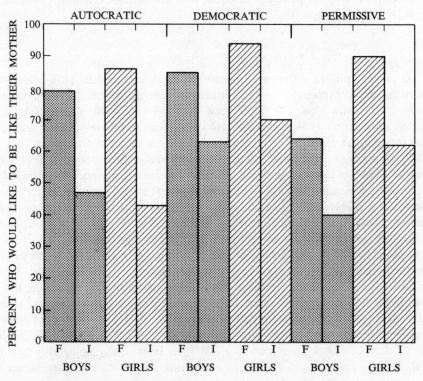

F = Frequent parental explaining
I = Infrequent parental explaining

resources, seems to be crucial in the development of masculine boys [43]. Particularly if the father left home before the boy was 5 years old, a masculine self concept in early adolescence is related to the mother's encouragement of aggression and masculine self concept [9].

The development of feminine girls is also highly dependent on the parents' interactions with each other and with their daughters. In his definition of masculine and feminine behavior to his daughter, and in his behavior as a husband with his wife, the father shows his daughter how to be a woman and how to interact with a man. The father's acceptance of the daughter as feminine facilitates her self-acceptance as feminine. Evidence suggests that father-absent girls are likely to show some maladjustment, since they are deprived of the father's important teaching and are likely to have mothers beset with the problems which burden single family heads [10]. The mother may also belittle the father because she has been hurt by his desertion and/or because he has not fulfilled the masculine role of provider. As with boys, the damaging effects of father absence may be mitigated by a strong, flexible mother and by help from male family members and friends.

## Positive Interactions

Much of what parents and adolescents do together is a give and take. Much of it is growth-promoting in the children and often in the parents, too.

### Instrumental and Expressive Behavior

Adolescents in Israel and the United States have been questioned as to how they perceive their parents in terms of instrumentality and expressivity [15, 22]. The mother was seen as more often expressive and the father more often instrumental.

Expressive and instrumental behavior during family interaction was the focus of an ingenious study [80]. The laboratory setting was a game using lights, pushers, and balls. The family was told that the problem was to figure out how to play the game and to exceed the average of other families who have played it. As they played, the individuals were scored for their attempts to control other members and for their expressions of support of other members. Class comparisons showed middle-class parents to be more controlling and more supportive of their children and of each other than were lower-class parents. Fathers tended to exercise more control over sons than daughters, but mothers used about the same control with girls and boys. Mothers were more supportive of daughters than of sons. Middle-class fathers were more instrumental and more supportive than middle-class mothers, but in the working class, there was little difference between parents in use of power and support.

### Communication

Any human relationship is enhanced by mutual understanding. Conflicts are stimulated and increased by not seeing one another's point of view. Sometimes it is

**Figure 15–2.** (*Facing page*) Strength of boys' and girls' desires to be like their parents, for three levels of parental power, taking amount of parental explaining into account.
SOURCE: Adapted from G. H. Elder, "Parental Power Legitimation and Its Effect Upon the Adolescent," *Sociometry*, **26**, 50–65.

hard for parents and children to put themselves in each other's shoes, but having lived together for between one and two decades, a parent and child know many ways of letting each other know what they are thinking and feeling. Facial expressions, posture, silences, tones of voices—all have meaning and add to the meaning of acts and spoken words. "Sorry, but you can't take the car tonight" may be interpreted as hostility, punishment, parental wisdom, or sincere regret, according to how it is said. A youngster's sudden seeking of a parent's company may tell the parent, without words, that the son or daughter has been rebuffed by friends.

Talking together is very necessary too, even though nonverbal communication may be quite meaningful. Foremost among problems cited by one sample of teen-agers was parents not listening to what children wanted to tell them about important matters [76]. As teachers of college freshmen, we have asked classes, "What do adolescents need most from parents?" Often the first answer is "Listen to them!" One would expect adolescents to be able to express themselves better than children, since they have more words at their command and a greater flexibility of thought. Why, then, do some parents and adolescents have great difficulty in understanding each other through talking? This question was approached with 100 college students, 99 of whom indicated some trouble in communicating with their parents [26]. These subjects said that lack of words had nothing to do with any difficulties they experienced in talking with parents. When asked which subject was most difficult to discuss with parents, boys and girls replied that sex was hardest to discuss, with mothers as well as with fathers. Girls had trouble talking with mothers about marriage and about misbehavior. Boys found it especially hard to talk about misbehavior and about failures and defeats. When asked why they found it hard to talk about these topics, the girls indicated that they often did not get enough opportunities to talk to their mothers or their fathers. Guilt too held them back. Both boys and girls were affected by fear of mothers nagging and fear that their mothers might not keep secrets. Respect for privacy is very important to adolescents and yet many parents pry too much [76]. Teen-agers object to parents listening to their telephone conversations and asking their friends what they do on dates.

Children's understanding of parents' motives was considered in a study [71] of 656 Swedish boys and girls, ages 11 through 15. As the children grew older, they were less acceptant of parental restriction that stemmed from authoritarian attitude and more acceptant of rationally or altruistically motivated restrictions. As the children increased in verbal intelligence, with age factor eliminated, they also were less acceptant of authoritarian-motivated restrictions. This study may indicate either that greater maturity brings increased understanding of parents' motivations, or greater maturity brings less tolerance for authoritarian restrictions, or both.

Searching for broad, general conditions which would lead to good communication in a family, parents' satisfactions with their children were compared with the ways in which children perceived the parents' satisfactions [32]. The subjects were boys and girls between 11 and 16 and their parents. A high level of accuracy in communication between parent and adolescent was found to exist in families where husband and wife communicated well with each other. That is, when the husband and wife agreed well on domestic values and on which roles they expected one another to play, then their children tended to understand clearly how well satisfied their parents were with them. High socioeconomic status was associated with good communication between parent and adolescent. (This finding is consistent with the fact that high socioeconomic status is associated with happy marriages and hence with good communication between husband and wife.)

The practical significance of these research results is varied. It does not help parents and children much to know that high socioeconomic status predicts good communication. Nor can children do a great deal about the clarity with which their parents understand each other. Parents can, of course, work to build a sound marriage which will serve as a foundation for communication with their children. Some of the more detailed research results could prove worthwhile in day-to-day family relationships. Realizing that their children may feel they have not enough chances to talk, parents could plan their time so as to make regular and frequent opportunities. Adolescents, too, could point out to their parents that they need more time together in order to understand one another. If mothers realized how important it is to keep confidences in order to continue to receive them, then surely they would be more reluctant to gossip and to share private information with friends. Both parents might try to be more acceptant and less critical of their children as persons, while still making clear their own values and standards of behavior. Can a parent change in the direction of being more rational and understanding with his child? Yes indeed, according to results from a study on changing attitudes through group discussion [41]. Not only did these parents change their attitudes toward their children, but the children also changed their behavior.

### Feelings of Love and Closeness

Attachment is of vital importance throughout life, although objects of attachment change [14, pp. 207–208]. Adults, as well as infants, seek proximity and contact with people they love at times when they feel threatened or weakened. Adolescents normally continue to be attached to their parents, but not so strongly as they were as children. Girls are often more strongly attached than boys. (This characteristic is seen in many animals, not only among primates, but in the herd animals, where sheep and goats are likely to stay close to their mothers throughout life.)

A previously mentioned study [54] of adolescents' feelings of closeness to parents revealed that 47 percent of the men and 58 percent of the women reported feeling very close to both parents before the age of 15. Similar findings on sex difference occurred in a study [25] of boys and girls from seventh to eleventh grades, in which girls reported receiving more love, affection, and nurturance from both parents than boys reported receiving. Boys saw themselves as being treated in more hostile, negative ways by both parents. Even though there is a statistically significant sex difference in this area, it is noteworthy that about half of the men and over half of the women did feel very close to their parents. Only 13 percent of the men and 7 percent of the women reported having felt neutral toward both parents. The remainder were close to one parent, more to the mother than to the father. A 4-year psychiatric study of suburban high school boys showed that the typical boy liked and admired his parents [67]. At 14, he felt closer to his mother but by 18 was more intimate with his father.

Further indication of love of parents by adolescents is from a study [39] of attitudes in which children from third grade through twelfth grade were asked to complete sentences beginning with "My father—" and "My mother—." Answers

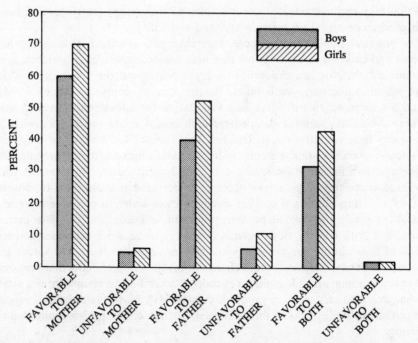

**Figure 15–3.** Responses of boys and girls to incomplete sentences, revealing attitudes toward parents. Favorable attitudes far outweigh unfavorable ones. Mothers receive a few more positive responses than fathers, from both boys and girls.

Source: Data from D. B. Harris and S. C. Tseng, "Children's Attitudes Toward Peers and Parents as Revealed by Sentence Completions," *Child Development*, **28**.

were classified into favorable, unfavorable, and neutral. While a favorable attitude may not be exactly the same as love, at least it is an indication of some sort of positive relationship. Figure 15–3 shows that adolescents held many more favorable than unfavorable attitudes toward their parents. Both sexes were more favorable to the mother than to the father, a fact compatible with the finding mentioned above, that adolescents were more likely to feel closer to the mother than to the father. During the high school years, boys' attitudes grew more favorable toward both the mother and father, while girls showed a larger increase in positive statements about the father than they did in regard to the mother. Considering the high level of acceptance of both parents by both sexes along with the increases in favorable attitudes as the adolescents grew older, it does not look as though the adolescent search for independence requires hostility toward parents.

**Perceived Similarity.** Positive personality characteristics in both young men and women are associated with their seeing themselves as similar to their fathers [47]. Studies [68, p. 254] contrasting normal and neurotic subjects demonstrated that normal young men identified more with their parents than did neurotic young men. The normal men saw their fathers as being closer to their ideals than did the neurotics. In another study [79] college students filled out a test (Minnesota Multiphasic Personality Inventory) for themselves; again, as they thought their fathers would respond; and again, as they thought their mothers would respond. The results showed that for both men and women normal personality characteristics were associated with seeing oneself as similar to one's father. This association was most clearly shown in women in the masculinity–femininity scale, while masculine women were less similar to their fathers than were feminine women.

**Similarity in Values.** When two generations hold the same values, however, it indicates harmony and positive interaction between them. Although a study of conflicts may give the impression that adolescents usually reject their parents' values, there is much evidence to show that parents and teen-agers are more alike than unlike in values [5]. The psychiatric study of high school boys showed them sharing their parents' outlook on life and holding the same middle-class values [67].

College students' values have been found quite similar to their parents' values, no matter whether the students are activists or not [85]. Values included dedication to causes, conventional moralism, intellectualism, and humanitarianism. Resemblances were greater for values than for other domains of personality, such as need for recognition or being self-critical. First-voters are likely to vote as their fathers do [59, p. 212]. When parents agree with each other on religion, most of their children, especially girls, follow the same ideology. A survey of college students' religion in relation to that of their parents showed only 17.8 percent disagreeing with parents, and many of the disagreements were minor [72]. Vocational ambitions and efforts are strongly affected by parents, as shown in an investigation of parental and peer influences on social mobility. While most working-class boys did not aspire to go to college, a minority of boys from blue-collar homes were in the college preparatory course, headed for middle-class occupations. Forty-three percent of these boys had been advised by their parents to enter professions, whereas of the remainder of the working class boys, only 16 percent had been advised by parents to enter professions. A similar contrast was shown for middle-class boys. Of those planning to enter professions, 53 percent had received such advice from parents, but only 21 percent in noncollege preparatory courses had been so advised [78]. While this research shows that adolescents' ambitions are affected by factors other than parents, it does indicate that parents have considerable influence on their sons' vocational values.

Even when teenagers disagree on values with their parents, there is evidence that as the children grow into adulthood, they tend to adopt the same attitudes toward adolescent behavior which their parents held toward them [4]. The areas in which 103 college girls conflicted most with their parents were discipline, responsibilities, and family rules and regulations. These girls were planning to bring up their own daughters in ways very similar to the methods their mothers had used.

## Parents Versus Other Influences

The many pulls upon adolescents include those exerted by their parents. Some conflicts are frankly between parents and children. Other problems are created by the opposition of parental and other influences, most important the influences of peers. Teachers and other adults in the community may also put adolescents into the position of having to choose between them and their parents. Other adults can be very influential on the adolescent while reinforcing values held by the parents or opening new vistas which the parents then endorse.

The adolescent realizes that the various meaningful persons in his life vary in the expectations that they hold for him [38]. He can see different sets of norms held by his parents, teachers, and peers. There is some evidence that this knowledge helps him to make his own decisions. That is, he can use the demands of his parents when he wishes to make some resistance to demands of peers or teachers, and vice versa.

## Parents and Other Adults

After parents, teachers have the greatest opportunities for significance in the lives of children. High school students have indicated that they consider it most important for teachers to be interested, understanding, and helpful to them [86]. Almost everyone knows at least one case where a teacher had a significant lifelong influence on an adolescent. Ellen's third grade teacher channeled her sensitivity to nature into careful observation. Her tenth grade biology teacher refined and deepened her knowledge and enjoyment with the result that she has become a botanist. Almost everyone knows at least one case of a child modeling himself after a teacher in direct contrast to the models available at home. Stan, a big, socially awkward boy, identified strongly with the high school football coach and rejected his librarian father. He is majoring in physical education. For many youngsters, a teacher or youth leader provides a welcome and healthy chance to explore a new identity and then to adopt it if it fits. With the variety of personalities, relationships, and situations possible in American life, parents cannot possibly open up to an adolescent sufficient choices of identity for him to be sure of finding what he needs. Part of the letting-go process which many parents find difficult is the acceptance of these other adult influences as essential relationships for their children.

Studies comparing the importance of parents and teachers in adolescence have generally awarded parents the first place. Senior high school students were asked, "Which things would make you the most unhappy? (a) If my parents did not like what I did. (b) If my (favorite) teacher did not like what I did. (c) If my best friend did not like what I did." [30]. Over 80 percent of boys and girls replied that they would be most concerned over parental disapproval. Teacher disapproval rated first with only 1 percent of girls and 4 percent of boys. Disapproval of the best friend would be most important to 18 percent of girls and 16 percent of boys. Thus teacher disapproval was shown to count for very little if matched against parents' disapproval or even against best friends'. And the importance of parents to adolescents is again highlighted.

Another comparison of adolescents' concepts of teachers and parents indicated that adolescents considered teachers to be more clever, skillful, persevering, rich, and knowledgeable than parents [87]. Parents were seen as more easygoing, trustful, happy, popular, and peaceful than teachers. The boys rated the teachers as less calm, strong, successful, and patient than their parents. A personality test (Cattell) showed that both boys and girls tended to be more strongly identified with parents than with teachers.

**Other Adults As Models.** A longitudinal adolescent study showed a number of clear-cut instances in which an adult outside the family who had a close relationship with the subject had served as a model. It happened as often with adolescents of low morality as with those of high. Using an Adult Guess-Who Test, the subjects were asked to write names of adults in the community who were community-minded, friendly to young people, trustworthy, good looking, or carefully dressed. The morally mature adolescents tended to name solid, reputable people in their neighborhoods. The low group gave more scattered responses, including some teachers but also some young adults of questionable reputation. Clergymen were almost never mentioned [69].

A successful program is the result of planned efforts to provide adult models for about 2500 black ghetto boys [58]. In the course of a year, each boy is given opportunities to meet, watch, and talk with 27 or more successful black men in blue-collar and white-collar occupations. IN stands for *Interested Negroes*, of whom more than 1000 are available to junior high school boys. IN finds out what kinds of work the boy would like to observe and sends him to a man doing that type of work. Often the successful man has come from a community similar to the one in which the boy lives. Thus the boy has a chance to identify with a man who looks like a hero whom he might dare to emulate.

## Parents and Peers

Peers are of tremendous importance in the lives of adolescents, but what of their influence as compared with that of parents? Coleman's subjects were almost equally divided as to which would be worse, disappointing a parent or breaking with a friend [21].

In some ways, adolescents become closer to their peers as they grow up; in other ways they remain fairly close to their parents. They want to spend more and more time with their friends and less at home. They often feel that friends understand them better and that they are more like their friends than they are like their parents. However, parents are still recognized as sources of guidance and authority.

Changes between the fourth and tenth grades are shown in an investigation of family and peer orientation [13]. The subjects were asked three types of questions. To find out which group they identified with most, they were asked whether friends or family understood them better and whether they wanted to be more like their parents or more like their friends when they grew up. Questions to explore association orientation were about which group they most enjoyed being with. Norm orientation was studied by asking whose ideas were more like theirs in regard to right and wrong, activities that are fun, and the importance of school. Table 15–1 shows family and peer orientation at the various grade levels for the three different areas. The trend is clearly from family to peer orientation. Although the family loses and peers gain in regard to identification, there are twice as many tenth graders with a family orientation as with a peer orientation. As for spending time with friends or family, three prefer friends to the one who prefers family. As for values and norms, peers made steady gains, ending in tenth grade with 50 percent of choices as compared with 30 percent for the family.

Studies on guidance and acceptance of authority show adolescents behaving realistically. The influence of parents was compared with that of peers by asking boys aged 14 to 16, in a national survey [82, p. 31], "Would you take the ideas of people your own age, or the ideas of your parents, on—?" On the question of what time to be in at night, 95 percent would pay attention to their parents, 1 percent to peers; on personal problems, 76 percent to parents, 8 percent to peers; on how to act with the gang, 62 percent to parents, 23 percent to peers; on joining clubs, 47 percent to parents, 34 percent to peers; on personal grooming, 45 percent to parents, 30 percent to peers. These answers give a rather surprising weight to parents' influence.

Table 15–1 Orientation to Family and Peers in Children from Fourth Through Tenth Grade

| Orientation Toward | Grade in School | | | | | | |
|---|---|---|---|---|---|---|---|
| | 4TH | 5TH | 6TH | 7TH | 8TH | 9TH | 10TH |
| *Combined Orientation* | | | | | | | |
| Family | 87.1 | 80.5 | 80.2 | 66.7 | 41.7 | 44.7 | 31.6 |
| Neutral | 6.9 | 12.2 | 11.2 | 9.3 | 18.3 | 22.4 | 20.2 |
| Peer | 5.9 | 7.3 | 8.6 | 24.1 | 40.0 | 32.9 | 48.1 |
| *Normative Orientation* | | | | | | | |
| Family | 82.2 | 64.6 | 69.8 | 51.9 | 33.0 | 42.4 | 30.4 |
| Neutral | 5.9 | 12.2 | 12.1 | 13.9 | 14.8 | 16.5 | 19.0 |
| Peer | 11.9 | 23.2 | 18.1 | 34.3 | 52.2 | 41.2 | 50.6 |
| *Association Orientation* | | | | | | | |
| Family | 75.2 | 65.9 | 62.1 | 51.9 | 20.9 | 21.2 | 15.2 |
| Neutral | 15.8 | 24.4 | 25.0 | 22.2 | 39.1 | 37.6 | 29.1 |
| Peer | 8.9 | 9.8 | 12.9 | 25.9 | 40.0 | 41.2 | 55.7 |
| *Identification* | | | | | | | |
| Family | 81.2 | 79.2 | 77.6 | 72.2 | 57.4 | 62.3 | 51.9 |
| Neutral | 13.8 | 18.3 | 18.1 | 18.5 | 24.3 | 24.7 | 21.5 |
| Peer | 5.0 | 2.4 | 4.3 | 9.2 | 18.2 | 13.0 | 26.6 |
| *N* | 101 | 82 | 116 | 108 | 115 | 85 | 79 |

SOURCE: Reprinted by permission from C. E. Bowerman and J. W. Kinch, "Changes in Family and Peer Orientation of Children between the Fourth and Tenth Grades," *Social Forces*, 37, Table 1, p. 208. Copyright © 1959, University of North Carolina Press.

Another attempt to assess the relative influence of parents and peers used stories about adolescent girls trying to solve conflicts in which one solution was favored by parents, another by peers [16]. Then ninth, tenth, and eleventh grade girls made their own choices as to solutions. The experimental group was then given a second form of the test, in which parents were credited with the solutions offered in the first test by peers, and vice versa. Thus a measure of shifting to parent or peer was obtained. Results indicated that the girls tended to see parents and peers as differing as to the areas where they were competent guides to behavior. In other words, the girls consistently chose parents' advice in any areas concerned with the larger society, such as jobs. They tended to take peers' advice in areas where peer conformity was important, such as how to dress for a party or football game. In consulting peers as to which course to take in school, they were not seeking vocational advice, but information which would prevent them from being separated from friends.

Where adolescents perceived themselves as more like peers than parents, they chose the peers' solutions, as in taste in clothes and feelings about school. Where they perceived themselves as more like parents, they chose parents' solutions, as in questions of moral behavior. Other data from the study suggested that the more difficult the choice, the more the girl referred to the parents' solution. Also, the girls often dealt with parent–peer cross-pressures by not communicating with their parents.

## The Peer Group

Sociologists debate the question of how distinctly adolescence and youth are defined and separated from the rest of American culture and whether it is accurate to call it a *subculture*. The sharpness with which adolescence is cut off from childhood and adulthood doubtless varies from one American situation to another.

For most adolescents, peers (age-mates) play an even more important part in life than they did during childhood. A few adolescents remain outside the social swim from preference, pursuing studies, hobbies, or athletics, perhaps with one or two friends. Some youngsters, rejected by the peer group, exist in isolation or with other isolates in twos or threes. Among peers, there are two main kinds of groups: crowds and cliques. Friends, of course, are individuals.

### The Crowd

Both boys and girls belong to "the crowd," but there are occasions when one sex gets together. The like-sex crowd is not always identical with the group of boys or girls which participates in the boy–girl crowd. Especially at the younger ages, late maturers and certain nonconforming, independent individuals are unacceptable or uninterested in boy–girl affairs, but they may be cherished members of a like-sex group. Within the crowd are cliques, small groups of close friends, and pairs of best friends.

The crowd is usually based on the school, although neighborhood has some influence. School is the place where most social interaction takes place, in the classroom and library, at basketball and football games, clubs, interest groups, parties, in the corridor and yard (or campus, as it is sometimes called).

One of the basic functions of the crowd is to provide a group identity which separates adolescent from parent, a "we" feeling apart from the family. Thus the adolescent strengthens his own sense of identity by being a member of a group which defines his difference from his parents. Joe gets his hair cut (or not cut) like the other boys do, but different from Dad's. The girls wear pretty much the same shade of lipstick and nail polish, as well as standardized coiffures, but if adults adopt those fashions, they are soon dead and replaced. Signs known to the crowd tell whether you are going steady, looking for a new steady, interested in playing the field or not interested. As adults catch on, the signs change. Language, music, and dancing are also exclusive as regards the older generation. While embracing the latest dance fashion, teen-agers are likely to register disgust when their parents do the same dance, even if they do it rather well. It is quite acceptable, even cute, for parents to do a similar dance, however, as long as it comes from their own adolescent days. In these and a thousand other ways adolescents reject their parents and their parents' generation. The crowd gives them strength for self-assertion and a new frame of reference from which to reject the old.

The crowd is also for fun and confortable feelings, for doing things together like bowling and strolling, for hanging around the soda fountain, for just talking and talking and talking. And giggling and shouting. The output in decibels is very large in comparison with the intellectual content of conversation, but with good reason. Everybody is trying out a variety of roles, uncertain and tentative as to what kind of person he can be. There is security and warmth in the company of people who face the same problems, feel the same way, behave the same way, and wear the same symbols of belonging. It feels good to giggle and shout, to be silly and to stand together against those who do not understand.

Table 15–2 shows how high school boys and girls say they like to spend their leisure time. Table 15–3 reveals the ways in which friends spend their time together.

It is based on answers to the question "What do you and the fellows (girls) you go around with here at school have most in common—what are the things you do together?"

Both tables point up the boys' greater participation in athletics and the greater variety of activities and interests which boys have as compared with girls. Girls reported "just being with the group," rather than specific activities, almost twice as often as boys.

**Table 15–2** Percentage of High School Boys and Girls Reporting Pleasure in Various Activities

|  | Boys (%) | Girls (%) |
|---|---|---|
| 1. Organized outdoor sports—including football, basketball, tennis, etc. | 22.0 | 6.9 |
| 2. Unorganized outdoor activities—including hunting, fishing, swimming, boating, horseback riding | 14.7 | 11.3 |
| 3. "Being with the group," riding around, going up town, etc. | 17.2 | 32.5 |
| 4. Attending movies and spectator events—athletic games, etc. | 8.5 | 10.4 |
| 5. Dating or being out with opposite sex | 13.6 | 11.6 |
| 6. Going dancing (girls only) |  | 12.0 |
| 7. Hobby—working on cars, bicycles, radio, musical instruments, etc. | 22.5 | 20.1 |
| 8. Indoor group activities—bowling, playing cards, roller skating, etc. | 8.0 | 8.1 |
| 9. Watching television | 19.4 | 23.6 |
| 10. Listening to records or radio | 11.2 | 31.7 |
| 11. Reading | 13.7 | 35.5 |
| 12. Other, e.g., talking on telephone | 7.1 | 9.3 |
| 13. No answer | 8.1 | 3.7 |
| *Number of Cases* | (4020) | (4134) |

SOURCE: Reprinted with permission of The Free Press from *The Adolescent Society* by J. S. Coleman. Copyright © 1961 by The Free Press Corporation.

**Table 15–3** High School Boys and Girls Report on How They Spend Time with Their Friends

|  | Boys (%) | Girls (%) |
|---|---|---|
| 1. Organized outdoor sports–including football, basketball, tennis, etc. | 34.5 | 8.2 |
| 2. Unorganized outdoor activities–including hunting, fishing, swimming, boating, horseback riding | 11.7 | 6.6 |
| 3. In-school activities, interests, clubs | 8.9 | 19.2 |
| 4. Attending spectator events |  |  |
| (a) School-related games and events | 5.4 | 22.1 |
| (b) Out-of-school–movies, etc. | 17.8 | 33.0 |
| 5. Eating together at lunch or taking classes together | 9.1 | 13.7 |
| 6. Dating together or going to dances together | 19.7 | 39.6 |
| 7. Having parties together (girls only) |  | 10.6 |
| 8. "Hanging around together," "going uptown" | 13.4 | 26.8 |
| *Number of Cases* | (4020) | (4134) |

* Listed in the table are all the categories of activities or interests mentioned by at least 10 percent of the boys or girls.

SOURCE: Reprinted with permission of The Free Press from *The Adolescent Society* by J. S. Coleman. Copyright © 1961 by The Free Press Corporation.

## The Clique

Smaller and more intimate than the crowd, although often called "the crowd" by its members, a clique is a highly selected group of friends. Usually alike in social background, interests, and experience, they are emotionally attached to each other. Members' feeling for one another is the basic factor holding them together. Some cliques become formalized into clubs, even fraternities and sororities, but most adolescent cliques remain informal and small. Just as the adolescent generation differentiates itself from adults by many symbols, and one crowd from another, so a clique is likely to have ways of proclaiming its difference from others and solidarity within itself. "Everybody" wears blue on Tuesdays. A fraternity pin. The turn of a phrase. A food fad.

Compared with boys, girls show a wider range of emotional needs in peer relationships [46] and a greater need for close friendships [24]. Girls are more cliquish than boys [21]. Belonging to a clique or peer group is more related to status values for girls than for boys [21, 46]. Since high status is relative, excluding others from a high-status clique can make the members feel important.

Erikson [31, pp. 92–93] tells how clique members can be petty, cruel, and intolerant in order to defend themselves against a sense of *identity diffusion*. By excluding others who are "different" in skin color, religion, class, abilities, or even such trivialities as dress and appearance, the youngster gains some sense of identity from the group to which he belongs. Erikson stresses the importance of understanding this mechanism without condoning the behavior. Adolescents have to be helped to grow beyond the point where they feel the necessity for defending themselves by these cruel methods. (These are the methods of totalitarian systems.) Erikson implies that it can be done by adults living so as to demonstrate "a democratic identity which can be strong and yet tolerant, judicious and still determined."

## Dominant Values in the Peer Culture

In every one of the ten high schools (chosen for diversity and representing the United States), boys chose the role of famous athlete as more desirable than jet pilot, with atomic scientist third and missionary far down at the bottom [21]. A more recent study on young adolescent boys (between 10 and 14) confirmed the importance of athletic ability for friendship choices and also indicated that conformity to adult standards was correlated with sociometric choice [52]. Girls in the ten representative high schools chose in this order: model, nurse, schoolteacher, actress (or artist). When asked how they would like to be remembered in high school, boys chose first athletic star, then brilliant student, and last, most popular. Girls preferred being a leader in activities, with popularity a close second and scholarship last. When asked about dating preferences, girls ranked brilliant students below athletic and good-looking boys, while boys registered even less desire to date brilliant girls, strongly preferring best-looking girls and preferring cheer leaders. Apparently, certain values have been stable since a generation ago when a popular song summed it up thus: "You gotta be a football hero, to get along with a beautiful girl."

Although the study does not yield information on what happened to individuals' values over the high school years, it does show group changes throughout the academic year based on questionnaires answered by 8000 youngsters. Although the

Robert J. Izzo

shifts are small, the image of the athletic star for boys becomes even more attractive, and for girls, the activities leader becomes more attractive. For both, the scholarship value loses appeal.

A very different picture of adolescent values emerges from a longitudinal, intensive study of character development in adolescence [69]. Of all the children born during one year in a carefully selected city, a third of these cases, selected to be representative, were studied in greater detail. When these youngsters evaluated one another, their judgments could be checked against the elaborate findings of the research staff. In judging and rewarding peers, the adolescents took into account both moral values and social skill values. They tended to reward peers who were honest, responsible, loyal, kind, and self-controlled. They also rewarded geniality and skill in games. Peers and research staff had high agreement on which adolescents showed the most desirable social behavior. As they grew older, the youngsters weighted character values more heavily in relation to surface values. Here is an example from this study, [69, p. 136]:

> "Earl Eddy" could do practically no wrong when he and his peers were in the early teens. He was highly active, socially visible, and good at games and dancing, well before most of the group had mastered these skills. This is a vivid illustration of the way somewhat superficial values can sometimes outweigh the virtues of good character in the eyes of uncertain adolescents, until they themselves have achieved solid competence. However, at the time he was seventeen, he was still relying on his old techniques. The group had mastered and outgrown these social and athletic skills as a primary basis for judging personal worth. At that point, they dramatically lost respect for him. He did not change, but the group outgrew his adolescent "techniques."

The results of these two studies do not conflict. Each touches upon peer group values from its point of view. Together, they give a more rounded picture than

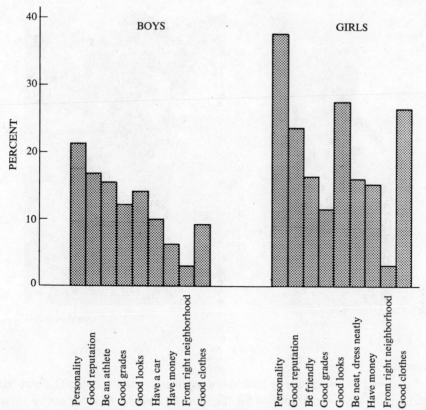

**Figure 15–4.** Categories of responses of high school students to the question, "What does it take to get into the leading crowd in this school?"

SOURCE: Reprinted with permission of The Free Press from *The Adolescent Society* by J. S. Coleman. Copyright © 1961 by The Free Press Corporation.

either yields by itself. They show adolescents saying they care more about looks, athletics, and activities than they do for academic achievement, and yet demonstrating respect for moral values and mature social behavior.

Values vary from one peer group to another. Coleman shows distinctive differences in the ways in which the various schools emphasized the values investigated. For instance, in Elmtown and Maple Grove, scholastic interests were combined with others, while Green Junction focused on the athletic and Marketville gave independent status to the athlete and scholar [21, p. 196]. The intensive longitudinal study indicated that the moral values held by deviant groups can result in rewards for stealing or cruelty [69, p. 139]. The values which an adolescent accepts as his own will come partly from his own crowd and the other groups he contacts (See Figure 15–4). The local variation of the general picture is the environment with which he will interact. What of the value system he makes his own will depend on many factors, such as his position in the peer social system, his own personality, and his family. The study of character development suggested that the family is on the average a more potent force than the peer group, which reinforces and crystallizes tendencies already present. It is possible, however, for peer group values to become the most important ones for an adolescent [69, pp. 140–141].

Ellen S. Smart

*Friends*

The term *best friend* usually indicates a member of the same sex. The best-friend relationship is an important one for the sense of identity, as anyone who shares a telephone with an adolescent will testify. The long conversations are between like-sex friends, especially best friends, and longer for girls than for boys. A best friend is the best audience on whom to project all the roles and identities that you want to test as possibilities, since this audience is just as concerned with testing and trying. A pair may try a role together. "We'd both look better minus 10 pounds. Let's go on the same diet! We just won't let each other eat more than eleven hundred calories a day." They may play at building a common identity, each gaining security from feeling stronger as a pair than as an individual. "Edna is part of me and I'm part of her. We think the same things. Each of us knows what the other one is thinking. We wear the same kind of clothes and we trade clothes." Communication is easy with someone who faces the same succession of disequilibria—fluctuations in physical balance, emotional upsets, new mental powers, problems with parents, and all the rest. Sometimes the communication is only partial, in that each is a sounding board for the other, not unlike the egocentric conversations of preschool children.

Best-friend relationships have been shown to be more stable with increasing age, from 11 to 18 as seen in Figure 15–5. In these studies [45, 84], it is implied, although not specifically stated, that the best friends chosen were members of the same sex. The same rate of increase has been found for stability in choices of favorite games and animals and similar increases for stability of choice of school subjects, leisure time activities, and occupational choice [62]. Choice stability probably reflects increasing personality maturity. In turn, stability in choice of friends makes possible more opportunities for development of the sense of intimacy, since intimacy grows within permanent relationships. Erikson writes of the

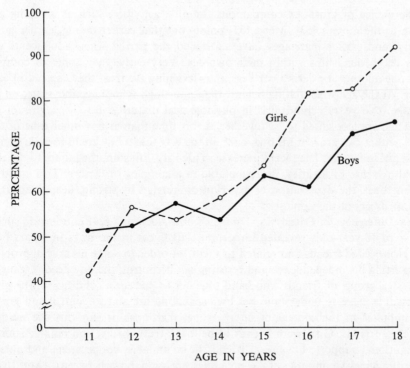

**Figure 15–5.** Increasing stability of friendships, as shown by percentages of boys and girls choosing the same person as "best friend" on two occasions two weeks apart.

Source: Reprinted by permission from G. G. Thompson and J. E. Horrocks, "A Study of the Friendship Fluctuations of Urban Boys and Girls," *Journal of Genetic Psychology*, **70**, 53–63. Copyright © 1947, The Journal Press.

sense of intimacy as "the condition of a true twoness in that one must first become oneself" [31, p. 95]. Just as all the senses have early beginnings before their periods of critical growth, so we would expect the sense of intimacy to show some expression in childhood and adolescence. In its fullest meaning, intimacy between two people exists on all planes of contact, including sexual, but here, in its beginning stage, it is largely a meeting of minds. Bob tells Tom what he thinks and feels, trying to express it in ways that Tom will understand. Tom listens carefully to Bob and asks pertinent questions, trying to put himself in Bob's place. Each tries to understand and to make himself understandable. Each cares what the other thinks and feels. The stronger a person's sense of identity, the more he can care about the other person's thoughts and feelings. Released from the constant necessity of searching for his identity, he is free to enter into an intimate relationship. Since identity develops slowly throughout the period of adolescence, it is reasonable that it should gradually make way for intimacy.

The years 1946 and 1947 were the dates of the studies showing that the best-friend relationship became more stable through the teen years. If the studies were to be repeated today, we wonder (1) would best friend still continue through the teens to mean a member of the same sex? and (2) would friendships with the same sex show increasing stability? Adolescents have less time and energy for like-sex best friends because they are turning increasingly to the opposite sex for companionship. Comparing adolescents of the 1940s and 1960s there is an increase in the choice of cross-sex companions for nine activities, such as studying and going to the movies [53]. Mead [63] points out that earlier dating, earlier going steady, and earlier marriages have shortened the period when adolescents can form deep friendships within their own sex. Very early, they come to compete with one another for dating partners, thus lessening the trust they can put in each other. At the age when dating begins, the junior high school age, boys are, on the average, two years behind girls in physiological maturity. Boys and girls of the same age are less suited to be together at this time than at any other time of life. Thus neither can grow at his own pace, in the way that a boy could in male society and a girl in female. The recent increase in identity diffusion, the failure to develop a healthy sense of identity, is attributable to a complex of factors. This could be one of them, the deprivation of a period dominated by strong, deep friendships with members of the same sex.

**Sex Differences in Friendship.** Douvan's and Adelson's [24] nationwide survey of 14- to 16-year-olds revealed important differences in the ways in which boys and girls needed friends and related to them. In order to solve his crucial problem of asserting his independence and resisting adult control, the boy needs a gang or at least a group of friends who band together to present a solid front. The girl's problem is more to understand her own sexual nature and to control and gratify her impulses in the context of interpersonal relationships; for this she needs a few close friends. Girls want friends to be loyal, trustworthy, and reliable sources of emotional support; boys want friends to be amiable, cooperative, and able to control aggressive impulses. Like preadolescent girls, boys between 14 and 16 are not concerned with warmth, sensitivity, and close relationships. The support that boys want from friends is against concrete trouble, especially conflicts with authority, whereas girls want help with their own emotional crises. Since the study did not go beyond age 16 with boys, it is possible that older boys change in the direction of developing warmer and closer relationships with friends.

**Popularity.** A popular person is one who is chosen or liked by many peers. A youngster may achieve popularity at some expense to his integrity since he may have to make many concessions in order to please a variety of people. He does not necessarily have a deeply satisfying "best friend" with whom he develops intimacy and strengthens his identity. Popularity is a strong value, however. We have already discussed some of the ways in which it is achieved. The study of 10 high schools gives some insight into the average criteria for popularity [21, pp. 43–50]. From the feminine point of view being a leader in activities and being in a leading crowd and cheer-leading were consistently important. Grades and family background were less important in popularity with boys than with girls. Nice clothes were more so. Since popularity with boys was important in the status system of girls, the importance of personal attractiveness was increased. Boys saw being an athlete, being in a leading crowd, and being an activities leader as important criteria. Scholarship, while relatively unimportant, appeared to boys as even less important in their popularity with girls, while having a nice car became more important in relation to girls.

The basis for sociometric choices was studied by factor analysis of the responses of 10- to 14-year-old boys in a camp [52]. Results showed the two main factors underlying popularity to be perceived athletic ability and perceived conformity to adult standards. The second factor is difficult to square with other investigators' findings as to the importance of friends for support against adults. Perhaps it meant that for these very young adolescent boys, conformity on the part of friends would not get them into trouble with adults.

To the extent that success is measured by popularity and membership in the leading crowd, there is widespread threat to the sense of adequacy of many youngsters. There are not enough places at the top. Nor is there free access to the top for anyone who is willing to work hard for it. The system does have its democratic aspects, however. Social position of families counts for considerably less than athletic achievement. Motor skill is distributed much more evenly throughout the socioeconomic hierarchy than is scholarship. If scholarship and class position were more important than athletics, then the youngsters from more privileged families would have a greater advantage than they do.

## The Opposite Sex

*Patterns of Association*

In the 1930s and 40s, research [20, 34] revealed the pubescent child as standing on the brink of heterosexual relationships. He was at the end of preadolescence, the time of life when boys and girls said they hated each other, when they played sex-appropriate games in like-sex groups, shunning the opposite sex vociferously. Preadolescent boys proclaimed their masculinity by being loud, aggressive, dirty, and rejecting of feminine values, many of which coincided with adult values. With pubescence came covert interest in the opposite sex, expressed by taking a quick look when others were not noticing, and by hostile, provocative, and teasing behavior. Groups of boys and groups of girls engaged in such exciting and enticing activity. The group hostility phase gradually gave way to group activities and group dating. After group dating came double-dating, and eventually pair dating.

Dating, a custom developed by middle-class North American youth, is more of a social relationship than a courtship one. A study on dating practices in a Midwestern high school [19] used the reports of seniors on their dating experience through high school. The reports showed 49 percent of girls and 36 percent of boys dating at age 13 indicating considerable boy–girl activity at the age when boys and girls used to be apart or only beginning tentative approaches to each other. Dating during the three years was thus: tenth grade, girls 85 percent, boys 71 percent; eleventh grade, girls 94 percent, boys 72 percent; twelfth grade, girls 89 percent, boys 85 percent. Douvan and Adelson [24] found that the most usual age for beginning dating is 14 for girls and 15 for boys [24]. Almost all American girls have dated by 17 and 30 percent of them have a steady boy friend. Young adolescent girls are defensive, suspicious, and manipulative toward boys, attributing popularity to specific skills, such as conversation and dancing. As they mature, they appreciate both boys and girls more as individuals, seeing popularity more as the product of sensitivity, understanding of the boy, and interest in him as a person.

Communication between the sexes was explored through a projective picture test used with boys and girls between 10 and 17 [17]. The pictures showed a boy and girl standing side by side, sitting side by side, the girl running after the boy, and the boy running after the girl. Figure 15–6 shows the stimulus pictures for adolescents. The subject was asked, "What is happening now? Why? What will happen next? How will the girl feel then? How will the boy feel then?" Most of the respondents saw the pair as having a romantic potential, although the younger

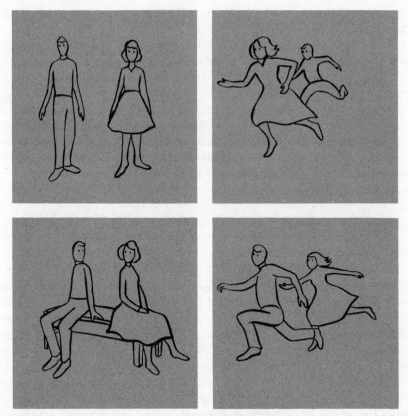

**Figure 15–6.** Stimulus pictures used in eliciting adolescents' interpretations of boy–girl relationships.

SOURCE: Reprinted by permission from Carlfred B. Broderick and Jean Weaver, "The Perceptual Context of Boy–Girl Communication," *Journal of Marriage and the Family*, **30**, 618–627. Copyright © 1968, by the National Council on Family Relations.

subjects emphasized this aspect less than the older ones did. About a quarter of the subjects saw the boy and girl as friends, while only a very few (none to 3 percent) saw them as hostile and exploitative. As the subjects increased in age, they saw communication between the boy and girl as having less to do with matters external to the pair and more with building, maintaining, or repairing romantic relationships.

Several important questions arise from the fact that dating begins earlier and happens more frequently than it used to do. First, what is the result in terms of personality development in both sexes? Second, what is happening to sex and love relationships of adolescents? These topics have been discussed at length by members of the clergy, sociologists, newspaper columnists, parents and adolescents. Research sheds some light on these questions but does not answer them clearly.

*Personality Development and Dating*

We have already mentioned Mead's concern over the detrimental effect of shortening the period of exclusive like-sex association. The education editor of the *New York Times* has registered disapproval of early dating, after pointing out that some children are dating at 9 years of age [40]. The Roman Catholic Church has taken a strong stand against early dating. A church-approved book for adolescents, *Dating for Young Catholics* [49, pp. 20–21], stresses the importance of learning appropriate sex-role behavior (which of course contributes to the sense of identity) through like-sex associations through adolescence: ". . . boys and girls who date too early and who spend a lot of time with the other sex, sometimes do not develop the characteristics of their own sex as fully as they should. They don't have as good an understanding as they might have of what will be expected of them as men or women for the rest of their lives."

Erikson's theory does not preclude the possibility of developing the sense of identity through association with the opposite sex. In fact, he describes such a boy–girl relationship: ". . . such attachment is often devoted to an attempt at arriving at a definition of one's identity by talking things over endlessly, by confessing what one feels like and what the other seems like, and by discussing plans, wishes and expectations" [31, p. 95]. The danger implied in a boy–girl relationship of this sort is not that it is inadequate for promoting identity, but that it may come to involve a sexual relationship before the pair are ready for intimacy. That is, before the sense of identity is sufficiently established.

Another point of view, one which has been widespread in textbooks on family relationships, is that dating is educational, giving adolescents experience in human relationships, promoting social skills, and enhancing their ability to choose a mate wisely [61]. If indeed variety in dating partners and a large number of dates actually do promote personality development and wise mate selection, then early dating is desirable, since it has been shown that early daters (beginning under 13) delay going steady for a longer time than do late daters [61]. Early beginners tend to play the field, have a try at going steady and then return to playing the field before going steady again. Thus they have considerable experience with the opposite sex before choosing a marriage partner and getting involved in a situation where a sense of intimacy is required for success. It may be inaccurate to think of early dating as a causal factor here, however. Early daters tend to be early maturers. Early maturing boys enjoy more favorable self concepts and other positive personality attributes than do late maturers [48, 66]. While early maturing girls do not evoke the social esteem or popularity granted to early maturing boys, they still have favorable self concepts, as compared with late maturing girls. It is likely that the youngsters with the most favorable personality characteristics have the most opportunity for dating, both in regard to early dating and number of partners throughout the dating period. (See pages 576–577 and Figure 15–4 for importance of personality factors in popularity.)

## Romantic Love

One of the effects of love is an emphasis on the loved one's favorable qualities and a playing down of his faults. Romantic love makes this emphasis to an extreme degree. Romantic love is embedded in a complex of beliefs and ideals in Western culture: for every individual there is an ideal mate; love hits suddenly, even at first sight; when ideal mates marry, they live happily ever after; nothing matters but love; fidelity is a natural part of love; moonlight, roses, music, and perfume symbolize and promote love. Large parts of the American economy reinforce these beliefs and ideals through advertising, movies, songs, and magazine stories.

Adolescents are fertile ground for the seeds of romance, although it is likely

Robert J. Izzo

that some recent cultural developments are causing a decrease in romantic love. In spite of its potential danger, that of leading to a marriage without a realistic basis, romantic love offers opportunities for personality growth, along with a deeply beautiful experience which is worthwhile in itself. Tom sees Alice, the girl of his dreams, as a perfect woman and a perfect person, embodying the qualities which he, in his imperfection, would like to achieve. And Alice loves him! To be loved by such a marvelous creature proves that he is more worthy than he had thought possible. What's more, since they are a pair (unique and perhaps predestined), he derives some good qualities from her. The qualities which Tom sees in Alice and then makes his own are his own ideals. His identity becomes firmer as he projects his ideals and then incorporates them, with Alice playing an essential reciprocal role. With Alice, of course, the same process can take place, resulting in a stronger sense of identity for her too.

Tom's and Alice's relationship may develop into one where the sense of intimacy is promoted. Tom may share thoughts and feelings with Alice as he does with Bob, in a search for real understanding of the other person. If Tom and Alice communicate realistically, they will discard some of their romantic patterns, but *after* romantic love has served its identity-building function. If their love affair does grow into a permanent one, they may retain some romantic patterns which can continue to serve each one's sense of identity. After all, none of the crises of personality growth is ever completely solved, and identity, like the other senses, continues to need strengthening throughout life.

### Sex Behavior

Until quite recently, many family life researchers maintained that there was no difference between the sex behavior of present-day adolescents and that of the

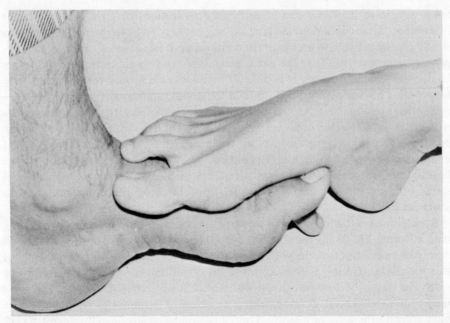

Craig Szwed

previous generation of adolescents. Others see a gradual but steady increase in liberalism, mainly in semipermanent premarital pairing [2]. Evidence of a change which took place in the mid-sixties comes from a study of college girls and what they did as teen-agers [6]. Although the sample was not large (only 205) and represented only one university, it was a well-controlled study. The same questionnaire and sampling was used with a group of girls in the same university, ten years earlier. While the percentages having premarital coitus while engaged was about the same in the two samples, the present group had double the rate of coitus while dating (23 percent versus 0) and going steady (28 percent versus 15), as compared with the earlier group. Among engaged girls who had had coitus, 75 percent had their first experience in the dating stage. Of those who had begun in the dating stage, 56 percent had more than one partner and 22 percent had five or more. Girls who had had their first date at 14 or younger had higher rates of coitus than girls who began to date at 15 or later, 31 percent versus 12 percent. High rates were also associated with dating a large number of boys (21 or more) and going steady several times.

**Sexual Codes.** Even though rates for premarital sex have increased, the study quoted above indicates that the majority of girls do not have coitus before marriage. Codes of teen-age sex behavior have been analyzed by Reiss [74]. The most popular code for teen-age girls, he says, is petting-with-affection. The linking of sex with mutual affection is a long-standing ideal in Western culture. The custom of petting-with-affection combines the sex-affection ideal with the standard of abstinence, since the couple stops short of full sex relations. They feel that it is right to pet when they are in love or very fond of each other. A few girls, especially younger teen-agers, permit only kissing and a few permit sexual intercourse. Girls who were devout in religion were found to be more conservative than average.

The double standard is still the most popular code among teen-age boys [74]. While a few, especially the highly educated, pay lip service to abstinence, still

# 582 The Adolescent

fewer adhere to it. Many accept petting-with-affection for girls and coitus for themselves. Although a double-standard boy may try to have intercourse with his steady girl, he is likely to break up the relationship if he succeeds, since he has thus proved her a bad girl. Thus the girl is encouraged to be a tease and sex is a game. Under these circumstances, it is difficult or impossible to link sex with affection. Lower-class boys are most likely to hold the double standard.

Another teen-age standard, popular with older adolescents, is permissiveness-with-affection [74]. This code permits coitus in a stable relationship, which may be strong affection, being in love, or being engaged. Although the majority of middle-class boys hold the double standard, a large proportion of them are more flexible and a minority accept permissiveness-with-affection. Boys of higher social status stress equality of the sexes and the importance of affection more than do lower-class boys.

Reiss estimates that increases in teen-age sex behavior have been more in petting than in coitus. He thinks that the basic attitudes toward sex are fairly well formed during the teens but that the young person is not yet ready to act upon them and that he has yet to learn how to combine his values into a coherent code of living [74]. The value of love-integrated-with-sex is highly consistent with Erikson's theory of psychosocial development. The sense of intimacy is an achievement built upon a firm sense of identity. Until a person has a strong and integrated self, fusion with another person threatens him with loss of self. When he has a firm conviction of self and accepts his meaning as a person, then he can forget himself in mental and physical intimacy with someone he loves. Because most teen-agers have a way to go in establishing a firm sense of identity, sex relations are rarely intimate relations, although they may indeed be accompanied by affection. Since boys experience intense sex tensions, coitus without intimacy is highly acceptable to many. For those boys and girls who feel disappointed in sex, it may well be that they expected intimacy and got only sensory experience.

New trends in relations between the sexes seem to show that a permanent monogamous commitment is not required as much as it used to be. The separation of sex and reproduction is one basic factor. So is the younger generation's seeking of honesty and love. Perhaps there are levels of intimacy appropriate to different levels of adolescent development. Probably petting-with-affection represents a very coherent code for the average adolescent. The double standard is obviously inconsistent with love, human dignity, and full enjoyment of sex.

**Masturbation.** Cultural interpretations of masturbation have followed such a confusing course that neither parents nor children know what to think about this common adolescent practice. While the old idea that masturbation is a shame and a sin is now outmoded, contemporary sex guides to youth still hint that it is not quite nice or at any rate, something to be indulged in as seldom as possible. Even while fully accepting the fact that masturbation has never been known to cause physical harm, many people have a nagging idea that there is something wrong with it psychologically. A psychiatrist [12, pp. 159–169] gives the psychoanalytic point of view that masturbation plays a necessary but temporary role in psychosexual development. Through masturbation, the adolescent integrates his childhood sex experience with his present and future. Infantile sexual pleasures become not ends in themselves but part of the mature heterosexual act, in foreplay. Through fantasy during masturbation, the adolescent connects the solitary sex experience with heterosexual acts. In this way, masturbation promotes development. If it becomes indispensable for releasing tension, then development has gone wrong and masturbation is pathological.

In addition to its function of integrating the total sex experience, masturbation helps to relieve the sexual tensions of individuals who are denied heterosexual outlets. Among such individuals are those who hold the ideal of love integrated with sex and who wish to avoid sexual intercourse until they can have it with a deeply loved, permanent partner. The effect of masturbation on these people is probably determined largely by whether they consider it shameful, sinful, and injurious or a natural, neutral substitute for a necessarily postponed activity.

## Sex Identity

The development of the sense of identity includes the development of identity as a man or a woman. As noted in previous chapters, sex typing occurs from birth onward. By the time a child reaches adolescence, he or she has done a great deal of growing in either a masculine or feminine direction.

The adolescent asks, "Just what does it mean to be an adult of my sex and what sort of acceptable adult am I capable of becoming?" Since the cultural prescription is not clear-cut and in fact permits many different interpretations, each young person has to select from the variety of possibilities, without the certainty of knowing that his choice is right. While freedom of choice is a cherished democratic right, it does carry the disadvantage of uncertainty and anxiety. Students reflect the strain of this burden in their current practice of dropping out for a semester or a year or two in order to "find themselves." Dropping out began with college students but is also done by high school students who "run away" if they have to in order to attain a moratorium from demands.

**Masculine Identity.** Since masculinity is defined in terms of activity and achievement, boys are encouraged to develop assertiveness and independence [24]. A boy has to come to terms with authority while maintaining his autonomy, neither submitting nor fighting too much. He has to come to terms with assertiveness, becoming neither timid nor cruel but controlled and purposeful. He has to come to terms with his sexuality, which he experiences directly as sexual desires. In order to control and gratify his sex impulses, he must loosen his family ties and make new ones. But before he can develop a sexual identity in relation to the opposite sex, he needs a foundation in the identity which requires achievement and assertiveness. Some sort of vocational success, perhaps a plan or commitment, will serve.

The adolescent boy knows and has known from early childhood that he must achieve and produce. Even though the high school peer group in general rewards athletes more than it does scholars, the adult male's vocational role is that of breadwinner, both before and after marriage. This fundamental is clear, even though expectations of husbands are not so definite. Also, there is continuity between the two roles. Research shows that husband–wife relationships are strongly influenced by the husband's vocational role. Men who were successful and competent in the work world exerted more power in making decisions at home than did men who were less adequate vocationally [11, p. 31]. The very importance of work as part of a man's role makes vocational decisions serious and problems anxiety-producing [81].

Another ingredient of masculine identity is the establishment of personal controls and standards. Douvan and Adelson found boys with well-internalized standards to be high in achievement striving, independence of judgment, energy level in work and play, self-confidence, self-criticism, organization of thought and capacity to bind present and future time [24, p. 116]. Boys with externalized standards were low in these types of ego strength.

There is evidence that the ideal male role is changing from the picture of a man as a go-getter, a competitive individual who initiates, invents, saves for the future, and pushes ahead. Modern bureaucratic society seems to influence men to be cooperative, relaxed group members, enjoying the present and letting the company take care of the future [64]. Mead [63] decries the shift from longtime goals to immediate gratification which means early marriage and early forcing into a pattern of domestication, focusing on earning a living instead of on ambitions for the future, curtailing the period of freedom in which a youth can dream. The more external aspects of masculine identity have undergone recent changes. Girls and boys dress much alike, and although girls have for many years worn male clothing on occasion, boys did not formerly wear pink shirts, flowered pants, and beads. While both sexes may have long hair, masculinity is unmistakable with beards and mustaches. Adults' overreaction to the new styles suggests that they suspect inner changes as well as outer. Is the cultural norm for masculine behavior being threatened by the young? Are young men relaxing in their attempts to internalize standards of control, to achieve and to assert themselves? While the majority of youth seem to maintain the general norms, a visible and vocal minority have developed different life styles in which the typical male role is modified.

**Feminine Identity.** Douvan and Adelson found girls' development of sex identity to be very different from that of boys. Autonomy, assertion, and occupational goals had no significance for the feminine identity. Interpersonal competence is critical for girls, and it is in a framework of interpersonal relations that they come to understand their sexuality. Girls are trained to cultivate sensitivity, warmth, and sympathy. Girls who measured high on a femininity test measured high on ego strength. Where the boy gained masculine identity by focusing on a future job, the girl gained feminine identity by projecting herself into the future as a wife and mother, carrying on nurturing interpersonal activities. Indications of high integration in feminine girls as compared with girls low in femininity included the following characteristics [24, p. 242]:

1. Much social activity, including many leisure pursuits, clubs and other voluntary organizations.
2. Planning and awareness of the future.
3. Poise, social skill, self-confidence, organized thinking.
4. More self-esteem and more sources of self-esteem.
5. An integrated ego ideal. The feminine girl knows an adult she would like to emulate.

Among not completely feminine girls, Douvan and Adelson distinguished five types: *ambivalent*, who score high on femininity but wish to be boys, envy boys, or choose masculine jobs, apparently feeling that feminine goals are neither full enough nor open enough to offer all that they want; *neutral*, who stress neither feminine nor masculine interests, showing immature social relationships and compliance and closeness to their families; *boyish*, who say they would like to be boys, enjoy team sports and active recreation, show an immature sort of concern with honesty, loyalty, and courage, and rebel against parents; *achievement-oriented*, who hold masculine occupational goals, often hold jobs, are not popular, look for social mobility which they expect will come more from work than from marriage, although marriage is not rejected; *antifeminine*, who do not want to marry. The last category includes only 5 percent of girls, the only group which shows severe psychological deviance. They are very constricted in all levels of ego functioning, particularly in imagination. Often these girls come from large, economically deprived families, where they were eldest. Most likely the girl was introduced early to the burdens of family life without the pleasures, perhaps with traditional, punitive parents. Quite logically, the boy's role looked more desirable to her and she had had her fill of housework and child care.

The clearly feminine girls were responding to the cultural stereotype of the woman as nurturant, centered on relationships involved in love, reproduction, homemaking, and dependent upon a man to define her status in society. This stereotype waxes and wanes in popularity in American culture. At present, it seems to be diminishing, as shown by Women's Liberation and other pressures for equal or improved status for women. Now that the population explosion threatens human existence, woman's reproductive role will have to shrink. Already the advertising industry has stopped trying to sell washing machines through pictures of women with ten children. When families with one or two children become the norm, then the feminine cultural role will doubtless encompass more than family relationships. There are already many women in the world who perform valuable services outside the family and yet retain a feminine way of feeling and relating. We expect the life style of such women to become incorporated more into the cultural ideal and as such to influence the feminine identity development of girls.

### Marriage

Americans marry relatively young, as Figure 15–7 will show. Average age at marriage gradually decreased from 1890 to 1950 while social change has been speeding up and the complexity of life increasing. Early marriage is a problem for the participants who are not mature enough to cope with the demands of marriage. While the nationwide average age of marriage has not decreased since 1950, as can be seen from Figure 15–7, the problems of youthful marriages are serious to the people involved and to society. The number of teen-age marriages has increased since mid-century, because the number of teen-agers has greatly increased. At present there are in the United States about 500,000 wives and 200,000 husbands under 19 years of age [35].

From the standpoint of personality development, one would expect adolescent marriages to be less satisfactory than those between adults. With one partner or both in the crisis of developing a sense of identity, the relationship cannot be one of mutuality and intimacy, which is the essence of the ideal American marriage. Both partners expect happiness from marriage, and yet their own immaturity prevents the establishment of the relationship which yields lasting happiness. The theory is borne out by statistics. A study [56, p. 130] of 1425 high school marriages showed that 20 percent of those occurring three years previously had already ended in annulment, divorce, or separation. This figure is nearly three times as large as the marriage dissolution rate for the general population for the first three years of

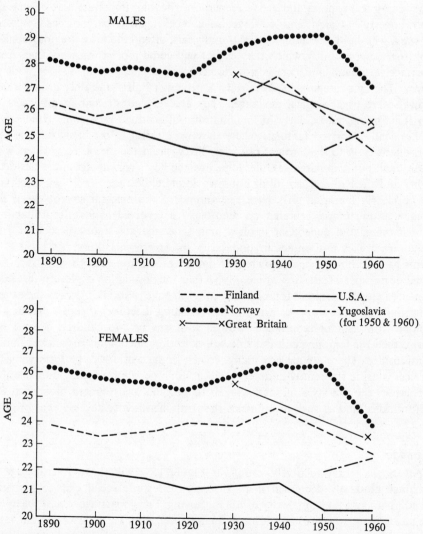

**Figure 15–7.** Average age at marriage over seven decades.
SOURCES: J. Moss, "Teen-age Marriage: Cross-National Trends and Sociological Factors," *Journal of Marriage and the Family*, **27**, 2, 230–242, and E. Venables, "Proposed Affinities in British-American Perspectives of Adolescence," *Journal of Marriage and the Family*, **27**, 2, 148–170.

marriage [7, p. 94]. Further evidence comes from census data on age at marriage and remarriage. Women still in their first marriage in a given year had been married at an average age of 21, while those already in their second marriage had contracted the first at 19 [37]. A study of divorced couples and happily married couples showed that as contrasted with the happily married, more of the divorced women had married before 18 and the men before 21 [60, pp. 101–102].

Conclusions from extensive research on young marriages indicate the factors contributing to early marriage [18]. The insecurity of modern life leads to a desire for loyalty, warmth, and affection which adolescents hope to find in marriage. Personal happiness is understood as inherent in family life. Sometimes marriage is used for avoiding the draft. A bandwagon effect may operate, as friends marry young. Marriage is overevaluated due to the romantic, glamorous image promoted by mass media. Economic restraints are reduced by prosperity, employment of wives, contribution of parents, and occupational fringe benefits. Increased heterosexual behavior at younger years, earlier dating and going steady, plus increased stimulation of sex drives by mass media, leads to increased premarital sexual intercourse, pregnancy, and forced marriages. Some early marriages are precipitated by the desire to escape from unhappy situations in home, school, or community or to solve other emotional problems.

Some of the outstanding characteristics of young marriages are as follows [18]. Most of them involve young brides and older grooms. Only 10 percent of high school brides marry high school students. High school students who marry are mostly juniors and seniors. One third to one half of high school brides are pregnant. One half to three quarters of high school grooms are involved in a premarital pregnancy. Premarital pregnancy rates are highest among couples where both are still in high school, lowest where both have finished high school. Most weddings are performed by clergymen. Young marriages involve more crossing of religious lines than do older marriages. Brides tend to come from lower- or working-class families.

**Problems Resulting from Early Marriage.** In addition to the disasters of marriage dissolution and the hazards to personality development already mentioned, young marrieds face curtailment of education and reduction of level of aspiration. (This problem is a serious one from the standpoint of society, as well as for the individuals involved, since it results in individuals less able to do society's productive and creative work.) Not only do married high school students face restrictions and some hostility from teachers and principals, but economic pressures may force them out of school. An analysis of 765 Pennsylvania high school marriages showed that two thirds of the married high school boys remained in school, while 90 percent of the girls dropped out [23]. A Minnesota study on teen-age marriages showed that 69 percent of these brides were pregnant and that most of them were required to drop out of school [3]. A more liberal policy exists in California, where only 9 percent of high schools reported that they suspended a married pregnant girl as soon as the pregnancy was known [55]. Even when pregnant teen-age brides are allowed to stay in school, they must stop to have their babies, and few ever return. Limited in education, and needing to take any sort of a job in order to make ends meet, the married adolescent may have to settle for a vocational identity which is a far cry from his dreams.

Most obvious of problems is children. The higher instability of teen-age marriages implies that they will involve more children in divorce than will other marriages. Thus the average adolescent is two stages behind the stage of maturity required by parenthood. Since most teen-agers are deeply involved in the identity crisis and barely started on the problems of intimacy, the sense of generativity is far beyond them. One has to grow far beyond mutual give and take, understanding, and communicating in order to nurture a completely dependent being, to fit one's own existence in with his, to enjoy giving without receiving immediate understanding and appreciation.

**Education for Marriage and Family.** Many high schools and colleges try to prepare their students for marriage through courses, as well as through lecture series and individual lectures, films, and discussions. The objectives of marriage education include giving adolescents knowledge of facts, behavior, development,

social norms and attitudes toward the self and other people, competence in interpersonal skills, and values in human development and relationships. Evaluations
of the results of marriage and family living courses have shown considerable
benefit to those students who have taken them, in terms of added knowledge,
understanding, attitudes, and abilities [27]. Cultural values, of course, influence the
content of courses preparing adolescents for future roles. While United States
courses tend to stress interpersonal relationships, New Zealand educators, through
the Plunket Society, emphasize nutritional preparation of adolescent girls for future
pregnancy. Ideally, both boys and girls would be educated for family living in its
social, psychological, and physical aspects.

## Summary

American parents and adolescents are likely to have considerable trouble with
each other as the child, in accordance with cultural demands, establishes his independence and sense of identity. Some of their conflicts are intensified by the
emotional concentration of the nuclear family, rapid social changes, and the
impact of mass media and easy travel. Some authorities consider conflict inevitable,
while others, noting the existence of many harmonious parent—adolescent relationships, doubt the necessity of conflict. Boys challenge parental authority more
than girls do. Adolescents generally like, love, and admire their parents, even
though they are concerned about problems regarding parents.

Parents usually have complex feelings about their teen-age children, often with
considerable ambivalence. Not only do they worry about the child's adequacy in
coping with his life but they also relive some of their own adolescent feelings and
problems. Parents often find it difficult to achieve a satisfactory balance between
controlling their almost-grown children and allowing them sufficient freedom.

Most adolescents have some trouble in communicating with parents, finding
certain topics, such as sex, misbehavior, and failure hard to discuss. When husband
and wife communicate well with each other, then parent–child communication
tends to be satisfactory, as well. From studies on feelings of closeness and on
attitudes toward parents, it seems that the search for independence does not
require most adolescents to feel hostile. The extent to which adolescents want to
be like their parents is affected by the family power structure, or the ways in which
decisions are made. Normal personality characteristics have been found related to
adolescents seeing themselves as similar to their fathers. Parents have considerable
effect upon their adolescents' values. The effect is more obvious when the children
become adults.

While adolescents are usually influenced more by their parents than by any
other adults, youngsters often use several adults for models. Teachers, youth
leaders and such people may build relationships which are important in adolescents' development. Although teen-agers move from family orientation toward
peer orientation, the family retains strongest influence in certain areas, while
peers become stronger in places where adolescents see them as knowing more than
parents.

The adolescent peer group is fairly distinct as a cultural group. Peer interaction
provides opportunities essential to the growth of the sense of identity. The crowd
offers the adolescent a group identity which helps him to separate himself from his
family, drawing a distinct line between generations. Because he feels comfortable

when identified with the crowd, he can try out a variety of roles. The clique is a small, select group of close friends, usually alike in interests and background, giving one another security and status, often behaving cruelly to outsiders.

A large survey by questionnaire indicated that dominant values for boys are athletic, for girls, social, with scholarship not only low on the list but actually losing value over time. A longitudinal study demonstrated adolescents' respect for moral values and mature social behavior. Adult values are accepted increasingly with age.

Friendship contributes to the sense of identity, especially close relationships such as "best friends" enjoy. When the sense of identity has reached a certain level of strength, friends can achieve true intimacy. It is easier and safer to develop the first intimate friendship with members of the same sex. Boys need a group of friends for support in resisting adult authority. Girls need close individual friends for emotional support in understanding themselves.

Greatly valued by many adolescents, popularity may exact a price of those who achieve it. Popularity, along with other attributes, gives high status. Many adolescents feel inadequate and inferior because they are assigned low or moderate statuses in systems which offer little room at the top.

Cross-sex friendships occur at earlier ages today than they did formerly. Earlier dating, going steady, and marriage also occur, threatening to restrict personality development. As adolescents mature, they increase in appreciation of one another as individuals and in understanding the role of interpersonal communication.

Romantic love is an aspect of American culture which sometimes confuses adolescents and yet also strengthens and beautifies their relationships with the opposite sex. Romantic love can promote the development of the sense of identity.

Although the limited available research indicates that the majority of adolescent girls do not have premarital coitus, it also suggests that coitus has increased in the dating and going-steady periods. The most usual code for girls is petting-with-affection and for boys, the double standard.

The development of a masculine identity requires a boy to come to terms with his assertiveness, independence, and sexuality. Vocational identity is basic. Internalized standards of control of behavior are typical of boys with strong egos and well-developed identity. Feminine identity develops as girls increase in interpersonal competence, which they use for understanding their sexuality. High femininity was associated with ego strength. Of all types of girls who are not highly feminine, the only pathological type is the antifeminine. There is evidence of recent change in cultural prescriptions for masculine and feminine roles.

Adolescent marriages have a poor chance for success, posing threats to the participants, their families, and the children who result from them. Personality immaturity, including educational and vocational immaturity, makes it difficult to achieve the high level of satisfaction which Americans demand of marriage. Education for marriage and family living has been found helpful to those adolescents who take such courses. Unfortunately, this type of education is not available to all.

## References

1. Adams, J. F. Adolescent personal problems as a function of age and sex. *J. Genet. Psychol.*, 1964, **104**, 207–214.

2. Adelson, J. What generation gap? *New York Times Magazine*, Jan. 18, 1970.
3. Anderson, W. J., & Latts, S. M. High school marriages and high school policies in Minnesota. *J. Marr. Fam.*, 1965, **27**, 266–270.
4. Bath, J. A., & Lewis, E. C. Attitudes of young female adults toward some areas of parent-adolescent conflict. *J. Genet. Psychol.*, 1962, **100**, 241–253.
5. Bealer, R. C., Willits, F. K., & Maida, P. R. The rebellious youth subculture—A myth. *Children*, 1964, **11**, 43–48.
6. Bell, R. R., & Chaskes, J. B. Premarital sexual experience among coeds, 1958 and 1968. *J. Marr. Fam.*, 1970, **32**, 81–84.
7. Bernard, J. Divorce and remarriage—Research related to policy. In E. M. Duvall & S. M. Duvall (Eds.), *Sex ways—In fact and faith*. New York: Association, 1961.
8. Biller, H. B. The mother–child relationship and the father-absent boy's personality development. *Merrill-Palmer Quart.*, 1971, **17**, 227–241.
9. Biller, H. B., & Bahm, R. N. Father-absence, perceived maternal behavior and masculinity of self-concept among junior high school boys. *Devel. Psychol.*, 1971, **2**, 178–181.
10. Biller, H. B., & Weiss, S. D. The father–daughter relationship and the personality development of the female. *J. Genet. Psychol.*, 1970, **116**, 79–93.
11. Blood, R. O., & Wolfe, D. M. *Husbands and wives*. Glencoe, Ill.: Free Press, 1960.
12. Blos, P. *On adolescence*. Glencoe, Ill.: Free Press, 1962.
13. Bowerman, C. E., & Kinch, J. W. Changes in family and peer orientations of children between fourth and tenth grades. *Soc. Forces*, 1959, **37**, 206–211.
14. Bowlby, J. *Attachment and loss*. Vol I: *Attachment*. London: Hogarth, 1969.
15. Breznitz, S., & Kugelmass, S. The perception of parents by adolescents: Consideration of the instrumentality–expressivity differentiation. *Hum. Relat.*, 1965, **18**, 103–113.
16. Brittain, C. V. Adolescent choices and parent–peer cross-pressures. *Am. Soc. Rev.*, 1963, **28**, 385–391.
17. Broderick, C. B. & Weaver, J. The perceptual context of boy-girl communication. *J. Marr. Fam.*, 1968, **30**, 618–627.
18. Burchinal, L. G. Young marriages—What we know about them. In E. M. Duvall & S. M. Duvall (Eds.), *Sex ways—In fact and faith*. New York: Association, 1961, pp. 69–83.
19. Cameron, W. J., & Kenkel, W. F. High school dating: A study in variation. *Mar. Fam. Living*, 1960, **22**, 74–76.
20. Campbell, E. H. The social-sex development of children. *Genet. Psychol. Mono.*, 1939, **21**, 461–552.
21. Coleman, J. S. *The adolescent society*. Glencoe, Ill.: Free Press, 1961.
22. Dahlem, N. W. Young Americans reported conceptions of their parents. *J. Psychol.*, 1970, **74**, 187–194.
23. de Lissovoy, V., & Hitchcock, M. E. High school marriages in Pennsylvania. *J. Marr. Fam.*, 1965, **27**, 263–265.
24. Douvan, E., & Adelson, J. *The adolescent experience*. New York: Wiley, 1966.
25. Droppelman, L. F., & Schaefer, E. S. Boys' and girls' reports of maternal and paternal behavior. *J. Abn. Soc. Psychol.*, 1963, **7**, 648–654.
26. Dubbe, M. C. What teen-agers can't tell parents and why. *The Coordinator*, 1956, **4**:3, 3–7.

27. Duvall, E. M. How effective are marriage courses? *J. Marr. Fam.*, 1965, **27**, 176–189.
28. Elder, G. H. Parental power legitimatization and its effect upon the adolescent. *Sociometry*, 1963, **26**, 50–65.
29. Emmerich, W. Family role concepts of children ages six to ten. *Child Devel.*, 1961, 32, 609–624.
30. Epperson, D. C. A reassessment of indices of parental influence in the adolescent society. *Am. Soc. Rev.*, 1964, **29**, 93–96.
31. Erikson, E. H. *Identity and the life cycle.* New York: International Universities, 1959.
32. Farber, B., & Jenne, W. C. Family organization and parent-child communication: Parents and siblings of a retarded child. *Mono. Soc. Res. Child Devel.*, 1963, **28**:7.
33. Freud, A. Adolescence. *Psychoan. Stud. Child*, 1958, **13**, 255–278.
34. Furfey, P. H. *The growing boy.* New York: Macmillan, 1930.
35. Gladden, J. W. Trends in high school marriages and public school policy in the United States. *Fam. Coord.*, 1968, **17**, 279–287.
36. Glassberg, B. Y. Sexual behavior patterns in contemporary youth culture— Implications for later marriage, *J. Marr. Fam.*, 1965, **27**, 190–192.
37. Glick, P. C. *American families.* New York: Wiley, 1957, pp. 56–68. Also, Stability of marriage in relation to age at marriage. In R. F. Winch, R. McGinnis & H. R. Barringer, *Selected studies in marriage and the family.* New York: Holt, 1962, pp. 622–626.
38. Goodman, N. Adolescent norms and behavior: Organization & conformity. *Merrill-Palmer Quart.*, 1969, **15**, 199–211.
39. Harris, D. B., & Tseng, S. C. Children's attitudes toward peers and parents as revealed by sentence completions. *Child Devel.*, 1957, **28**, 401–411.
40. Hechinger, G. Slowing down the social pace. *New York Times Magazine*, April 14, 1963.
41. Hereford, C. F. *Changing attitudes through group discussion.* Austin: University of Texas Press, 1963.
42. Hess, R. D., & Torney, J. V. Religion, age and sex in children's perceptions of family authority. *Child Devel.*, 1962, **33**, 781–789.
43. Hilgard, J. R., Neuman, M. F., & Fisk, F. Strength of adult ego following bereavement. *Am. J. Orthopsychiat.*, 1960, **30**, 788–798.
44. Hoffman, M. L. Childrearing practices and moral development: Generalizations from empirical research. *Child Devel.*, 1963, **34**, 295–318.
45. Horrocks, J. E., & Thompson, G. G. A study of the friendship fluctuations of rural boys and girls. *J. Genet. Psychol.*, 1946, **69**, 189–198.
46. Horrocks, J. E., & Weinberg, S. A. Psychological needs and their development during adolescence. *J. Psychol.*, 1970, **74**, 51–69.
47. Johnson, M. M. Sex-role learning in the nuclear family. *Child Devel.*, 1963, **34**, 319–333.
48. Jones, M. C., & Mussen, P. H. Self-conceptions, motivations and interpersonal attitudes of early- and late-maturing girls. *Child Devel.*, 1958, **29**, 491–501.
49. Kelly, G. A. *Dating for young Catholics.* Garden City, N.Y.: Doubleday, 1963.
50. King, K. Adolescent perception of power structure in the Negro family. *J. Marr. Fam.*, 1969, **31**, 751–764.

51. Knox, D. H. Conceptions of love at three developmental levels. *Fam. Coord.*, 1970, **19**, 151–157.
52. Krieger, L. H., & Wells, W. D. The criteria for friendship. *J. Soc. Psychol.*, 1969, **78**, 109–112.
53. Kuhlen, R. G., & Houlihan, N. B. Adolescent heterosexual interest in 1942 and 1963. *Child Devel.*, 1965, **36**, 1049–1052.
54. Landis, J. T. A re-examination of the role of the father as an index of family integration. *Marr. Fam. Living*, 1962, **24**, 122–128.
55. Landis, J. T. High school student marriages, school policy and family life education in California. *J. Marr. Fam.*, 1965, **27**, 271–280.
56. Landis, J. T., & Landis, M. G. *Building a successful marriage* (4th edition). Englewood Cliffs, N.J.: Prentice-Hall, 1963.
57. Levy, J., & Munroe, R. *The happy family*. New York: Knopf, 1949.
58. Lewis, E. A new set of heroes. *Am. Educ.*, 1970, **6**:1, 23.
59. Lipset, S. M. *Political man*. Garden City, N.Y.: Doubleday, 1960.
60. Locke, H. J. *Predicting adjustment in marriage*. New York: Holt, 1951.
61. Lowrie, A. H. Early and late dating: Some conditions associated with them. *Marr. Fam. Living*, 1961, **23**, 284–290.
62. McKinney, J. P. The development of choice stability in children and adolescents. *J. Genet. Psychol.*, 1968, **113**, 79–83.
63. Mead, M. The young adult. In E. Ginzberg (Ed.), *Values and ideals of American youth*. New York: Columbia University Press, 1961, pp. 37–51.
64. Miller, D. R., & Swanson, G. E. *The changing American parent*. New York: Wiley, 1958.
65. Moore, B. M., & Holtzman, W. H. *Tomorrow's parents*. Austin: University of Texas Press, 1965.
66. Mussen, P. H., & Jones, M. C. Self-conceptions, motivations and interpersonal attitudes of late- and early-maturing boys. *Child Devel.*, 1957, **28**, 243–256.
67. Offer, D., Marcus, D. & Offer, J. L. A longitudinal study of normal adolescent boys. *Am. J. Psychiat.*, 1970, **126**, 917–924.
68. Osgood, C., Suci, G., & Tannenbaum, P. H. *The measurement of meaning*. Urbana: University of Illinois, 1957.
69. Peck, R. F., & Havighurst, R. J. *The psychology of character development*. New York: Wiley, 1960.
70. Pedersen, F. A. Relationships between father-absence and emotional disturbance in male military dependents. *Merrill-Palmer Quart.*, 1966, **12**, 321–331.
71. Pikas, A. Children's attitudes toward rational versus inhibiting parental authority. *J. Abn. Soc. Psychol.*, 1961, **62**, 315–321.
72. Putney, S., & Middleton, R. Rebellion, conformity and parental religious ideologies. *Sociometry*, 1961, **24**, 125–135.
73. Rainwater, L. Crucible of identity: The Negro lower-class family. In A. E. Winder & D. L. Angus (Eds.), *Adolescence: Contemporary studies*. New York: American Book, 1968, pp. 166–181.
74. Reiss, I. L. *The social context of premarital permissiveness*. New York: Holt, Rinehart & Winston, 1967.
75. Schlesinger, B. *The one parent family*. Toronto: University of Toronto Press, 1969.
76. Schmuck, R. Concerns of contemporary adolescents. *Bull. Nat. Assoc. Secondary-School Principals*, 1965, **49**, 19–28.

77. Shellow, R., Schamp, J. R., Liebow, E., & Unger, E. Suburban runaways of the 1960's. *Mono. Soc. Res. Child. Devel.*, 1967, **32**:3.
78. Simpson, R. L. Parental influence, anticipatory socialization, and social mobility. *Am. Soc. Rev.*, 1962, **27**, 517–522.
79. Sopchak, A. L. Parental "identification" and "tendency toward disorders" as measured by the MMPI. *J. Abn. Soc. Psychol.*, 1952, **47**, 159–165.
80. Straus, M. A. The influence of sex of child and social class on instrumental and expressive family roles in a laboratory setting. *Sociol. Soc. Res.*, 1967, **52**, 7–21.
81. Strodbeck, F. L. Family interaction, values and achievement. In R. F. Winch, R. McGinnis & H. R. Barringer, *Selected studies in marriage and the family.* New York: Holt, 1962, pp. 355–376.
82. Survey Research Center. *A study of adolescent boys.* Ann Arbor: University of Michigan Press, 1956.
83. Sutton-Smith, B., Rosenberg, B. G., & Landy, F. Father-absence effects in families of different sibling compositions. *Child Devel.*, 1968, **39**, 1213–1228.
84. Thompson, G. G., & Horrocks, J. E. A study of the friendship fluctuations of urban boys and girls. *J. Genet. Psychol.*, 1947, **70**, 53–63.
85. Troll, L. E., Neugarten, B. L., & Kraines, R. J. Similarities in values and other personality characteristics in college students and their parents. *Merrill-Palmer Quart.*, 1969, **15**, 323–336.
86. Won, G., & Yamamura, D. Expectations of youth in relating to the world of adults. *Fam. Coord.*, 1970, **19**, 219–224.
87. Wright, D. S. A comparative study of the adolescent's concepts of his parents and teachers. *Educ. Rev.*, 1962, **14**, 226–232.

# Chapter 16

Robert J. Izzo

# Growth in Self-Direction

The development of the sense of ego identity involves a search for something to which one can be true. *Fidelity* is a virtue which adolescents have to achieve in order to move forward in psychosocial development. "... fidelity is that virtue and quality of adolescent ego strength which belongs to man's evolutionary heritage but which—like all basic virtues—can arise only in the interplay of a life stage with the individuals and the social forces of a true community." [15, p. 235]. Bowlby [5, p. 207] describes these phenomena in terms of attachment. During adolescence, as the bonds to parents grow weaker, the individual's attachment behavior is directed not only to other people but to institutions other than the family, such as schools, colleges, and political and religious organizations. Thus the attachment behavior and resulting fidelity to institutions and groups are expressions of the growing sense of ego identity and contributors to it.

Not only does the young person seek cultural values worthy of his commitment but he also needs a conviction of autonomy, the feeling that he is in charge. Convictions of adequacy and achievement are also basic, for one must have personal resources in order to offer himself in commitment. Adolescence can be viewed through a series of developing goals and values and as attempts to reach the goals and to be true to the values.

## Responsibility and Achievement

Boys and girls at every age level from 12 through 20 indicated a strong desire to be self-directing, to establish and work for worthwhile goals, and to be productive [31]. The subjects answered a questionnaire consisting of portrayals of social roles. For example, "Nothing stops Caroline from doing the best she can." After each item, the subject answers two questions: Am I like her (him)? Do I want to be like her? Answers at all ages showed significant interest in work-success, indicated by choice of goals in which initiative and action were involved. The young people showed eagerness to put forth their best efforts and to reach high goals. They were not looking for material rewards but the satisfaction of attaining their own goals and meeting their own standards for achievement. Self concept and self-evaluation are closely associated with these goals. Since the goals were held by the youngest subjects studied, it seems that the desire for a more effective, adequate self is already established by the age of 12 or 13. Erikson's theory is thus confirmed in that the development of a sense of industry and resulting feelings of adequacy are crucial during the elementary school years. The development of responsibility and achievement motivation can be seen as further development of the sense of industry and as essential to the sense of ego identity.

### Responsibility

A responsible person is one who consistently does his work, contributes his share, and carries his load without being watched or coerced by someone else. In their answers to questions about goals, adolescents showed that they wanted to conform to standards set by home and other institutions at the same time that they wanted to be independent and adequate [31]. A goal called *adequacy–self-assertion*, important to girls over 16 and boys over 17, is illustrated by these items: the people at home treat Steve like a grown man; Janet is seldom shy with a boy. The investigators suggest that a major change in adolescence is the acquisition of social skills which serve goals already established: the internalized values for mastery of the environment.* Thus the child begins adolescence knowing that he wants to be ade-

* The alert reader may notice some contradiction between this section and the discussion of masculine and feminine identity on pages 583–585. Douvan and Adelson found that masculine identity required assertiveness, achievement, and internalization of standards, while feminine

quate and to achieve, but he has to learn to do so with and through other people. In indicating that he wants to conform to established standards, he shows that he wants to achieve within the cultural framework. Fair success in so doing would normally be called *responsibility* by parents and other adults. Responsibility in tenth graders was shown to be positively associated with having companionship with their parents, and negatively associated with parental rejection and neglect [7]. This does not say what caused children to be responsible, or that rejecting, neglectful parents caused irresponsibility. More likely, a certain quality of interaction between parent and child builds companionship, mutual involvement, and responsibility.

A sex difference in responsible behavior showed up when teachers' ratings of tenth grade boys and girls were compared [7]. Teachers considered girls more responsible than boys, although they rated boys higher in leadership. If adequacy–self-assertion, as defined in the study of adolescent values [31] is related to responsibility, then we might expect tenth grade boys to lag behind girls, since the former developed the adequacy–self-assertion goal about a year later. Another explanation for teachers' finding boys less responsible is Douvan and Adelson's statement that the development of masculine identity requires rebellion against adults [12]. The comparison of tenth grade boys' and girls' responsibility included a survey of their parents behavior. Parents of girls had given them more affection, praise, and companionship than they had given their sons. In matters of discipline they were more love-oriented with girls, using more reasoning, appealing, showing disappointment, and threatening to withdraw love, while with boys they tended more toward physical punishment. Here then is further evidence that companionship and loving concern are related to the development of responsibility in adolescents.

Although parent attitudes and family relationships have much to do with it, the giving of specific jobs by parents was not found to be associated with responsibility in the child. Social responsibility on the part of the parents was, however, related to socially responsible attitudes in the children [23]. Probably the meaning of his work to the adolescent has a great deal to do with the responsibility he feels and shows. A serious, significant, and demanding job is likely to evoke more responsible effort and more satisfaction than is a simple routine task. Compare lifeguarding with tidying the garage, or making a wedding cake with doing a week's ironing! Paid work outside the home tends to give the youngster a greater feeling of responsibility than does working for his family, since in the former situation, he is judged entirely on his own performance, whereas his family has to keep him anyway. Responsibility is shown also in school, with friends and in the community work and play. This topic will be touched upon again under the heading "Moral Development."

**Independence.** Independence or self-reliance is a characteristic which can be seen early in life, probably in infancy. From preschool years through adolescence, it is

---

identity required interpersonal competence. Perhaps the difference between the two studies lies in the study on values being concerned with all aspects of the development of the self and identity, while Douvan and Adelson focused on masculinity and femininity. Perhaps self-assertion is relevant to developing a whole sense of identity but not important to the feminine aspects of it. Perhaps masculine identity does not require achieving within a framework of interpersonal competence, but being a whole person requires some development of feminine characteristics in a man and masculine ones in a woman.

a fairly stable characteristic, more so for girls than boys [35]. The investigators who studied independence defined its opposite, dependency, in terms of passive behavior in the face of obstacles or stress; seeking support, nurturance, and help when under stress; seeking affection and emotional support from female adults; seeking help with specific problems. Dependency in adults was rated on seeking dependent gratifications in choice of an occupation; dependent behavior toward a love object (sweetheart, husband, wife); dependent behavior with parents; dependent behavior with nonparents; withdrawing in face of failure; conflict over dependent behavior. Relating childhood behavior to adult behavior, results showed that girls who were generally dependent as children tended to be dependent adults, but boys often changed during childhood. Probably these findings reflect the pressure that is placed upon boys to become more and more independent as they grow up. College freshmen's capacity for autonomous behavior has been found to be related to their parents' behavior as autonomous people with inner-directed standards of action [45].

## Achievement

Children develop standards of performance for themselves from their parents' expectations of them, depending on the ways in which the parents encourage children, set tasks for them, and make demands upon them. Children doubtless take parents as models for achievement behavior and aspirations, just as they do in other areas.

Success or failure at school contributes also to aspirations. By the time the child reaches adolescence, he has many experiences which affect his desire for excellence, his definition of it, and his expectations as to what he will be able to accomplish. Achievement expectations and life span expectations were compared in two groups of adolescents, one white and upper-middle-class, the other largely black and lower-class [76]. Both groups saw themselves as having lived about a third of their lives, thus underestimating their biological futures. The lower-class boys and girls saw their present achievements representing 43 percent of their total life's achievements, whereas the other group saw present achievements as 31 percent of the whole. Ideal achievement scores (what they would like to achieve) were quite similar for the two groups. Other studies confirm the finding that disadvantaged adolescents would like to achieve just as much as the more privileged ones. A survey of Job Corps adolescents indicated that they would like to lead a middle-class style of life [21]. Discrepancy in actual expectations between privileged and disadvantaged probably represents realistic thinking in both groups.

**Attitudes Related to School Success.** Although successful students are more likely to come from middle-class homes than from disadvantaged, there are some advantaged students who do poorly in school and some from poor backgrounds who do well. When certain attitudes were explored in over 1000 Grade 10 students, some conditions for success in school were discovered [24]. Successful students from both types of background shared three conditions and in these they differed from the unsuccessful students from both types of background. Successful students believed that it is possible for man to gain control of his environment. This finding is consistent with the importance of children's belief in an internal locus of control, as discussed on page 418. The significance of this attitude for school success is very understandable. A student who believes that a person can control his environment would logically try to gain mastery of his own.

The second significant attitude was the position that it is worthwhile to associate with formal and informal school groups. A student holding this belief would, of course, share interests and activities related to the school. A third important dimension was believing that one's peer group valued education. The student agreed with items such as "Most of your friends will probably go on to college."

An attitude which did not distinguish between successful and unsuccessful students was that education is important. Students generally admitted that education is important. The extent to which they were able to make use of school was apparently much more related to the other three dimensions of attitudes and beliefs. One of the most interesting results of the study was that home background was significant only because of the differences in peer group attitudes. Advantaged students were more convinced than disadvantaged that their peers valued education highly. The study did not explore all aspects of home background and does not prove that no other differences exist. It only shows that among the dimensions studied, only one difference was significant.

**Stability of Achievement Behavior.** At the Fels Foundation, 71 subjects were followed from birth to early adulthood [44]. Ratings of achievement behavior at age 10 to 14 showed significant relationships to ratings of adult achievement behavior, particularly in the intellectual sphere. In this area, ratings at 10–14 accounted for at least a quarter of the variation in ratings in adulthood. The true figure may be greater than 25 percent, since other kinds of observations, interviews, and ratings might reveal more. Even if childhood experience determined as much as half of the adult achievement behavior, there is still room for the adolescent years to be extremely important in the development of achievement motivation.

**Parental Influence.** When parent–adolescent relationships are studied for insight into achievement behavior, one has to consider that some of the measured results will be due to past parent–child relationships rather than to only the present situation. With this limitation in mind, let us see what is offered by some research on parents and adolescents. In general, when parents demand high achievement, adolescents, as well as children, are likely to deliver it [9]. This statement is deceptively simple. If it were that easy to build achievement motivation, the world might be overrun with eager beavers. Many other influences interact with parental demands.

Achievement motivation is closely related to independence. The settings in which parents communicate their expectations make a difference in children's reactions to those expectations. Children tend to develop high levels of aspiration when their parents make appropriate demands at appropriate times, rewarding success liberally, and holding standards of excellence for them while also giving them freedom to work out their own problems in their own ways [72]. Both of these conditions seem to be necessary for high achievement motivation: a demand for achievement, and plenty of opportunities for independent work and decision making. Parental faith is implicit. The youngster and everyone else must realize that if a parent expects his offspring to do well, while giving him autonomy within wide limits, then the parent believes strongly in the child. Such a relationship has meaning for an adolescent's sense of identity, as well as for his desire to excel. He is faced with the problem of believing in himself, his abilities and potential, with the questions of whether he will be able to play the roles in life that he wants to play and of what *are* the roles he would like to play. The demonstrated faith of parents shows him that significant people are sure he can accomplish what he must.

*Background Factors*

What kinds of settings produce the types of parent–child relationships which lead to high-achievement motivation? Research shows that culture, class, family size, position in the family, and family structure all have some bearing on the question.

**Cultural Differences.** Achievement motivation of boys in 11 different nations was studied by comparing their vocational aspirations with the occupational statuses of the fathers [40]. If the boy chose an occupation higher than his father's, he received a higher score for achievement motivation than if his choice were on the same level as the father's or lower. The boys were of normal intelligence, from lower- or middle-class families and of three age levels, 6, 10, and 14 years. The high scores, in order and starting with the highest, were in Turkey, Lebanon, French Canada, Israel, the Bantu sample, Brazil, and the United States. Low scores, starting with the lowest, occurred in Japan, Germany, France, and English Canada. The average score for a national group probably reflects that nation's attitude toward members of the younger generation getting ahead or maintaining the *status quo* of their families. If getting ahead is a national value, then most parents would promote this goal with their children. Further evidence suggests that the vocational aspiration scores do actually reflect national values. A study of motivation themes in children's readers (mentioned on page 438) assigned motivation scores to 9 of the 11 countries represented in the present study. The correlation between aspiration scores and the textbook achievement scores was 0.87, indicating a strong relationship between textbook themes and boys' desires to get ahead vocationally. Most likely the two scores reflect general cultural attitudes toward achievement.

Cultural differences in training for independence and achievement were found in a study which compared six racial and ethnic groups living in the United States [52]. The groups differed in social mobility and achievement motivation. High-achievement motivation was more characteristic of Greeks, Jews, and white Protestants than of Italians, French-Canadians, and Negroes.

**Race Differences.** Southern white and black adolescents (ages 14 to 17), of low socioeconomic status, were compared on two dimensions which are related to school success [77]. *Delay of gratification* was tested by offering real choices, such as one candy bar now or a box of candy bars three weeks from today. The white students were more likely to wait three weeks for a larger reward. *Internal versus external control* was assessed by a questionnaire which measured the extent to which the adolescent believed in luck, chance, fate, or powers beyond his control rather than in his own abilities and activities. For example, one question was, "When somebody gets mad at you, do you feel that there is nothing you can do about it?" White students were much more likely than black students to locate the source or control inside themselves. The authors point out that a recent study of preschool children of low socioeconomic status showed no difference between blacks and whites in locus of control. Therefore, they say, significant differences in experience occur during the elementary school years, convincing the black students that they have little control over what happens to them and that it is better to take a small reward now than to trust others to deliver a larger reward promised for later.

**Class Differences.** Comparisons show the middle class to be most concerned with achievement and most intent upon training its children thus. The successful middle-class parent serves as a model of academic and occupational achievement, actively perpetuating middle-class behavior in his child. One investigator [7] compared upper-middle-class parent–adolescent relationships with those in the lower-middle-class and commented on the results in both boys and girls. Independence training was greater for upper-middle-class girls than for lower, with the former showing more initiative. For boys, the reverse was true, with lower-middle-class boys being controlled less by their parents and showing more achievement aspiration.

The joint effects of social class and family size have been studied for boys only [53]. Although the middle class averaged the highest achievement scores, scores within a given class varied greatly with the sizes of the families. The lowest aspiration levels were seen in large lower-class families, the next lowest in large upper-class families. Medium-sized upper-class families produced about the same aspiration levels as middle-class families. Tables 16–1 and 16–2 show the contrasts and similarities between the different classes and family sizes.

**Position in the Family.** Ordinal position makes a difference in achievement orientation. The popular notion is that eldest children are most ambitious. When class and family size are also taken into account, the eldest child does not always

**Table 16–1** Achievement Aspiration Scores of Boys, According to Family Size and Social Class

| | Sample A* | | | | Sample B† | | | |
|---|---|---|---|---|---|---|---|---|
| | FAMILY SIZE | | | | FAMILY SIZE | | | |
| Social Class | Small | Medium | Large | $\bar{x}$ | Small | Medium | Large | $\bar{x}$ |
| I–II | 5.20 | 6.41 | 2.33 | 5.46 | 7.28 | 7.93 | 2.25 | 7.11 |
| III | 6.49 | 6.14 | 5.83 | 6.28 | 7.67 | 7.36 | 6.13 | 7.32 |
| IV | 5.06 | 3.40 | 2.82 | 4.00 | 6.33 | 6.15 | 7.29 | 6.29 |
| V | 4.57 | 3.67 | 1.48 | 3.31 | 4.15 | 5.00 | 2.00 | 4.69 |
| $\bar{x}$ | 5.43 | 4.64 | 2.48 | | 6.61 | 6.57 | 6.22 | |
| N | 178 | 193 | 54 | | 155 | 166 | 45 | |

* Information lacking for two cases.
† Information lacking for one case.
SOURCE: Reprinted by permission from B. C. Rosen, "Family Structure and Achievement Motivation," *American Sociological Review*, **26**:4, Table 1, p. 585. Copyright © 1961, American Sociological Association.

**Table 16–2** Achievement Aspiration Scores of Boys, According to Birth Order, Family Size and Social Class

| | Social Class I–II–III | | | Social Class IV–V | | |
|---|---|---|---|---|---|---|
| | FAMILY SIZE | | | FAMILY SIZE | | |
| Birth Order | Small | Medium | Large | Small | Medium | Large |
| Oldest | 5.82 | 7.52 | 5.75 | 4.31 | 2.86 | 1.00 |
| Intermediate | * | 5.44 | 10.00 | * | 3.43 | 1.96 |
| Youngest | 5.94 | 5.21 | 2.00 | 5.93 | 3.90 | 2.84 |

* There are, of course, no intermediate children in a two-child family.
SOURCE: Reprinted by permission from B. C. Rosen, "Family Structure and Achievement Motivation," *American Sociological Review*, **26**:4, Table 3, p. 578. Copyright © 1961, American Sociological Association.

show up as the one most interested in achievement, although he often does. The study from which these tables come indicates that the highest achievement scores of all belong to children born into intermediate positions in large families of the upper and middle classes. Eldest children score high in medium-sized families in the upper and middle class. The youngest child in a small upper- or middle-class family is likely to be just as achievement-oriented as the eldest. Least ambitious of all is the eldest in a large lower-class family. Second place for lack of achievement motivation goes to the youngest in a large upper or middle-class family.

The effect of power structure on achievement motivation is significant. Power structure can be described in terms of who dominates the family, who makes most of the decisions, and whether and how people cooperate. In a study [62] of aspiration and actual school achievement of urban high school boys, families were classified into four types: father-dominant, mother-dominant, conflicting, and autonomic (cooperating smoothly). Scholastic achievement was about the same for boys from mother-dominated and autonomic families, lower for those from father-dominated, and lowest for those from conflicting families. There was a difference in the emotional patterns of the first two groups, even though they achieved about the same. The boys from mother-dominated families showed much more anxiety and tension than did their scholastic equals from autonomic families. When the subjects were compared in level of aspiration, those from conflicting families were considerably lower than the rest. The other three groups did not differ greatly, although the highest average score came from the autonomic group. In this respect, the lowest socioeconomic group differed from the whole group, in that mother-dominated families produced the highest levels of aspiration, father-dominated next, and autonomic third highest. Thus it can be seen that the relationships between husband and wife create a family atmosphere which affects the children's aspirations and their actual achievements. This study suggests that the democratic, equalitarian family is just as efficient as a mother- or father-dominated family in producing go-getters and that the democratic family is best of all in building healthy personalities at the same time.

While the family is extremely influential in childhood achievement motivation, with the school the second important factor, the adolescent interacts with a wider world of which family and school are only parts. He has a broader base on which to build his level of aspiration, since it is part of the identity which he is working to achieve. He seeks this part of himself through relationships with peers, while he works and earns money, when he tastes the pleasures of recreation and acquisition which achievement makes possible, when he reads about heroes and failures, when he creates and enjoys the arts, when he contemplates good and bad in the world.

## Vocational Development

A major concern of adolescents is the choosing of a vocation and getting established in it. A firm sense of identity requires successful working and producing a role acceptable to the young person and to the adults and peers important to him [59]. In contrast to the situation in simple societies, where there is little choice of occupation, modern youth is faced with a bewildering array of possibilities. Even though his parents may be ready with advice or even urging, the young person feels the necessity for self-direction in choosing his occupation. To be adequate and successful in an acceptable work role is usually a requirement of adulthood. In actually doing adult work, a young person learns to distinguish between what he thinks and hopes he might become, and what he hopes and thinks he could do in order to make a better world [33].

The background for vocational choice lies in the development of the sense of industry, in the stage previous to adolescence, for here is where work skills and attitudes take on great importance. The child identifies with his parents as workers and with older children and with other workers. He begins to learn to organize his time and to put work ahead of play appropriately. He experiments with different vocational roles, observing, learning about them, sometimes choosing one. Thus he shapes his concept of himself as a potential worker [4].

Vocational guidance means helping with both the choosing and the preparation. In a broad sense, all of education is preparation for work roles. The youngster's interaction with his school depends upon many influences, including the important ones of his desire for achievement and his intellectual resources. Educational achievement and vocational preparation depend also on the opportunities offered.

**Opportunities for Education.** A society expresses important beliefs and values in the educational system it maintains. In a project sponsored by UNESCO and the International Association of Universities [6] educational selection processes in 12 countries were studied. About three quarters of the world's education systems, which enroll about half of the world's students, follow the European plan. The other quarter, enrolling the other half of the students, uses the American plan, or what the Russians call the Russian plan. The European system channels children at 10 to 12 years into those who may go to university and those who will not. The former are permitted to study in preparation for higher education. The latter receive a different kind of education, with emphasis on the vocational. Further selective processes operate on the first group. Eventually, 1 to 8 percent of an age group go to university, having passed a final examination which makes them eligible.

The American plan permits everyone who wishes to do so to take a college preparatory course in secondary school. Completion of such a course does not grant automatic entrance to college. The institutions of higher learning apply their own systems of selection. For many years, it has been possible for anyone who could pay, to get into a college, not necessarily the one of his first choice. The state of California has practiced open access for some time, admitting all high school graduates who desired it, to a two-year college, all those in the upper third of the high school class to a state college, and those in the upper 12 percent to a state university. More open access is desired by students throughout the country. At present, the American 18- through 20-year-old population has this educational status: 60,000 have less than nine years of education; 2.9 million have had one to three years of high school; 7 million have completed four years of high school; half of the last group, 3.5 million, are enrolled in college [27]. In the Soviet Union, 900,000 places in universities are available to the 3 million new high school graduates [28]. Genuine open access means that ability to pay will not be a criterion for entrance. The average cost of American undergraduate education has doubled in the past ten years [8]. The average cost in private institutions is over four times that in public institutions, showing that the public actually does support higher education to a large degree. It is still not enough, however, for many students who have no financial support from their families. Children from a family with an income of over $15,000 are five times as likely to enter college as those from families earning less than $3000 [27].

The American plan also includes terminal education for those electing it in high school, with preparation for some vocations possible. The junior high school is an American invention designed to accommodate to the variety of physical, intellectual, and emotional growth encountered in people between about 11 and 15. Ideally, the junior high provides a time and a place where the young adolescent can explore vocational identities and find at least the broad outlines of the one that fits, if not the exact form. Guided by teachers and counselors, he tests himself as to interests, talents, and achievements. With self-knowledge in these areas, he is helped to choose the high school course which will lead him to an appropriate work role. Whether the junior high school is fulfilling its obligations or not, some sort of system like this is required by the basic values in American democracy.

Probability of going to college is greater for low-achieving boys than for low-achieving girls, but chances are the same for high achievers of both sexes [74]. When fathers were associated with academia, offspring had similar attendance rates. Birth order is also associated with college opportunities [22]. First-borns are more likely than others to go to college.

**Education Required by Various Occupations.** Educational level is related to occupational level. As one ascends the occupational scale, more and more years of academic achievement are required, with the professions necessitating education that extends into adulthood. A college education has become almost essential for success in the professions and management occupations. The average professional or technical worker has had more than four years of college. In some jobs, the worker can learn while doing, through an apprenticeship, an in-service training program, or a probationary period after an appropriate amount of formal education. Such jobs include many skilled crafts, salesclerk, policeman, and college professor. For other jobs, especially those where licensing is required, an institutional training period and examination are required before the worker is allowed to operate. Examples of these occupations are hairdresser, optometrist, schoolteacher, and physician. The increasing technological complexity of the modern world creates an increased demand for workers who are competent in using various scientific techniques. Many technicians are trained by the companies who need them, others by educational institutions. In addition to finding out which work roles he wants and which he could achieve, the adolescent has to find and obtain the education necessary for the job. Many young people also face the problem of being educated for jobs which do not exist.

**Intellectual Factors.** Intelligence as measured by IQ tests is positively related to occupational level, but correlations between intelligence and success on the job are quite low. For high school boys who were not going to college, good predictors of occupation were grade point average and post high school education [26]. The occupations can be arranged in a hierarchy according to average intelligence of those following them, but with each occupation, there is a wide range of intelligence scores, with considerable overlapping between levels [69]. For example, a teacher with a score of 110 scored higher than 10 teachers out of 100, while a lumberjack with a score of 60 scored higher than 10 lumberjacks out of 100. The top 10 percent of lumberjacks, however, scored higher than the bottom 10 percent of teachers.

An analysis of test scores of 10,000 people in 22 occupations yields Figure 16–1.

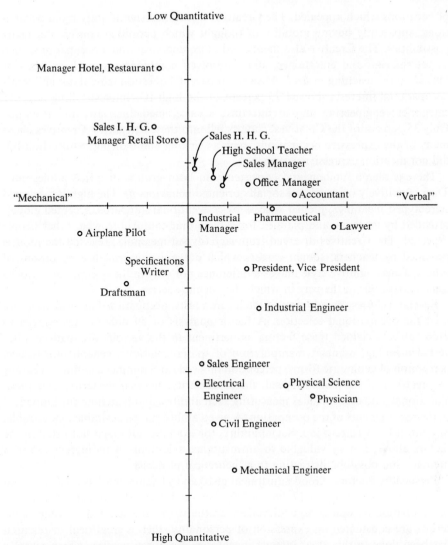

**Figure 16–1.** Quantitative, mechanical, and verbal requirements of various occupations, shown by the location of the occupation in the quadrants. The quantitative dimension is represented by the vertical axis, the mechanical-verbal dimension by the horizontal.

Source: Reprinted by permission from R. L. Thorndike and E. Hagen, *Ten Thousand Careers*. New York: John Wiley & Sons, Inc., 1959. Copyright © 1959, John Wiley & Sons, Inc.

Arrangement along the quantitative axis shows the relative requirements of the various occupations for quantitative and mathematical performance. The horizontal axis shows relative requirements for mechanical and verbal skills and knowledge. The diagram suggests how requirements are combined in various jobs. It is easy to pick out each type of combination by quadrants. Occupations placed near one another are close in requirements. See Figure 16–1.

Occupational choice was found to be related to style of cognitive functioning in high school students. When the occupational aspirations of highly creative adolescents were compared with those of high intelligent (high IQ) adolescents, [18] striking differences occurred between the two groups in both quantity and quality of vocations which appealed. The Creatives mentioned significantly more occupations, apparently having mobility of thought which permitted considering many possibilities. The Creative also mentioned more unconventional occupations, such as veterinarian and entertainer, and unresolved combinations, such as "law or music" and "teaching or art." Answers to parents' questionnaire about children's occupational interests showed 75 percent of the high IQs interest falling into five categories: engineering and architecture, science, medicine, law, and teaching. Only 35 percent of the Creatives' choices fell into these categories. Creatives chose many of the expressive occupations, such as writing and dancing, while High IQs did not mention expressive careers.

There is then a fundamental consistency in both groups of gifted adolescents. Their cognitively oriented and socially oriented behaviors *fit*. The high IQs selected stereotyped meanings, judged success by conventional standards, accepted models provided by teachers, and planned for careers that conform to what other people expected. The Creatives diverged from stereotyped meanings, rejected the models provided by teachers, sought careers which did not conform to expectations of others. Thus cognitive style makes a difference not only in the occupations adolescents choose but in the way in which they define success.

**Special Abilities.** In addition to intelligence tests, occupational aptitude tests are used for occupational selection. A factor analysis of 59 different tests given to 2156 subjects yielded these factors as pertinent in the various occupations [51]: verbal meaning, number, manipulation of spatial relations, general intelligence, perception of geometric forms, perception of words and numbers, aiming, accuracy or precision of movement, speed, finger dexterity, manual dexterity, and logic. Vocational guidance includes measuring such abilities and matching the individual to the requirements of the occupation. A given ability can be desirable, undesirable, or neutral for a certain job. Social ability, for example, although not listed in the factors above, is very valuable to an insurance salesman, of indifferent use to a fireman, and possibly distracting to a theoretical physicist.

**Personality Factors.** Good adjustment at 10 and 11 years predicts education and vocational achievement at 17 and 18 [10]. Personality factors contribute to choice of occupation as well as to achievement in the work role selected. Insofar as interests are considered an expression of personality, then a great deal of research has been done in this area. Interest inventories are questionnaires which reveal a pattern of interests. The pattern is then matched to the interest pattern of people engaged in a certain occupation. In the Strong Vocational Interest Test, for example, occupations are grouped by similarity of interest pattern, and the individual's test results are examined to see which group or groups they fit. Thus a person may find that his pattern fits that of Group IX, consisting of sales manager, real-estate salesman, and life insurance salesman. Or he may go into Group II, mathematician, engineer, chemist, physicist. When the results of interest tests are factor-analyzed, these broad types of interest show up as distinct: scientific, linguistic, social, and business [51, p. 86]. Interests in children are quite unstable. Interest patterns increase in permanence as adolescents progress through high school and college. A longitudinal study concludes that the interests characteristic of scientists become crystallized in boys between ages 10 and 14, but that the temperamental pattern basic to the interests becomes established much earlier. Girls who are interested in careers, as contrasted with those who are not, show certain characteristics. The career girls scored higher on scales measuring responsibility, self-control, and achievement. Their career interests began to take shape at or before the age of 14 [71].

**Cultural and Family Influences.** Vocational plans will naturally be affected by cultural values and by the type of jobs available in the country to which the adolescent belongs. The occupational aspiration research [40], mentioned on page 600, showed that engineering, medicine, and mechanical occupations were popular among boys in most of the 11 countries. Exceptions occurred among Bantu boys, who chose clerk and teacher; in Germany, where manual occupations were preferred; and in Japan, where boys wanted most to be clerks and merchants.

The higher the socioeconomic level of the family, the better are the children's chances of going to college, graduating from college, achieving high-level occupations, and achieving eminence. The reasons for these conditions are complex. They include differences in all sorts of opportunities as well as the personality structure produced by middle- and upper-class families and the values held. Studies of eminence and achievement at high levels usually show a larger-than-chance proportion of first-borns and only children. The same is true in studies of gifted children and children with high IQs [51, 66].

The effects upon adult roles of experiences with siblings have been explored by using a vocational interest test (Strong) with 20-year-olds [65]. A child's sex and ordinal position influence not only the ways in which his parents treat him but also the interactions between him and his siblings. What is more, these interactions continue to occur while the nuclear family lasts. They are not merely a matter of infancy and early childhood. In this article, only twosomes are considered, the effect of the relationship on each member of the pair being considered. The analysis of interest patterns as related to role situation led to these conclusions:

First-borns, especially girls, tended to choose teaching occupations more than did second-borns. This finding fits with other research which suggests that they have higher responsibility training, being more often put in charge of younger children and playing adult surrogate roles.

The all-boy twosome had the most masculine scores and preferred the conventional economic activities of producing, buying, and selling: life insurance salesman, buyer, real-estate salesman, banker, purchasing agent, production manager, farmer, accountant, sales manager, and president of a manufacturing company. Of all the girls, the girl with the older brother showed the highest interest in the economic activities of buyer and life insurance salesman.

In the all-boy pair, the first-born tends to choose occupations where achievement is by strategy, the second-born achievement by power. Jobs involving strategy are production manager, personnel director, public administrator, YMCA secretary, school administrator, social worker, CPA, accountant, office man, purchasing agent, banker, sales manager, lawyer, president of manufacturing concern. Occupations requiring applications of physical power to persons, animals, and things are physician, osteopath, dentist, veterinarian, farmer, policeman, mortician, and YMCA physical director.

The all-girl pair did not show such definite trends as the all-boy. Preferences as to power strategy were the reverse of the boys, the first-born girls preferring occupations involving physical power and the second-borns preferring strategic jobs. The authors suggest that the first-born girl is encouraged and approved by her mother when she takes physical care of her siblings and acts as a parent surrogate. Therefore, she has little need to develop strategic ways of coping with siblings.

Two-sex twosomes preferred the most expressively creative occupations of artists, music performer, author, and architect. The highest-scoring boy was the boy with a younger sister, while the highest-scoring girl was the one with an older brother. This twosome, older boy–younger girl, was therefore the most creative. When the technically creative professions were considered—psychologist, physicist, mathematician, engineer, and chemist—it was found that the older brother of a girl tended to express greatest interest.

This study is significant in its illumination of the processes by which people come to assume the great variety of work roles offered in a society. The number of reciprocal roles which siblings can play is large, and this research is only beginning in delineating their influence upon the adult work roles which the individual chooses.

**Vocational Maturity.** Based on the idea that growth occurs through solving certain problems at each age, a project called the Career Pattern Study is concerned with finding out what is appropriate vocational behavior at various ages. Selecting and preparing for an occupation is one of the essential tasks of adolescents. In order to understand better how this task is achieved, and thus to know better how to help adolescents with it, the investigators started with the handling of the task in early adolescence, using boys entering the ninth grade [64]. They were concerned with the competence of these adolescents as to making important decisions about their vocational futures. From analyses of tests and interviews and a factor analysis, the following vocational maturity in ninth grade was defined. The essence of vocational maturity was *planfulness*, a looking ahead in preparation for vocational choice. Planfulness was the general factor in the four kinds of behavior which indicated vocational maturity, planning orientation, and taking the long view ahead, the short view ahead, and the intermediate view. Wisdom of choice was not characteristic of boys this age. Almost half the subjects had vocational preferences which were inappropriate for their intelligence levels. Almost half chose vocations which did not agree with the interest patterns as shown on a standard vocational interest test.

Those who did express wise preferences, however, were more likely to be among the more successful young men at age 25, as shown by a follow-up study of the ninth grade boys [63]. Other ninth grade predictors of success at age 25 were concerned with education and vocational choices, acceptance of responsibility for choice and planning, planning itself, consistency of field preferred, parental occupational and educational levels, cultural stimulation, out-of-school activities, and high school grades.

This research shows, then, that at the beginning of adolescence, vocational maturity is an expression of the whole personality rather than a narrow part of it. Preparation for taking adult roles has a broad base. The study also yields evidence that it is unwise to let boys this age make vocational choices which will limit their experience and education, since they tend not to choose appropriately.

Another study of vocational choice dealt with 929 high school students [47]. Questionnaires were administered to the tenth, eleventh, and twelfth grades. Although this inquiry was neither as deep nor as thorough as the one described above, its conclusions give some information about the problems adolescents face in trying to find suitable occupations. The subjects did not know enough about the various vocational possibilities to be able to choose wisely. They often did not know why they chose certain work roles. They received little useful guidance from adults. The authors concluded that these facts were the reasons why the subjects had not gone far in developing long-range vocational objectives.

**An Example of Vocational Development: The Growth of Scientists.** A study [50] of the development of scientists offers insight into the making of a scientist but also into some of the ways in which background, experiences, relationships, and abilities influence the adolescent's work roles. Sixty-four eminent scientists were chosen for careful individual study on the bases of membership in learned societies and ratings by scientists in important positions. The subjects were biologists, physicists, and social scientists (psychologists and anthropologists). Although the report goes into what the scientists were like as adults, our interest here is in how they came to be scientists.

Most of the families were upper-middle-class, with an economic range from relatively poor to very well-to-do and none extremely wealthy. Fifty-three percent of the fathers were professional men. In most of the homes, learning was valued for its own sake, and the interests of many of the subjects took an intellectual form at an early age. Many were first-borns or only children, and many of those who had siblings were in positions similar to those of first or only children.

Certain home situations occurred more often in this group than in the normal population. One such event was the early death of a parent. Fifteen percent lost a parent by death before the age of 10, whereas of a group of 624 college students, only 6.3 percent had lost a parent by age 10. There were significant differences between the three groups. Twenty-five percent of biologists, 13 percent of physicists, and 9 percent of social scientists had lost a parent by age 10. The author mentions a corroborating study which showed that 25 percent of mathematicians and physicists lost a parent before age 10. The author suggests that the effects of parental death included stimulating the boys to greater independence. She also tries to explain the differential effects. The problem of facing death, she speculates, turned the boys to a deep concern with the mechanisms of life, and for some, this concern developed into a generalized interest in biology.

Social isolation and some disinterest in persons were often felt by the physicists and to a slightly lesser extent by the biologists. These men had tended to have cordial but rather distant relationships with their fathers, apparently identifying comfortably with them, respecting them, and not being pressured by them. They tended not to have close relations with siblings and to have only a few friends rather than a crowd or gang. They were slow in dating, often starting in the later years of college. They found satisfaction in things outside the human realm. The social scientists, in contrast to the others, were more involved with family relationships and pressures. They more often conflicted with their fathers and found their fathers unsatisfactory persons with whom to identify. Their families tended to feel superior, and to strive to isolate themselves from other families. Boys growing up in such families would understandably place great importance on interpersonal relationships and, if they acquired a scientific attitude, would generalize the problems they encountered and try to solve them as social scientists. Half of them started dating in high school. They dated more extensively than did the other two groups.

A number of scientists had unusual physical conditions which may have contributed to feeling isolated. There were extremes of height, a few were abnormally small and a few unusually weak. Only 3 of the 12 theoretical physicists had generally good health and normal physical development. Such physical difficulties probably helped to make these boys avid readers.

The majority went to public schools, although all but two of the anthropologists went to private schools. Most of them liked school, got along well with teachers, and did a great deal of reading. The different subgroups had different reading patterns, the theoretical physicists being very omnivorous readers. The physicists, and not the others, carried on great activity with gadgets, radio, meccano sets, and such. Half of the biologists showed interest in natural history as children, the other half becoming interested during adolescence in chemistry, agriculture, and what science their schools offered. The social scientists showed early interest in literature and the classics.

The decision to become a certain kind of scientist was made by a few in child-hood, by over half during the junior and senior years in college, and by some in the second year of graduate school. The social scientists were most often late in choosing, often because they did not know enough about their fields to have become interested in them earlier. Several social scientists switched from English because they became disillusioned with it as a way of understanding human behavior. Although physicists found out early about the possibilities of research, the others often came upon it as an exciting discovery when they did their own first research. One of them expressed it thus: "One of the professors took a group of us and he thought if we wanted to learn about things, the way to do it was to do research. My senior year I carried through some research. That really sent me, that was the thing that trapped me. After that there was no getting out."

Curiosity was always characteristic of the scientists. Instead of losing their childish curiosity as many people do, they developed it into a system of thinking in a question–answer way. They settled upon their particular fields as objects of curiosity. The experience of doing research showed them how to spend their lives finding out the things they wanted to know.

**Sex and Cultural Differences in Vocational Goals.** Most of the available re-search on vocations concerns boys and men, a reflection of the general traditional attitude that men's work is more important than women's. Vocational goals as indications of self concept were studied in boys and girls from 16 to 19 years of age, in the United States, both Germanies, Chile, Poland, and Turkey [58]. Samples were equalized for educational level and socioeconomic background. Subjects reported their vocational goals for after graduation. Goals were classified as major professional (such as medicine and architecture), minor professional (such as nursing and photography), clerical-commercial, and undecided. Girls, in com-parison with boys, were much more likely to choose minor rather than major pro-fessional goals. This sex difference was even more striking in the United States than in other countries. American students set lower goals for themselves than did any of the others measured, and American girls set the lowest. This finding suggests that American women are still responding to the traditional expectation that girls make a career of domesticity, using jobs outside the home as short-time stopgaps. Although American girls are supposed to have equal opportunities with men, they do not pick up the option. The authors point out that in many cases, women's so-called emancipation means only adding an outside job to a full-time domestic load, amounting to a new type of double standard.

The cross-cultural findings may be misleading. While Americans were seen to have lower occupational aspirations than students in the other countries, the result may be due to a difference in samples. Since large numbers of Americans go to college, this group is not very similar to the small elite groups who have access to higher education in other countries. Even though the investigators equated fathers' occupational backgrounds, it is possible that social-class differences were great enough to influence the results.

## Moral Development

Increasing self-direction is possible through the development of moral judgment and moral action. The sense of identity includes a concept of oneself as a moral person, behaving responsibly and acceptably in his own eyes and in the eyes of his fellow men. The adolescent, then, is concerned with what is right and with doing right. Moral knowledge and moral actions are not the same, although both are essentials of morality.

**Moral Structure.** As the child interacts with a social and moral environment, he constructs and reconstructs the thought processes with which he thinks about moral issues, comes to decisions, and carries out actions. "These changing structures represent successive transformations of ways of thinking and feeling about the social world, about right and wrong, and about the self in relation to these" [70]. "Moral development involves a continual process of matching a moral view to one's experience of life in a social world" [39]. Because he experiences conflict, the child changes his moral structures in an effort to make them fit with reality as he knows it. Achievement of formal thought and broader experience make possible a more comprehensive kind of thinking about morality. The adolescent can think more objectively than the child, who is more influenced by his own needs and desires. Greater flexibility of thought makes it possible to go beyond the immediate situation to consider many factors that might have bearing on the question. Therefore he can judge an act right or wrong or in-between in terms of the intentions and the setting in which it happened, whereas a child is more likely to judge in terms of results and to declare it good or bad rather than shaded. An adolescent can accept, understand, and invent flexible rules because he is flexible in thought. His ability to control thought empowers him to hold different aspects of a conflict situation in mind while considering all, and thus to avoid the conflicting statements often produced by younger children. His potential for independence in moral thinking (as in all thinking) contrasts with the dependency of the child, who thinks that rules are unchangeable, given by adults or by God, or by some obscure and rigid agent. An adolescent can easily take the role of another. He can understand duty and obligation as based on reciprocal rights and expectations which people have of one another, whereas the childish concept of duty is obedience to a rule or to an adult. Children are likely to believe in eye-for-an-eye, tooth-for-a-tooth type of justice, in which people must pay for their misdeed by enduring inevitable punishment given by some authority. Adolescents can grasp a concept of justice based on making amends for misdeeds, repairing, restoring what has been spoiled or taken away by the wrongdoing. They can conceive of individual responsibility, equality before the law, and impartiality in justice [38].

This is not to say that all adolescents think in the most mature ways possible at their age, nor to say that children do not occasionally think on the levels designated as adolescent. Everyone has heard of a little child making an extraordinarily sage moral comment and everyone knows that adolescents (and adults) sometimes think childishly. Rather, there are typical levels of moral structure at different ages.

There are also wide individual differences at each age. An individual generally prefers a judgment or explanation of the highest level that he is capable of understanding and not necessarily capable of producing [49].

### Sequential Development of Moral Structures

Kohlberg's studies [37, 39] show growth trends from childhood into adulthood. In intensive interviews he discussed stories posing moral conflicts. The first story is about Heinz, the husband of a woman close to death from cancer. A special drug discovered by the local druggist might cure her, but Heinz did not have the money to buy it. Should he steal it from the druggist, who was trying to make a huge profit on the drug? An analysis of the answers showed a sequence of age-related changes from age 7 through 16. Later studies [39] showed no further stages at later ages, although there were changes in individuals as they matured. The level of morality a subject accepted was closely related to his level of understanding of moral concepts. Moral internalization was not a simple cognitive learning of cultural norms, however, nor only a matter of mental age, as defined by intelligence tests. Level of moral judgment was found to be related to IQ, but even more to chronological age, or to age-linked experience.

Six types of moral judgment were distinguished. Each of the moral ideas expressed by every subject was designated as one of six types. Then it was possible to show proportions of various kinds of moral thinking for each subject and for each age level. Growth trends could thus be plotted. In order to understand Figure 16–2, which shows those trends, it is necessary to define the six types of moral judgment. They are grouped in twos, making three general levels of moral development thus:

I. *Preconventional level, on which impulse gratification is modified by rewards and punishments.*

Stage 1. Punishment and obedience orientation. The reason for doing anything or for not doing something is to avoid punishment. "Being right" means obeying an authority. There is no concept of *a* right.

Stage 2. Instrumental relativist orientation. The reason for behavior is to get pleasure for oneself, often in the form of rewards from another person. Everyone has a right to do what he wants with himself and his possessions, even though his behavior conflicts with the rights of others. Reciprocity is pragmatic and has nothing to do with loyalty or gratitude or justice.

II. *Conventional level where conduct is controlled by the anticipation of social praise and blame. Meeting the expectations of family or nation and maintaining such groups is valuable regardless of consequences.*

Stage 3. Good-boy, nice-girl morality, or maintaining good relationships and the approval of other people. Conformity to stereotyped notions of majority or "natural" behavior. Intention becomes important in judging behavior. The concept of everyone's rights is the same as in Stage 2, with the addition that nobody has the right to do evil.

Stage 4. "Law and order" orientation. Right behavior consists of following fixed rules, respecting authority, maintaining the established social order for its own sake. When legitimate authorities disapprove or punish, the youngster feels guilty. A right is a claim on the actions of others, usually an earned claim, such as payment for work.

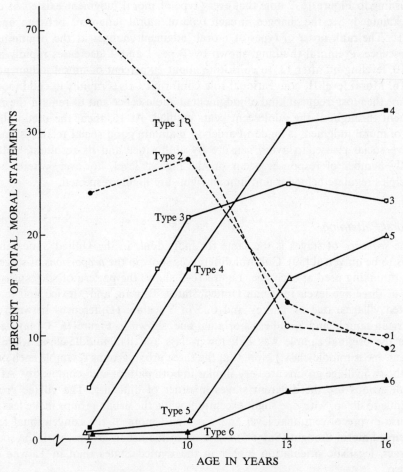

**Figure 16–2.** Frequency of use of six types of moral judgment by boys at ages 7, 10, 13, and 16.

SOURCE: Reprinted by permission from L. Kohlberg, "The Development of Children's Orientations Toward a Moral Order: I. Sequence in the Development of Moral Thought," *Vita Humana*, **6**, 11–33. Copyright © 1963, S. Karger, Basel/New York.

III. *Postconventional, autonomous, principled level. Morality of self-accepted moral principles, in which the person regulates his behavior by an ideal which he holds, regardless of immediate social praise and blame.*

Stage 5. Social-contract legalistic orientation. Morality of contract and of democratically accepted law. Community respect and disrespect are powerful motivators. The concept of human rights emerges here. There are rights linked to role and status and also unearned, universal, individual rights as a human being.

Stage 6. Morality of individual principles of conscience. Motivation is feeling right with oneself. The idea of rights includes all that expressed in Type 5 plus the notion that the life and personality of every individual is to be respected. Acceptable principles, such as the Golden Rule, have logical comprehensiveness, universality, and consistency.

Turning to Figure 16–2 note that every type of moral judgment existed at each age examined. See the changes in each type of moral judgment between ages 7 and 16. The rank order of types of moral judgment changes at the beginning of adolescence. Premoral thinking, shown by Types 1 and 2, decreases rapidly after age 10, leveling off after 13, to constitute about 20 percent of moral judgments at age 16. Moral level II, conventional role conformity, rises rapidly in childhood to become the most frequent kind of judgment at adolescence and to remain the most frequent throughout the adolescent years studied. At 16, then, the predominant type of moral judgment is made in order to maintain good social relationships, to receive social praise, to avoid censure by authorities and its resultant guilt. A goodly number of responses occur on the highest level, however, where moral principles regulate behavior and human rights are highly respected.

*Cultural Patterning*

The *sequence* of stages is the same for individuals in the United States and it seems to be universal [39]. Cultural differences show in the *proportions* of stages of moral thinking used at each age. Figure 16–3 shows the pattern of stages used by boys at three age levels in urban United States, Taiwan, and Mexico and in two isolated villages, one in Turkey and one in Yucatan. (Differences between this American sample and Kohlberg's original one, shown in Figure 16–3, may be because the original sample was half lower-class and half middle-class, while the present one is middle-class.) Note that the three urban groups resemble each other and the two village groups are very similar in both pattern and complexity. At age 10, all groups use the different stages in order of difficulty. The village groups continue to do so, with one slight exception, while the urban groups make less and less use of preconventional level and more and more of the conventional level. Principled moral thought (Stage 5) increases in the urban groups, with the social-contract, legalistic orientation higher in the United States than in Taiwan and Mexico.

A class comparison in the United States used older adolescents and young adults. The middle-class subjects made much more use of Stage 5 than did the lower-class young men. Lower-class subjects were higher in the use of Stage 2. Stage 5 thinking seems to stabilize during the high school years. Although the principled level is not used to a great extent by any group studied, there was an almost significant increase in Stage 6 thinking between ages 16 and 25. People who operate predominantly in Stage 6 constitute about 4 percent of the sample in several urban studies.

Another age trend is for *consistency* in thinking. While children tend to use several different stages of moral thinking, older adolescents and adults operate more in a preferred stage. Development in moral thinking goes on through conflict and attempts to resolve it. Conflict causes disequilibrium in existing structures, as the child is unable to assimilate his experiences. He explores another structure which is close to what he has. If it fits, he accommodates his structure and moves to a new equilibrium, a new stage of moral development [70]. The more complex the culture, the more one would expect the child to encounter conflicts and hence to experience more disequilibrium, more attempts to accommodate, and more transformations of moral structures. Thus the individual growing up in an urban setting would logically develop and use more complex stages of moral thought than would the child growing up in a simple culture.

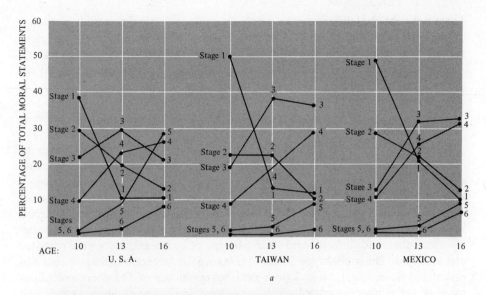

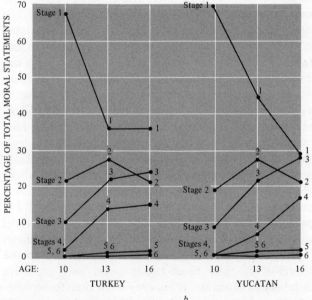

**Figure 16–3.** (*Above*) Middle-class urban boys in the United States, Taiwan, and Mexico, showing proportions of moral thinking in Kohlberg's six stages, at three levels. (*Below*) Proportions of stages in moral thinking by boys of three age levels in two isolated villages.

SOURCE: Reprinted from "Continuities and Discontinuities in Childhood and Adult Moral Development," by L. Kohlberg and R. Kramer, *Human Development*, 1969, **12**, 93–120. Published by S. Karger, Basel/New York. By permission.

Details within one stage, as well as patterning of stages, will differ from one culture to another. For example, the development of the concept of individual and government rights was explored among adolescents ages 11 through 18, in the United States, England, and Germany [17]. With increasing age came greater awareness of the reciprocal nature of individual and state rights. The youngsters gradually came to realize that the growth of a sense of community furthers individual rights.

There were national differences on emphasis on rights. Americans were most concerned with individual liberties. The British, more than the other two, evaluated polices in terms of benefit or cost to the individual rather than to the community. The Germans most often saw themselves as subjects who obeyed the rules of the state in return for security and protection.

### Family Influences

Since a child is likely to restructure moral thinking on a higher level when he faces conflict and the opportunity to transform his modes of thought, one would expect the family to influence the level he achieves. This rationale promoted a study of eighth graders and their parents in an upper-middle-class and upper-class community near San Francisco [30]. Using Kohlberg's stories, children and parents were tested for level of moral thinking. Then they were asked to discuss two stories on which they had differed, and their patterns of communication were recorded and analyzed. The modal type of moral thinking for fathers was Stage 4 (law and order) and for mothers, Stage 3 (nice-girl). Seventeen out of 53 fathers and 12 out of 53 of the mothers operated on the principled level. The children were almost equally distributed between the preconventional and conventional levels. The child's level was found strongly related to the mother's. Children's levels correlated strongly with fathers' when the fathers were warm and involved with their sons and daughters but not when fathers were cold and distant and the wives complained that their husbands were overdemanding and strict with the children.

Parent–child patterns of communication were examined for encouragement of the child in taking part in decision making. Conventional parents were less likely to encourage decision making than were principled parents. Children with low-encouraging parents were much more likely to operate on a preconventional level than were children whose parents gave strong encouragement for decision making.

Another measure of parent–child interaction gave further understanding of the link between parents' and children's moral levels. Parental encouragement was strongly related to the percentage of family discussion time used by the child. No child of low-encouraging parents used more than 20 percent of the discussion time, while over half of the highly encouraged children used up to 40 percent of the time. Amount of time used for family discussion was related to the moral level of the parents and to the moral level of the child. Since higher moral levels are more complex, taking in more dimensions of reality, it requires more time to consider them and to resolve conflicts. The advanced parents offer the child advanced levels to think about and time and encouragement to do so.

### Correlates of High Moral Development

Since moral judgment involves more and more flexible and abstract thinking as higher levels are attained, it seems reasonable that intelligence should be correlated with moral judgment. Kohlberg [38] found a correlation of .31 between intelligence and stage of moral development. A higher correlation (.59) appeared between age and moral development with mental age controlled, suggesting the great importance of age-linked experience in making moral judgments. These findings support a concept of moral development as taking place through not only cognitive learning but also social learning [46].

Insight into such cognitive and social learning comes from a comparison of high school students who were judged to be high in moral behavior and judgment with a group judged high in adjustment [18]. (Those high in both were eliminated from the comparison.) Although the two groups were about the same in IQ, the first did significantly better on achievement tests, both numerical and verbal. They were less satisfied with their performance, however, than the second group. The high moral group was also less satisfied with the school and the teachers. When they thought about school, they reflected on its intellectual aspects in contrast to the highly adjusted group, who thought first of social and personal aspects. Learning, to the high moral adolescents, was a personal, serious, individual experience, in which the learner attacked a problem and with which other people tended to interfere. To the others, learning was more a shared enterprise than a solitary one, and other people often helped. Socially, the high moral people were on the fringe, having placed other values ahead of success and popularity.

## Values and the Social Order

The virtue of fidelity, a product of the developing sense of ego identity, requires a community to which the young person can be true. The adolescent has to examine his social order, to make sense out of it, to accept or reject, commit himself or withdraw. Cognitive development makes a large contribution to this process, just as it does to the closely allied process of moral development. Information and experiences are processed to produce a transformed view of the family, politics, law, religion, and other institutional aspects of his community. His concept of community is restructured as he moves from a concrete, face-to-face notion to one of a social order. If a child lives in a complex culture, he may alter his concept of community as neighborhood to community as the world. (Not necessarily, though. We knew an 18-year-old ricksha driver in Banaras, a most complex culture, who had never heard of Delhi or Calcutta.)

*Attitudes Toward Foreign People*

Television brings the whole world to the children of many nations. By the time they reach the teen years, they are well aware of belonging to a country which occupies a certain position in relation to other countries and whose people have certain distinctive characteristics. The study referred to in Chapter 12, in which children's views of foreign people were explored, included 14-year-olds [40]. At this age, children were found to express more stereotyped notions of other countries than they did at earlier ages. There was some cross-national variation in friendliness, Americans showing the greatest expression of affection, and Japanese, Turks, and Israelis the least. The 14-year-olds were given a test of ethnocentrism in order to measure attitudes of prejudice and distrust toward people who did not belong to the subject's group but to other groups who were alien as to nation, region, or religion. (For example, a question from the test is, "Do you think people of different races and religions would get along better if they visited each other and shared things?") The highest ethnocentrism scores went to Bantus and Brazilians and the lowest to American, English-Canadian, French-Canadian, Japanese, and French.

A small proportion of the world's adolescents take part in the Experiment for International Living, an organization which arranges and supervises visits in other countries and living for extended periods of time with families in foreign countries. Thus there is interaction between different nationals on a very personal level. On the college level there are many opportunities for study abroad, often including possibilities for living with foreign families. Youth hostels and international student organizations encourage student travel by making it cheap and convenient and giving young people easy ways of meeting each other. The Peace Corps and its counterparts in other countries have shown the great involvement of many older youth in promoting the well-being of people outside their own national groups. Another demonstration of youth's concern for other countries, and their own country's position in relation to them, is opposition to the war in Vietnam.

In Europe and the United States, explorations of adolescent fears have revealed young people's awareness of and disturbance over what is going on in the whole world. A South Dakota group showed that teen-agers became more afraid with increasing age of war and of Communists' taking over [11]. Dutch adolescents expressed anxiety over the future of mankind [43]. They were afraid of destruction by scientific means and of automatization and other dehumanizing influences. Compared with younger children's fears about home, school, personal relations, and more concrete items, the fears of adolescents show much broader involvement in the social order.

*Politics and Law*

A child has a concrete concept of his community, country, and government. He cannot imagine an abstract collectivity. An example from a study [29] of 17,000 elementary school children is the answer of 7-year-old Tommy to the question "What is the government?"

> The government is like the president but he isn't actually a president. The builders, the street makers and all these people work for the government. The sidewalks and streets are the government's property and he lets people walk in them.
> He has a moneymaking machine and he makes a lot of money, but he doesn't use it. I think he uses money for decoration—some money is put on necklaces with little things.
> . . . Probably he works in the capital, like the President. He does! He lives in Washington. He doesn't live in the White House. He has his own home.
> He's the judge of the wildlife service. I sent him a letter about banding birds and he told the wildlife service to send me that pamphlet . . .

The young child views the president as personal, nurturant, benevolent, and very powerful [29]. He sees his country and language as superior. National symbols, especially the flag and Statue of Liberty, are points of attachment. By eighth grade, the concept of nation has some abstraction and ideological content. When asked why they were proud to be American, "freedom" and "the right to vote" became frequent answers by eighth graders. Also at this age, our country was seen as part of a larger, organized system of countries. A child's political knowledge is understandably influenced by current events, and his answers to questions reflect the imminence of an election, the shooting of a president or candidate, and the turmoil over a war [48].

Even in early adolescence, between 13 and 15, the child understands government in terms of its concrete agents, such as the police, the mayor, and the president [2]. In later adolescence, he grasps the structure and processes of the community. He comes to realize that the agents of the government are servants of the social order, and that politics involves interactions of citizens and community.

Concepts of law undergo significant transformations during the adolescent years. Adelson and associates [2] interviewed 120 subjects between 10 and 18 years of age, beginning with the premise that 1000 people had moved to a Pacific Island to build a community. Questions dealt with a wide range of political and legal topics. Answers showed the years from 13 to 15 to be the time when the following important changes occurred:

1. *From a concrete to abstract level of discourse.* When asked, "What is the purpose of laws?" a typical 13-year-old response was, "To keep people from doing things they're not supposed to do, like killing people and like . . . if you're in the city, like speeding in the car and things like that."

   A 15 year-old said, "To keep us safe and free," while an 18-year-old answered, ". . . to set up a standard of behavior for people, for society living together so that they can live peacefully and in harmony with each other."

2. *From a restrictive to a beneficial view of the law.* The examples above also show the change from emphasis on constraint to appreciation of the positive, constructive aspects of law. The younger adolescent thinks in terms of restrictions because he himself is controlled by benign authority at home and at school, and also because he thinks of individual conduct rather than of total community. The older adolescent can conceive of community needs and processes, past, present, and future. Although he realizes that law inhibits for the common good, he sees that law fulfills many social functions.

3. *From an absolute to a functional view of the law.* The younger subjects tended to think that existing laws should be upheld, no matter how involved enforcement was. Adolescents over 15 were more likely to revise an unworkable law, reflecting their increased flexibility of thought.

4. *From concern with outer effects to concern with inner effects.* Younger subjects saw the law in terms of restraining external conduct. When asked what would happen if there were no laws, they suggested pillage, chaos, and the rule of the strong and evil. Older subjects mentioned this sort of result but stressed inner corruption, such as personal confusion and dwindling of moral capacity.

The older adolescents saw the law as a human product, made to serve the social and spiritual good. With formal thought at their disposal, they were able to criticize a proposal from many angles, recognizing many of man's foibles and anticipating future results from one or another course of action. They understood that the law must accommodate competing interests and must balance short-term against long-term effects. Thus does an adolescent come to know his community in the complexity of its political and legal institutions, and on this basis he can and will pledge his fidelity.

### Religion

In developing his sense of identity, the adolescent has important interactions with the religious institution of his culture. He asks, "Who am I?" and "To what and whom can I be true?" His religion answers, "A child of God" and "To God and Jesus" or "To Buddha's teachings" or "To the god of your choice—Shiva, Vishnu, Durga, Sarasvati—as you decide." His church confirms his identity as a child of God through a confirmation ceremony. If the church waits for confirmation until the child has achieved some facility with formal thought, then his asking of questions and pondering on conflicts and issues will make the church pertinent to his developing sense of identity [61, p. 294]. Initiation ceremonies typically take place at puberty, in order to establish an individual as an adult in his own eyes and in the eyes of God and the social order.

Just as increased cognitive and social growth underlie the moral development of adolescence, so they also contribute to religious and philosophical development. The adolescent, in his urge for self-direction, tries to find out for himself the meaning of life. To find his identity involves placing himself in new relationships. What eventually results from a successful search is called by Erikson the sense of integrity [14, pp. 268, 269].

**Typical Concepts.** Studies on children of three denominations have already been reported (pages 435–436). Adolescents between 11 and 14 showed differentiated and abstract conceptions of their denominations, seeing them as systems-among-systems. Such concepts were seen as typical of Piaget's stage of formal operations. Religious beliefs and practices were explored in the context of personality development in 30 young adolescents who were subjects of a longitudinal study at the Menninger Foundation [61]. Table 16–3 summarizes their basic beliefs. The adolescents had clearer beliefs about Jesus than about God. God was personal and somewhat physical to a third of the subjects and abstract to another third. Moralistic teaching shows in their beliefs about heaven, hell, right, and wrong. Seeing God primarily as lawgiver and judge seems to be related to the young adolescent's being under the control of parents and teachers. This finding is consistent with those of the studies on adolescents' conceptions of law, described above.

Four religious orientations were distinguished in the Menninger group of adolescents. The largest number were traditional, accepting the forms of the church with little question, integrating it weakly into their lives. The second group was conventional, echoing parents, pastors, and priests, maintaining a childhood orientation. The third group conformed to peers, believing much that was neither traditional nor conventional. The fourth group held beliefs which resulted from their own struggles in coping with the environment. This group led the investigator to the conclusion that vulnerability or openness to stress is an important predisposition to religious experience. As the adolescent tries actively to cope with conflict in solving identity problems, he is likely to recall symbols, myths, and rituals, and to appeal to loyalties larger than his immediate group and to open himself to novelty, mystery, and creative life forces.

**Intellectual and Sex Differences.** Some differences in religious experience between honor students and average students emerged in the study of adolescent religious experiences [13]. An analysis of the compositions written by 144 ninth graders showed that the honor students (with presumably higher intelligence) had more experience of feeling close to God when alone than did the average students. The average ones had more experience than the honor students of feeling close to God when in church. The authors suggest this explanation of the result: because of higher intelligence and the ability to think more abstractly, the honor students could conceive God in broader terms and in more situations than could the average students. Since curiosity and independence were most likely more characteristic of the honor students than of the average, the former would be expected to resist the conformity required by church. Resisting church and conceiving God broadly,

**Table 16–3** Basic Religious Beliefs of 30 Young Adolescents Showing Numbers and Percentages Subscribing to Each

| | Group of Thirty—Basic Beliefs | | |
|---|---|---|---|
| God | Quasi-physical | 6 | 20% |
| | Person | 5 | 16.6% |
| | Power | 8 | 26.6% |
| | Abstraction | 3 | 10% |
| | Confused | 6 | 20% |
| | Unreal | 2 | 7% |
| Christ | Mystical reality | 5 | 16.6% |
| | Historical model | 7 | 23% |
| | Theological abstraction | 8 | 26% |
| | Distant story | 7 | 23% |
| | Matter of indifference | 1 | 3.3% |
| | Matter of hostility | 2 | 7% |
| Church | One true church | 6 | 20% |
| | Mediator, God and men | 6 | 20% |
| | For "saved" believers | 5 | 16.6% |
| | Fellowship of growing Christians | 5 | 16.6% |
| | Social group | 4 | 13.3% |
| | Indifferent | 4 | 13.3% |
| Heaven and Hell | Geographical place | 5 | 16.6% |
| | Reward and punishment | 9 | 30% |
| | Relationship with God | 5 | 16.6% |
| | State of mind | 6 | 20% |
| | Uncertain | 2 | 7% |
| | Unreal | 2 | 7% |
| Right and Wrong | Law of parents | 5 | 16.6% |
| | Law of church | 7 | 23% |
| | Peers' standards | 7 | 23% |
| | Thoughtful codes | 6 | 20% |
| | Confused | 2 | 7% |
| | Rebellious rē authority | 3 | 10% |
| Prayer | Person to person | 8 | 26.6% |
| | Harmony with power | 5 | 16.6% |
| | Reflective planning | 3 | 10% |
| | Rote recital | 7 | 23% |
| | Indifference (no practice) | 5 | 16.6% |
| | Hostile to idea | 2 | 7% |

From *Adolescent Religion* by Charles William Stewart. Copyright © 1967 by Abingdon Press. Used by permission.

they would experience Him more in solitary situations than would the average adolescent.

Some sex differences in adolescent religious experience were also reported. Girls were much more likely than boys to experience God in solitary situations. For example, "I think the time when I feel closest to God is at night when my brothers and sisters are sleeping and the house is quiet. . . ."

Girls were more likely than boys to experience God when they were feeling anxiety of fear. "I feel close to God when someone I love is in danger."

Boys more often than girls felt that they contacted God in situations involving moral action. "I feel closest to God whenever I do something for someone else. I don't need any reward; the feeling I get is all I need."

In the type of religious experience called *acute*, there were no significant differences between honor and average students, nor were there between boys and girls. Although the study did not show whether these experiences distinguished between adolescents and younger children, we could expect at least two of them, meditation and initiation, to be typically adolescent. Meditation experiences which brought an acute awareness of God were occasions of quiet, solitary thinking, often with heightened awareness of self and surroundings. They sound much like the self-cognition described in Chapter 14 as an essential in the establishment of the sense of identity. This example is given: "I had gone into the woods as I often did, but for some reason, I felt more alone. I began to think of what had brought me back to camp that year and my motives and how right or wrong they were. The way in which I answered my own questions seemed to go deeper than my own personal thoughts. . . . I felt He had been a guiding influence in my decision."

**Trends in Importance of Religion.** Reports vary on the significance of religion to adolescents. A survey of about 1000 high school students in Georgia showed 85 percent of both black and white groups claiming that religion was important to them [55]. An English survey of 2000 indicated that churchgoing decreased as children became older [32]. When Dutch adolescents wrote statements about their future life, religion was rarely mentioned [43]. The investigator concludes that the church and religion, as traditional mediators of values, have little effect on youth. A 37-year span was covered in an inquiry into religious attitudes of students at Harvard and Clark Universities [34]. Comparing today's freshmen with those of 37 years ago, it was clear that attitudes toward the church had become less favorable. For example, 78 percent of the early group and 17 percent of the present group agreed with the item, "I think that the church is a divine institution and it commands my highest loyalty and respect."

Over the 37-year period, freshmen decreased a small but significant amount in their belief in the reality of God. Of the most recent groups, 25 percent thought of God as a personal being, 60 percent as impersonal, and 15 percent disclaimed any belief. Attitudes toward religion were found to be specific rather than generalized. Between 25 and 30 percent said that religion had little or no influence on their standards of ethical conduct. Even though subjects felt much less favorable toward the church then they did 10, 20, 30 years ago, the disaffection was more for the established church than for religion in general. Students seemed to be disillusioned with the church's beliefs and preachings in relation to current social, civic, and economic problems. This conclusion is supported by the fact that adolescents and youth are showing interest in a variety of religions and religious experiences. While we have no information on numbers of participants, we know young Americans who are Vedantists, Zen Buddhists, Mahayana Buddhists, Hindus, Ba'hai, and Moslems. The "Jesus People" are a growing number of adolescents and youth who are developing a contemporary fundamentalist Christian religion. The rejection of traditional American forms of religion does not necessarily mean rejection of religion.

## Life Style

For almost every statement one can make about adolescence, a contradiction can be found. They get along very well with their parents; they rebel against their parents. There is a large generation gap; there is no generation gap. Adolescents are increasingly active sexually; they are no different from the way their parents were at their age. Some authors consider adolescent culture sick, while others applaud their rejection of the adult sick society.

It looks to us as though the continuity with past generations of adolescents is in terms of freedom to try out a variety of roles and opportunities to develop new patterns of feelings, thought, and action. Some adolescents have more freedom than others and some make more use of it than others. The majority, as previous chapters have shown, do not stray very far from the parental modes, graduating from adolescence into adulthood. Some deviate from the social order to the culture of delinquency and crime. We shall discuss this group briefly. Some others graduate from adolescence to youth and some live as adolescents in a youth culture.

### Delinquents

Technically, a juvenile delinquent is one whose behavior is brought to the attention of law enforcement agencies because it endangers the juvenile, other individuals, or the community [57, p. 352]. Thus identical pieces of behavior may or may not be legally delinquent. In terms of life style, it may be more useful to think of delinquency as a kind of deviancy from the dominant middle-class behavior norms.

The hard-core lowest socioeconomic level generates delinquent gang behavior as a product of its culture [42]. The behavior labeled delinquent is deviant from middle-class behavior but good adjustment in the lower-class setting, where prestige accrues from "getting into trouble," being tough, and being smart. The excitement of potential danger lends spice to an often dull existence. Belief in fate and luck is strong. Attitudes toward personal autonomy are ambivalent, with authority often rejected verbally and yet covertly equated with nurturance, protection, and care. Desires for belonging and status are answered by the peer group. In the process of conforming to peer group demands for toughness, smartness, and so on, the adolescent violates middle-class norms or laws. His alienation from the dominant culture is because he never belonged in the first place, having been born into another culture.

The hard-core lower-class culture cannot account for delinquency at other socioeconomic levels. Many theories and many research projects have sought for reasons why some adolescents violate laws and norms of the mainstream social order. Results show many factors involved. The age group under 15 has had the highest recent increase in crime. Crime has increased in all areas but more in suburban than in rural and urban areas [57, pp. 357–364]. Studies of opportunities of deviant youth tend to show them deprived as to education, recreation, and employment. Thus they do not have means to achieve their goals in socially acceptable ways. They may be materially well off but lacking in care and protection. Needs for dependency, submission, and being cared for were emphasized in the early recollections of delinquent boys and girls [75]. Sometimes delinquency in middle-class children is an attempt, perhaps an unconscious one, to make their parents pay attention to them or to express dissatisfaction or desperation with school. Of about 1000 runaway adolescents, a small minority were seriously disturbed, and the large majority (40 percent girls, 60 percent boys) were much like adolescents who had not run away [60]. Many runaways were trying to change relationships with their parents, not to deny them. Some wanted a little rest before engaging in further interaction with parents, teachers, or friends. Widespread dissatisfaction with inadequate school experiences was disruptive of parent–child relationships and thus provided a double reason for running away. Delinquents' perceptions of factors promoting happy-successful living revealed emphasis on dominance, aggression, and exhibition [67]. Nondelinquents put more stress on the value of nurturant, deferent, affiliative behavior.

Family studies show personal and marital inadequacy in parents associated with inadequacy in children. For example, delinquent boys are more likely to have emotionally disturbed fathers than are normal boys. An investigation of this question showed 44 percent of delinquent boys, as contrasted with 18 percent of a normal group, to have disturbed fathers [20]. A scale of parental behavior revealed significant differences between the parents of a group of normal boys and girls and a group of 81 institutionalized delinquent 12- to 18-year-old boys [56]. The parents of delinquents were more likely to grant extreme autonomy and to provide lax discipline. Delinquent boys' fathers were less positive and less loving, while mothers were more positive and more loving than those of normal youngsters.

If the family is so important an influence, how can one family produce both a delinquent and a civically responsible adolescent? The answer is twofold. Siblings do not have identical experiences with their family, nor with any situation. Siblings are different individuals, different in physical constitution as well as in life experience. A classic [25] study on delinquent and nondelinquent pairs of brothers concludes that the delinquent boy had had little satisfaction from his family relationships, while his brother had had a much more fulfilling family life. The former was likely to feel rejected, unloved, deprived, insecure, blocked, jealous, guilty, and confused. He was often intensely unhappy over family shortcomings, such as lack of harmony and parental mistakes and misconduct.

Physical constitution has been found to have a bearing on delinquency in boys [9, 19, 20]. Delinquents were more likely to be solid, muscular, closely knit, rather than linear and fragile. The interplay between physical, social and psychological factors is shown in the series of studies from which this information comes. For example, linear and fragile boys tended to be more sensitive and responsive to the environment than did chubby types, who were more solid and matter-of-fact. When a linear boy has an emotionally disturbed father, he was more likely to be delinquent than was a chubby boy with an emotionally disturbed father.

Limited moral development, as expressed in delinquency, is the result of a complex of interactions between the individual and the environment. This topic constitutes a whole area of specialized study.

*Youth*

Keniston uses the term *youth* to mean those who "after adolescence and before adulthood enter a further stage of development." Although the years of youth can be fixed roughly from 18 to the mid or late twenties, or perhaps under 30, youth is "a state of mind, a set of questions, and a trajectory of psychological change"

Courtesy the Peace Corps by Rowland Scherman

[36, p. 267]. The majority of individuals move directly from adolescence into adulthood, while a few have youth available to them, and only some of those people choose to live as youth. Adolescence is recognized and accepted by society, even though it is often considered puzzling or problematic. Youth is little recognized or institutionalized, although some cultures and institutions require service at this point. Compulsory military service for all youth is an example. The Mormon church sends all of its young men into the world as missionaries. Many different countries offer service opportunities to their young people through organizations similar to the Peace Corps. In these organizations, as in the hippy movement and in the New Left, young men and women postpone entering established society while they examine society and their relationship to it. College graduate schools are also used by youth for their special developmental purposes. Some individuals in the Peace Corps, college, hippy groups (and so on) are still coping with adolescent problems and thus are not really youth.

A youth, according to Keniston, has solved the major problems for developing the sense of identity. He has finished rebelling against his parents and has come to terms with his emotional dependence on them. He has achieved mutuality and intimacy with the opposite sex, although he has not entered a permanent relationship. He knows what kind of person he is, what he can do, and what he wants to do. He remains flexible, leaving doors open, exploring, evaluating, testing. The successful ending of youth results in an articulation of self and society while acknowledging the claims of both. The happy ending means discovering a social role through which the person can preserve his commitments and express what he is.

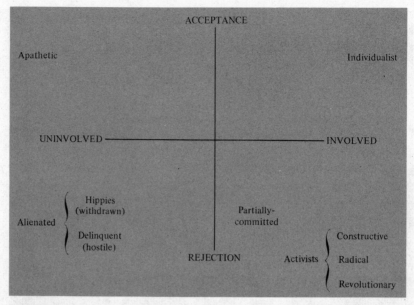

**Figure 16–4.** Types of youth arranged on two dimensions of attitudes toward society.

Youth are an elite and minority [36, p. 273]. Coming from economically comfortable, liberal, intellectual, loving parents, youth are privileged and often very talented. Although there are many variations on youth, Keniston sees two main kinds: those who try to change society, and those who reject it and/or withdraw from it. Young radicals try to change it; hippies reject and withdraw. We recognize that some 18- to 24-year-olds are not entitled to be called *youth* in Keniston's terms, and that some chronological and technical adolescents participate in some of the following life styles. The life styles are outcomes of adolescent experiences. To the present generation of young adolescents, the styles of youth represent choices to be made.

Figure 16–4 shows a way of classifying youth on two dimensions of attitudes toward the social order, following a study of Berkeley students [3]. The first dimension, shown on the horizontal line, is concerned with the degree to which the individual is involved with politico-social issues. The vertical line represents the degree to which the individual accepts or rejects the dominant values of society and conforms to the behavior norms of its institutions.

*Apathetic Youth*

Located in the upper left corner of the figure are apathetic youth, young people who are uninvolved with social and political issues. They accept the societal *status quo* and the values of their parents. Their interests are career, success, marriage, family, and financial security. From his analysis of data from a Fortune poll, Adelson [1] estimates this majority to be around 80 percent of 18- to 24-year-olds. It would be a mistake to call them *youth* in Keniston's sense, because they are not in a further stage of personality development between adolescence and adulthood. They have arrived at adulthood except for the economic vocational aspects.

Perhaps they should be called *apathetic young adults*. Some of the apathetic are occasionally moved to join in campus demonstrations or outpourings of a stimulating nature.

### Individualist Youth

The upper right corner of Figure 16–4 indicates acceptance of the societal *status quo* and involvement with keeping it. That is, this group is conservative. These young people are politically active, often well organized, working within legal limits to preserve the traditional forms of society. Autonomy and individual liberty are usually important, although there may be an authoritarian, hierarchical structure. Young Americans for Freedom and Young Conservatives are examples of individualist youth organizations.

Conservative students tend to be more submissive to authority and to control impulse and anxiety more firmly than the average student. Conservatives describe themselves as independent, uncompromising, egocentric, and unconventional. Their ideals are more concerned with personal integrity and individualism than with interpersonal relationships. They show less interest in altruistic and humanistic values than do others. Parents of individualists have been found to emphasize achievement and goodness, using guilt for control and showing anger and disappointment when children indicated resentment and feelings of failure.

### Alienated Youth

On the low end of both dimensions, individuals reject social values and institutions, adopting a different set of values and even building their own institutions. Alienated youth include disaffiliates or hippies, who withdraw from the social order, and delinquents, who fight it, not in order to change it but to provide satisfaction for themselves.

**Hippies**. Disaffiliates are alienated from their families and from society. Keniston [36] studied a special group of alienated young men at Harvard and found the source of their estrangement to be in relationships with their parents, especially with cold, status-oriented fathers. Subsequent experiences built upon the alienation began in the family context.

A more complete withdrawal from societal values and involvement is seen in hippies who have left high school or college and who live in their own communities or communes. Their institutions include a different kind of family and religion, their values a different kind of love, dress, food, and time orientation. They hate hypocrisy, artificiality, and materialism which they often see as embraced by their parents. (Their parents are usually middle class and "successful".) They choose not to fight the way of life which is dominated by the industrial–military complex, but to get away from it. They focus on the present, trying to fill it with love and beauty, using the resources of nature, art, and drugs. Virtues include kindness, mildness, nonviolence, acceptance of individual differences, sharing, equality, naturalness, sincerity, and honesty.

Probably the most basic contradiction in the hippy way of life is dependence on the technological society that the hippy rejects. The existence of youth as a stage of life is a result of the affluent society. Many hippies live on money earned by their

Ellen S. Smart

parents, who work in the rejected materialistic, military–industrial affluent society. Others live on welfare payments, also earned by workers in that society. Although hippies also work at low-level jobs or in the work of a commune, they continue to use some of the fruits of the technological society, such as cars, radios, musical instruments, drugs, and medical services. This discrepancy probably bothers the members of the mainstream more than it does the hippies themselves, since the latter are focused on the immediate present and care more for intuition and mystic experience than for rational deduction.

### Activists

The lower right of the figure denotes involvement with the social order and rejection of it. The activist tries to change what he does not like in his society. The most rejecting is the revolutionary; the least rejecting the constructive activist, who works within existing societal framework to make right what is wrong. The young radical, according to Keniston [36, pp. 253–256], opposes violence, cruelty, and power-seeking while he tries to change the world through peaceful revolution. The partially committed occupy a position on the *rejection* end of the vertical, and closer to *involvement* than to uninvolvement. A study of Civil Rights workers [54] revealed some workers who went on just a few Freedom Rides without giving up their other interests or doing further work for the cause. The Berkeley study also turned up some dissenters who participated in protests but in nothing else.

**Constructive Activists.** Volunteer workers typify this type of activists. They work in the Peace Corps, in VISTA, mental hospitals, tutoring programs, and environmental improvement programs. While they are very much involved with alleviating human ills and making a better world, they do not challenge the social order and the adults who are in charge. While working altruistically instead of furthering his own career, the volunteer has opportunities for self-discovery and evaluation. While achieving fidelity to certain of society's ideals, he prepares for further investment of himself, for broader and deeper fidelity.

There is no clear division between constructivist activists and radicals. Some volunteer workers also engage in protest and political action. One condition common to both is experience with parents who were rational, democratic, and humanistic. Such parents focus the child's attention on the results of his actions upon other people and upon himself, encouraging him to feel responsible and able to influence what happens to himself and to others. This finding has resulted in all the studies that have focused on the parent–child relations of activists. Children apparently grow up able and eager to resist arbitrary and "hypocritical" authority when they have participated in a democratic authority structure with parents who were highly educated and politically liberal [16]. These offspring expect institutions as well as individuals to accommodate to reason and truth.

**Young Radicals.** The essential of being a radical is the systematic effort to change and reform society. Radicals are very receptive to change in the world and changes in themselves [36, pp. 274–290]. The future is open and of indeterminate length. The focus is on the present. Identification is with the same generation rather than with leaders, making for a feeling of disconnection with other generations and ideologies.

Young radicals try to include the alien, as long as it is contemporary. Psychological inclusiveness involves accepting and integrating all of one's feelings, impulses, and fantasies rather than repressing, denying, and rejecting. Interpersonal inclusiveness means accepting and respecting peasants, nonwhites, the deprived, the deformed. In fact, it seems to include everyone except middle-class Americans of another generation.

Personalism is a prime value, being one's own individual self, being honest with other people, amd promoting a world in which people will be good to each other. Sex is seen as good when it expresses intimacy, mutuality, and caring; bad when it is exploitative or deceptive. Marriage is considered more an institution for having children than for having sex. The importance of the individual also requires that he takes part in making decisions.

Nonviolence is perhaps the most crucial value. Young radicals, along with the rest of youth, are opposed to war, interpersonal violence, exploitation, and domination.

### The Influence of Youth

Rejecting youth, both uninvolved and involved, are changing our society. They are changing adults and established institutions and they are influencing adolescents and children. They are even changing their apathetic contemporaries. Both hippies and radicals demonstrate a way of life and offer an array of values. Through their being and through the purposive efforts of the activists, they have contributed to these changes [41]: the demand for relevance in education and some movement toward it; increasing autonomy in matters of appearance, taste, morals, and values; resistance to militarization of life and war as an instrument of foreign policy; efforts to alleviate the plight of the poor; a personalist-command orientation which rejects competitiveness; a questioning of tradition and history.

The influence of radicals and hippies is out of proportion to their numbers. Adelson believes that youth represents the current mood of society. Some of the figures are passive and gentle—the flower children; others are active and angry, assaulting the system—the delinquents and radicals. Adelson says:

> In these images, and in our tendency to identify ourselves with them, we can discover the alienation within all of us, old and young. We use the young to represent our despair, our violence, our often forlorn hopes for a better world. Thus, these images of adolescence tell us something true and something false about the young; they may tell us even more about ourselves.

## Summary

Fidelity is a virtue developed by the adolescent as he seeks and finds ways of committing himself as a participant in his community. Adolescents want to be self-directing, productive, responsible, and yet cooperative with expectations at home and at school. Achievement within the cultural framework is seen as responsibility by parents and teachers. The assumption of responsibility in adolescence seems to be related to warmth, friendliness, and companionship of the home in which the adolescents grew up. Girls have been found to be rated as more responsible than boys and to be given more love-oriented discipline. Girls tend to maintain about the same level of dependency on others as they grow up, but boys often change, probably because the culture calls for more independence from adolescent and adult males.

Achievement is related to standards and attitudes developed by the adolescent in the various contexts of his life. Success or failure at school influences what the child expects of himself, although what he would like to achieve may be far beyond what he thinks he can actually do. Success in school is related to perceptions of the peer group's evaluation of education. Motivation to achieve is related to the extent to which parents have expected achievement from their children and given them chances to achieve on their own. Cultural background and class position of the family are related to adolescents' measured need for achievement. Democratic, equalitarian families tend to produce children with a high need for achievement. Factors which help to build a strong sense of identity also bring about the building of independence, responsibility, and drive for achievement because of the relationship of the latter characteristics to a sense of identity. Race differences which are significant for achievement motivation include willingness to delay present gratification for future rewards and the belief in internal rather than external control of events.

In the American culture adolescents are expected not only to prepare for a vocation, as is true in all cultures, but to decide from a vast array of vocations which one to prepare for. Because some vocations demand education beyond high school, vocational choice and preparation are related to educational achievement and aspirations. Although individuals in any occupation differ widely in intellectual capacity, it is possible to arrange occupations from low to high as to average level of intelligence of people engaged in them.

Intellectual level therefore is one of the factors involved in occupational choice. Cognitive style, particularly creativity, is another such factor. Specific abilities are required in differing degrees in various occupations. Not only are specific interests important in occupational success, but patterns of interests have been found to be so related. These patterns of interests are unstable in childhood, but are very stable from late adolescence onward through adulthood.

Family background is related to vocational success, not only because of differences in wealth and prestige, but also because of differences in personality of the children. One study has shown interesting differences in the interest patterns related to vocational success between children who occupied different positions among their siblings.

Many adolescents state vocational choices which are inappropiate for them as to their intelligence level or interest patterns. The earlier a wise choice is made, the more likely the adolescent is to become successful in his vocation in young adulthood. The wisdom of choice can be increased by greater knowledge of vocational possibilities and greater insight into one's own abilities. Adolescents can be helped to achieve both of these by sympathetic guidance from adults.

Background and personality characteristics of groups of eminent biologists, physicists, and social scientists were found in one study to differ among the three groups and from more unselected groups of individuals. This study shows not how to bring about eminence in these fields, but the fact that the development of personal characteristics is a dynamic, coherent process.

Moral development proceeds through the development of thought processes which are moral structures of schemas. These structures are built and successively transformed as the child interacts with a social and moral environment. Six stages, grouped into three levels of moral development, have been delineated by Kohlberg. Patterns of moral behavior can be shown for individuals, age levels, and cultures.

Moral judgments made by individuals are related to the level and kind of intellectual processes of which they are capable. The development of flexibility of thought during adolescence makes possible the holding of relative standards of morality and the recognition of extenuating circumstances. Although individuals of all ages make some moral judgments at all levels of thought, older people give more judgments which show the development of and adherence to individual standards. Moral judgment and moral behavior are positively related to each other, but it is obvious that people behave immorally even when they "know better." The general level of moral development of adolescents is related to the kind of family in which they have grown up.

In developing the virtue of fidelity, the adolescent chooses values and makes them his own. The more complex his community, the more opportunities he may have for complex interactions, leading to abstractions in values. He develops attitudes toward foreign people, toward his own country, and toward himself as a member of the nation. As he structures and restructures his concepts of law and politics, he makes value judgments and commitments. He examines and chooses in the field of religion, influenced by the religion of his family and by his education, intelligence, and sex.

Commitment to a life style takes various forms. The majority of adolescents pass into an adulthood resembling that of their parents. Delinquents from all social levels deviate from the mainstream of society. The hard-core poor were never in the mainstream. The middle-class delinquents appear to reject the mainstream, but often their misbehavior represents a cry for help and attention. *Youth* is a stage of further development after adolescence and before adulthood, a moratorium made possible by the affluent, highly technological society. Varieties

## 632 The Adolescent

of youth include the *alienated*, of which hippies are one type; *individualists*, who are traditional, conservative, and politically active; *constructive activists*, who work within the social system to try to improve it; and *radicals* who seek to make large changes in the social order. Apathetic young people, who constitute a large share of the age group between 18 and 24, are concerned with family, job, and security rather than with the social order and world problems. Adults have much to learn from the alienated, the constructivists, and the radicals.

## References

1. Adelson, J. What generation gap? *New York Times Magazine*, January 18, 1970.
2. Adelson, J., Green, B., & O'Neil, R. Growth of the idea of law in adolescence. *Devel. Psychol.*, 1969, **1**, 327–332.
3. Block, J. H., Haan, N., & Smith, M. B. Activism and apathy in contemporary adolescents. In J. F. Adams (Ed.), *Understanding adolescence*. Boston: Allyn & Bacon, 1968, pp. 198–231.
4. Borow, H. The adolescent in a world of work. In J. F. Adams (Ed.), *Understanding Adolescence*. Boston: Allyn & Bacon, 1968, pp. 337–360.
5. Bowlby, J. *Attachment and loss*. Vol. I: *Attachment*. London: Hogarth, 1969.
6. Bowles, F. *Access to higher education*. Paris, United Nations Educational, Scientific and Cultural Organization and the International Association of Universities, 1963.
7. Bronfenbrenner, U. Some familial antecedents of responsibility and leadership in adolescents. In L. Petrullo & B. M. Bass (Eds.), *Leadership and interpersonal behavior*. New York: Holt, 1961, pp. 239–271.
8. Carlson, N. A. Higher costs in higher education. *Am. Educ.*, 1970, **6**:1, 37.
9. Clarke, H. H., & Olson, A. L. Characteristics of 15-year-old boys who demonstrate various accomplishments or difficulties. *Child Devel.*, 1965, **36**, 559–567.
10. Crites, J. O. & Semlar, I. J. Adjustment, educational achievement and vocational maturity as dimensions of development in adolescence. *J. Couns. Psychol.*, 1967, **15**, 489–496.
11. Croake, J. W. Adolescent fears. *Adolescence*, 1967, **2**, 459–468.
12. Douvan, E. & Adelson, J. *The adolescent experience*. New York: Wiley, 1966.
13. Elkind, D., & Elkind, S. Varieties of religious experience in young adolescents. *J. Sci. Stud. Religion*, 1962, **2**, 102–112.
14. Erikson, E. H. *Childhood and society*. New York: Norton, 1963.
15. Erikson, E. H. *Identity: Youth and crisis*. New York: Norton, 1968.
16. Flacks, R. The liberated generation: An exploration of the roots of student protest. *J. Soc. Issues*, 1967, **23**, 52–75.
17. Gallatin, J. E. The development of the concept of rights in adolescence. Unpublished Ph.D thesis, Ann Arbor: University of Michigan, 1967.
18. Getzels, J. W., & Jackson, P. W. *Creativity and intelligence*. New York: Wiley, 1962.
19. Glueck, S., & Glueck, E. *Physique and delinquency*. New York: Harper, 1956.
20. Glueck, S., & Glueck, E. *Family environment and delinquency*. Boston: Houghton Mifflin, 1962.

21. Gottlieb, D. Poor youth do want to be middle class but it's not easy. *Personnel Guidance J.*, 1967, **46**, 116–122.
22. Greene, R. L., & Clark, J. R. Birth order and college attendance in a cross-cultural setting. *J. Sociol. Psychol.*, 1968, **75**, 289–290.
23. Harris, D. B. Work and the adolescent transition to maturity. *Teachers College Record*, 1961, **63**, 146–153.
24. Harrison, F. I. Relationship between home background, school success, and adolescent attitudes. *Merrill-Palmer Quart.*, 1968, **14**, 331–334.
25. Healy, W., & Bronner, A. F. *New light on delinquency and its treatment.* New Haven: Yale University Press, 1936.
26. Heath, B. R. G., & Strowing, R. W. Predicting occupational status for non-college-bound males. *Personnel Guidance J.*, 1967, **14**, 144–149.
27. Hechinger, F. Taking the politics out of open access. *New York Times*, March 15, 1970.
28. Hechinger, F. It's college time for Russians, too. *New York Times*, August 30, 1970.
29. Hess, R. D., & Torney, J. V. *The development of political attitudes in children.* Chicago: Aldine, 1967.
30. Holstein, C. E. The relation of children's moral judgment level to that of their parents and to communication patterns in the family. In Smart, R. C. & Smart, M. S. (Eds.), *Readings in Child Development and Relationships*, Macmillan, 1972.
31. Horrocks, J. E., & Weinberg, S. A. Psychological needs and their development during adolescence. *J. Psychol.*, 1970, **74**, 51–71.
32. Hyde, K. E. *Religious learning in adolescence.* London: Oliver and Boyd, 1965.
33. Inhelder, B., & Piaget, J. *The growth of logical thinking from childhood to adolescence.* New York: Basic Books, 1958.
34. Jones, V. Attitudes of college students and their changes: A 37-year study. *Genet. Psychol. Mono.*, 1970, **81**, 3–80.
35. Kagan, J., & Moss, H. A. The stability of passive and dependent behavior from childhood through adulthood. *Child Devel.*, 1960, **31**, 577–591.
36. Keniston, K. *Young radicals.* New York: Harcourt, Brace & World, 1968.
37. Kohlberg, L. The development of children's orientations toward a moral order. I: Sequence in the development of moral thought. *Vita Humana*, 1963, **6**, 11–13.
38. Kohlberg, L. Moral development and identification. In H. W. Stevenson (Ed.), *Child psychology*, The Sixty-second Yearbook of the National Society for the Study of Education. Chicago: University of Chicago Press, 1963, pp. 277–332.
39. Kohlberg, L., & Kramer, R. Continuities and discontinuities in childhood and adult moral development. *Human Devel.*, 1969, **12**, 93–120.
40. Lambert, W. E., & Klineberg, O. *Children's views of foreign peoples.* New York: Appleton-Century-Crofts, 1967.
41. McDonald, D. Youth. *Center Magazine*, 1970, **3**:4, 22–23.
42. Miller, W. B. Lower class culture as a generating milieu of gang delinquency. In A. E. Winder & D. L. Angus (Eds.), *Adolescence: Contemporary studies.* New York: American Book, 1968.
43. Mönks, F. Future time perspective in adolescents. *Human Devel.*, 1968, **11**, 107–123.

44. Moss, H. A., & Kagan, J. Stability of achievement and recognition-seeking behaviors from early childhood through adulthood. *J. Abn. Soc. Psychol.*, 1961, **62**, 504–513.

45. Murphey, E. B., Silber, E., Coelho, G. V., Hamburg, D. A., & Greenberg, I. Development of autonomy and parent–child interaction in late adolescence. *Am. J. Orthopsychiat.*, 1963, **33**, 643–652.

46. Peck, R. F., & Havighurst, R. J. *The psychology of character development.* New York: Wiley, 1960.

47. Powell, M., & Bloom, V. Development of and reasons for vocational choices of adolescents through the high school years. *J. Educ. Res.*, 1962, **56**, 126–133.

48. Rebelsky, F., Conover, C., & Chafetz, P. The development of political attitudes in young children. *J. Psychol.*, 1969, **73**, 141–146.

49. Rest, J. R. Developmental hierarchies of comprehension and preference in moral thinking. Paper presented at the meeting of the Society for Research in Child Development, Santa Monica, Calif., March 28, 1969.

50. Roe, A. *The making of a scientist.* New York: Dodd, Mead, 1953.

51. Roe, A. *The psychology of occupations.* New York: Wiley, 1956.

52. Rosen, B. C. Race, ethnicity and the achievement syndrome. *Am. Soc. Rev.*, 1959, **24**, 47–50.

53. Rosen, B. C. Family structure and achievement motivation, *Am. Soc. Rev.*, 1961, **26**, 574–585.

54. Rosenhan, D. The kindnesses of children, *Young Children*, 1969, **25**:1, 30–44.

55. Schab, F. Adolescence in the south: A comparison of white and Negro attitudes about home, school, religion and morality. *Adolescence*, 1968, **3**, 33–38.

56. Schaefer, E. S. Children's reports of parental behavior: An inventory, *Child Devel.*, 1965, **36**, 414–424.

57. Sebald, H. *Adolescence: A sociological analysis.* New York: Appleton-Century-Crofts, 1968.

58. Seward, G. H., & Williamson, R. C. A cross-national study of adolescent professional goals. *Human Devel.*, 1969, **12**, 248–254.

59. Shacter, B. Identity crisis and occupational processes: An intensive exploratory study of emotionally disturbed male adolescents. *Child Welfare*, 1968, **47**, 26–37.

60. Shellow, R., Schamp, J. R., Liebow, E., & Unger, E. Suburban runaways of the 1960's. *Mono. Soc. Res. Child Devel.*, 1967, **32**:3.

61. Stewart, C. W., *Adolescent religion.* New York: Abingdon Press, 1967.

62. Straus, M. A. Conjugal power structure and adolescent personality. *Marr. Fam. Living*, 1962, **24**, 17–25.

63. Super, D. E. Ninth grade vocational maturity and other predictors of career behavior and occupational criteria at age 25. Paper presented at the meeting of the American Psychological Association, August 30, 1963.

64. Super, D. E., & Overstreet, P. L. *The vocational maturity of ninth-grade boys.* New York: Columbia University Press, 1960.

65. Sutton-Smith, B., Roberts, J. M., & Rosenberg, B. G. Sibling associations and role involvement. *Merrill-Palmer Quart.*, 1964, **10**, 25–38.

66. Taft, R. A note on the characteristics of the members of MENSA, a potential subject pool. *J. Soc. Psychol.*, 1971, **83**, 107–111.

67. Thompson, G. G., & Gardner, E. F. Adolescents' perceptions of happy-successful living. *J. Genet. Psychol.*, 1969, **115**, 107–120.

68. Thorndike, R. L., & Hagen, E. *Ten thousand careers.* New York: Wiley, 1959.

69. Thorndike, R. L., & Hagen, E. *Measurement and evaluation in psychology and education.* New York: Wiley, 1961.
70. Turiel, E. Developmental processes in the child's moral thinking. In P. H. Mussen, J. Langer, & M. Covington (Eds.), *Trends and issues in developmental psychology.* New York: Holt, Rinehart and Winston, 1969, pp. 92–131.
71. Tyler, L. E. The antecedents of two varieties of vocational interests. *Genet. Psychol. Mono.*, 1964, **70**, 177–227.
72. Veroff, J. Theoretical background for studying the origins of human motivational dispositions. *Merrill-Palmer Quart.*, 1965, **11**, 3–18.
73. Wall Street Journal. Hip culture discovers a new trip. March 2, 1971.
74. Werts, C. E. A comparison of male vs. female college attendance probabilities. *Sociol. Educ.*, 1968, **41**, 103–110.
75. Wolman, R. N. Early recollections and the perception of others: A study of delinquent adolescents. *J. Genet. Psychol.*, 1970, **116**, 157–163.
76. Zelen, S. L., & Zelen, G. J. Life-span expectations and achievement expectancies of underprivileged and middle-class adolescents. *J. Soc. Psychol.*, 1970, **80**, 111–112.
77. Zytkoskee, A., Strickland, B. R., & Watson, J. Delay of gratification and internal versus external control among adolescents of low socioeconomic status: *Devel. Psychol.*, 1971, **4**, 93–98.

# Part V
# Summary

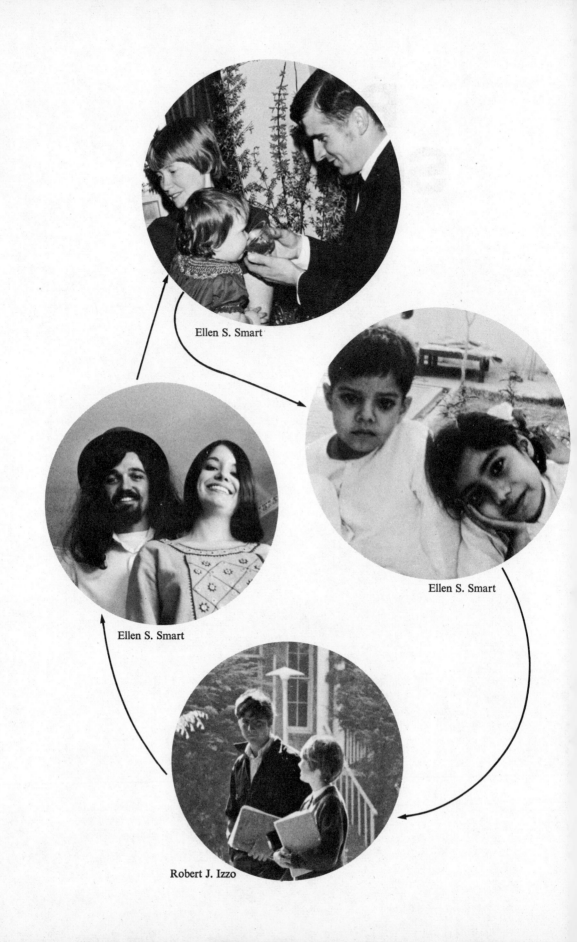

Ellen S. Smart

Ellen S. Smart

Ellen S. Smart

Robert J. Izzo

# Chapter 17

Courtesy the Peace Corps by Ray Witlin

## An Overview of Human Life and Growth

All of existence is continuous and related. A search for beginnings and causes of life reveals psychological, physiological, biological, biochemical, and physical structures built upon and of each other.

Every organism and its environment have dynamic, reciprocal relationships. Affecting each other and being affected by each other, neither can be understood without the other, nor can either be what it *is* without the other. The cool air under the tree does not exist without the tree, nor would the tree exist without air. An

639

interesting interaction between plants and landscape can be seen in coastal areas where conservation projects are carried out. A beach which was washed away by a hurricane now stretches smoothly into the Atlantic, backed by sand dunes built by plants. The plants were dead Christmas trees stuck into the sand and then reinforced by living plants which, finding nutrients and moisture enough in the sand, sent down a network of tough roots, which held the sand in the dunes.

More remarkable even than the building of beaches is the interaction of the human baby with his environment, his family. A human baby grows into a human child as he lives in a human family, calling forth maternal and paternal responses from two adults whose behavior could not be parental if he were not there.

## Varieties of Interaction Between the Individual and His World

The story of child development begins with the interactions of a small package of DNA and ends with an adult human being living in a complex social network. Everyone has some beliefs and hypotheses as to how these many changes take place. Nobody has explained it all in a comprehensive theory, but many theorists have described and explained parts of it. A theory depends first of all on the point of view from which the observer looks at the human scene and consequently on the phenomena which he observes. Theories of growth and development usually have a biological flavor. Learning experiments may suggest the influence of physics. Research in social relationships often involves sociology and perhaps anthropology. This chapter deals with six types of interactions which represent different ways of looking at human phenomena. They are: equilibration, growth and development, learning, maturation, evolutionary adaptation, and heredity.

## Equilibration

The organism constantly regulates its life processes so as to maintain physical and mental states within certain limits.

### Homeostasis

Homeostasis is a balance which the organism maintains within itself during the processes of living and as environmental influences affect its internal conditions. Since the balance is continually upset and re-created, through a complex of interactions, it can be called a dynamic equilibrium. Through activities that are mostly unconscious, the individual keeps his blood sugar at a definite level, his water content within a given range, his oxygen content just so. Breathing and heartbeat speed up or slow down from their average rates to restore disturbed balances. The mechanisms of homeostasis regulate sleeping and waking states, activity and rest. Pressures and depleted tissues may register consciously as felt needs, leading to such purposeful interactions with the environment as eating, drinking, and eliminating.

Looming large in the life of a newborn infant, the problems of homeostasis dwindle throughout infancy and childhood. By about 3 months of age basic physiological processes are well controlled. At any time throughout the life span, however, when the balance is seriously threatened, when biological demands become crucial or urgent, the individual drops his higher-order activities, such as giving a lecture or playing tennis, in order to restore the balance within his body.

### Psychological Equilibrium

The search for balance occurs in the mental realm as well as in the physical. Equilibration is the process of achieving a state of balance. Sooner or later, the state of equilibrium is upset and a new one must be created. Equilibration includes selecting stimuli from the world, seeking this or that kind, more or less, paying attention to some of them and using some in more complex mental operations. When you consider all the sounds, sights, tastes, and other perceptions available, it follows that a person could not possibly attend to all of them at once. There must be ways of selecting stimuli and avoiding or reducing psychological conflict. In Walter's words: ". . . there are mechanisms within the brain which act like traffic cops for information and actually damp down and modify the action of the receptors themselves. It has been shown that the information which is allowed to reach the brain from the outside world is a function of its novelty and significance. The level of the receptor itself, the actual eye or ear, is cut down, as though the central nervous system were to say: 'I'm not interested in what you're sending me'" [48, p. 109]. What Walter is describing is very much akin to homeostasis of physiological functions, the maintenance of satisfactory internal conditions.

Equilibration is one of Piaget's principles of mental development [34, pp. 5–8]. Action can be provoked when equilibrium is upset by finding a new object, being asked a question, identifying a problem; in fact, by any new experience. Equilibrium is reestablished by reaching a goal, answering a question, solving a problem, imitating, establishing an effective tie or any other resolution of the difference between the new factor or situation and the mental organization already existing. Equilibration results in the successive stages of intelligence which Piaget describes.

Equilibration, in Piaget's theory, includes two complementary processes through which the person proceeds to more complex levels of organization—*assimilation*, which is the taking in from the environment what the organism can deal with and *accommodation*, the changing of the organism to fit external circumstances. Just as the body can assimilate foods and not other substances, so the mind can take in certain aspects and events in the external world and not others. Existing structures or *schemas* incorporate experiences which fit them or which almost fit them.

A schema is a pattern of action and/or throught. A baby develops some schemas before he is born and has them for starting life as a newborn. With simple schemas, he interacts with his environment, working toward equilibration. He achieves equilibrium over and over again, by using the schemas available to him at the moment. For example, a baby has a furry toy kitten which he knows as *kitty*. When given a small furry puppy he calls it *kitty*, strokes it and pats it, assimilating the puppy to an existing schema. A new little horse on wheels requires accommodation, since it is too different to be assimilated into the schema for dealing with *kitty*. It looks different; it feels different; it is not good for stroking and patting, but something can be done with the wheels which cannot be done with *kitty*. A new pattern of action is required. The child accommodates by changing and organizing existing schemas to form a schema for dealing with *horsey*. Thus the child grows in his understanding of the world and his ability to deal with his experiences in meaningful ways. Assimilation conserves the structural systems that he has while accommodation effects changes through which he copes more adequately with his environment and behaves in increasingly complex ways.

When homeostasis presents no problems, such as hunger, thirst, or fatigue, a person looks for something to do, something interesting, a new experience. If equilibrium were completely satisfying in itself, then surely he would sit or lie quietly doing nothing. In looking for action, the child seems to be trying to upset his state of equilibrium, as though equilibration were fun! And so it is. Activity is intrinsic in living tissue, brain cells included. Curiosity, exploration, competence, and achievement motivation are all outgrowths of the human propensity for enjoying the process of equilibration. The first stage of the process, perception of a problem, an incongruity or discrepancy, involves tension and a feeling of incompleteness. Something is missing or something is wrong.

The baby pushes himself forward to grasp a toy that is out of reach. The 4-year-old makes a mailbox which is necessary for his game of postman. The first grader sounds out a new word. Each child reduces a feeling of tension as he creates a new equilibrium. The equilibration (achievement of new balance) makes him into a slightly different person from what he has been, a person who can move forward a bit, a person who has made his own mailbox and can therefore make other things, a person who can read another word. Thus equilibration is a way of describing behavior development. New and more complex behavior occurs as it is demanded by the person's relationship with his surroundings.

When a person's schemas are adequate to deal with the situation in which he finds himself, he reacts automatically. For example, the response of a hungry breast-fed baby of 3 months would be quite automatic when offered his mother's breast. A 10-year-old would automatically answer the question "What is two times two?" When the schemas are not quite adequate to the situation, the child uses what he has, changing them slightly into actions which do solve the problem. For instance, the baby would change his behavior sufficiently to cope with a bottle and the 10-year-old with "$2x = 4$. What does $x$ equal?" The change which takes place at the same time within the child is the development of a new behavior pattern or schema. A pleasant feeling of curiosity and satisfaction accompanies successful adjustments to demands for new behavior.

A person feels uneasy when he encounters a situation in which his resources are very inadequate. In order to provoke uneasiness, the problem must be somewhat similar to those which a person can solve, but not similar enough for him to succeed with. Such a problem for the baby mentioned might be a cup of milk. For the 10-year-old it might be an equation such as $5x - 49/x = 20x/5$. If the situation is so far removed from a person's past experience that his schemas for dealing with it are extremely inadequate, then he will have no reaction to it. He will not notice it. He will not select from the environment the stimuli which would pose the problem. The baby will not try to drink out of a carton full of cans of milk. The child won't attempt to solve $xY - x5 - 144 = 1062 + 2300$.

Familiar objects in unfamiliar guise produce unpleasantness, uneasiness, or even fear. (Chimpanzees are afraid of the keeper in strange clothes, an anesthetized chimp, a plaster cast of a chimp's head. Human babies are afraid of strangers.) In order to be frightened or to get the unpleasant feeling, the subject must first have residues of past experience with which to contrast the present experience. Thus does incongruity arise, with its accompanying unpleasant feeling tone. If the individual can cope with the situation successfully, he achieves equilibration and its accompanying pleasant feeling tone. Stimuli preferred and chosen are those that are slightly more complex than the state of equilibrium that the individual has already reached. Thus he moves on to a new state of equilibrium [36].

## Growth and Development

The child's body becomes larger and more complex while his behavior increases in scope and complexity. If any distinction is made between the two terms, growth refers to size, and development to complexity. However, the two are often used interchangeably and this is what we have done. The terms *growth* and *development* were borrowed from the physical field, but they are commonly understood in connection with mental and personality characteristics. One can say, "He has grown mentally," or "He has developed mentally." The statement means "He is now functioning on a more complex intellectual level." Or one can speak of growth of personality and development of attitudes. Listening in on second grade and fifth grade classrooms in the same school building will reveal differences in subject matter interests and in mode of thinking.

Growth or development can be shown to have taken place either by comparing younger and older individuals at the same moment of time or by comparing the same individuals at two different points of time. When the measures of some characteristic of a number of individuals are averaged by age groups, the averages of the successive age groups show what growth has taken place. If each individual is measured only once, that is, if there are different people at each age, the study is *cross-sectional*. If the same individuals are measured at each successive age, the study is *longitudinal*. If some individuals do not remain available for continued study and new ones are added, the study is called *mixed longitudinal*. In a cross-sectional study, growth status at each age is investigated, and inferences regarding growth are drawn from *differences* between any groups. *Change* in status from age to age can be inferred only if the individuals at the two ages can be assumed to be comparable in all relevant ways. In a longitudinal study both growth status at each age and change in status from age to age can be investigated more precisely, because the same individuals are involved and actual growth patterns are established for individuals.

### Principles of Growth

There are a number of generalizations about growth which are more apparent with respect to physical growth but which, as far as research can show, are also true for psychological growth. We will elaborate on nine such statements about growth at this point, some of them with subheadings.

**Variation of Rates.** Rates of growth vary from one individual to another, and they vary within one individual. An organism grows at varying rates, from one time to another. The organs and systems grow at varying rates, at different times. There is a sex difference in rates and terminals. Various group differences can be shown. It is no wonder that comparisons of growth require facts obtained by highly controlled methods.

An organism and its parts grow at rates which are different at different times. The body as a whole, as measured by height and weight, shows a pattern of velocity that is fast in infancy, moderate in the preschool period, slow during the school

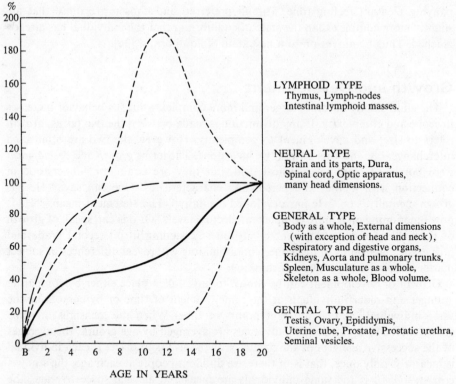

**Figure 17–1.** Growth curves of the body as a whole and of three types of tissue. Values at each age are computed as percentages of values for total growth.

Source: Reproduced by permission from J. A. Harris, C. M. Jackson, D. G. Paterson, and R. E. Scammon, *The Measurement of Man*. Minneapolis: University of Minnesota Press, 1930.

years, and fast in the beginning of adolescence. Figure 17–1 illustrates growth velocities of different types of tissue, expressed as percentages of maturity for each age. The general type of growth, which represents not only height and weight, but muscles, skeleton, and most of the internal organs, is illustrated by a sigmoid curve, an elongated S. The brain and related tissues grow in a different pattern of velocity, very fast during the first 2 years, moderately until about 6, and very little after that. The growth curve for genital tissue is almost the reverse of that of neural tissue. The genital system grows very little during infancy and childhood and very fast in adolescence. The fourth curve in Figure 17–1 represents the lymph system which grows rapidly throughout infancy and childhood, reaches a peak just before puberty, and then decreases in size throughout adolescence.

There are sex differences in rates. Early in fetal life, girls show evidence of maturing faster than boys, especially in skeletal development. At birth, girls are four weeks ahead of boys skeletally. Boys' skeletal development is about 80 percent of that of girls' from birth to maturity [44, p. 43]. Girls are ahead of boys in dentition, as measured by eruption of permanent teeth. Although sex differences in height and weight before the preadolescent growth spurt are very slight, favoring boys, sexual maturity and its antecedent growth spurt occur in girls about two years before they do in boys. Therefore, there is a period of about two years when girls are taller and heavier than boys. At all ages, girls are more mature physiologically.

**Individual Differences in Terminals.** It is obvious, yet it is essential in understanding growth, to recognize that for different people maturity comes at different points. You have only to walk down the street to observe that some people grow until they are over 6 feet tall, others stop at 5 feet, and most people stop in between. Measurable mental growth stops at different times for different individuals too. The average girl reaches height and weight terminals before the average boy. Little is known about mental growth terminals.

**Dynamic Interrelations in Growth.** It would be surprising if different measures of growth were not related to each other. A tremendous number of studies have probed into the question of interrelationships of growth-controlling and regulating mechanisms.

Correlations between measures of growth can be between measures in the same field (physical–physical, mental–mental, and so on), or in different fields (physical–mental, mental–emotional). Skeletal development, assessed by X rays of the wrist, is at present the best indicator of physiological maturity, although if body proportions could be quantified and scaled in some manageable way, this might prove even more useful. Fat thickness in childhood is also a measure of general physiological maturity [16]. Sexual maturity and eventual height can be predicted with good accuracy from measurements of skeletal maturity. A general factor of bodily maturity operating throughout the growth period influences the child's growth as a whole, including his skeleton, size, physiological reactions, and possibly intelligence. Influencing factors of more limited scope operate independently of the general factor and of each other. One of these limited factors controls baby teeth, another permanent teeth, another the ossification centers in the skeleton and probably several others regulate brain growth. This is why various measures of physical growth have low positive correlations with each other. If there were only one controlling factor, then the different measures would presumably all correlate highly or even perfectly with one another [44].

Studies of the relation between physical and mental growth show a small but consistent positive correlation, bearing out the hypothesis of a general factor which influences all growth processes. This relationship has been studied from age 6½ onward, comparing the mental ages or academic achievement, or both, of early maturing youngsters with those of late maturers [1, 24, 39, 40, 42]. A study of children at the extremes of distributions of mental traits showed gifted boys to be significantly ahead of retarded boys in measures of physical growth [24]. A small positive correlation between mental ability and size is also found in adults [45]. As an example of the relationships between growth and personality, there is good evidence that early maturers feel more adequate and more comfortable about themselves than do late maturers [23, 31].

**Optimal Tendency.** An organism behaves as though it were seeking to reach its maximum potential for development in both structure and function. Even though growth is interrupted, such as in periods of inadequate food supply, the child (or organism) makes up for the lean period as soon as more and better food is available, returning to his characteristic pattern of growth. Only if the deprivation is severe, or if it occurs throughout a critical period, will he show permanent effects from it.

During the deprivation period, the organism adapts by slowing growth and cutting down on the use of energy.

All sorts of adaptive arrangements are worked out when there are interferences with the normal course of development, as though the child is determined to reach his best potential by another route when one is blocked. The child with poor eyesight seeks extra information from his other senses. Babies with a tendency toward rickets drink cod liver oil freely if permitted to, selecting their own diets from a wide variety of simple foods [7]. For northern white children, the characteristics of the home were found to be most important in determining how well the child did at school, but for southern black children the characteristics of the school were more important than those of the home. "It is as if the child drew sustenance from wherever it was available. When the home had more to offer, it became more determining; but when the school could provide more stimulation than the home, then the school became the more influential factor." [5, p. 106].

"Every breach in the normal complex of growth is filled through regenerative, substantive, or compensatory growth of some kind. . . . Insurance reserves are drawn upon whenever the organism is threatened. . . . Herein lies the urgency, the almost irrepressible quality of growth" [18, p. 165]. This principle has been recognized as working in physical realms as well as organic, where there seems to be a self-stabilizing or target-seeking property of certain systems [48].

**Differentiation and Integration.** From large global patterns of behavior, smaller, more specific patterns emerge. Later the small, specific patterns can be combined into new, complicated, larger patterns. For example, a photographic study of human beginnings shows an $11\frac{1}{2}$ weeks' fetus reacting to being stroked on the right cheek [18, p. 25]. The fetus contracted the muscles of his neck, trunk, and shoulder, causing his whole body to bend away from the stimulus and the arms and hands to move backward. When a newborn infant is stroked on the cheek he turns toward the stimulus, pursing his lips and opening his mouth when his lips touch something. Thus he shows a new, specialized response pattern which involves a small part of his body instead of the whole. As he grows older, the rooting response changes and becomes integrated with other behavior patterns. Instead of turning toward food when he is touched near the mouth, he turns toward the breast or bottle when he sees it. His hands come into play in guiding food toward his mouth. Later he uses a knife and fork. He is integrating behavior patterns of eyes and hands with the rooting pattern, forming a smoothly functioning whole.

Examples can also be taken from purely intellectual fields, such as mathematics. There is a stage of maturity at the end of infancy when a child knows *one, two* and *a-lot-of*. At 5, he has differentiated *three* and *four* out of *a-lot-of*. By 6, numbers up to ten have true meaning. Using these differentiated concepts, he next combines them in addition and subtraction to form new and more complicated concepts. Conceptual differentiation and integration are at work as the student moves up through algebra and geometry into higher mathematics. There remains an undifferentiated sphere where each person stops in his progress in mathematics.

**Developmental Direction.** Certain sequences of development take place in certain directions, in reference to the body. The motor sequence takes two such directions, cephalocaudal (head to tail) and proximodistal (midline to outer extremities). Like all animals, the child grows a relatively large, complex head region early in life, whereas the tail region or posterior is small and simple. As he becomes older, the region next to the head grows more, and finally, the end region grows. Coordination follows the same direction, the muscles of the eyes coming under control first, then the neck muscles, then arms, chest, and back, and finally the legs. The motor sequence illustrates the proximodistal direction by the fact that the earliest controlled arm movements, as in reaching, are large movements, controlled mostly by shoulder muscles. Later the elbow is brought into play in reaching, then the wrist, and then the fingers.

**Normative Sequence.** The sequence of motor development has long been noticed and understood as one of the ways of nature. "A child must creepe ere he walke."

As the structures of the body mature in their various sequences, they function in characteristic ways, provided that the environment permits appropriate interaction. The resulting behavior patterns appear in an orderly sequence. Sequences have been described for locomotion, use of hands, language, problem solving, social behavior, and other kinds of behavior [6, 19, 20]. During the decade of the thirties, the bulk of research in child development was normative, delineating sequences of development and designating average ages for the patterns observed. The classic viewpoint, exemplified by Gesell, stressed normative sequences as an unfolding. Although the role of the environment was implicit in these early writings, the focus was on regulation from innate forces. Today interaction between organism and environment is emphasized as basic to development. The change in viewpoint has come about to some extent because of the broadening of areas of child study to include a variety of cultures, at home and abroad. Although child development continues to take place in orderly sequences, exceptions can be found [8]. Hence normative sequences cannot be considered as universal, but must be understood as occurring in particular kinds of environments.

**Epigenesis.** Growth takes place upon the foundation which is already there. New parts arise out of and upon the old. Although the organism becomes something new as it grows, it still has continuity with the past and hence shows certain consistencies over time. Through interactions with the environment, the organism continues to restructure itself throughout life, being at each moment the product of the interaction which took place in the previous moment between organism and environment. A toddler's body results from interactions of a baby's body with food, water, and air. The motor pattern of walking is derived and elaborated from creeping and standing. Writing is built from scribbling.

**Critical Periods.** There are certain limited times during the growth period of any organism when it will interact with a particular environment in a specific way. The result of interactions during critical periods can be especially beneficial or harmful. The prenatal period includes specific critical periods for physical growth. The first three months are critical for the development of eyes, ears, and brain, as shown by defects in children whose mothers had German measles during the first three months of pregnancy. Apparently those organs are most vulnerable to the virus of German measles when they are in their periods of rapid growth.

Experiments on vision with human and animal infants reveal critical ages for the development of visual responses, times when the infant will either show the response without experience or will learn it readily [14]. If the visual stimulus is not given at the critical age (as when baby monkeys are reared in darkness), the animal later learns the response with difficulty, or not at all.

Psychological development also shows critical periods in the sense that certain behavior patterns are acquired most readily at certain times of life. Critical periods in personality development include the period of primary socialization, when the infant makes his first social attachments [38] and develops basic trust [11]. A warm relationship with a mother figure is thought to be essential among the experiences which contribute to a sense of trust [4]. This type of critical period is probably not so final and irreversible as is a critical period for the development of an organ in the embryo. If the term "critical period" is applied to the learning of skills such as swimming and reading, then it should be understood that it signifies the most *opportune* time for learning and not the only one [30].

### Stage Theories of Development

The last three principles of growth are incorporated in theories of child development which present growth occurring in stages. Each stage is created through epigenesis, behavior patterns being organized and reorganized in an orderly sequence. Thus past, present, and future development are related and can be understood as an ongoing process. Small pieces of behavior can be interpreted in terms of the stage when they occur instead of being invested with one meaning. For example, crying at 1 month of age was seen to be an active attempt to overcome interference with sucking, whereas crying at 1 year of age was found to be a passive mode of response to environmental frustration [26]. Stage theories encourage research which establishes ways of predicting future development [22].

This book is organized in stages of development, leaning heavily on two stage theories: Erikson's theory of personality growth, and Piaget's theory of the growth of intelligence. The ages which correspond with the various stages are only approximations or rough landmarks. While it is useful to be able to anchor stage concepts to some sort of chronology, it is important to realize that stages are only age-related and not age-determined. The growth principle, *variation of rates*, applies here.

**Erikson's Stages.** Erikson's theory might be called epigenetic in a double sense. Not only does it portray epigenetic stages, but it was built upon Freud's theory and yet is a new organization and a unique creation. Freud proposed psychosexual stages of development, each of which used a certain zone of the body for gratification of the id (the unconscious source of motives, strivings, desires, and energy). The ego, which mediates between the demands of the id, the outside world, and the superego, "represents what may be called reason and common sense, in contrast to the id, which contains the passions" [15, p. 15]. The superego or ego ideal corresponds roughly to *conscience*. Freud's psychosexual stages are: *oral*, when the mouth is the main zone of satisfaction, about the first year; *anal*, when pleasure comes from anal and urethral sensations, the second and third years; *phallic*, the third and fourth years, a time of pleasure from genital stimulation; *oedipal*, also genital but now, at 4 and 5 years, the child regards the parent of the opposite sex as a love object and the same-sex parent as a rival; *latency*, from 6 to around 11, when sexual cravings are repressed (made unconscious) and the child identifies with the parent and peers of his own sex; *puberal* when mature genital sexuality begins.

Erikson uses Freud's concepts in his theory of psychosocial development, adding to the complexity of each stage and also adding three stages above the puberal, thus dealing with adulthood as a time for growth. Progress through the stages takes place in an orderly sequence. In making his stages psychosocial as well as psychosexual, Erikson recognizes the interaction between individual and culture as contributing to personal growth. While Freud's theory has a great deal to say about pathology, Erikson's offers a guide to both illness and health of personality. For each stage, there are problems to be solved within the cultural context. Thus each stage is a critical period for development of certain attitudes, convictions, and abilities. After the satisfactory solution of each crisis, the person emerges with an increased sense of unity, good judgment and capacity to "do well" [12, p. 92]. The conflicts are never completely resolved nor the problems disposed of forever. Each stage is described with a positive and negative outcome of the crisis involved. The stages are [11, pp. 247–274]:

1. *Basic trust versus basic mistrust.* Similar to Freud's oral stage, the development of a sense of trust dominates the first year. Success means coming to trust the world, other people, and himself. Since the mouth is the main zone of pleasure, trust grows on being fed when hungry, pleasant sensations when nursing, and the growing conviction that his own actions have something to do with pleasant events. Consistent, loving care is trust-promoting. Mistrust develops when trust-promoting experiences are inadequate, when the baby has to wait too long for comfort, when he is handled harshly or capriciously. Since life is never perfect, shreds of mistrust are woven into the fabric of personality. Problems of mistrust recur and have to be solved later, but when trust is dominant, healthy personality growth takes place.

2. *Autonomy versus shame and doubt.* The second stage, corresponding to Freud's anal period, predominates during the second and third year. Holding on and letting go with the sphincter muscles symbolizes the whole problem of autonomy. The child wants to do for himself with all of his powers: his new motor skills of walking, climbing, manipulating; his mental powers of choosing and deciding. If his parents give him plenty of suitable choices, times to decide when his judgment is adequate for successful outcomes, then he grows in autonomy. He gets the feeling that he can control his body, himself, and his environment. The negative feelings of doubt and shame arise when his choices are disastrous, when other people shame him or force him in areas where he could be in charge.

3. *Initiative versus guilt.* The Oedipal part of genital stage of Freudian theory, 4 and 5 years, is to Erikson the stage of development of a sense of initiative. Now the child explores the physical world with his senses and the social and physical worlds with his questions, reasoning, imaginative, and creative powers. Love relationships with parents are very important. Conscience develops. Guilt is the opposite pole of initiative.

4. *Industry versus inferiority.* Solutions of problems of initiative and guilt bring about entrance to the stage of developing a sense of industry, the latency period of Freud. The child is now ready to be a worker and producer. He wants to do jobs well instead of merely starting them and exploring them. He practices and learns the rules. Feelings of inferiority and inadequacy result when he feels he cannot measure up to the standards held for him by his family or society.

5. *Identity versus role diffusion.* The Freudian puberal stage, beginning at the start of adolescence, involves resurgence of sexual feelings. Erikson adds to this concept his deep insights into the adolescent's struggles to integrate all the roles he has played and hopes to play, his childish body concept with his present physical development, his concepts of his own society and the value of what he thinks he can contribute to it. Problems remaining from earlier stages are reworked.

6. *Intimacy versus isolation.* A sense of identity is the condition for ability to establish true intimacy, "the capacity to commit himself to concrete affiliations and partnerships and to develop the ethical strength to abide by such commitments" [11, p. 263]. Intimacy involves understanding and allowing oneself to be understood. It may be, but need not be, sexual. Without intimacy, a person feels isolated and alone.

7. *Generativity versus self-absorption.* Involvement in the well-being and development of the next generation is the essence of generativity. While it includes being a good parent, it is more. Concern with creativity is also part of it. Adults need to be needed by the young, and unless the adults can be concerned and contributing, they suffer from stagnation.

8. *Ego integrity versus despair.* The sense of integrity comes from satisfaction with one's own life cycle and its place in space and time. The individual feels that his actions, relationships, and values are all meaningful and acceptable. Despair arises from remorseful remembrance of mistakes and wrong decisions plus the conviction that it is too late to try again.

Figure 17–2 shows the normal timing of Erikson's stages of psychosocial development. The critical period for each stage is represented by a swelling of the rope which stretches throughout life. The ropes indicate that no crisis is ever solved completely and finally, but that strands of it are carried along, to be dealt with at different levels. As one rope swells at its critical period, the other ropes are affected and interact. As Chapter 16 showed, solutions to identity problems involve problems in all the other stages. The metaphor of the rope can also be extended by thinking of the personalities of a family's members as being intertwined ropes. When the parents' Generativity strands are becoming dominant, the infant's Trust strand is dominant. The two ropes fit smoothly together, indicating a complementary relationship between the personalities of infant and parents.

**Piaget's Stages.** Figure 17–2 shows Piaget's stages in the development of intelligence. Piaget is concerned with the nature of knowledge and how it is acquired. His studies of infants and children have revealed organizations of structures by which the child comes to know the world. The structural units are *schemas*, patterns of action and/or thought. As the child matures, he uses his existing schemas to interact, transforming them through the process of equilibration. Each stage of development is an advance from the last one, built upon it by reorganizing it and adapting more closely to reality. Reorganization and adaptation go on continuously, but from one time to another the results differ from each other. Piaget has broken this series of organizations of structures into units called periods and stages. There are three periods, each of which extends the previous one, reconstructs it, and surpasses it [35, pp. 152–159]. Periods are divided into stages which have a constant sequence, no matter whether the child achieves them at a slow or fast pace. Progress through the periods and stages is affected by organic growth, exercise and experience, social interaction or equilibration. The periods are:

1. *Sensorimotor.* Lasting from birth until about 2, sensorimotor intelligence exists without language and symbols. Practical and aimed at getting results, it works through action-schemas [35, p. 4]. Beginning with the reflex patterns present at birth, the baby builds more and more complex schemas through a succession of six stages. Figure 17–2 lists the names of the stages. They are described in Chapter 3. During this period the baby constructs a schema of the permanence

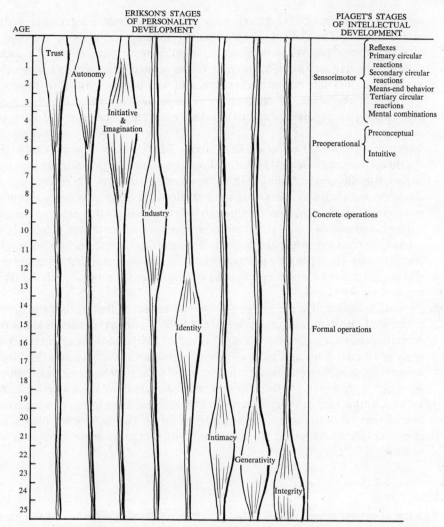

**Figure 17–2.** Schematic representation of Erikson's stages of psychosocial development, with names of Piaget's stages of the development of intelligence.

of objects. He comes to know that things and people continue to exist even when he cannot see them and he realizes that they move when he is not looking. He learns control of his body in space. He begins to use language to imitate and to make internal representations of reality.

2. *Preoperational.* Sometimes this period, from about 2 to 7, is considered a sub-period of the whole time from 2 to 11. It is distinctly different, however, from the sensorimotor period and the period which comes around 7, the period of concrete operations. Two stages, preconceptual and intuitive thought, are included. The preoperational period is marked by the *semiotic* function and imitation. The semiotic function, often called symbolizing, is the use of an indicator or sign as distinct from the object or event to which it refers [35, pp. 52–91]. For example, the bell that announces dinner is perceived as distinct from the food but as indicating food. Achievements show much use of his new representational abilities, in deferred imitation (imitation starting after the

model has disappeared), symbolic play, drawing, mental images, and verbal representation. The child thinks that names are essential parts of the objects to which they refer. When he gives a reason, it is in terms of how he wants things to be. He sees no need to come to the same conclusions as anyone else because he does not realize the existence of viewpoints other than his own. Throughout this stage the child becomes more flexible in his thinking, more able to use past experience and to consider more than one aspect of an event at a time.

3. *Concrete operations.* The period from about 7 to 11 years of age is essentially the time when the child can think about real, concrete things in systematic ways, although he has great difficulty in thinking about abstractions. He orders, counts, classifies, and thinks in terms of cause and effect. He develops a new concept of permanence, called *conservation*, through which he realizes that amount, weight, volume, and number stay the same when outward appearances of objects or groups are changed. Although he finds it difficult to change his hypotheses, he learns to take other people's points of view and comes to feel that his reasoning and his solutions to problems should check with other people's. His thinking has become socialized.

4. *Formal operations.* The period of formal operations or logical thought begins at about 11 and continues to develop until about 15, when the individual has the mental operations for adult thinking. Instead of having to think about concrete objects, he can think and reason in purely abstract terms. He can think systematically, combining all factors in a situation so as to exhaust all possibilities. He makes hypotheses and tests them. This type of thinking is basic to logic and to the scientific method. The limitation of this stage is a confusion of what could and should be with what is practically possible. The adolescent resists the imperfections in the world when he can construct ideal arrangements in his mind.

## Learning

Learning occurs when behavior changes as a result of experience. Experiments on newborn infants have demonstrated learning. As children grow older and their behavior more complex, the variables which influence behavior also increase in number and complexity. Thus different types of learning are described.

### Conditioning

Conditioning, or learning by association, is the establishing of a connection between a stimulus and a response. In *classical conditioning*, the kind made famous by Pavlov, a neutral stimulus is presented with another stimulus which elicits an innate response. After several such presentations, the neutral stimulus is given without the other stimulus and the response occurs. Pavlov sounded a buzzer when he gave food to his dog. Eventually the dog salivated at the sound of the buzzer.

Operant, or instrumental, conditioning is done by rewarding the desired response whenever it occurs. Operant conditioning techniques have been developed for use in a wide variety of situations, with animal and human subjects. By rewarding small pieces of behavior, complex patterns can be built up, thus "shaping" or modifying the behavior of the subject. This technique has proved very useful in treating behavior disorders in infants, children, retardates, and the mentally ill.

Conditioning has been used to explore the abilities of infants and to show that newborn babies do learn [27]. Papoušek taught newborn babies to turn their heads to the sound of a buzzer by using a combination of classical and operant conditioning methods [32]. A bell was sounded and if the infant turned to the left, he was given milk. If he did not turn, head-turning was elicited by touching the corner of his mouth with a nipple. Then he was given milk. Newborns were slow to condition, taking an average of 18 days, whereas at 3 months, only 4 days were required and by 5 months, 3 days. Two-month-old infants learned to operate a mobile by means of head-pressing on their pillows [49]. Until recently, the problem for experimenters was to find a way of delivering rewards which would be contingent on a response that the infant was able to make. The ingenious arrangement of the mobile and an activating device in the pillow revealed not only that infants could learn instrumentally (by operant conditioning) but also that they showed enormous involvement and pleasure in the process of controlling stimulation.

### Reinforcement

One of the laws of learning which Thorndike formulated in 1905 is the law of effect: "Any act which in a given situation produces satisfaction becomes associated with that situation, so that when the situation occurs, the act is more likely to recur also" [46, p. 203]. This principle is the basis of learning through reinforcement or rewards and punishment. Rewards and punishments, or positive and negative reinforcements, can be given to oneself or to others. It is not always possible to predict what will be rewarding and punishing, since previous experience and the state of the person at the time contribute to the meaning the particular reinforcement has. Havighurst has shown that rewards and punishments change with the age and maturity of the individual and that the development of the reward-punishment system varies from one culture to another [21]. These findings have important implications for educating children from minority subcultures.

Different schedules of reinforcement have different effects on learning by operant conditioning. Response strength is measured by the number of nonreinforced trials required to extinguish the behavior. Intermittent (random) reinforcement results in a much stronger response than does continuous reinforcement. This finding has practical implications for parents and teachers. For example, if the child finds that whining is never rewarded, he will soon stop whining, but if his parents give in occasionally and reward him with what he wants, then whining will be strengthened [41].

Punishment can be very effective in controlling children's behavior, but used without understanding of its complexity, punishment can have undesired effects. Important variables are timing, intensity, relationship between agent and recipient, cognitive structure (reasoning), and consistency [33].

### Verbal Mediation

After the child acquires language, he grows in the ability to use words in solving problems and learning. By 5 or 6 years, the ability can be demonstrated by the child's solution of problems which are most easily done with the aid of a principle such as "Always choose the big one" or "It's the color that counts in finding the answer."

### Observational Learning

Children learn many behavior patterns through watching and listening and then patterning their behavior according to what they have observed. Social learning, especially, is facilitated by modeling or imitating. Bandura and his associates have done many experiments to show the conditions under which children will learn through observation. One important finding is that children will imitate without any external reinforcement being given. That is, modeling is its own reward. Bronfenbrenner [5] has summarized information on factors affecting the modeling process, under three headings:

**Characteristics of the Subject.** The child must be able to perceive and to perform the actions and to be interested in observing and imitating.

**Characteristics of the Stimulus Act.** It is easier to imitate a complex action if it is broken into a series of components and labeled. The child then takes part in increasingly complex interactions.

**Characteristics of the Model.** The power of the model to induce imitation increases as:

1. The child sees the model as competent, high in status and controlling resources.
2. The child has already experienced the model as rewarding and nurturant.
3. The model is an important source of the child's comfort and support, such as parents, peers, and older children.
4. The child sees the model as similar to himself.
5. Several models show the same behavior.
6. The behavior demonstrated is typical of a group to which the child belongs or wants to belong.
7. The child sees the model rewarded for his behavior. (If he sees the model punished, he is likely not to imitate the behavior unless he gets into a situation where he does not anticipate punishment for performing the actions.)

Bronfenbrenner points out that the Soviets employ all of these principles of modeling in their educational system, where great use is made of the peer group for inducing adult-approved behavior in children. The teacher serves as a competent, high-status, resource-controlling model. The other characteristics of potent models are exemplified by peers.

### Social Learning

When a child learns how to think, feel and behave as a member of a certain group, or in a particular role, the process is called social learning. *Socialization* refers to the teaching done by members of the groups or institution in order that social learning may occur in the child. Social learning occurs in people of all ages, but much of it takes place in childhood, as the individual learns appropriate values, attitudes and behavior patterns. Parents are the primary socializers. Siblings and other family members also teach. Teachers and peers are important socializing agents, and then other members of the community.

Socialization refers to both the present and the future. The child learns to behave appropriately as the child he now is, but he also learns attitudes, values and skills that he will use in the future. From interacting with his father, he learns the father role as well as the son role. Similarly, he observes his various socializers as worker, manager, host, citizen, teacher, and in all the many roles that they play in his society. His socializers make varying use of the different methods of teaching implied by the types of learning sketched above. The child learns some specific information and skills, as well as values and attitudes. Thus he is gradually socialized into his family, community and nation through a process which maintains the values and behavior patterns of that group.

## Maturation

As the child's bodily structures grow, they change in size and complexity, becoming more and more the way they will be in the mature state. Bodily functions likewise change as the structures do. The whole process is called maturation. Although maturation is controlled by hereditary factors, the environment must be adequate to support it. The growth principle of normative sequence is reflected in maturation, since structures and functions mature in an orderly, irreversible sequence. Since maturation is little affected by experience, its effects are the same throughout a species. An impoverished environment slows the process of maturation more than it changes quality or sequence.

Certain behavior patterns are due to maturation more than to learning because they are relatively independent of experience. Many developmental processes involve both maturation and learning. Examples of processes which are largely maturational are the motor sequence and the emergence of language. In all but the most abnormal environments, infants go through regular sequences of raising the head, raising the chest, sitting, creeping, standing with support, and so on.

Some theories of development stress the role of maturation in determining behavior. Gesell is one of the best known of these theorists, since his writings had a great deal of influence on parents and child care authorities of his time. Gesell's descriptions of behavior stages led many parents to feel that they could do little to influence their children's behavior and that they must enjoy his good stages and wait patiently while he grew out of unattractive, annoying, or disturbing stages. While Piaget recognizes the importance of maturation, he also stresses the necessity for the child to interact, explore, and discover for himself in order to build his mental structures. Mental growth cannot be forced or hurried, however, since its counterpart is physical maturation. "Mental growth is inseparable from physical growth: the maturation of the nervous and endoctrine systems, in particular, continues until the age of sixteen" [35, p. vii].

## Evolutionary Adaptation

The behavior patterns which develop through maturation can be traced back in the history of the species or the phylum. These fixed action patterns evolved as the animal adapted to a certain environment. *Ethology* is the study of the relation between animal behavior and environment. Ethology has influenced the study of human development, offering insight into certain kinds of behavior which cannot be explained as learning or fully understood as maturation. Lorenz pointed out the implications of ethology for understanding certain forms of human behavior [28]. Bowlby has integrated psychoanalytic theory with ethology [4]. Ainsworth [2] has done extensive research on attachment behavior, the main focus of the ethological approach to human development.

The adaptive behavior pattern becomes fixed in form, appearing as an innate skill in every member of a species, even though he has not had opportunities to learn [9]. A specific stimulus from the environment activates the particular behavior pattern, as though it were a key, unlocking the mechanism. Thus the behavior is sometimes called an *innate response mechanism*, or IRM. For example, a toad's catching response is released by a small, moving object, a 9-week-old gosling gives an intense fear reaction to his first sight of a hawk, and a stickleback fish will attack a red spot that resembles the red underbelly of another stickleback.

Bowlby points out that the environment to which a species is adapted is the environment in which it evolved into its present form [4, p. 59]. Most likely, when man first emerged as a distinct species, he lived by hunting and gathering in a savannah environment, much like today's most primitive societies and not unlike the ground-dwelling primates [2]. Mother–infant reciprocal behavior was adapted to protecting the infant so as to insure his survival. The baby's unlearned, spontaneous patterns of crying, clinging, and sucking brought him (and still bring him) into contact with the mother. Other aspects of attachment behavior, maturing a little later, serve to maintain and strengthen the contacts with the mother, who was (and still is) adapted or genetically programmed to respond with specific action patterns. In the urban environment of today, close physical contact of mother and baby is not necessary for protecting the baby from predators, but babies still behave as though it were and mothers still respond to their infants' behavior with innate action patterns. Closeness of mother and baby has other advantages, however, in terms of normal development.

Human behavior is largely labile, with relatively few fixed action patterns. The individual can make many adaptations, can learn a great deal. He is equipped with a few innate behavior mechanisms, such as attachment behavior and certain patterns of fear behavior, which have various kinds of value.

## Heredity

While most students of child development will study the mechanisms of heredity in a biology course, we include a brief account here. After all, the mechanisms of heredity are what start the child developing and what control the course of development.

### Biological Inheritance

The human being is composed of two main types of cells. By far the larger number of cells are the *body* cells. These are the cells which compose the skeleton, skin, kidneys, heart, and so on. A minority of cells are the *germ* cells. In the male, germ cells are called *spermatazoa* (the singular is spermatazoon), usually shortened to *sperm*: in the female, the germ cells are *ova* (the singular is *ovum*).

Each body cell is composed of several different parts, the most important of which for our present discussion are the *chromosomes*, of which there are 46, arranged in 23 pairs. The sizes and shapes of the chromosomes can be determined by viewing a prepared cell through an electron microscope. Twenty-two of the pairs of chromosomes are composed of two highly similar chromosomes, though each pair differs in certain respects from every other pair. These 22 pairs are similar

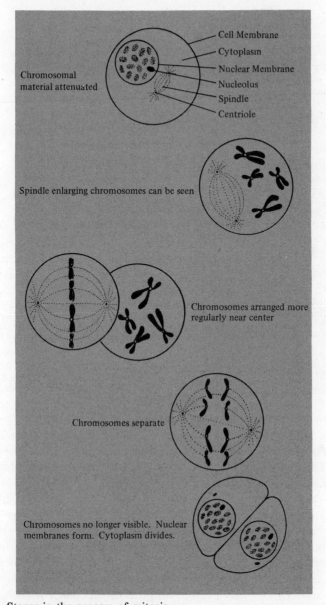

Cell Membrane
Cytoplasm
Nuclear Membrane
Nucleolus
Spindle
Centriole

Chromosomal material attenuated

Spindle enlarging chromosomes can be seen

Chromosomes arranged more regularly near center

Chromosomes separate

Chromosomes no longer visible. Nuclear membranes form. Cytoplasm divides.

**Figure 17–3.** Stages in the process of mitosis.

SOURCE: Adapted from P. A. Moody, *Genetics of Man*, Figure 3.2, p. 28. W. W. Norton, 1967.

in males and females. In males, the twenty-third pair is composed of two chromosomes which are unequal in size. The larger one is an *X chromosome*; the smaller is a *Y chromosome*. In females, the twenty-third pair is composed of two X chromosomes. When, in the course of growth, a body cell divides to form two new cells, it goes through the process of *mitosis*. The result of mitosis is that each of the new cells has exactly the same kind and number of chromosomes as the first cell had before it divided. Figure 17–3 shows the process of mitosis.

DNA, a substance in the chromosomes, is the carrier of the genetic code which transmits characteristics from one generation to the next. Figure 17–4 shows a

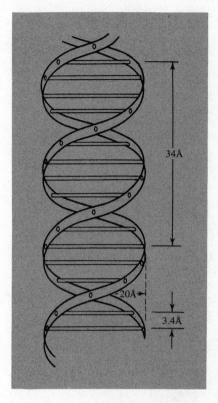

**Figure 17–4.** DNA takes the form of a double helix.

SOURCE: Adapted from G. W. Burns, *The Science of Genetics*. New York: The Macmillan Company, 1969, Figure 14–9, p. 258.

model of the DNA molecule, in the shape of a double helix or spiral ladder. The genes, carriers of specific instructions for growth, are arranged in linear order on the spirals. The two spirals can come apart like a zipper. Then each half produces another half.

**Dominant and Recessive Genes.** A recent story [43], which might be called *science prediction* rather than *science fiction*, went like this: a young couple had been quietly holding hands in a secluded corner of the campus. Then one of them said, "Let's match cards." Each pulled out a printed card containing a few holes. They put one on top of the other. None of the holes matched. They embraced happily. Like most human beings, each carried a few dangerous recessive genes out of the thousand or more which can cause birth defects. Since it takes a recessive gene from each parent to produce a characteristic which does not show in either parent, the young couple could safely plan to have children. Or if not with complete assurance, at least they would know that they were not endangering their future children as far as their own dangerous recessives were concerned. Suppose two of the holes had matched. Each of the couple was carrying a recessive gene for cystic fibrosis. For each conception, chances would be one in four for a child with two recessives and hence having cystic fibrosis, two in four for a child carrying one recessive, like the parents, and not showing the defect, and one in four for a normal child with two normal genes. And suppose they conceived a defective embryo. It could be diagnosed early in pregnancy and aborted, if they so chose.

Although at the moment when this is being written, the story is only prediction, the technology on which it is based is of the present. Many physical characteristics, including a large number of defects, are inherited according to simple Mendelian law, as illustrated in our story. Some other defects, such as color-blindness, are sex linked, which means that they are dominant in the male and recessive in the female. A male shows the defect when he carries only one gene for it, but the female does not suffer unless she has two such genes.

Heredity works in more complicated ways, also. Genes work in concert with one another and with the environment. The mechanisms of *crossing over* and *independent assortment* add enormously to the variety of genetic combinations possible. Genes "turn on" and off at various times during the life cycle. For example, the control of sexual maturation is considerably influenced by heredity.

**Gene Blends.** Many characteristics are the results of more than one pair of genes. Skin color in human beings is such a characteristic. It is not determined in all-or-none way, as is seed color in peas. Rather, in spite of popular belief to the contrary, a child's skin color is almost never darker than the skin of the darker parent, nor lighter than the skin of the lighter parent. If the child's skin is darker than either parent's, it is only a shade darker. At least two pairs of genes are considered to be active in determining skin color; there may be three or more.

Standing height is another human characteristic which is the result of many different genes working at least in part in a literally additive way, although blending of the kind which determines skin color may also be operating. A human being's height is the sum of the lengths of many different bones and many pieces of cartilage. Each bone's length is probably determined by one or more genes, and varies somewhat independently of the length of every other bone. Height is therefore a *polygenic* trait. (In addition, of course, the variation in heights of a group of individuals is affected by environmental factors such as diet and disease.)

**Meiosis.** Although each individual receives the chromosomes from germ cells of the parents, the offspring of the same parents do not receive identical chromosomes. The explanation of this difference between brothers and sisters lies in the process of *miosis*, the formation of germ cells, sperm, and ova.

Figure 17–5 shows the development of sperm which contain only 2 single chromosomes, since to show 23 would be unnecessarily complicated. In the diagram the primordial germ cell, the *spermatogonium*, is shown as containing two pairs of chromosomes. In the process of meiosis, the spermatogonium divides into two cells called *secondary spermatocytes*, each of which has one of the members of each pair of chromosomes. Each chromosome is composed of two *chromatids*. Each spermatocyte divides into two *spermatids*, each of which has one of the chromatids from the eight chromatids which are shown to have been in the original spermatogonium. From each spermatid develops a sperm. Therefore, from each male primordial germ cell result four sperm, each containing 23 single chromosomes.

The development of each ovum is similar to the development of each sperm, except that from each female primordial germ cell (called an *obgonium*) there result not four ova, but one. But it, like each sperm, contains 23 chromatids from among the 92 chromatids present in the obgonium. Since the obgonium begins meiosis with two X chromosomes, every ovum contains an X chromosome. The spermatogonium, which begins meiosis with one X and one Y chromosome, results in four sperms, two of which contain an X apiece and two a Y. If an X-bearing sperm fertilizes an ovum, the new individual will have two X chromosomes, and will be female. If a Y-bearing sperm fertilizes an ovum, the new individual will have one Y chromosome and one X chromosome, and will be a male.

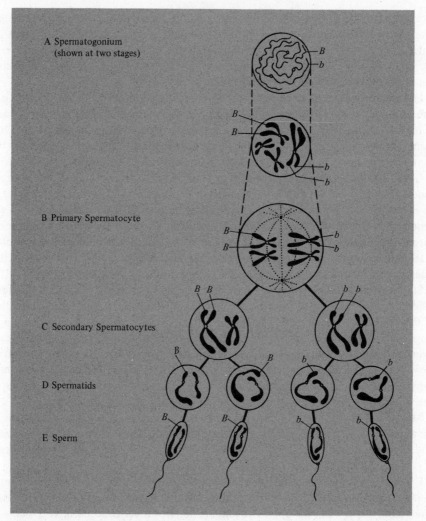

A Spermatogonium
(shown at two stages)

B Primary Spermatocyte

C Secondary Spermatocytes

D Spermatids

E Sperm

**Figure 17–5.** Meiosis provides the mechanism by which a heterozygous male produces sperm of two kinds: half of them containing the dominant gene, *B*, half of them containing its recessive allele, *b*.

SOURCE: Adapted from P. A. Moody, *Genetics of Man*, Figure 3.7, p. 34. W. W. Norton, 1967.

In the same way, if one parent has two genes for any trait, each offspring will receive from that parent the same kind of genetic material as any other offspring. But if a parent has unlike genes for a trait, half of the offspring (other things being equal, which they often are not) will receive one kind of gene (e.g., the dominant gene) and half will receive the other. The process of meiosis explains part of the genetic difference between brothers and sisters, including the fact that a given father and mother are likely to have both sons and daughters.

*Behavior Genetics*

Not only are body form and coloration inherited from generation to generation, but different kinds of functioning are, also. The ability to roll the tongue is one of these functions. One of the authors of this book (MCS) can roll her tongue; RCS cannot. All three of their daughters can. Since this ability is known to be a dominant characteristic, we know that RCS is homozygous recessive. Some of our grand-children may turn out to be like Grandpa. Our daughters are heterozygous for this characteristic. If their husbands are also heterozygous, we could predict that our grandchildren will be tongue-rollers in the ratio of 3:1.

(Incidentally, the genetic ratios hold only for large populations, not for small samples. Since we expect that the total number of our grandchildren will be six, they might all be tongue-rollers.)

The inheritance of certain defects in mental functioning can be described in terms of chromosomes [29]. Down's syndrome (Mongolism), a type of mental retardation accompanied by distinctive physical anomalies, occurs when an extra chromosome is attached to the chromosome numbered 21, making a total of 47 instead of the normal 46 chromosomes. Klinefelter's syndrome, incomplete sexual development along with lowered intelligence in males, involves two X chromosomes in addition to a Y. Turner's syndrome, in which females have only one X chromosome, includes defective spatial abilities. Males with an XXY condition are more likely than normals to be tall, aggressive, and mentally defective.

The transmission of all-or-none traits, such as tongue-rolling and Down's syndrome, can be explained by basic rules of genetics. When many genes are involved and when the characteristic is highly complex, such as intelligence or emotional stability, *heritability* is studied by *quantitative genetics*. Heritability of a charac-teristic can be estimated by comparing correlations between groups of known genetic similarity. Since the heredity of animals can be controlled, they can be used for experimental work in heredity. In working with humans, investigators have to use groups which vary in known degrees, from identical twins to unrelated persons. Results of many studies on inheritance of intelligence and personality indicate that there are indeed significant hereditary components in both [47].

**Intelligence.** Figure 17–6 shows median (average) sizes of correlations between measured intelligence of persons of different degrees of genetic similarity [13]. Unrelated persons living apart show no correlation (−.01). Identical twins reared together are very similar (.87). Identical twins reared apart are more closely correlated than those in any other relationship group (.75). Intelligence of parents and children correlates significantly (.50). Heredity components have been found in the following intellectual abilities, listed in order of weight of influence by heredity: word fluency, verbal ability (including spelling and grammar), spatial ability, clerical speed and accuracy, reasoning, number ability, and memory [47].

**Personality.** There is evidence for heritability of several dimensions of per-sonality, the main ones of which are usual activity level; expression of emotions frankly in interpersonal relationships; degree of planning ahead rather than behaving impulsively [47]; extraversion–introversion [37].

**Age Trends.** Correlations between intelligence of children and parents are low negative in early infancy, zero at around a year, low positive at the end of the second year, and moderate (.5) in early childhood and thereafter [10]. This pattern is true of children and parents living apart, as well as of those living together. Correlations between stature of parents and children also increase throughout the early preschool years [17].

**Sex Differences in Heritability.** There is evidence that girls are controlled by heredity more than boys are, most likely because the X chromosome, of which girls have two and boys one, carries more hereditary material than does the Y

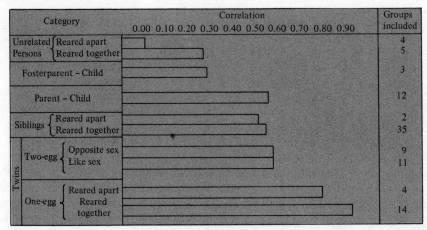

**Figure 17–6.** Median correlation coefficients for intelligence test scores showing degree of similarity between performances of people of varying degrees of relatedness under different and similar environmental conditions.

SOURCE: Data from L. Erlenmeyer-Kimling and L. F. Jervik. *Science*, 1964, **142**, 1477–79.

chromosome. After age 13, measurements of stature correlate more highly for father–daughter than for father–son and for mother–daughter than for mother–son [17]. Data from the Berkeley Growth Study indicated that girls' intellectual functioning is more genetically determined than boys and that the impact of the environment is greater upon boys than upon girls [3]. High school boys and girls, studied by a twin control method, showed stronger heritability for girls than for boys on a battery of tests of achievements and aptitudes [25].

## Summary

A baby, like all organisms, interacts continuously with his environment. He and his parents influence each other and change each other. Child development is described from different theoretical viewpoints, offering different ways of interpreting and understanding. Six types of interaction are described briefly in this chapter.

Equilibration is a process of regulation which the organism carries on in physical and intellectual modes. Homeostasis is the maintaining of the organism within certain physical limits such as those of chemical content and temperature. Psychological equilibrium involves regulating stimulation to an optimal level and also progressing toward more complex levels of mental organization. Piaget's notion of equilibration includes two complementary processes, accommodation and assimilation. Assimilation is the taking in and using of material from the environment; accommodation is changing the schemas to adjust to reality as it is experienced. Equilibration is enjoyable, as shown by children's curiosity and exploration, looking for problems and incongruities to be solved.

Growth and development, terms which can be used interchangeably, refer to increasing size and complexity of structure and function. The following principles or generalizations hold for many kinds of growth and development: variation in rates between individuals, between sexes, within the organism and of the organism in time; individuals differ in time of reaching maturity; measures of growth are interrelated; organisms behave as though they were seeking to achieve maximum potential, searching for substitute sources of nurture when the usual ones are not available; specific patterns of behavior are differentiated out of larger, global patterns, and then specific patterns are integrated into larger, complex patterns; certain sequences of physical and motor development take place in directions (cephalo-caudal and proximo-distal) in relation to the body; certain behavior patterns mature in orderly sequences; growth is based on a foundation, the organism interacting with the environment to transform itself; critical periods are specific times when the organism will interact with the environment in specific ways which may be harmful or beneficial.

Stage theories, including Erikson's and Piaget's, explain development as proceeding epigenetically, being reorganized on more and more complex levels which occur in an orderly sequence. Erikson's psychosocial theory uses Freud's psychosexual stages as a base and develops a theory of the healthy personality. The eight stages of man's development involve the development of basic trust versus basic mistrust; autonomy versus doubt and shame; initiative versus guilt; industry versus inferiority; identity versus role diffusion; intimacy versus isolation; generativity versus self-absorption; ego integrity versus despair. Piaget shows how children develop intelligence in the process of dealing with the world and coming to know it. His sensorimotor period, spanning infancy, is subdivided into six stages. The preoperational period, from around 2 to 7, includes the stages of preconceptual and intuitive thought. The period of concrete operations comprises the school years, and the period of formal operations (logical thought), adolescence.

Learning is the change in behavior due to experience. Different methods of learning include classical conditioning, when a neutral stimulus becomes associated with a response due to pairing of the neutral stimulus with a stimulus which normally elicits the response; operant conditioning, when a response is established as a result of rewarding it, a method used widely for shaping behavior; verbal mediation, the use of words in problem solving or self-instruction; observational learning, a complex process of imitating some of the behavior of other people, according to the characteristics of the child himself, the stimulus, and the model. Reinforcement includes rewards and punishments, both of which operate in complex ways.

Maturation is the growth toward maturity of the body, its structures, and functions—growth which is relatively independent of experience. Most developmental processes involve both maturation and learning.

Evolutionary adaptation accounts for certain behavior patterns which mature quickly into a complex and relatively fixed form. The environment to which a species is adapted is the one in which it emerged in its present form. Attachment behavior in the human infant is most easily understood in terms of evolutionary adaptation.

Hereditary characteristics in human beings are sometimes the result of single pairs of genes, but often of numbers of genes working together. Most human beings carry several dangerous recessive genes, which will do no harm unless matched with the same dangerous genes from the partner in reproduction. Birth defects can be predicted on a chance basis, and some with certainty. An ovum contains an X chromosome, a sperm either an X or a Y. The source of sex differences is in the X and Y chromosomes, including differences in heritability, females being more influenced by heredity. These functions include intelligence and many of its components and also certain personality dimensions. Correlations between physical and mental measurements of parents and children increase during the preschool period.

# References

1. Abernethy, E. M. Relationships between physical and mental growth. *Mono. Soc. Res. Child Devel.*, 1936, **1**:7.
2. Ainsworth, M. D. S. Object relations, dependency and attachment: A theoretical review of the infant–mother relationship. *Child Devel.*, 1969, **40**, 969–1025.
3. Bayley, N., & Schaefer, E. S. Correlations of maternal and child behaviors with the development of mental abilities: Data from the Berkeley growth study. *Mono. Soc. Res. Child Devel.*, 1964, **29**:6.
4. Bowlby, J. *Attachment and loss.* Vol. I: *Attachment.* London: Hogarth, 1969.
5. Bronfenbrenner, U. *Two worlds of childhood.* New York: Russell Sage Foundation, 1970.
6. Bühler, C. *The first year of life.* New York: Day, 1930.
7. Davis, C. M. Self-selection of diet by newly weaned infants. *Am. J. Dis. Child.*, 1928, **36**, 651–679.
8. Dennis, W. Causes of retardation among institutional children: Iran. *J. Genet. Psychol.*, 1960, **96**, 46–60.
9. Eibl-Eibesfeldt, I. Concepts of ethology and their significance in the study of human behavior. In H. W. Stevenson, E. H. Hess, & H. L. Rheingold (Eds.), *Early behavior.* New York: Wiley, 1967, pp. 127–146.
10. Eichorn, D. H. Developmental parallels in the growth of parents and their children. In *Newsletter of Division on Devel. Psychol.*, Washington, D. C.: *American Psychological Association*, Spring, 1970.
11. Erikson, E. H. *Childhood and society.* New York: Norton, 1963.
12. Erikson, E. H. *Identity, youth and crisis.* New York: Norton, 1968.
13. Erlenmeyer-Kiling, L. K., & Jarvik, L. F. Genetics and intelligence: A review. *Sci.*, 1964, **142**, 1477–1479.
14. Fantz, R. L. The origin of form perception. *Sci. Am.*, 1961, **204**, 66–72.
15. Freud, S. *The ego and the id.* New York: Norton, 1962.
16. Garn, S. M. Fat thickness and developmental status in childhood and adolescence. *J. Am. Medic. Assoc.*, 1960, **99**, 746–751.
17. Garn, S. M. Body size and its implications. In L. W. Hoffman & M. L. Hoffman (Eds.), *Review of child development research.* Vol. 2. New York: Russell Sage Foundation, 1966, pp. 529–561.
18. Gesell, A. *The embryology of behavior.* New York: Harper, 1945.
19. Gesell, A., & Thompson, H. *The psychology of early growth.* New York: Macmillan, 1938.
20. Halverson, H. M. An experimental study of prehension in infants by means of systematic cinema records. *Genet. Psychol. Mono.*, 1931, **10**, 107–286.
21. Havighurst, R. J. Minority subcultures and the law of effect. *Am. Psychol.*, 1970, **25**, 313–322.
22. Hunt, J. M., & Bayley, N. Explorations into patterns of mental development and prediction from the Bayley scales of infant development. Paper presented at the Fifth Minnesota Symposium on Child Psychology, Minneapolis, May 2, 1970.

23. Jones, M. C., & Mussen, P. H. Self-conceptions, motivations, and interpersonal attitudes of early- and late-maturing girls. *Child Devel.*, 1958, **29**, 492–501.
24. Ketcham, W. A. Relationship of physical and mental traits in intellectually gifted and mentally retarded boys. *Merrill-Palmer Quart.*, 1960, **6**, 171–177.
25. Klinger, R. Sex differences in heritability assessed by the Washington pre-college test battery of achievement/aptitude measures. Paper presented at the meeting of the Society for Research in Child Development, Santa Monica, Calif., March 27, 1969.
26. Lewis, M. The meaning of a response, or why researchers in infant behavior should be oriental metaphysicians. *Merrill-Palmer Quart.*, 1967, **13**, 7–18.
27. Lipsitt, L. P. Learning in the human infant. In H. W. Stevenson, E. H. Hess, & H. L. Rheingold (Eds.), *Early behavior.* New York: Wiley, 1967, pp. 225–247.
28. Lorenz, K. *King Solomon's ring.* New York: Crowell, 1952.
29. McClearn, G. E. Behavioral genetics: An overview. *Merrill-Palmer Quart.*, 1968, **14**, 9–24.
30. McGraw, M. B. Major challenges for students of infancy and early childhood. *Am. Psychol.*, 1970, **25**, 754–756.
31. Mussen, P. H., & Jones, M. C. The behavior-inferred motivations of late- and early-maturing boys. *Child Devel.*, 1958, **29**, 61–67.
32. Papoušek, H. Experimental studies of appetitional behavior in human new-borns and infants. In H. W. Stevenson, E. H. Hess, & H. L. Rheingold (Eds.), *Early behavior.* New York: Wiley, 1967, pp. 249–277.
33. Parke, R. D. Effectiveness of punishment as an interaction of intensity, timing, age, nurturance and cognitive structuring. *Child Devel.*, 1969, **40**, 213–235.
34. Piaget, J. *Six psychological studies.* New York: Random House, 1967.
35. Piaget, J., & Inhelder, B. *The psychology of the child.* New York: Basic Books, 1969.
36. Sackett, G. P. Effects of rearing conditions upon the behavior of rhesus monkeys (Macca Mulatta). *Child Devel.*, 1965, **36**, 855–868.
37. Scarr, S. Social introversion-extraversion as a heritable response. *Child Devel.*, 1969, **40**, 823–832.
38. Scott, J. P. Early experience and the organization of behavior. Belmont, Calif.: Brooks/Cole. 1968.
39. Shuttleworth, F. K. The physical and mental growth of girls and boys age six to nineteen in relation to age at maximum growth. *Mono. Soc. Res. Child Devel.*, 1939, **4**:3.
40. Simon, M. D. Body configuration and school readiness. *Child Devel.*, 1959, **30**, 493–512.
41. Stevenson, H. W. Learning and reinforcement effects. In T. D. Spencer & N. Kass (Eds.), *Perspectives in child psychology.* New York: McGraw-Hill, 1970, pp. 325–355.
42. Stone, C. P., & Barker, R. G. Aspects of personality and intelligence in post-menarcheal and premenarcheal girls of the same chronological age. *J. Comp. Psychol.*, 1937, **23**, 439–455.
43. Sullivan, W. If we master the gene. *New York Times,* June 14, 1970.
44. Tanner, J. M. *Education and physical growth.* London: University of London Press, 1961.

45. Tanner, J. M. Relation of body size, intelligence test scores and social circumstances. In P. Mussen, J. Langer, & M. Covington (Eds.), *Trends and issues in developmental psychology.* New York: Holt, Rinehart and Winston, 1969.
46. Thorndike, E. L. *The elements of psychology.* New York: Seiler, 1905.
47. Vandenberg, S. G. Human behavior genetics: Present status and suggestions for future research. *Merrill-Palmer Quart.,* 1969, **15,** 121–154.
48. Walter, G. Comments in J. M. Tanner & B. Inhelder (Eds.), *Discussions on child development.* Vol. I. New York: International Universities, 1953.
49. Watson, J. S., & Ramey, C. T. Reactions to response-contingent stimulation in early infancy. Unpublished paper. University of California at Berkeley, 1970.

# Appendixes

# Appendix A  Recommended Daily Dietary Allowances, Revised 1968

| | Age* Years From–Up to | Weight kg | Weight lbs | Height cm | Height in. | K calories | Protein gm | Fat Soluble Vitamins — Vitamin A Activity I.U. | Vitamin D I.U. | Vitamin E Activity I.U. |
|---|---|---|---|---|---|---|---|---|---|---|
| Infants | 0–1/6 | 4 | 9 | 55 | 22 | kg × 120 | kg × 2.2† | 1500 | 400 | 5 |
| | 1/6–1/2 | 7 | 15 | 63 | 25 | kg × 110 | kg × 2.0† | 1500 | 400 | 5 |
| | 1/2–1 | 9 | 20 | 72 | 28 | kg × 100 | kg × 1.8† | 1500 | 400 | 5 |
| Children | 1–2 | 12 | 26 | 81 | 32 | 1100 | 25 | 2000 | 400 | 10 |
| | 2–3 | 14 | 31 | 91 | 36 | 1250 | 25 | 2000 | 400 | 10 |
| | 3–4 | 16 | 35 | 100 | 39 | 1400 | 30 | 2500 | 400 | 10 |
| | 4–6 | 19 | 42 | 110 | 43 | 1600 | 30 | 2500 | 400 | 10 |
| | 6–8 | 23 | 51 | 121 | 48 | 2000 | 35 | 3500 | 400 | 15 |
| | 8–10 | 28 | 62 | 131 | 52 | 2200 | 40 | 3500 | 400 | 15 |
| Males | 10–12 | 35 | 77 | 140 | 55 | 2500 | 45 | 4500 | 400 | 20 |
| | 12–14 | 43 | 95 | 151 | 59 | 2700 | 50 | 5000 | 400 | 20 |
| | 14–18 | 59 | 130 | 170 | 67 | 3000 | 60 | 5000 | 400 | 25 |
| | 18–22 | 67 | 147 | 175 | 69 | 2800 | 60 | 5000 | 400 | 30 |
| | 22–35 | 70 | 154 | 175 | 69 | 2800 | 65 | 5000 | — | 30 |
| | 35–55 | 70 | 154 | 173 | 68 | 2600 | 65 | 5000 | — | 30 |
| | 55–75+ | 70 | 154 | 171 | 67 | 2400 | 65 | 5000 | — | 30 |
| Females | 10–12 | 35 | 77 | 142 | 56 | 2250 | 50 | 4500 | 400 | 20 |
| | 12–14 | 44 | 97 | 154 | 61 | 2300 | 50 | 5000 | 400 | 20 |
| | 14–16 | 52 | 114 | 157 | 62 | 2400 | 55 | 5000 | 400 | 25 |
| | 16–18 | 54 | 119 | 160 | 63 | 2300 | 55 | 5000 | 400 | 25 |
| | 18–22 | 58 | 128 | 163 | 64 | 2000 | 55 | 5000 | 400 | 25 |
| | 22–35 | 58 | 128 | 163 | 64 | 2000 | 55 | 5000 | — | 25 |
| | 35–55 | 58 | 128 | 160 | 63 | 1850 | 55 | 5000 | — | 25 |
| | 55–75+ | 58 | 128 | 157 | 62 | 1700 | 55 | 5000 | — | 25 |
| Pregnancy | | | | | | +200 | 65 | 6000 | 400 | 30 |
| Lactation | | | | | | +1000 | 75 | 8000 | 400 | 30 |

* Entries on lines for age range 22–35 years represent the reference man and woman at age 22. All other entries represent allowances for the midpoint of the specified age range.

† Assumes protein equivalent to human milk. For proteins not 100 percent utilized factors should be increased proportionately.

## Water Soluble Vitamins / Minerals

| | Ascorbic Acid mg | Folacin‡ mg | Niacin mg equiv.§ | Riboflavin mg | Thiamine mg | Vitamin B₆ mg | Vitamin B₁₂ µg | Calcium gm | Phosphorus gm | Iodine µg | Iron mg | Magnesium mg |
|---|---|---|---|---|---|---|---|---|---|---|---|---|
| **Infants** | 35 | 0.05 | 5 | 0.4 | 0.2 | 0.2 | 1.0 | 0.4 | 0.2 | 25 | 6 | 40 |
| | 35 | 0.05 | 7 | 0.5 | 0.4 | 0.3 | 1.5 | 0.5 | 0.4 | 40 | 10 | 60 |
| | 35 | 0.1 | 8 | 0.6 | 0.5 | 0.4 | 2.0 | 0.6 | 0.5 | 45 | 15 | 70 |
| **Children** | 40 | 0.1 | 8 | 0.6 | 0.6 | 0.5 | 2.0 | 0.7 | 0.7 | 55 | 15 | 100 |
| | 40 | 0.2 | 8 | 0.7 | 0.6 | 0.6 | 2.5 | 0.8 | 0.8 | 60 | 15 | 150 |
| | 40 | 0.2 | 9 | 0.8 | 0.7 | 0.7 | 3 | 0.8 | 0.8 | 70 | 10 | 200 |
| | 40 | 0.2 | 11 | 0.9 | 0.8 | 0.9 | 4 | 0.8 | 0.8 | 80 | 10 | 200 |
| | 40 | 0.2 | 13 | 1.1 | 1.0 | 1.0 | 4 | 0.9 | 0.9 | 100 | 10 | 250 |
| | 40 | 0.3 | 15 | 1.2 | 1.1 | 1.2 | 5 | 1.0 | 1.0 | 110 | 10 | 250 |
| **Males** | 40 | 0.4 | 17 | 1.3 | 1.3 | 1.4 | 5 | 1.2 | 1.2 | 125 | 10 | 300 |
| | 45 | 0.4 | 18 | 1.4 | 1.4 | 1.6 | 5 | 1.4 | 1.4 | 135 | 18 | 350 |
| | 55 | 0.4 | 20 | 1.5 | 1.5 | 1.8 | 5 | 1.4 | 1.4 | 150 | 18 | 400 |
| | 60 | 0.4 | 18 | 1.6 | 1.4 | 2.0 | 5 | 0.8 | 0.8 | 140 | 10 | 400 |
| | 60 | 0.4 | 18 | 1.7 | 1.4 | 2.0 | 5 | 0.8 | 0.8 | 140 | 10 | 350 |
| | 60 | 0.4 | 17 | 1.7 | 1.3 | 2.0 | 5 | 0.8 | 0.8 | 125 | 10 | 350 |
| | 60 | 0.4 | 14 | 1.7 | 1.2 | 2.0 | 6 | 0.8 | 0.8 | 110 | 10 | 350 |
| **Females** | 40 | 0.4 | 15 | 1.3 | 1.1 | 1.4 | 5 | 1.2 | 1.2 | 110 | 18 | 300 |
| | 45 | 0.4 | 15 | 1.4 | 1.2 | 1.6 | 5 | 1.3 | 1.3 | 115 | 18 | 350 |
| | 50 | 0.4 | 16 | 1.4 | 1.2 | 1.8 | 5 | 1.3 | 1.3 | 120 | 18 | 350 |
| | 50 | 0.4 | 15 | 1.5 | 1.2 | 2.0 | 5 | 1.3 | 1.3 | 115 | 18 | 350 |
| | 55 | 0.4 | 13 | 1.5 | 1.0 | 2.0 | 5 | 0.8 | 0.8 | 100 | 18 | 350 |
| | 55 | 0.4 | 13 | 1.5 | 1.0 | 2.0 | 5 | 0.8 | 0.8 | 100 | 18 | 300 |
| | 55 | 0.4 | 13 | 1.5 | 1.0 | 2.0 | 5 | 0.8 | 0.8 | 90 | 18 | 300 |
| | 55 | 0.4 | 12 | 1.5 | 1.0 | 2.0 | 6 | 0.8 | 0.8 | 80 | 10 | 300 |
| **Pregnancy** | 60 | 0.8 | 15 | 1.8 | +0.1 | 2.5 | 8 | +0.4 | +0.4 | 125 | 18 | 450 |
| **Lactation** | 60 | 0.5 | 20 | 2.0 | +0.5 | 2.5 | 6 | +0.5 | +0.5 | 150 | 18 | 450 |

‡ The folacin allowances refer to dietary sources as determined by *Lactobacillus casei* assay. Pure forms of folacin may be effective in doses less than ¼ of the RDA.
§ Niacin equivalents include dietary sources of the vitamin itself plus 1 mg equivalent for each 60 mg of dietary tryptophan.

# Appendix B

## Height-Weight Interpretation Folders for Boys and Girls*

*Uses of folder.* This folder (1) provides each child a personal chart designed to accompany him from grade to grade and give a graphic record of his growth in height and weight, (2) furnishes the teacher a guide for interpreting each pupil's height and weight records as indicators of growth status and growth progress, and (3) brings the attention of school health workers to certain height and weight findings suggestive of deviations from satisfactory health.

*Determining weight.* Obtain the weight of each pupil in September, January, and May. Wherever possible use beam-type, platform scales. Before each weighing period check the scales; if they do not balance correctly, adjust them. Have the child remove his shoes and as much other clothing as practicable (the weight measures used in developing the chart were taken on children wearing underclothing only). With the child standing near the center of the platform of the scales, his hands hanging free, determine weight to the nearest one-half pound.

*Determining height.* Use a metric measure fixed in the upright position, and a wood headpiece. The measure may be a yardstick, metal tape, or paper scale; it should be fastened firmly to an upright board or to a smooth wall with no wainscoting. (An accurate paper scale may be purchased from the Institute of Child Behavior and Development, State University of Iowa.) Although a chalk box can serve as the headpiece, this is not recommended for regular use. A more satisfactory headpiece is easily made in the school workshop by joining at right angles the shorter edges of two pieces of seasoned wood 7 inches × 5 inches, and mounting within the 90° angle a triangular wood brace having an opening for insertion of the fingers.

Measure height with shoes removed. Have the child stand with heels, buttocks, and upper part of back in contact with the wall or board; feet almost together but not touching each other; arms hanging at the sides; heels in firm contact with the floor; head facing straight forward; and chin lifted but not tilted up. When he is positioned, place one face of the headpiece against the upright scale and bring the other face down, keeping it horizontal, until it crushes the child's hair and makes contact with the top of his head. Take two separate measurements and record height to the nearest one-fourth inch.

* Prepared for the Joint Committee on Health Problems in Education of the NEA and AMA by Howard V. Meredith and Virginia B. Knott, State University of Iowa. Copies may be secured through the order departments of the American Medical Association, 535 N. Dearborn St., Chicago, Illinois 60610, or of the National Education Association, 1201 Sixteenth St., N.W. Washington, D.C. 20036.

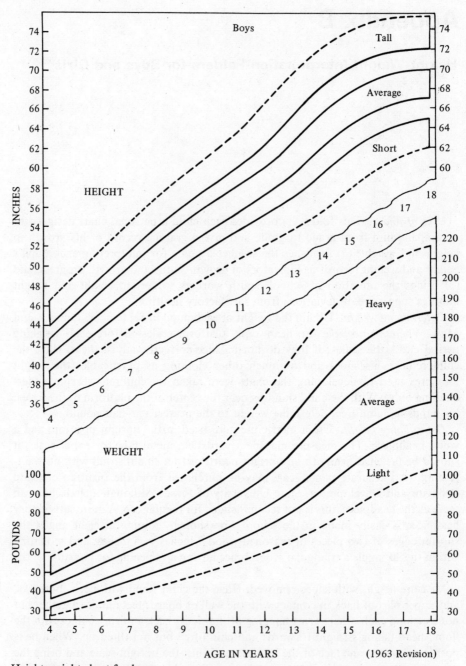

Height-weight chart for boys.

SOURCE: Reprinted with the permission of the American Medical Association.

*Registering height and weight status.* Assume you have determined the height and weight of Ned Barth. Ned weighs 50 pounds, is 45 inches in height, and will have his fifth birthday tomorrow. Find age 5 below the *height* portion of the boys' chart and 45 inches along its left-hand margin. Plot a point above 5 years and opposite 45 inches. Below this dot on the height portion of the chart write "45.0."

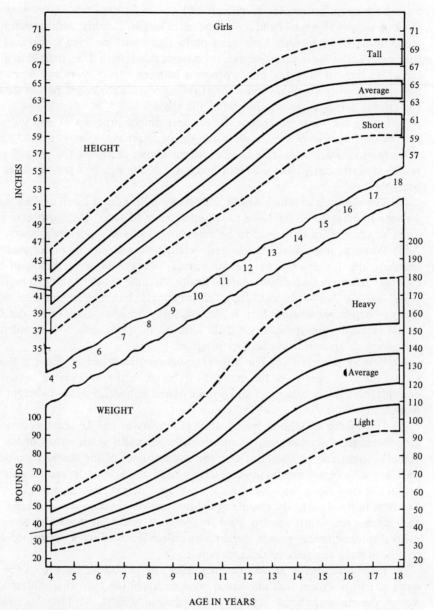

Height-weight chart for girls.

SOURCE: Reprinted with the permission of the American Medical Association.

Next, find age 5 years below the *weight* portion of the chart and 50 pounds along its left-hand margin. Plot a point above 5 years and opposite 50 pounds. Above this mark in the weight portion of the chart write " 50.0."

With the completion of these directions, the height and weight status of Ned Barth at age 5 years is fully registered. At any age from 4 years to 18 years, the status of other children can be registered similarly. Girls' measurements should be entered on the chart provided for girls.

*Registering height and weight progress.* Assume Ned is now one year older. At age 5 years 4 months he weighed 52 pounds and had a height of 46 inches, at age

5 years 8 months he weighed 55 pounds and was 46.5 inches tall, and now at age 6 years he weighs 58 pounds and is 47.5 inches in height. Further, assume that points representing these records have been plotted correctly on Ned's chart. Having status records at more than one age, it becomes possible to draw *individual growth curves*, or lines of progress. Ned's progress between ages 5 years and 6 years can be depicted by drawing lines connecting (a) his points in the height part of the chart and (b) his points in the weight part of the chart.

Following the same procedure, height and weight progress of any individual may be portrayed over part or all of the period from age 4 years to age 18 years.

*Interpreting status.* (1) The figures written above or below the plotted points readily describe each child's overall body size at the age or ages measures have been obtained.

(2) The channels in which height and weight points for a given age are located indicate standings with reference to schoolmates of like age. The illustrative values given at age 6 years show Ned to be moderately tall and moderately heavy.

(3) When an individual's height and weight points do not lie in corresponding channels, the discrepancy may denote normal slenderness or stockiness of build, or it may reflect an undesirable state of health. Assume the chart shows a new pupil to be "average" in height and "light" in weight. He should be screened for medical study to determine whether he is a "satisfactorily healthy" child of slender build, or a "medically unsatisfactory" child with an incipient infection, a nutritional deficiency, or an unsuitable activity program.

*Interpreting progress.* (1) The difference between recorded heights (or weights) at two different ages gives the amount of change in the intervening period. For example, Ned Barth between 5 and 6 years of age gained 2.5 inches in height and 8 pounds in weight.

(2) During the childhood span from age 4 years to age 11 years normality of growth progress is indicated by approximately parallel relationship of the individual's height and weight lines with the channel lines of the chart. Suppose that Paul Stone has been measured successively from age 6 years to age 10 years. His height line runs along the middle of the "average" height channel, while his weight line runs fairly close to the middle of the average weight channel until age 9 years then takes a steep turn upward. Paul should be screened for medical investigation —his disproportionate gain in weight may reflect the need for a prescribed diet, a change in daily regimen, or drug therapy.

(3) Interpretations of growth progress after age 11 years are made on the same basis as earlier except that allowance must be made for individual differences in age of the circumpuberal "spurt" in height and weight. Suppose (a) Eric and Gerald are nearly alike in height and weight at each age from 5 to 11 years, and (b) the time of rapid adolescent growth in these measures begins before 13 years for Eric and after 15 years for Gerald. In the early teens when Gerald is continuing to grow in height and weight at childhood rates, this growth should not be appraised as "unsatisfactory."

*About the chart.* The height and weight measurements for constructing the chart were collected in 1961–1963 on white boys and in 1961 for white girls attending public and private schools in Iowa City, Iowa. To obtain the channels, age distributions for height and weight were subdivided as follows: Upper 10 percent (Tall, Heavy), next 20 percent, middle 40 percent (Average), next 20 percent, and lower 10 percent (Short, Light).

# Appendix C

## Characteristics of Children Under Age 14, United States

NUMBER OF CHILDREN UNDER AGE 14
United States, 1940–1969

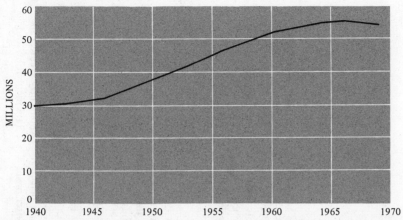

SOURCE: From *Statistical Bulletin*, 1970, **51**, p. 10. Courtesy of Metropolitan Life Insurance Company.

| Characteristic | Age Group | | | |
| --- | --- | --- | --- | --- |
| | Under 14 | Under 5 | 5–9 | 10–13 |
| Number in thousands (July 1) | | | | |
| 1940 | 30,657 | 10,627 | 10,699 | 9,331 |
| 1960 | 53,349 | 20,364 | 18,825 | 14,160 |
| 1966 | 56,355 | 19,811 | 20,813 | 15,731 |
| 1969 | 55,291 | 17,960 | 20,827 | 16,504 |
| Sex (1969)—percent | 100.0 | 100.0 | 100.0 | 100.0 |
| Male | 51.0 | 51.0 | 51.0 | 50.8 |
| Female | 49.0 | 49.0 | 49.0 | 49.2 |
| Race (1969)—percent | 100.0 | 100.0 | 100.0 | 100.0 |
| White | 84.2 | 82.8 | 84.4 | 85.6 |
| All other | 15.8 | 17.2 | 15.6 | 14.4 |
| Living arrangement (1969)—percent | 100.0 | 100.0* | 100.0* | 100.0 |
| In families | 99.3 | 99.4 | 99.4 | 98.9 |
| Living with both parents | 85.5 | 86.6 | 85.6 | 83.9 |
| Living with mother only | 10.7 | 9.8 | 11.0 | 11.7 |
| Living with father only | 0.9 | 0.5 | 1.0 | 1.3 |
| Living with relative other than parent | 2.2 | 2.5 | 1.8 | 2.0 |
| Not in families | 0.7 | 0.6 | 0.6 | 1.1 |
| School enrollment (1968)—percent | 100.0† | 100.0† | 100.0 | 100.0 |
| Enrolled in school | 82.5 | 15.7 | 94.6 | 99.1 |
| Not enrolled in school | 17.5 | 84.3 | 5.4 | 0.9 |

\* Relates to ages under 6 and 6–9, respectively.
† Excludes ages under 3.

Source of basic data. Reports by the Bureau of the Census.

Statistical Bulletin, 1970, **51** (July). Reprinted by permission of the Metropolitan Life Insurance Company.

# Appendix D Communicable Diseases of Childhood

| | Chickenpox | Diphtheria | German Measles | Infantile Paralysis | Measles |
|---|---|---|---|---|---|
| **Cause** | A virus: Present in secretions from nose, throat, mouth of infected people. | Diphtheria bacillus: Present in secretions from nose, throat, and skin of infected people and carriers. | A virus: Present in secretions from nose and mouth of infected people. | 3 strains of polio virus have been identified. Present in discharges from nose, throat, bowels of infected people. | A virus: Present in secretions from nose and throat of infected people. |
| **How spread** | Contact with infected people or articles used by them. Very contagious. | Contact with infected people and carriers or articles used by them. | Contact with infected people or articles used by them. Very contagious. | Primarily, contact with infected people. | Contact with infected people or articles used by them. Very contagious. |
| **Incubation period** (from date of exposure to first signs) | 13 to 17 days. Sometimes 3 weeks. | 2 to 6 days. Sometimes longer. | 14 to 21 (usually 18) days. | Usually 7 to 14 days. | About 10 to 12 days. |
| **Period of communicability** (time when disease is contagious) | From about 1 day before, to 6 days after first appearance of skin blisters. | From about 2 to 4 weeks after onset of disease. | From 7 days before to 5 days after onset of symptoms. | Apparently greatest in late incubation and first few days of illness. | From 4 days before until about 5 days after rash appears. |

676

| | | | | | |
|---|---|---|---|---|---|
| **Most susceptible ages** | Under 15 years. | Under 15 years. | Young children, but also common in young adults. | Most common in children 1 to 16 years. | Common at any age during childhood. |
| **Seasons of prevalence** | Winter. | Fall and spring. | Spring and winter. | Summer. | Mainly spring. Also fall and winter. |
| **Prevention** | No prevention. | Vaccination with diphtheria toxoid (in triple vaccine for babies). | German measles (rubella) vaccine. | Polio vaccine. | Measles vaccine. |
| **Control** | Exclusion from school for 1 week after eruption appears. Avoid contact with susceptibles. Cut child's fingernails short and keep clean. Immunity usual after one attack. | Antitoxin and antibiotics used in treatment and for protection after exposure. One attack does not necessarily give immunity. | Isolation when necessary, for 5 days after onset. Immunity usual after one attack. | Isolation for about one week from onset, for duration of fever. Immunity to infecting strain of virus usual after one attack. | Isolation until 5 days after appearance of rash. Immune globulin between 3 and 6 days after exposure can lighten attack. Antibiotics for complications. Immunity usual after one attack. |

* Based on The Control of Communicable Diseases, American Public Health Association, 1965, and Report of Committee on Control of Infectious Diseases, American Academy of Pediatrics, 1969.
Courtesy of Metropolitan Life Insurance Company, 1971.

| | Mumps | Rheumatic Fever | Smallpox | Tetanus | Strep Infections | Whooping Cough |
|---|---|---|---|---|---|---|
| **Cause** | A virus. Present in saliva of infected people. | Direct cause unknown. Precipitated by a strep infection. | A virus: Present in skin pocks and discharges from mouth, nose, throat of infected people. | Tetanus bacillus: Present in a wound so infected. | Streptococci of several strains cause scarlet fever and strep sore throats: Present in secretions from mouth, nose, ears of infected people. | Pertussis bacillus: Present in secretions from mouth and nose of infected people |
| **How spread** | Contact with infected people or articles used by them. | Unknown. But the preceding strep infection is contagious. | Contact with infected people or articles used by them. | Through soil, contact with horses, street dust, or articles contaminated with the bacillus. | Contact with infected people, rarely from contaminated articles. | Contact with infected people and articles used by them. |
| **Incubation period** (from date of exposure to first signs) | 14 to 21 (commonly 18) days | Symptoms appear about 2 to 3 weeks after a strep infection. | From 10 to 14 (usually 12) days. | 3 days to 3 weeks. Sometimes longer. Average about 8 days. | 2 to 5 days. | From 5 to 10 days. |
| **Period of communicability** (time when disease is contagious) | From about 7 days before symptoms to 9 days after. Principally at about time swelling starts. | Not communicable. Preceding strep infection is communicable. | From 2 to 3 days before rash, until disappearance of all pock crusts. | Not communicable from person to person. | Greatest during acute illness (about 10 days). | From onset of first symptoms to 4th week of the disease. |

| | | | | | | |
|---|---|---|---|---|---|---|
| **Most susceptible ages** | Children and young people | All ages; most common from 6 to 12 years. | All ages. | All ages. | All ages. | Under 7 years. |
| **Seasons of Prevalence** | Winter and spring. | Mainly winter and spring. | Usually winter, but anytime. | All seasons, but more common in warm weather. | Late winter and spring. | Late winter and early spring. |
| **Prevention** | Mumps vaccine. | No prevention, except proper treatment of strep infections. See Strep infections. | Vaccination. | Immunization with tetanus toxoid (in triple vaccine for babies). | No prevention. Antibiotic treatment for those who have had rheumatic fever. | Immunization with whooping cough vaccine (in triple vaccine for babies). |
| **Control** | Mumps immune globulin for exposed susceptibles (those who have not been vaccinated or had mumps). Immunity usual after one attack but second attacks can occur. | Use of antibiotics. One attack does not give immunity. | Vaccinia immune globulin may prevent or modify smallpox if given within 24 hours after exposure. Isolation until all pock crusts are gone. Immunity usual after one attack. | Booster dose of tetanus toxoid for protection after a wound. Antitoxin used in treatment and for temporary protection for child not immunized. One attack does not give immunity. | Isolation for about 1 day after start of treatment with antibiotics—used for about 10 days. One attack does not necessarily give immunity. | Booster doses (next page). Pertussis immune globulin can lighten attack or give protection after exposure in infants under 2 years. Isolation from susceptible infants for about 3 weeks from onset or until cough stops. Immunity usual after one attack. |

# Appendix E

## Vaccination Schedule

This schedule for first vaccinations is based on recommendations of the American Medical Association and the American Academy of Pediatrics. Mumps vaccine is not suggested for infants and children, but it is advised especially for boys nearing adolescence, who have not had mumps. Your physician may suggest a slightly different schedule suitable for your individual child. Recommendations change from time to time, as science gains new knowledge.

| Disease | Age for first dose | No. of doses | Boosters |
|---|---|---|---|
| **Diphtheria Whooping cough Tetanus** | 6 weeks to 2 months | 3 shots, about one month apart | At 1 year and again at 3 to 6 years; before school entrance. Repeated as recommended by physician |
| **Polio** | 6 weeks to 3 months | Oral vaccine: 3 doses, four to six weeks apart | At about 1 year; before school entrance and as recommended by physician |
| **Smallpox** | 15 to 18 months | 1 vaccination | Every 3 to 5 years, and if exposed |
| **German measles** | No earlier than 12 months | 1 vaccination | As yet, no recommendation |
| **Measles** | 12 months | Live-type: 1 vaccination | As yet, no recommendation |
| **Mumps** | Preadolescence (especially for boys) | 1 vaccination | As yet, no recommendation |

Courtesy of Metropolitan Life Insurance Company

# Author Index

Entries in *italics* refer to pages on which bibliographic references are given.

Abernethy, E. M., 645, *664*
Abravanal, E., 396, *413*
Acker, M., 419, *448*
Adams, A. O., 69, *83*
Adams, G., 63, *82*
Adams, J. F., 555, *589*
Adamson, J. M., 319, *338*
Adelson, J., 552, 554, 555, 571, 576, 577, 581, 583, 584, *590,* 597, 618, 619, 626, 630, *632*
Ainsworth, M. D. S., 106, 117, 123,*131,* 143, 152, 154, 157, 158, 159, 163,' 166, *182,* 307, 308, *334,* 655, 656, *664*
Albert, J., 393, 396, *414*
Albino, R. C., 102, *131*
Allen, L., 250, *270*
Allinsmith, W., 440, *447*
Almy, M., 276, *301,* 392, *413*
Alpert, R., 434, *449*
Altman, L. K., 213, *226*
Amatora, M., 437, *445*
Amatruda, C. S., 104, 107, 116, 129, *133,* 247, *270*
Ames, L. B., 129, *131,* 239, 240, *269,* 326, *334*
Anastasiow, N., 463, *485*
Anderson, W. J., 587, *590*
Angel, K., 513, *527*
Anisfeld, M., 259, *269,* 281, *301*
Apgar, V., 56, *82*
Appel, G., 75, *82*
Applebaum, R. M., 139, *182*
Applefeld, S. W., 289, *303*
Araki, C. T., 522, *527*
Archer, M., 526, *528*
Aronfreed, J., 320, *334*
Aronoff, F. W., 289, *301*
Asch, H., 398, *416*
Astrand, P. O., 517, *527, 529*
Atkinson, J. W., 421, *448*
Ausubel, D. P., 470,*482,* 494, 512,*527,* 536, *549*

Bachtold, L. M., 408, *416,* 545, *550*
Bacon, M. K., 328, *335*
Bahm, R. N., 561, *590*
Baird, D., 37, *50*
Baker, C. T., 250,*272,* 420,*448,* 463,*486*
Baker, H. V., 477, *482*
Bakwin, H., 74, *82*
Baldwin, A. L., 315, *334,* 479, *482*
Baldwin, C. P., 479, *482*
Bales, R. F., 461, *485*
Balfour, G., 243, *269*
Ball, R. S., 129, *136*
Bandura, A., 313, 331,*334,335,* 431,*446*
Barker, R. G., 425, *446,* 645, *665*
Barnicot, N. A., 57, *83*
Barocas, R., 532, *548*
Barrett, I. M., 26, *52*
Barron, F., 404, *413,* 542, 544, 545, *548*
Barry, H., 328, *335*
Barton, S., 72, *82*
Baruch, D. W., 306, *335*
Bassett, E., 369, *378*
Bath, J. A., 565, *590*
Baumrind, D., 196, *226,* 309, *335*
Bayley, N., 106, 128, 129,*131,135,* 150, 168, *182, 185,* 253, *269,* 525, 526, *527, 528,* 648, 662, *664*
Beal, V. A., 26, *50*
Bealer, R. C., 565, *590*
Becker, W. C., 140, 168, *182*
Bee, H. L., 254, 266, *269,* 463, *482*
Béhar, M., 74, *82,* 204, 206, *226*
Bell, R. Q., 72, *82,* 110, 112, *133,* 150, *182,* 216, *229,* 309, *338*
Bell, R. R., 456, *482,* 581, *590*
Bell, S. M., 117, 123,*131,* 143, 155, 156, 157, 158, 159, *182*
Beller, E. K.,*338,* 434, 435, 437,*448,449*
Bellugi-Klima, U., 263, 264, 265, *269*
Belmont, L., 223, *226,* 374, 375, *378*
Benenson, A. S., 360, *378*
Bentler, P. M., 392, *414*

681

# Subject Index

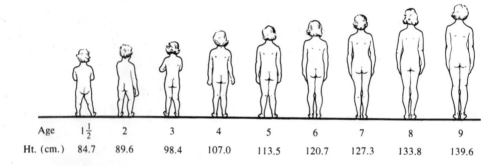

| Age | $1\frac{1}{2}$ | 2 | 3 | 4 | 5 | 6 | 7 | 8 | 9 |
|---|---|---|---|---|---|---|---|---|---|
| Ht. (cm.) | 84.7 | 89.6 | 98.4 | 107.0 | 113.5 | 120.7 | 127.3 | 133.8 | 139.6 |

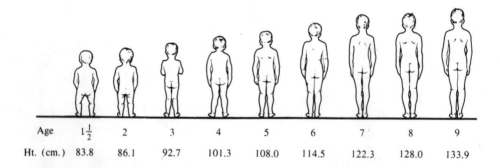

| Age | $1\frac{1}{2}$ | 2 | 3 | 4 | 5 | 6 | 7 | 8 | 9 |
|---|---|---|---|---|---|---|---|---|---|
| Ht. (cm.) | 83.8 | 86.1 | 92.7 | 101.3 | 108.0 | 114.5 | 122.3 | 128.0 | 133.9 |